PowerPoint® 2007
Bible

PowerPoint® 2007
Bible

Faithe Wempen

Wiley Publishing, Inc.

PowerPoint® 2007 Bible

Published by
Wiley Publishing, Inc.
10475 Crosspoint Boulevard
Indianapolis, IN 46256
www.wiley.com

Copyright © 2007 by Wiley Publishing, Inc., Indianapolis, Indiana

Published simultaneously in Canada

ISBN: 978-0-470-04368-4

Manufactured in the United States of America

10 9 8 7 6 5 4 3

For general information on our other products and services or to obtain technical support, please contact our Customer Care Department within the U.S. at (800) 762-2974, outside the U.S. at (317) 572-3993 or fax (317) 572-4002.

Library of Congress Cataloging-in-Publication Data

Wempen, Faithe.
    Microsoft PowerPoint 2007 bible / Faithe Wempen.
        p. cm.
    Includes indexes.
    ISBN-13: 978-0-470-04368-4 (paper/cd-rom)
    ISBN-10: 0-470-04368-7 (paper/cd-rom)
  1. Presentation graphics software.   2. Microsoft PowerPoint (Computer File)
I. Title.
    T385.W4673 2007
    005.5'8—dc22   2006103085

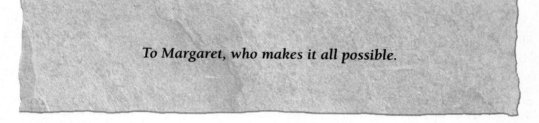

To Margaret, who makes it all possible.

About the Author

Faithe Wempen, M.A., is an A+ Certified hardware guru, Microsoft Office Specialist Master Instructor, and software consultant with over 90 computer books to her credit. She has taught Microsoft Office applications, including PowerPoint, to over a quarter of a million online students for corporate clients including Hewlett Packard, CNET, Sony, Gateway, and eMachines. When she is not writing, she teaches Microsoft Office classes in the Computer Technology department at Indiana University-Purdue University at Indianapolis (IUPUI), does private computer training and support consulting, and owns and operates Sycamore Knoll Bed and Breakfast in Noblesville, Indiana (www.sycamoreknoll.com).

Credits

Senior Acquisitions Editor
Jim Minatel

Development Editor
Maureen Spears

Technical Editor
Echo Swinford

Production Editor
Felicia Robinson

Copy Editors
Mildred Sanchez
Marylouise Wiack

Editorial Manager
Mary Beth Wakefield

Production Manager
Tim Tate

**Vice President and Executive Group
Publisher**
Richard Swadley

Vice President and Executive Publisher
Joseph B. Wikert

Project Coordinator
Jennifer Theriot

Graphics and Production Specialists
Carrie A. Foster
Shawn Frazier
Denny Hager
Joyce Haughey
Jennifer Mayberry
Heather Ryan
Rashell Smith
Ronald Terry

Quality Control Technicians
John Greenough
Christy Pingleton

Media Development Project Supervisor
Laura Carpenter VanWinkle

Media Development Specialist
Laura Adkinson

Book Designer
Elizabeth Brooks

Proofreading and Indexing
Sherry Massey
Techbooks

Contents at a Glance

Contents

Contents

Contents

Part II: Using Graphics and Multimedia Content   261

Chapter 10: Drawing and Formatting Objects 263

Contents

Contents

Part III: Interfacing with Your Audience   507

Chapter 19: Creating Support Materials 509

Chapter 20: Preparing for a Live Presentation 531

Contents

Contents

Part V: Appendixes   727

Preface

Some books zoom through a software program so fast it makes your head spin. You'll come out dizzy, but basically able to cobble together some sort of result, even if it doesn't look quite right. This is not one of those books.

The *Microsoft PowerPoint 2007 Bible* is probably the only PowerPoint book you will ever need. In fact, it might even be the only book on giving presentations you'll ever need. No, seriously! I mean it.

As you probably guessed by the heft of the book, this is not a quick-fix shortcut to PowerPoint expertise. Instead, it's a thoughtful, thorough educational tool that can be your personal trainer now and your reference text for years to come. That's because this book covers PowerPoint from "cradle to grave." No matter what your current expertise level with PowerPoint, this book brings you up to the level of the most experienced and talented PowerPoint users in your office. You might even be able to teach those old pros a thing or two!

But this book doesn't stop with PowerPoint procedures. Creating a good presentation is much more than just clicking a few dialog boxes and typing some text. It requires knowledge and planning—lots of it. That's why this book includes a whole chapter on planning a presentation, and another whole chapter on the practical issues involved in presenting one. You learn things like the following:

- How to select the best color schemes for selling and informing
- How to gauge the size of the audience and the meeting room when selecting fonts
- How to arrange the tables and chairs in the meeting room to encourage (or discourage) audience participation
- How to choose what to wear for a live presentation
- How to overcome stage fright

And lots more! When you finish this book, you will not only be able to build a presentation with PowerPoint, but you'll also be able to explain why you made the choices you did, and you'll deliver that presentation smoothly and with confidence.

If you are planning a presentation for remote delivery (for example, posting it on a Web site or setting up a kiosk at a trade show), you'll find lots of help for these situations too. In fact, an entire section of the book is devoted to various nontraditional presentation methods, such as live Internet or network delivery, trade show booths, and interactive presentation distribution on a disk or CD.

How This Book Is Organized

This book is organized into parts, which are groups of chapters that deal with a common general theme. Here's what you'll find:

- **Part I: Building Your Presentation.** In this part, you start building a robust, content-rich presentation by choosing a template, entering your text, and applying text formatting, both manually and via PowerPoint 2007's new Themes feature.

- **Part II: Using Graphics and Multimedia Content.** This part teaches you how to import and create various types of graphical and multimedia content including clip art, diagrams, photos, charts, sound effects, movies, and music. You'll also learn here how to create movement with animation effects and transitions.

- **Part III: Interfacing with Your Audience.** This part helps you prepare your presentation for various delivery scenarios, including printing handouts for a live audience, running a live show on a computer screen, designing visual aids for user-interactive or self-running presentation, and sharing a collaborating with others.

- **Part IV: Project Labs.** This part provides four step-by-step walkthroughs that demonstrate how to create some of the most powerful and sought-after PowerPoint effects and projects, including creating navigation systems, classroom games, complex animations, and graphically presented text.

- **Appendixes.** At the end of the book you'll find information about customizing PowerPoint and checking out the new features in PowerPoint 2007.

What's on the companion CD-ROM

The CD-ROM included with PowerPoint 2007 Bible contains more than 500 PowerPoint templates and backgrounds that you can use to design your own PowerPoint presentations. If you aren't familiar with how to choose a background or template for your presentation, be sure to read Chapter 3 in this book which discusses templates and Chapter 5 which includes the backgrounds discussion before attempting to use the CD-ROM. Please see Appendix C for more information on the professional designers who supplied the templates for your use. The CD-ROM also contains author files for use in the Project Labs in Part IV.

Special Features

Every chapter in this book opens with a quick look at what's in the chapter and closes with a summary. Along the way, you also find icons in the margins to draw your attention to specific topics and items of interest.

Here's what the icons mean:

 These icons point you to chapters or other sources for more information on the topic under discussion.

 Notes provide extra information about a topic, perhaps some technical tidbit or background explanation.

Expert Tips offer ideas for the advanced user who wants to get the most out of PowerPoint.

Cautions point out how to avoid the pitfalls that beginners commonly encounter.

Good luck with PowerPoint 2003! I hope you have as much fun reading this book as I had writing it. If you would like to let me know what you thought of the book, good or bad, you can e-mail me at faithe@wempen.com. I'd like to hear from you!

Acknowledgments

Some books zoom through a software program so fast it makes your head spin. You'll come out dizzy, but basically able to cobble together some sort of result, even if it doesn't look quite right. This is not one of those books.

The *Microsoft PowerPoint 2007 Bible* is probably the only PowerPoint book you will ever need. In fact, it might even be the only book on giving presentations you'll ever need. No, seriously! I mean it.

As you probably guessed by the heft of the book, this is not a quick-fix shortcut to PowerPoint expertise. Instead, it's a thoughtful, thorough educational tool that can be your personal trainer now and your reference text for years to come. That's because this book covers PowerPoint from "cradle to grave." No matter what your current expertise level with PowerPoint, this book brings you up to the level of the most experienced and talented PowerPoint users in your office. You might even be able to teach those old pros a thing or two!

But this book doesn't stop with PowerPoint procedures. Creating a good presentation is much more than just clicking a few dialog boxes and typing some text. It requires knowledge and planning—lots of it. That's why this book includes a whole chapter on planning a presentation, and another whole chapter on the practical issues involved in presenting one. You learn things like the following:

- How to select the best color schemes for selling and informing
- How to gauge the size of the audience and the meeting room when selecting fonts
- How to arrange the tables and chairs in the meeting room to encourage (or discourage) audience participation
- How to choose what to wear for a live presentation
- How to overcome stage fright

And lots more! When you finish this book, you will not only be able to build a presentation with PowerPoint, but you'll also be able to explain why you made the choices you did, and you'll deliver that presentation smoothly and with confidence.

If you are planning a presentation for remote delivery (for example, posting it on a Web site or setting up a kiosk at a trade show), you'll find lots of help for these situations too. In fact, an entire section of the book is devoted to various nontraditional presentation methods, such as live Internet or network delivery, trade show booths, and interactive presentation distribution on a disk or CD.

Part I

Building Your Presentation

Chapter 1

A First Look at PowerPoint

PowerPoint 2007 is a member of the Microsoft Office 2007 suite of programs. A *suite* is a group of programs designed by a single manufacturer to work well together. Like its siblings Word (the word processor), Excel (the spreadsheet), Outlook (the personal organizer and e-mail manager), and Access (the database), PowerPoint has a well-defined role. It creates materials for presentations.

A *presentation* is any kind of interaction between a speaker and audience, but it usually involves one or more of the following visual aids: 35mm slides, overhead transparencies, computer-based slides (either local or at a Web site or other network location), hard-copy handouts, and speaker notes. PowerPoint can create all of these types of visual aids, plus many other types that you learn about as we go along.

Because PowerPoint is so tightly integrated with the other Microsoft Office 2007 components, you can easily share information among them. For example, if you have created a graph in Excel, you can use that graph on a PowerPoint slide. It goes the other way, too. You can, for example, take the outline from your PowerPoint presentation and copy it into Word, where you can dress it up with Word's powerful document formatting commands. Virtually any piece of data in any Office program can be linked to any other Office program, so you never have to worry about your data being in the wrong format.

In this chapter you'll get a big-picture introduction to PowerPoint 2007, and then we'll fire up the program and poke around a bit to help you get familiar with the interface. You'll find out how to use the tabs and panes, and how to get help and updates from Microsoft.

IN THIS CHAPTER

Who uses PowerPoint and why?

What's new in PowerPoint 2007?

Learning your way around PowerPoint

Changing the view

Zooming in and out

Displaying and hiding screen elements

Working with window controls

Getting help and updates

Who Uses PowerPoint and Why?

PowerPoint is a popular tool for people who give presentations as part of their jobs, and also for their support staff. With PowerPoint, you can create visual aids that help get the message across to an audience, whatever that message may be and whatever format it may be presented in. Although the traditional kind of presentation is a live speech presented at a podium, advances in technology have made it possible to give several other kinds of presentations, and PowerPoint has kept pace nicely. The following list outlines the most common PowerPoint formats:

- **Podium:** For live presentations, PowerPoint helps the lecturer emphasize key points through the use of overhead transparencies, 35mm slides, or computer-based shows.
- **Kiosk shows:** These are self-running presentations that provide information in an unattended location. You have probably seen such presentations listing meeting times and rooms in hotel lobbies and giving sales presentations at trade show booths.
- **Internet formats:** You can use PowerPoint to create a show that you can present live over a network or the Internet with a program such as Microsoft NetMeeting, while each participant watches from his or her own computer. You can even store a self-running or interactive presentation on a Web site and make it available for the public to download and run on the PC.

When you start your first PowerPoint presentation, you may not be sure which delivery method you will use. However, it's best to decide the presentation format before you invest too much work in your materials, because the audience's needs are different for each medium.

CROSS-REF   You learn a lot more about planning your presentation in Chapter 2.

Most people associate PowerPoint with sales presentations, but PowerPoint is useful for people in many other lines of work as well. The following sections present a sampling of how real people just like you are using PowerPoint in their daily jobs.

Sales

More people use PowerPoint for selling goods and services than for any other reason. Armed with a laptop computer and a PowerPoint presentation, a salesperson can make a good impression on a client anywhere in the world. Figure 1-1 shows a slide from a sample sales presentation.

Sales possibilities with PowerPoint include the following:

- Live presentations in front of clients with the salesperson present and running the show. This is the traditional kind of sales pitch that most people are familiar with.
- Self-running presentations that flip through the slides at specified intervals so that passersby can read them or ignore them as they wish. These types of presentations are great for grabbing people's attention at trade show booths.
- User-interactive product information demos distributed on CD or disk that potential customers can view at their leisure on their own PCs. This method is very inexpensive, because you can create a single presentation and distribute it by mail to multiple customers.

FIGURE 1.1

PowerPoint offers unparalleled flexibility for presenting information to potential customers.

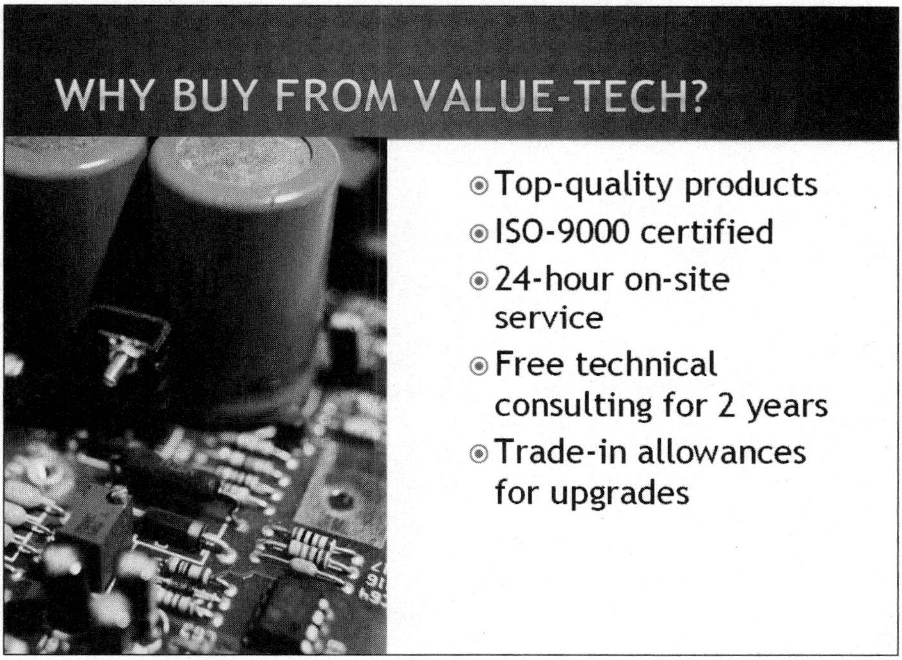

CROSS-REF See Chapter 20 to learn about controlling a live presentation. You create a self-running presentation show in Chapter 21. You learn how to create a user-interactive show in Chapter 22.

Marketing

The distinction between sales and marketing can be rather blurred at times, but marketing generally refers to the positioning of a product in the media rather than its presentation to a particular company or individual. Marketing representatives are often called upon to write advertising copy, generate camera-ready layouts for print advertisements, design marketing flyers and shelf displays, and produce other creative selling materials.

PowerPoint is not a drawing program per se, and it can't substitute for one except in a crude way. However, by combining the Office 2007 clip art collection and drawing tools with some well-chosen fonts and borders, a marketing person can come up with some very usable designs in PowerPoint. Figure 1-2 shows an example. You learn about clip art in Chapter 12.

FIGURE 1.2

PowerPoint can generate camera-ready marketing materials, although they can't substitute for the tools that professional advertising companies use.

Human Resources

Human resources personnel often find themselves giving presentations to new employees to explain the policies and benefits of the company. A well-designed, attractive presentation gives the new folks a positive impression of the company they have signed up with, starting them off on the right foot.

One of the most helpful features in PowerPoint for the human resources professional is the Organization Chart tool. With it, you can easily diagram the structure of the company and make changes whenever necessary with a few mouse clicks. Figure 1-3 shows an organization chart on a PowerPoint slide. You can also create a variety of other diagram types. Organization charts and other diagrams are covered in Chapter 11.

FIGURE 1.3

Microsoft's Organization Chart lets you easily create organizational diagrams from within PowerPoint.

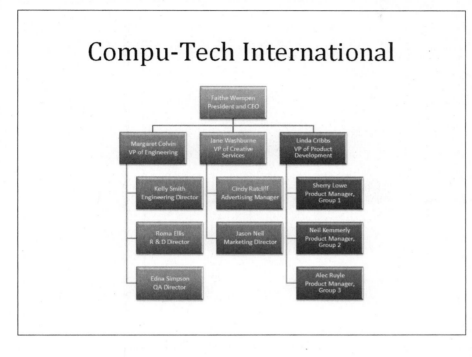

Education and Training

Most training courses include a lecture section in which the instructor outlines the general procedures and policies. This part of the training is usually followed up with individual, hands-on instruction. PowerPoint can't help much with the latter, but it can help make the lecture portion of the class go smoothly.

Using a third-party scanning program, or the Scanner and Camera Wizard in Windows, you can scan in diagrams and drawings of the objects you are teaching the students to use. You can also use computer-generated images, such as screen captures, to teach people about software.

PowerPoint's interactive controls even let you create quizzes that each student can take on-screen to gauge his or her progress. Depending on the button the student clicks, you can set up the quiz to display a "Yes, you are correct!" or "Sorry, try again" slide. See Figure 1-4. I explain this procedure in more detail in Chapter 21 and in Lab 4 in the Project Labs section at the end of the book.

FIGURE 1.4

Test the student's knowledge with a user-interactive quiz in PowerPoint.

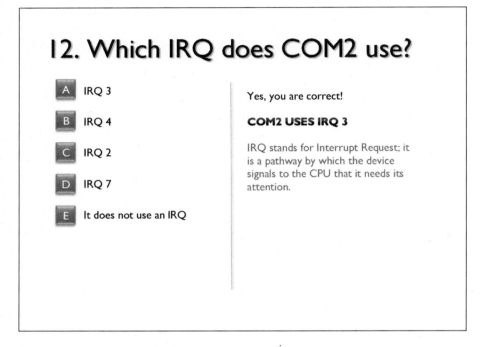

Hotel and Restaurant Management

Service organizations such as hotels and restaurants often need to inform their customers of various facts but need to do so unobtrusively so that the information will not be obvious except to those looking for it. For example, a convention center hotel might provide a list of the meetings taking place in its meeting rooms, or a restaurant might show pictures of the day's specials on a video screen in the waiting area.

In such unattended situations, a self-running (kiosk) presentation works best. Typically the computer box and keyboard are hidden from the passersby, and the monitor displays the information.

CROSS-REF You learn more about kiosk setups in Chapter 21.

Clubs and Organizations

Many nonprofit clubs and organizations, such as churches and youth centers, operate much the same way as for-profit businesses and need sales, marketing, and informational materials. But clubs and organizations often have special needs too, such as the need to recognize volunteers for a job well done. PowerPoint provides a Certificate template that's ideal for this purpose. Figure 1-5 shows a certificate generated in PowerPoint.

FIGURE 1.5

With PowerPoint, you can easily create certificates and awards.

What's New in PowerPoint 2007?

Like other programs in the Office 2007 suite, PowerPoint 2007 takes a radical and innovative new approach to its user interface. Although it's very convenient to use once you master it, even experienced users of earlier versions might need some help getting started. Here's a quick summary of the new features you'll encounter.

Tabs and the Ribbon

Instead of using a complex menu system, PowerPoint 2007 relies on a graphical *Ribbon* with multiple tabbed pages (referred to as *tabs)*. Each tab is like a toolbar, with buttons and lists you can select or open.

Tabs are not easily customizable as toolbars were in earlier versions, but the *Quick Access Toolbar* provides a home for any custom buttons or shortcuts you would like to keep readily available. You can add almost any button or command to the Quick Access Toolbar by right-clicking it and choosing Add to Quick Access Toolbar. See Figure 1-6.

FIGURE 1.6

The Ribbon and its tabbed pages of command groups enable users to select commands and apply formatting.

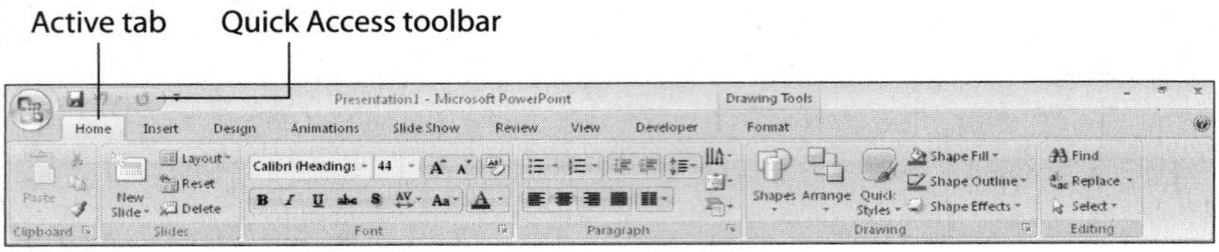

Active tab   Quick Access toolbar

Office Menu

One menu remains: the Microsoft Office menu (abbreviated in this book as *Office menu*). You can access it by clicking the Microsoft Office button (again, abbreviated in this book as *Office button*), the big round button in the top-left corner of the screen. See Figure 1-7.

FIGURE 1.7

The Office button opens a menu of commands similar to those that were on the File menu in previous versions of PowerPoint.

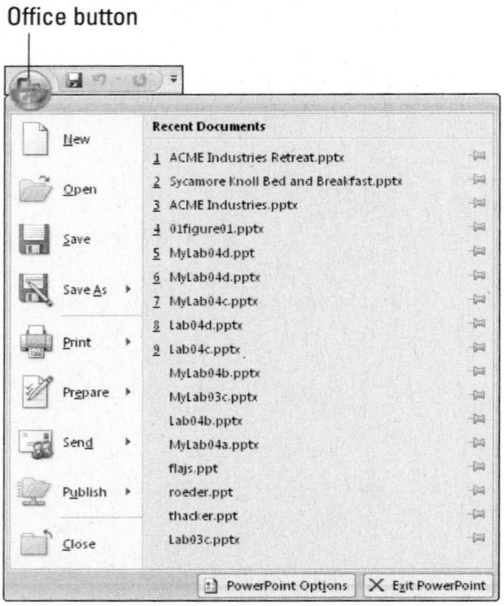

Office button

The commands on the Office menu are for working with the file itself: saving, printing, opening, closing, and so on. These commands were on the File menu in earlier PowerPoint versions (and in fact, some people actually still call the Office menu the "File menu").

Styles for Graphics and Text

If you've worked with Microsoft Word, you are probably familiar with the concept of styles. A *style* is a saved formatting specification that you can apply to multiple blocks of text in Word, to ensure consistency. For example, to ensure that all of your headings are formatted the same way, apply a Heading style to each one.

PowerPoint 2007 extends the concept of styles to cover graphic objects such as pictures, drawn lines, and shapes as well as text. For example, suppose you want each photo to have a beveled edge effect; you can simply apply a picture style that contains the desired edge type to each picture. No more manual formatting of multiple graphic objects!

Styles are found in various parts of PowerPoint, depending on the object type. For example, Figure 1-8 shows the Picture Styles section of the Format tab, available when a picture is selected. Shape Styles (for drawn lines and shapes) and WordArt Styles (for text) are also available.

FIGURE 1.8

You can apply styles to easily and consistently format graphic objects.

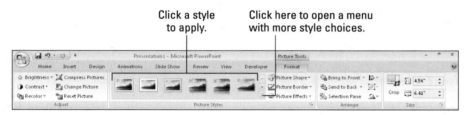

More Drawing and Photo Formatting Choices

Drawn objects (formerly called AutoShapes, now called Office Art graphics) are much improved in PowerPoint 2007. You can not only apply basic colors and fills to them, but you can add shadows, glows, surfaces, and 3-D tilt and rotation. In earlier versions, the 3-D option simply enabled you to extend perspective to create "sides" on a flat object. In PowerPoint 2007, the 3-D option now enables you to tilt the entire object. Figure 1-9 shows examples of some of the new effects.

All of the new effects for drawn objects can also be applied to the borders of other graphics, such as imported pictures. There are also some new tools for working with photos, including applying a tint to a picture and changing the shape of the photo frame.

FIGURE 1.9

Many more effects are available for drawn lines and shapes.

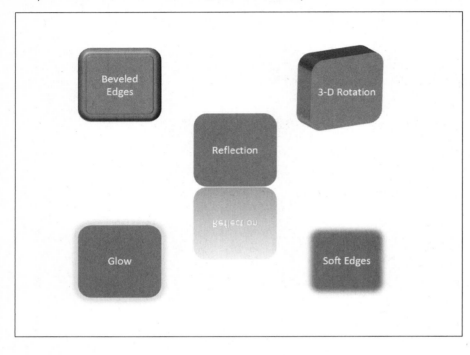

More Text Formatting Options

PowerPoint 2007 adds several new text formatting capabilities to help users further polish their work. For example, you can now control character spacing and kerning, use different underline styles and colors, and make all characters in a line equal height.

Perhaps the most significant improvement in text formatting, however, is the ability to format any text using the full range of WordArt formatting tools. WordArt (a.k.a. shaped text) has been around in Office programs for years, but there has always been a strict differentiation between regular text and WordArt. Regular text (that is, text appearing in the presentation outline) could not receive WordArt formatting such as reshaping, stretching, and distortion.

PowerPoint 2007 loses the differentiation between WordArt text and regular text, so the full gamut of formatting features is available to all text, regardless of position or usage. You can format individual words as separate pieces of WordArt, or entire text boxes by using a common WordArt style. In Figure 1-10, the slide title "Green Hill Shelties" is regular text and appears on the presentation outline, but it also benefits from WordArt formatting effects.

FIGURE 1.10

WordArt can now be applied to regular text, including slide titles.

Color, Font, and Effect Themes

Styles can automate the formatting of individual objects, but you can also apply overall themes to the entire presentation to change all of the formatting at once. A *theme* is a set of formatting specifications that are applied to objects and text consistently throughout the presentation (except in cases where an object has manual formatting applied that overrides the theme).

There are three elements to a theme: the colors, the fonts, and the effects. Colors are applied via a set of placeholders, as they were in PowerPoint 2003, but now you can apply tints or shades of a color much more easily. Whenever you open a list or menu that contains a color picker, you select from a palette like the one in Figure 1-11. The top row contains swatches for the colors in the current theme, and beneath them are various tints (lighter versions) and shades (darker versions) of the colors. By applying theme colors instead of fixed colors, you enable objects to change color automatically when you switch to a different theme.

FIGURE 1.11

Choose colors for text and graphic objects from a color picker that focuses on theme-based color choices.

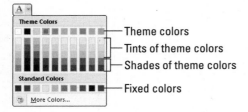

Theme colors
Tints of theme colors
Shades of theme colors
Fixed colors

Font themes apply one font for headings and another for body text. In PowerPoint 2007 it is usually best not to apply a specific font to any text, but instead to apply either (Body) or (Heading) to it. Then you can let the font theme dictate the font choices, so that they will update automatically when you chose a different theme. On the Font drop-down list, the top choices are now (Body) and (Heading), as shown in Figure 1-12. The font listed next to them is the font that happens to be applied with the current theme.

FIGURE 1.12

When you apply (Body) and (Heading) as the font choices rather than a specific font, you enable formatting via font themes.

Apply placeholders for theme fonts

Calibri	44

Theme Fonts
Calibri	(Headings)
Calibri	(Body)

All Fonts
- Agency FB
- **Aharoni** אבגד הוז
- **ALGERIAN**
- Andalus أبجد هوز
- Angsana New ชื่อ
- AngsanaUPC ชื่อ
- Arabic Typesetting أبجد هوز
- Arial
- **Arial Black**
- Arial Narrow
- **Arial Rounded MT Bold**
- Arial Unicode MS
- AvantGarde
- Baskerville Old Face
- Batang
- BatangChe
- **Bauhaus 93**

Effect themes apply shadows and 3-D effects to graphic objects. PowerPoint 2007's new gallery of effects are impressive and can make plain lines and shapes appear to pop off the screen with textures that simulate glass, metal, or other surfaces.

CROSS-REF   For more on font themes, see Chapter 5.

SmartArt

SmartArt uses groups of lines and shapes to present text information in a graphical, conceptually meaningful way. Experts have been saying for years that people respond better to information when it is presented graphically, but the difficulty in constructing attractive diagrams has meant that most people used plain bulleted lists for everything. SmartArt can convert a bulleted list into a conceptual diagram in just a few clicks.

Figure 1-13 shows a plain bulleted list (left) and a SmartArt diagram constructed from it. The SmartArt is not only more interesting to look at, but it also conveys additional information — it shows that the product life cycle repeats continuously.

FIGURE 1.13

SmartArt diagrams are easy to create and make information more palatable and easy to understand.

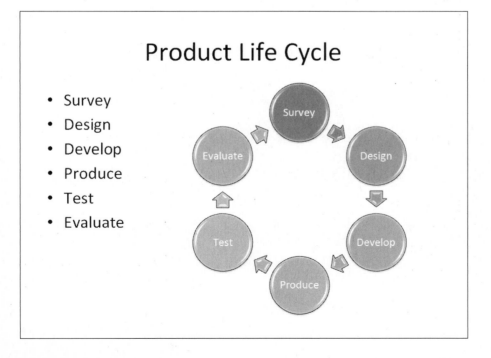

NOTE   SmartArt is similar to the Diagrams feature found in PowerPoint 2003 but is based on a new graphics engine from Microsoft called Escher 2.0. (Charts also use this same graphics engine, and share the same formatting capabilities.)

Better Charting Tools

In earlier Office versions, Excel had a great charting feature, but the other applications suffered along with an inferior tool called Microsoft Graph. PowerPoint 2007 includes a great, all-new charting tool, the same one that's in Excel 2007. Like SmartArt, it is integrated with the new Escher 2.0 graphics engine, and you can format the charts with a variety of theme effects. Figure 1-14 shows a typical chart.

FIGURE 1.14

You can construct charts more easily with better formatting and layout options in PowerPoint 2007.

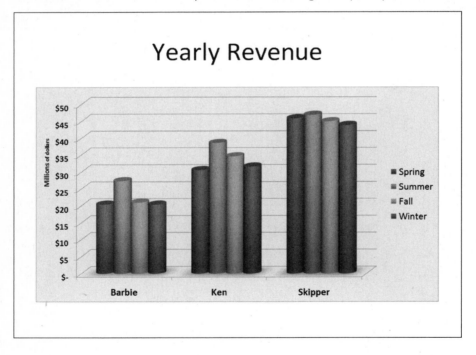

Custom Slide Layouts

In earlier versions of PowerPoint, you were stuck with the slide layouts that came with PowerPoint. In PowerPoint 2007, you can create your own slide layouts, complete with content placeholders, and apply them as easily as you can apply the built-in ones. This makes it easy to reuse complex layouts without having to resort to manually created text frames each time. Custom layouts are configured from within the expanded and improved Slide Master view.

Learning Your Way Around PowerPoint

Now that you have seen some of the potential uses for PowerPoint, and toured the new features, let's get started using the program.

PowerPoint is one of the easiest and most powerful presentation programs available. You can knock out a passable presentation in a shockingly short time by skimming through the chapters in Parts I and II of the book, or you can spend some time with PowerPoint's advanced features to make a complex presentation that looks, reads, and works exactly the way you want.

Starting and Exiting PowerPoint

You can start PowerPoint just like any other program in Windows: from the Start menu. Follow these steps:

1. Click the Start button. The Start menu opens.
2. Click All Programs.
3. Click Microsoft Office.
4. Click Microsoft Office PowerPoint 2007. The program starts.

If you have opened PowerPoint before, a shortcut to it might appear in the Recently Used Programs list, which is directly above the All Programs command on the Start menu. See Figure 1-15. If you use other applications more frequently than PowerPoint, PowerPoint may scroll off this list and you therefore have to access it via the All Programs menu.

EXPERT TIP If you don't want to worry about PowerPoint scrolling off the list of the most frequently used programs on the Start menu, right-click PowerPoint's name on the Start menu and choose Pin to Start Menu. PowerPoint will then appear on the list at the top of the left column of the Start menu. To remove it from there later, right-click it and choose Unpin from Start Menu.

FIGURE 1.15

A shortcut to PowerPoint might appear on the top level of the Start menu.

PowerPoint shortcut

When you are ready to leave PowerPoint, select Office ➪ Exit or click the Close (X) button in the top-right corner of the PowerPoint window. (The Office button is the round button in the top left corner.) If you have any unsaved work, PowerPoint asks if you want to save your changes. Because you have just been playing around in this chapter, you probably do not have anything to save yet. (If you do have something to save, see Chapter 3 to learn more about saving.) Otherwise, click No to decline to save your changes, and you're outta there.

Understanding the Screen Elements

PowerPoint's interface is typical of any Windows program in many ways, but as you learned earlier in the chapter it also has some special Office 2007 specific features as well. The PowerPoint window contains these elements, pointed out in Figure 1-16:

- **Title bar:** Identifies the program running (PowerPoint) and the name of the active presentation. If the window is not maximized, you can move the window by dragging the title bar.

- **Ribbon:** Functions as a combination of menu bar and toolbar, offering tabbed "pages" of buttons, lists, and commands.

- **Office button:** Opens the Office menu, from which you can open, save, print, and start new presentations.

- **Quick Access Toolbar:** Contains shortcuts for some of the most common commands. You can add your own favorites here as well.

- **Minimize button:** Shrinks the application window to a bar on the taskbar; you click its button on the taskbar to reopen it.

- **Maximize/Restore button:** If the window is maximized (full screen), changes it to windowed (not full screen). If the window is not maximized, clicking here maximizes it.

- **Close button:** Closes the application. You may be prompted to save your changes, if you made any.

- **Work area:** Where active PowerPoint slide(s) appear. Figure 1-17 shows it in Normal view, but other views are available that make the work area appear differently.

CROSS-REF See the section "Changing the View" later in this chapter for details.

- **Status bar:** Reports information about the presentation and provides shortcuts for changing the view and the zoom.

NOTE I don't dwell on the Windows controls in detail because this isn't a Windows book, but if you're interested in learning more about Windows-based programs in general, pick up *Windows Vista For Dummies* or *The Windows Vista Bible*, also published by Wiley.

Working with the Ribbon

As mentioned earlier in the chapter, PowerPoint 2007's user interface is based on the Ribbon, which is a bar across the top of the window that contains tabbed pages of commands and buttons. Rather than opening a menu and selecting a command, you click a tab and then click a button or open a list on that tab.

FIGURE 1.16

The PowerPoint window is a combination of usual Windows features and unique Office 2007 elements.

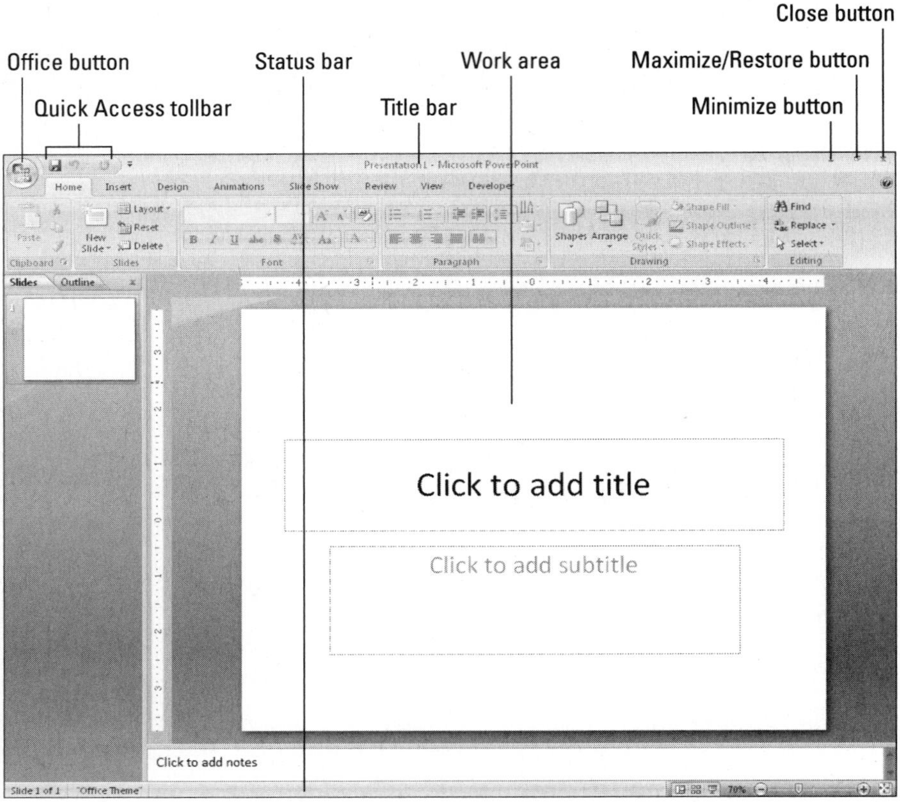

Here are some important terms you need to know when working with tabs:

- **Ribbon**: The whole bar, including all of the tabs.

- **Office button**: A button that opens an Office menu, from which you can choose to start a new presentation, save, print, and perform other file-related activities. See Figure 1-7 for this button's location.

- **Quick Access Toolbar**: A small toolbar adjacent to the Office button from which you can select commonly used commands.

EXPERT TIP To add a command to the Quick Access Toolbar, right-click it and choose Add to Quick Access Toolbar. To remove the command from there, right-click it and choose Remove from Quick Access Toolbar.

- **Tab**: A tabbed page of the Ribbon. Figure 1-17 shows the Home tab, for example.

- **Contextual tab**: A tab that appears only when certain content is selected, such as a graphic or a chart. The context name appears above the tab name. In Figure 1-17, Drawing Tools is the context name for the Format tab.

- **Group**: A section of a tab. The Home tab shown in Figure 1-17 has the following groups: Clipboard, Slides, Font, Paragraph, WordArt Styles, and Editing.

- **Dialog box launcher**: A small icon in the bottom-right corner of a group, from which you can open a dialog box related to that group.

NOTE To find out what a toolbar button does, point the mouse at it. A ScreenTip pops up explaining it.

FIGURE 1.17

The Ribbon is PowerPoint 2007's primary user interface.

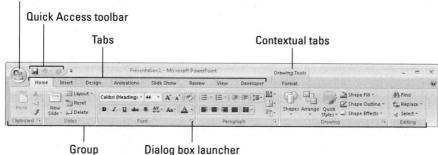

Office button

Quick Access toolbar

Tabs

Contextual tabs

Group   Dialog box launcher

Working with Collapsible Tab Groups

Within a tab, groups can expand or collapse depending on the width of the PowerPoint window. When the window is large enough (somewhere around 1100 pixels), everything within each group is fully expanded, so that each item has its own button. When the window is smaller, groups start collapsing so that all groups remain visible. At first, large buttons get smaller and stack vertically; if that's not enough, then groups collapse into single large buttons with drop-down lists from which you can select the individual commands. Figure 1-18 shows the same tab in three different widths for comparison.

CAUTION Because of the Ribbon's collapsing ability, the exact steps for performing certain procedures depend on the active PowerPoint window's width. A small window may require an extra step of opening a button's menu to select a command, for example. For a large window, each command appears directly on the tab. This book assumes an average window size of 1024 x 768 pixels; if you run PowerPoint at a smaller resolution, you may occasionally have an extra step to access a command.

FIGURE 1.18

The size of the PowerPoint window determines how much the groups are collapsed or expanded on the Ribbon.

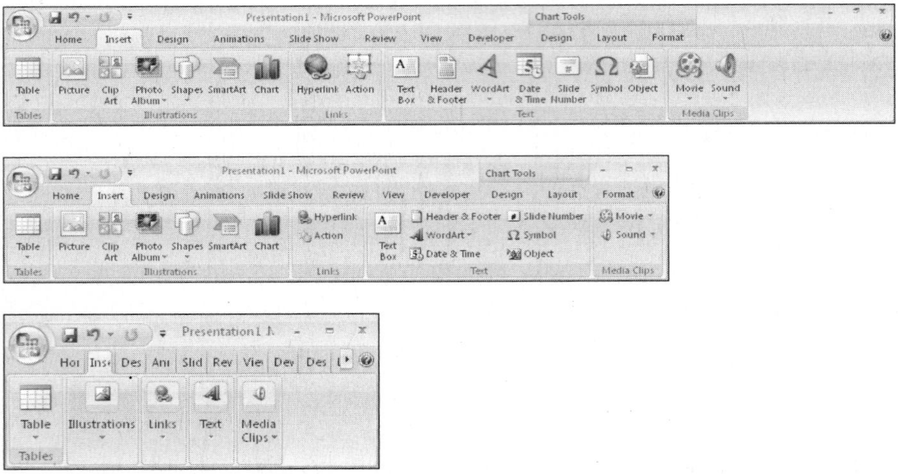

Working with Office Menu Submenus

On the Office menu, some of the commands have arrows next to them. Clicking one of these arrows opens a submenu in the right side of the Office menu with additional choices. For example, Figure 1-19 shows the submenu for Print.

Notice in Figure 1-19 that the arrow next to the Print command on the Office menu is actually a separate button from Print itself. The Print command can also be individually clicked to open the Print dialog box, without opening the submenu. The Save As command has the same functionality; you can either select Save As directly from the first level, or you can open its submenu.

Not all of the arrows are like that, though. The Finish, Send, and Publish commands do not have separate top-level functions; clicking any of those simply opens their submenu.

Working with Dialog Boxes

Dialog boxes are PowerPoint's (and Windows') way of prompting you for more information. When you issue a command that can have many possible variations, a dialog box appears so you can specify the particulars.

FIGURE 1.19

Some of the commands on the Office menu have submenus.

The Print dialog box (File ⇨ Print) is an excellent example of a dialog box because it has so many kinds of controls. Here are some of the controls you see on the Print dialog box shown in Figure 1-20:

- **Check box:** These are individual on/off switches for particular features. Click to toggle them on or off.

- **Option buttons:** Each section of the dialog box can have only one option button chosen at once. When you select one, the previously selected one becomes deselected, like on a car radio. Click the one you want.

- **Text box:** Click in a text box to place an insertion point (a vertical line) there, and then type.

- **Increment buttons:** Placed next to a text box, these buttons allow you to increment the number in the box up or down by one digit per click.

- **Drop-down list:** Click the down arrow next to one of these to open the list, and then click your selection from the menu that appears.

- **Command button:** Click one of these big rectangular buttons to jump to a different dialog box. OK and Cancel are also command buttons; OK accepts your changes and Cancel rejects them.

FIGURE 1.20

The Print dialog box is an excellent study in dialog box controls.

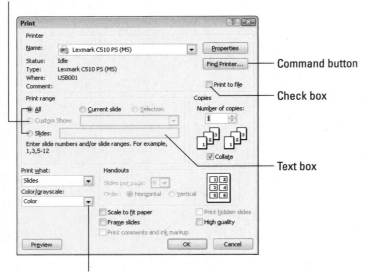

Option buttons

Command button

Check box

Text box

Drop-down list

You might also sometimes see tabs at the top of a dialog box; this occurs when the dialog box has more controls than will fit on one screen. To move to a tabbed page, click the tab.

CROSS-REF Dialog boxes that open or save files have some special controls and icons all their own, but you learn about those in more detail in Chapter 3, where you also learn to open and save your files.

Changing the View

A *view* is a way of displaying your presentation on-screen. PowerPoint comes with several views because at different times during the creation process, it is helpful to look at the presentation in different ways. For example, when you add a graphic to a slide, you need to work closely with that slide, but when you rearrange the slide order, you need to see the presentation as a whole.

PowerPoint offers the following views:

- **Normal:** A combination of several resizable panes, so you can see the presentation in multiple ways at once. Normal is the default view.

- **Slide Sorter:** A light-table-type overhead view of all the slides in your presentation, laid out in rows, suitable for big-picture rearranging.

- **Notes Page:** A view with the slide at the top of the page and a text box below it for typed notes. (You can print these notes pages to use during your speech.)

- **Slide Show:** The view you use to show the presentation on-screen. Each slide fills the entire screen in its turn.

CROSS-REF This chapter covers only the four regular views. The Master views are discussed in Chapter 5.

There are two ways to change a view: click a button on the View tab, or click one of the view buttons in the bottom-right corner of the screen. See Figure 1-21. All of the views are available in both places except Notes Page, which you can access only from the View tab.

FIGURE 1.21

Select a view from the View tab or from the viewing controls in the bottom-right corner of the screen.

View buttons

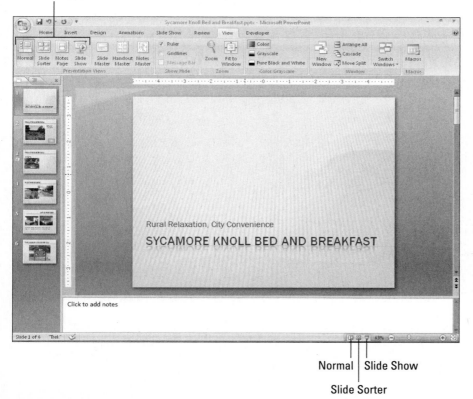

Normal | Slide Show

Slide Sorter

EXPERT TIP When you save, close, and reopen a file, PowerPoint opens the same view in which you left the file. To have the files always open in a particular view, choose Office ⇨ PowerPoint Options ⇨ Advanced, and open the Open All Documents Using This View list and select the desired view. The options on this list include some custom versions of Normal view that have certain panes turned off. For example, you can open all documents in Normal – Outline and Slide view to always start with the Notes pane turned off.

Normal View

Normal view, shown in Figure 1-22, is a very flexible view that contains a little of everything. In the center is the active slide, below it is a Notes pane, and to its left is a dual-use pane with two tabs: Outline and Slides. (Figure 1-21 shows Slides, and Figure 1-22 shows Outline.) When the Outline tab is selected, the text from the slides appears in an outline form. When the Slides tab is selected, thumbnail images of all the slides appear (somewhat like Slide Sorter view, which you will see later in this chapter).

FIGURE 1.22

Normal view, the default, offers access to the outline, the slide, and the notes all at once.

Slides/Outline pane   Slides pane

RELAX AT SYCAMORE KNOLL!

Looking for that special getaway for the weekend?

More Information

Make sure to tell the audience that this photo was taken on the grounds of Sycamore Knoll and shows how the gardens typically look in June or July.

Notes pane

Each of the panes in Normal view has its own scroll bar, so you can move around in the outline, the slide, and the notes independently of the other panes. You can resize the panes by dragging the dividers between the panes. For example, to give the notes area more room, point the mouse pointer at the divider line between it and the slide area so that the mouse pointer becomes a double-headed arrow, and then hold down the left mouse button as you drag the line up to a new spot.

The Slides/Outline pane is useful because it lets you jump quickly to a specific slide by clicking on it. For example, in Figure 1-21 you can click on any of the slide thumbnails on the Slides tab to display it in the Slide pane. Or in Figure 1-22 you can click some text anywhere in the outline to jump to the slide containing that text.

EXPERT TIP   In earlier versions of PowerPoint, an Outlining toolbar was available when working with the Outline tab. In PowerPoint 2007, you can right-click anywhere in the outline to access some of those same tools on a context menu.

You can turn the Slides/Outline pane off completely by clicking the X button in its top-right corner. This gives maximum room to the Slides pane. When you turn it off, the Notes pane disappears too; they cannot be turned on/off separately. To get the extra panes back, reapply Normal view.

Slide Sorter View

If you have ever worked with 35mm slides, you know that it can be helpful to lay the slides out on a big table and plan the order in which to show them. You rearrange them, moving this one here, that one there, until the order is perfect. You might even start a pile of backups that you will not show in the main presentation, but will hold back in case someone asks a pertinent question. That's exactly what you can do with Slide Sorter view, shown in Figure 1-23. It lays out the slides in miniature, so you can see the big picture. You can drag the slides around and place them in the perfect order. You can also return to Normal view to work on a slide by double-clicking the slide.

Slide Show View

When it's time to rehearse the presentation, nothing shows you the finished product quite as clearly as Slide Show view does. In Slide Show view, the slide fills the entire screen. You can move from slide to slide by pressing the Page Up or Page Down keys, or by using one of the other movement methods available.

CROSS-REF   You learn about these other movement methods in Chapter 20.

You can right-click in Slide Show view to display a menu that enables you to control the show without leaving it. To leave the slide show, choose End Show from the menu or just press the Esc key.

EXPERT TIP   When entering Slide Show view, the method you use determines which slide you start on. If you use the Slide Show View button in the bottom-right corner of the screen, the presentation will start with whatever slide you have selected. (You can also press Shift+F5 to do this, or choose Slide Show ➪ From Current Slide.) If you use the View ➪ Slide Show or Slide Show ➪ From Beginning command, or press F5, the presentation will start at the beginning.

FIGURE 1.23

Use Slide Sorter view for a birds-eye view of the presentation.

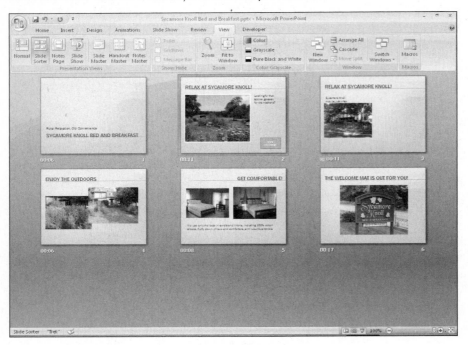

FIGURE 1.24

Slide Show view lets you practice the presentation in real life.

Previous slide or animation

Open slide navigation menu

Next slide or animation

Open pointer control menu

Notes Page View

When you give a presentation, your props usually include more than just your brain and your slides. You typically have all kinds of notes and backup material for each slide — figures on last quarter's sales, sources to cite if someone questions your data, and so on. In the old days of framed overhead transparencies, people used to attach sticky notes to the slide frames for this purpose and hope that nobody asked any questions that required diving into the four-inch-thick stack of statistics they brought.

Today, you can type your notes and supporting facts directly in PowerPoint. As you saw earlier, you can type them directly into the Notes pane below the slide in Normal view. However, if you have a lot of notes to type, you might find it easier to work with Notes Page view instead.

Notes Page view is accessible only from the View tab. In this view, you see a single slide (uneditable) with a text area, called the *notes placeholder*, below it for your notes. See Figure 1-25. You can refer to these notes as you give an on-screen presentation, or you can print notes pages to stack neatly on the lectern next to you during the big event. If you have trouble seeing the text you're typing, zoom in on it, as described in the next section.

FIGURE 1.25

Notes Page view offers a special text area for your notes, separate from the slides.

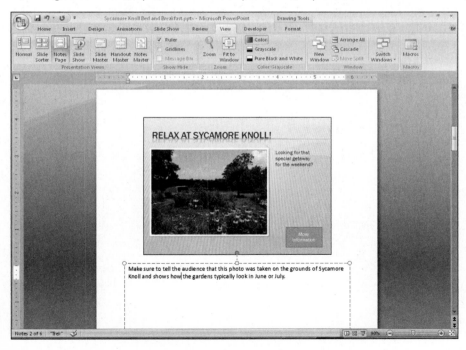

Zooming In and Out

If you need a closer look at your presentation, you can zoom the view in or out to accommodate almost any situation. For example, if you have trouble placing a graphic exactly at the same vertical level as some text in a box next to it, you can zoom in for more precision. You can view your work at various magnifications on-screen without changing the size of the surrounding tools or the size of the print on the printout.

In Normal view, each of the panes has its own individual zoom. To set the zoom for the Slides/Outline pane only, for example, select it first; then choose a zoom level. Or to zoom only in the Slide pane, click it first. In a single-pane view like Notes Page or Slide Sorter, a single zoom setting affects the entire work area.

The larger the zoom number, the larger the details on the display. A zoom of 10% would make a slide so tiny that you couldn't read it. A zoom of 400% would make a few letters on a slide so big they would fill the entire pane.

The easiest way to set the zoom level is to drag the Zoom slider in the bottom-right corner of the PowerPoint window, or click its plus or minus buttons in increment the zoom level. See Figure 1-26.

To resize the current slide so that it is as large as possible while still fitting completely in the Slides pane, click the Fit Slide to Current Window button, or click the Fit to Window button in the Zoom group on the View tab.

FIGURE 1.26

Zoom in or out to see more or less of the slide(s) at once.

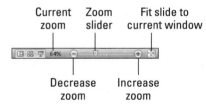

Another way to control the zoom is with the Zoom dialog box. On the View tab, in the Zoom group, click the Zoom button. (You can also open that dialog box by clicking the % next to the Zoom slider.) Make your selection, as shown in Figure 1-27, by clicking the appropriate button, and then click OK. Notice that you can type a precise zoom percentage in the Percent text box. You can specify any percentage you like, but some panes and views will not go higher than 100%.

FIGURE 1.27

You can zoom with this Zoom dialog box rather than the slider if you prefer.

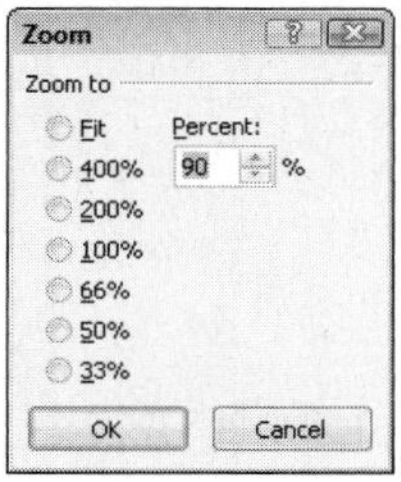

Enabling Optional Display Elements

PowerPoint has a lot of optional screen elements that you may (or may not) find useful, depending on what you're up to at the moment. The following sections describe them.

Ruler

Vertical and horizontal rulers around the slide pane can help you place objects more precisely. To toggle them on or off, mark or clear the Ruler check box on the View tab. Rulers are available only in Normal and Notes Page views.

The rulers help with positioning no matter what content type you are working with, but when you are editing text in a text frame they have an additional purpose as well. The horizontal ruler shows the frame's paragraph indents and any custom tab stops, and you can drag the indent markers on the ruler just like you can in Word.

NOTE The ruler's unit of measure is controlled from the Regional Settings in the Control Panel in Windows.

EXPERT TIP The vertical ruler is optional. To disable it while retaining the horizontal ruler, choose Office ➪ PowerPoint Options, click Advanced, and in the Display section, clear the Show Vertical Ruler check box.

Gridlines

Gridlines are non-printing dotted lines at regularly spaced intervals that can help you line up objects on a slide. Figure 1-28 shows gridlines (and the ruler) enabled.

To turn gridlines on or off, use any of these methods:

- Press Shift+F9.
- On the View tab, in the Show/Hide group, mark or clear the Gridlines check box.
- On the Design tab, in the Arrange group, choose Align ➪ Show Gridlines.

FIGURE 1.28

Gridlines and the ruler help align objects on a slide.

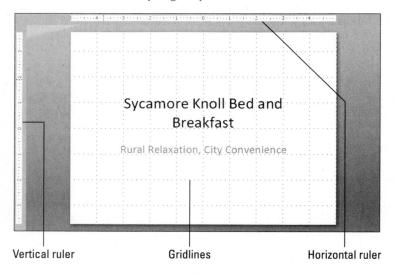

Vertical ruler   Gridlines   Horizontal ruler

There are many options you can set for the gridlines, including whether objects snap to it, whether the grid is visible, and what the spacing should be between the gridlines. To set grid options, follow these steps:

1. On the Home tab, in the Drawing group, choose Arrange ➪ Align ➪ Grid Settings, or right-click the slide background and choose Grid and Guides. The Grid and Guides dialog box opens (see Figure 1-29).

2. In the Snap To section, mark or clear these check boxes:

   - Snap Objects to Grid: Specifies whether or not objects will shift automatically align with the grid.

   - Snap Object to Other Objects: Specifies whether or not objects will automatically align with other objects.

3. In the Grid Settings section, enter the amount of space between gridlines desired.

4. Mark or clear the Display Grid On Screen check box to display or hide the grid. (Note that you can make objects snap to the grid without the grid being displayed.)

5. Click OK.

FIGURE 1.29

Set grid options and spacing.

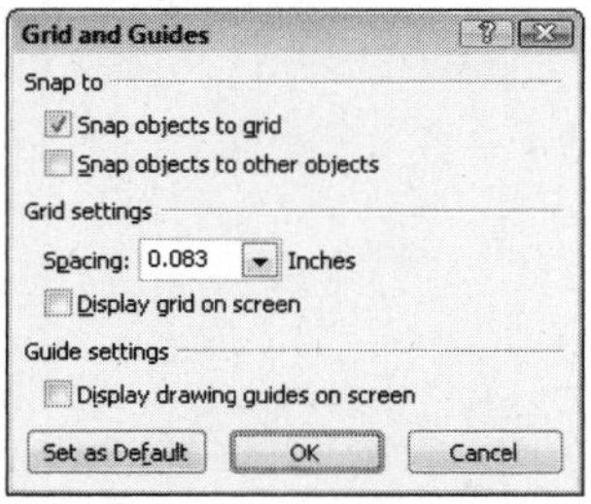

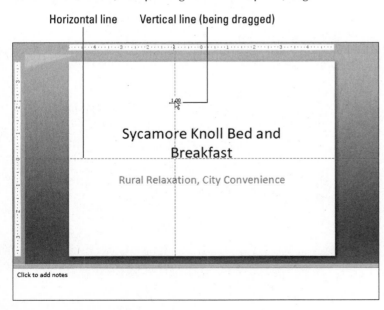

Guides

Guides are like gridlines except they are individual lines, rather than a grid of lines, and you can drag them to different positions on the slide. As you drag a guide, a numeric indicator appears to let you know the ruler position. See Figure 1-30. Use the Grid and Guides dialog box shown in Figure 1-29 to turn guides on/off, or press Alt+F9.

FIGURE 1.30

Guides are movable, non-printing lines that help with alignment.

You can create additional sets of guide lines by holding down the Ctrl key while dragging a guide (to copy it). You can have up to eight horizontal and vertical guides, all at positions you specify.

Color/Grayscale/Pure Black and White Views

Most of the time you will work with your presentation in color. However, if you plan to print the presentation in black and white or grayscale (for example, on overhead transparencies or black-and-white handouts), you should check to see what it will look like without color.

EXPERT TIP This Color/Grayscale/Pure Black and White option is especially useful when you are preparing slides that will eventually be faxed, because a fax is pure black and white in most cases. Something that looks great on a color screen could look like a shapeless blob on a black-and-white fax. It doesn't hurt to check.

Click the Grayscale or the Pure Black and White button on the View tab to switch to one of those views. When you do so, a Grayscale or Black and White tab becomes available, as shown in Figure 1-31. From its Setting group, you can fine-tune the grayscale or black-and-white preview. Choose one that shows the object to best advantage; PowerPoint will remember that setting when printing or outputting the presentation to a grayscale or black-and-white source.

FIGURE 1.31

Select a grayscale or a black-and-white preview type.

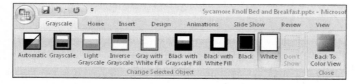

When you are finished, click the Back to Color View button on the Grayscale tab. Changing the Black and White or Grayscale settings doesn't affect the colors on the slides; it only affects how the slides will look and print in black and white or grayscale.

Opening a New Display Window

Have you ever wished you could be in two places at once? Well, in PowerPoint, you actually can. PowerPoint provides a way to view two spots in the presentation at the same time by opening a new window.

To display a new window, display the View tab and click New Window in the Window group. Then use Arrange All or Cascade to view both windows at once.

You can use any view with any window, so you can have two slides in Normal view at once, or Slide Sorter and Notes Pages view, or any other combination. Both windows contain the same presentation, so any changes you make in one window are reflected in the other window.

Arranging Windows

When you have two or more windows open, whether they are for the same presentation or different ones, you need to arrange them for optimal viewing. You saw earlier in this chapter how to resize a window, but did you know that PowerPoint can do some of the arranging for you?

When you want to arrange the open windows, do one of the following:

- **Tile**: On the View tab, click Arrange All to tile the open windows so there is no overlap.
- **Cascade**: On the View tab, click Cascade to arrange the open windows so the title bars cascade from upper-left to lower-right on the screen. Click a title bar to activate a window.

These commands do not apply to minimized windows. If you want to include a window in the arrangement, make sure you restore it from its minimized state first.

Switching among Windows

If you have than one window open and can see at least a corner of the window you want, click it to bring it to the front. If you have one of the windows maximized, on the other hand, or if another window is obscuring the one you want, click Switch Windows (on the View tab) and select the window you want to view.

Using the Help System

The PowerPoint Help system is like a huge instruction book in electronic format. You can look up almost any PowerPoint task you can imagine and get step-by-step instructions for performing it.

To open the PowerPoint Help window, press F1 or click the Help icon (the question mark) in the upper-right corner of the PowerPoint window. See Figure 1-32.

To look up information in the Help system, you can:

- Click one of the topics on the default Browse PowerPoint 2007 Help page shown in Figure 1-32, and then keep clicking subtopics to narrow down the search until you arrive at what you want.
- Type a keyword or phrase in the Search box, and then click Search or press Enter to find all help articles that contain it.

FIGURE 1.32

Get help with PowerPoint via the PowerPoint Help window.

Browse help by topic

Type a word search or phrase here

Click here to open the PowerPoint Help window

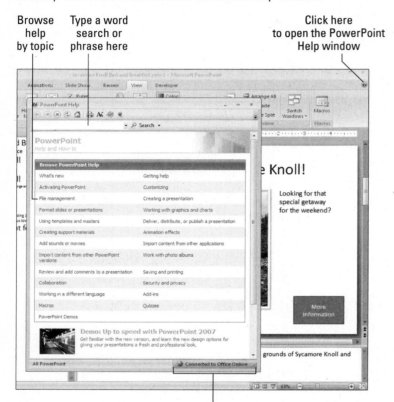

This shows the connection status indicator

EXPERT TIP Much of the Office 2007 Help system relies on an Internet connection. By default, Office 2007 applications automatically connect to Microsoft's servers online to gather additional Help information. If you have a slow Internet connection, and find that searches are slow, try disabling online Help so that PowerPoint just uses the Help files installed on your PC. To do this, from the PowerPoint Help window, click the connection status indicator (see Figure 1-32), and from the menu that appears, choose Show Content Only From This Computer.

When you browse or search the Help system, a list of articles matching the topic or search term appears. Click an article to read it. Figure 1-33 shows an article on saving files, for example.

FIGURE 1.33

A typical article in the Help system contains some background information and step-by-step instructions.

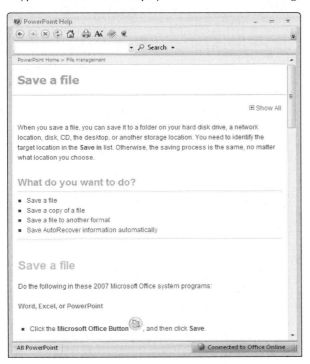

The PowerPoint Help window's toolbar contains the buttons shown in Table 1-1.

TABLE 1-1

Help Toolbar Buttons

Button(s)	Name	Description
← , →	Back and Forward	These are just like in Internet Explorer; Back goes back to a previously viewed topic and Forward goes forward again afterward.
✖	Stop	Stops Web content from loading. Useful if it is loading very slowly and you want to give up.
↻	Refresh	Reloads content from the Web.

continued

Button(s)	Name	Description
TABLE 1.1 (continued)		
	Home	Returns to the default list of topics (Figure 1-32).
	Print	Prints the currently displayed article.
	Change Font Size	Opens a menu from which you can select the size of the text that appears in the Help system. This setting also affects text in Internet Explorer.
	Show Table of Contents	Toggles an extra pane to the left of the main Help window that contains the top-level list of topics.
	Keep on Top	Keeps the Help window on top of all other windows.

Using PowerPoint Support Resources

Microsoft provides a variety of support tools for PowerPoint in addition to the Help system. You can diagnose problems with your PowerPoint installation, for example, download update, register your copy of PowerPoint, and more.

To access these tools, follow these steps:

1. Click the Office button, and then click PowerPoint Options.
2. Click Resources. A list of resource topics appears, as in Figure 1-34.
3. Click the button for the type of help you need. Each of these options is described in Table 1-2.

TABLE 1-2

PowerPoint Resources

Resource	Description
Get Updates	Connects to the Office Web site, runs a utility that evaluates the dates on your current Office files, and downloads and installs updates if available.
Office Diagnostics	Runs a utility that checks Office files and reinstalls any that have become corrupted or changed.
Contact Us	Opens a Web page listing contact information for Microsoft.
Activate Microsoft Office	Opens a utility that activates your copy of PowerPoint. (See the following section for details.)

Resource	Description
Register for Online Services	Opens a window that enables you to send your contact information to Microsoft and receive free online services in return
About Microsoft Office PowerPoint 2007	Provides version information for your copy of PowerPoint.

FIGURE 1.34

Support tools for PowerPoint appear in the Resources section of the PowerPoint Options dialog box.

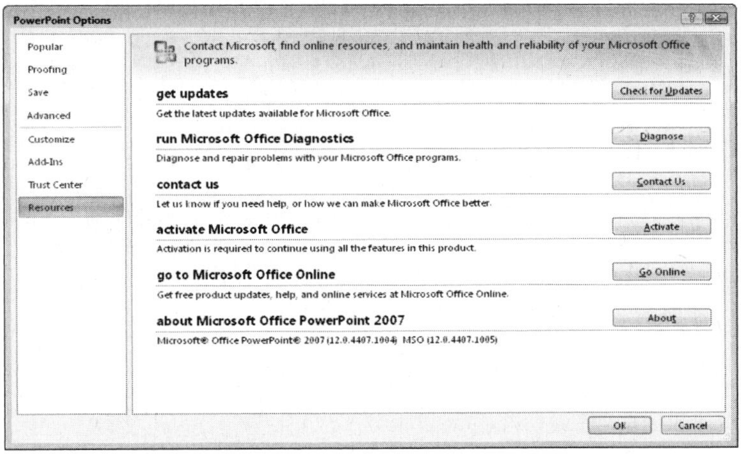

Understanding Product Activation

All Office 2007 products must be activated after a certain number of days or a certain number of uses. This is a simple matter if you have an Internet connection. Every time you start an Office 2007 application, a reminder to activate appears. Follow the prompts to activate it. You do not have to give any personal information.

So what is this activation, and why is it required? Activation locks your copy of Office (or PowerPoint, if you bought it separately) to the hardware configuration in your computer, so that it can't be installed on any other PC.

The activation utility surveys a sampling of your PC's hardware (around a dozen different components), and based on their models, serial numbers, and so on, it comes up with a number. Then it combines that number mathematically with the 24-digit installation key code you entered when you installed the software, to produce a unique number that represents that particular copy of Office combined with that particular PC. It then sends that number off to an activation database at Microsoft, along with the original installation key code.

So how does this prevent illegal software copying? Two ways. One is that the installation key code is locked to that hardware ID, so that if you install the same copy on a different PC, it can't be activated there. (This is not the case for some corporate and volume-licensed copies.) The other is that it prevents you from radically changing the hardware in the PC without contacting Microsoft for reactivation authorization. For example, you could not take the hard disk out of the PC and put it in another PC without reactivating Office.

It is this second point that has been an issue of conflict between Microsoft and users, because many users like to tinker with their hardware and they do not want to have to contact Microsoft every time they make hardware changes. According to Microsoft documentation, the change of one or two pieces of hardware will not trigger the need for reactivation, but your experience may differ.

There are two situations in which you might not have to activate:

- When you buy a new PC with Office preinstalled. Office will already have been activated, so you do not have to go through the process.

- If you work for a company or attend a school that has a licensing agreement with Microsoft for a certain number of copies. You might have a version of Office that does not contain the activation requirement.

When you go through the activation process, you are also asked whether you want to register your copy of the software. Activation by itself sends no identifying information about you or your PC to Microsoft; if you want to be on the Microsoft mailing list for update information, you must go through the additional process of registration.

Adjusting Privacy Settings

In some situations, it is advantageous for your copy of PowerPoint to communicate with Microsoft over the Internet. For example, when you use the Help system, you get better results if you are connected, and when inserting clip art, you have more images to choose from if you are connected.

It's a two-way street: your copy of PowerPoint can also help Microsoft by sending information to the company about your usage habits. For example, when Microsoft is developing a new version of PowerPoint, they look at usage data to determine which features of the program people are using the most and the least. This program for gathering user data is the Customer Experience Improvement Program, and participation in it is optional.

To control whether — and how — your copy of PowerPoint interacts online with Microsoft, follow these steps to configure Privacy Options:

1. Choose Office ➪ PowerPoint Options.
2. Click Trust Center, and then click the Trust Center Settings button. The Trust Center dialog box opens.

3. Click Privacy Options, and then mark or clear any of the check boxes in the Privacy Options section. See Figure 1-35. To get information about each of the options, point to the "i" symbol to its right.

4. Click OK, and then OK again to close all open dialog boxes.

FIGURE 1.35

Choose how your copy of PowerPoint will interact with Microsoft via the Internet.

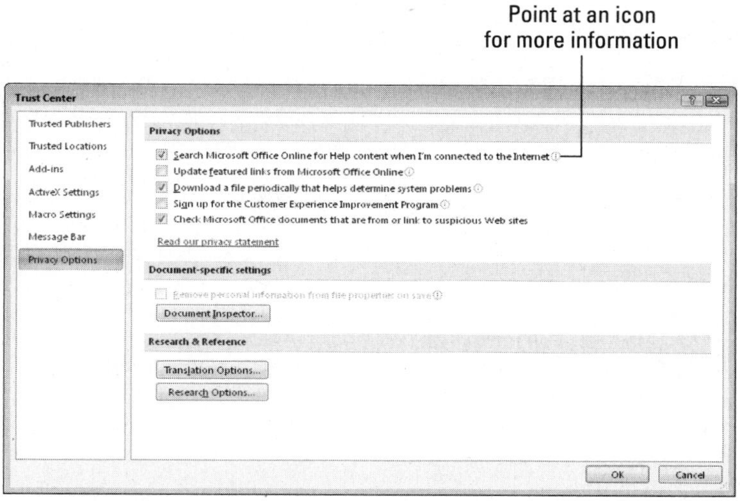

Point at an icon
for more information

Summary

This chapter provided an introduction to PowerPoint. You learned about PowerPoint 2007's new features, how to navigate the new user interface, how to control the view of the PowerPoint window, and how to get help and support. In the next chapter, you'll learn about the "soft skills" involved in planning and executing a successful presentation.

Chapter 2

What Makes a Great Presentation?

*W**ow! What a great presentation!** That's what you want your audience to come away thinking, right?

Most people won't be nit-picky enough to pinpoint exactly what they loved about the experience. Nobody is likely to say, "Weren't the colors in that pie chart on slide 43 artfully chosen?" or "Did you see his tie? I wonder where I can buy one just like it." Instead, you'll leave your audience with an overall impression that they gather from a host of little details, from the color scheme on your slides to the anecdotes and jokes you tell.

You can turn off your computer for this chapter, because you won't need it to follow along. In this chapter, I'll present some strategies for planning the best presentation ever. I'll provide an 11-point action plan for building your presentation file, and address some of the "soft" topics that can make or break a show, such as how to arrange a room, what to wear, where to stand, and more.

Qualities of an Effective Presentation

What separates an effective presentation from an ineffective one? No, it's not just a gut feeling; there are proven attributes for which you can strive. The rest of this chapter elaborates on these points, but here's a quick overview of what to work on.

An effective presentation:

- Is designed and formatted appropriately for the audience and the medium.

- Is tightly focused on its subject, with extraneous facts trimmed away or hidden for backup use.

- Uses the right PowerPoint theme, with colors and fonts chosen to reinforce the message of the presentation.

- Includes the right amount of text on each slide, without overcrowding.

- Uses artwork purposefully to convey information and create an overall visual impression.

- Uses charts rather than raw columns of numbers to present financial or numeric information.

- Employs sound and video to create interest where needed, but does not allow the effects to dominate the show.

- Uses animations and transitions if appropriate for the audience and message, but does not allow them to dominate.

- Offers the audience handouts that contain the information they will want to take with them.

- Leaves time at the end for a question-and-answer session so the audience members can clarify any points they were confused about.

Now that you know what the goal is, how do you get there? The following section outlines a precise, step-by-step action plan for developing a presentation that has these qualities.

Developing Your Presentation Action Plan

Can you guess what the single biggest problem is when most people use PowerPoint? Here's a hint: It's not a problem with the software at all. It's that they don't think things through carefully before they create their presentation, and then they have to go back and make major modifications later. You've probably heard the saying, "If you don't have time to do it right, how are you going to find time to do it over?" This sentiment is certainly applicable to creating presentations.

In the following sections, I outline a strategy for creating the appropriate PowerPoint presentation right from the start. By considering the issues addressed here, you can avoid making false assumptions about your audience and their needs, and so avoid creating a beautiful presentation with some horrible flaw that makes it unusable. By spending a half-hour or so in this chapter, you can save yourself literally days in rework later.

Step 1: Identifying Your Audience and Purpose

Before you can think about the presentation you need to create, you must first think of your audience. As you probably already know from real-life experience, different audiences respond to different presentation types. For example, a sales pitch to a client requires a very different approach than an informational briefing to your coworkers. Ask yourself these questions:

- **How many people will be attending the presentation?** The attendance makes a difference because the larger the group, the larger your screen needs to be so that everyone can see. If you don't have access to a large screen, you have to make the lettering and charts big and chunky so that everyone can read your presentation.

- **What is the average age of the attendees?** Although it's difficult to generalize about people, it's especially important to keep your presentation light and entertaining when you're presenting to a very young audience (teens and children). Generally speaking, the older the audience, the more authoritative you need to be.

- **What role will the audience take in relation to the topic?** If you are rolling out a new product or system, the managerial staff will likely want a general overview of it, but the line workers who will actually be operating the product need a lot of details. Generally speaking, the higher the level of managers, the more removed they will be from the action, and the fewer details of operation they need.

- **How well does the audience already know the topic?** If you are presenting to a group that knows nothing about your topic, you want to keep things basic and make sure that you define all of the unfamiliar terms. In contrast, with a group of experts, you are likely to have many follow-up questions after the main presentation, and so you should plan on having some hidden backup slides ready in anticipation of those questions. See Chapter 20 for more on hiding slides for backup use.

- **Does the audience care about the topic?** If the topic is personally important to the attendees (such as information on their insurance benefits or vacation schedule), they will likely pay attention even if your presentation is plain and straightforward. However, if you must win them over, you need to spend more time on the bells and whistles.

- **Are the attendees prejudiced either positively or negatively toward the topic?** Keeping in mind the audience's preconceived ideas can make the difference between success and failure in some presentations. For example, knowing that a client hates sales pitches can help you to tailor your own presentation to be out of the ordinary.

- **Are the attendees in a hurry?** Do your attendees have all afternoon to listen to you, or do they need to get back to their regular jobs? Nothing is more frustrating than sitting through a leisurely presentation when you're watching precious minutes tick away. Know your audience's schedule and their preference for quick versus thorough coverage.

Next, think about what you want the outcome of the presentation to be. Although you might want more than one outcome, you should try to identify the primary one as your main goal. Some outcomes to consider include the following:

- **Audience feels good about the topic.** Some presentations are strictly cheerleading sessions, designed to sway the audience's opinion. Don't discount this objective — it's a perfectly legitimate reason to make a presentation! For example, suppose a new management staff has taken over a factory. The new management team might want to reassure the workers that everything is going to be okay. A feel-good, *Welcome to the Team* presentation, complete with gimmicks such as company T-shirts or hats, can go a long way in this regard.

- **Audience is informed.** Sometimes you need to convey information to a group of people, and no decision is involved on their part. For example, suppose your company has switched insurance carriers and you want to let all of the employees know about their new benefits. An informational presentation can cover most of the common questions and save your human resources people a lot of time in answering the same questions over and over.

- **Audience members make individual decisions.** This presentation is a kind of sales pitch in which you are pitching an idea or product to a group, but each person says yes or no individually. For example, suppose you are selling timeshare vacation condos. You may give a presentation to a group of 100 people in an attempt to sell your package to at least a few members of the group.

  This presentation type can also have an informational flavor; you are informing people about their choices without pushing one choice or the other. For example, if your employees have a choice of health plans, you might present the pros and cons of each plan and then leave it to each employee to make a selection.

- **Audience makes a group decision.** This is the kind of presentation that scares a lot of people. You face a group of people who will confer and make a single decision, based on the information you present. Most sales pitches fall into this category. For example, you might be explaining your product to a group of managers to try to get their company to buy it.

Think about these factors carefully and try to come up with a single statement that summarizes your audience and purpose. Here are some examples:

- *I am presenting to 100 factory workers to explain their new health insurance choices and teach them how to fill out the necessary forms.*

- *I am presenting to a group of six to ten mid-level managers, trying to get them to decide as a group to buy my product.*

- *I am presenting to a group of 20 professors to convince at least some of them to use my company's textbooks in their classes.*

- *I am presenting to individual Internet users to explain how my company's service works.*

Let's take that first example. Figure 2.1 shows some notes that a presenter might make when preparing to explain information about employee benefits enrollment to a group of factory workers. Jot down your own notes before moving to step 2.

FIGURE 2.1

Make notes about your presentation's purpose and audience.

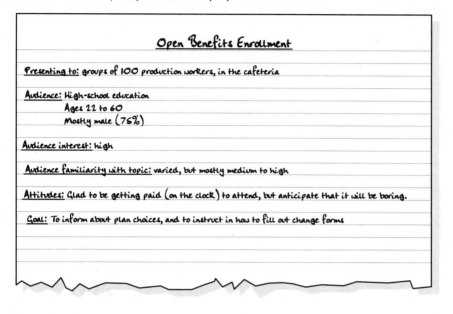

> ## Open Benefits Enrollment
>
> **Presenting to:** groups of 100 production workers, in the cafeteria
>
> **Audience:** High-school education
> Ages 22 to 60
> Mostly male (75%)
>
> **Audience interest:** high
>
> **Audience familiarity with topic:** varied, but mostly medium to high
>
> **Attitudes:** Glad to be getting paid (on the clock) to attend, but anticipate that it will be boring.
>
> **Goal:** To inform about plan choices, and to instruct in how to fill out change forms

Step 2: Choosing Your Presentation Method

You essentially have three ways to present your presentation to your audience, and you need to pick the way that you're going to use up front. These methods include speaker-led, self-running, and user-interactive. Within each of those three broad categories, you have some additional choices. Before you start creating the presentation in PowerPoint, you should know which method you are going to use because it makes a big difference in the text and other objects that you put on the slides.

Speaker-Led Presentations

The speaker-led presentation is the traditional type of presentation: you stand up in front of a live audience (or one connected through teleconferencing) and give a speech. The slides that you create in PowerPoint become your support materials. The primary message comes from you, and the slides and handouts are just helpers.

With this kind of presentation, your slides don't have to tell the whole story. Each slide can contain just a few main points, and you can flesh out each point in your discussion. In fact, this kind of presentation works best when your slides don't contain a lot of information, because people pay more attention to you, the speaker, if they're not trying to read at the same time. For example, instead of listing the top five reasons to switch to your service, you might have a slide that just reads: *Why Switch? Five Reasons.* The audience has to listen to you to find out what the reasons are.

This kind of presentation also requires some special planning. For example, do you want to send each audience member home with handouts? If so, you need to prepare them. They may or may not be identical to your PowerPoint slides; that's up to you. You also need to learn how to handle PowerPoint's presentation controls. It can be really embarrassing to be fiddling with the computer controls in the middle of a speech, and so you should *practice, practice, practice* ahead of time.

CROSS-REF Handouts and other support materials (such as cards for speaker notes) are covered in Chapter 19. For more on PowerPoint presentation controls, see Chapter 20.

Self-Running Presentations

With a self-running presentation, all of the rules change. Instead of using the slides as teasers or support materials, you must make the slides carry the entire show. All of the information must be right there, because you won't be looking over the audience's shoulders with helpful narration.

In general, self-running presentations are presented to individuals or very small groups. For example, you might set up a kiosk in a busy lobby or a booth at a trade show and have a brief but constantly running presentation of perhaps five slides that explains your product or service.

Because there is no dynamic human being keeping the audience's attention, self-running presentations must include attention-getting features. Sounds, video clips, interesting transitions, and prerecorded narratives are all good ways to attract viewers.

You must also consider the timing in a self-running presentation. Because there is no way for a viewer to tell the presentation, "Okay, I'm done reading this slide; bring on the next one," you must carefully plan how long each slide will remain on-screen. This kind of timing requires some practice!

CROSS-REF Part III explains how to use sounds, videos, and other moving objects in a presentation to add interest. Chapter 21 deals with timing issues that are associated with a self-running presentation, as well as how to record voice-over narration.

User-Interactive Presentations

A user-interactive presentation is like a self-running presentation, except that the viewer has some input. Rather than standing passively by, the viewer can tell PowerPoint when to advance a slide. Depending on the presentation's setup, viewers may also be able to move around in the presentation (perhaps to skip over topics that do not interest them) and request more information. This type of presentation is typically addressed to a single user at a time, rather than a group, and is usually distributed over the Internet, a company intranet, or via CD.

The user runs the presentation using either PowerPoint or a free program called PowerPoint Viewer that you can provide for download. You can also translate a PowerPoint presentation to HTML format (the native format for World Wide Web pages), so that anyone with a Web browser can view it. However, presentations usually lose some of their features when you save them in Web format, so consider the decision carefully.

CROSS-REF Chapter 21 explains how to place action buttons on slides so that the viewer can control the action. Chapter 22 covers some of the issues involved in preparing a presentation for mass distribution.

Step 3: Choosing Your Delivery Method

Whereas the presentation method is the general conceptual way that the audience interacts with the information, the delivery method is the way that you *deliver* that interaction. It's a subtle but important difference. For example, suppose that you have decided to use a speaker-led presentation method. That's the big picture, but how will you deliver it? Will you present from a computer, or use 35mm slides, or overhead transparencies, or just plain old handouts? All of these methods fall under the big umbrella of "speaker-led."

PowerPoint gives you a lot of options for your delivery method. Some of these options are more appropriate for speaker-led shows, while others can be used for any presentation method. Here are some of the choices:

- **Computer show through PowerPoint.** You can use PowerPoint's Slide Show view to play the slides on a computer screen. If necessary, you can also hook up a large, external monitor to the PC so that the audience can see it better. This setup requires that PowerPoint (or the PowerPoint Viewer utility) be installed on the computer at the presentation site. This method works for speaker-led, self-running, or user-interactive shows.

- **Computer show through a Web site.** You can save your presentation in Web format and then publish it to a Web site. You can use this method for speaker-led, self-running, or user-interactive shows, and no special software is required — just a Web browser. However, you lose some of the cool graphical effects, including some transitions and animation effects. Web delivery is used mostly for self-running or user-interactive shows.

- **Computer show on CD.** You can create a CD that contains both the presentation and the PowerPoint Viewer utility. The presentation starts automatically when the viewer inserts the CD into a PC. This method is most useful for self-running or user-interactive shows.

- **Overhead transparencies.** You can create overhead transparencies, which are just clear sheets, on most printers. During your presentation, you place them on an overhead projector one at a time.

CAUTION Be careful that the transparencies that you buy are designed for your printer! For example, inkjet transparencies will melt in a laser printer.

- **35mm slides.** These are more expensive to create than transparencies, but the resolution is a bit higher and the image quality is better. Slides transport well in carousels, and you don't have to fumble with placing them manually on the projector. Of course, you lose all of the special effects, such as animations and sounds, just as you do with overheads.

- **Paper.** If there is no projection media available, then your last resort is to distribute your slides to the audience on paper. If you give them handouts, these handouts should be a supplement to an on-screen show, and not the main show themselves.

CROSS-REF Chapter 19 covers printing, both on paper and on transparencies. See Chapter 21 for more on self-running presentations.

Step 4: Choosing a Theme That Matches Your Medium

PowerPoint comes with so many themes and templates that you're sure to find one that is appropriate for your situation. A *theme* is a set of design settings: background, fonts, colors, and graphic effects. PowerPoint 2007 has many built-in themes that are available in every presentation, and you can also create your own themes and use themes that others have created and stored in theme files. A *template* is a full-fledged PowerPoint file that has been designated as a sample from which you can create new presentations. It contains everything that a presentation requires, including sample slides. A template can also contain multiple themes that are piggybacked onto slide masters within the template. When you start a new presentation, you do so from a template, and you inherit any themes and sample slides in that template, in addition to having the built-in themes available.

EXPERT TIP You aren't stuck with the color scheme or design that comes with a particular theme or template. As you learn in Chapter 5, you can apply different color, font, and effects themes separately from the overall theme.

What's the best theme to use? What are the best colors? It all depends on the situation, and on your presentation medium. Here are some tips.

Overhead projector

Using an overhead projector is never anyone's first choice, but sometimes it may be all that is available. An overhead projector image is medium-sized (probably about 36"x36"), but often of poor quality. You will probably be fighting with room lighting, and so your slides may appear washed out. Here are some tips for preparing slides that you will be showing with overhead projectors:

- **Fonts:** For headings, choose chunky block fonts, such as Arial Black, that can stand up to a certain amount of image distortion. For small type, choose clear, easy-to-read fonts such as Arial or Times New Roman.

- **Text color:** Black letters on a light background stand out well. Avoid semi-dark lettering, such as medium-blue, because it easily washes out under an overhead projector's powerful light.

- **Background color:** Avoid dark backgrounds. You probably will not position each slide perfectly on the overhead projector, and the white space around the edges is distracting if your transparencies have a dark background. Consider using a simple white background when you know that you're going to be using transparencies, and *especially* when you want to write on the transparencies.

- **Content:** Keep it simple. Overheads are best when they are text-heavy, without a lot of fancy extras or clipart. The overhead projector is an old technology, and slides that are too dressy seem pretentious.

35mm slides on a slide projector

Here are some guidelines for formatting slides that are destined to be 35mm slides:

- **Fonts:** You can use almost any readable font. If your audience will sit far away from the screen, stick with plain fonts such as Arial and Times New Roman for the body text.

- **Text color:** Go for contrast. Try light text on a dark background. My personal favorite for 35mm slides is bright yellow text on a navy blue background.

- **Background color:** Keep it dark — but not black. Light colors make the screen too bright. Dark blues, greens, and purples are all good choices. Stick with solid backgrounds to compensate for any image distortion that occurs on-screen. You should avoid patterned, shaded, or clip art backgrounds.

- **Content:** You can use any combination of text and graphics with success, but it has to be static. Animations and transitions don't work with 35mm slides. For example, if you have a bulleted list, don't build the bulleted list one bullet at a time from slide to slide. It looks awkward.

Computer-Driven Presentations

If you are lucky enough to have access to a computer-based presentation system, you can show your slides on a PC monitor or TV screen. Some large meeting facilities even have projection TVs that let you project the image onto very large screens.

Here are some guidelines for formatting for this medium:

- **Fonts:** The image on a computer screen is usually nice and sharp, and so you can use any font. However, you should first test your presentation on the computer from which you'll be presenting, as some fonts may look more jagged than others. If you are presenting to a large group on a small screen, make sure that you keep all of the lettering rather large. Also make sure that the font is available on the presentation computer; if it's not there, your text and bullets may not look the way you anticipated.

- **Text color:** As with 35mm slides, go for contrast. Both dark text on a light background and light text on a dark background work well.

- **Background color:** Dark backgrounds such as dark blue, green, or purple are a good choice if the room is not too dark. Light backgrounds can add ambient light to the room, which can sometimes be helpful. You are also free to use gradients, shading, patterns, pictures, and other special backgrounds because all of these elements display nicely on most monitors.

- **Content:** You can go all out with your content. Not only can you include both text and graphics, but also animations, transitions, sounds, and videos.

Step 5: Developing the Content

Your slides should say to the audience, "I had you in mind when I created this," and, "Relax; I'm a professional, and I know what I'm doing." Good-looking, appropriate slides can give the audience a sense of security, and can lend authority to your message. On the other hand, poorly done or inconsistent slides can tell the audience, "I just slapped this thing together at the last minute," or, "I don't really know what I'm doing."

Only after you have made all of the decisions in steps 1 through 4 can you start developing your content in a real PowerPoint presentation. Now comes the work of writing the text for each slide, which most people prefer to do in Normal view. Type the text on the outline or on the text place-holder on the slide itself, and you're ready to roll.

Developing your content may include more than just typing text. For example, your content may include charts that you created in PowerPoint or imported from another program such as Excel, pictures, and other elements.

CROSS-REF Chapter 4 guides you through the process of creating slides and text boxes. You learn about graphical content in Part II of this book. In Lab 1, you learn how to present content without bulleted lists.

Avoiding Information Overload

When presenting, you want to give the audience exactly the information that they need and no more. You don't want them to leave clutching their heads and saying, "Wow! That was too much to absorb!" or, "What a waste of time!" You may have a great deal of information that you need to convey to the audience in a very short time. To ensure that they absorb it all without feeling over-whelmed, here are a few ideas:

- **Before you give your presentation, analyze it closely to make sure that you only cover the essential topics.** By trimming some nonessential topics, you make more room to cover the important themes in enough detail.

- **Don't try to cram every detail onto your slides.** Use the slides for general talking points, and then fill in the discussion with your speech.

- **Use SmartArt to replace bullets.** As you will learn in Chapter 11, you can easily use the new SmartArt diagrams in PowerPoint 2007 in place of a plain bulleted list to make the information more memorable and easier to understand.

- **Provide detailed handouts that elaborate on your slides.** Ensure that the audience receives them at the beginning of the presentation. Then, refer to the handouts throughout the presentation, letting the audience know that they can read all of the details later.

- **Summarize at the end of the presentation with a few simple slides**. These should contain bullet points that outline what the audience should have learned. You might even want to use interim summary slides throughout a complex presentation.

Step 6: Creating the Visual Image

The term *visual image* refers to the overall impression that the audience gets from watching the presentation. You can create a polished, professional impression by making small tweaks to your presentation after you have decided on the content.

You can enhance the visual image by making minor adjustments to the slide's design. For example, you can give a dark slide a warmer feel by using bright yellow instead of white for lettering. Repositioning a company logo and making it larger may make the headings look less lonely. You can use WordArt effects to dress up some text and make it look more graphical. A product picture is more attractive in a larger size or with a different-colored mat around it. All of these little touches take practice and experience.

Audiences like consistency. They like visual elements that they can rely on, such as a repeated company logo on every slide, accurate page numbering on handouts, and the title appearing in exactly the same spot on every slide. You can create a consistent visual image by enforcing these rules in your presentation development. It's easier than you might think, because PowerPoint provides a slide master specifically for images and text that should appear on each slide.

CROSS-REF You'll work with slide masters and learn more about the benefits of consistency in Chapter 5.

Step 7: Adding Multimedia Effects

If you're creating a self-running presentation, multimedia effects are extremely important for developing audience interest. Flashy videos and soundtracks can make even the most boring topic fun to hear about, especially for young audiences. How about a trumpet announcing the arrival of your new product on the market, or a video of your CEO explaining the reasoning behind the recent merger?

CAUTION Even if you are going to be speaking live, you still might want to incorporate some multimedia elements into your show. However, be careful not to let them outshine you or to appear gratuitous. Be aware of your audience (see step 1), and remember that older and higher-level managers want less flash and more substance.

All kinds of presentations can benefit from slide animations and transitions. *Animations* are simple movements of the objects on a slide. For example, you can make the bullet points on a list fly onto the page one at a time, and discuss each one on its own. When the next bullet flies in, the previous ones can turn a different color so that the current one stands out. You might also animate a picture of a car so that it appears to "drive onto" the slide, accompanied by the sound of an engine revving. You can also animate charts by making data series appear one at a time, so that it looks like the chart is building. *Transitions* are animated effects for moving from slide to slide. The most basic and boring transition is to simply remove one slide from the screen and replace it with another. However, you can also use many alternative effects such as zooming the new slide in, sliding it from the top, bottom, left, or right, or creating a fade-in transition effect.

CROSS-REF Chapters 16 and 17 deal with the mechanics of placing sound and video clips into a presentation and controlling when and how they play. You learn about animations and transitions in Chapter 18.

Step 8: Creating the Handouts and Notes

This step is applicable only to speaker-led presentations. With a live audience, you may want to provide handouts so that they can follow along. You can make handouts verbatim copies of your slides, or abbreviated versions with only the most basic information included as a memory-jogger. Handouts can be either black and white or in color, and PowerPoint provides several handout formats. For example, you can print from one to nine slides per printout, with or without lines for the audience to write additional notes.

EXPERT TIP A continual debate rages in the professional speakers' community over when to give out handouts. Some people feel that if you distribute handouts beforehand, people will read them and then not listen to the presentation. Others feel that if you distribute handouts after the presentation, people will frantically try to take their own notes during the presentation or will not follow the ideas as easily. There's no real right or wrong answer, it seems, and so you should distribute them whenever it makes the most sense for your situation.

As the speaker, you may need your own special set of handouts with your own notes that the audience should not see. PowerPoint calls these Notes Pages, and there is a special view for creating them. (You can also enter notes directly into the Notes pane in Normal view.)

CROSS-REF Notes are covered, along with handouts, in Chapter 19, which also guides you through selecting the appropriate size and format, as well as working with your printer to get the best results for your handouts.

Step 9: Rehearsing the Presentation

No matter which type of presentation you are creating (speaker-led, self-running, or user-interactive), you need to rehearse it. However, the goals for rehearsing are different for each type.

Rehearsing a Live Presentation

When you rehearse a live presentation, you check the presentation slides to ensure that they are complete, accurate, and in the right order. You may need to rearrange them and hide some of them for backup-only use.

You should also rehearse using PowerPoint's presentation controls, which display each slide on a monitor and let you move from slide to slide, take notes, assign action items, and even draw directly on a slide. Make sure that you know how to back up, how to jump to the beginning or end, and how to display one of your backup slides.

CROSS-REF You can learn about navigation skills in Chapter 20.

Rehearsing a Self-Running Presentation

With a speaker-led presentation, the presenter can fix any glitches that pop up, or explain away any errors. With a self-running presentation, you don't have that luxury. The presentation itself is your emissary. Therefore, you must go over it repeatedly, checking it many times to make sure that it is perfect before distributing it. Nothing is worse than a self-running presentation that doesn't run, or one that contains an embarrassing error.

The most important feature in a self-running presentation is *timing*. You must make the presentation pause for the correct amount of time so that the audience can read the text on each slide. The pause must be long enough so that even slow readers can catch it all, but short enough so that fast readers do not become bored. You can now see how difficult this can be to make perfect.

PowerPoint has a Rehearse Timings feature that is designed to help you with this task. It lets you show the slides and advance them manually after the correct amount of time has passed. The Rehearse Timings feature records how much time you spend on each slide, and gives you a report so that you can modify the timing if necessary. For example, you may be working on a presentation that is supposed to last ten minutes, but with your timings, it comes out to only nine minutes. You can add additional time for each slide to stretch it out to last the full ten minutes. You may also want to record voice-over narration for your presentation. You can also rehearse this, to make sure that the voice matches the slide that it is supposed to describe (which is absolutely crucial, as you can imagine!).

CROSS-REF Chapter 16 covers timing as well as voice-overs.

Rehearsing a User-Interactive Presentation

In a user-interactive presentation, you provide the readers with on-screen buttons that they can click to move through the presentation, so that timing is not an issue. The crucial factor with a user-interactive presentation is link accuracy. Each button on each slide is a link. When your readers click a button for the next slide, it must take them to the next slide and not to somewhere else. And if you include a hyperlink to a Web address on the Internet, when the readers click it, the Web browser should open and that page should appear. If the hyperlink contains a typo and the readers see File Not Found instead of the Web page, the error reflects poorly on you. Chapter 21 covers creating and inserting these links.

If you are planning to distribute your presentation through the Internet, you have a big decision to make. You can distribute the presentation in its native PowerPoint format and preserve all of its more exciting features, such as animations and videos. However, not everyone on the Internet owns a copy of PowerPoint, and so you are limiting your audience. Although PowerPoint supplies a free program, called the PowerPoint Viewer that you can post for downloading on your Web page, not everyone will take the time to download and install it, and so you may turn off potential viewers before you start.

The other option is to save the presentation in HTML (Web) format. When you save in HTML format, you convert each of the slides to a Web page, and you add links (if you didn't already have them) that move the viewer from slide to slide. You lose many of the animations, transitions, sounds, videos, animated graphics, and other extras, but you retain your text and most static elements of the presentation. The advantage is that everyone with a Web browser can view your presentation with no special downloads or setup.

CROSS-REF You learn more about preparing a presentation for the Internet, using either method, in Chapter 21.

Step 10: Giving the Presentation

For a user-interactive or self-running presentation, giving the presentation is somewhat anticlimactic. You just make it available and the users watch it. Yawn.

However, for a speaker-led presentation, giving the speech is the highlight, the pinnacle, of the process. If you've done a good job rehearsing, you are already familiar with PowerPoint's presentation controls. You should be prepared to back up, to skip ahead, to answer questions by displaying hidden slides, or to pause the whole thing (and black out the screen) so that you can hold a tangential discussion.

CROSS-REF Chapter 20 covers all of these situations in case you need to review them.

What remains now? Nothing, except for setting up the room and overcoming your stage fright. Later in this chapter, you'll get some tips about using a meeting room most effectively and being a dynamic speaker. Check them out — and then go get 'em!

Step 11: Assessing Your Success and Refining Your Work

If giving a presentation is a one-time thing for you — great. It's over, and you never have to think about it again. However, it is more likely that you will have to give another presentation someday, somewhere, and so you shouldn't drive the experience out of your mind just yet. Perhaps you learned something that might be useful to you later. Immediately after the presentation, while it is still fresh in your mind, jot down your responses to the following questions. Then keep them on file to refer to later, the next time you have to do a presentation!

- Did the colors and design of the slides seem appropriate?
- Could everyone in the audience read the slides easily?
- Did the audience look mostly at you, at the screen, or at the handouts? Was that what you intended?
- Did the audience take notes as you were speaking? If so, did you give them handouts with note-taking lines to write on?
- Was the length of the presentation appropriate? Did the audience become bored or restless at any point?
- Were there any slides that you wished you had prepared but didn't?

- Were there any slides that you would omit if you were doing it over?

- Did your speaker notes give you enough help that you could speak with authority?

- Did the transitions and animations add to the entertainment value, or were they distracting or corny?

- Did the sound and video clips play with adequate quality? Were they appropriate and useful?

Choosing and Arranging the Room

Are you giving a live presentation? The choice of room—and its arrangement—can make a big difference in your success. If you have any say in it, make sure that you get an appropriate size of room for the presentation. For example, a room that is too small makes people feel uncomfortable and seems crowded, whereas a room that is too large can create a false formality and distance that can cause people to lose focus. You also don't want to have to shout to be heard.

CAUTION To avoid having to shout during your presentation, make sure that there is a working sound system, with a microphone and amplifier available, if necessary. If possible, check this detail a few days ahead of time, to avoid scrambling for one at the last minute.

Next, make sure that tables and chairs are set up appropriately. Figures 2.2 through 2.5 illustrate several setups, each of which is appropriate for a certain kind of presentation:

- For a classroom setting where the audience will take a lot of notes, give them something to write on, as in Figure 2.2. This arrangement works well when the audience will be listening to and interacting with you, but not with one another.

FIGURE 2.2

In a classroom arrangement, each audience member has plenty of room to write and work.

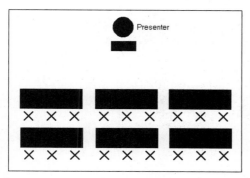

- If the audience is not expected to take notes while you are giving the speech, consider an auditorium setup, as in Figure 2.3. This arrangement is also good for fitting a lot of people into a small room. (This is also known as theater-style seating.)

FIGURE 2.3

An auditorium setup (or theater-style seating) fits a lot of people into a small space; it's great for large company meetings.

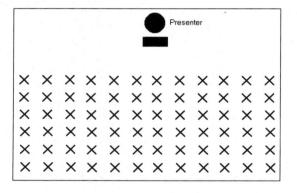

- If you want the audience to interact in small groups, you should set up groups where people can see each other and still see you. Figure 2.4 shows a small-group arrangement.

FIGURE 2.4

Having small groups clustered around tables encourages discussion and works well for presentations that incorporate hands-on activities.

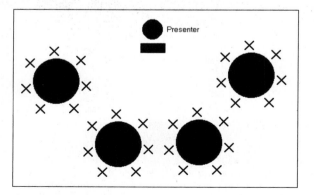

■ To make it easier for the entire group to interact with one another as a whole, use a U-shape, as in Figure 2.5.

FIGURE 2.5

Arrange the room in a U-shape if you want participants to have discussions as a large group.

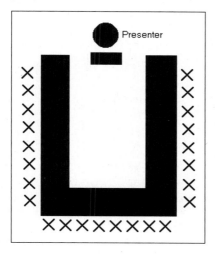

Choosing Your Attire

The outfit that you choose for the presentation should depend on the expectations of the audience and the message that you want to send to them. Before you decide what to wear, ask yourself, "What will the audience be wearing?" Choose one of these classifications:

■ **Very informal:** Jeans, shorts, T-shirts

■ **Informal:** Nice jeans, polo shirts

■ **Business casual:** Dress slacks and oxfords, with or without a tie, for men; dress slacks or a skirt and a dressy, casual shirt (sweater, silk blouse, vest) for women

■ **Business:** Dress slacks and a shirt and tie, with or without a jacket, for men; dress or skirt (blazer optional) for women

■ **Business formal:** Suit and tie for men; suit or conservative dress for women

Now, shape your own choice of attire, depending on the impression that you want to convey. To convey authority, dress one level above your audience. Use this attire any time your audience does not know who you are and when you need to establish yourself as the leader or the expert. (Most teachers fall into this category.) For example, if your audience is dressed informally, you should wear a dress shirt and tie (for men) or a skirt and sweater (for women). (If you're female and will be seated on a stage, you might want pants or a very long skirt.) However, you should not dress more than two levels above your audience because it makes them feel intimidated. For example, if you are presenting to factory workers who are dressed in very informal clothing, you should not wear a business suit.

To convey teamwork and approachability, dress at the same level as the audience, or slightly (no more than one level) above. For example, if you are a CEO visiting a factory that you manage, the workers already recognize your authority — you don't have to prove it. Instead, you want to appear approachable, and so if they are wearing informal clothing, you might wear dress slacks and a dress shirt (but no tie) for a man, or slacks and a sweater for a woman.

Avoid dressing below the audience's level. This is almost never a good idea. If you do not know what the audience will be wearing, err on the side of formality. It is better to look a little stiff than it is to look less professional than your audience.

Keeping the Audience Interested

There are no miracle cures here — some people are naturally better, more interesting speakers than others. However, there are definite steps that all speakers can take to stack the odds in their favor when it comes to giving a successful live presentation.

Speech Techniques

Here are some strategies for improving your speaking style:

- **Plant your feet firmly; don't pace.** Pacing makes you appear nervous, and people have to constantly follow you with their eyes. However, you should keep your upper body mobile, and should not be afraid to use arm gestures.

- **Use gestures to support your voice.** If you are talking about three different points, then hold up fingers to illustrate one, two, and three points. If you are talking about bringing things together, bring your hands together in front of you to illustrate. Don't freeze your hands at your sides.

- **Don't memorize your speech.** If someone asks a question, it will throw you off and you'll forget where you were.

- **Conversely, don't read the speech word for word from your notes.** Notes should contain keywords and facts, but not the actual words that you will say.

- **Don't talk with your face in your notes.** Make eye contact with an audience member before you begin speaking.

- **Pick a few people in the audience, in different places in the room, and make direct eye contact with each of them, in turn, as you speak.** Talk directly to a single person for the duration of the point that you are making and then move on. Also, don't forget to smile!

- **Don't be afraid to pause.** Speaking slowly, with pauses to look at your notes, is much more preferable than rushing through the presentation. Keep in mind that pauses that might seem very long to you really aren't.

- **Don't stare at or read your slides.** Focus your attention on your audience, and pay as little attention to the support materials as possible while you speak. You want to engage directly with your audience to deliver your message in your own words.

- **Emphasize verbs and action words in your presentation**. Remember that the verb is the most powerful element in the sentence.

Content tips

Consider these content techniques:

- If the audience is not in a hurry and you are not rushed for time in your presentation, start with some kind of icebreaker, like an anecdote or joke.

CAUTION Be careful with humor. Analyze the joke that you plan to tell from all angles, making very sure that it does not offend any race, ethnic group, gender, sexual orientation, or class of workers. It is *much* worse to tell a joke that hurts someone's feelings — even one person — than it is to tell none at all.

- Include the audience in interactive exercises that help to firm up their understanding of the topic.

- Ask questions to see whether the audience understood you, and give out small prizes to the people who give correct answers. Nothing energizes an audience into participation more than prizes, even if they are cheap giveaways like key chains and bandannas.

- If possible, split the presentation into two or more sessions, with a short break and question-and-answer period between each session.

- During the Q&A portion, turn off the slide projector, overhead, or computer screen so that people focus on you and on the question, not on the previous slide. If turning off the equipment isn't practical, consider inserting a simple Q&A Session title slide or a blank slide that displays during the Q&A.

Managing Stage Fright

Even if you're comfortable with the PowerPoint slides that you've created, you still might be a little nervous about the actual speech that you're going to give. This is normal. In fact, a study from a few years ago showed that public speaking is the number-one fear among businesspeople. Fear of death came in second. That should tell you something.

It's okay to be a little bit nervous because it gives you extra energy and an edge that can actually make your presentation better. However, if you're too nervous, it can make you seem less credible.

One way to overcome stage fright is to stop focusing on yourself, and instead focus on your audience. Ask yourself what the audience needs and how you are going to supply that need. Become their caretaker. Dedicate yourself to making the audience understand you. The more you think of others, the less you think of yourself.

Summary

Although this chapter had little to do with PowerPoint *per se*, it focused on making successful presentations using your PowerPoint slides as a tool. The information that you learned here can help a beginning presenter look more experienced, or help a more experienced presenter polish his or her skills to perfection.

Chapter 3

Creating and Saving Presentation Files

I f you're an experienced Windows and PowerPoint user, starting new presentations and saving files may be second nature to you. If so — great! You may not need this chapter. On the other hand, if you aren't entirely certain about some of the finer points, such as saving in different formats or locations, stick around.

Even people who consider themselves "advanced" users may benefit from this chapter, because it looks at some of the unique advanced saving features of Office applications and explains how to secure files with passwords.

Starting a New Presentation

You can start a blank presentation from scratch, or you can base the new presentation on a template or on another presentation. Using a template or existing presentation can save you some time. However, if you have a specific vision you're going for, starting a presentation from scratch gives you a clean canvas to work from.

Starting a Blank Presentation from Scratch

When you start PowerPoint, a new blank presentation begins automatically with one slide. Just add your content to it, add more slides if needed, change the formatting (as you'll learn in upcoming chapters), and go for it.

If you need to start another blank presentation, follow these steps:

1. Choose Office ➪ New. The New Presentation dialog box opens. See Figure 3.1.

Select Blank Presentation from the New Presentation dialog box.

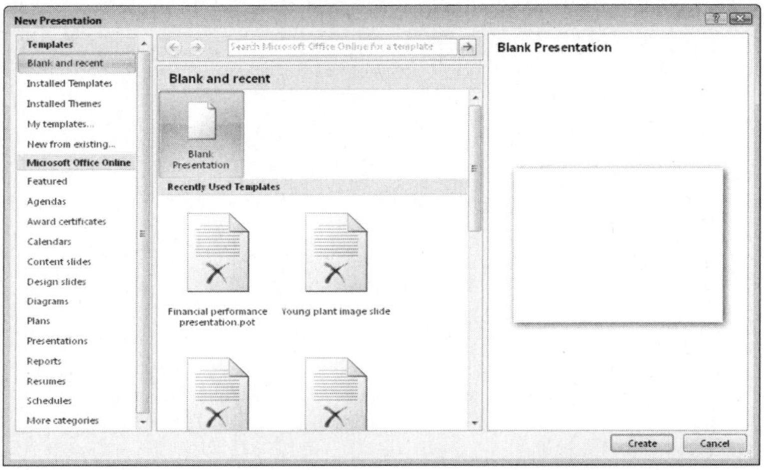

2. Blank Presentation is already selected. Click Create.

EXPERT TIP Press the Ctrl+N shortcut key to start a new presentation.

Starting a Presentation from a Template

A *template* is a file that contains starter settings — and sometimes starter content — on which you can base new presentations. Templates vary in their exact offerings, but can include sample slides, a background graphic, custom color and font themes, and custom positioning for object placeholders.

When selecting a template, you can choose from these categories:

- **Installed Templates:** Microsoft-provided templates that come preinstalled with PowerPoint.
- **My Templates:** Templates that you have created and saved yourself and templates that you previously downloaded from Microsoft Office Online

■ **Microsoft Office Online templates:** Microsoft-provided templates that you download from Microsoft on an as-needed basis

NOTE Also under Templates in Figure 3.1 is *Installed Themes.* Themes are not exactly templates, but they are similar. Chapter 1 explained the difference. You can start a new presentation based on a theme as an alternative to using a template. Such a presentation starts with defined color, font, and effect settings.

Using an Installed Template

There are only a few installed templates because Microsoft assumes that most people have an always-on Internet connection these days. Each installed template demonstrates a special-purpose type of presentation, such as a photo album, pitchbook, or quiz show. There is one Corporate Presentation template as well, but if you are interested in standard corporate presentation templates, you might prefer to look at the online offerings instead.

Follow these steps to start a presentation based on an installed template:

1. Choose Office ➪ New. The New Presentation dialog box opens.

2. In the Templates list, click Installed Templates. A list of the installed templates appears.

3. Click a template to see a preview of it.

4. Select the template you want and click Create. A new presentation opens based on that template.

Using a Saved Template

When you start a new presentation with an online template, as in the preceding section, PowerPoint copies that template to your hard disk so you can reuse it in the future without connecting to the Internet. It is stored, along with any custom template you have created, in the My Templates folder.

To access these downloaded and custom templates, follow these steps:

1. Choose Office ➪ New. The New Presentation dialog box opens (see Figure 3.1).

2. Click My Templates. A different New Presentation dialog box appears containing templates that you have downloaded or created. See Figure 3.2.

3. Click OK. A new presentation opens based on that template.

EXPERT TIP Recently used template names appear on the right side of the New Presentation dialog box when it opens initially. You can select a template from there and click Create. To remove an item from the Recently Used Templates, right-click the item and choose Remove Item from List. To clear the whole list at once, right-click any entry and choose Remove All Items from List.

FIGURE 3.2

Choose a previously used or custom template.

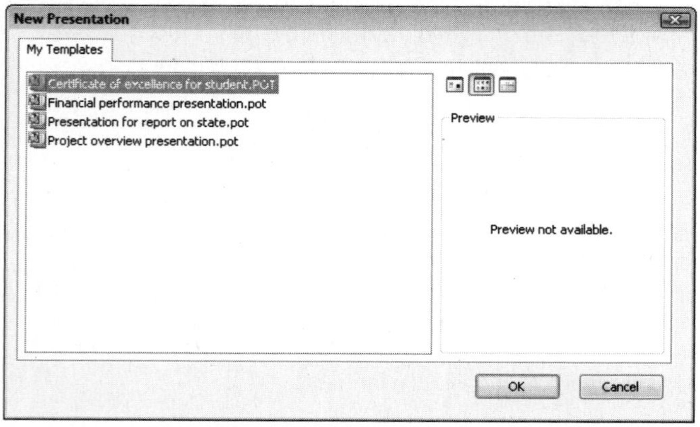

Using an Online Template

The bulk of the templates for presentations are available online. You can access the library of online templates without leaving PowerPoint. Follow these steps:

1. Choose Office ⇨ New. The New Presentation dialog box opens.

2. In the Templates list, in the Microsoft Office Online section, click the category of template you want. If you want standard business presentations, click Presentations; most of the other categories have special purposes.

3. Depending on the category you choose, a subcategory list might appear in the center pane. If it does, click the subcategory that you want.

4. Click a template to see a preview of it.

5. Select the template that you want and click Download. A new presentation opens based on that template.

EXPERT TIP Spend some time exploring the templates available on Microsoft Office Online. There's a lot here! For example, Design Slides has templates that don't contain any sample content — just design elements. This category has subcategories for earlier versions of PowerPoint, so if there was a particular design template you loved in, say, PowerPoint 2000, you can find it again here.

Basing a New Presentation on an Existing One

If you already have a presentation that's similar to the new one you need to create, you can base the new presentation on the existing one.

Follow these steps to use an existing presentation as a template:

1. Choose Office ➪ New. The New Presentation dialog box opens.
2. Click New from Existing. The New from Existing Presentation dialog box opens. See Figure 3.3.

FIGURE 3.3

Select an existing presentation to use as a template.

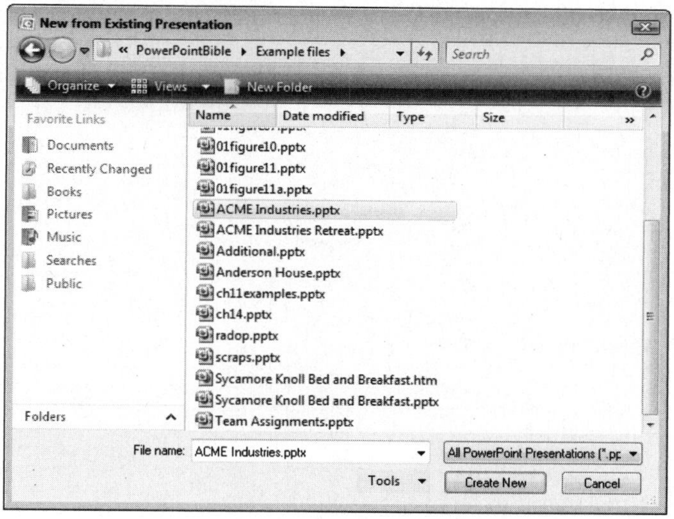

3. Navigate to the location containing the existing presentation and select it. When you select a presentation, the Open button changes to a Create New button.
4. Click Create New.

Basing a New Presentation on Content from Another Application

PowerPoint can open files in several formats other than its own, so you can start a new presentation based on some work you have done elsewhere. For example, you can open a Word outline in PowerPoint. The results might not be very attractive — but you can fix that later with some text editing, slide layouts, and design changes.

To open a file from another application, do the following:

1. Choose Office ➪ Open. The Open dialog box appears.
2. Click the File Type button (or Files of Type in Windows XP) and choose the file type. For example, to open a text file, choose All Outlines. See Figure 3.4.

Select a data file from some other program as the basis of a new presentation.

File type button

3. Select the desired file, and then click Open.
4. Save your work as a PowerPoint file by choosing File ➪ Save As.

CROSS-REF See the section "Saving Your Work" for more details on saving. You can also import a Word outline into an existing presentation.

Saving Your Work

PowerPoint is typical of most Windows programs in the way it saves and opens files. The entire PowerPoint presentation is saved in a single file, and any graphics, charts, or other elements are incorporated into that single file.

The first time you save a presentation, PowerPoint opens the Save As dialog box, prompting you for a name and location. Thereafter, when you save that presentation, PowerPoint uses the same settings and does not prompt you for them again.

Saving for the First Time

If you haven't previously saved the presentation you are working on, Save and Save As do the same thing: They open the Save As dialog box. From there, you can specify a name, file type, and file location. Follow these steps:

1. Choose Office ➪ Save. The Save As dialog box appears.
2. Enter a filename in the File name box. See Figure 3.5.

FIGURE 3.5

Save your work by specifying a name for the presentation file.

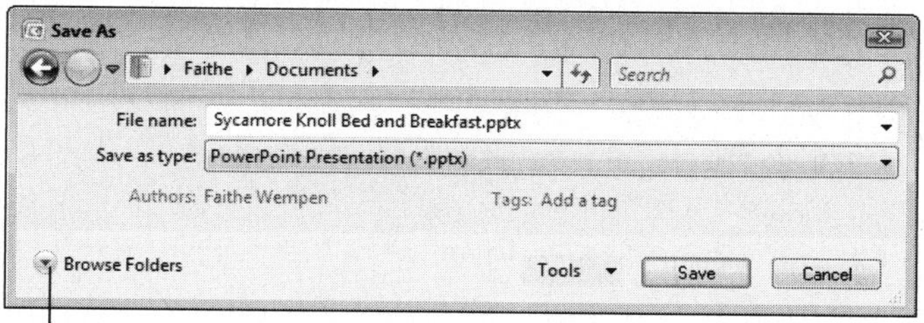

Click here to expand
the dialog box

NOTE   In Windows Vista, the Save As dialog box does not show the existing content of the current location by default. To view it, click the Browse Folders arrow in the bottom-left corner of the dialog box.

CROSS-REF   To save in a different location, see the section "Changing Drives and Folders." To save in a different format, see the section "Saving in a Different Format."

3. Click Save. Your work is saved.

Filenames can be up to 255 characters. For practical purposes, however, keep the names short. You can include spaces in the filenames and most symbols except <, >, ?, *, /, and \. However, if you plan to post the file on a network or the Internet at some point, you should avoid using spaces; use the underscore character instead to simulate a space if needed. There have also been problems reported with files that use exclamation points in their names, so beware of that. Generally it is best to avoid punctuation marks in names.

EXPERT TIP If you want to transfer your presentation file to a different computer and show it from there, and that other computer does not have the same fonts as your PC, you should embed the fonts in your presentation so the desired fonts are available on the other PC. To embed fonts from the Save As dialog box, click the Tools button, choose Save Options, and mark the Embed Fonts in the File check box. This option makes the saved file larger than normal, so choose it only when necessary. For more information on advanced saving features, see the section "Specifying Save Options."

Saving Subsequent Times

After you have once saved a presentation, you can resave it with the same settings (same file type, name, and location) in any of the following ways:

- Choose Office ⇨ Save.
- Press Ctrl+S.
- Click the Save button on the Quick Access Toolbar.

If you need to save your presentation under a different name, as a different file type, or in a different location, use the Save As command instead. This reopens the Save As dialog box, as in the preceding steps, so that you can save differently. The originally saved copy will remain under the original name, type, and location.

EXPERT TIP If you frequently use Save As, you may want to place a button for it on the Quick Access Toolbar. To do this, right-click the Save As command and choose Add to Quick Access Toolbar.

Changing Drives and Folders

By default, all files in PowerPoint (and all of the Office applications) are saved to the Documents folder (or My Documents under Windows XP) for the current user. Each user has his or her own version of this folder, so that each person's documents are kept separate depending on who is logged in to the PC.

The Documents folder is a convenient save location for beginners, because they never have to worry about changing the drive or folder. However, more advanced users will sometimes want to save files to other locations. These other locations can include floppy disks, other hard disks in the same PC, hard disks on other PCs in a network, hard disks on Web servers on the Internet, or writeable CDs.

EXPERT TIP Each user has a Documents or My Documents folder in his or her own profile. The actual location of that folder depends on the Windows version. For example, if Mary is logged in, the path would be C:\Users\Mary\Documents. In Windows XP, the path would be C:\Documents and Settings\Mary\My Documents. If your usual PowerPoint files seem to be missing at some point, make sure you are logged in under your usual username.

Throughout all of the Office programs, the dialog boxes that save and open files are different depending on the operating system you are using.

Changing the Save Location (Windows Vista)

Windows Vista's Save As dialog box offers several alternatives for navigating between locations. Here's a summary:

■ **Browse Folders:** By default a compact version of the Save As dialog box appears, as in Figure 3.5. To see the full version, as in Figure 3.6, click the Browse Folders arrow.

FIGURE 3.6

Jump to a desired location using the Favorite Links and/or Folders lists.

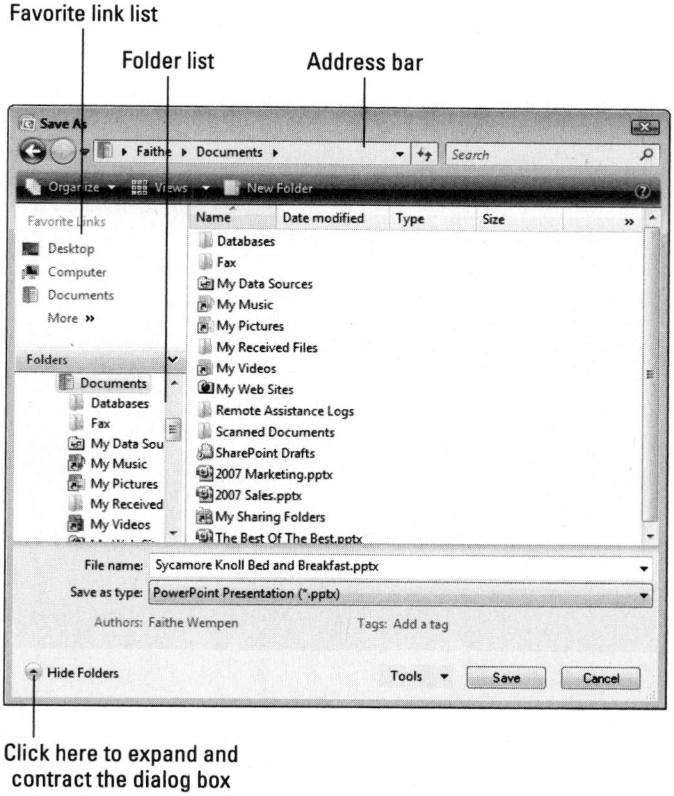

Favorite link list

Folder list   Address bar

Click here to expand and contract the dialog box

■ **Favorite Links list:** This area displays shortcuts for popular locations such as Documents and Desktop. Double-click a shortcut here to jump to the desired location. This area does not appear unless Browse Folders is turned on.

EXPERT TIP   Add your own favorite locations to the Favorite Links list by dragging their icons into the Favorite Links pane.

■ **Folders list:** This area displays a folder tree of locations, similar to the folder list in a Windows Explorer window. See Figure 3.6. To display the Folders list if it does not already appear, click the up arrow to the right of Folders (below the Favorite Links list). To hide the Folders list, click the down arrow (which replaces the up arrow).

EXPERT TIP   Drag the divider line between the Favorite Links and Folders lists to adjust their relative sizes. Drag the vertical divider line between them and the file listing to make the Favorite Links and Folders panes wider or narrower. You can also enlarge the whole Save As dialog box if needed by dragging its border.

■ **Address bar:** This area shows the path to the currently displayed location. You can jump directly to any of those levels by clicking the name there. This is similar to the "Up One Level" feature from Windows XP style dialog boxes except you are not limited to going up a single level at a time — you can go directly up to any level. You can also click the right-pointing arrow to the right of any level to see a menu of other folders within that location, and jump to any of them from the menu. See Figure 3.7.

FIGURE 3.7

Click an arrow on the Address bar to see a menu of locations at the chosen level within the current path.

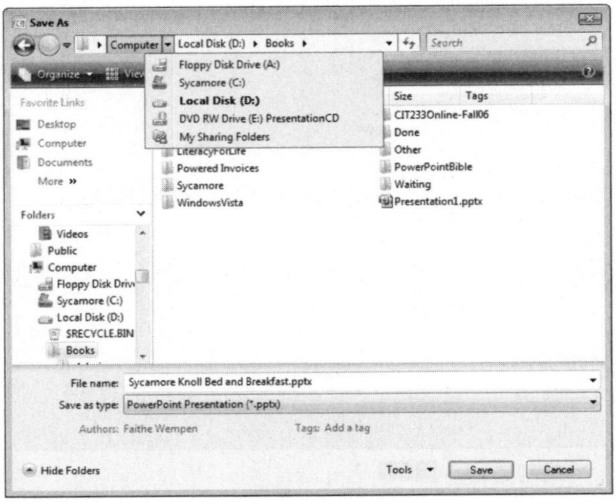

Changing the Save Location (Windows XP)

Under Windows XP, the Save In list shows the top-level locations on the system, including each drive, My Documents, and My Network Places. Open the list, as shown in Figure 3.8, and select the location in which you want to start. Then double-click folder icons in the file listing to drill down to the location in which you want to save. To go back up one level, click the Up One Level button. See Figure 3.8.

FIGURE 3.8

Select a top-level location from the Save In list and then double-click folders to work your way through to the desired location.

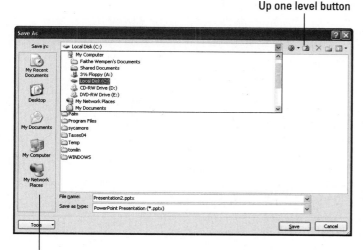

Up one level button

Places bar

Along the left side of the Save As dialog box is the *Places Bar.* It's roughly equivalent to the Favorite Links list in Windows Vista. You can click a folder to jump to the desired location to save a file.

EXPERT TIP If you consistently want your PowerPoint files saved into a different folder, change the default file location. Choose Office ➪ PowerPoint Options and click Save. Then type a new file location in the Default File Location text box. You cannot browse for it; you must know the full path name. Separate the parts of the path with \ symbols, like this: C:\Books\PowerPoint\ PPBible.

Saving in a Different Format

PowerPoint 2007 has a new XML-based file format, like the other Office 2007 applications. XML stands for eXtensible Markup Language; it is a text-based coding system similar to HTML that describes formatting by using inline bracketed codes and style sheets. XML-based data files are smaller than the data files from earlier PowerPoint versions, and they support all of the latest PowerPoint 2007 features. For best results, use this format whenever possible.

There are also several variants of this format for specialty uses. For example, there's a macro-enable version with a .pptm extension. There are also "show" variants (.ppsx and .ppsm) that open in Slide Show view by default, and template variants (.potx and .potm) that function as templates.

EXPERT TIP PowerPoint 2007 does not include macro recording functionality, so why is there a macro-enabled file format? It's because of Visual Basic for Applications (VBA). From the Developer tab, you can access a VBA editor, which lets you embed VBA code inside a PowerPoint presentation file (provided it is in a macro-enabled format).

However, not everyone has PowerPoint 2007, and only PowerPoint 2007 can open files with these new formats. (You can download a compatibility pack for earlier PowerPoint versions that will allow them to accept the new files, but you can't assume that everyone who has an earlier version of PowerPoint will download it.) Therefore you might need to save presentations in other file formats in order to share files with other people.

The available formats are shown in Table 3.1. In the Save As dialog box, open the Save as Type drop-down list and select the desired format. See Figure 3.9.

FIGURE 3.9

Choose a different format, if needed, from the Save As Type drop-down list.

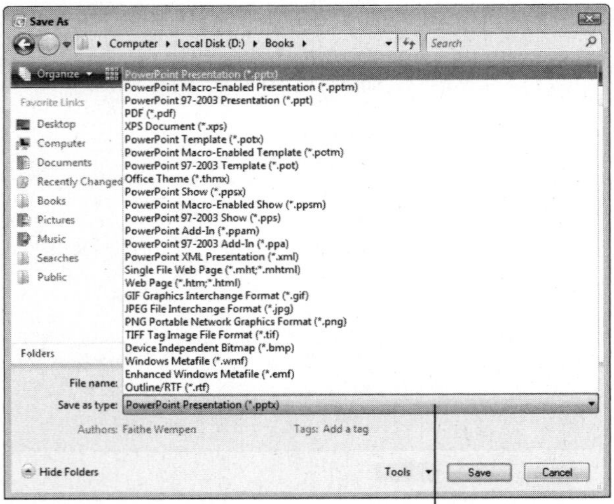

Click here to open the list

TABLE 3.1

PowerPoint Save As Formats

Presentations:

Format	Extension	Usage Notes
PowerPoint Presentation	.pptx	The default; use in most cases. Can open only in PowerPoint 2007 (or on an earlier version with a conversion add-on installed).
PowerPoint Macro-Enabled Presentation	.pptm	Same as above except it supports the storage of VBA or macro code.
PowerPoint 97-2003 Presentation	.ppt	A backward-compatible format for sharing files with users of PowerPoint 97, 2000, 2002 (XP), or 2003.
PowerPoint Template	.potx	A 2007-format template file.
PowerPoint Macro-Enabled Template	.potm	A 2007-format template file that supports the storage of VBA or macro code.
PowerPoint 97-2003 Template	.pot	A backward-compatible template file, also usable with PowerPoint 97, 2000, 2002 (XP), or 2003.
PowerPoint Show	.ppsx	Just like a regular PowerPoint file except it opens in Slide Show view by default; useful for distributing presentations to the audience on disk.
PowerPoint Macro-Enabled Show	.ppsm	Same as above except it supports the storage of VBA or macro code.
PowerPoint 97-2003 Show	.pps	Same as a regular backward-compatible presentation file except it opens in Slide Show view by default.
PowerPoint XML Presentation	.xml	A presentation in XML format, suitable for integrating into an XML information storage system.
Single File Web Page	.mht, .mhtml	A complete presentation stored in a single file that can be displayed in most modern Web browsers. Suitable for posting on a Web site or sending via e-mail.
Web Page	.htm, .html	A typical text HTML file with each graphic element in a separate file. Suitable for posting on a Web site.

Graphics/Other:

Format	Extension	Usage Notes
PDF	.pdf	Produces files in Adobe PDF format, which is a hybrid of a document and a graphic. It shows each page exactly as it will be printed, and yet allows the user to mark up the pages with comments and to search the document text. Available only after downloading PDF and XPS support from Office Online. You must have a PDF reader such as Adobe Acrobat to view PDF files.

continued

TABLE 3.1   *(continued)*

Graphics/Other:

Format	Extension	Usage Notes
XPS	.xps	Much the same as PDF except it's a Microsoft format. Windows Vista comes with an XPS viewer application.
Office Theme	.thmx	Somewhat like a template, but it contains only theme settings (fonts, colors, and effects). Use this if you want to apply the colors, fonts, and effects from the current presentation to other presentations but you don't want to save any of the content or layout.
PowerPoint Add-In	.ppam	A file containing executable code (usually VBA) that extends PowerPoint's capabilities.
PowerPoint 97-2003 Add-In	.ppa	Same as above except the add-in is backward-compatible.
GIF Graphics Interchange Format	.gif	Static graphic. GIFs are limited to 256 colors.
PNG Portable Network Graphics Format	.png	Static graphic. Similar to GIF except without the color depth limitation. Uses lossless compression; takes advantage of the best features of both GIF and JPG.
JPEG File Interchange Format	.jpg	Static graphic. JPG files can be very small, making them good for Web use. A lossy format, so picture quality may not be as good as with a lossless format.
TIFF Tagged Image File Format	.tif	Static graphic. TIF is a high-quality file format suitable for slides with high-resolution photos. A lossless compression format.
Device Independent Bitmap	.bmp	Static graphic. BMP is the native format for Windows graphics, including Windows background wallpaper.
Windows Metafile	.wmf	Static graphic. A vector-based format, so it can later be resized without distortion. Not Mac-compatible.
Enhanced Windows Metafile	.emf	Enhanced version of WMF; not compatible with 16-bit applications. Also vector-based and non-Mac-compatible.
Outline/RTF	.rtf	Text and text formatting only; excludes all non-text elements. Only text in slide placeholders will be converted to the outline. Text in the Notes area is not included.

EXPERT TIP   If you consistently want to save in a different format from PowerPoint 2007, choose Office ⇨ PowerPoint Options and click Save. Then, choose a different format from the Save Files in this Format drop-down list. This makes your choice the default in the Save As Type drop-down list in the Save As dialog box. Not all of the formats are available here; your choices are PowerPoint Presentation (the default), PowerPoint Macro-Enabled Presentation, and PowerPoint 97-2003.

Table 3.1 lists a lot of choices, but don't let that overwhelm you. You have three main decisions to make:

- **PowerPoint 2007 format or backward-compatible with PowerPoint 97-2003.** Unless compatibility is essential, go with the 2007 format because you get access to all of the new features. (See Table 3.2 to learn what you'll lose with backward-compatibility.) If you use a backward-compatible format, some of the features described in this book work differently or aren't available at all.

- **Macro-enabled or not.** Most people will never need to create a macro-enabled presentation. PowerPoint 2007 does not support macro recording, so the only macros you would have would be written in VBA, and most PowerPoint users aren't fluent in VBA programming.

- **Regular presentation or PowerPoint Show.** The "show" variant starts the presentation in Slide Show view when it is loaded in PowerPoint; that's the only difference between it and a regular presentation. You can build your presentation in a regular format, and then save in show format right before distribution.

Most of the other choices from Table 3.1 are special-purpose and not suitable for everyday use. The following sections explain some of those special types.

TABLE 3.2

PowerPoint 2007 Features Not Supported in Previous PowerPoint Versions

Feature	Issues
SmartArt Graphics	Converted to uneditable pictures
Charts (except Microsoft Graph charts)	Converted to editable OLE objects, but the chart might appear different
Custom Slide Layouts	Converted to multiple masters
Drop Shadows	Soft shadows converted to hard shadows
Equations	Converted to uneditable pictures
Heading and body fonts	Converted to static formatting
New effects:	Converted to uneditable pictures
■ 2-D or 3-D text	
■ Gradient outlines for shapes or text	
■ Strikethrough and double-strikethrough	
■ Gradient, picture, and texture fills on text	
■ Shadows, soft edges, reflections	
■ Most 3-D effects	

continued

TABLE 3.2 *(continued)*	
Feature	**Issues**
Themes	Converted to styles
Theme colors	Converted to styles
Theme effects	Converted to styles
Theme fonts	Converted to regular font usage

Saving for Use on the Web

To share your presentation on the Web with people who don't have PowerPoint, you can save in one of the Web Page formats.

You have two choices for Web format: Web Page or Single File Web Page. Web Page creates an HTML document that has links to the slides, and then the slides and their graphics are stored in a separate folder. This would be suitable for posting on a Web site. Single File Web Page creates a single .mht document that contains all of the HTML codes and all of the slides. This would be suitable for e-mailing, for example. (In fact, the "M" in the name format is short for "mail," because this format was originally designed for e-mail use.) However, with both of these Web formats, you lose some of the special effects, so you might prefer to distribute the presentation in a different way on the Web. If keeping the full effect of all the effects is important, consider saving in one of the PowerPoint Show formats and then make the PowerPoint Viewer utility available for free download from the same Web page.

CROSS-REF See Chapter 22 for details about the PowerPoint Viewer.

Saving Slides as Graphics

If you save your presentation in one of the graphic formats shown in the Graphics/Other section of Table 3.1, the file ceases to be a presentation and becomes a series of unrelated graphic files, one per slide. If you choose one of these formats, you're asked whether you want to export the current slide only or all slides. If you choose all slides, PowerPoint creates a new folder in the selected folder with the same name as the original presentation file and places the graphics files in it.

Saving Slide Text Only

If you want to export the text of the slides to some other application, consider the Outline/RTF format, which creates an outline similar to what you see in the Outline pane in PowerPoint. This file can then be opened in Word or any other application that supports RTF text files. Only text in placeholders is exported, though, not text in manually inserted text boxes.

Specifying Save Options

The Save Options enable you to fine-tune the saving process for special needs. For example, you can employ Save Options to embed fonts, to change the interval at which PowerPoint saves AutoRecover information, and more.

There are two ways to access the Save options:

■ Choose Office ➪ PowerPoint Options and click Save.

■ From the Save As dialog box, click Tools ➪ Save Options.

The PowerPoint Options dialog box appears, as in Figure 3.10.

FIGURE 3.10

Set Save Options to match the way you want PowerPoint to save your work.

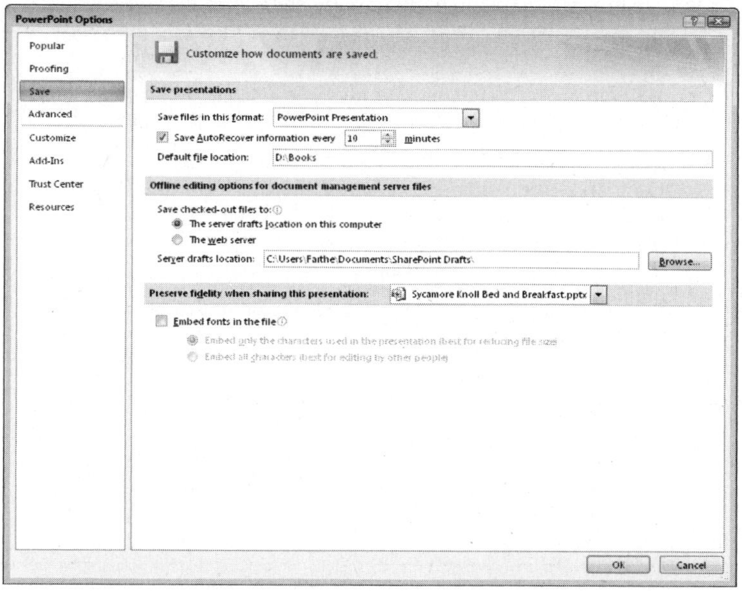

Then set any of the options desired. They are summarized in Table 3.3. Click OK when you are finished.

One of the most important features described in Table 3.3 is AutoRecover, which is turned on by default. This means if a system error or power outage causes PowerPoint to terminate unexpectedly, you do not lose all of the work you have done. The next time you start PowerPoint, it opens the recovered file and asks if you want to save it.

CAUTION AutoRecover is *not* a substitute for saving your work the regular way. It does not save in the same sense that the Save command does; it only saves a backup version as PowerPoint is running. If you quit PowerPoint normally, that backup version is erased. The backup version is available for recovery only if PowerPoint terminates abnormally (because a system lockup or a power outage, for example).

TABLE 3.3

Save Options

Feature	Purpose
Save Files in This Format	Sets the default file format to appear in the Save As dialog box. Your choices are a regular presentation, a macro-enabled presentation, or a 97-2003 backward-compatible presentation.
Save AutoRecover info every ___ minutes	PowerPoint saves your work every few minutes so that if the computer has problems and causes PowerPoint to terminate abnormally, you do not lose much work. Lower this number to save more often (for less potential data loss) or raise it to save less often (for less slowdown/delay related to repeated saving).
Default file location	Specify the location that you want to start from when saving with the Save As dialog box. By default it is your Documents (or My Documents) folder.
Save Checked-Out Files To	Sets the location in which any drafts will be saved that you have checked out of a Web server library such as SharePoint. If you choose The Server Drafts Location on This Computer, then you must specify what that location will be in the Server Drafts Location box. If you choose to save to The Web Server, it's not an issue because every save goes immediately back to the server.
Preserve Fidelity When Sharing This Presentation	This drop-down list enables you to select from among all the open presentation files for the following setting to affect.
Embed Fonts in the File	Turn this on if you are saving a presentation for use on a different PC that might not have the fonts installed that the presentation requires. You can choose to embed the characters in use only (which minimizes the file size, but if someone tries to edit the presentation they might not have all of the characters out of the font that they need), or to embed all characters in the font set. Unlike the others, this setting applies only to the current presentation file.

Setting Passwords for File Access

If a presentation contains sensitive or confidential data, you can encrypt the file and protect it with a password. Encryption is a type of "scrambling" done to the file so that nobody can see it, either from within PowerPoint or with any other type of file-browsing utility.

You can enter two separate passwords for a file: the Open password and the Modify password. Use an Open password to prevent unauthorized people from viewing the file at all. Use a Modify password to prevent people from making changes to the file.

You can use one, both, or neither of the password types. For example, suppose you have a personnel presentation that contains salary information. You might use an Open password and distribute that password to a few key people in the Human Resources department who need access to it. But then you might use a Modify password to ensure that none of those people make any changes to the presentation as they are viewing it.

For the Open password, you can specify an encryption method and strength. Many encryption codes are available, and the differences between them are significant mostly to high-end technical users. However, if you do have a preference, you can choose it when you choose the Open password.

To manage a file's passwords and other security settings, do the following:

1. Save the file as you normally would from the Save As dialog box.
2. Click Tools, and choose General Options. The General Options dialog box opens. See Figure 3.11.

FIGURE 3.11

Set a password to prevent unauthorized access.

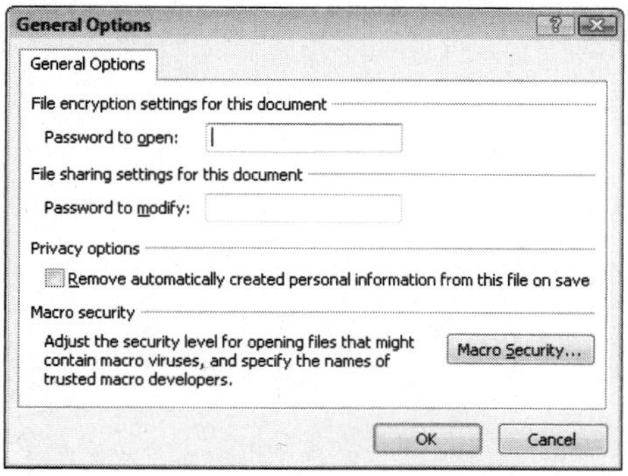

3. If you want an Open password, enter it in the Password to Open box.
4. If you want a Modify password, enter it in the Password to Modify box.
5. (Optional) If you want your personal information stripped from the file, such as your name removed from the Author field of the Properties box, mark the Remove Automatically Created Personal Information from This File On Save check box.

6. *(Optional)* If desired, adjust the macro security level for PowerPoint (all files, not just this one) by clicking the Macro Security button and making changes to the settings in the Trust Center; then click OK to return to the General Options dialog box.

7. Click OK.

8. If you specified a password in step 3, a confirmation box appears for it. Retype the same password and click OK.

9. If you specified a password in step 4, a confirmation box appears for it. Retype the same password and click OK.

10. Continue saving normally.

When you (or someone else) open the file, a Password prompt appears. The Open password must be entered to open the presentation file. The Modify password will *not* work. After that hurdle, if you have set a separate Modify password, a prompt for that appears. Your choices are to enter the Modify password, to cancel, or to click the Read Only option to open the presentation in Read Only mode.

Closing and Reopening Presentations

You can have several presentation files open at once and switch freely between them, but this can bog down your computer's performance somewhat. Unless you are doing some cut-and-paste work, it's best to have only one presentation file open — the one you are actively working on. It's easy to close and open presentations as needed.

Closing a Presentation

When you exit PowerPoint, the open presentation file automatically closes, and you're prompted to save your changes if you have made any. If you want to close a presentation file without exiting PowerPoint, follow these steps:

1. Choose Office ⇨ Close.

   If you have not made any changes to the presentation since the last time you saved, you're done.

2. If you have made any changes to the presentation, you're prompted to save them. If you don't want to save your changes, click No, and you're done.

3. If you want to save your changes, click Yes. If the presentation has already been saved once, you're done.

4. If the presentation has not been saved before, the Save As dialog box appears. Type a name in the File Name text box and click Save.

Opening a Presentation

To open a recently used presentation, select it from the right side of the Office menu. Although only one file appears in Figure 3.12, up to nine can appear by default.

FIGURE 3.12

Close the presentation via the Office menu.

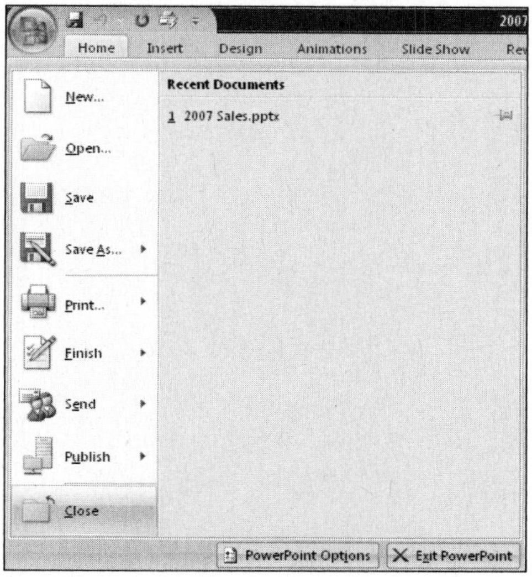

EXPERT TIP To pin a certain file to the Office menu's list so that it never scrolls off, click the push-pin icon to the right of the file's name on the menu. You can increase or decrease the number of recently used files that appear on the Office menu. Choose Office ➪ PowerPoint Options, click Advanced, and in the Display section, set the Number of Documents in the Recent Documents List.

If the presentation you want to open does not appear on the Office menu, follow these steps to find and open it:

1. Choose Office ➪ Open. The Open dialog box appears.

2. Choose the file you want. If necessary, change the location to find the file.

CROSS-REF See the section "Changing Drives and Folders" earlier in this chapter if you need help.

3. Click Open. The presentation opens.

To open more than one presentation at once, hold down the Ctrl key as you click each file you want to open. Then, click the Open button and they all open in their own windows. For more information, see the "Working with Multiple Presentations" section later in this chapter.

The Open button in the Open dialog box has its own drop-down list from which you can select commands that open the file in different ways. See Figure 3.13, and refer to Table 3.4 for an explanation of the available options.

FIGURE 3.13

The Open button's menu contains several special options for opening a file.

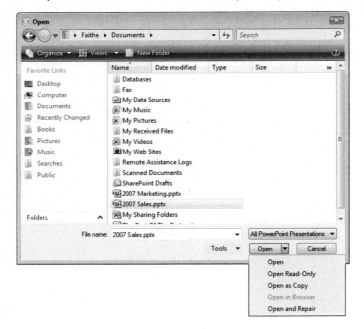

TABLE 3.4

Open Options

Open Button Setting	Purpose
Open	The default, simply opens the file for editing.
Open Read-Only	Allows changes but prevents those changes from being saved under the same name.
Open Copy	Opens a copy of the file, leaving the original untouched.

Open Button Setting	Purpose
Open in Browser	Applicable only for Web-based presentations, opens it for viewing in a Web browser.
Open and Repair	Opens the file, and identifies and repairs any errors it finds in it.
Show Previous Versions	Applicable only if the presentation file is stored on an NTFS volume under Windows Vista. See the next section for details.

Opening a File from a Different Program

Just as you can save files in various program formats, you can also open files from various programs. PowerPoint can detect the type of file and convert it automatically as you open it, so you do not have to know the exact file type. (For example, if you have an old PowerPoint file with a .ppt extension, you don't have to know what version it came from.) The only problem is with files that don't have extensions that PowerPoint automatically recognizes. In that case, you must change the File Type setting in the Open dialog box to All Files so that the file to be opened becomes available on the file list. See Figure 3.14. This change is valid for only this one use of the Open dialog box; the file type reverts to All PowerPoint Presentations, the default, the next time you open it.

FIGURE 3.14

To open files from different programs, change the File Type setting to All Files.

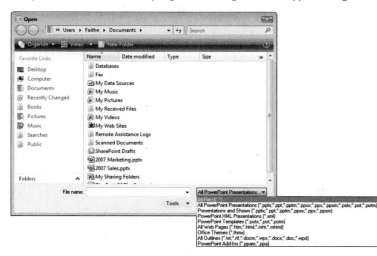

CAUTION   PowerPoint opens only presentation files and text-based files such as Word outlines. If you want to include graphics from another program in a PowerPoint presentation, copy-and-paste them into PowerPoint or insert them using the Picture command on the Insert tab. Do not attempt to open them with the Open dialog box.

Finding a Presentation File to Open

If you have forgotten where you saved a particular presentation file, you're not out of luck. The Open dialog box (under Windows Vista) includes a Search box that can help you locate it. See Figure 3.15.

To search for a file, follow these steps:

1. Choose Office ➪ Open to display the Open dialog box.
2. Navigate to a location that you know the file is in. For example, if you know it is on the C: drive, click Computer in the Favorite Links list and then double-click the C: drive.

FIGURE 3.15

Use the Search box in the Open dialog box (Windows Vista only) to look for a file.

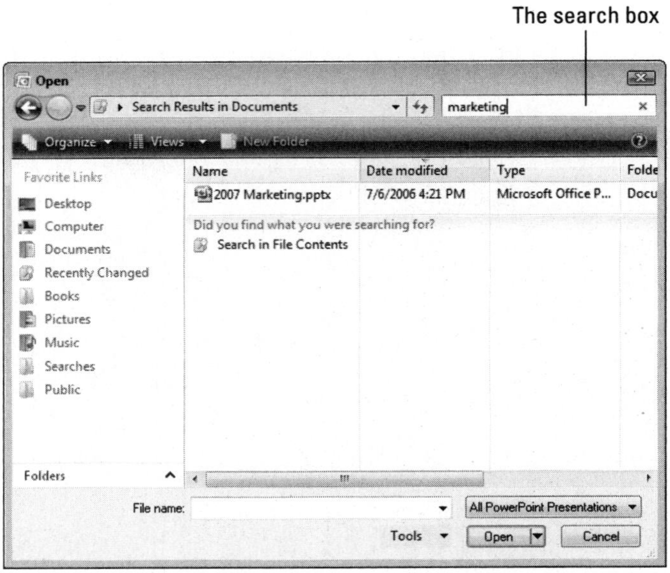

The search box

3. Click in the Search box and type part of the filename (if you know it) or a word or phrase used in the file.

4. Press Enter. A list of files appears that match that specification.

5. Open the file as you normally would.

NOTE You can also use the Search utility from outside of PowerPoint. In Windows, click Start and choose Search. Although the Search utility in Windows Vista is different from the one in Windows XP, both can find a file by name, content, author, date, or many other properties.

Setting File Properties

File properties are facts about each file that can help you organize them. If you have a lot of PowerPoint files, using file properties can help you search intelligently for them using the Search feature you learned about in the preceding section. For example, you can specify an author, a manager, and a company for each file, and then search based on those values.

You can set a file's properties while it is open in PowerPoint by doing the following:

1. Choose Office ➪ Prepare ➪ Properties. A Properties ribbon appears above the presentation window.

2. Fill in any information you want to store about the presentation. See Figure 3.16.

FIGURE 3.16

Enter information to store in the file's properties.

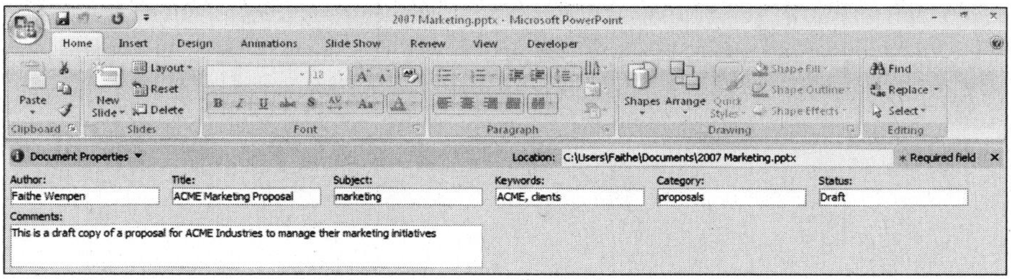

3. Click the down arrow to the right of Standard in the Properties ribbon, and choose Advanced Properties. The Properties dialog box for the file appears.

4. Click the Summary tab, and confirm/change any information there. This is the same information that you entered in the Properties ribbon, with the addition of a couple of other fields. See Figure 3.17.

FIGURE 3.17

The Summary tab has many of the same fields as the ribbon.

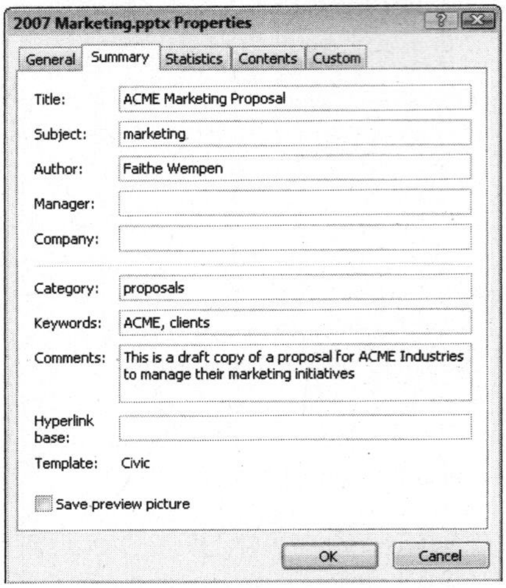

5. Click the Custom tab, shown in Figure 3.18, and choose any additional fields you need and set values for them. For example, click the Client field on the Name list, and type a value for it in the Value text box. Repeat this for any of the other custom fields.

FIGURE 3.18

The Custom tab enables you to set custom properties based on your tracking needs.

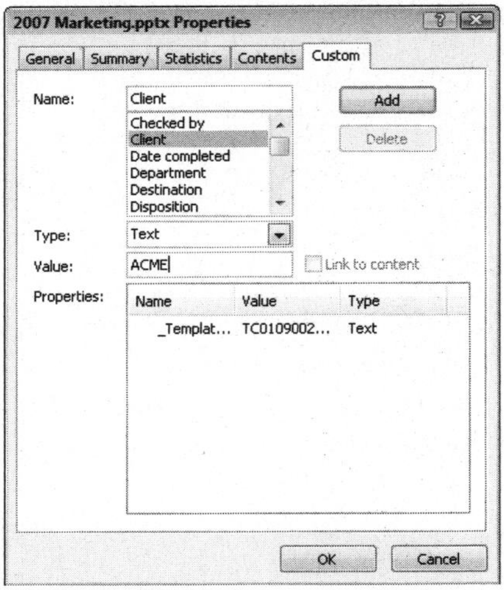

Working with Multiple Presentations

You will usually work with only one presentation at a time. But occasionally you may need to have two or more presentations open at once — for example, to make it easier to copy text or slides from one to the other.

To open another presentation, choose Office ⇨ Open and select the one you want, the same as usual.

When more than one presentation is open, you can switch among them by selecting the one you want to see from the taskbar in Windows. Alternatively, you can click the Switch Windows button on the View tab and select any open presentation from there as shown in the following figure.

Switch between open windows of all applications — not just PowerPoint — by pressing Alt+Esc repeatedly to cycle through them, or by holding down the Alt key and pressing Tab to browse thumbnails of open windows.

6. Review the information on the Statistics and Contents tab if desired. (You can't change that information.)

7. Click OK.

Now you can use the contents of the properties fields when performing a search.

Managing Files from Within PowerPoint

To save yourself some time, you can perform certain file management tasks without leaving PowerPoint. Any dialog box that enables you to select a file to open — such as the Open dialog box — or enables you to save a file — such as the Save As dialog box — can also be used to copy, delete, and rename files.

Creating a New Folder

When saving files, you might want to create a new folder to put them in. To create a new folder in a Windows Vista style dialog box, click New Folder in the command bar. See Figure 3.19. To create a new folder in Windows XP, click the New Folder button in the row of buttons that appears across the top of the Save As dialog box. See Figure 3.20.

FIGURE 3.19

Create a new folder from a Windows Vista style dialog box.

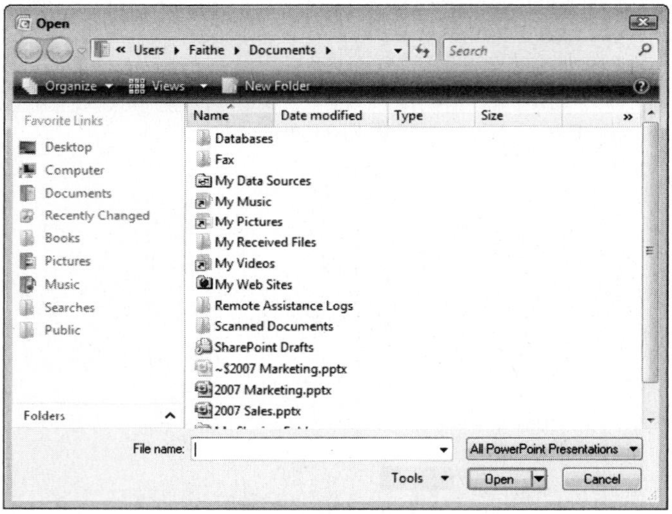

Copying a Presentation

One way to copy a presentation is to open it and then save it under a different name. (You learned to do this earlier in this chapter.) But here's a method that enables you to copy without having to first open the file:

1. From the Open dialog box, select the file you want to copy. (You can also use the Save As dialog box if you enable Browse Folders so you see the file listing.)

2. Right-click the file and choose Copy from the shortcut menu.

3. If necessary, change to a different drive and/or folder.

4. Right-click an empty area in the list of files.

FIGURE 3.20

Create a new folder from a Windows XP style dialog box.

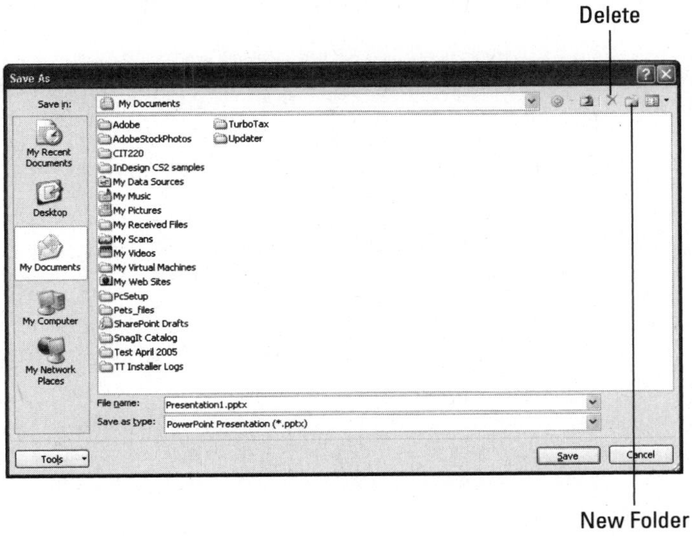

5. Choose Paste from the shortcut menu. The file appears. If you pasted it into the same folder as the original, the new one has the words *Copy of* at the beginning of its name to differentiate it. Rename it if desired.

CROSS-REF For more on renaming, see the section "Renaming a Presentation" later in this chapter.

6. Click Cancel to close the dialog box.

Deleting a Presentation

Just as you can copy a file, you can delete a presentation file from Windows itself, bypassing PowerPoint altogether. Just select the file in Windows Explorer or My Computer and press the Delete key, or drag it to the Recycle Bin on the Windows desktop.

To delete a file from within PowerPoint, select it from the Save As or Open dialog box and press the Delete key on the keyboard or right-click it and choose Delete. (Or in a Windows XP style dialog box, you can click the Delete button on the toolbar.) You cannot delete a file that is currently open.

NOTE If you accidentally delete a file, you can get it back if you deleted from Windows; just open the Recycle Bin and drag it back out.

Renaming a Presentation

To rename a file from within the Save As or Open dialog boxes, click it, and then press F2, or right-click it and choose Rename from the shortcut menu. Then type the new name and press Enter.

If you have the display of file extensions for known file types turned off in Windows (the default), you do not need to type the .pptx extension when renaming files. In fact, if you do type it, the file may end up with a double extension, like myfile.pptx.pptx. On the other hand, if you have the display of file extensions turned on, you must type the file extension while renaming a file.

EXPERT TIP To change the setting that governs whether or not file extensions are displayed, open the Computer window in Windows Vista and choose Organize ⇨ Folder Options or open the My Computer window in Windows XP and choose Tools ⇨ Folder Options. Then click the View tab and mark or clear the Hide extensions for known file types check box.

Mapping a Network Drive

This assigns a drive letter to a folder on a remote PC. This might be useful if you save frequently to a network location and you don't want to have to wade through multiple levels of folders each time to find it. (But you can also accomplish the same thing by creating a shortcut in My Network Places.)

To map the currently displayed folder as a network drive, open the Tools menu from either the Open or Save As dialog box and choose Map Network Drive. This opens a dialog box that lets you associate a drive letter with the location.

Summary

This chapter made you a master of files. You can now confidently create new presentations, and save, open, close, and delete PowerPoint presentation files. You can also save files in different formats, search for missing presentations, and lots more. This is rather utilitarian knowledge and not very much fun to practice, but later you will be glad you took the time to learn it, when you have important files you need to keep safe.

In the next chapter, you learn about slide layouts and text-based presentations. You also learn how to create your own layouts, and how to use the Outline pane to create the text that will form the basis of your message.

Chapter 4

Creating Slides and Text Boxes

<table>
<tr><td>IN THIS CHAPTER</td></tr>
</table>

PowerPoint makes it easy to create consistent, attractive slides that use standard preset layouts. You just choose the layout that you want for a particular slide and then fill in its placeholders with text, graphics, or other content.

In this chapter, you'll learn how to build a simple text-based presentation by creating new slides and entering text on them. You'll learn how to import content from other programs, and how to create, size, and position text boxes to hold the text for your presentation.

IN THIS CHAPTER

Creating new slides

Inserting content from external sources

Managing slides

Using content placeholders

Creating text boxes manually

Working with text boxes

Creating New Slides

Different templates start a presentation with different numbers and types of slides. A blank presentation has only a single slide, and you must create any others that you want.

There are several ways to create new slides. For example, you can type new text in the outline and then promote it to slide status, or you can add slides with the New Slide button that is on the Insert tab. You can also copy existing slides, either within the same presentation or from other sources. The following sections outline these procedures in more detail.

Creating New Slides from the Outline Pane

As discussed in Chapter 1, the Outline pane shows the text from the presentation's slides in a hierarchical tree, with the slide titles at the top level (the slide level) and the various levels of bulleted lists on the slides displaying as subordinate levels. Text that you type in the Outline pane appears on the slide, and vice versa, as shown in Figure 4.1.

> **NOTE** The Outline pane doesn't actually show all of the text in all cases; see "Creating Text Boxes Manually" later in this chapter to find out why text in some text boxes does not appear in the Outline pane.

Follow these steps to create a new slide from the Outline pane:

1. Switch to Normal view.
2. Right-click the existing line on the Outline pane that the new slide should follow.
3. Click New Slide. A new line appears in the Outline pane, with a slide symbol to its left.
4. Type the title for the new slide. The title appears both in the Outline pane and on the slide.

FIGURE 4.1

When you type text into the Outline pane, it automatically appears on the current slide.

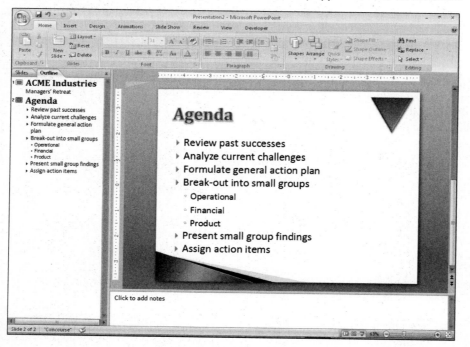

You can also create a new slide by starting a new line in the Outline pane and then promoting it to slide level by pressing Shift+Tab. Follow these steps to insert a new slide in this way:

1. Position the insertion point at the end of the last line of the slide that the new slide should follow, and press Enter to start a new line.

2. Press Shift+Tab to promote the new line to the highest level (press it multiple times if needed), so that a slide icon appears to its left.

3. Type the title for the new slide. The title appears both in the Outline pane and on the slide.

After creating the slide, you can continue creating its content directly in the Outline pane. Press Enter to start a new line, and then use Tab to demote, or Shift+Tab to promote, the line to the desired level. You can also right-click the text and choose Promote or Demote. Promoting a line all the way to the top level changes the line to a new slide title.

Creating a Slide from the Slides Pane

Here's a very quick method for creating a new slide, based on the default layout. It doesn't get much easier than this:

1. In Normal view, in the Slides pane, click the slide that the new slide should follow.

2. Press Enter. A new slide appears using the Title and Content layout.

The drawback to this method is that you cannot specify the layout. To choose a layout other than the default one, see the next section.

Creating a Slide from a Layout

A *slide layout* is a layout guide that tells PowerPoint what placeholder boxes to use on a particular slide and where to position them. Although slide layouts can contain placeholders for text, they also contain graphics, charts, tables, and other useful elements. After you create a new slide with placeholders, you can click a placeholder to open whatever controls you need to insert that type of object.

CROSS-REF See the section, "Using Content Placeholders" for more information on inserting objects.

When you create new slides using the outline method described in the preceding section, the new slides use the Title and Content layout, which consists of a slide title and a single, large placeholder box for content. If you want to use another layout, such as a slide with two adjacent but separate frames of content, you must either switch the slide to a different layout after its creation (using the Layout menu on the Home tab), or you must specify a different layout when you initially create the slide.

To specify a certain layout as you are creating a slide, follow these steps:

1. In Normal or Slide Sorter view, select or display the slide that the new one should follow.

   You can select a slide by clicking its thumbnail image in Slide Sorter view or on the Slides pane in Normal view. You can also move the insertion point to the slide's text in the Outline pane.

2. On either the Home tab, do one of the following:

   ■ To add a new slide using the default Title and Content layout, click the top (graphical) portion of the New Slide button.

   ■ To add a new slide using another layout, click the bottom (text) portion of the New Slide button and then select the desired layout from the menu, as shown in Figure 4.2.

FIGURE 4.2
_____

Create a new slide, based on the layout of your choice.

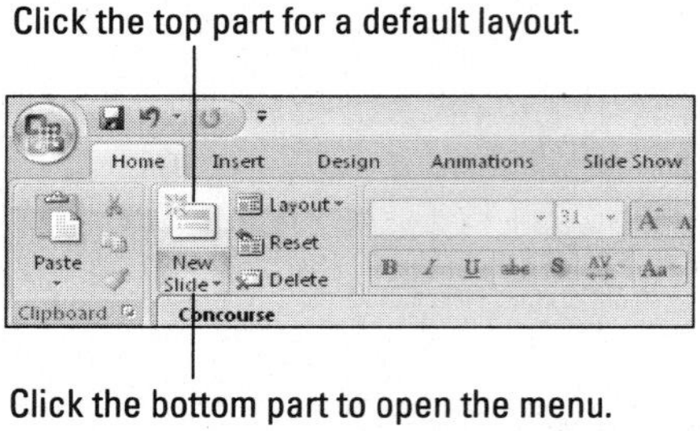

Click the top part for a default layout.

Click the bottom part to open the menu.

EXPERT TIP The layouts that appear on the menu come from the slide master. To customize these layouts, click Slide Master on the View tab. You will learn more about the slide master and about changing layouts in Chapter 5.

Copying Slides

Another way to create a new slide is to copy an existing one in the same presentation. This is especially useful when you are using multiple slides to create a progression because one slide is typically identical to the next slide in a sequence, except for a small change. (You can also build effects within a single slide using PowerPoint's animation effects, as you will learn in Chapter 18.)

There are several ways to copy one or more slides. One way is to use the Windows Clipboard, as in the following steps:

1. Select the slide or slides that you want to copy. See "Selecting Slides" later in this chapter for more information about selecting slides.

CAUTION If you select from the Outline pane, make sure that you click the icon to the left of the slide's title so that the entire slide is selected; if you select only part of the text on the slide, then only the selected part is copied.

2. Press Ctrl+C. You can also click the Copy button on the Home tab, or right-click the selection and click Copy.

3. Select the slide that the pasted slide or slides should follow. Alternately, in the Outline pane, click to place the insertion point where you want the insertion.

4. Press Ctrl+V. You can also click the Paste button on the Home tab, or right-click the destination and click Paste.

PowerPoint also has a Duplicate Slides command that does the same thing as a copy-and-paste command. Although it may be a little faster, it gives you less control as to where the pasted copies will appear:

1. Select the slide or slides to be duplicated.

2. On the Home tab, click the bottom part of the New Slide button to open its menu.

3. Click Duplicate Selected Slides.

   PowerPoint pastes the slides immediately after the last slide in the selection. For example, if you selected slides 1, 3, and 6, then the copies are placed after slide 6.

EXPERT TIP To make duplication even faster, you can place the Duplicate Selected Slides command on the Quick Access toolbar. To do that, right-click the command on the menu and choose Add to Quick Access Toolbar.

Inserting Content from External Sources

Many people find that they can save a lot of time by copying text or slides from other programs or from other PowerPoint presentations to form the basis of a new presentation. There's no need to reinvent the wheel each time! The following sections look at various ways to bring in content from external sources.

Copying Slides from Other Presentations

There are several ways to copy slides from other presentations. You can:

■ Open the presentation, save it under a different name, and then delete the slides that you *don't* want, leaving a new presentation with the desired slides ready for customization.

■ Open two PowerPoint windows side-by-side and drag-and-drop slides between them.

■ Open two PowerPoint presentations, copy slides from one of them to the Clipboard (Ctrl+C), and then paste them into the other presentation (Ctrl+V).

■ Use the Reuse Slides feature in PowerPoint, as described next.

To reuse slides from other presentations with the Reuse Slides feature, follow these steps:

1. On the Home tab, click the lower portion of the New Slide button to open its menu.

2. Click Reuse Slides. The Reuse Slides pane appears.

3. Click Open a PowerPoint File.

   OR

   Click the Browse button and then click Browse File.

4. In the Browse dialog box, select the presentation from which you want to copy slides, and click Open. Thumbnail images of the slides in the presentation appear in the Reuse Slides pane, as shown in Figure 4.3.

5. (Optional) If you want to keep the source formatting when copying slides, select the Keep Source Formatting check box at the bottom of the task pane.

6. (Optional) You can move the cursor over a slide to see an enlarged image of it.

FIGURE 4.3

Choose individual slides to copy to the current presentation.

7. Do any of the following:

   ▪ To insert a single slide, click it.

   ▪ To insert all slides at once, right-click any slide and choose Insert All Slides.

   ▪ To copy only the theme (not the content), right-click any slide and choose Apply Theme to All Slides, or Apply Theme to Selected Slides.

CAUTION Copying the theme with the Apply Theme to All Slides or Apply Theme to Selected Slides command does not copy the background graphics, layouts, or anything else other than the three elements that are included in a theme: font choices, color choices, and effect choices. If you want to copy all of the formatting, select the Keep Source Formatting check box (step 5) and insert one or more slides.

Inserting New Slides from an Outline

All of the Microsoft Office applications work well together, and so it's easy to move content between them. For example, you can create an outline for a presentation in Microsoft Word and then import it into PowerPoint. PowerPoint uses the heading styles that you assigned in Word to decide which items are slide titles and which items are slide content. The top-level headings (Heading 1) form the slide titles.

To try this out, open Word, switch to Outline view (from the View tab), and then type a short outline of a presentation. Press Tab to demote, or Shift+Tab to promote, a selected line. Then save your work, go back to PowerPoint, and follow these steps to import it:

1. On the Home tab, click the lower portion of the New Slide button to open its menu.

2. Click Slides from Outline. The Insert Outline dialog box opens.

3. Select the file containing the outline text that you want to import.

4. Click Insert. PowerPoint imports the outline.

If there were already existing slides in the presentation, they remain untouched. (This includes any blank slides, and so you might need to delete the blank slide at the beginning of the presentation after importing.) All of the Heading 1 lines from the outline become separate slide titles, and all of the subordinate headings become bullet points in the slides.

Tips for Better Outline Importing

Although PowerPoint can import any text from any Word document, you may not always get the results that you want or expect. For example, you may have a document that consists of a series of paragraphs with no heading styles applied. When you import this document into PowerPoint, it might look something like Figure 4.4.

FIGURE 4.4

A Word document consisting mainly of plain paragraphs makes for an unattractive presentation.

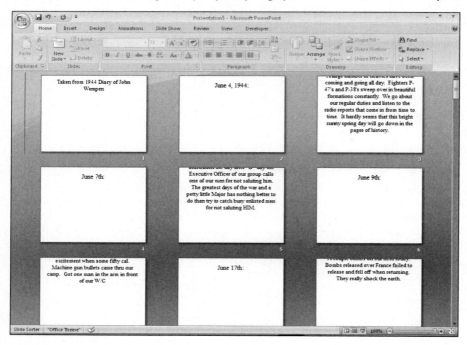

Figure 4.4 is a prime example of what happens if you don't prepare a document before you import it into PowerPoint. PowerPoint makes each paragraph its own slide. It can't tell which ones are actual headings and which ones aren't because there are no heading styles in use. The paragraphs are too long to fit on slides, and so they are truncated off the tops of the slides. Extra blank lines are interpreted as blank slides. Quite a train wreck, isn't it? Figure 4.4 also illustrates an important point to remember: regular paragraph text does not work very well in PowerPoint. PowerPoint text is all about short, snappy bulleted lists and headings. The better that you prepare the outline before importing it, the less cleanup you will need to do after importing. Here are some tips:

- Non-headings in Word do not import into PowerPoint unless you use no heading styles at all in the document (as in Figure 4.4). Apply heading styles to the text that you want to import.

- Stick with basic styles only in the outline: for example, just Heading 1, Heading 2, and so on.

- Delete all blank lines above the first heading. If you don't, you will have blank slides at the beginning of your presentation.

- Strip off as much manual formatting as possible from the Word text, so that the text picks up its formatting from PowerPoint. To strip off formatting in Word, select the text and press Ctrl+spacebar.

- Do not leave blank lines between paragraphs. These will translate into blank slides or blank bulleted items in PowerPoint.

- Delete any graphic elements, such as clip art, pictures, charts, and so on. They will not transfer to PowerPoint anyway and may confuse the import utility.

Importing from Other Text-Based Formats

In addition to Word, PowerPoint also imports from plain-text files, from WordPerfect (5.x or 6.x), from Microsoft Works, and from Web pages. The procedure is the same as in the preceding steps. If the file does not appear in the Insert Outline dialog box, change the file type to the desired file type.

If you are setting up a plain-text file for import, you obviously won't have the outlining tools from Word at your disposal. Instead, you must rely on tabs. Each line that should be a title slide should start at the left margin; first-level bullet paragraphs should be preceded by a single tab; second-level bullets should be preceded by two tabs, and so on.

Post-Import Cleanup

After importing text from an outline, there will probably be a few minor corrections that you need to make. Run through this checklist:

- The first slide in the presentation might be blank. If it is, then delete it.

- The Title Slide layout may not be applied to the first slide; apply that layout, if necessary. (You can use the Layout list on the Home tab.)

- A theme may not be applied; choose one from the Design tab, if necessary.

CROSS-REF See Chapter 5 for more information on working with themes.

- Some of the text might contain manual formatting that interferes with the theme formatting and creates inconsistency. Remove any manual formatting that you notice. (One way to do this is to select all of the text in the Outline pane by pressing Ctrl+A and then stripping off the manual formatting by pressing Ctrl+spacebar.)

- If some of the text is too long to fit comfortably on a slide, change to a different slide layout, such as a two-column list, if necessary. You might also need to split the content into two or more slides.

- There might be some blank bullet points on some slides (if you missed deleting all of the extra paragraph breaks before the import). Delete these bullet points.

Opening a Word Document as a New Presentation

Instead of importing slides from a Word document or other text-based document, as described in the preceding section, you can simply open the Word document in PowerPoint. PowerPoint starts a new presentation file to hold the imported text. This saves some time if you are starting a new presentation anyway, and you don't have any existing slides to merge with the incoming content.

To open a Word document in PowerPoint, follow these steps:

1. Choose Office ➪ Open. The Open dialog box appears.
2. Change the file type to All Outlines.
3. Select the document.
4. Click Open. The document outline becomes a PowerPoint presentation, with all Heading 1 paragraphs becoming title slides.

> **CAUTION** You can't open or insert a Word outline in PowerPoint if it is currently open in Word. This limitation is an issue only for Word files, not plain text or other formats.

Importing Text from Web Pages

PowerPoint accepts imported text from several Web-page formats, including HTML and MHTML (Single File Web Page). It is helpful if the data is in an orderly outline format, or if it was originally created from a PowerPoint file, because there will be less cleanup needed.

There are several ways to import from a Web page:

- Open a Web-page file as you would an outline (see the preceding section), but set the file type to All Web Pages.
- Insert the text from the Web page as you would a Word outline (in the Home tab, click New Slide ➪ Slides from Outline).
- Reuse slides from a Web presentation as you would from any other presentation (in the Home tab, click New Slide ➪ Reuse Slides).

> **CAUTION** You should use one of the above methods rather than pasting HTML text directly into PowerPoint. This is because when you paste HTML text, you might get additional HTML tags that you don't want, including cross-references that might cause your presentation to try to log onto a Web server every time you open it.

When importing from a Web page, don't expect the content to appear formatted the same way that it was on the Web page. We're talking strictly about text import here. The formatting on the Web page comes from HTML tags or from a style sheet, neither of which you can import. If you want an exact duplicate of the Web page's appearance, take a picture of the page with the Shift+PrintScreen command, and then paste it into PowerPoint (Ctrl+V) as a graphic.

If you are importing an outline from an MHTML-format Web page that contains pictures, the pictures are also imported into PowerPoint. If importing from a regular HTML file, you cannot import the pictures.

EXPERT TIP If you need to show a live Web page from within PowerPoint, try Shyam Pillai's free Live Web add-in, found at `www.mvps.org/skp/liveweb.htm`.

Managing Slides

After inserting a few slides into a presentation, and perhaps building some content on them, you might decide to make some changes, such as rearranging, deleting, and so on. The following sections explain how to manage and manipulate the slides in a presentation.

Selecting Slides

Before you can issue a command that acts upon a slide or a group of slides, you must select the slides that you want to affect. You can do this from either Normal or Slide Sorter view, but Slide Sorter view makes it easier because you can see more slides at once. From Slide Sorter view, or from the Slides pane in Normal view, you can use any of these techniques to select slides:

- To select a single slide, click it.
- To select multiple slides, hold down the Ctrl key as you click each one. Figure 4.5 shows slides 1, 3, and 6 selected, as indicated by the shaded border around the slides.

FIGURE 4.5

Select slides in Slide Sorter view by holding down the Ctrl key and clicking each slide.

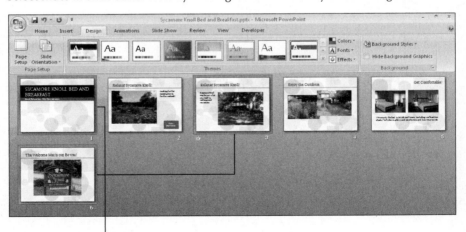

Selected Slides

■ To select a contiguous group of slides (for example, slides 1, 2, and 3), click the first slide, and then hold down the Shift key as you click the last one. All of the slides in between are selected as well.

To cancel the selection of multiple slides, click anywhere outside of the selected slides.

To select slides from the Outline pane in Normal view, click the slide icon to the left of the slide's title; this selects the entire slide, as shown in Figure 4.6. It's important to select the entire slide and not just part of its content before issuing a command such as Delete, because otherwise, the command only affects the portion that you selected.

Select slides in the Outline pane by clicking the slide icon to the left of the slide title.

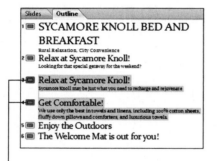

Slide icons

Deleting Slides

You may want to get rid of some of the slides, especially if you created your presentation using a template that contained a lot of sample content. For example, the sample presentation may be longer than you need, or you may have inserted your own slides instead.

Select the slide or slides that you want to delete, and then do any of the following:

■ On the Home tab, click Delete.

■ Right-click the selection and choose Delete Slide.

■ Press the Delete key on the keyboard.

Undoing Mistakes

Here's a command that can help you in almost all of the other chapters in this book: undoing. The Undo command allows you to reverse past actions. For example, you can use it to reverse all of the deletions that you made to your presentation in the preceding section. The easiest way to undo a single action is to click the Undo button on the Quick Access toolbar or press Ctrl+Z. You can click it as many times as you like; each time you click it, you undo one action.

EXPERT TIP   By default, the maximum number of Undo operations is 20, but you can change this. Choose Office ➪ PowerPoint Options, then click Advanced, and in the Editing Options section, change the Maximum Number of Undos setting. Keep in mind that if you set the number of undos too high, it can cause performance problems in PowerPoint.

You can undo multiple actions at once by opening the Undo button's drop-down list, as shown in Figure 4.7. Just drag the mouse across the actions that you want to undo (you don't need to hold down the mouse button). Click when the desired actions are selected, and presto, they are all reversed. You can select multiple actions to undo, but you can't skip around. For example, to undo the fourth item, you must undo the first, second, and third ones, as well.

FIGURE 4.7

Use the Undo button to undo your mistakes and the Redo button to reverse an Undo operation.

The Redo command is the opposite of Undo. If you make a mistake with the Undo button, you can fix the problem by clicking the Redo button. Like the Undo button, it has a drop-down list, and so you can redo multiple actions at once.

The Redo command is available only immediately after you use the Undo command. If Redo isn't available, a Repeat button appears in its place. The Repeat command enables you to repeat the last action that you performed (and it doesn't have to be an Undo operation). For example, you can repeat some typing, or some formatting. Figure 4.8 shows the Repeat button.

The Repeat button appears when Redo is not available, and enables you to repeat actions.

Repeat

Rearranging Slides

The best way to rearrange slides is to do so in Slide Sorter view. In this view, the slides in your presentation appear in thumbnail view, and you can move them around on the screen to different positions, just as you would manually rearrange pasted-up artwork on a table. Although you can also do this from the Slides pane in Normal view, you are able to see fewer slides at once. As a result, it can be more challenging to move slides around, for example, from one end of the presentation to another. To rearrange slides, use the following steps:

1. Switch to Slide Sorter view.

2. Select the slide that you want to move. You can move multiple slides at once if you like.

3. Drag the selected slide to the new location. The mouse pointer changes to a little rectangle next to the pointer arrow as you drag. A vertical line also appears where the slide will go if you release the mouse button at that point, as shown in Figure 4.9.

4. Release the mouse button. The slide moves to the new location.

FIGURE 4.9

As you drag a slide, its new position is indicated by a vertical line.

Vertical line shows destination

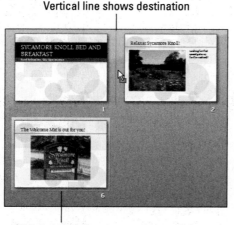

Slide beige dragged

You can also rearrange slides in the Outline pane in Normal view. This is not quite as easy as using Slide Sorter view, but it's more versatile. Not only can you drag entire slides from place to place, but you can also move individual bullets from one slide to another.

Follow these steps to move content in the Outline pane:

1. Switch to Normal view and display the Outline pane.

2. Position the mouse pointer over the slide's icon. The mouse pointer changes to a four-headed arrow.

3. Click on the icon. PowerPoint selects all of the text in that slide.

4. Drag the slide's icon to a new position in the outline. As you drag, a horizontal line appears to indicate where the slide will go, as shown in Figure 4.10.

FIGURE 4.10

Drag a slide's icon to move it up or down in the Outline pane.

Selected slide

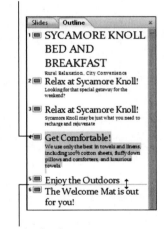

Line shows destination

5. Release the mouse button when the horizontal line is in the right place. All of the slide's text moves with it to the new location.

There are also keyboard shortcuts for moving a slide up or down in the Outline pane that may be faster than clicking the toolbar buttons. You can press the Alt+Shift+Up arrow keys to move a slide up, and the Alt+Shift+Down arrow keys to move the slide down.

These shortcuts work equally well with single bullets from a slide. Just click to the left of a single line to select it, instead of clicking the Slide icon in step 3.

Using Content Placeholders

Now that you know something about inserting and managing entire slides, let's take a closer look at the content within a slide. The default placeholder type is a multi-purpose content placeholder, as shown in Figure 4.11.

FIGURE 4.11

A content placeholder can contain a variety of different elements.

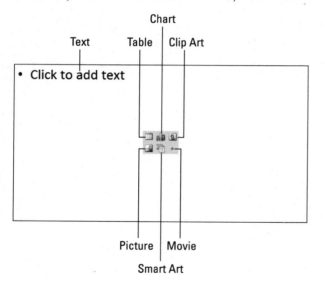

Inserting Content into a Placeholder

To type text into a content placeholder, click inside the placeholder box and start typing. You can enter and edit text as you would in any word-processing program. To insert any other type of content into a placeholder, click one of the icons shown in Figure 4.12. A dialog box opens to help you select and insert that content type.

CROSS-REF Chapters 6 and 7 cover the various formatting that you can apply to text on a slide. You will learn about these various content types later in the book:

- Tables: Chapter 9

- SmartArt: Chapter 11

- Clip art: Chapter 12

- Pictures (from files): Chapter 13

- Charts: Chapter 14

- Movies: Chapter 17

A content placeholder can hold only one type of content at a time. If you click in the placeholder and type some text, the icons for the other content types disappear. To access them again, you must delete all of the text from the placeholder.

Placeholders vs. Manually Inserted Objects

You can insert content on a slide independently of a placeholder by using the Insert tab's buttons and menus. This technique allows you to insert an item in its own separate frame on any slide, to coexist with any placeholder content. You can learn how to insert each content type in the chapters in which they are covered (see the preceding list).

Creating Text Boxes Manually

The difference between a placeholder-inserted object and a manually inserted one is most significant with text boxes. Although you might think that a text box would create consistent results, there are actually some significant differences between placeholder text boxes and manually inserted ones.

Here are some of the characteristics of a text placeholder:

- You cannot create new text placeholder boxes on your own, except in Slide Master view.

CROSS-REF You learn how to use Slide Master view to create your own layouts that contain custom text placeholders in Chapter 5.

- If you delete all of the text from a text placeholder, the placeholder instructions return (in Normal view).

- A text placeholder box has a fixed size on the slide, regardless of the amount or size of text that it contains. You can resize it manually, but if you reapply the layout, the placeholder box snaps back to the original size.

- AutoFit is turned on by default in a text placeholder, so that if you type more text than will fit, or resize the frame so that the existing text no longer fits, the text shrinks in size.

- The text that you type in a text placeholder box appears in the Outline pane.

A manual text box, on the other hand, is one that you create yourself using the Text Box tool on the Insert tab. Here are some characteristics of a manual text box:

- You can create a manual text box anywhere, and you can create as many as you like, regardless of the layout.

- If you delete all of the text from a manual text box, the text box remains empty or disappears completely. No placeholder instructions appear.

- A manual text box starts out small vertically, and expands as you type more text into it.

- A manual text box does not use AutoFit by default; the text box simply becomes larger to make room for more text.

- You cannot resize a manual text box so that the text that it contains no longer fits; PowerPoint refuses to make the text box shorter vertically until you delete some text from it. (However, you can decrease its horizontal width.)

- Text typed in a manual text box does not appear in the Outline pane.

Figure 4.12 shows two text placeholders (one empty) and a text box. Notice that the empty placeholder contains filler text to help you remember that it is there. Notice also that only the text from the placeholder appears in the Outline pane; the text-box text does not. Empty text boxes and placeholders do not show up in Slide Show view, so you do not have to worry about deleting any unneeded ones.

When Should You Use a Manual Text Box?

Graphical content such as photos and charts can work well either in placeholders or as manually inserted objects. However, when it comes to text, you should stick with placeholders as often as possible. Placeholder text appears in the Outline pane, whereas text in a manually inserted text box does not. When the bulk of a presentation's text is in manually created text boxes, the outline becomes less useful because it doesn't contain the presentation text. In addition, when you change to a different formatting theme that includes different positioning for placeholders — for example, to accommodate a graphic on one side — the manual text boxes do not shift. As a result, they might end up overlapping the new background graphic with unattractive results. In a case such as this, you would need to manually go through each slide and adjust the positioning of each text box.

However, there are times when a manually created text box is preferable or even necessary. For example, suppose that you have a schematic diagram of a machine and you need to label some of the parts. Manually placed text boxes are perfect for these little snippets of text that are scattered over the surface of the picture. Manual text boxes are also useful for warnings, tips, and any other information that is tangential to the main discussion. Finally, if you want to vary the placement of the text on each slide (consciously circumventing the consistency provided by layouts), and you want to precisely position each box, then manual text boxes work well because they do not shift their position when you apply different themes or templates to the presentation.

FIGURE 4.12

Two text placeholders and a text box.

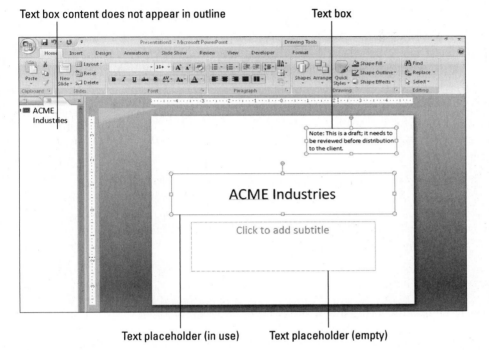

Text box content does not appear in outline

Text box

Text placeholder (in use)   Text placeholder (empty)

EXPERT TIP If you insert text in a placeholder and then change the slide's layout so that the slide no longer contains that placeholder (for example, if you switch to Title Only or Blank layout), the text remains on the slide, but it becomes an *orphan*. If you delete the text box, then it simply disappears; a placeholder does not reappear. However, it does not become a manual text box, because its content still appears in the Outline pane, while a manual text box's content does not.

Creating a Manual Text Box

To manually place a text box on a slide, follow these steps:

1. If necessary, reposition the existing placeholders or objects on the slide to make room for the new text box.

2. On the Insert tab, click Text Box. The mouse pointer turns into a vertical line.

3. Do either of the following:

   ▪ To create a text box that automatically enlarges itself horizontally as you type more text, but does not automatically wrap text to the next line, click once where you want the text to start, and begin typing.

■ To create a text box with a width that you specify, and that automatically wraps text to the next line and grows in height as needed, click and drag to draw a box where you want the text box to be. Its height will initially snap back to a single line's height, regardless of the height that you initially draw; however, it will grow in height as you type text into it.

4. Type the text that you want to appear in the text box.

Working with Text Boxes

Text boxes (either placeholder or manual) form the basis of most presentations. Now that you know how to create them, and how to place text in them, let's take a look at how to manipulate the boxes themselves.

CROSS-REF Are you looking for information about formatting text boxes — perhaps to apply a background color or a border to one? See the formatting text boxes discussion in Chapter 7.

Selecting Text Boxes

On the surface, this topic might seem like a no-brainer. Just click it, right? Well, almost. A text box has two possible "selected" states. One state is that the box itself is selected, and the other is that the insertion point is within the box. The difference is subtle, but it becomes clearer when you issue certain commands. For example, if the insertion point is in the text box and you press Delete, PowerPoint deletes the single character to the right of the insertion point. However, if you select the entire text box and press Delete, PowerPoint deletes the entire text box and everything in it.

To select the entire text box, click its border. You can tell that it is selected because the border appears as a solid line. To move the insertion point within the text box, click inside the text box. You can tell that the insertion point is there because you can see it flashing inside, and also because the box's border now consists of a dashed line. Figure 4.13 shows the difference between the two borders.

FIGURE 4.13

The border of a text box is different when the box itself is selected (left) and when the insertion point is in the box (right).

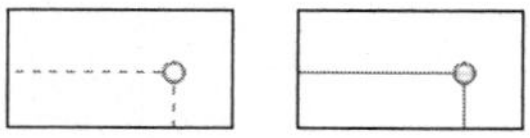

In the rest of this book, when you see the phrase "select the text box," it means in the first way; the box itself should be selected, and the insertion point should *not* appear in it. For most of the upcoming sections it does not make any difference, although in a few cases it does.

EXPERT TIP When the insertion point is flashing in a text box, you can press Esc to select the text box itself.

You can select more than one text box at once by holding down the Shift key as you click additional text boxes. This technique is useful when you want to select more than one text box, for example, so that you can format them in the same way, or so that you can resize them by the same amount.

Sizing a Text Box

The basic techniques for sizing text boxes in PowerPoint are the same for every object type (for that matter, they are also the same as in other Office applications). To resize a text box, or any object, follow these steps:

1. Position the mouse pointer over a selection handle for the object. The mouse pointer changes to a double-headed arrow.

   If you want to resize proportionally, make sure that you use a corner selection handle, and hold down the Shift key as you drag.

2. (Optional) To resize proportionally, hold down the Shift key.

3. Click and drag the selection handle to resize the object's border.

CAUTION Allowing PowerPoint to manage placeholder size and position through layouts ensures consistency among your slides. When you start changing the sizes and positions of placeholders on individual slides, you can end up creating consistency problems, such as headings that aren't in the same spot from slide to slide, or company logos that shift between slides.

You can also set a text box's size from the Size group on the Drawing Tools Format tab. When the text box is selected, its current dimensions appear in the Height and Width boxes, as shown in Figure 4.14. You can change the dimensions within these boxes.

FIGURE 4.14

You can set an exact size for a text box from the Format tab's Size group.

Height Width

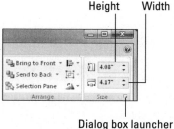

Dialog box launcher

You can also set the size of a text box from the Size and Position dialog box:

1. Click the dialog box launcher in the Size group on the Drawing Tools Format tab, as shown in Figure 4.14. The Size and Position dialog box opens.

2. On the Size tab, set the height and width for the text box, as shown in Figure 4.15.

FIGURE 4.15

You can adjust the size of the text box from the Size and Position dialog box.

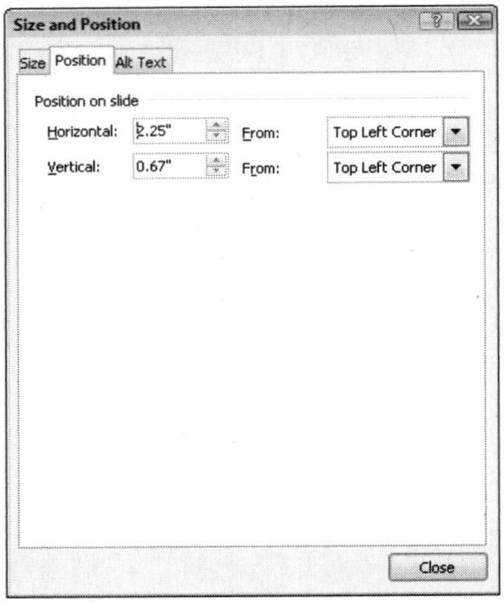

To keep the size proportional, select the Lock Aspect Ratio check box in the Scale section before you start adjusting the height or width.

3. Click Close to close the dialog box.

EXPERT TIP The Size and Position dialog box is *non-modal*. This means that you can leave it open and continue to work on your presentation. It also means that any changes that you make in this dialog box are applied immediately; there is no Cancel button in the dialog box to cancel your changes. To reverse a change, you can use the Undo command (Ctrl+Z).

Positioning a Text Box

To move an object, simply drag it by any part of its border other than a selection handle. Select the object, and then position the mouse pointer over a border so that the pointer turns into a four-headed arrow. Then drag the object to a new position. With a text box, you must position the mouse pointer over a border and not over the inside of the frame; with all other object types, you don't have to be that precise; you can move an object by dragging anywhere within it.

To set an exact position, use the Size and Position dialog box:

1. Click the dialog box launcher in the Size group on the Drawing Tools Format tab, as shown in Figure 4.14. The Size and Position dialog box opens.

2. On the Position tab, shown in Figure 4.16, set the horizontal and vertical position, and the point from which it is measured. By default, measurements are from the top-left corner of the slide.

FIGURE 4.16

You can adjust the position from the Size and Position dialog box.

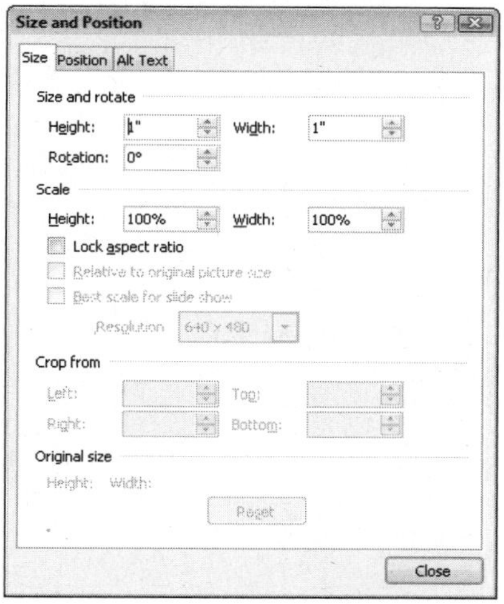

3. Click Close to close the dialog box.

Changing a Text Box's AutoFit Behavior

When there is too much text to fit in a text box, there are three things that may happen:

- **Do Not AutoFit:** The text and the box can continue at their default sizes, and the text can overflow out of the box or be truncated.
- **Shrink Text on Overflow:** The text can shrink its font size to fit in the text box. This is the default setting for placeholder text boxes.
- **Resize Shape to Fit Text:** The text box can enlarge to the size needed to contain the text. This is the default setting for manual text boxes.

Whenever there is too much text in a placeholder box, the AutoFit icon appears in the bottom-left corner. Click that icon to display a menu, as shown in Figure 4.17. From that menu, you can turn AutoFit on or off.

FIGURE 4.17

You can use the AutoFit icon's menu to change the AutoFit setting for a text box.

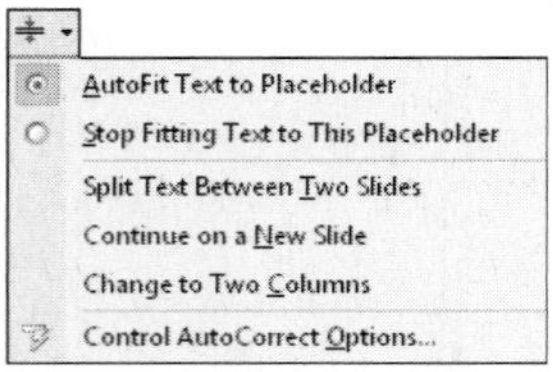

With a manual text box, the AutoFit icon does not appear, and so you must adjust the AutoFit behavior in the text box's properties. The following method works for both manual and place-holder boxes:

1. Right-click the border of the text box and choose Format Shape.
2. Click Text Box.
3. In the Autofit section, choose one of the Autofit options, as shown in Figure 4.18.
4. Click Close.

FIGURE 4.18

You can set AutoFit properties in the Format Shape dialog box.

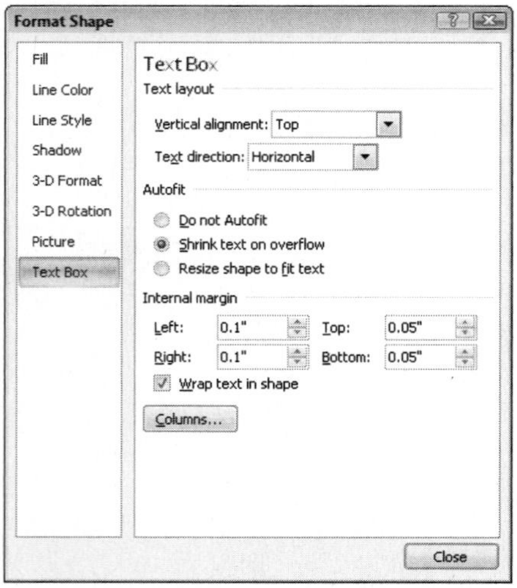

One other setting that also affects AutoFit behavior is the Wrap Text in Shape option. This on/off toggle enables text to automatically wrap to the next line when it reaches the right edge of the text box. By default, this setting is On for placeholder text boxes and for manual text boxes that you create by dragging. However, it is Off by default for manual text boxes that you create by clicking. You can change the setting by displaying the text box's properties, as shown in Figure 4.18, and selecting or deselecting the Wrap Text in Shape check box.

Table 4.1 summarizes the various AutoFit behaviors and how they interact with one another.

TABLE 4.1

AutoFit and Resize Shape to Fit Text Behaviors

Setting	Default For	When Wrap Text in Shape Is On	When Wrap Text in Shape Is Off
Do Not Autofit	n/a	Text overflows at bottom of text box only	Text overflows at right and bottom of text box
Shrink Text on Overflow	Placeholders	Text shrinks to fit	Text shrinks to fit
Resize Shape to Fit Text	Manual text boxes	Text box expands vertically only (default for manual text box that you create by dragging)	Text box expands vertically and horizontally (default for manual text box that you create by clicking). However, if you clicked to create the text box initially, the width keeps expanding until you press Enter.

Summary

In this chapter, you learned how to create new slides, either from scratch or from outside sources. You learned how to select, rearrange, and delete slides, and how to place content on a slide. Along the way, you learned the difference between a content placeholder and a manually inserted object, and how to create your own text boxes, move and resize objects, and find or replace text. These are all very basic skills, and perhaps not as interesting as some of the more exciting topics to come, but mastering them will serve you well as you build your presentation.

In the next chapter, you'll learn about themes and layouts, two of the innovative features in PowerPoint 2007 that make it such an improvement over earlier versions. You'll find out how a theme differs from a template and how it applies font, color, and effect formatting to a presentation. You will then apply layouts and create your own custom layouts and themes.

Chapter 5

Working with Layouts, Themes, and Masters

Most presentations consist of multiple slides, so you'll need a way of ensuring consistency among them. Not only will you want each slide (in most cases) to have the same background, fonts, and text positioning, but you will also want a way of ensuring that any changes you make to those settings later automatically populate across all your slides.

To accomplish these goals, PowerPoint offers layouts, themes, and masters. *Layouts* determine the positioning of placeholders; *themes* assign color, font, and background choices; and *masters* transfer theme settings to the slides and provide an opportunity for repeated content, such as a logo, on each slide. In this chapter you learn how to use layouts, themes, and masters to create a presentation that is attractive, consistent, and easy to manage.

Understanding Layouts and Themes

As you learned in Chapter 4, a *layout* is a positioning template. The layout used for a slide determines what content placeholders will appear and how they will be arranged. For example, the default layout, called Title and Content, contains a placeholder for a title across the top of the slide and a multipurpose placeholder for body content in the center.

A *theme* is a group of design settings. It includes color settings, font choices, object effect settings, and in some cases also a background graphic. In Figure 5.1 later in the chapter, the theme applied is called Concourse, and it is responsible for the colored swoop in the corner, the color of that swoop, and the fonts used on the slide. A theme is applied to a *slide master*, which is a sample slide and not part of the regular presentation, existing only behind-the-scenes to provide its settings to the real slides. It holds the formatting that you want to be consistent among all the slides in the presentation (or at least a group of them, because a presentation can have multiple slide masters). Technically, you do not apply a theme to a slide; you apply a theme to a slide master, and then you apply a slide master to a slide. That's because a slide master can actually contain some additional elements besides the formatting of the theme such as extra graphics, dates, footer text, and so on.

Themes versus Templates

PowerPoint 2007 handles themes, layouts, and slide masters very differently from earlier versions, and this can take some getting used to if you're upgrading.

In PowerPoint 2003, you applied a *design template* (not a theme) to the slide master. A design template was a regular PowerPoint template file (.pot extension) with color choices, font choices, and background graphics. You could have multiple slide masters in a single presentation, so you could base some slides on a different design template than others. PowerPoint 2007 still uses templates, but its primary means of changing the presentation's look and feel is to apply different *themes* to the slide master rather than different templates to the presentation as a whole.

A PowerPoint 2007 template contains at least one slide master, and that slide master has a theme applied to it, so technically every template contains at least one theme. A template with multiple slide masters can therefore carry multiple themes. However, when you apply a template to an existing presentation, only the theme associated with its default (first) slide master is applied. If you start a new presentation based on that template, though, and the template contains more than one theme, you have access to all the stored themes within it.

A theme is both simpler than and more complex than a template. It is simpler in that it cannot hold some of the things a real template can hold. A theme can provide only font, color, effect, and background settings to the presentation. (It can in some cases also provide slide layouts, but let's postpone that discussion for a bit.) And a theme can contain only one set of settings, whereas a template that has multiple slide masters can contain multiple sets of settings. On the other hand, a theme can also do *more* than a PowerPoint template; you can apply a theme saved as a separate file to other Office applications, so you can share its color, font, and effect settings with Word or Excel, for example.

Where Themes Are Stored

A theme is an XML file (or a snippet of XML code embedded in a presentation or template file). A theme can come from any of these sources:

- **Built-in:** Some themes are embedded in PowerPoint itself and are available from the Themes gallery on the Design tab regardless of the template in use.
- **Custom (automatically loaded):** The default storage location for theme files in Windows Vista is C:\Users*username*\AppData\Roaming\Microsoft\Templates\Document Themes.

For Windows XP, it is C:\Documents and Settings\username\Application Data\Microsoft\ Templates\Document Themes. All themes (and templates containing themes) stored here are automatically displayed among the gallery of theme choices on the Design tab, in a Custom category.

- **Inherited from starting template:** If you start a presentation using a template other than the default blank one, that template might have one or more themes included in it.

- **Stored in current presentation:** If you modify a theme in Slide Master view while you are working on a presentation, the modified code for the theme is embedded in that presentation file.

- **Stored in a separate file:** If you save a theme (using any of a variety of methods you'll learn later in this chapter), you create a separate theme file with a .thmx extension. These files can be shared among other Office applications, so you can standardize settings such as font and color choices across applications. (Some of the unique PowerPoint portions of the theme are ignored when you use the theme in other applications.)

Themes, Layouts, and Slide Master View

In PowerPoint 2003, slide layouts were almost completely separate from slide masters and were completely separate from design templates. PowerPoint 2003 provided noncustomizable layouts you could apply to change the placeholder types and positions, and these layouts were largely unaffected by the design applied to the slider master. The slide master consisted of a single slide defining generic placement for all the title and content placeholders, with an optional second slide to separately define the placement for title slides.

In PowerPoint 2007, the slide master has separate layout masters for each layout, and you can customize and create new layouts. For example, Figure 5.1 shows Slide Master view (View ➪ Slide Master). Notice along the left side that there is a different, separately customizable layout master for each available layout, all grouped beneath the slide master. Any changes you make to the slide master trickle down to the individual layout masters, but you can also customize each of the individual layout masters to override a trickle-down setting. For example, on a particular layout you can choose to omit the background graphic to free up its space on the slide for extra content.

Are Layouts Stored in Themes?

Yes and no. Yes, custom layouts are stored with theme files, but they are not always immediately available when you apply that theme to a presentation. It depends on how you apply the theme. If you start a new presentation based on a template that contains a certain theme, then whatever custom layouts are defined for that theme in the template are automatically made available. However, if you apply the theme to the presentation later, then the custom layouts don't carry over — you only get the colors, fonts, effects, and backgrounds. We'll look at some ways to get around this later in the chapter, in the section "Customizing and Creating Layouts."

FIGURE 5.1

In Slide Master view, notice that each layout has its own customizable layout master.

Slide master

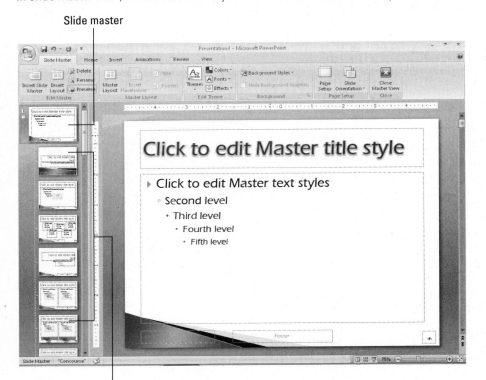

Subordinate master for each layout

A *master* is a set of specifications that govern formatting and appearance. PowerPoint actually has three masters: the Slide Master (for slides), the Handout Master (for handouts), and the Notes Master (for speaker notes). This chapter deals only with the Slide Master.

CROSS-REF For more on the Handout and Notes Masters, see Chapter 19.

The *slide master* holds the settings from a theme and applies them to one or more slides in your presentation. A slide master is not exactly the same thing as a theme because the theme can also be external to PowerPoint and used in other programs, but there's a rough equivalency there. A slide master is the representation of a particular theme applied to a particular presentation.

Which themes appear in Slide Master view?: the ones you have applied to at least one slide in the presentation, plus any custom themes copied from another presentation (see the section "Copying a Theme from Another Presentation" for more details) and any themes inherited from the template used to create the presentation. The built-in themes do not show up here unless they are in use.

When you make changes to a slide master, those changes trickle down to the individual layout masters associated with it. When you make changes to an individual layout master, those changes are confined to that layout in that master only.

To enter Slide Master view, choose View ➪ Slide Master. When you do so, a Slide Master tab appears. To exit from Slide Master view, choose Slide Master ➪ Close or select a different view from the View tab.

Changing a Slide's Layout

Although earlier versions of PowerPoint had many different layouts, they were all mostly the same but with different types of content placeholders. In PowerPoint 2007, there are fewer layouts, but the placeholders on them are much more accommodating to different types of content. For example, the default layout, called Title and Content, has placeholders for a slide title plus a single type of content — text, a table, a chart, a picture, a piece of clip art, a SmartArt diagram, or a movie. That's a big improvement because now you can choose based on the layout you want and not the type of content you might decide to put into it.

When you change the layout, you change the type and/or positioning of the placeholders on it. If the previous placeholders had content in them, that content shifts to a new location on the slide to reflect the different positioning for that placeholder type. If the new layout does not contain a placeholder appropriate for that content, the content remains on the slide but becomes *orphaned*. That means it is a free-floating object, outside of the layout. You need to manually position an orphaned object if it's not in the right spot. However, if you later apply a different layout that does contain a placeholder for the orphaned object, it snaps back into that placeholder.

To switch a slide to a different layout, follow these steps:

1. Select the slide(s) to affect.
2. On the Home tab, click Layout. A menu of layouts appears. See Figure 5.2.
3. Click the desired layout.

CROSS-REF If you want to modify a built-in layout, or create your own layouts, see "Customizing and Creating Layouts" later in this chapter.

When a presentation has more than one slide master defined, separate layouts appear for each of the slide master themes. Figure 5.3 shows the Layout menu for a presentation that has two slide masters.

FIGURE 5.2

Switch to a different layout for the selected slide(s).

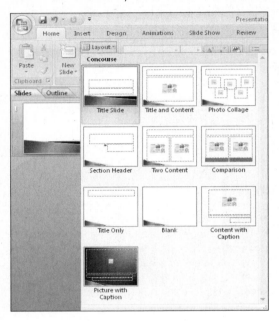

FIGURE 5.3

When there are multiple slide masters, each one's layout is separate.

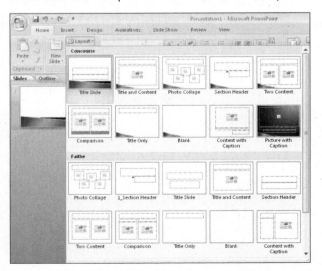

Applying a Theme

As you learned in "Understanding Layouts and Themes" at the beginning of this chapter, themes are the PowerPoint 2007 way of applying different designs to the presentation. A theme includes a background graphic (usually), color and font choices, and graphic effect settings. A theme can also include custom layouts, although these are not available when you apply the theme to an existing presentation. (More on that quandary later in the chapter.)

The method for applying a theme depends on whether that theme is already available in the current presentation or not. Some themes are built into PowerPoint so that they are always available; other themes are available only when you use certain templates, or when you specifically apply them from an external file. The following sections explain each of those possibilities.

NOTE *Themes*, **also called** *design themes*, **contain a combination of colors, fonts, effects, backgrounds, and layouts. There are also more specialized themes: color themes, font themes, and effect themes. When this book uses the term "theme" alone, it's referring to a design theme. Where there is potential for confusion, the book calls it a design theme to help differentiate it from the lesser types of themes.**

Applying a Theme from the Gallery

A *gallery* in PowerPoint is a menu of samples from which you can choose. The Themes gallery is a menu of all of the built-in themes plus any additional themes available from the current template or presentation file.

To select a theme from the gallery, follow these steps:

1. (Optional) If you want to affect only certain slides, select them. (Slide Sorter view works well for this.)

2. On the Design tab, in the Themes group, if the theme you want appears, click it, and skip the rest of these steps. If the theme you want does not appear, you will need to open the gallery. To do so, click the down arrow with the line over it, as shown in Figure 5.4.

   The Themes gallery opens, as you see in Figure 5.5. The gallery is divided into sections based upon the source of the theme. Themes stored in the current presentation appear at the top; custom themes you have added appear next. Built-in themes appear at the bottom.

FIGURE 5.4

Open the Themes gallery by clicking the down arrow with the line above it.

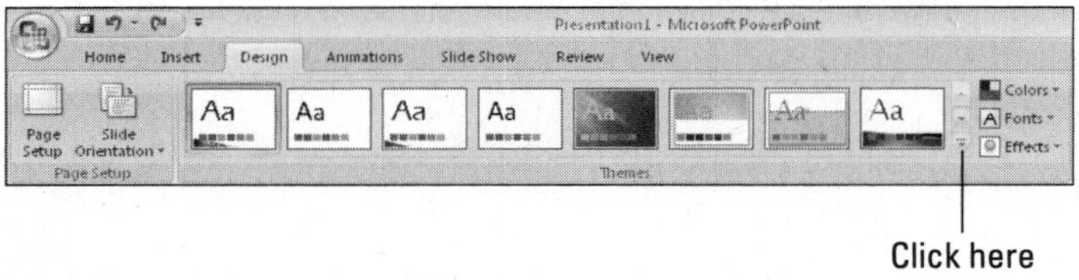

Click here

EXPERT TIP You can drag the bottom-right corner of the menu to resize the gallery. To filter the gallery so that only a certain category of theme appears, click the down arrow to the right of All Themes at the top and select a category from the menu that appears.

FIGURE 5.5

Select the desired theme from the menu.

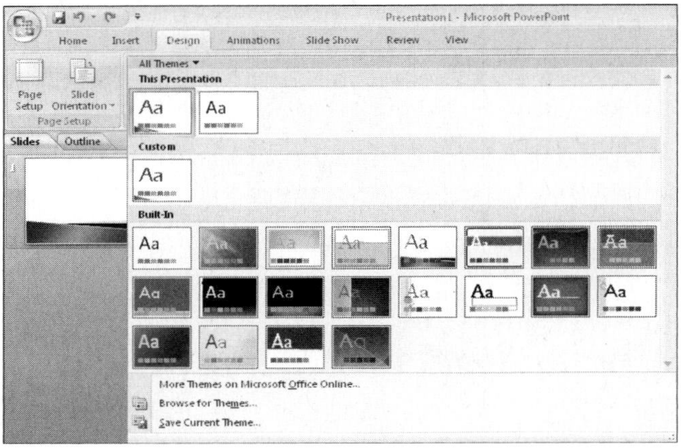

3. Click the theme you want to apply.

   ▢ If you selected multiple slides in step 1, the theme is applied only to them.

   ▢ If you selected a single slide in step 1, the theme is applied to the entire presentation.

EXPERT TIP To override the default behavior in step 3, so that you can apply a different theme to a single slide, right-click instead of clicking in step 3 and choose Apply to Selected Slide(s) from the shortcut menu.

Applying a Theme from a Theme or Template File

You can open and use externally saved theme files in any Office application. This makes it possible to share color, font, and other settings between applications to create consistency between documents of various types. You can also save and load themes from templates.

CROSS-REF To create your own theme files, see "Creating a New Theme" later in this chapter.

To apply a theme to the presentation from a theme or template file, follow these steps:

1. On the Design tab, open the Themes gallery (see Figure 5.5) and click Browse for Themes. The Choose Theme or Themed Document dialog box opens.

   2. Navigate to the folder containing the file and select it.

   3. Click Apply.

A theme file contains only one theme, but a template file can potentially contain multiple themes.
So how does PowerPoint know which one you want to apply if you apply from a template? If the
template file contains any slides, the theme that the first slide uses is applied. Otherwise the first
theme in the template (as determined by the order in Slide Master view) is applied.

Applying a Theme to a New Presentation

Applying a theme from a theme or template file to an existing presentation, as in the preceding
section, applies only the formatting; it does not copy any custom slide layouts you might have
created. To copy the custom layouts, you must start a new presentation based on the theme.

To start a new presentation based on the theme, follow these steps:

   1. Choose Office ➪ Open. The Open dialog box appears.

   2. Open the File Type list and choose Office Themes.

   3. Navigate to the location containing the theme and select it. Custom themes are stored by
   default in C:\Users*username*\AppData\Roaming\Microsoft\
   Templates\Document Themes for Windows Vista or C:\Documents and Settings\user-
   name\Application Data\Microsoft\Templates\Document Themes for Windows XP.

   4. Click Open. PowerPoint starts a new presentation based on that theme and any custom
   layouts that the theme includes.

Changing Colors, Fonts, and Effects

In addition to overall themes, which govern several types of formatting, PowerPoint also provides
many built-in color, font, and effect themes that you can apply separately from your choice of overall theme. So, for example, you can apply a theme that contains a background design you like, and
then change the colors and fonts for it.

In the following sections, you'll learn how to apply some of these built-in color, font, and effect settings to a presentation without changing the overall theme. Then later in the chapter you will learn
how to save these customized settings as new themes and even how to create your own custom
color and font settings in a theme.

Understanding Color Placeholders

To understand how PowerPoint changes colors via a theme, you must know something about how it handles color placeholders in general. PowerPoint uses a set of color placeholders for the bulk of its color formatting. Because each item's color is defined by a placeholder, and not as a fixed color, you can easily change the colors by switching to a different color theme. That way if you decide, for example, that you want all the slide titles to be blue rather than green, you make the change once and it is applied to all slides automatically.

A group of colors assigned to preset placeholders is a *color theme*. PowerPoint contains 20+ built-in color themes that are available regardless of the overall theme applied to the presentation. Because most design themes use placeholders to define their colors, you can apply the desired design theme to the presentation and then fine-tune the colors afterward by experimenting with the built-in color themes.

How many color placeholders are there in a color theme? There are actually 12, but sometimes not all of them are available to be applied to individual objects. When you choose a color theme (Design ➪ Colors), the gallery of themes from which you choose shows only the first 8 colors of each color theme. It doesn't matter so much here because you can't apply individual colors from there anyway. When selecting colors from a color picker (used for applying fill and border color to specific objects), as in Figure 5.6, there are 10 theme swatches. And when you define a new custom color scheme, there are 12 placeholders to set up. The final 2 are for visited and unvisited hyperlinks; these colors aren't included in a color picker.

FIGURE 5.6

PowerPoint uses color pickers such as this one to enable you to easily apply color placeholders to objects.

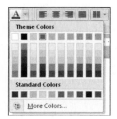

Switching Color Themes

After applying the overall theme you want, you might want to apply different colors. To switch to a different color theme, follow these steps:

1. (Optional) To apply a different color theme to a slide master other than the default one, open Slide Master view (View ➪ Slide Master) and click the desired slide master. Otherwise, the color change will apply to all slides that use the default slide master. The default slide master is the first one listed in Slide Master view.

2. On the Design tab (or the Slide Master tab if in Slide Master view), click Colors. A gallery of color themes opens.

3. (Optional) Point to a color theme and observe the preview on the slide behind the list.

4. Click the desired color theme. See Figure 5.7.

FIGURE 5.7

Select the desired theme from the dialog box.

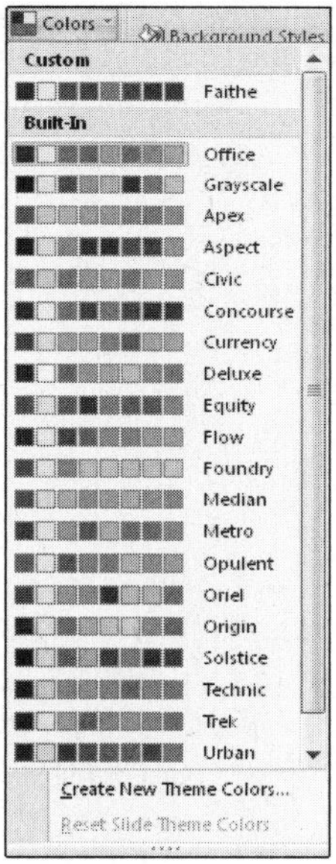

CROSS-REF You can also create custom color themes; see the section "Creating a Custom Color Theme" later in this chapter for details.

Understanding Font Placeholders

By default in most themes and templates, text box fonts are not set to a specific font, but to one of two designations: Heading or Body. Then a *font theme* defines what specific fonts to use. To change the fonts across the entire presentation, all you have to do is apply a different font theme.

A *font theme* is an XML-based specification that defines a pair of fonts: one for headings and one for body text. Then that font is applied to the text boxes in the presentation based on their statuses of Heading or Body. For example, all of the slide titles are usually set to Heading, and all of the content placeholders and manual text boxes are usually set to Body.

In a blank presentation (default blank template), when you click inside a slide title placeholder box, you see Calibri (Headings) in the Font group on the Home tab. Figure 5.8 shows that the current font is Calibri, but that it is being used only because the font theme specifies it. You could change the font theme to Verdana/Verdana, for example, and then the font designation for that box would appear as Verdana (Headings).

FIGURE 5.8

When some text is using a font placeholder rather than a fixed font, (Headings) or (Body) appears after its name in the Font group on the Home tab.

In some font themes, the same font is used for both headings and body. In a default blank presentation both fonts are Calibri, for example, and the Verdana/Verdana set is an additional example. In many other font themes, though, the heading and body fonts are different.

Switching Font Themes

After applying an overall theme, you might decide you want to use different fonts in the presentation. To switch to a different font theme, follow these steps:

1. (Optional) To apply a different font theme to a slide master other than the default one, open Slide Master view (View ➪ Slide Master) and click the desired slide master. Otherwise, the font change will apply to all slides that use the default slide master. The default slide master is the first one listed in Slide Master view.

2. On the Design tab (or Slide Master tab, if in Slide Master view), click Fonts. A gallery of font themes opens.

3. (Optional) Point to a font theme and observe the change on the slide behind the list.

4. Click the desired font theme. See Figure 5.9.

Changing the Effect Theme

Effect themes apply to several types of drawings that PowerPoint can construct, including SmartArt, charts, and drawn lines and shapes. They make the surfaces of objects formatted with 3-D attributes look like different textures (more or less shiny-looking, colors more or less deep, and so on).

To change the effect theme, follow these steps:

1. On the Design tab, click Effects. A gallery of effect themes opens.

2. (Optional) Point to a theme and observe the change on the slide behind the list. (This works only if you have an object on that slide that is affected by the effect theme; see the sidebar "Setting Up a Graphic on Which to Test Effect Themes" to set up such an object.)

3. Click the desired effect theme. See Figure 5.10.

FIGURE 5.9

Select the desired font theme.

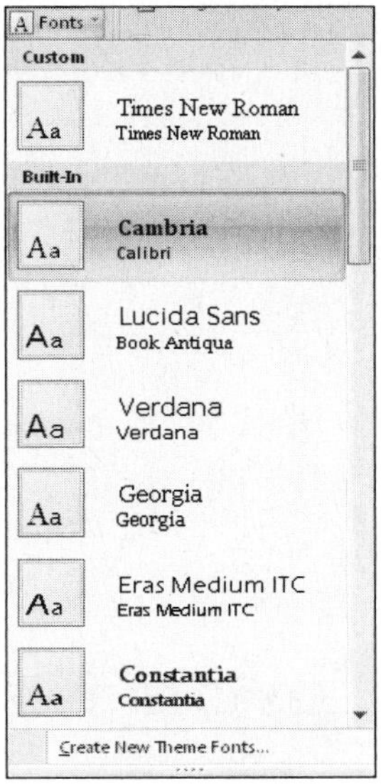

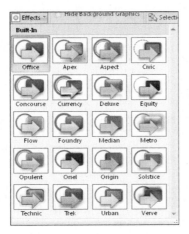

FIGURE 5.10

Select the desired effect theme.

Setting Up a Graphic on Which to Test Effect Themes

Because you haven't worked with any of these graphics yet in this book, you haven't had an opportunity to try them out yet. Effect themes are most evident when there are colorful 3-D graphics in use, so do the following to construct a dummy diagram that you can use to try out effect themes:

1. On the Insert tab, click SmartArt.

2. Click Cycle, click the top left diagram, and click OK.

3. On the SmartArt Tools Design tab, click Change Colors, and click the first sample under Colorful.

4. On the Smart Art Tools Design tab, open the SmartArt Styles gallery and click the first sample under 3-D.

Now you have a diagram on which you can see the effect themes applied.

Creating and Managing Custom Color and Font Themes

You can define your own custom color themes and font themes, and save them for reuse in other presentations. By default these are saved in the personal folders for the logged-in user on the local PC, and they remain available to that user regardless of the theme or template in use.

These custom color and font themes are also included if you save the overall theme as a separate theme file (.thmx), as you will learn to do later in this chapter, so that you can take those settings to another PC or send them to some other user.

Creating a Custom Color Theme

A custom color theme defines specific colors for each of the 12 color placeholders (including the 2 that you can't directly use — the ones for hyperlinks). To create a custom color theme, first apply a theme to the current presentation that is as close as possible to the theme you want. This makes it easier because you have to redefine fewer placeholders. Then follow these steps:

1. On the Design tab, open the Colors list and choose Create New Theme Colors. The Create New Theme Colors dialog box opens.

2. Type a name for the new color theme in the Name box, replacing the default name (Custom 1, or other number if there is already a Custom 1).

3. Click a color placeholder and open its menu. See Figure 5.11.

FIGURE 5.11

Select the color for the chosen placeholder.

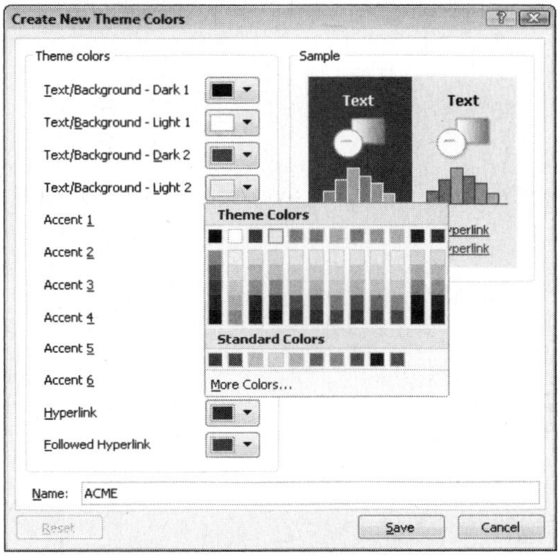

4. Click a color. Alternatively, you can click More Colors, select a color from the Colors dialog box (Figure 5.12), and click OK. The Colors dialog box has two tabs: The Standard tab has color swatches, and the Custom tab enables you to define a color numerically by its RGB (Red Green Blue) or HSL (Hue Saturation Lightness).

FIGURE 5.12

Choose a custom color if none of the standard colors is appropriate.

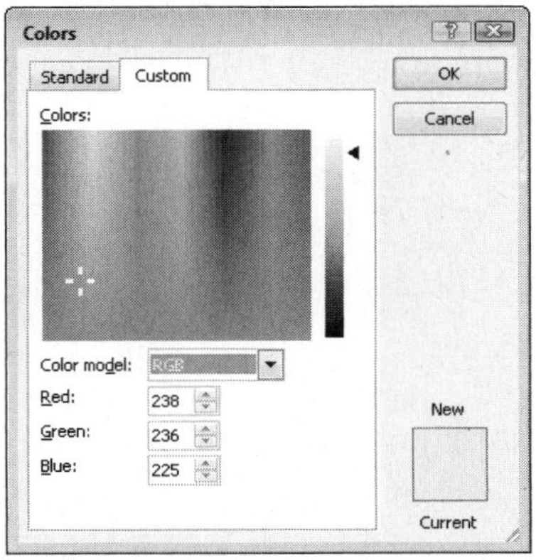

5. (Optional) Click the Preview button to see the effect of the change on the current slide.

6. Redefine any other colors as needed.

7. Click Save. The color scheme is saved, and now appears at the top of the Colors gallery, in the Custom area.

Sharing a Custom Color Theme with Others

A custom color scheme is available only to the currently logged-in user on the PC on which it is created. If you want to share it with another user on the same PC, you can copy it into his or her user folder:

- In Windows Vista:

  C:\Users*username*\AppData\Roaming\Microsoft\Templates\Document Themes\Theme Colors

  where *username* is that user's login name.

- In Windows XP:

  C:\Documents and Settings*username*\Application Data\Microsoft\Templates\Document Themes\Theme Colors.

- The default color themes are located in:

  C:\Program Files\Microsoft\Office\Document Themes 12\Theme Colors regardless of the operating system version.

Another way to share a custom color theme is to create the new color theme and then save the (overall) theme to a theme file (.thmx). See "Creating a New Theme" later in this chapter. The resulting theme file will contain the custom colors, as well as the usual theme content.

Deleting a Custom Color Theme

A custom color theme remains until you delete it from the Theme Colors folder for your user profile. To delete a theme color, use Windows Explorer to navigate to this folder:

C:\Users*username*\AppData\Roaming\Microsoft\Templates\Document Themes\Theme Colors

where *username* is your login name, and you'll find an .xml file for each of your custom color themes. Delete the files for the color themes that you want to delete. You can also right-click the color theme in the Gallery, click Edit, and then click the Delete button in the Edit Theme Colors dialog box.

EXPERT TIP If you don't want to delete a custom color theme, but you also don't want it showing up on your Colors menu in PowerPoint all the time, move the file to a folder outside of the Document Themes folder hierarchy. For example, create an Unused Themes folder on your hard disk and move it there until you need it. When you want to use the custom color theme again, move the file back to its original location

If you don't want to leave PowerPoint to delete the color theme, you can take advantage of the fact that you can use most dialog boxes in PowerPoint that save or open files to manage files in general. Follow these steps:

1. Open any dialog box that saves or opens files. For example, on the Design tab, open the Themes gallery and choose Browse for Themes.

2. Navigate to the location of the color themes:

   C:\Users*username*\AppData\Roaming\Microsoft\Templates\Document Themes\Theme Colors

3. Open the File Type list and choose All Files so that all of the files appear.

4. Select the file for the color theme that you want to delete and press the Delete key on the keyboard.

5. Click Cancel to close the dialog box.

Creating a Custom Font Theme

You can create your own custom font themes, which are then available in all presentations. A custom font theme defines two fonts: one for headings and one for body text. To create a custom font theme, follow these steps:

1. On the Design tab, open the Fonts list and choose Create New Theme Fonts. The Create New Theme Fonts dialog box opens, as shown in Figure 5.13.

2. Type a name for the new font theme in the Name box, replacing the default text there.

3. Open the Heading Font drop-down list and select the desired font for headings.

4. Open the Body Font drop-down list and select the desired font for body text.

5. Click Save. The font theme is saved, and now appears at the top of the Fonts list, in the Custom area.

FIGURE 5.13

Create a new custom font theme by specifying the fonts to use.

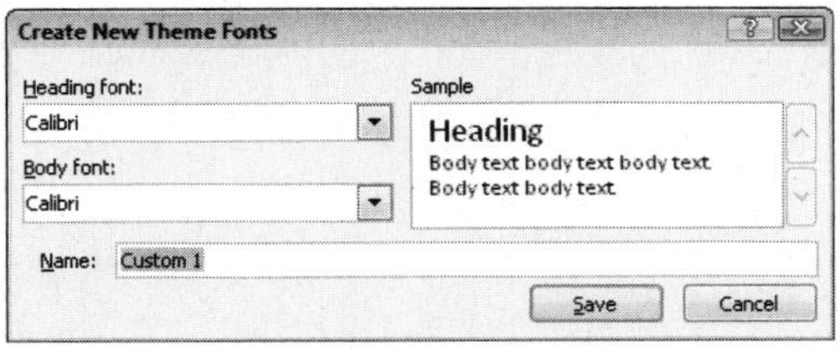

Sharing a Custom Font Theme with Others

A custom font theme is available only to the currently logged-in user on the PC on which it is created. If you want to share it with another user on the same PC, you can copy it into his or her user folder:

- In Windows Vista:

  C:\Users*username*\AppData\Roaming\Microsoft\Templates\Document Themes\Theme Fonts

  where *username* is that user's login name.

- In Windows XP:

  C:\Documents and Settings*username*\Application Data\Microsoft\Templates\Document Themes\Theme Fonts

You can also share a custom font theme by creating it and then saving the (overall) theme as a new theme (.thmx) file. Then you can share that theme file with others via e-mail, disk, or other distribution methods.

CROSS-REF   To save your theme as a new theme, see the section "Creating a New Theme."

Deleting a Custom Font Theme

A custom font theme remains until you delete it from the Theme Fonts folder for your user profile. To delete a font theme, use Windows Explorer to navigate to this folder:

- In Windows Vista:

  C:\Users*username*\AppData\Roaming\Microsoft\Templates\Document Themes\Theme Fonts

- In Windows XP:

  C:\Documents and Settings*username*\Application Data\Microsoft\Templates\Document Themes\Theme Fonts

  where *username* is your login name, and you'll find an .xml file for each of your custom font themes. Delete the files for the font themes that you want to delete.

You can also delete it from within PowerPoint by browsing for the file with any dialog box that saves or opens files, or by right-clicking the font theme in the Gallery, clicking Edit, and then clicking Delete in the Edit Theme Fonts dialog box.

CROSS-REF   Deleting a custom font theme from a dialog box is essentially the same as deleting a custom color theme. See the section "Deleting a Custom Color Theme" for more details.

Changing the Background

The *background* is the color, texture, pattern, or image that is applied to the entire slide (or slide master), on which everything else sits. By its very definition, it applies to the entire surface of the slide; you cannot have a partial background. However, you can have a *background graphic* overlaid on top of the background. A background graphic is a graphic image placed on the slide master that complements and works with the background.

It's important to understand the distinction between a background and a background graphic because even though most themes contain both, they are set up differently, and making the change you want to the overall appearance of your slides often involves changing both. For example, Figure 5.15 shows the Concourse theme applied to a slide master. The slide background is pure white, and a blue and black background graphic is overlaid on it.

Most themes consist of both background formatting (even if it is just a solid color) and a background graphic. The background graphics included in the built-in themes in PowerPoint are unique to those themes, and not available as separate graphics outside of them. So, for example, if you want the colored swoop shown in Figure 5.14, the only way to get it is to apply the Concourse theme. Because the decorative background graphics are unique to each theme, many people choose a theme based on the desired background graphic, and then customize the slide master's appearance to modify the theme as needed.

FIGURE 5.14

A slide's background is separate from its background graphic(s) if any are present.

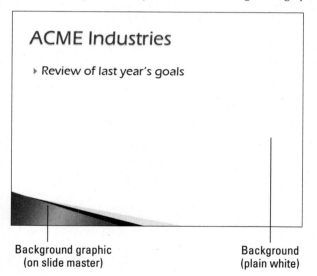

Background graphic
(on slide master)

Background
(plain white)

137

EXPERT TIP To use a background graphic from one template with the look-and-feel of another, apply the first theme to a slide, and then in Slide Master view copy the background graphic to the Clipboard. Then apply the second theme and paste the graphic from the clipboard into the slide master.

Applying a Background Style

Background styles are preset background formats that come with the built-in themes in PowerPoint. Depending on the theme you apply, different background styles are available. These background styles all use the color placeholders from the theme, so their color offerings change depending on the color theme applied.

To apply a background style, follow these steps:

1. (Optional) To affect only certain slides, select them.
2. On the Design tab, click Background Styles. A gallery of styles appears. See Figure 5.15.
3. Click the desired style to apply it to the entire presentation. Alternatively, you can right-click the desired style and choose Apply to Selected Slides.

FIGURE 5.15

Apply a preset background style.

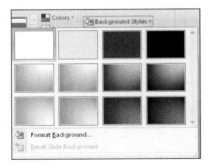

You cannot customize background styles or add your own custom background styles; there are always 12 of them, and they are always determined by the theme. If you need a different background, you can choose Format Backgrounds and then customize the background settings as described in the following sections.

Applying a Background Fill

A custom background fill can include solid colors, gradients, textures, or graphics. Because Chapter 10 covers these in more detail, this section covers how to specify your own background fill, which involves the following steps:

1. (Optional) To affect only certain slides, select them.

2. On the Design tab, click Background Styles. The Background Styles gallery opens.

3. Click Format Background. The Format Background dialog box opens.

4. Choose the option button that best describes the type of fill you want. See Figure 5.16.

5. Set the options for the fill type that you chose. For example, in Figure 5.16, click the Color button and choose a solid color. The changes you make apply immediately.

CROSS-REF See Chapter 10 for details about these fill types and how to configure their options.

FIGURE 5.16

Select a background fill type, and configure the options for the type you chose.

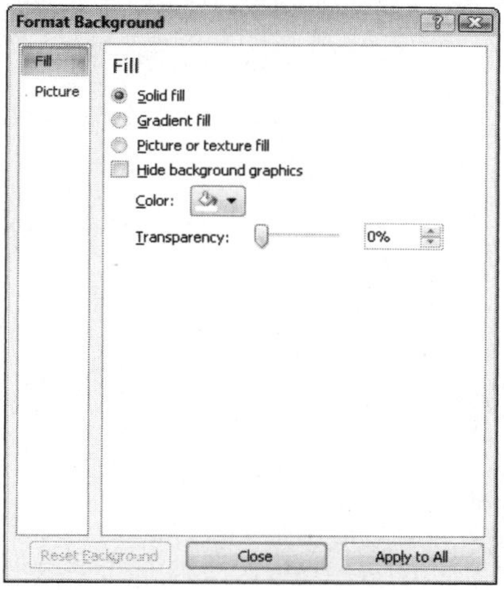

6. (Optional) To apply the change to all slides, click Apply to All. Otherwise the change will apply only to the slides you selected in step 1.

7. (Optional) To apply a different background to some other slides, select them and repeat steps 4 and 5. The Format Background dialog box is nonmodal, so its changes are applied immediately and you can select things in the presentation file without closing it.

8. Click Close to exit the dialog box.

Working with Background Graphics

In the preceding steps, one of the fill types you could choose was Picture or Texture Fill. This type of fill covers the entire background with the picture or texture that you specify.

This is not a background graphic, however. A *background graphic* is an object or a picture overlaid on top of the background on the slide master. It complements the background, and it might or might not cover the entire background.

 Some theme-provided background graphics actually consist of multiple shapes grouped together. You can ungroup them, as shown in Chapter 10, so that you can modify or remove only a portion of the background graphic.

Displaying and Hiding Background Graphics

Sometimes a background graphic can get in the way of the slide's content. For example, on a slide that contains a large chart or diagram, a background graphic around the border of the slide can overlap the content. You don't have to delete the background graphic entirely to solve this problem; you can turn it off for individual slides. To hide the background graphics on one or more slides, follow these steps:

1. Select the slide(s) to affect.
2. On the Design tab, mark the Hide Background Graphics check box.

Clear the check box to redisplay the background graphics later as needed.

Deleting Background Graphics

The background graphics reside on the slide master, so to remove one, you must use Slide Master view. Follow these steps:

1. On the View tab, click Slide Master. Slide Master view opens.
2. Select the slide master or layout master that contains the graphic to delete.
3. Click the background graphic to select it.
4. Press the Delete key on the keyboard.

EXPERT TIP Some background graphics are on the slide master itself, and others are on individual layout masters. The background graphics on the slide master trickle down to each of its layout masters, but can't be selected/deleted from the individual layout masters.

To use a background graphic only on certain layouts, cut it from the slide master to the Clipboard (Ctrl+X), and then paste it individually onto each layout master desired (Ctrl+V). Alternatively, turn on the background graphic for the slide master and then use Hide Background Graphics on individual layout masters that should not contain it.

Adding Your Own Background Graphics

You can add your own background graphics, either to the slide master or to individual layout masters. This works just like adding any other graphic to a slide (see Chapter 13) except you add it to the master instead of to an individual slide.

Inserting pictures is covered in greater detail in Chapter 13, but here are the basic steps for adding a background graphic:

1. Display the slide master or layout master on which you want to place the background graphic.

2. Do any of the following:

   ▪ On the Insert tab, click Picture. Select a picture to insert and click Open.

   ▪ On the Insert tab, click Clip Art. Search for a piece of clip art to use, and insert it on the master.

   ▪ In any application (including PowerPoint), copy any graphic to the Clipboard by pressing Ctrl+C; then display the master and paste the graphic by pressing Ctrl+V.

EXPERT TIP Most of the background graphics that come with the built-in themes are either semi-transparent or use one of the placeholder colors for their fill. Therefore changing the color theme also changes the color of the background graphic. Keep that in mind if you are creating your own background graphics; it's better to use theme colors or transparency than to use fixed colors that might clash with a color theme that you later apply.

Working with Preset Placeholders

As a review, to enter Slide Master view, display the View tab and click Slide Master. One or more slide masters appear in the left pane, with its own subordinate layout masters. A slide master has five preset placeholders that you can individually remove or move around. Figure 5.18 points them out on a slide master with the Concourse theme applied, but they might be in different locations in other themes:

- **Title:** The placeholder for the title on each slide
- **Text:** The main content placeholder on each slide
- **Date:** The box that displays the current date on each slide
- **Slide number:** The box that displays the slide number on each slide
- **Footer:** A box that displays repeated text at the bottom of each slide

These elements are all enabled by default, but the Footer is empty by default so it is not visible on individual slides unless you type some text into it in Slide Master view or add text to it using Insert Header and Footer. Each of these elements trickles down to the layout masters beneath it, so formatting, moving, or deleting one of these elements from the slide master also changes it on each of the layouts. See Figure 5.17 for an example of the various placeholders.

Each slide master contains these placeholders (or can contain them)

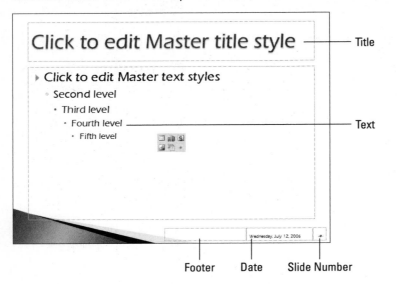

Formatting a Preset Placeholder

You can format the text in each of the placeholders on the slide master just like any regular text, and that formatting carries over to all slides and layouts based on it. For example, if you format the code in the Slide Number box with a certain font and size, it will appear that way on every slide that uses that slide master. You can also format the placeholder boxes just like any other text boxes. For example, you can add a border around the page number's box, and/or fill its background with color.

EXPERT TIP If you want to make all the text in a heading all-caps or small-caps, use the Font dialog box. From the Home tab, click the dialog box launcher in the Font group and mark the Small Caps or All Caps check box there.

CROSS-REF See Chapters 6 and 7 to learn how to format text. See Chapter 7 for more information about formatting text boxes.

Moving, Deleting, or Restoring Preset Placeholders

You can move each of the placeholders on the slide master or an individual layout master. For example, you might decide you want the Footer box at the top of the slide rather than the bottom, or that you want to center the slide number at the bottom of the slide. To move a placeholder, click it to select it and then drag its border, just as you did with text boxes in Chapter 4.

To delete one of the placeholders on the slide master, select its box and press the Delete key on the keyboard. Deleting it from the slide master deletes it from all of the associated layouts as well.

To restore deleted placeholders on the slide master, follow these steps:

1. In Slide Master view, select the slide master (not a layout).

2. On the Slide Master tab, click Slide Layout. The Master Layout dialog box opens. Check boxes for already displayed elements are marked and unavailable. Check boxes for previously deleted elements are available as shown in Figure 5.18.

3. Mark the check boxes for the elements that you want to restore.

4. Click OK.

FIGURE 5.18

Restore deleted placeholders from the slide master.

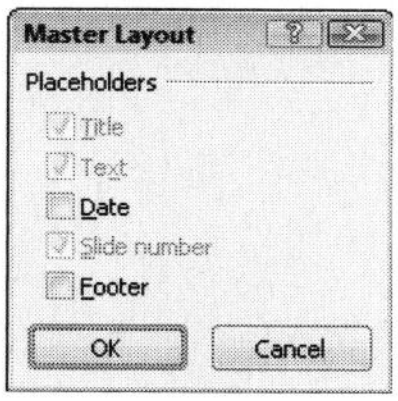

CAUTION　Restored placeholders might not appear in the same spots as they did originally; you might need to move them. To put the placeholders back to their original locations, reapply the theme from the Themes button on the Slide Master tab.

Here are some more details you should remember about deleting and restoring:

■ On an individual layout master, you can quickly delete and restore the Title and Footer placeholders by marking or clearing the Title and Footers check boxes on the Slide Master tab. The "footer" that this check box refers to is actually all three of the bottom-of-the-slide elements: the actual footer, the date box, and the slide number box.

■ You can also individually delete the placeholders from a layout master, the same as on a slide master. Just select a placeholder box and press the Delete key.

■ You can restore all of the placeholders, except Text, by marking the aforementioned check boxes on the Slide Master tab. Whenever any of the three footer boxes are missing, the Footers check box becomes cleared, and you can restore the missing box(es) by re-selecting the check box.

■ You cannot restore the Text placeholder, however, on an individual layout master. You must recreate it with the Insert Placeholder command.

CROSS-REF　For more on the Insert Placeholder command, see the section, "Customizing and Creating Layouts."

Displaying the Date, Number, and Footer on Slides

Even though the placeholders for Date, Number, and Footer might appear on the slide master, they do not appear on the actual slides in the presentation unless you enable them. This might seem counterintuitive at first, but it's actually a benefit. PowerPoint enables you to turn the date, number, and footer on and off without having to delete, recreate, or reformat their placeholders. You can decide at the last minute whether you want them to display or not, and you can choose differently for different audiences and situations.

All three areas are controlled from the Header and Footer dialog box. To open it, from the Insert tab click Header and Footer. (Clicking Date and Time or clicking Number opens the same dialog box.) Then on the Slide tab, mark the check boxes for each of the three elements you want to use. See Figure 5.19.

FIGURE 5.19
_____

Choose which of the footer elements should appear on slides.

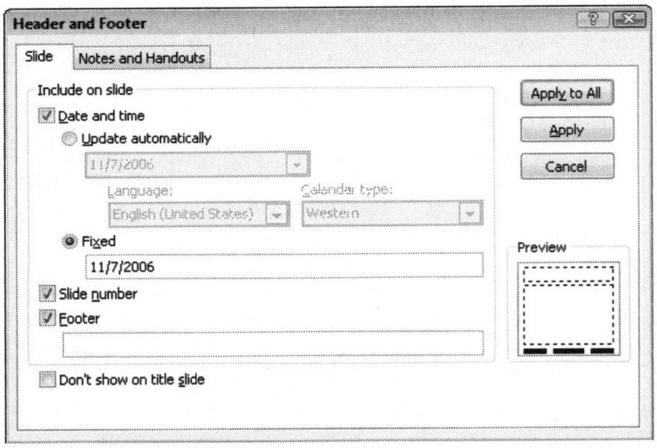

Date and Time

You can set Date and Time either to Update Automatically or to Fixed:

- Update Automatically pulls the current date from the computer's clock and formats it in whatever format you choose from the drop-down list. You can also select a language and a Calendar Type (although unless you are presenting in some other country than the one for which your version of PowerPoint was developed, this is probably not an issue.)

- Fixed prints whatever you enter in the Fixed text box. When Fixed is enabled, it defaults to today's date in the m/dd/yyyy format.

EXPERT TIP In addition to (or instead of) placing the date on each slide, you can insert an individual instance of the current date or time on a slide, perhaps as part of a sentence. To do so, position the insertion point inside a text box or placeholder and then on the Insert tab, click Date and Time. Select the format you want from the dialog box that appears and click OK.

Slide Number

This option shows the slide number on each slide, wherever the Number placeholder is positioned. You can format the Number placeholder on the master slide with the desired font, size, and other text attributes

CROSS-REF See Chapter 6 for more on formatting.

By default, slide numbering starts with 1. You can start with some other number if you like by following these steps:

1. Close Slide Master view if it is open. To do so, click the Close button on the Slide Master tab.

2. On the Design tab, click the dialog box launcher in the Page Setup group. The Page Setup dialog box opens.

3. In the Number Slides From box, increment the number to the desired starting number.

4. Click OK.

EXPERT TIP You can insert the slide number on an individual slide, either instead of or in addition to the numbering on the Slide Master. Position the insertion point, and then on the Insert tab, click Slide Number. If you are in Slide master view, this places a code on the Slide Master for the slide number that looks like this: <#>. If you are on an individual slide, it inserts the same code but the code itself is hidden and the actual number appears.

Footer

The footer is blank by default. Mark the Footer check box, and then enter the desired text in the Footer box. You can then format the footer text from the slide master as you would any other text (see Chapter 6). You can also enter the footer text in the Header and Footer dialog box's Footer text box.

Don't Show on Title Slide

This check box in the Header and Footer dialog box suppresses the date/time, page number, and footer on slides that use the Title Slide layout. Many people like to hide those elements on title slides for a cleaner look and to avoid repeated information (for example, if the current date appears in the subtitle box on the title slide).

Customizing and Creating Layouts

In addition to customizing the slide master (including working with its preset placeholder boxes, as you just learned), you can fully customize the individual layout masters. This very useful capability is brand new in PowerPoint 2007.

A layout master takes some of its settings from the slide master with which it is associated. For example, by default it takes its background, fonts, color scheme, and preset placeholder positioning from the slide master. But it also can be individually customized; you can override the slide master's choices for background, colors, and fonts, and you can create, modify, and delete various types of content placeholders.

Understanding Content Placeholders

There are seven basic types of content you can insert on a PowerPoint slide: Text, Picture, Chart, Table, Diagram, Media (video or sound), and Clip Art. A placeholder on a slide master or layout master can specify one of these types of content that it will accept, or you can designate it as a Content placeholder, such that it will accept any of the seven types. Most of the layouts that PowerPoint generates automatically for its themes use the Content placeholder type because it offers the most flexibility. By making all placeholders Content, PowerPoint can get by with fewer separate layout masters because users will choose the desired layout based on the positioning of the placeholders, not their types.

A Content placeholder appears as a text placeholder with a small palette of icons in the center, one for each of the content types. Each content placeholder can hold only one type of content at a time, so as soon as the user types some text into the content placeholder or clicks one of the icons in the palette and inserts some content, the placeholder becomes locked into that one type of content until the content is deleted from it.

NOTE On a slide that contains a placeholder that contains some content (any type), selecting the placeholder and pressing Delete removes the content. To remove the placeholder itself from the layout, select the empty placeholder and press Delete. If you then want to restore the placeholder, reapply the slide layout to the slide.

You can move and resize a placeholder on a layout master as you would any other object. Drag a selection handle on the frame to resize it, or drag the border of the frame (not on a selection handle) to move it.

CROSS-REF The Content placeholders were identified back in Chapter 4 in Figure 4.12. You can also see Chapter 4 for more on moving and resizing an object.

Adding a Custom Placeholder

You can add a placeholder to either the slide master or to an individual layout master. If you add it to the slide master, it will repeat on every layout master, it's more common to add placeholders to individual layouts.

To add a placeholder, follow these steps:

1. In Slide Master view, select the layout master (or slide master) to affect.
2. On the Slide Master tab, click the bottom part of the Insert Placeholder button to open its menu.

3. Click Content to insert a generic placeholder, or click one of the specific content types. See Figure 5.20. The mouse pointer becomes a cross-hair.

FIGURE 5.20

Create a new placeholder on a slide.

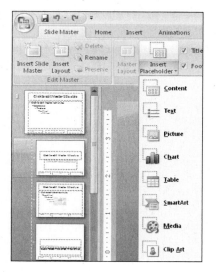

4. Drag on the slide to draw the placeholder box of the size and position desired. A blue box appears showing where the placeholder box will go. When you release the mouse button, the new placeholder appears on the slide.

Deleting and Restoring a Custom Placeholder

To delete a custom placeholder, select it and press the Delete key, just as you learned to do earlier with the preset placeholders.

The difference between custom and preset placeholders is not in the deleting, but rather in the restoring. You can immediately undo a deletion with Ctrl+Z, but you cannot otherwise restore a deleted custom placeholder from a layout master. PowerPoint retains no memory of the content placeholders on individual layouts. Therefore, you must recreate any content placeholders that you have accidentally deleted.

EXPERT TIP To restore one of the built-in layouts, copy it from another slide master. See the sections "Duplicating and Deleting Layouts," and "Copying Layouts Between Slide Masters" later in this chapter.

Overriding the Slide Master Formatting for a Layout

You can apply formatting to a layout in almost exactly the same ways as you apply formatting to a regular slide or to a slide master. Only a few things are off-limits:

- You cannot apply a different theme to one layout. To use a different theme for some slides, create a whole new slide master (covered later in this chapter).

- You cannot apply a different font, color, or effect theme, because these are related to the main theme and the slide master. If you need different fonts or colors on a certain layout, specify fixed font formatting for the text placeholders in that layout, or specify fixed color choices for objects.

CROSS-REF   For more on slide masters, see the section "Managing Slide Masters." For more on formatting text placeholders, see Chapter 6. For more on specifying colors for objects, see Chapter 10.

- You cannot delete a background graphic that is inherited from the slide master; if you want it only on certain layouts, delete it from the slide master, and then paste it individually onto each layout desired, or select Hide Background Graphics from the Slide Master tab and then deselect Hide Background Graphics from certain layouts.

- You cannot change the slide orientation (portrait or landscape) or the slide size.

So what *can* you do to an individual layout, then? Plenty. You can do the following:

- Apply a different background.

- Reposition, resize, or delete preset placeholders inherited from the slide master.

- Apply fixed formatting to text placeholders, including different fonts, sizes, colors, attributes, indents, and alignment.

- Apply fixed formatting to any placeholder box, including different fill and border styles and colors.

- Create manual text boxes and type any text you like into them. You might do this to include an explanatory note on certain slide layouts, for example.

- Insert pictures or clip art that should repeat on each slide that uses a certain layout.

Creating a New Layout

In addition to modifying the existing layouts, you can create your own brand-new layouts, defining the exact placeholders you want. To create a new layout, follow these steps:

1. From Slide Master view, click the slide master with which to associate the new layout.

2. Click Insert Layout. A new layout appears. Each new layout you create starts with preset placeholders inherited from the slide master for Title, Footer, Date, and Slide Number.

3. (Optional) Delete any of the preset placeholders that you don't want.

4. Insert new placeholders as needed.

5. (Optional) Name the layout.

CROSS-REF To insert a placeholder, see the section "Adding a Custom Placeholder" earlier in the chapter. To name the layout, see the next section "Renaming a Layout."

NOTE The new layout is part of the slide master, but not part of the theme. The theme is applied to the slide master, but at this point their relationship ends; and changes that you make to the slide master do not affect the theme. To save your custom layout(s), you have two choices: You can save the presentation as a template, or you can save the theme as a separate file. You learn more about saving themes in "Managing Themes" later in this chapter.

Renaming a Layout

Layout names can help you determine the purpose of a layout if it is not obvious from viewing its thumbnail image.

To change the name of a layout, or to assign a name to a new layout you've created, follow these steps:

1. In Slide Master view, right-click the layout and choose Rename Layout. The Rename Layout dialog box opens.

2. Type a new name for the layout, replacing the existing name. See Figure 5.21.

3. Click Rename.

FIGURE 5.21

Change the name of a layout to clarify its purpose.

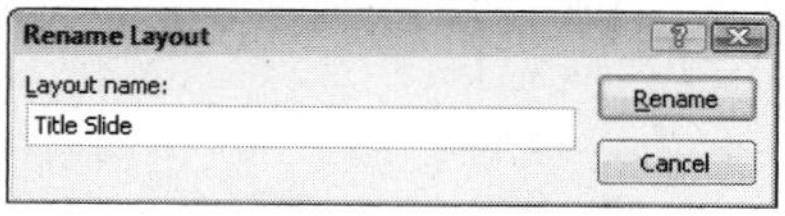

Rename Layout

Layout name:
Title Slide

Rename
Cancel

Duplicating and Deleting Layouts

You might want to copy a layout to get a head start on creating a new one. To copy a layout, right-click the layout in Slide Master view and choose Duplicate Layout. A copy of the layout appears below the original.

If you are never going to use a certain layout, you might as well delete it; every layout you can delete makes the file a little bit smaller. To delete a layout, right-click the layout in Slide Master view and choose Delete Layout.

Copying Layouts Between Slide Masters

When you create additional slide masters in the presentation, any custom layouts you've created for the existing slide masters do not carry over. You must manually copy them to the new slide master.

To copy a layout from one slide master to another, follow these steps:

1. In Slide Master view, select the layout to be copied.
2. Press Ctrl+C.
3. Select the slide master under which you want to place the copy.
4. Press Ctrl+V.

You can also copy layouts between slide masters in different presentations. To do so, open both presentation files, and then perform the above steps. The only difference is that after step 2, you must switch to the other presentation's Slide Master view.

Managing Slide Masters

Let's review the relationship one more time between slide masters and themes. A theme is a set of formatting specs. Themes are not applied directly to slides — they are applied to slide masters, which are then in turn applied to slides. The slide masters exist within the presentation file itself. You can change them by applying different themes, but they are essentially "built in" to the presentation file.

When you change to a different theme for all of the slides in the presentation, your slide master changes its appearance. You can tweak that appearance in Slide Master view. As long as all of the slides in the presentation use the same theme, you need only one slide master. However, if you apply a different theme to some of your slides, you need another master, because a master can have only one theme applied to it at a time. PowerPoint automatically creates the additional master(s) for you, and they are all available for editing in Slide Master view.

If you later reapply a single theme to all of the slides in the presentation, you do not need multiple masters anymore, so the unused one is automatically deleted. In addition to all this automatic creation and deletion of slide masters, you can also manually create and delete slide masters on your own. Any slide masters that you create manually are automatically preserved, even if they aren't always in use. You must manually delete them if you don't want them anymore.

In the following sections, you learn how to create and delete slide masters manually, and how to rename them. You also learn how to lock one of the automatically created slide masters so that PowerPoint does not delete it if it falls out of use.

Creating and Deleting Slide Masters

To create another slide master, click Insert Slide Master on the Slide Master tab. It appears below the existing slide master(s) in the left pane of Slide Master view. From there, just start customizing it. You can apply a theme to it, modify its layouts and placeholders, and all the usual things you can do to a slide master. Another way to create a new slide master is to duplicate an existing one. To do this, right-click the slide master and choose Duplicate Master.

To delete a slide master, select it in Slide Master view (make sure you select the slide master itself, not just one of its layouts) and press the Delete key. If any of that slide master's layouts were applied to any slides in the presentation, those slides automatically convert to the default slide master's equivalent layout. If no exact layout match is found, PowerPoint does its best: It uses its default Title and Content layout and includes any extra content as orphaned items.

Renaming a Slide Master

Slide master names appear as category headings on the Layout list as you are selecting layouts. For example, in Figure 5.22, the slide master names are Faithe and Concourse.

FIGURE 5.22

Slide master names form the category titles on the Layout list.

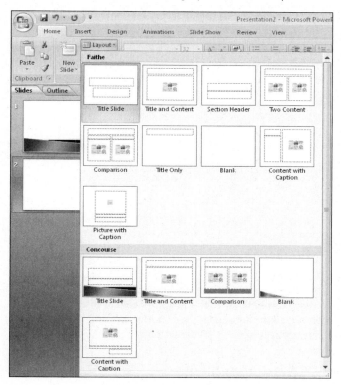

To rename a slide master, follow these steps:

1. In Slide Master view, right-click the slide master and choose Rename Master. The Rename Master dialog box opens.

2. Type a new name for the master, replacing the existing name.

3. Click Rename.

Preserving a Slide Master

Unless you have created the slide master yourself, it is temporary. Slide masters come and go as needed, as you format slides with various themes. To lock a slide master so that it doesn't disappear when no slides are using it, right-click the slide master and choose Preserve Master. A check mark appears next to Preserve Master on its right-click menu, indicating it is saved. To unpreserve it, select the command again to toggle the check mark off. See Figure 5.23.

FIGURE 5.23

The Preserve Master command saves a slide master so that PowerPoint cannot automatically delete it.

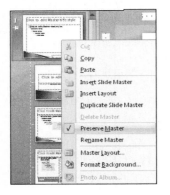

Managing Themes

As you learned earlier in the chapter, themes are applied to slide masters to create the background, color, font, and effect formatting for a presentation. Some themes are built into PowerPoint, and you can also create and save your own themes as separate files and apply them to other presentations or even to other Office documents, such as in Word and Excel. In this section you learn how to create new themes, manage theme files, and apply themes across multiple presentations.

Creating a New Theme

To create a new theme, first format a slide master exactly the way you want, including any custom layouts, backgrounds, colors, and font themes. Then save the slide master's formatting as a new theme by following these steps:

1. On the Slide Master or the Design tab, click Themes, and click Save Current Theme. The Save Current Theme dialog box opens.

   ▪ The default location shown in the Save Current Theme dialog box under Windows Vista is C:\Users*username*\AppData\Roaming\Microsoft\Templates\Document Themes.

   ▪ For Windows XP, it is C:\Documents and Settings*username*\Application Data\Microsoft\Templates\Document Themes.

2. Type a name for the theme file in the File Name text box.

3. Click Save. The new theme is saved to your hard disk.

The new theme is now available from the Themes button's menu in all presentations you create while logged in as the same user on the same PC. All of its formatting is available, including any custom color or font themes it includes.

EXPERT TIP As noted earlier, if the saved theme includes any custom layouts, PowerPoint does not make them available automatically when you apply the theme to an existing presentation. If you start a new presentation based on the theme, though, they are available. To start a new presentation based on a theme, open the theme file (Office ⇨ Open). PowerPoint does not actually open the theme file, but instead it starts a new presentation based on it.

Renaming a Theme

You can rename a theme file by renaming the .thmx file from Windows Explorer, outside of PowerPoint. You can also rename a theme file from inside PowerPoint by using any dialog box that saves or opens files. For example, to use the Choose Theme or Themed Document dialog box to rename a theme, follow these steps:

1. From the Design or Slide Master tab, click Themes, and choose Browse for Themes. The Choose Theme or Themed Document dialog box opens.

2. Navigate to the folder containing the theme file to rename.

   ▪ By default, theme files are stored under Windows Vista in: C:\Users*username*\AppData\Roaming\Microsoft\Templates\Document Themes.

   ▪ For Windows XP, it is C:\Documents and Settings*username*\Application Data\Microsoft\Templates\Document Themes.

3. Right-click the theme file and choose Rename.

4. Type the new name for the theme and press Enter.

5. Click Cancel to close the dialog box.

Deleting a Theme

A custom theme file continues appearing on the Themes button's menu indefinitely. If you want to remove it from there, you must delete it from the Document Themes folder, or move it to some other location for storage. To delete a theme, follow these steps:

1. From the Design or Slide Master tab, click Themes, and choose Browse for Themes. The Choose Theme or Themed Document dialog box opens.

2. Navigate to the folder containing the theme files:

   - In Windows Vista: C:\Users*username*\AppData\Roaming\Microsoft\Templates\Document Themes.

   - In Windows XP: C:\Documents and Settings*username*\Application Data\Microsoft\Templates\Document Themes.

3. Right-click the theme file and choose Delete.

4. At the Delete File confirmation box, click Yes.

5. Click Cancel to close the dialog box.

Copying a Theme from Another Presentation

A presentation file "contains" themes in that the themes are applied to its slide masters. (That's how a template contains themes too.) As you learned earlier, you can preserve a slide master in Slide Master view so that it doesn't get deleted automatically when there are no slides based on it; by creating new slide masters, applying themes to them, and then preserving them, you can create a whole library of themes in a single presentation or template file. Then to make this library of themes available in another presentation, you simply base the new presentation on that existing presentation (or template).

However, if you did not initially base the new presentation on the template or presentation that contains the theme you want, you can apply the theme from it after-the-fact. One way to do this is to copy-and-paste (or drag-and-drop) the slide master from one file's Slide Master view to the other's.

Follow these steps to copy a slide master (and thereby copy its theme) to another presentation:

1. Open both presentations.

2. In the presentation that contains the theme, enter Slide Master view (View ➪ Slide Master).

3. Select the slide master (top slide in the left pane) and press Ctrl+C to copy it.

4. Switch to the other presentation (View ➪ Switch Windows).

5. Enter Slide Master view (View ➪ Slide Master).

6. Press Ctrl+V to paste the slide master (and its associated theme and layouts).

Summary

In this chapter you learned how themes and slide masters make it easy to apply consistent formatting in a presentation, and how layout masters are associated with slide masters and provide consistent layouts for the slides based on them. You learned how to create, edit, rename, and delete themes and layouts, and how to copy themes between presentations.

Now that you know how to format entire presentations using themes, you're ready to start learning how to make exceptions to the formatting rules that the themes impose. In the next chapter you will learn how to format text in PowerPoint, and apply different fonts, sizes, attributes, and special effects. You can use this knowledge to make strategic changes to the text placeholders on slide masters to further customize your themes, or you can make changes to text on individual slides on a case-by-case basis to make certain slides stand out from the rest.

Chapter 6

Formatting Text

Text formatting is formatting that you can apply to individual characters of text. It includes font (typeface), size, attributes such as bold and underline, fill color, and border color. (Formatting that affects entire paragraphs only, such as indentation or bullet style, is called *paragraph formatting*, not text formatting, and is covered in Chapter 7.)

As you learned in Chapter 5, PowerPoint automates text formatting by applying themes to slide masters. The slide masters then dictate the default text size, font, color, and attributes that should be used on slides. By applying text formatting through the slide masters, rather than to individual slides, you ensure consistency and make it much easier to make global font changes later on.

However, you may need to change the formatting of some text. For example, the font size for titles on the slide master may be a bit too large; in this case, you can decrease the font size for the Title placeholder, and this change will apply to all of the layouts for that master. You can even save the changes to a new theme file so that you can reuse the theme with the smaller title text later on.

In some cases, you might need to manually change the text formatting for an individual text box, or even an individual paragraph or word. For example, you may create text boxes manually that label the parts of a diagram; in this case, you would probably want to use a fixed font and size for those labels, so that they do not change if you switch themes later on.

Changing the Font

There are several ways to change the font that is used in a presentation. Whenever possible, in order to maintain consistency, you should use the method that affects an entire slide master. However, in some cases, you may need to change the font in an individual text box, or even individual characters within the text box. Office 2007 comes with a lot of different fonts, and you may also have acquired some additional fonts by installing other programs. A *font* is a typeface, or a style of lettering. To see an example of two different font styles, compare the lettering of the above heading to the lettering in this paragraph.

NOTE In the past, when most fonts were not scalable, a distinction was sometimes drawn between the term "typeface" — referring to a certain style of lettering — and the term "font" — which referred to a specific typeface used at a certain size, with a certain combination of attributes, such as bold and italic. Nowadays, however, the terms font and typeface are synonymous for all practical purposes.

Windows fonts are generic — that is, they work with any program. For example, a font that came with WordPerfect also works with Microsoft Word and with PowerPoint. Within PowerPoint, you have access to all of the installed Windows fonts on your system.

The majority of the fonts that come with Windows and Office are scalable, OpenType or TrueType fonts. These are *outline fonts*, which means that they consist of unfilled mathematically created outlines of each character. When you assign a size, you are sizing the outline; each outline is then filled in with black (or whatever color you choose) to form each character. As a result, these fonts look good at any size. PowerPoint's Font list does not differentiate between OpenType and TrueType fonts, and both are marked with TT icons to their left, as shown in Figure 6.1.

Depending on the default printer, PowerPoint's Font list may also contain fonts that have printer icons to their left. These are *printer-resident* fonts, and they are built into the default printer that you have set up in Windows. Figure 6.1 shows one such font, AvantGarde. You should not use these fonts in a presentation that you plan to show on another computer, or to distribute to others electronically, because not everyone will have these fonts available.

In terms of appearance, there are two basic groups of fonts: *serif* (those with little tails on each letter, such as the small horizontal lines at the bases of the letters i and t) and *sans-serif* (those without the tails). The headings and regular paragraph text in this book are a serif font. If you flip back to the first page of this chapter and look for the words "IN THIS CHAPTER," this is an example of a sans-serif font.

FIGURE 6.1

Fonts appear on the Fonts list on the Home tab.

Choosing the Right Fonts

A font can make a tremendous difference in the readability and appeal of your presentation, so selecting the right ones is very important. But how do you choose from among all of the fonts that are installed on your system? Here are some general rules:

- Strive for consistency. (Yes, I keep harping on that, but it's important.) You should avoid changing the font on an individual slide, and instead, make font changes to the slide master, or, in some cases, to a master layout.

- Whenever possible, rather than choosing a fixed font, use the (Headings) or (Body) placeholders at the top of the Font menu (Figure 6.1). You can then redefine those placeholders using a font theme. This makes it much easier to change the fonts for the entire presentation later on.

CROSS-REF For more on font themes, see Chapter 5.

- Try to use a sans-serif font for the "Headings" font, because sans-serif is easier to read at large sizes.

- Use serif fonts for the body if the presentation is very text-heavy, because serif fonts are easier to read in long paragraphs (such as in this book).

- Avoid script fonts in presentations, because they are hard to read.

- Avoid novelty fonts, because they take the focus away from your message.

Another consideration when choosing fonts is whether the PC on which you present the show is likely to have the same fonts installed. If you stick with Windows-supplied fonts such as Arial and Times New Roman, which are available in both Windows XP and Windows Vista, this is a non-issue. However, if you use a font that came with Office 2007, such as Calibri, but you plan on presenting on a PC that uses an earlier version of Office, then you might want to embed the fonts in the presentation when you are saving it. If you present or edit the show on a PC that does not have the right fonts, and the fonts are not embedded, then PowerPoint will use fonts that are as close as possible to a match. Although this is helpful, it can also cause strange and unexpected line breaks in your text.

EXPERT TIP To embed fonts when saving the presentation, choose Tools ➪ Save Options in the Save As dialog box. Select the Embed Fonts in the File check box, and click OK.

EXPERT TIP If you end up on the other side of that equation, and are stuck with a presentation that uses fonts that your system doesn't have, use Replace Fonts to replace all instances of the missing font with one that is available on your PC. It's easier, of course, if all fonts are specified from slide masters, rather than on individual slides because then you have to make the change only on the master, not on each slide.

Changing the Font Theme

Choosing a different font theme was covered in Chapter 5 because of the connection between themes and fonts, but let's have another look at it here in the context of font formatting. A font theme is a specification that names two fonts: one for headings (titles) and one for body text (everything else). Font themes apply to all text that uses the font placeholders rather than a fixed font. To switch to a different font theme, follow these steps:

1. On the Design tab, click Fonts. The Fonts menu opens to display samples of the available themes. These include both built-in font themes and any custom themes that you've created.

2. Hover the mouse pointer over a theme to see it previewed on the slide.

3. Click the font theme that you want.

CROSS-REF To create your own custom font themes, see Chapter 5.

EXPERT TIP You apply the font theme to the slide master that the current slide uses. If you have other slides in the presentation that use different slide masters, the change does not affect them. To apply the change to all slide masters, instead of clicking the font theme in step 3, right-click it and choose Apply to All Slides from the menu that appears.

Applying a Fixed Font

If you apply a specific font to some text, that text will no longer use the font that is specified by the font theme. That font will not change when you change the presentation's overall font theme.

If this is what you want, then you have two ways to apply a specific font: from the Home tab or from the mini toolbar.

To apply a font from the Home tab, follow these steps:

1. Select the text to be formatted. It can be on a slide master (most preferable), on a layout master, or on an individual slide.

2. On the Home tab, in the Font group, open the Font drop-down list.

3. Point to a font other than the ones designated (Headings) and (Body). The selected text is previewed in that font, as shown in Figure 6.2.

4. Click the font that you want. PowerPoint applies the font to the text.

FIGURE 6.2

Apply a font from the Font list on the Home tab.

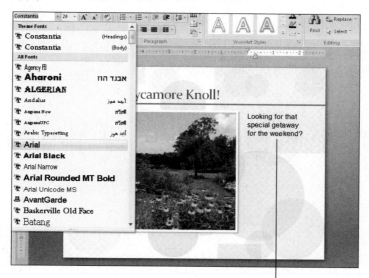

Selected font
is previewed
on the slide

If you want to return to using the theme fonts, select the "Headings" or the "Body" font from the top of the menu.

The *mini toolbar* is just what it sounds like — a small toolbar. It appears above and to the right of selected text. When the mouse pointer is directly on top of the selected text, the mini-toolbar appears dimmed, but if you move your mouse up to the mini-toolbar, it becomes fully visible.

To apply a font from the mini toolbar, follow these steps:

1. Select the text to be formatted. It can be on a slide master (most preferable), on a layout master, or on an individual slide.

2. Hover the mouse pointer over the selection so that the mini toolbar appears, as shown in Figure 6.3. If it does not appear, right-click the selection.

3. On the mini toolbar, open the Font drop-down list.

4. Point to a font other than the ones marked (Headings) or (Body). The selected text is previewed in that font.

5. Click the font that you want. PowerPoint applies the font to the text.

FIGURE 6.3

Use the mini toolbar to apply a font.

Using the Font Dialog Box

The Font dialog box (shown in Figure 6.4) provides a third way of changing the font. It also gives you access to the controls for setting font size, color, and attributes, all of which you will learn about later in this chapter. To open the Font dialog box, click the dialog box launcher in the Font group on the Home tab. Then make your selections in the dialog box, just as you would from the Home tab's Font group. Notice in Figure 6.4 that the Font drop-down list is labeled Latin Text Font. In this case, "Latin" just means regular text characters.

Replacing Fonts

If you restrain yourself from using a lot of manual text formatting, and rely on the theme to handle it, you should not have a problem with inconsistent font usage. Whenever you need to make a change, you can do it once on the slide master and be done with it.

FIGURE 6.4

The Font dialog box provides access to many different text-formatting controls, as well as the font list.

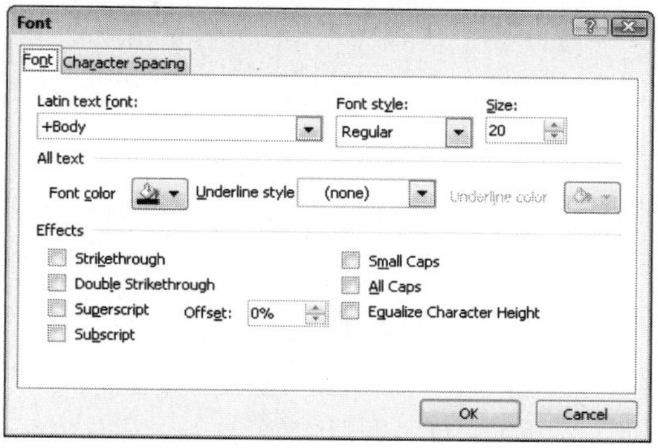

However, not everyone can be counted on to show such discipline and good design sense as you. Suppose your coworker created a long presentation in which he sporadically applied a certain font for some special elements. Now you need to work on that presentation, but you don't have that font. You will need to go through and hunt for all instances of that font and change them to some other font. Fortunately, PowerPoint has a Replace Fonts feature that can help you to find all of these instances. Follow these steps:

1. On the Home tab, in the Editing group, click the down arrow for the Replace button and choose Replace Fonts. The Replace Font dialog box appears, as shown in Figure 6.5.

2. In the Replace drop-down list, select the font that you want to replace. Only the fonts that are currently in use in the presentation appear on this list, and so it's easy to navigate.

3. In the With drop-down list, select the desired replacement font. All of the available fonts on your system appear here.

4. Click Replace. All of the instances of that font are replaced.

5. Repeat steps 2 to 4 to replace another font, or click Close when you're finished.

FIGURE 6.5

Replace all instances of one font with another.

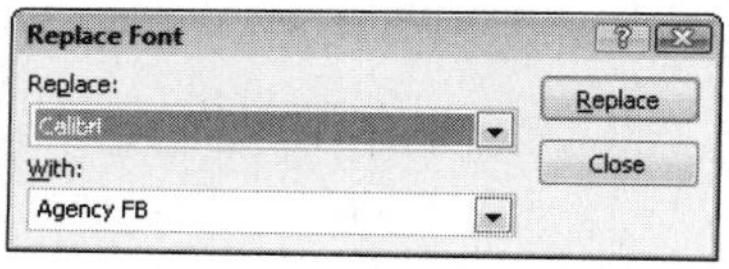

CAUTION Replacing the theme fonts makes the placeholders no longer respond to font theme changes. You have to reset the Slide Master by reapplying a theme font there if you "un-theme" them using Replace Fonts.

Changing the Font Size

Each theme has a specified font size that it uses for titles and for body text, with different sizes typically used for different levels of bulleted lists. You can use the default settings, or you can edit the placeholders on the slide master to change them. In some cases, you might also need to change the size of an individual block of text on an individual slide.

NOTE As you learned at the end of Chapter 4, PowerPoint has an AutoFit feature that you can turn on or off for each text box. When enabled, AutoFit permits the text size to shrink so that the text fits into the text box, or it permits the text box to grow so that the text fits at its current size. However, AutoFit does not change the text's font size as applied by the Font Size setting; if you enlarge the text box, the text goes back to its regular size.

Choosing the Right Sizes

The size of the text is just as important as the font. If the text is too large, it looks unattractive and amateurish, but if it's too small, the people in the back row won't be able to follow along.

Font size is measured in points, and each point measures 1/72 of an inch when printed. However, PowerPoint slides are usually shown on a screen rather than printed, and so the appropriate font size depends mainly upon the presentation medium. For example, a 72-point letter on a 15" monitor is very different than a 72-point letter on a 12-foot projection screen.

The default sizes that are specified in the built-in themes provide you with a good starting point. You can increase or decrease the sizes on the slide masters as necessary. Here are some things to consider when choosing font size:

- The farther away the audience will be sitting from the slides, and the smaller the display screen, the larger the text should be.

- Very thick and very thin letters are harder to read at small sizes. A font of moderate thickness is most readable.

- Very tight spacing can make thick letters difficult to read; on the other hand, very loose spacing can emphasize the individual letters to the point where the words they comprise are not as obvious. (Character spacing adjustment is a new feature in PowerPoint 2007, and is controlled through the Character Spacing button on the Home tab.)

- If any of your slide titles are so long that they wrap to an additional line within the title placeholder box, consider slightly decreasing the font size for the title placeholder on the slide master so that the wrapping doesn't occur. Make your changes to the slide master — not the individual slide on which the problem occurs. This is because audiences find it jarring when the slide title is not in the same place or not the same size on every slide.

Specifying a Font Size

The Font Size drop-down list, shown in Figure 6.6, is on the Home tab and is actually also an input box. You can click it and type a font size directly into the text box, or you can open the drop-down list and select a value. Typing your own value is useful if the size that you want doesn't appear on the list. At the smaller sizes, the list increments by one point, but at the larger sizes, it makes bigger jumps, and so not all values are available.

Select a font size from the drop-down list, or click in the Font Size text box and type a value.

Font size text box and list

Decrease font size

Increase font size

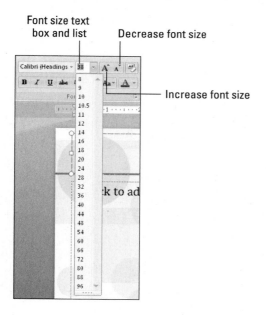

> **NOTE** The same Font Size drop-down list is also available in the mini toolbar and in the Font dialog box.

As a shortcut, you can also use the Increase Font and Decrease Font buttons, which are available both on the Home ribbon and on the mini toolbar. They are shown in Figure 6.6, and they increase or decrease the font size by one position on the Font Size list. (As noted earlier, for the smaller sizes, the increment occurs at one point at a time, but for larger sizes there is more of a jump between sizes.) You can also use the following keyboard shortcuts:

- Increase Font: Ctrl+Shift+>
- Decrease Font: Ctrl+Shift+<

Adjusting Character Spacing

Character spacing is the amount of blank space between individual letters. You can adjust this spacing to make more or less text fill a text box. Character spacing can affect the appearance and readability of both titles and body text, and Figure 6.7 shows examples of the various character spacing presets that are available with examples of how it affects your text.

FIGURE 6.7

Character spacing, which you set from the Home tab, affects the appearance and readability of your text.

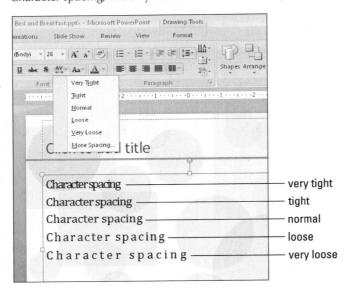

To adjust character spacing, select the text and then choose a setting from the Character Spacing drop-down menu on the Home tab.

To set custom spacing, choose More Spacing from the drop-down menu. This opens the Font dialog box to the Character Spacing tab, as shown in Figure 6.8.

To set custom spacing, choose either Expanded or Condensed from the Spacing list, and then enter a number of points by which to expand or condense. As a point of reference, Table 6.1 lists the presets from Figure 6.7 and their expand/condense values; use these as a basis for fine-tuning.

FIGURE 6.8

Adjust character spacing and kerning using custom settings in the Font dialog box.

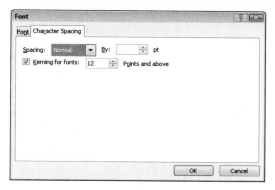

TABLE 6.1

Equivalent Expanded/Condensed Settings for Character Spacing Presets

Preset	Custom Spacing Equivalent
Very Tight	Condense by 3 points
Tight	Condense by 1.5 points
Normal	Normal
Loose	Expand by 3 points
Very Loose	Expand by 6 points

You can also adjust kerning in the Font dialog box. *Kerning* decreases the amount of space between two letters, based upon their shapes. For example, when capital letters A and V appear next to each other, you can reduce the space between them without them overlapping because of their shapes. Kerning takes the shapes of the letters into account as it selectively tightens the spacing. Kerning looks best when you apply it to large text, and so the Kerning for Fonts setting enables you to specify a minimum font size, as shown in Figure 6.8, below which text is not kerned.

Changing Font Color/Text Fill

To set the font color for individually selected text, use the Font Color button on the Home tab, or use the Text Fill button on the Drawing Tools Format tab in the WordArt Styles group. Why are there two buttons that do the same thing? Well, they don't do *exactly* the same thing. The Font

Color button on the Home tab applies only simple, solid-color formatting, and is available even in legacy presentations. The Text Fill button has a wider array of fill options, including gradients, textures, and even picture fills. It is available only in a PowerPoint 2007 presentation. Figure 6.9 shows these two buttons and their menus.

FIGURE 6.9

The Font Color button (left) and the Text Fill button (right) are both located on the Home tab. They can both apply solid-color formatting, but only the Text Fill button can apply special fill effects.

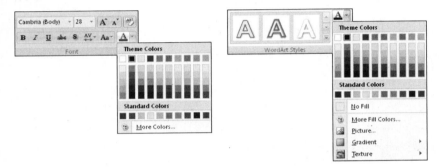

For text color and fill, as with the colors of all objects, it is usually best to stick with the theme color placeholders rather than using fixed colors. This way, if you want to change the color theme or the overall theme later on, the colors will automatically update. This doesn't necessarily mean that you have to forego special fill effects; you just have to base them on theme colors. For example, if you're creating a gradient effect, you should use two theme colors for the gradient.

 **For more on color placeholders, see Chapter 5. For more on special fill effects, see Chapter 10.**

Applying a Text Outline

One of the major improvements in PowerPoint 2007 is the ability to apply graphics-like formatting to any text. For example, you can apply outlines to text, just as you can apply borders to drawn shapes, text boxes, or other objects. In PowerPoint 2003 and earlier, this was possible only with WordArt text (that is, text treated as an internal graphic) and not as regular text. Figure 6.10 shows some text with an outline.

FIGURE 6.10

You can now apply borders to regular text.

By default, text has no outline. To apply an outline, select the text and then choose a color from the Text Outline button in the WordArt Styles group on the Home tab. You can choose either a theme color or a standard (fixed) color. You can also choose an outline weight from the Weight submenu, as shown in Figure 6.11. Chapter 10 covers object outlines (borders) in more detail.

FIGURE 6.11

You can apply a text outline color, as well as a different line thickness, or weight.

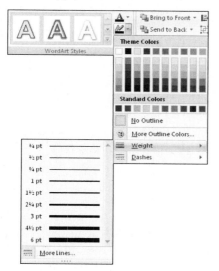

 **NOTE**   You can also apply dashes to the text outline, although this is usually not a good idea for text. Dashes are more suitable for the borders of larger objects.

Applying Text Attributes

Text attributes are modifiers that you apply to the text, such as bold, italics, underline, strikethrough, shadow, and so on. PowerPoint offers several attributes, as shown in Figure 6.12.

FIGURE 6.12

Text attributes that are available in PowerPoint 2007.

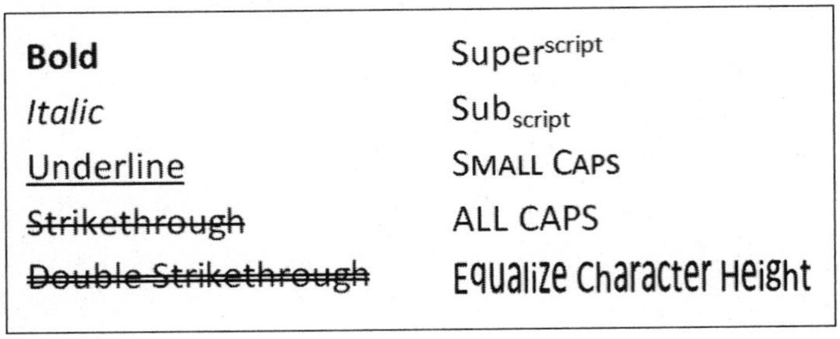

Bold	Super^{script}
Italic	Sub_{script}
Underline	SMALL CAPS
Strikethrough	ALL CAPS
Double Strikethrough	Equalize Character Height

There are actually several types of text attributes, and they can be divided into the following major groups:

- Bold and italic are actually considered *font styles*. You can apply one of these four styles to your text: Regular, Bold, Italic, or Bold Italic. In some fonts, each of these styles is formed with a separate character set that is embedded in the font file, and the letters are actually different shapes. However, in other fonts, bold is simulated by making each character a little thicker, and italics is simulated by tilting each character to the right. Figure 6.13 shows the difference between these font types.

FIGURE 6.13

Some fonts use different character sets for bold and italic, while others do not.

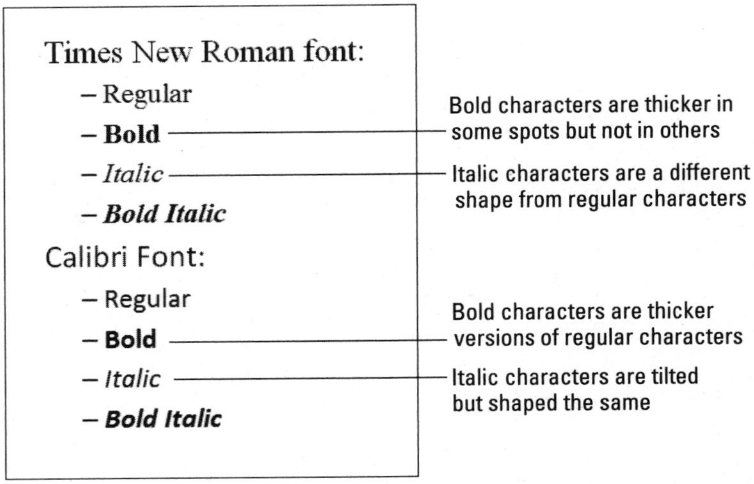

Times New Roman font:
— Regular
— **Bold** ——————— Bold characters are thicker in some spots but not in others
— *Italic* ——————— Italic characters are a different shape from regular characters
— ***Bold Italic***

Calibri Font:
— Regular
— **Bold** ——————— Bold characters are thicker versions of regular characters
— *Italic* ——————— Italic characters are tilted but shaped the same
— ***Bold Italic***

- Some attributes apply an effect on top of — or in addition to — the text. These include underlining, strikethrough, and double strikethrough.

- Superscript and Subscript attributes are used for setting off symbols and numbers for footnotes, chemical notations, exponents, and so on. They raise or lower the affected text and also shrink it by about 30 percent (this is the default setting, although you can also customize the percentage).

- Shadow formatting takes two forms. If you apply it with the button in the Font group, then it is available in all presentations, even legacy ones, and it simply places a slightly offset gray copy behind the characters. You can also apply shadow formatting from the WordArt Styles group to create different types of shadows.

- All Caps formatting appears to change lowercase letters to their uppercase equivalents. However, they are not really uppercase; they're just formatted this way. Removing the All Caps attribute returns the text to their normal appearance.

- Small Caps formatting is similar to All Caps except that letters that are normally lowercase appear slightly smaller than letters that were already uppercase to begin with.

NOTE Small Caps formatting was not available in earlier versions of PowerPoint, and if you save the presentation in PowerPoint 97-2003 format and open it in an earlier version, the Small Caps attribute is removed.

- Equalize character height formatting forces each letter to be the full height that is allotted for capital letters. This distorts the letters and is most useful when working with shaped WordArt text (which is covered later in this chapter).

As shown in Figure 6.14, the five most popular text attributes appear as toggle buttons in the Font group on the Home tab. They are Bold, Italic, Underline, Shadow, and Strikethrough.

FIGURE 6.14

Use the Font group's buttons for these five attributes.

Bold   Shadow

Italic | Strike through

Underline

The other attributes are available in the Font dialog box. You can access them by following these steps:

1. On the Home tab, click the dialog box launcher in the Font group. The Font dialog box opens, as shown in Figure 6.15.

2. In the Font Style drop-down list, choose the combination of bold and italic that you want: Regular, Bold, Italic, or Bold and Italic.

3. Choose a text color from the Font Color drop-down list. (We'll look at font color as a separate topic later in this chapter.)

4. If you want underlined text, choose an Underline Style from the drop-down list. The default color for an underline is the same as the color of the text; if you want a different color, you can choose it from the Underline Color drop-down list.

5. In the Effects section, select or deselect the check boxes for any attributes that you want. Some of these attributes are mutually exclusive, and so one is deselected when you select the other:

   - Strikethrough and Double-strikethrough
   - Superscript and Subscript
   - All Caps and Small Caps

6. Click OK to apply your choices.

FIGURE 6.15

Choose font attributes from the Font dialog box.

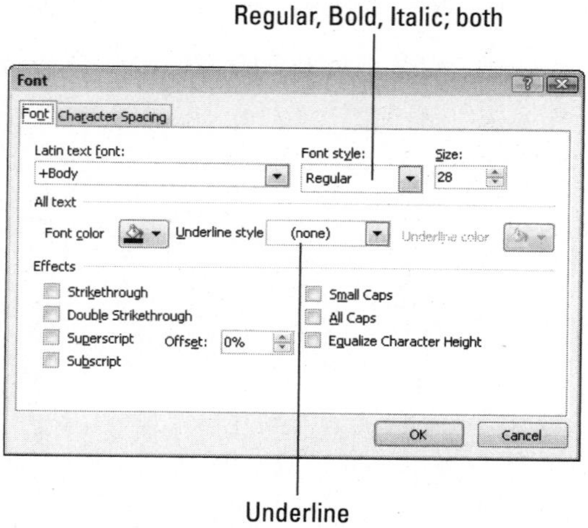

Regular, Bold, Italic; both

Underline

Changing Text Case

Each character has a numeric value stored in the presentation file, and uppercase character numbers are completely different from their lowercase counterparts. For example, a capital B is not just formatted differently from a lowercase b — it is a different character.

As you learned in the preceding section, you can apply the All Caps attribute to some text to force it to appear in all uppercase format, but this is just an illusion. The identifying numbers for the characters have not changed; they're just wearing a mask. When you remove the attribute, the characters go back to the way they normally look.

If you want to *really* change the case of some text, including changing the numeric identifiers for the characters behind the scenes, then you must either retype the text or use the Change Case feature. You can access the Change Case attribute in the Font group on the Home tab, as shown in Figure 6.16. Change Case enables you to set a block of text to any of the following settings:

- **Sentence case:** Capitalizes the first letter of the first word in the sentence, and the first letter of the first word after a sentence-ending punctuation mark such as a period.
- **Lowercase:** Converts all characters to lowercase that are not already so. (It does not do anything to numbers or symbols.)
- **Uppercase:** Converts all characters to uppercase that are not already so. (It does not do anything to numbers or symbols.)
- **Capitalize each word:** Capitalizes the first letter of each word.
- **Toggle case:** Reverses the case of every letter. For example, it would change "Smith" to "sMITH."

FIGURE 6.16

Change the case of the selected text by selecting a Change Case option from the menu.

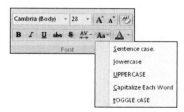

When you use the Change Case attribute, the text retains no memory of its previous capitalization state. For example, if you used the Capitalize Each Word option on the word "PowerPoint," it would convert to "Powerpoint." If you wanted to re-capitalize the middle P, then you would have to manually retype it (or select only that P and choose Change Case ⇨ Uppercase).

EXPERT TIP Most style guides dictate that you should capitalize all important words in titles, but not *every* word. For example, in the title "The Best of the Best," you do not capitalize the words "of" and "the." Unfortunately, the Capitalize Each Word option in Word cannot make that distinction for you, and so you must make those changes manually. However, Word's grammar checker does identify and fix these capitalization errors. If you have a long, text-heavy presentation, you might find it worthwhile to export the text to Word, perform a grammar check, and then re-import it.

Applying WordArt Styles

WordArt enables you to apply formatting features to text that would normally be used only with graphics, such as special fills, outlines, glows, reflections, and other special effects. It's pretty amazing stuff, as you'll see in the following sections, especially with the all-new effects that PowerPoint 2007 provides.

Up until PowerPoint 2007, WordArt has always been a rather compartmentalized specialty feature. However, in PowerPoint 2007, you can apply WordArt Styles to *all* text. There is no distinction between WordArt and regular text, and so you do not have to choose between cool special effects and including text in the outline and spell checks.

A *WordArt Style* is a preset combination of fill color, outline color, and text effects. WordArt Styles are built into PowerPoint — you can't customize them or add to them. However, you can apply one and then make changes to it.

CROSS-REF For more on text effects, see the section, "Applying WordArt Styles."

To apply a WordArt Style, follow these steps:

1. (Optional) To make the style apply to certain text, select that text.

2. On the Drawing Tools Format tab, in the WordArt Styles group, open the WordArt Styles gallery. Notice in Figure 6.17 that there are two categories of styles. Some apply only to selected text, and others apply to the entire text box (object).

3. Hover the mouse pointer over the styles to preview them on the text on the slide.

4. Click the desired style to apply it. To remove a previous WordArt effect, click Clear Wordart.

If you choose a WordArt style that is supposed to apply only to the selected text, but you have not selected any text, then PowerPoint applies it to the word at the insertion point's location. The insertion point can be at the beginning of the word or anywhere within it, but not following the word. If the insertion point follows a word, PowerPoint tries to apply the style to text that is to the right of the word. If this is a blank space, the style applies to the blank space and the change is not apparent.

FIGURE 6.17

Select a WordArt Style.

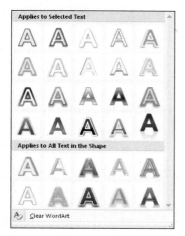

CAUTION When you save a presentation in PowerPoint 97-2003 format, any text box that contains text with WordArt formatting applied is converted to a graphic that you cannot edit. If you need to edit the text in PowerPoint 2003 or earlier, make sure that you remove the WordArt effects before saving in that format.

Applying Text Effects

The text effects that you apply using the Text Effects button in the WordArt Styles group — Shadow, Reflection, Glow, Bevel, 3-D Rotation, and Transform — are similar to regular attributes such as bold, italic, and underline, in that they apply modifiers to the basic text to produce some special appearance. However, this chapter looks at these effects separately because they are part of the new WordArt functionality in Office 2007, and apply only to text in PowerPoint 2007 presentations (as opposed to legacy presentations).

NOTE When working with text for backward-compatible presentations, stick with the effects that you can access from the Font group.

All of these effects, except for Transform, are also available for formatting graphics objects such as drawn shapes, SmartArt, and charts.

CROSS-REF To customize and fine-tune each of these effects, see Chapter 10.

Shadow

There are two ways of applying a shadow — one is available in all cases and the other is available only with PowerPoint 2007 presentations. The Shadow button in the Font group applies a default shadow to any text, and you can use it even in a backward-compatible presentation. Its shadow appears slightly below and to the right of the text, and the shadow color is automatically based on the background color.

For more flexibility, in the WordArt Styles group, click Text Effects and then select Shadow to open a gallery of shadow presets. These presets are divided into categories, including Outer (the default type), Inner, and Perspective, as shown in Figure 6.18. You can scroll down in the gallery to access more presets.

FIGURE 6.18

Select a shadow preset.

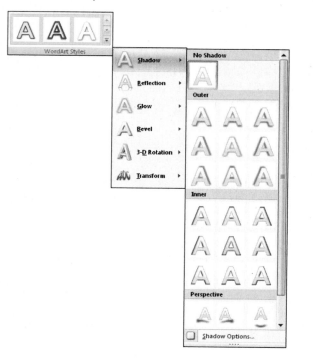

You can also customize the shadow by choosing Shadow Options, which opens the Format Text Effects dialog box. You can then fine-tune the shadow by changing its color, transparency, size, and so on.

CROSS-REF Chapter 10 looks at each of the shadow settings in detail.

CAUTION The WordArt gallery and its effects are not available when working in Compatibility mode (that is, on a PowerPoint 97-2003 format presentation).

Reflection

Reflection creates a partial mirror image of the text beneath the original, making it appear as if it were looking into a reflecting pool. Figure 6.19 illustrates the effect.

Choose a reflection preset from the Reflection submenu of the Text Effects menu, as shown in Figure 6.19. There are no custom options that you can set for text reflection; you're limited to the presets that are provided. To remove the reflection effect, choose No Reflection from the top of the gallery menu.

FIGURE 6.19

Select a reflection preset to apply a Reflection effect to text.

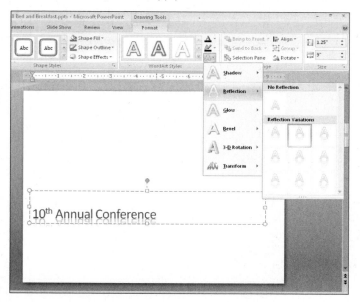

Glow

Glow appears as a soft halo effect around the text. You can choose from four levels of thickness for the glow, as well as any glow color. Figure 6.20 shows a glow effect. Notice that when you apply a glow to text that has a reflection, the glow also applies to the reflection.

FIGURE 6.20

This text has a Glow effect applied to it.

You can choose a glow preset from the Glow submenu of the Text Effects menu. You must first select the level that you want by clicking one of the presets in the gallery. Then, if you cannot find the desired color, you can reopen the submenu and choose More Glow Colors. You can then click the color that you want from the color picker, as shown in Figure 6.21. To remove the glow, choose No Glow from the top of the gallery menu.

FIGURE 6.21

You can select a glow preset, as well as a different color.

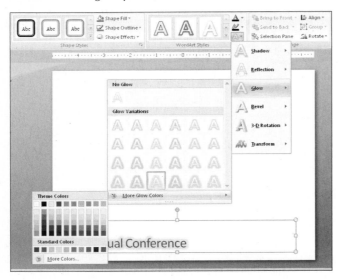

Bevel (3-D format)

A *bevel* is a slanting, curving, or rounding off of the edges of an object. It is not a very obvious effect when applied to most text, and so it's mostly for larger, drawn objects and pieces of charts and diagrams. However, on large, thick letters in light colors, beveling is sometimes useful to create a raised or textured effect. For example, in Figure 6.22, a bevel effect adds a raised appearance to the letters.

FIGURE 6.22

You can select a bevel present and add depth or texture to text.

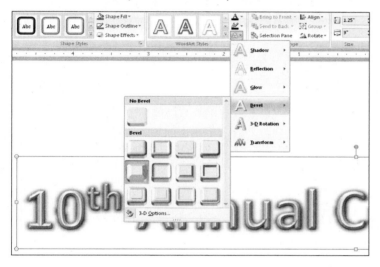

NOTE Bevel effects are not easily visible at the default zoom in Normal view. To really see the bevel effect, zoom in on the letters to at least 300 percent.

Choose a bevel preset from the Bevel submenu of the Text Effects menu, as shown in Figure 6.22.

Beveling is a subset of a larger category of formatting known as 3-D Format. With 3-D Format, you can apply not only bevels to the edges, but also depth, contours, and surface effects. 3-D Format effects are not as effective with text as with other types of objects because text is relatively small and thin, and the effects are not readily visible.

CROSS-REF For more on depth, contours, and surface effects, see Chapter 10.

To access the advanced options, choose More 3-D Settings from the gallery menu. The Format WordArt dialog box opens with the 3-D Format settings displayed, as shown in Figure 6.23. From here you can adjust the width and height of the top and bottom bevel effect (in points), and you can also experiment with the colors and sizes of the depth and contour settings, as well as the 3-D lighting and surface effects.

Fine-tune the bevel settings in the Format Text Effects dialog box.

Format Text Effects		
Text Fill	**3-D Format**	
Text Outline	Bevel	
Outline Style	Top:	Width: 3 pt / Height: 3 pt
Shadow	Bottom:	Width: 0 pt / Height: 0 pt
3-D Format	Depth	
3-D Rotation	Color:	Depth: 4.5 pt
Text Box	Contour	
	Color:	Size: 0 pt
	Surface	
	Material:	Lighting:
		Angle: 0°
	Reset	Close

EXPERT TIP The Contour section governs the outline that appears around the text when you apply beveling. If you do not want the beveled text to have an outline, set the Size to 0 points in the Contours section, as shown in Figure 6.23.

The Depth setting in the Format WordArt dialog box controls the length of the 3-D effect that is applied to the text. It doesn't do anything until you apply a Rotation setting, which is covered in the next section. However, when you rotate the text, it shows "sides" according to its depth setting. For example, in Figure 6.24, the text has a five-degree X rotation and a depth of 60 points.

The Depth setting sets the length of the sides of the text. These sides are visible only when you apply a rotation to the text.

3-D Rotation

The 3-D Rotation effect slants, tilts, or otherwise manipulates the text so that it looks as if it is being viewed at an angle. Earlier versions of PowerPoint had a very basic 3-D effect that kept the faces of the characters forward but added some perspective slant to the "sides" of the text. However, in PowerPoint 2007, you can actually slant and tilt the letters themselves, as shown in Figure 6.25.

The 3-D rotation effect makes text appear to tilt, slant, and rotate.

There are four factors that make up a 3-D rotation setting:

- **X:** left-to-right rotation
- **Y:** Top-to-bottom rotation
- **Z:** Rotation around a center point
- **Perspective:** The height at which you are viewing (above or below)

The 3-D rotation presets combine these factors to create commonly used effects. Select a rotation preset from the 3-D Rotation submenu of the Text Effects menu, as shown in Figure 6.26.

To adjust each of the four factors separately, choose More 3-D Settings from the bottom of the submenu and set the angles for each factor in the Format WordArt dialog box. By combining them with the 3-D Format settings in the Format WordArt dialog box, you can create almost any effect that you want.

CROSS-REF For more on the various rotation settings, see Chapter 10.

FIGURE 6.26

FIGURE 6.26

Choose a 3-D rotation preset.

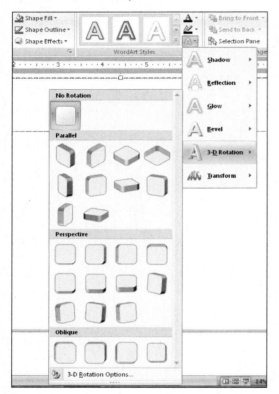

Transform

Transform settings are just for text and are not available for graphic objects such as drawn shapes. You can think of transformations — which were called WordArt Shapes in earlier versions of PowerPoint — as "molds" into which you squeeze text in order to change its shape. Figure 6.27 shows some examples of various transformations that are not rotated. However, you can combine a transformation with 3-D rotation to create some even more unusual effects.

Applying a Transformation

There are two categories of transformation: Follow Path and Warp. Follow Path is the "traditional" type of WordArt transformation, squeezing the text into various shapes. Follow Path does not reshape the text itself, but makes the characters hug a curved path. The bottom-right example in Figure 6.27 is a Follow Path effect; the others are Warp effects.

FIGURE 6.27

Some examples of transformation effects.

To apply a transformation effect, select it from the Transform submenu of the Text Effects menu, as shown in Figure 6.28. To remove a transformation effect, choose No Transform.

Modifying a Transformation

After applying a transformation, you might be able to modify its shape somewhat, depending on the transformation that you have chosen. Once you select the WordArt, look for a purple diamond in the WordArt text. You can drag this diamond to reshape the effect, making it more or less dramatic. You can drag the purple diamond in the center of the WordArt to stretch or compress the center. Lines appear as you drag to show the new position.

NOTE You can also rotate the WordArt by dragging the green circle at the top. This works just like rotating any other object and is covered in Chapter 10.

Tips for Using the Follow Path Transformations

The Follow Path transformations are a bit different from the Warp transformations, and so it might not be obvious how to manipulate them. Here are some tips:

- If the text seems to follow the path in a lopsided manner (especially common with short text phrases), set the text's horizontal alignment to Center. To do this, use the Center button in the Paragraph group on the Home tab.

CROSS-REF For more on text alignment, see Chapter 7.

FIGURE 6.28

Choose a transformation effect.

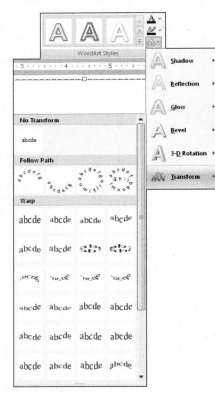

FIGURE 6.29

Modify the shape of the transformation effect by dragging a purple diamond.

- The third Follow Path transformation (Circle) makes text appear in a circle. Where it starts depends on the horizontal alignment setting for the text. You can set horizontal alignment using the buttons in the Paragraph group on the Home tab. If you set the text to be left-aligned, it starts at the left; if you center the text, the text bends around the right side as a center point. If you use right alignment, the text starts upside-down.

- The fourth Follow Path transformation (Button) makes text appear above a center line, on a center line, and then below a center line. To indicate what text should appear where, press Enter to insert paragraph breaks between the text segments.

Copying Formatting with Format Painter

Once you have formatted text exactly the way you want it, you might want to copy it to other blocks of text. To do this, you can use the Format Painter tool. Format Painter picks up the formatting of any object (including text) and "paints" it onto other objects.

To use Format Painter, follow these steps:

1. Select the text or other object whose formatting you want to copy.

2. On the Home tab, click the Format Painter icon in the Clipboard group, as shown in Figure 6.30. The mouse pointer changes to a paintbrush. If you want to copy the formatting onto more than one object or section of text, double-click the Format Painter icon instead of just clicking it.

FIGURE 6.30

Format Painter copies formatting, not only for text but also for other objects.

Format Painter

3. Click the object, or drag across the text, to which you want to apply the formatting.

4. (Optional) If you double-clicked the Format Painter icon in step 2, Format Painter is still enabled; click additional objects to apply the formatting. Press Esc to cancel the Format Painter when you are finished.

NOTE To clear the formatting from a block of text, click the Clear All Formatting button in the Font group on the Home tab.

Summary

In this chapter, you learned many techniques for formatting text. You learned how to apply different fonts, sizes, colors, and attributes, and how to bend and shape text with 3-D effects and WordArt transformations. In the next chapter, we'll continue to look at text formatting, focusing on paragraph-wide effects such as bulleted and numbered lists, indentation, and alignment.

Chapter 7

Formatting Paragraphs and Text Boxes

I n the previous chapter you learned how to format text by applying fonts, sizes, colors, attributes, and WordArt special effects. Now that your text is looking its best, you can expand the focus to the next level: paragraphs.

What can you do to an entire paragraph, as opposed to an individual text character? Plenty. For example, you can define multiple levels of bulleted and numbered lists, and you can adjust the tab stops, indentations, line spacing, and horizontal alignment for each paragraph.

All of these things happen within the context of text boxes, of course, because PowerPoint places all text in text boxes. So this chapter also takes a look at text box formatting, including fills, borders, vertical alignment, and rotation.

Formatting Bulleted Lists

For better or for worse, most PowerPoint presentations contain a lot of bulleted lists. In previous chapters, you've seen how easy it is to create a bulleted list in PowerPoint. When you create a slide based on a layout that includes a bullet list, or when you type a new slide in the outline pane, you get bullets automatically.

CROSS-REF See Chapter 2 for an analysis of why this is sometimes not the best way to go, and see Lab 1 at the end of the book to learn about alternatives.

CAUTION If you apply text formatting such as bold to a paragraph, the bullet character will also be affected. To avoid this, leave a blank space after the final character in the paragraph and then make sure you select only the text, not the entire paragraph, before applying text effects.

Bullets and the Slide Master

You can apply the bulleted list changes you learn about in the following sections to individual paragraphs, but your best bet is to apply them to the slide master, or at least to individual layout masters. That way, you ensure consistency throughout the presentation. On the slide master, five levels of bullets are defined, as shown in Figure 7.1. (You can add additional levels by pressing Enter and then Tab after the last level.) You can customize any of these levels individually. Here's a high-level overview of the process:

1. On the View tab, click Slide Master.
2. Click the top slide in the left pane, selecting the slide master itself (not one of its subordinate layouts).
3. Click on the slide, in the "Click to edit Master text styles" line.
4. Customize the bullet character, as in the following sections.
5. Click in the "Second level" line, and customize it.

FIGURE 7.1

To ensure consistency, make bullet format changes on the slide master.

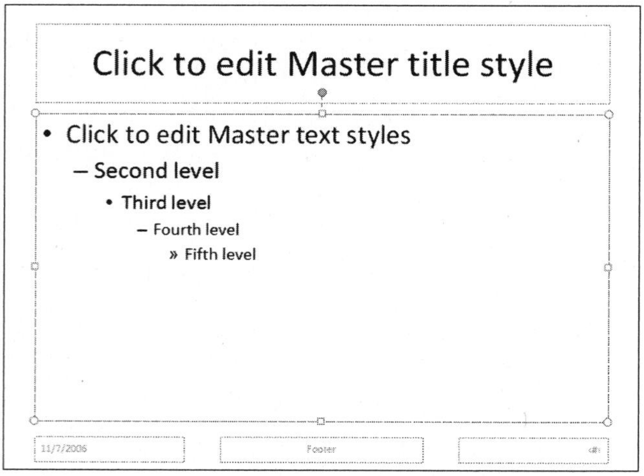

6. Repeat for other levels you want to customize. (If you do not plan to use all nine levels, you do not need to make changes to them.)

7. On the Slide Master tab, click Close.

Using Bullet Presets

You can turn off the bullets for any paragraph(s) or text placeholder by selecting them and clicking the Bullets button on the Home tab (or the Edit Master tab) to toggle the bullet(s) off. In that same way, you can apply bullets to paragraphs or text placeholders that don't currently have them.

NOTE When you are working in Slide Master view, an Edit Master tab replaces the Home tab, but they both have the same commands and buttons.

The default bullet character depends on the theme but is usually one of the presets on the Bullets button's menu, as shown in Figure 7.2. To switch among the presets, select the paragraph(s) to affect, open the button's menu, and click a different preset. The menu also has a None command, an alternative for toggling bullets off.

FIGURE 7.2

Click the Bullets button to toggle bullets on/off or open its drop-down list.

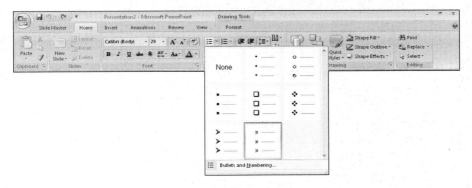

CAUTION When you turn the bullet character off in PowerPoint, the indentation of the paragraph does not change, so you're left with a first line that hangs out to the left of any other lines in a multiline paragraph. To fix this, see the section "Setting Tabs and Indents" later in this chapter.

Each of those seven presets is a placeholder. By default, each placeholder is populated with a certain symbol, but you can modify any or all of the placeholders to be different sizes or colors, and you can even replace the characters with your own choices of symbols or graphics. In the following sections you learn how to select your own bullet characters.

Changing Bullet Size and Color

Each of the bullet presets (see Figure 7.2) is actually a character from a symbol font. It is text—and as such, you can format it like text. You can increase or decrease its size, and you can change its color. To change a bullet's size and color, follow these steps:

1. Select the paragraph(s) to affect. For best results, make the change on the slide master to ensure consistency.

2. Open the Bullets button's menu and choose Bullets and Numbering. The Bullets and Numbering dialog box appears with the Bulleted tab displayed.

3. In the Size box, use the increment buttons to increase or decrease the size. The size is in relation to the text size of the paragraph.

4. Click the Color button, and select a color from the Color Picker. See Figure 7.3.

FIGURE 7.3

Change bullet size and color.

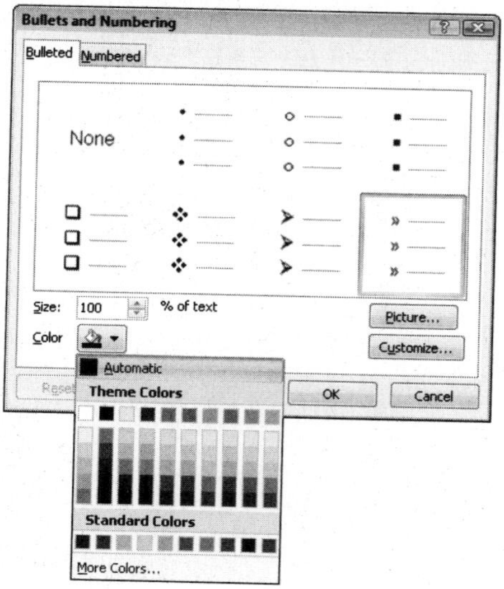

5. Click OK to apply the changes.

NOTE   The color and size changes you make in the Bullets and Numbering dialog box affect all presets.

Changing the Bullet Symbol

If you do not like any of the preset bullets, you can change that preset position to a different character. You can use any character from any font installed on your system, including any letter or number.

CROSS-REF   If you want a numbered list, see the section "Formatting Numbered Lists" later in this chapter.

To select a different bullet symbol, follow these steps:

1. Select the paragraph(s) to affect. For best results, make the change on the slide master to ensure consistency.

2. Open the Bullets button's menu and choose Bullets and Numbering. The Bullets and Numbering dialog box appears with the Bulleted tab displayed, as shown in Figure 7.3.

3. Click the preset that you want to replace, and then click Customize. The Symbol dialog box opens. See Figure 7.4.

FIGURE 7.4

Select an alternative symbol to use as a bullet.

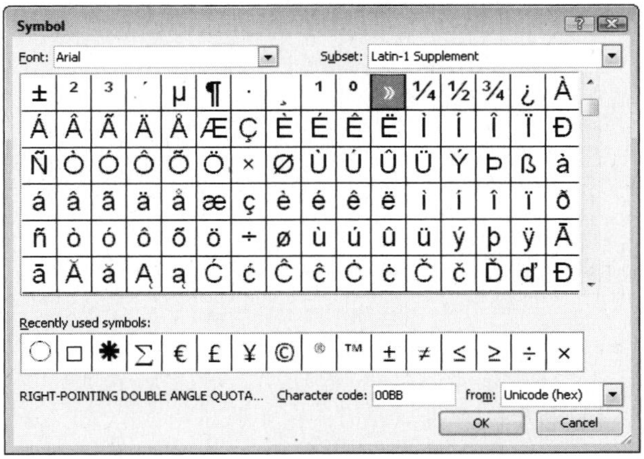

4. Select the desired font from the Font list. Although all fonts are available, most of the characters suitable for bullets are in the Wingdings fonts.

5. Click the desired character. Notice the scroll bar to the right of the characters; there are more characters than can be displayed at once.

6. Click OK. The new symbol appears on the Bulleted tab.

7. (Optional) Change the new symbol's size and color if desired, as in the preceding section.

8. Click OK to apply the new symbol to the selected paragraph(s). It also now appears on the Bullets button's list, in place of the previous preset that you selected in step 3.

Resetting a Preset

After you have customized a bullet preset, you might decide you want to go back to its original setting. To reset it, follow these steps:

1. Open the Bullets button's menu and choose Bullets and Numbering. The Bullets and Numbering dialog box appears with the Bulleted tab displayed, as shown in Figure 7.3.

2. Click the preset that you want to reset.

3. Click the Reset button. The position is reset.

4. Click OK to apply the reset character. Do not click Cancel or the reset will be cancelled. If you don't actually want to apply the character, change it afterward.

EXPERT TIP   If the Reset button is unavailable, try clicking another preset, and then clicking back to the desired one again.

Using a Picture Bullet

The Clip Organizer contains many small graphics that work well as bullets. Such graphics have a keyword of "bullet" assigned to them. The Picture Bullet dialog box, which you can access by clicking the Picture button in the Bullets and Numbering dialog box, is a special simplified version of the Clip Organizer that shows only clips that have "bullet" as one of their keywords.

To use a picture bullet from the Clip Organizer, follow these steps:

1. Select the paragraph(s) to which you want to apply the picture bullet. For best results, make the change on the slide master to ensure consistency.

2. Open the Bullets button's menu and choose Bullets and Numbering. The Bullets and Numbering dialog box appears with the Bulleted tab displayed.

3. Click the preset that you want to replace, and then click Picture. The Picture Bullet dialog box opens. See Figure 7.5.

4. Select the desired graphic.

5. Click OK. The graphic appears in the preset position that you chose in step 3.

6. Click OK to apply the graphic to the selected paragraphs as a bullet.

EXPERT TIP   To see more bullet graphics, mark the Include Content from Office Online check box. Then close and reopen the Picture Bullet dialog box. Be aware, however, that with a slow Internet connection, this might dramatically decrease the performance of this dialog box, making scrolling and picture preview very sluggish.

FIGURE 7.5

Choose a picture bullet from the Clip Organizer.

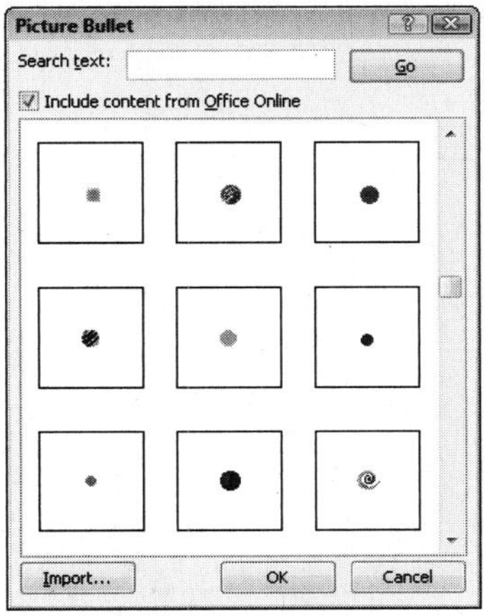

NOTE   The bullets with yellow stars in the bottom-right corner have special animation effects when you display them in Slide Show view. Bullets with a blue globe in the bottom-left corner are from the Web collection.

Most of the picture bullets are a fixed color; they do not change color when you change the theme, and they are not affected by the Color setting in the Bullets and Numbering dialog box.

You can also add your own pictures as bullets. For best results, stick with very small, simple graphics. A detailed photo might look great as a full-screen image, but as a bullet it will probably look blurry and unrecognizable. To import your own picture, follow these steps:

1. Select the paragraph(s) to which you want to apply the picture bullet. For best results, make the change on the slide master to ensure consistency.

2. Open the Bullets button's menu and choose Bullets and Numbering. The Bullets and Numbering dialog box appears with the Bulleted tab displayed.

3. Click the preset that you want to replace, and then click Picture. The Picture Bullet dialog box opens. See Figure 7.5.

4. Click Import. The Add Clips to Organizer dialog box opens.

5. Select the graphic you want to use and click Add. The picture appears as a thumbnail in the Picture Bullet dialog box.

6. Select the newly imported picture and click OK to apply the graphic as a bullet to the selected paragraph(s).

EXPERT TIP   If the picture bullet is too small, reopen the Bullets and Numbering dialog box and increase the Size setting.

Formatting Numbered Lists

Numbered lists are very similar to bulleted ones except instead of using the same character for each item they use sequential numbers or letters. Use a numbered list whenever the order of the items is significant.

Using Numbering Presets

To switch from bullets to numbering, or from neither to numbering, click the Numbering button on the Home tab — or on the Edit Master tab if you're in Slide Master view. This applies the default numbering style — the one in position #1 of the presets.

Like the Bullets button, the Numbering button also has a drop-down list with seven preset formats plus None. See Figure 7.6. You can apply any of those presets from the menu.

EXPERT TIP   You usually don't want to apply numbering to the slide master, because it's not the norm — bullets are. In addition, the optimal amount of space between paragraphs is often different when using numbered lists. Consider creating a special master layout for numbered lists and applying your number formatting to that layout in Slide Master view.

FIGURE 7.6

Click the Numbering button to toggle numbering on/off or open its drop-down list and select a preset.

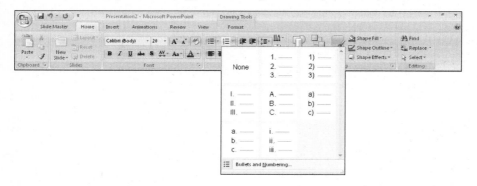

Changing Number Size and Color

Numbers can have different sizes and colors in relation to the rest of the paragraph text, just as bullets can. Using a different size and/or color can make the numbers stand out. To change a number's size and color, follow these steps:

1. Select the paragraph(s) to affect. If you want to create a layout master to store the numbering formatting, switch to Slide Master view and work on that layout master.

2. Open the Numbering button's menu and choose Bullets and Numbering. The Bullets and Numbering dialog box appears with the Numbered tab displayed.

3. In the Size box, use the increment buttons to increase or decrease the size. The size is in relation to the text size of the paragraph, as shown in Figure 7.7.

FIGURE 7.7

Change numbering size and color.

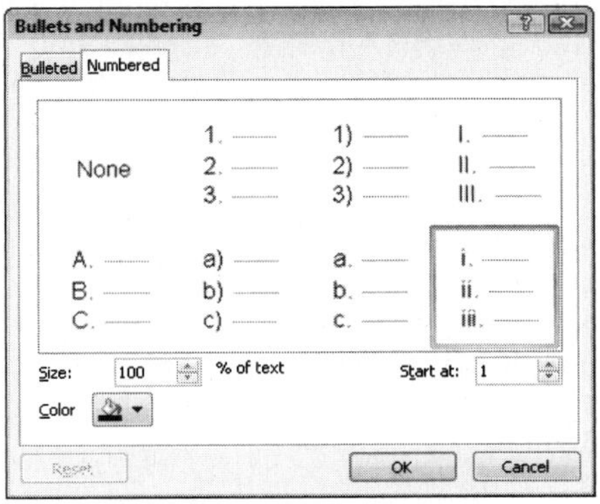

4. Click the Color button, and select a color from the Color Picker.

5. Click OK to apply the changes.

NOTE The color and size changes you make in the Bullets and Numbering dialog box affect all seven presets.

Changing the Start Number

To start the numbered list at some other number than 1, change the Start At value in the Bullets and Numbering dialog box (see Figure 7. 7). You might do this, for example, if a numbered list continues from one slide or one text box to the next.

Setting Tabs and Indents

In PowerPoint 2003 and earlier, you applied tabs and indents to entire text boxes only; you could not set them for individual paragraphs, like in Word. In PowerPoint 2007, however, you can set them for each paragraph, so you have more control.

Working with Indents

Each level of bullet (or numbering) on the Slide Master has a preset indent defined for it. There are two separate indents: one for the first line of the paragraph, and another for subsequent lines. They are represented on the ruler by triangles:

- **First line indent:** This down-pointing triangle represents the positioning of the first line of the paragraph. Because bulleted lists are the default, and the bullet character hangs to the left of the rest of the paragraph, by default, the first line indent is set to be farther to the left.

- **Hanging indent:** This up-pointing triangle represents the positioning of the second and subsequent lines in a multiline paragraph. If it is a single-line paragraph, this indent is ignored.

- **Left indent:** This rectangle controls both of the triangles as a single unit. If you want to move both triangles and maintain the spacing between them, you would drag this rectangle.

You can drag these symbols on the horizontal ruler to change their positions, as shown in Figure 7-8. You can also click the Increase Indent or Decrease Indent buttons in the Paragraph group (on the Home tab or the Edit Master tab) to change the overall left indent.

FIGURE 7.8

Adjust the indents by dragging their markers.

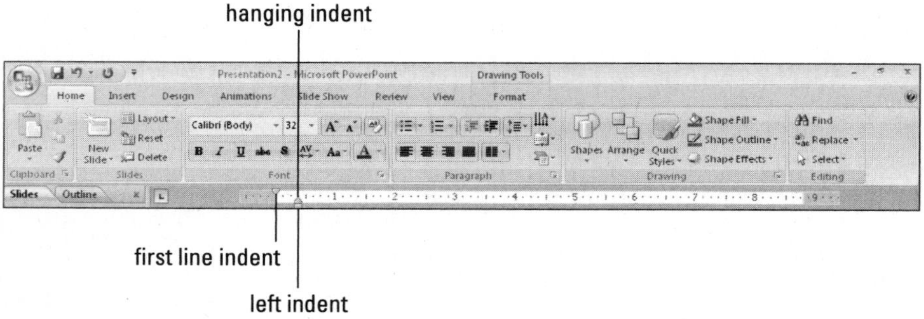

You can also control indentation more precisely by using the Paragraph dialog box's Indentation controls. These controls let you specify indentation at intervals as small as $\frac{1}{10}$ of an inch, but they do not have an exact one-to-one relationship with the indent markers on the ruler, so you have to do a bit of mental translation.

There are three indentation settings in the Paragraph dialog box, as shown in Figure 7. 9. Open this dialog box by clicking the dialog box launcher in the Paragraph group on the Home tab. The settings are as follows:

- **Before Text:** This is a general left indent setting. It sets both the hanging indent marker and the left indent marker.

- **Special:** This controls what happens to the first line. The choices are Hanging, First Line, or None. To indent the first line to the left of the others, choose Hanging. If you want the first line to the right of the others, choose First Line.

- **By:** If you chose Hanging or First Line, this sets the amount by which the first line will be offset from the Before Text setting.

FIGURE 7.9

You can set up indentation via the Paragraph dialog box.

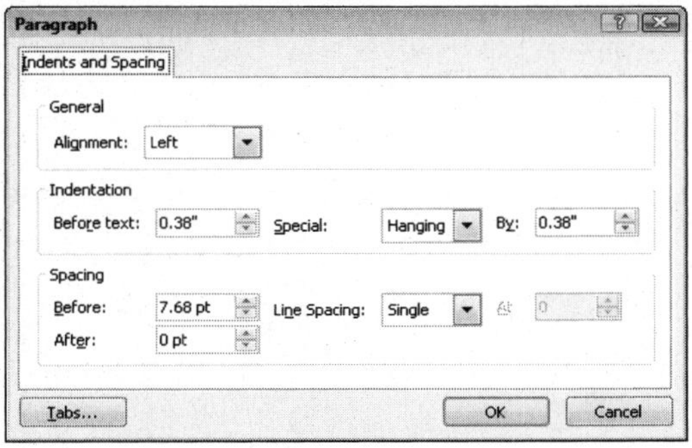

 Unlike in Word, there is no right indent marker for paragraphs in PowerPoint.

Working with Tabs

Default tab stops occur every 1" on the ruler. Each time you press the Tab key (except at the beginning of a paragraph), the insertion point moves to the next tab stop. If you press tab at the beginning of a paragraph, the paragraph is demoted one outline level. (Usually that demotion also involves an indentation as well, but the indentation is defined on the Slide Master in that case.)

In PowerPoint 2007, each paragraph can have its own separate custom tab stops set. (Earlier versions defined a single set of tab stops for the entire text box.) To set tab stops, follow these steps:

1. View the slide containing the text box in Normal or Slide view.
2. If the Ruler does not appear, choose View ➪ Ruler.

3. Click inside the text box for which you want to set tabs.

4. Click the Ruler where you want to set the tab. A little L appears, showing that you've just placed a left tab stop.

You can also set centered, right-aligned, or decimal-aligned tab stops. To set one of these, click the Tab Type button at the far left of the Ruler. Each time you click this button, it cycles through the available tab stop types as shown in Table 7.1.

TABLE 7.1

Tab Stop Types

L	Left
⊥	Center
⅃	Right
⅃•	Decimal

To get rid of a tab stop, drag and drop it off the Ruler.

New in PowerPoint 2007, you can also set tab stops via a Tabs dialog box for more precision. To access the Tabs dialog box, follow these steps:

1. Select the paragraph(s) to affect. To affect all slides, select the placeholders on the Slide Master in Slide Master view.

2. On the Home tab (or the Edit Master tab), click the dialog box launcher in the Paragraph group. The Paragraph dialog box opens.

3. Click the Tabs button. The Tabs dialog box opens as shown in Figure 7.10. From the Tabs dialog box, you can do any of the following:

   ▪ Set a Tab Stop: Type a number in the Tab Stop Position box to represent the number of inches from the left edge of the text box. Click the button in the Alignment section that represents the desired alignment, and then click Set.

   ▪ Clear a Tab Stop: To clear just one stop, select the stop to clear and then click the Clear button. To clear all custom tab stops, click Clear All.

   ▪ Change the Default Tab Stop Interval: The default interval is 1". To change that, increment or decrement the value in the Default Tab Stops box, or type a new value directly into the box.

FIGURE 7.10

FIGURE 7.10

Set or clear tab stops in the Tabs dialog box.

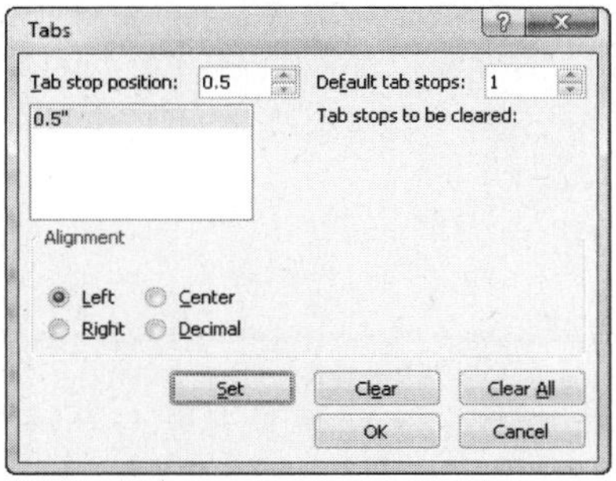

Adjusting Line Spacing

Depending on the theme, PowerPoint leaves varying amounts of space between lines and between paragraphs. The default blank theme leaves some extra space between each paragraph to make the divisions between them clearer; other themes tighten this up.

If the chosen theme doesn't provide the line spacing you want, open it up in Slide Master view and make changes to the text placeholders on the slide master(s). For example:

- If most of your bulleted lists are single-line, you might want to eliminate any extra space between paragraphs to make them seem closer together.
- If most of your bulleted lists are multiline paragraphs, you might want to add space between paragraphs to help differentiate them.
- If you want to make a large paragraph easier to read, you might add extra space between the lines.

To set basic line spacing, open the Line Spacing button's menu in the Paragraph group (Home tab or Edit Master tab) and select one of the presets. See Figure 7.11.

FIGURE 7.11

Choose a line spacing preset from the button's menu.

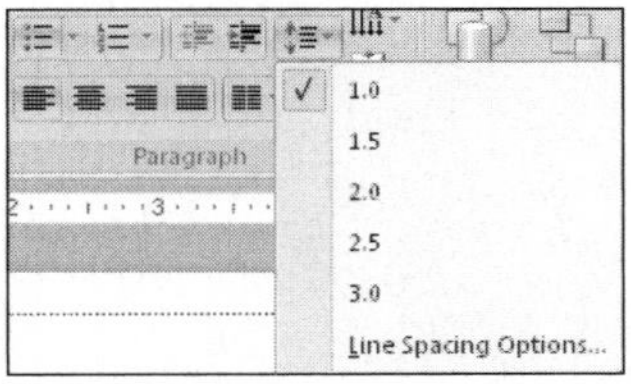

If you want more line spacing options, click the dialog box launcher for the Paragraph group on the Home tab (or the Edit Master tab). The Paragraph dialog box contains the line spacing controls, as shown in Figure 7.12. There are three line spacing settings you can adjust:

- **Before:** Space before the paragraph
- **After:** Space after the paragraph
- **Line Spacing:** Space between the lines within the paragraph

FIGURE 7.12

Adjust line spacing in the Paragraph dialog box.

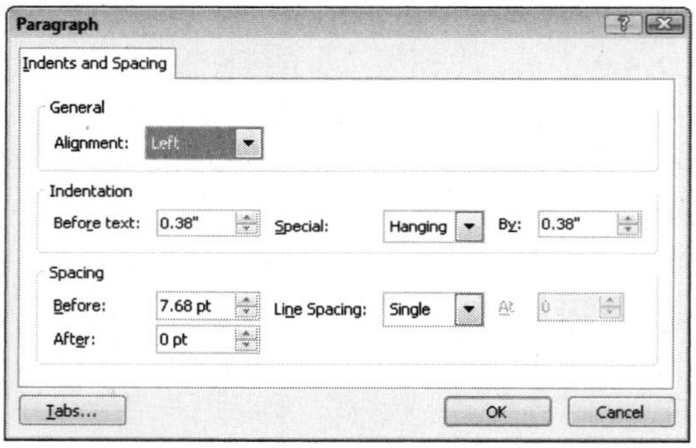

Before and After are pretty straightforward; you can set their values in points. (Remember, one point is $\frac{1}{72}$ of an inch on a printed page.) It may be helpful to think about the spacing in relation to the font size that you are using. For example, if you are using 24-point text, an After setting of 8 points would leave $\frac{1}{3}$ of a line between paragraphs.

You can set the Line Spacing to a preset value of Single, 1.5 Lines, or Double. You can also set it to Multiple and then enter a custom value in the At box. For example, a Multiple value of 1 is single spacing; a Multiple value of 0.9 is slightly less than single spacing, for just a bit of extra tightness in the layout.

All of the previously mentioned line spacing values are based on the text size in the paragraph, and not fixed amounts. As the text size changes, the line spacing will adjust automatically. If you need fixed line spacing that does not change when the font changes, choose Exactly from the Line Spacing list. Then you can enter an exact number of points for the spacing in the At box.

Changing Horizontal Alignment

You can set horizontal alignment on a paragraph-by-paragraph basis. The default alignment is Left, but you can also have Centered, Right, Justified, and Distributed:

- **Left, Centered, and Right:** These are fairly self-explanatory. They refer to the point at which each line of text aligns with the other lines of text. For example, the text in this book is left-aligned; the left edge of the paragraph is uniform and the right edge is ragged.

- **Justified:** Aligns with both the right and left margins of the text box. Space is added between words and letters to make that happen. The final line of the paragraph is not justified; it is left-aligned. Many newspapers use this alignment. It works best for long lines of text where there is a lot of text in which to spread out the extra spacing. Although justify looks good with large paragraphs, it is of limited usefulness for the brief bullet points that are the hallmark of most slides because it does not affect the last line, and in brief bullets the first line *is* the last line.

- **Distributed:** This is just like Justified except it includes the last line of the paragraph. You can use it to apply the Justified look to a single-line paragraph.

The Paragraph group on the Home tab (or the Edit Master tab) contains buttons for Left, Centered, Right, and Justified. Click a button to change the alignment of the selected paragraph(s), as shown in Figure 7.13.

FIGURE 7.13

Click a button on the Paragraph group to set alignment.

Left   Right

Centered

Justified

To use Distributed alignment, you must use the Paragraph dialog box. Click the dialog box launcher for the Paragraph group, and then choose the alignment from the Alignment drop-down list. Distributed appears on that list along with the other alignments.

EXPERT TIP *Alignment* refers to the text's position in its text box, not on the slide. If you want a text box centered on the slide, but the text is left-aligned within the box, simply move the text box where you want it. To align objects, rather than individual text paragraphs, see "Aligning and Distributing Objects" in Chapter 11.

Formatting Text Boxes

In addition to formatting the paragraphs within a text box, you can also format the text box itself. In Chapter 4 you learned how to create, resize, and move text boxes; now it's time to find out how to change their appearances.

Applying Fills and Outlines

Text boxes are just like any other object in their fill and outline formatting. You get the full details of object formatting in Chapter 10, but here's a quick look.

The *fill* is the center of the text box, and the *outline* is the border. Each can have separate formatting. For example, you can have a transparent fill with a solid border or vice versa. You can apply one of the Shape Styles presets from the Format tab to apply both at once, or you can adjust them separately with their respective menus on the Format tab. See Figure 7.14.

FIGURE 7.14

Format a text box using the Shape Styles group on the Format tab.

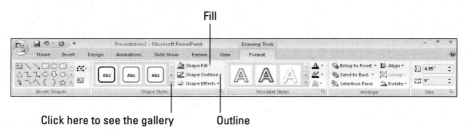

Fill

Click here to see the gallery   Outline

To apply one of the presets, click it, or open the gallery if the one you want doesn't appear. At the bottom of the gallery is Other Theme Fills, as shown in Figure 7.15. The fills on this submenu are the same as the background fills available from the Design tab, covered in Chapter 5. If you switch themes such that the background fill presets change, the background of the text box changes, too, if it is formatted with one of these.

The Shape Fill and Shape Outline buttons, and their respective menus, are familiar if you've reviewed Chapter 6, as they're very much the same as for text (WordArt). For the fill, you can choose a solid color, a gradient, a picture, or a texture. For the outline, you can select a color, thickness, and dash style. See Chapter 10 for the full details on fills and outlines.

FIGURE 7.15

Choose Other Theme Fills to select one of the theme's backgrounds for the fill of the text box.

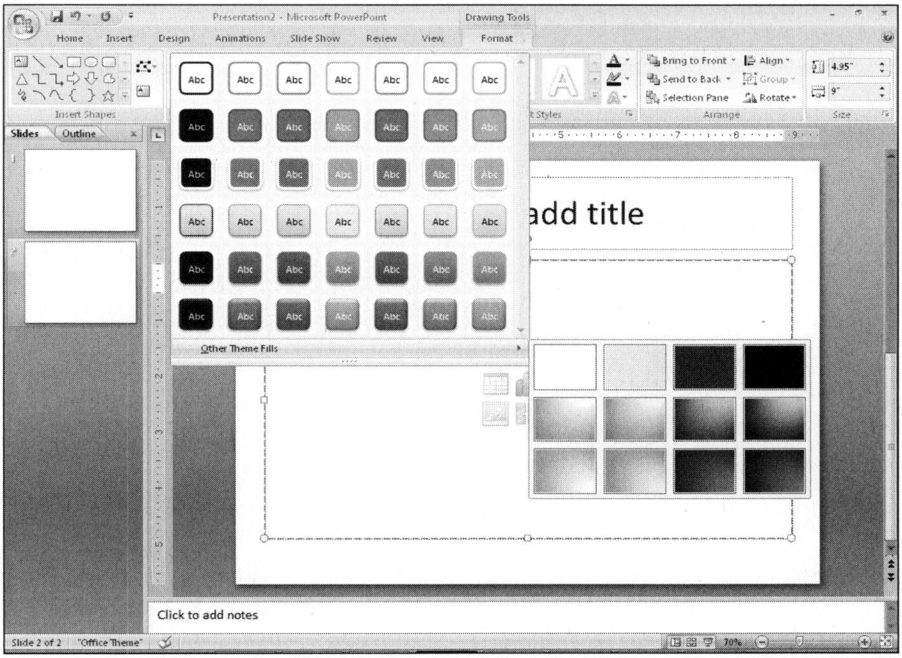

Selecting one of the background fills in Figure 7.15 fills the text box separately with one of the background presets. It does not necessarily pick the *same* background preset as is applied to the slide master. If you want the text box to always have the same fill as the current background, you can either leave it set to No Fill (the default fill), or you can set its fill to match the background:

1. Right-click the text box and choose Format Shape.
2. Click Fill if it is not already selected.
3. Click Slide Background Fill.
4. Click OK.

There are two differences between No Fill and a Slide Background Fill. One is that if the fill is a gradient, Slide Background fills the text box separately, so the text box's edges are still apparent, as in Figure 7.16. The other is that if there are any objects stacked behind the text box, the text box obscures them when set to Background, but shows them when set to No Fill.

FIGURE 7.16

The same fill has been applied both to the background and to the text box.

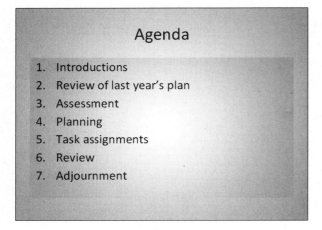

CAUTION After you've set the text box's fill to Background, the Shape Styles presets no longer work on it until you go back into the Format Shape dialog box and set the fill to Solid Fill or one of the other fills.

Setting Fill Transparency

Fill transparency determines how much of the background (or whatever is layered behind the text box) shows through it. By default, it is set to 0, which means the text box is not transparent at all when it has a fill assigned to it. To set the fill transparency, follow these steps:

1. Apply the desired fill.
2. Right-click the text box and choose Format Shape. The Format Shape dialog box opens.
3. Click Fill if the fill controls are not already displayed. See Figure 7.17.
4. Drag the Transparency slider or enter a percentage in its text box.

EXPERT TIP If the fill is a gradient, you must set the transparency separately for each of the gradient stops. (A stop is a color in the gradient.) Set the Gradient Stops drop-down list to Stop 1, adjust the transparency, set it to Stop 2, adjust the transparency, and so on. Chapter 10 explains gradients in more detail.

There is another way to set transparency, but it only works when you are applying solid fixed colors as follows:

1. Select the text box.
2. On the Drawing Tools Format tab, click Shape Fill and choose More Fill Colors.

FIGURE 7.17

Set a text box's transparency in the Format Shape dialog box.

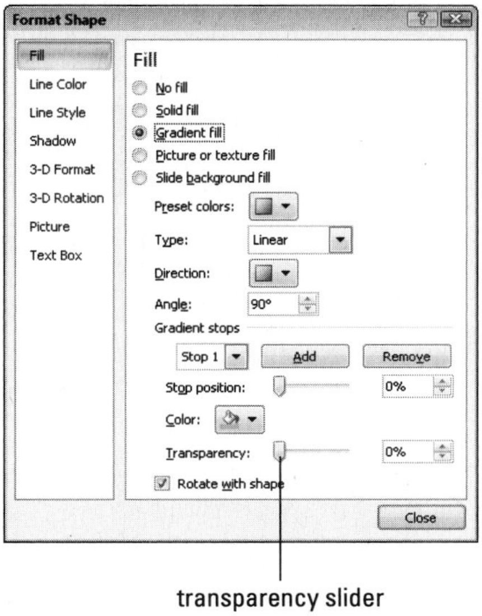

transparency slider

3. In the Colors dialog box, click the Custom tab.

4. Select the desired color.

5. Drag the Transparency slider at the bottom of the dialog box to a new value.

6. Click OK.

Controlling Vertical Alignment

The vertical alignment is the positioning of the text vertically within the text box. The default vertical alignment is Top, which means that if there is extra space in the text box, it congregates at the bottom.

For the main text placeholders in a presentation, Top alignment is usually the best because it prevents the first line of text on each slide from looking like it is inconsistently placed. However, for a manual text box on an individual slide, Middle alignment often looks better, especially in a text box that has an outline or fill defined.

You can choose Top, Middle, or Bottom alignment, or centered versions of each (Top Centered, Middle Centered, or Bottom Centered). The centered versions center the text horizontally within the text box, but it's not the same thing as horizontal alignment on a paragraph level. The text remains left-aligned with itself, but it scoots over to the center of the text box. Figure 7.18 shows the difference.

FIGURE 7.18

Vertical centering combinations with paragraph-level horizontal alignment.

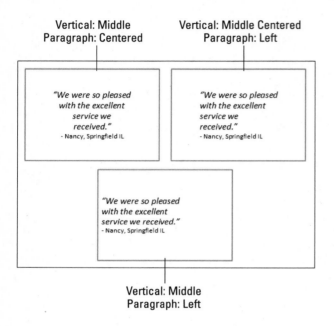

If you want one of the basic three alignments, click Align Text in the Paragraph group on the Home tab and select Top, Middle, or Bottom. See Figure 7.19.

FIGURE 7.19

Select a vertical alignment from the Align Text button's menu.

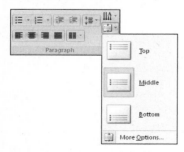

If you want one of the centered-type alignments, you must use the Paragraph dialog box. Follow these steps:

1. Right-click the text box and choose Format Shape to open the Format Shape dialog box.
2. Click Text Box.
3. In the Text Layout section, choose a Vertical Alignment setting. See Figure 7.20.

FIGURE 7.20

Choose a vertical alignment option.

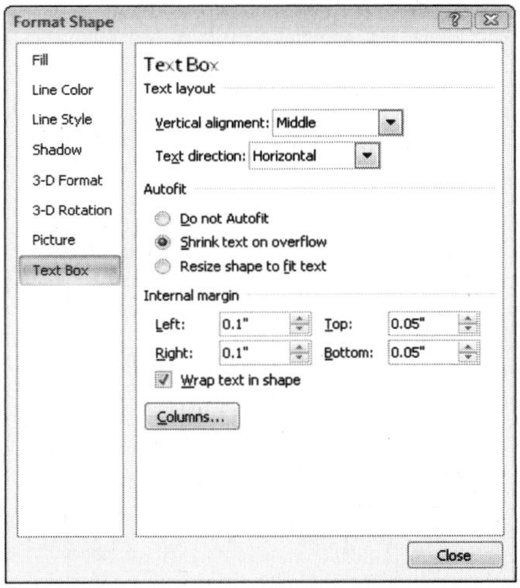

4. In the AutoFit section, choose Do Not Autofit or Shrink Text on Overflow.

   If Resize Shape to Fit Text is selected here, the text box can't be made any taller than is necessary to accommodate the text in it, so there will be no blank space to allocate vertically and no difference between the vertical alignment settings.

5. Click Close.

Changing Text Box Rotation

PowerPoint 2007 provides several types of rotation. You can spin things around a center point (the traditional 2-D type of rotation), or you can apply several 3-D rotation effects. However, the 3-D type is not well suited for text boxes because it tends to distort the text.

CROSS-REF See Chapter 10 to learn more about the 3-D type and to experiment with a text box. See Chapter 6 for 3-D type as it pertains to WordArt.

You can rotate a text box in 2-D by dragging its rotation handle, the green circle at the top of the text box. The text stays with it, so you can create upside-down text, sideways text, or text at whatever angle you like this way, as shown in Figure 7.21.

FIGURE 7.21

Rotate a text box by dragging its rotation handle.

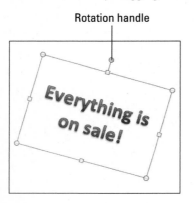

Rotation handle

If you want to rotate the text box only, but not the text within it, here's how to accomplish that:

1. Right-click the text box and choose Format Shape.
2. Click 3-D Rotation.
3. Mark the Keep Text Flat check box.
4. Click the buttons on the Z: row to rotate the text box while leaving the text as is.
5. Click Close.

EXPERT TIP   If you use the Z: setting to spin a text box without using Keep Text Flat, the text goes along with it, but the text is slightly fuzzier compared to when you use the rotation handle method.

Changing Text Direction

Instead of rotating the text box, you might prefer to just rotate the text within it. Text can run vertically on its side, facing either to the left or right, or the letters can be at normal orientation individually but stacked vertically. To set a text direction, use the Text Direction button in the Paragraph group on the Home tab (or the Edit Master tab). Figure 7.22 shows the menu and some examples of the text direction settings.

FIGURE 7.22

You can set text direction separately from text box rotation.

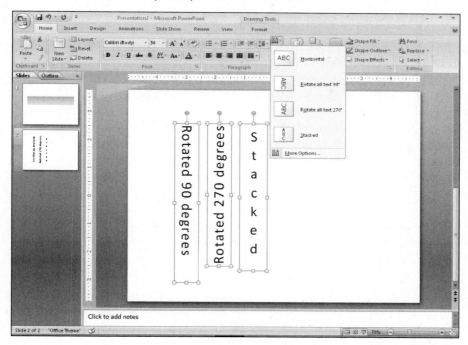

CAUTION After changing the text direction, you might need to resize the text box so that the text flows in the new direction.

EXPERT TIP When text is rotated 90 or 270 degrees, as in Figure 7.22, it often looks better if you use the Character Spacing button in the Font group to set its spacing to Loose. Conversely, Stacked text often looks better when set to Very Tight.

Setting Internal Margins

A text box's internal margins control the amount of blank space between the edge of the box and the text inside it. It's just like the margins in a word processing document except that each text box has its own individual margin settings. To set a text box's internal margins, follow these steps:

1. Right-click the text box's border and choose Format Shape. The Format Shape dialog box opens.

2. Click Text Box. The Text Box settings appear as shown in Figure 7.20.

3. In the Internal Margin section, change the Left, Right, Top, and Bottom settings as needed.

4. Click Close.

Creating Multiple Columns

In earlier versions of PowerPoint, if you wanted two columns of text, you had to place them in separate text boxes. This was awkward because the text boxes were not linked, so if you added or deleted in one box, the text did not flow into the other. In PowerPoint 2007, you can set up a text box to create multiple linked columns within a single text frame. This provides an easy way to convert a single-column layout into a multicolumn one, and solves the problem with awkward editing. To adjust the number of columns used in a text box, follow these steps:

1. Select the text box.

2. Click the Columns button in the Paragraph group on the Home tab (or the Edit Master tab).

3. Select a number of columns from the menu. See Figure 7.23.

FIGURE 7.23

Choose a number of columns for the text box.

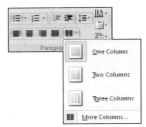

If you need a different number of columns, or you want to specify the spacing between them, choose More Columns from the menu. Then in the Columns dialog box (see Figure 7.24), enter a Number to specify the number of columns, and set an amount of spacing in inches.

FIGURE 7.24

Use the Columns dialog box to enter a larger number of columns than 3, or to adjust spacing between columns.

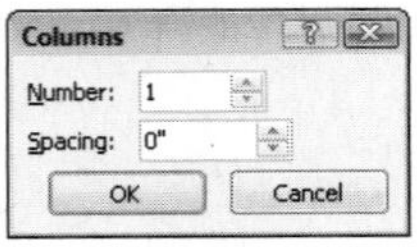

Summary

In this chapter, you learned how to format text boxes and the paragraphs within them. You learned about bulleted and numbered lists, tabs and indents, vertical and horizontal alignment, and more. Now you have the tools you need to set up a text-based presentation. (Don't worry, graphics are coming up in Part II of the book!)

But what good is nice-looking text if it's inaccurate or contains spelling errors? In the next chapter you learn how to make corrections to text with the spelling checker and the research tools, and you learn how to automate certain types of corrections.

Chapter 8

Correcting and Improving Text

PowerPoint contains many tools that can help you avoid embarrassing mistakes in your presentation's text, and this chapter takes a look at some of them. You'll learn how to replace one text string with another, perform a spelling check, set up PowerPoint to correct your most common errors automatically, and use the research tools in PowerPoint, including encyclopedias, translation guides, and thesauruses.

Finding and Replacing Text

Like all Microsoft applications, PowerPoint has a built-in Find tool, which lets you search for — and, optionally, replace — a string of text anywhere in your presentation. This feature works in all views except for Slide Show, in which it isn't applicable. However, in Slide Sorter view, it finds and replaces all instances only; you cannot interactively confirm each instance.

We will first take a look at the Find function. For example, let's say that Bob Smith was fired this morning. (Poor Bob.) Now you need to go through your presentation and see whether Bob's name is mentioned so that you can take out any lines that refer to him. Follow these steps to find a text string (such as *Bob Smith*):

1. Click Find on the Home tab, or press Ctrl+F. The Find dialog box appears.

2. Type what you want to find in the Find What text box, as shown in Figure 8.1. If you want to find a text string that you have searched for before, open the Find What drop-down list and select it. This is sometimes faster than retyping.

IN THIS CHAPTER

Finding and replacing text

Correcting your spelling

Setting the language

Using AutoCorrect to fix common problems

Using AutoFormat as you type

Using smart tags

Using the research tools

Type what you want to find, and then click the Find Next button.

3. If you want to find only whole words or to match the case, select the appropriate check box.

4. Click Find Next. The display jumps to the first instance of the text in your presentation, starting from the insertion point, working downward through the presentation, and then looping back to the top.

5. If the found instance was not the one that you were looking for, or if you want to see if there are other instances, then click the Find Next button again. You can continue clicking the Find Next button until you have seen all of the instances. When PowerPoint cannot find any more instances, a message appears — The search text was not found — and you must click OK to clear the message.

6. Click Close when you are finished.

You can also perform a replace, which adds functionality to the Find feature. This action finds the specified text and then replaces it with other text that you specify. For example, suppose that you are preparing a presentation for the Acme Corporation's sales staff. Two days before the presentation, you find out that the Primo Corporation has purchased Acme. You now need to go through the entire presentation and change every instance of Acme to Primo.

EXPERT TIP While you are using the Find feature, as explained in the preceding steps, you can switch to the Replace dialog box by clicking the Replace button. When you do so, your Find string transfers over to the Replace dialog box, so that you don't have to retype it.

To find and replace a text string, follow these steps:

1. Click Replace on the Home tab, or press Ctrl+H. The Replace dialog box appears.

NOTE The Replace button has a drop-down list. From this list, you can tell Replace Fonts to do a find-and-replace for certain font usage. You'll learn more about this in Chapter 6.

2. Type the text that you want to find in the Find What text box. If you have previously used Find or Replace, the most recent text that you found appears in the text box.

3. Type the new text in the Replace With text box. For example, if you were replacing **lay-offs** with **downsizing**, it would look like Figure 8.2.

FIGURE 8.2

Enter what you want to find and what you want to replace it with.

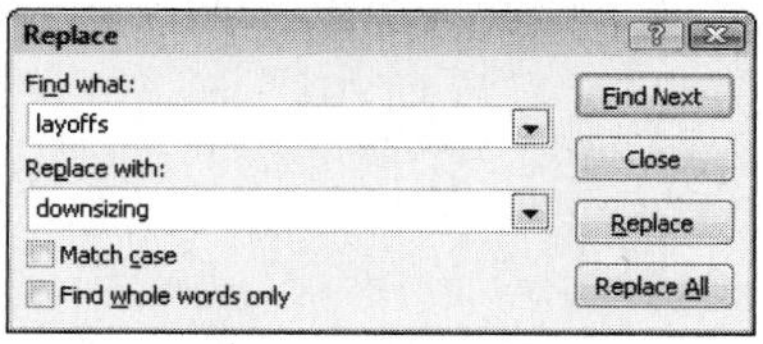

4. If you want whole words only or a case-sensitive search, select the appropriate check box.

5. Click Find Next to find the first instance.

6. If you want to replace that instance, click the Replace button. The next instance appears automatically. After this, click Find Next to go on.

7. Repeat step 6 to check and selectively replace each instance, or click the Replace All button to change all instances at once.

8. When you are finished, click Close. You may have to click OK first to clear a dialog box telling you that the specified text was not found.

Correcting Your Spelling

If you think that a spelling check can't improve the look of your presentation, just think for a moment how ugly a blatant spelling error would look in huge type on a five-foot projection screen. Frightening, isn't it? If that image makes you nervous, it should. Spelling mistakes can creep past even the most literate people, and pop up where you least expect them, often at embarrassing moments.

Fortunately, like other Microsoft Office programs, PowerPoint comes with a powerful spelling program that can check your work for you at any time, minimizing the number of embarrassing spelling mistakes. The Office programs all use the same spelling checker, and so if you are familiar with it in another Office application, you should be able to breeze through a spell check in PowerPoint with no problem.

CAUTION When PowerPoint marks a word as misspelled, it really just means that the word is not in its dictionary. Many words, especially proper names, are perfectly okay to use, even though they are not in PowerPoint's dictionary, so don't believe PowerPoint against your own good judgment.

Checking an Individual Word

As you work, PowerPoint underlines words that aren't in its dictionary with a red, wavy line. Whenever you see a red-underlined word, you can right-click it to see a list of spelling suggestions, as shown in Figure 8.3. Click the correction that you want, or click one of the other commands:

- **Ignore All:** Ignores this and all other instances of the word in this PowerPoint session. If you exit and restart PowerPoint, the list is wiped out.
- **Add to Dictionary:** Adds this word to PowerPoint's custom dictionary. (You learn more about the custom dictionary later in this chapter.)
- **Spelling:** Opens the spelling checker, described in the next section.

FIGURE 8.3

Right-click a red-underlined word for quick spelling advice.

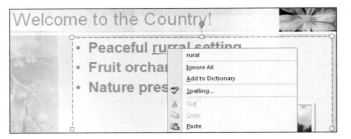

EXPERT TIP If you don't want to see the red, wavy underlines on-screen, you can turn the feature off by selecting Office ➪ PowerPoint Options, and then clicking Proofing. Click the Hide Spelling Errors check box and click OK. This just turns the underlines off; it doesn't stop PowerPoint from checking spelling as you type. A separate Check Spelling As You Type check box, in the same location, does that. Turning off Check Spelling as You Type relieves PowerPoint of a small processing burden, making it run a bit faster.

Checking the Entire Presentation

If your presentation is long, it can become tiresome to individually right-click each wavy-underlined word or phrase. In such cases, it's easier to use the spell-check feature in PowerPoint to check all of the words in the presentation.

To begin the spell check, click the Spelling button on the Review tab, or press F7. If there are no misspelled words in your presentation, PowerPoint presents a dialog box telling you that your spell check is complete. Click OK to close this dialog box. If, on the other hand, PowerPoint finds a misspelled word, you can choose from several options, as shown in Figure 8.4:

- **Not in Dictionary text box:** Shows the misspelled word.
- **Change To text box:** Shows what the spelling will be changed to if you click the Change or Change All buttons. You can choose a word from the Suggestions list or type your own correction here.

- **Suggestions text box:** Lists words that are close to the spelling of the word that you actually typed. Choose the one you want by clicking it; this moves it to the Change To text box.

- **Ignore button:** Skips over this occurrence of the word.

- **Ignore All button:** Skips over all occurrences of the word in this PowerPoint session only.

- **Change button:** Changes the word to the word shown in the Change To text box.

- **Change All button:** Changes all occurrences of the word in the entire presentation to the word in the Change To text box.

- **Add button:** Adds the word to PowerPoint's custom dictionary so that it is recognized in the future.

- **Suggest button:** Displays the suggestions in the Suggestions text box if you have set the spell checker's options so that suggestions do not automatically appear.

- **AutoCorrect button:** Adds the word to the AutoCorrect list so that if you misspell it the same way in the future, PowerPoint automatically corrects it as you type. See the "Using AutoCorrect to Fix Common Problems" section later in this chapter.

- **Close button:** Closes the Spelling dialog box.

FIGURE 8.4

When PowerPoint finds a misspelled word with the spell checker, you can respond to it using these controls.

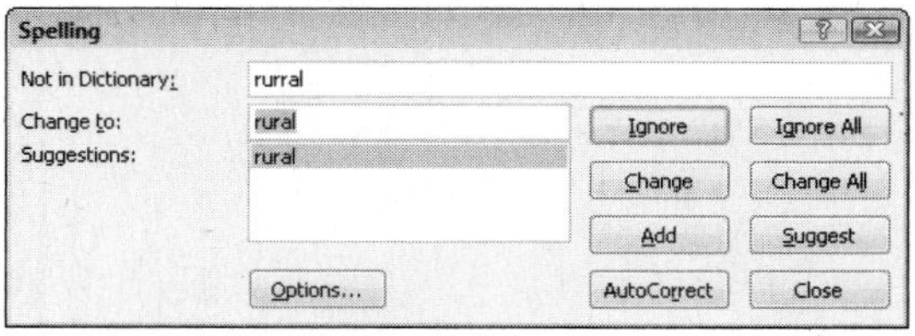

When PowerPoint can't find any more misspelled words, it displays a dialog box to let you know this; click OK to close it.

EXPERT TIP If you have more than one language dictionary available (for example, if you use PowerPoint in a multilingual office and have purchased multiple language packs from Microsoft), then you can specify which language's dictionary to use for which text. To do so, select the text that is in a different language than the rest of the presentation, and then click Set Language on the Review tab. Select the appropriate language from the list and click OK.

Setting Spelling Options

To control how (and whether) the spell checker operates, do the following:

1. Choose Office ⇨ PowerPoint Options, and click Proofing. The Proofing options appear, as shown in Figure 8.5.

FIGURE 8.5

You can set spelling options here.

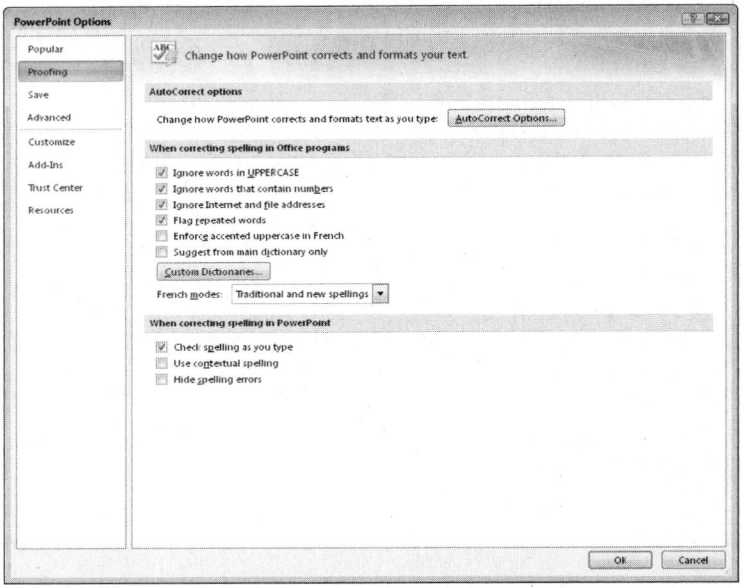

2. Select or deselect any of the check boxes as desired in the When Correcting Spelling in Office Programs section:

   Ignore Words in UPPERCASE: Prevents the spell checker from flagging acronyms.

   Ignore Words That Contain Numbers: Prevents the spell checker from noticing words with digits in them, such as license plate numbers or model numbers.

   Ignore Internet and File Addresses: Prevents the spell checker from flagging Web or e-mail addresses, network paths, or file paths.

   Flag Repeated Words: Flags second and subsequent instances of the same word in a row, preventing you from making mistakes like writing "the the."

Suggest From Main Dictionary Only: Ignores any custom spelling dictionaries if any are present.

Always Suggest Corrections: This option is selected by default. It allows suggestions to appear in the Suggestions text box in the Spelling dialog box (Figure 8-4). You can turn this option off for a very small improvement in performance. If you then want a suggestion as you are checking the spelling, you can click the Suggest button.

> **NOTE** The options in the When Correcting Spelling in Office Programs section apply across all Office programs, including Word and Excel.

3. Select or deselect any of the check boxes as desired in the When Correcting Spelling in PowerPoint section:

Check Spelling As You Type: This option is on by default. Turning it off prevents the spell checker from noticing and underlining words in red that it can't find in its dictionary. This can cause a small improvement in performance on a slow computer; you will not notice the difference on a fast computer.

Use Contextual Spelling: Allows PowerPoint to flag possible errors in context. For example, when this feature is on, PowerPoint identifies "I will go their." as a misspelling for the word "there." This feature also uses some memory, and so it can affect performance on a slow computer.

Hide Spelling Errors: This option is off by default. Selecting this check box prevents the red, wavy underline from appearing beneath misspelled words. It does not prevent the spell checker from checking them; you can right-click a misspelled word to see suggestions for it, as you normally would.

4. Click OK to accept the new settings.

Working with Custom Dictionaries

The main spelling dictionary in PowerPoint is read-only, and so when you add words to the dictionary, these words have to be stored somewhere else. This is where custom dictionaries come in. A custom dictionary contains a list of words that should not be flagged as misspellings. It can include proper names, acronyms, abbreviations, or any other codes or text strings that you frequently type.

> **NOTE** PowerPoint shares custom dictionaries with the other Office 2007 applications, and so you can use these dictionaries in PowerPoint or in one of the other applications.

The default custom dictionary is called custom.dic, and it's stored in a separate folder for each local user. If you are running Windows Vista, it's in Users\username\AppData\Roaming\Microsoft\UProof. If you are running Windows XP, it's in Documents and Settings\username\Application Data\ Microsoft\UProof. Because it is unique to the logged-in user, each user can have his or her own custom dictionary.

EXPERT TIP If there is a custom.dic file in a folder called Proof (as opposed to UProof), it's left over from an earlier version of Office. If you upgraded to Office 2007, any words that you already set up in it were copied over to the version in the UProof folder. Leave it in place if you still run an older version of Office, as well. Otherwise, you can delete it or leave it as you want.

Editing the Custom Dictionary

As you are spell checking, one of the options that you can use is Add to Dictionary — mentioned earlier in the chapter — which adds the word to the default custom dictionary. By default, this file is custom.dic. You'll learn how to create additional custom dictionaries later in this chapter.

You can also add words to the custom dictionary without having to type them in the presentation and then spell-check them. Follow these steps to add words:

1. Choose Office ⇨ PowerPoint options.
2. Click Proofing.
3. Click Custom Dictionaries.
4. Select the desired custom dictionary from the list. In Figure 8.6, only the default custom.dic dictionary appears.

FIGURE 8.6

Edit custom dictionaries from the Custom Dictionaries dialog box.

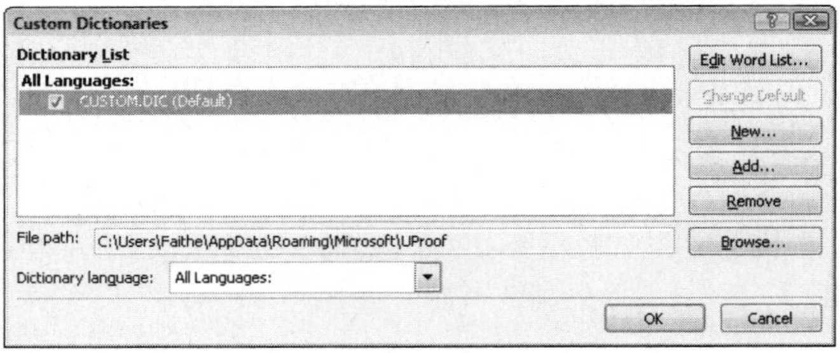

5. Click Edit Word List. A dialog box appears, listing all of the words that are currently in that dictionary.
6. To add a new word, type it in the Word(s) text box and click Add. Words can be no longer than 64 characters.
7. To delete a word, select it and click Delete. To clear the entire custom dictionary, click Delete All.
8. Click OK when you are finished editing the custom dictionary.

CAUTION The custom dictionary accepts multi-word entries, but you must enter them as separate words in the list; it does not recognize spellings that consist of only part of the word. For example, you could enter Shawna Browslawski, but the spell checker would not recognize Shawna or Browslawski by themselves. However, if you enter them as separate words, they are accepted either individually or together.

If you have a lot of words to add to the dictionary, you might prefer to edit the dictionary file manually. Dictionary files are plain-text files, and so you can edit them in Notepad. You can even combine two or more separate dictionary files into a single file by copying and pasting lists of words between them. To edit a dictionary file, open it in a text editor such as Notepad. Remember, the paths for the dictionary files are:

- Windows Vista: Users\username\AppData\Roaming\Microsoft\UProof
- Windows XP: Documents and Settings\username\Application Data\Microsoft\UProof

Creating a New Custom Dictionary

A custom dictionary file can be as large as 64KB in size, or 5,000 words. If you need a larger custom dictionary than this, you must create another dictionary file. You might also want additional custom dictionaries to keep sets of words separate for different clients or projects. For example, when working for a client with many trademarked product names that consist of non-traditional spellings of common words, you might want to set those names as correctly spelled, but when working for another client who does not use those names, you might want those words to be flagged as possible misspellings. You can enable or disable each custom dictionary, and so you can enable only the dictionaries that apply to the present project.

EXPERT TIP All spell checks use the main dictionary as well as all of the dictionaries that are selected in the Dictionary List. To disable a certain dictionary from being used, deselect its check box in the Custom Dictionaries dialog box.

To create a custom dictionary, follow these steps:

1. Choose Office ➪ PowerPoint options.
2. Click Proofing.
3. Click Custom Dictionaries.
4. Click New. The Create Custom Dictionary dialog box appears.
5. Navigate to the location in which you want to store the dictionary. The location where you store it depends on who you want to be able to access it:
   - To make the dictionary accessible to all users of your PC, store it in Program Files\Microsoft Office\OFFICE12\Dictionaries.
   - To make the dictionary accessible to only the current Windows user, store it in the default custom dictionary location:

     Windows Vista: Users\username\AppData\Roaming\Microsoft\UProof

     Windows XP: Documents and Settings\username\Application Data\Microsoft\UProof

221

6. Type a name for the dictionary in the File name text box.

7. Click Save.

The new dictionary appears in the Dictionary List in the Custom Dictionaries dialog box.

EXPERT TIP All enabled custom dictionaries are checked automatically during the spell-check process, but newly added words are placed only in the default custom dictionary. To set the default dictionary, select a custom dictionary in the Custom Dictionaries dialog box and then click the Change Default button.

Setting the Language

PowerPoint performs spell check using the native language for your copy of Word. For example, if you bought your copy in the United States, then English (U.S.) is the default language. It is important that you select the correct country as well as the correct language because some countries have different spellings for the same language than others. For example, in the United Kingdom, "s" substitutes for the American "z" in words like realize/realise. The Language setting is also used by some of the research tools, which are covered later in this chapter.

To mark a passage of text as a certain language (and country if applicable), follow these steps:

1. Select the text that you want to mark. To mark text on more than one slide, select the text from the Outline pane.

2. On the Review tab, click Language. The Language dialog box opens.

3. Select the language and country from the list, as shown in Figure 8.7.

FIGURE 8.7

Select a language for the text.

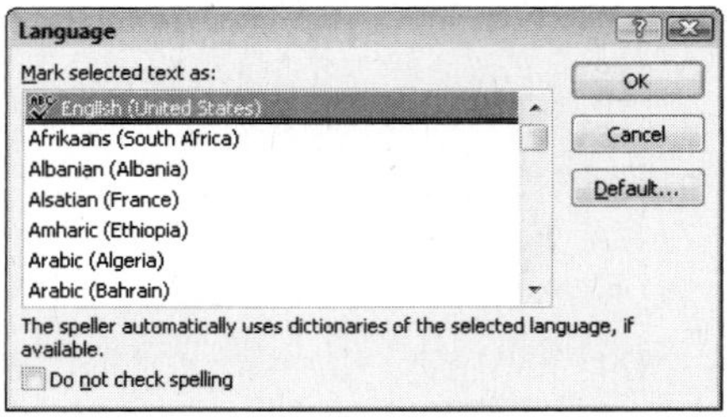

4. (Optional) To set a certain language as the default, select it and click Default; then click Yes to confirm.

5. Click OK.

Using AutoCorrect to Fix Common Problems

With AutoCorrect, PowerPoint can automatically correct certain common misspellings and formatting errors as you type. One way to add a word to the AutoCorrect list is to click the AutoCorrect button in the Spelling dialog box. Another way is to directly access the AutoCorrect options. To access AutoCorrect, follow these steps:

1. Choose Office ➪ PowerPoint Options.

2. Click Proofing.

3. Click AutoCorrect Options. The AutoCorrect dialog box opens.

4. If it is not already displayed, click the AutoCorrect tab, as shown in Figure 8.8.

FIGURE 8.8

Set up the corrections that you want PowerPoint to handle as you type.

5. Select the options that you want. At the top of the dialog box is a series of check boxes that help you to fine-tune some other corrections that AutoCorrect makes in addition to spelling corrections:

   ▪ **Show AutoCorrect Options Buttons:** This option controls whether a button is available to reverse an AutoCorrect action after the action occurs. (For more on how to use this button, see the end of this section.)

   ▪ **Correct Two Initial Capitals:** If you accidentally hold down the Shift key too long and type two capital letters in a row (such as MIcrosoft), PowerPoint corrects this error if you leave this option selected.

▦ **Capitalize First Letter of Sentences:** Leave this option selected to have PowerPoint capitalize the first letter of the first word after a sentence-ending punctuation mark, such as a period, or to capitalize the first letter of the word that occurs at the beginning of a paragraph.

EXPERT TIP Click the Exceptions button to open an AutoCorrect Exceptions dialog box. Here, you can enter a list of capitalization exceptions, such as abbreviations that use periods but aren't at the end of a sentence (for example, approx. and Ave.). You can also set up a list of Two Initial Capitals exceptions.

▦ **Capitalize First Letter of Table Cells:** Leave this option selected to capitalize the first letter of the first word within a table cell. Otherwise, PowerPoint does not treat text in a table as a sentence for capitalization purposes.

▦ **Capitalize Names of Days:** Leave this option selected to make sure that the names of days, such as Sunday, Monday, and so on, are capitalized.

▦ **Correct Accidental Use of Caps Lock Key:** If you accidentally leave the Caps Lock on, PowerPoint can sometimes detect it and fix this problem. For example, if you type the sentence, "hE WAS GLAD TO SEE US," PowerPoint may conclude that the Caps Lock is inappropriately on, and so it turns the Caps Lock off for you and fixes the sentence.

▦ **Replace Text As You Type:** This option activates the main portion of AutoCorrect, the word list. You must leave this option selected if you want AutoCorrect to correct spelling as you are typing. For example, if you type "yoiu," PowerPoint automatically changes it to "you."

6. Add items that you commonly misspell to the Replace/With list at the bottom of the dialog box. By default, this list already contains a number of word and symbol pairs. To the left is the common misspelling, and to the right is the word that PowerPoint substitutes in its place. Scroll through this list to see the types of corrections that PowerPoint makes. To add a word pair to the list, type the misspelling in the Replace text box and then type the replacement in the With text box. Then click the Add button. You can also add corrections through the Spelling dialog box.

EXPERT TIP You can use AutoCorrect to insert typographical symbols. The (C) entry is already set up to insert a copyright symbol, for example, and the (R) entry will insert a registered trademark symbol. If there is a symbol you use frequently yourself, feel free to set up an AutoCorrect entry to insert it more easily.

If PowerPoint insists on making a correction that you do not want, you can delete that correction from the list. Simply select it from the list and click Delete. For example, one of my clients likes me to code certain headings with (C) in front of them, and so the first thing that I do in any Office program is to remove the AutoCorrect entry that specifies that (C) must be converted to a copyright symbol ((c)).

7. When you are finished, click OK to close the AutoCorrect dialog box.

CAUTION Don't use AutoCorrect for misspellings that you may sometimes want to change to some other word, or you may introduce embarrassing mistakes into your document. For example, if you often type "pian" instead of "pain," and you also sometimes type "pian" instead of "piano," don't tell PowerPoint to always AutoCorrect to "pain," or you may find that PowerPoint has corrected your attempt at typing *piano* and made it a *pain*!

When an AutoCorrect action occurs, provided you have not turned off the icon, a small, blue rectangle appears when you point at the AutoCorrected word. Place your cursor over it to display an icon, and then click the icon to see a menu, as shown in Figure 8.9. From here, you can reverse the action, disable that particular correction, or open the AutoCorrect Options dialog box.

FIGURE 8.9

You can reverse an action, disable a correction, or open the AutoCorrect Options dialog box.

Using AutoFormat As You Type

The AutoFormat As You Type feature enables PowerPoint to convert certain letter combinations to typographical characters that look nicer on a slide than plain text. For example, one of the AutoFormat As You Type actions is to convert two dashes (--) into a single long dash (—).

Other actions include automatic bulleted and numbered lists. For example, in a manual text box, you may type a 1, press Tab, and type a paragraph, then type 2, press Tab, and type another paragraph. In this case, PowerPoint would guess that you want a numbered list and would apply the Numbering format to those paragraphs (just as if you had clicked the Numbering button on the toolbar). Figure 8.10 shows all of the AutoFormat As You Type options.

FIGURE 8.10

You can select the AutoFormat As You Type options that you want in this dialog box.

To change the AutoFormat As You Type settings, follow these steps:

1. Choose Office ➪ PowerPoint Options.
2. Click Proofing, and then click AutoCorrect Options.
3. Click the AutoFormat As You Type tab.
4. Select or deselect the options for the features that you want.
5. Click OK.

CROSS-REF For more on the AutoFit title text and body text feature as well as changing a text box's AutoFit behavior in general, see Chapter 4.

Using Smart Tags

When you move your mouse over certain types of text, a *smart tag* appears. Depending on the text, a smart tag might offer to perform a variety of actions on that text, such as looking up an address, scheduling a meeting, or getting a stock quote. Smart tags are "smart" in that PowerPoint is able to determine the type of content by its format and then offer appropriate choices. For example, PowerPoint can distinguish dates and telephone numbers from ordinary numbers, based on their patterns.

You can control the specific Smart Tag labels through the AutoCorrect dialog box. Here you can choose what types of recognizers you want to use. A *recognizer* is a type of data, such as Date,

Financial Symbol, Place, and so on. The types of tags depend on what is installed on your PC. By default, PowerPoint includes the following recognizers:

- **Measurement converter:** Identifies measurements and offers to convert them to other units.

- **Dates:** You can display the Outlook calendar and schedule a meeting.

- **Financial symbols:** You can get stock quotes, company reports, and business news from MSN MoneyCentral.

- **People's names:** You can send e-mail or instant messages, schedule meetings, open the person's contact information in Outlook (or create a new entry), and insert addresses.

A smart tag appears in a document as a dotted purple underline with an "i" icon. Click this icon for a menu of actions that you can perform, as shown in Figure 8.11.

FIGURE 8.11

Use a smart tag by clicking its button and selecting from its menu.

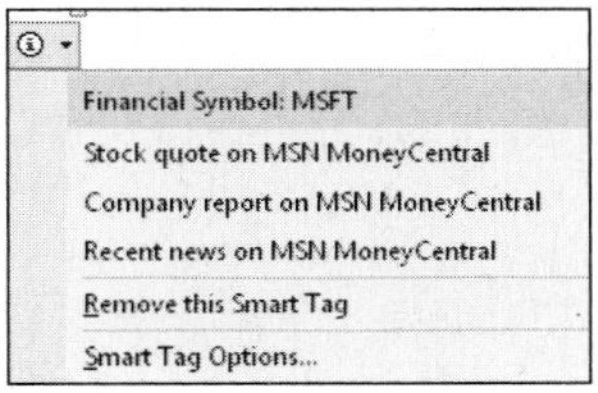

Smart tags are not enabled by default, and so you must turn them on if you want to use them. At the same time, you can also configure the tags, and add new tags if desired, by following these steps:

1. Choose Office ➪ PowerPoint Options.

2. Click Proofing.

3. Click AutoCorrect Options. The AutoCorrect dialog box opens.

4. Click the Smart Tags tab.

5. To turn the Smart Tag labels on or off, select or deselect the Label Text with Smart Tags option.

6. Select or deselect the options for each individual recognizer type, as shown in Figure 8.12.

7. After enabling or disabling the desired smart tags, click Check Presentation. PowerPoint re-checks the presentation for eligible text.

8. A confirmation box appears when the check is finished; click OK.

9. Browse through the presentation and look for the Smart Tag icon; when you see it, you can click it to access the smart tag.

FIGURE 8.12

Configure smart tags from the AutoCorrect dialog box.

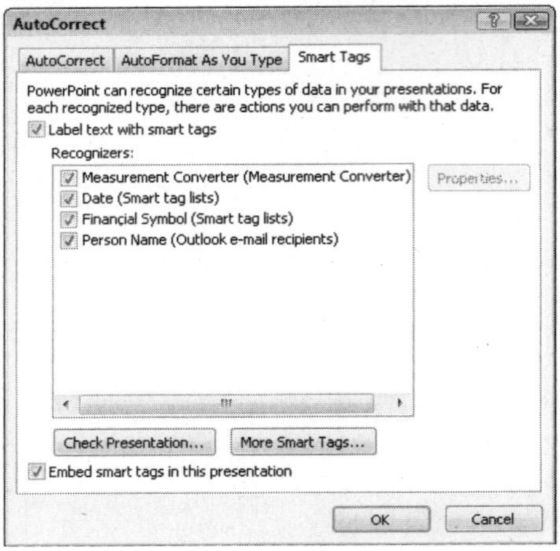

Other smart tags are available, some for free and some for an additional charge. To see what's available, click the More Smart Tags button on the Smart Tags tab of the AutoCorrect dialog box (Figure 8.12). Then follow the hyperlinks to the various services to learn about their benefits and costs. After you install new smart tags, these new tags might not be available until you exit and restart PowerPoint.

Using the Research Tools

The Research feature is available in most of the Office applications, including PowerPoint. It enables you to connect with various online and offline data stores to look up information. This may include online encyclopedias, dictionaries, and news services.

The available tools are divided into three broad categories of sites: *reference, research,* and *business/financial.* Reference sites include dictionaries, thesauruses, and translation utilities; research sites include encyclopedias and news services; business and financial information includes stock quotes and company profiles.

You can consult all of the reference sites as a group, or you can consult an individual tool. For example, you can look up a word in the dictionary, thesaurus, or translator all at once, or you can just use the thesaurus.

Looking up a Word in a Dictionary

To get a simple, concise definition of a word, a dictionary is your best bet. Here's how to use the dictionary in PowerPoint:

1. On the Review tab, click Research. The Research task pane opens.

2. Open the drop-down list of references at the top of the task pane and choose Encarta Dictionary: English (North America), or whatever language and country is appropriate.

3. In the Search For text box, type the word that you want to look up, and either press Enter or click the green arrow icon. A definition of the word appears, as shown in Figure 8.13.

FIGURE 8.13

Look up a word in the Encarta Dictionary.

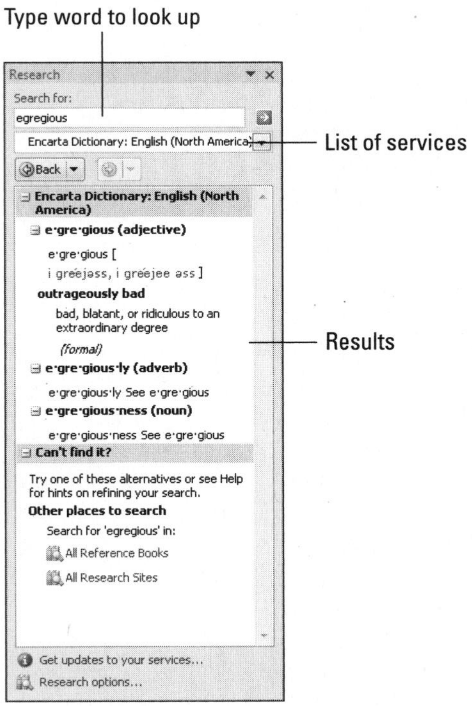

Type word to look up

- List of services
- Results

EXPERT TIP There are multiple dictionaries available; click the Research Options link at the bottom of the task pane to open a dialog box from which you can select other dictionaries. For example, the English version of Office comes with both North American and United Kingdom dictionaries, although only one is enabled by default (depending on the country in which you purchased Office).

Finding Synonyms and Antonyms with the Thesaurus

The thesaurus feature works just like a hardbound thesaurus book. It lets you look up synonyms and antonyms for a word so that you can make your vocabulary more varied and colorful.

> **NOTE** A *synonym* is a word that has a similar meaning to another word. An *antonym* is a word that has the opposite meaning.

To look up a word in the thesaurus, follow these steps:

1. Select a word that you want to look up.

2. On the Review tab, click Thesaurus. The Research task pane opens with the word's synonyms and antonyms displayed.

   Synonyms are grouped by general meaning. Antonyms are followed by the word (Antonym).

   Notice that the Thesaurus button opens the same task pane as the Research button, but with the Thesaurus tool selected.

> **NOTE** If the word that you want to look up does not already appear in the presentation, skip step 1, and then, after clicking the Thesaurus button, type the desired word in the Search For text box. Then press Enter or click the green arrow icon.

3. To insert a word into the presentation, do the following:

   a. Position the insertion point where you want to insert the found word, or select the word that you want to replace (if you did not select it already in step 1).

   b. Open the task pane menu for the word that you want to insert. (Move your cursor over the word to display a down arrow, and then click the down arrow.)

   c. Click Insert. As you can see in Figure 8.14, you can also click Copy (to copy it to the Clipboard for later insertion) and Look Up (to look up that word in the thesaurus).

FIGURE 8.14

Select a word in the thesaurus, and then insert it, copy it, or look it up.

Translating Text into Another Language

Translation helps you to translate text into a variety of languages. It's not a perfect translation by any means, so don't embarrass yourself and try to translate your entire presentation for a foreign audience. However, for simple words and phrases, as well as rough approximations of meaning, it can serve you well. To translate a passage of text in your presentation, follow these steps:

1. Select the text to be translated.

2. On the Review tab, click Translate. The Translation tools appear in the Research task pane.

3. Select the desired languages in the From and To drop-down lists, as shown in Figure 8.15.

4. Click the green arrow icon. A translation appears for the selected text.

FIGURE 8.15

Translate a word or phrase from your language to another language, or vice versa.

Using Research Sites

The research sites are sources that provide more in-depth information about a particular word or phrase, such as encyclopedias and news services. To use one of these services, follow these steps:

1. Select the word or phrase that you want to look up.

2. On the Review tab, click Research. The Research task pane opens. If it was already open, it closes; click the Research button again to reopen it.

3. Open the list of services and choose All Research Sites (or a particular site, if desired).

4. In the results that appear, click a hyperlink to read its information, as shown in Figure 8.16. Depending on what you select, a separate Web browser window may open.

FIGURE 8.16

Find in-depth information about a term or phrase with the Research group of sources.

CAUTION   Keep in mind that proper attribution of sources is a must. If you copy information from an online source such as an encyclopedia or news service, you must cite your source. Also, depending on the source, you might need to get written permission to use the data. This is especially true with photographs. Very few news services permit you to reuse their photos without permission.

Using Business and Financial Sites

The business and financial sites work just like research sites, except that they provide information that would be of more use to a businessperson evaluating a company. For example, Figure 8.17 shows the business summary that is provided for Microsoft. You can use these sites in the same way as in the preceding steps, except that you must choose All Business and Financial Sites in step 3.

Find important information about a business with the business and financial sites sources.

Summary

In this chapter, you learned how to use the spelling, proofing, and reference tools in PowerPoint to make a good impression on your audience. You learned how to find and replace text, how to look up reference information online without leaving PowerPoint, and even how to create custom dictionaries to use for different clients. Now you can present with confidence!

In the next chapter, you'll learn how to create and manage tables in PowerPoint. The table feature has undergone some changes since PowerPoint 2003, and I think you'll be surprised and pleased with what you can now do with them.

Chapter 9

Creating and Formatting Tables

You can type tabular data — in other words, data in a grid of rows and columns — directly into a table or import it from other applications. You can also apply much of the formatting that you learned about in Chapters 6 and 7, but there are some special methods that you must consider when working with tabular data. In this chapter, you'll learn how to create and manage PowerPoint tables and how to insert tabular data from other sources.

Creating a New Table

A table is a great way to organize little bits of data into a meaningful picture. For example, you might use a table to show sales results for several salespeople or to contain a multicolumn list of team member names.

> **NOTE** Text from a table does not appear in the presentation's outline.

There are several ways to insert a table, and each method has its purpose. The following sections explain each of the table creation methods. (Methods that involve using other programs, such as Word or Excel are covered later in the chapter, in the sections "Using Tables from Word" and "Integrating Excel Cells into PowerPoint.")

A table can be part of a content placeholder, or it can be a separate, free-floating item. If the active slide has an available placeholder that can accommodate a table, and there is not already content in that placeholder, the table is placed in it. Otherwise the table is placed as an independent object on the slide and is not part of the layout.

EXPERT TIP Depending on what you want to do with the table, it could be advantageous in some cases to *not* have the table be part of the layout. For example, perhaps you want the table to be a certain size and to not change when you apply a different theme. To ensure that the table is not part of the layout, start with a slide that uses a layout that contains no table-compatible placeholder, such as Title Only.

NOTE In earlier versions of PowerPoint, an AutoLayout feature changed the layout to one that contained a table placeholder if none were available. A lot of people found that annoying, though, and PowerPoint 2007 does not do it.

Creating a Table with the Insert Table Dialog Box

To create a basic table with a specified number of rows and columns, you can use the Insert Table dialog box. You can open it in either of two ways (see Figure 9.1):

■ In a content placeholder, click the Table icon.

■ On the Insert tab, choose Table ➪ Insert Table.

FIGURE 9.1

Open the Insert Table dialog box from either the Table menu or a content placeholder.

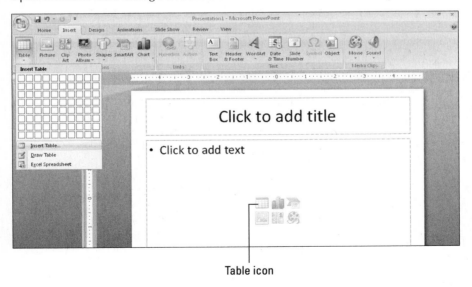

Table icon

In the Insert Table dialog box shown in Figure 9.2, specify a number of rows and columns and click OK. The table then appears on the slide.

FIGURE 9.2

Enter the number of rows and columns to specify the size of the table that you want to create.

Creating a Table from the Table Button

When you opened the Table button's menu (see Figure 9.1) in the preceding section, you probably couldn't help but notice the grid of white squares. Another way to create a table is to drag across this grid until you select the desired number of rows and columns. The table appears immediately on the slide as you drag, so you can see how it will look, as shown in Figure 9.3.

Other than the method of specifying rows and columns, this method is identical to creating a table via the dialog box, because the same issues apply regarding placeholders versus free-floating tables. If a placeholder is available, PowerPoint uses it.

FIGURE 9.3

Drag across the grid in the Table button's menu to specify the size of the table that you want to create.

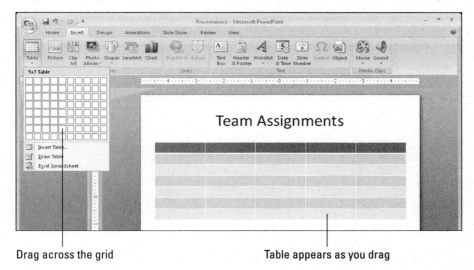

Drag across the grid   Table appears as you drag

NOTE When you create a table with this method and the preceding one, the table is automatically formatted with one of the preset table styles. You learn how to change this later in the chapter.

Drawing a Table

I've saved the most fun method for last. Drawing a table enables you to use your mouse pointer like a pencil to create every row and column in the table in exactly the positions you want. You can even create unequal numbers of rows and columns. This method is a good one to use whenever you want a table that is nonstandard in some way — different row heights, different column widths, different numbers of columns in some rows, and so on. To draw a table, follow these steps:

1. From the Insert tab, click Table, and choose Draw Table. The mouse pointer turns into a pencil.

2. Drag to draw a rectangle representing the outer frame of the table. Then release the mouse button to create the outer frame and to display the Design tab.

3. The mouse pointer remains a pencil; drag to draw the rows and columns you want. You can draw a row or column that runs all the way across or down the table's frame, or you can stop at any point to make a partial row or column. See Figure 9.4. When you begin to drag vertically or horizontally, PowerPoint locks into that mode and keeps the line exactly vertical or horizontal and straight. (Exception: It allows you to draw a diagonal line between two corners of existing cells.)

FIGURE 9.4

You can create a unique table with the Draw Table tool.

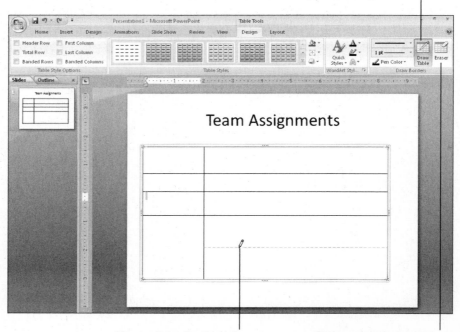

Toggles drawing mode on and off

Move pointer drawing a line   Changes cursor to an eraser

4. (Optional) To erase a line, click the Eraser button on the Table Tools Design tab, and then click the line to erase. Then click the Draw Table button on the Design tab to return the mouse pointer to its drawing (pencil) mode.

5. When you finish drawing the table, press Esc or click Draw Table again to toggle the drawing mode off.

EXPERT TIP If you need a table that is mostly uniform but has a few anomalies, such as a few combined cells or a few extra divisions, create the table using the Insert Table dialog box or the grid on the Table button, and then use the Draw Table and/or Eraser buttons on the Design tab to modify it.

Moving Around in a Table

Each cell is like a little text box. To type in a cell, click in it and type. It's pretty simple! You can also move between cells with the keyboard. Table 9.1 lists the keyboard shortcuts for moving the insertion point in a table.

TABLE 9.1

Moving the Insertion Point in a Table

To move to:	Press this:
Next cell	Tab
Previous cell	Shift+Tab
Next row	Down arrow
Previous row	Up arrow
Tab stop within a cell	Ctrl+Tab
New paragraph within the same cell	Enter

Selecting Rows, Columns, and Cells

If you want to apply formatting to one or more cells, or issue a command that acts upon them such as Copy or Delete, you must first select the cells to be affected, as in Figure 9.5:

- **A single cell:** Move the insertion point by clicking inside the desired cell. At this point, any command acts on that individual cell and its contents, not the whole table, row, or column. Drag across multiple cells to select them.

■ **An entire row or column:** Click any cell in that row or column and then open the Select button's menu on the Layout tab and choose Select Column or Select Row. Alternatively, position the mouse pointer above the column or to the left of the row, so that the mouse pointer turns into a black arrow, and then click to select the column or row. (You can drag to extend the selection to additional columns or rows when you see the black arrow.)

FIGURE 9.5

Select a row or column with the Select button's menu, or click above or to the left of the column or row.

Click above a column to select it

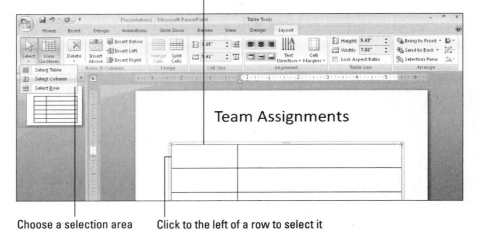

Choose a selection area   Click to the left of a row to select it

There are two ways to select the entire table — or rather, two senses in which the entire table can be "selected":

■ **Select all table cells:** When you select all of the cells, they all appear with shaded backgrounds, and any text formatting command that you apply at that point affects all of the text in the table. To select all cells, do any of the following:

▪ Choose Select Table from the Select button's menu, shown in Figure 9.5.

▪ Drag across all of the cells in the entire table.

▪ Click inside the table, and then press Ctrl+A.

- **Select the entire table:** When you do this, the table's frame is selected, but the insertion point is not anywhere within the table and cells do not appear with a shaded background. You do this kind of selection before moving or resizing the table, for example. To select the entire table, do any of the following:

    - Click the frame of the table.

    - Click inside the table, and then press Esc once.

    - Right-click the table and choose Select Table.

- **Drag a marquee around the table:** You can use the mouse to drag a marquee (a box) around the table. This is also called *lassoing*. When you release the mouse button, everything inside the area is selected.

Editing a Table's Structure

Now that you've created a table, let's look at some ways to modify the table's structure, including resizing the entire table, adding and deleting rows and columns, and merging and splitting cells.

Resizing the Overall Table

As with any other framed object in PowerPoint, dragging the table's outer frame resizes it. Position the mouse pointer over one of the selection handles (the dots on the sides and corners) so that the mouse pointer becomes a double-headed arrow, and drag to resize the table. See Figure 9. 6.

FIGURE 9.6

To resize a table, drag a selection handle on its frame.

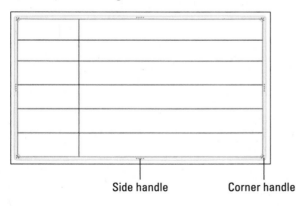

Side handle   Corner handle

 If you drag when the mouse pointer is over any other part of the frame, so that the mouse pointer becomes a four-headed arrow, you move the table rather than resize it.

To maintain the aspect ratio (height to width ratio) for the table as you resize it, hold down the Shift key as you drag a corner of the frame. If maintaining the aspect ratio is not critical, you can drag either a corner or a side.

All of the rows and columns maintain their spacing proportionally to one another as you resize them. However, when a table contains text that would no longer fit if its row and column were shrunken proportionally with the rest of the table, the row height does not shrink fully; it shrinks as much as it can while still displaying the text. The column width does shrink proportionally, regardless of cell content.

You can also specify an exact size for the overall table frame by using the Table Size group on the Layout tab, as shown in Figure 9.7. From there you can enter Height and Width values. To maintain the aspect ratio, mark the Lock Aspect Ratio check box *before* you change either the Height or Width settings.

FIGURE 9.7

Set a precise height and width for the table from the Table Size group.

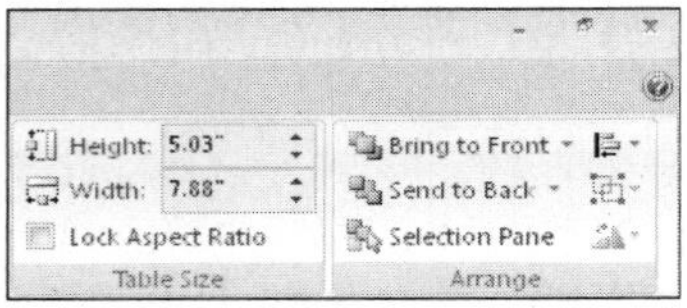

Inserting or Deleting Rows and Columns

Here's an easy way to create a new row at the bottom of the table: Position the insertion point in the bottom-right cell and press Tab. Need something more complicated than that? The Layout tab contains buttons in the Rows & Columns group for inserting rows or columns above, below, to the left, or to the right of the selected cell(s), as shown in Figure 9. 8. By default, each button inserts a single row or column at a time, but if you select multiple existing ones beforehand, these commands insert as many as you've selected. For example, to insert three new rows, select three existing rows and then click Insert Above or Insert Below.

FIGURE 9.8

Insert rows or columns by using these buttons on the Layout tab.

Alternatively, you can right-click any existing row or column, point to Insert, and choose one of the commands on the submenu. These commands are the same as the names of the buttons in Figure 9.8.

CAUTION Adding new rows increases the overall vertical size of the table frame, even to the point where it runs off the bottom of the slide. You might need to adjust the overall frame size after adding rows. On the other hand, inserting columns does not change the overall frame size; it simply resizes the existing columns so that they all fit and are all a uniform size (unless you have manually adjusted any of them to be a custom size).

To delete a row or column (or more than one of each), select the row(s) or column(s) that you want to delete, and then open the Delete button's menu on the Layout tab and choose Delete Rows or Delete Columns.

NOTE You cannot insert or delete individual cells in a PowerPoint table. (This is unlike in Excel, where you can remove individual cells and then shift the remaining ones up or to the left.)

Merging and Splitting Cells

If you need more rows or columns in some spots than others, you can use the Merge Cells and Split Cells commands. Here are some ways to merge cells:

- Click the Eraser button on the Design tab, and then click the line you want to erase. The cells on either side of the deleted line are merged.
- Select the cells that you want to merge and click Merge Cells on the Layout tab.
- Select the cells to merge, right-click them, and choose Merge Cells.

Here are some ways to split cells:

- Click the Draw Table button on the Design tab, and then drag to draw a line in the middle of a cell to split it.
- Select the cell that you want to split, right-click it, and choose Split Cells. In the Split Cells dialog box (see Figure 9.9), select the number of pieces in which to split in each direction, and click OK.
- Select the cell to split, and then click Split Cells on the Layout tab. In the Split Cells dialog box (see Figure 9.9), select the number of pieces in which to split in each direction, and click OK.

FIGURE 9.9

Specify how the split should occur.

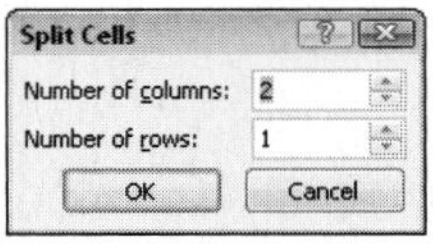

Applying Table Styles

The quickest way to format a table attractively is to apply a table style to it. When you insert a table using any method except drawing it, a table style is applied to it by default; you can change to some other style if desired, or you can remove all styles from the table, leaving it plain black-and-white.

When you hover the mouse pointer over a table style, a preview of it appears in the active table. The style is not actually applied to the table until you click the style to select it, however.

If the style you want appears on the Table Tools Design tab without opening the gallery, you can click it from there. If not, you can scroll row by row through the gallery by clicking the up/down arrow buttons, or you can open the gallery's full menu as shown in Figure 9.10.

FIGURE 9.10

Apply a table style from the gallery.

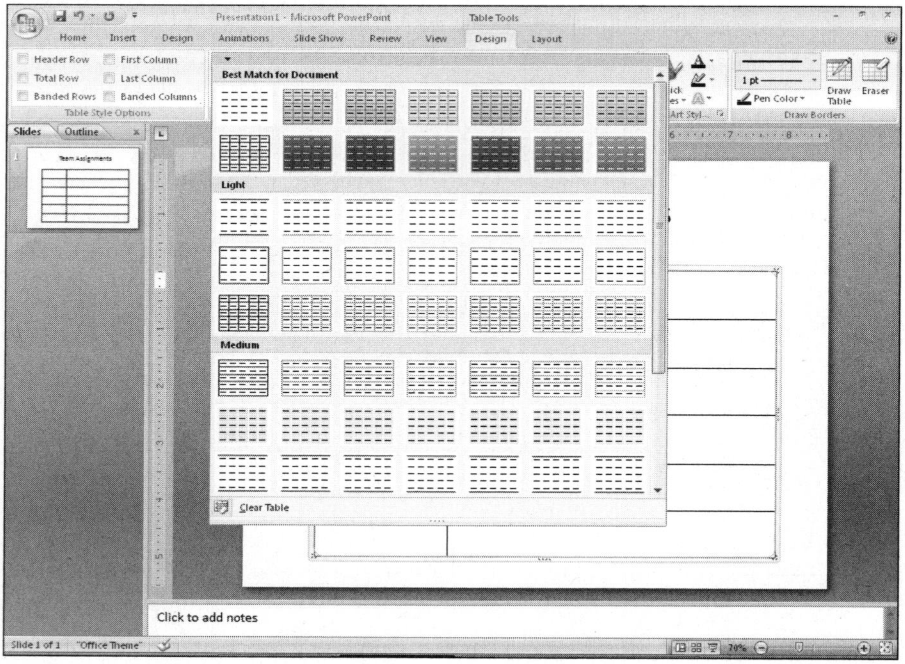

To remove all styles from the table, choose Clear Table from the bottom of the gallery menu. This reverts the table to default settings: no fill, and plain black 1-point borders on all sides of all cells.

The table styles use theme-based colors, so if you change to a different presentation theme or color theme, the table formatting might change. (Colors, in particular, are prone to shift.)

By default, the first row of the table (a.k.a. the *header row*) is formatted differently from the others, and every other row is shaded differently. (This is called *banding*.) You can control how different rows are treated differently (or not) from the Table Style Options group on the Table Tools Design tab. There is a check box for each of six settings:

- Header row: The first row
- Total row: The last row
- First column: The leftmost column
- Last column: The rightmost column
- Banded rows: Every other row formatted differently
- Banded columns: Every other column formatted differently

CAUTION With some of the styles, there is not a whole lot of difference between some of the settings. For example, you might have to look very closely to see the difference between First Column being turned on or off; ditto with Last Column and Total Row.

Formatting Table Cells

Although table styles provide a rough cut on the formatting, you might like to fine-tune your table formatting as well. In the following sections you learn how to adjust various aspects of the table's appearance.

Changing Row Height and Column Width

You might want a row to be a different height or a column a different width than others in the table. To resize a row or column, follow these steps:

1. Position the mouse pointer on the border below the row or to the right of the column that you want to resize. The mouse pointer turns into a line with arrows on each side of it.
2. Hold down the mouse button as you drag the row or column to a new height or width. A dotted line appears showing where it will go.
3. Release the mouse button.

You can also specify an exact height or width measurement using the Height and Width boxes in the Cell Size group on the Layout tab. Select the row(s) or column(s) to affect, and then enter sizes in inches or use the increment buttons, as shown in Figure 9.11.

Set a precise size for a row or column.

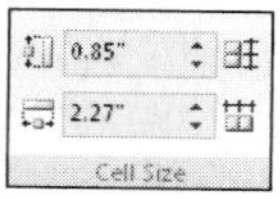

The Distribute Rows Evenly and Distribute Columns Evenly buttons in the Cell Size group (see Figure 9.11) adjust each row or column in the selected range so that the available space is occupied evenly among them. This is handy especially if you have drawn the table yourself rather than allowed PowerPoint to create it initially. If PowerPoint creates the table, the rows and columns are already of equal height and width by default.

Table Margins and Alignment

Remember, PowerPoint slides do not have any margins per se; everything is in a frame. An individual cell does have *internal* margins, however.

You can specify the internal margins for cells using the Margins button on the Layout tab, as follows:

1. Select the cells to which the setting should apply. To apply settings to the entire table, select the entire table.

2. On the Layout tab, click the Margins button. A menu of margin presets opens.

3. Click one of the presets or choose Custom Margins, and then follow these steps:

   a. In the Cell Text Layout dialog box, set the Left, Right, Top, and Bottom margin settings, as shown in Figure 9.12.

   b. Click OK.

FIGURE 9.12

You can set the internal margins on an individual cell basis for each side of the cell.

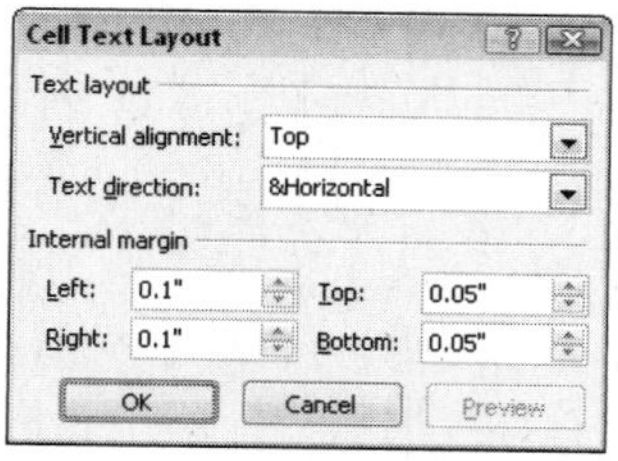

Applying Borders

The border lines around each cell are very important because they separate the data in each cell. By default (without a table style) there's a 1-point border around each side of each cell, but you can make some or all borders thicker, a different line style (dashed, for example), a different color, or remove them altogether to create your own effects. Here are some ideas:

- To make items appear to "float" in multiple columns on the slide (that is, to make it look as if they are not really in a table at all — just lined up extremely well), remove all table borders.

- To create a header row at the top without using the Quick Style Options, make the border beneath the first row of cells darker or thicker than the others.

- To make certain rows or columns appear as if they are outside of the table, turn off their borders on all sides except the side that faces the other cells.

- To make certain items appear as if they have been crossed off a list, format those cells with diagonal borders. This creates the effect of an X running through each cell. These diagonal lines are not really borders in the sense that they don't go around the edge of the cell, but they're treated as borders in PowerPoint.

When you apply a top, bottom, left, or right border, those positions refer to the entire selected block of cells if you have more than one cell selected. For example, suppose you select two adjacent cells in a row and apply a left border. The border applies only to the leftmost of the two cells. If you want the same border applied to the line between the cells too, you must apply an inside vertical border.

To apply a border, follow these steps:

1. Select the cell(s) that you want to affect.

2. In the Draw Borders group on the Table Tools Design tab, select a line style, width, and color from the Pen Style, Pen Weight, and Pen Color drop-down lists. See Figure 9.13.

FIGURE 9.13

Use the Draw Borders group's lists to set the border's style, thickness, and color.

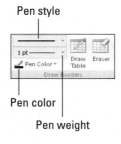

Pen style

Pen color

Pen weight

EXPERT TIP Try to use theme colors rather than fixed colors whenever possible, so that if you change to a different color theme later, the colors you choose now won't clash.

3. Open the Borders button's menu in the Table Styles group and choose the sides of the selected area to which the new settings should apply. See Figure 9.14. For example, to apply the border the bottom of the selected area, click Bottom Border.

If you want to remove all borders from all sides, choose No Border from the menu.

4. If necessary, repeat step 3 to apply the border to other sides of the selection. Some of the choices on the Borders button's menu apply to only one side; others apply to two or more at once.

FIGURE 9.14

Select the side(s) to apply borders to the chosen cells.

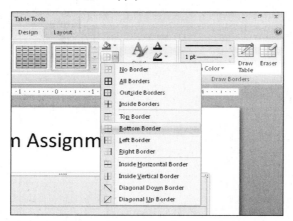

Applying Fills

By default, table cells have a transparent background so that the color of the slide beneath shows through. When you apply a table style, as you learned earlier in the chapter, the style specifies a background color — or in some cases, multiple background colors depending on the Quick Style Options you choose for special treatment of certain rows or columns.

You can also manually change the fill for a table to make it either a solid color or a special fill effect. You can apply this fill to individual cells, or you can apply a background fill for the entire table.

Filling Individual Cells

Each individual cell has its own fill setting; in this way a table is like a collection of individual object frames, rather than a single object. To set the fill color for one or more cells, follow these steps:

1. Select the cell(s) to affect, or to apply the same fill color to all cells, select the table's outer frame.

2. On the Table Tools Design tab, click the down arrow next to the Shading button to open its palette.

3. Select the desired color or fill effect. See Figure 9.15.

FIGURE 9.15

Apply a fill effect to the selected cell(s).

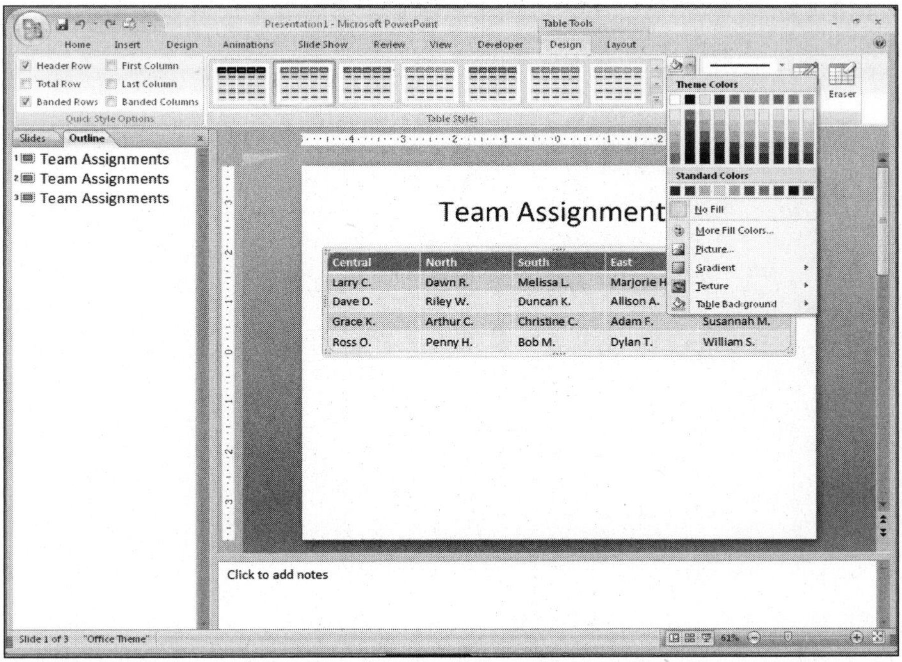

CROSS-REF For more on the various effects, see Chapter 10. Also see "Filling a Table with a Picture" later in this chapter for some issues involving picture fills specific to tables.

EXPERT TIP For a semi-transparent, solid-color fill, first apply the fill and then right-click the cell and choose Format Shape. In the Format Shape dialog box, drag the Transparency slider. For some types of fills, you can also set the transparency when you initially apply the fill.

Applying an Overall Table Fill

New in PowerPoint 2007, you can apply a solid color fill to the entire table that is different from the fill applied to the individual cells. The table's fill color is visible only in cells in which the individual fill is set to No Fill (or a semi-transparent fill, in which case it blends).

To apply a fill for the entire table, open the Shading button's menu and point to Table Background, and then choose a color, as shown in Figure 9.16.

FIGURE 9.16

Apply a fill to the table's background.

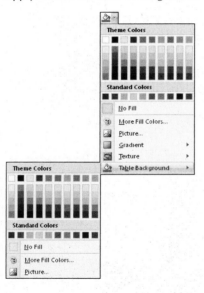

To test the new background, select some cells and choose No Fill for their fill color. The background color appears in those cells. If you want to experiment further, try applying a semi-transparent fill to some cells, and see how the color of the background blends with the color of the fill.

Filling a Table with a Picture

When you fill one or more cells with a picture, each cell gets its own individual copy of it. For example, if you fill a table with a picture of a dog, and the table has six cells, you get six dogs as shown in Figure 9.17.

If you want a single copy of the picture to fill the entire area behind the table, there are two ways you can do this. One is to set the picture to be tiled like a texture. Follow these steps:

FIGURE 9.17

When you apply a picture fill to a table, each cell gets its own copy.

1. Apply the picture to all of the cells in the table, or to the range of cells in which you want it to appear. To do this:

   a. Select the cells, and then right-click the selection and choose Format Shape.

   b. Click Fill, and then click Picture or Texture Fill.

   c. Click the File button, select the picture file, and click Insert.

2. Mark the Tile Picture as Texture check box. See Figure 9.18.

FIGURE 9.18

Set the picture to be tiled as a texture.

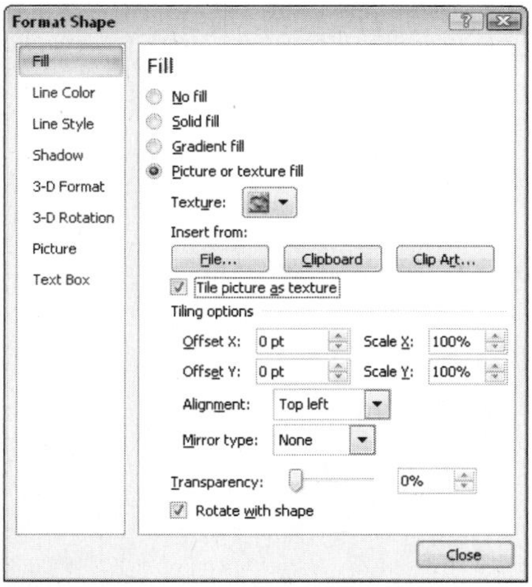

At this point, the picture fills the table without regard for cell borders, but it probably doesn't fill it exactly. Depending on the original size of the graphic and the size of the table, you probably either see a truncated version of the picture or a tiled version that does not match up with the cell borders. Figure 9.19 shows some examples.

FIGURE 9.19

The picture is too large (top) or too small (bottom) for the table fill.

To adjust the picture, use the Tiling Options in the Format Shape dialog box, shown in Figure 9.18:

- Adjust the position of the picture within the table by changing the Offset X and Offset Y values. These are measured in points, and move the picture to the right (X) and down (Y).

- Change the sizing of the picture by adjusting the Scale X and Scale Y values. The smaller the number, the smaller the picture — but don't go too small or the picture will start to tile (unless that's what you want, of course).

- Change the way the picture aligns in the table by changing the Alignment.

- (Optional) Set a mirror type if desired so that if you do have multiple copies tiled within the frame, each copy is flipped horizontally and/or vertically. (This is not common.)

It can take some time to get the picture optimally adjusted so that it exactly fits in the allotted space. If all of that seems like more than you want to mess with, there is an alternative method: make the table transparent and place the picture behind it on the slide. Here's how:

1. Place the picture on the slide by choosing Insert ➪ Picture.

2. Select the picture and choose Format ➪ Send to Back. (If the picture is the only object on the slide, this command is unavailable, but the command is unnecessary in that case.)

3. Create a plain unformatted table on top of the picture.

4. Set the table's fill to No Fill if it is not already transparent.

5. Resize the table and the picture as needed so they are both the same size. You might need to crop the picture to keep the right aspect ratio. Figure 9.20 shows a table overlaid over a photo in this way.

FIGURE 9.20

A picture placed behind a transparent table appears to fill its background.

Applying a Shadow to a Table

New in PowerPoint 2007, you can apply a shadow effect to a table. You can make it any color you like, and adjust a variety of settings for it.

NOTE If the cells have no fill, the shadow will apply to the gridlines, not to the table as a whole object.

To apply a shadow to a table, follow these steps:

1. Select the table's outer frame, and then right-click the frame and choose Format Shape.

2. Click Shadow, and then choose a preset and a color. See Figure 9.21.

3. (Optional) If desired, drag any of the sliders to fine-tune the shadow. These are covered in greater detail in Chapter 10.

4. Click Close to close the Format Shape dialog box when you are finished.

FIGURE 9.21

Apply a shadow to a table.

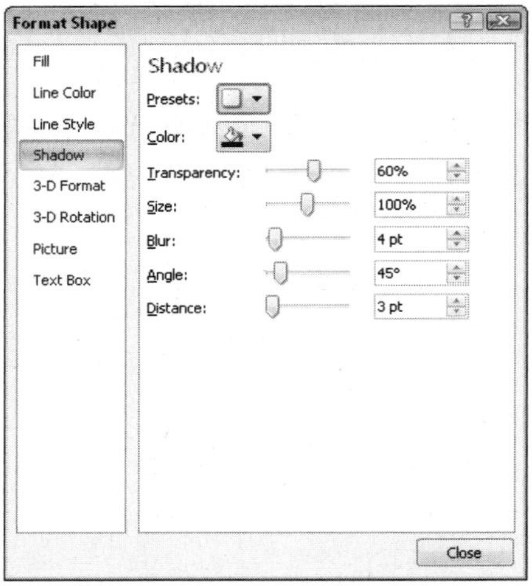

Applying a 3-D Effect to a Table

PowerPoint does not enable you to apply 3-D effects to tables, so you have to fudge that by creating the 3-D effect with rectangles and then overlaying a transparent table on top of the shapes. As you can see in Figure 9.22, it's a pretty convincing facsimile.

FIGURE 9.22

This 3-D table is actually a plain table with a 3-D rectangle behind it.

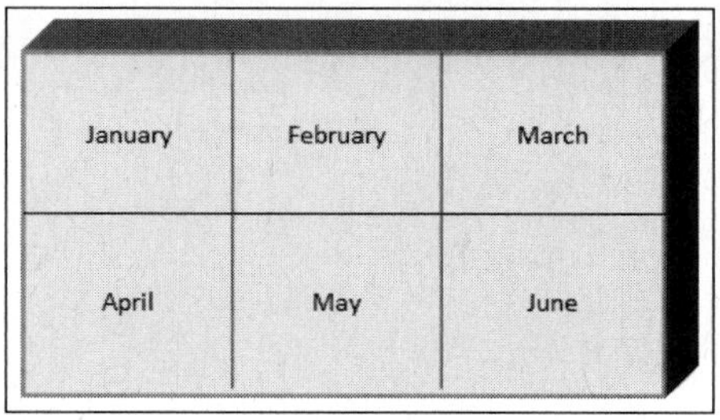

You might need to read Chapter 10 first to do some of these steps, but here's the basic procedure:

1. Create a rectangle from the Shapes group on the Insert tab, and apply a 3-D effect to it. Use any effect you like. To create the traditional "box" appearance as in Figure 9.22, apply the second Oblique preset and then in the 3-D Format options, increase the Depth setting to about 100 points.

2. Size the rectangle so that its face is the same size as the table.

3. On the Format tab, click Send to Back to send the rectangle behind the table.

4. Set the table's fill to No Fill if it is not already transparent.

5. (Optional) Set the table's outer frame border to None to make its edges appear to blend with the edges of the rectangle. To do that, open the Borders button's menu and select Outside Border to toggle that off.

Changing Text Alignment

If you followed the preceding steps to create the effect shown in Figure 9.22, you probably ran into a problem: Your text probably didn't center itself in the cells. That's because by default each cell's vertical alignment is set to Top, and horizontal alignment is set to Left.

Although the vertical and horizontal alignments are both controlled from the Alignment group on the Layout tab, they actually have two different scopes. Vertical alignment applies to the entire cell as a whole, whereas horizontal alignment can apply differently to individual paragraphs within the cell. To set vertical alignment for a cell, follow these steps:

1. Select one or more cells to affect. To affect only one cell, you do not have to select it; just click inside it.

2. On the Layout tab, in the Alignment group, click one of the vertical alignment buttons: Align Top, Center Vertically, or Align Bottom. See Figure 9.23.

Set the vertical and horizontal alignment of text from the Alignment group.

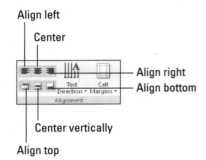

To set the horizontal alignment for a paragraph, follow these steps:

1. Select one or more paragraphs to affect. If you select multiple cells, all paragraphs within those cells are affected. If you click in a cell without selecting anything, the change only affects the paragraph in which you clicked.

2. On the Layout tab, in the Alignment group, click one of the horizontal alignment buttons: Align Left, Center, or Align Right. See Figure 9.23. You can also use the paragraph alignment buttons on the Home tab for horizontal alignment, or the buttons on the mini toolbar.

EXPERT TIP The horizontal alignments all have keyboard shortcuts: Ctrl+L for left, Ctrl+E for center, and Ctrl+R for right.

Changing Text Direction

The default text direction for table cells is Horizontal, which reads from left to right (at least in countries where that's how text is read). Figure 9.24 shows the alternatives.

To change the text direction for a cell, follow these steps:

1. Select the cell(s) to affect. To affect only a single cell, move the insertion point into it.

2. On the Layout tab, click Text Direction.

3. Select a text direction from the menu that appears.

NOTE You cannot set text direction for individual paragraphs; the setting applies to the entire cell.

FIGURE 9.24

You can set types of text direction.

Horizontal	Rotate all text 90	Rotate all text 270	Stacked

Using Tables from Word

If a table already exists in Word, you can copy it into PowerPoint. PowerPoint will convert the Word table to a PowerPoint table. From that point on, it is a part of the presentation, and maintains no relationship to Word. You can edit its text directly in PowerPoint.

To paste a table from Word to PowerPoint, copy it to the Clipboard (Ctrl+C) in Word, and then paste it onto a slide in PowerPoint (Ctrl+V). The resulting table appears in the center of the slide.

NOTE   You might need to increase the font size; Word's default size for body text is great for printed documents, but too small for most PowerPoint slides.

A pasted Word table is placed into a content placeholder on the slide if an appropriate one is available. Here are the basic rules for what goes on:

- If the slide has an appropriate content placeholder that is empty, the table is placed into it but retains its own size and shape.

- If the slide does not have a usable content placeholder at all (for example, a Title Only slide), a placeholder is created for it. (You can tell the table is in a placeholder because when you change layouts, the table travels into the new layouts.)

- If the slide already has content placeholders, but they are not empty, the table is inserted as a free-floating object, unrelated to any placeholders.

Word's table feature is somewhat more robust than PowerPoint's. If you want to maintain all the Word capabilities in the table, paste the table as a Word object instead of doing a regular paste. Follow these steps:

1. Copy the table in Word (Ctrl+C).

2. In PowerPoint, display the slide on which the table should be pasted.

3. On the Home tab, open the Paste button's menu and click Paste Special. The Paste Special dialog box opens.

4. Click the Paste option button.

5. In the As list, choose Microsoft Office Word Document Object.

6. Click OK. The table appears as a free-floating object (not in any placeholder).

The resulting table is an embedded object, and not directly editable using PowerPoint's table feature. To edit the object, you must double-click it to open it in Word.

EXPERT TIP To maintain a dynamic link between the Word file and the PowerPoint presentation, choose Paste Link instead of Paste in step 4. However, be aware that if you move the Word file, an error will appear in PowerPoint when it cannot find the file referenced in the link. See Chapter 15 for more information about linking and embedding.

Integrating Excel Cells into PowerPoint

If you need the calculating capabilities in a table, consider embedding Excel cells into the slide instead of using a traditional PowerPoint table.

Object linking and embedding is covered in detail in Chapter 15, but here's a quick look at how to use Excel from within PowerPoint:

1. Display the slide on which you want to place the Excel table.

2. If desired, select a placeholder into which it should be placed.

3. On the Insert tab, click the Table button, and on its menu, choose Excel Spreadsheet. A small frame with a few cells of an Excel spreadsheet appears, and the Ribbon changes to the tabs and tools for Excel. See Figure 9.25.

FIGURE 9.25

An Excel object can substitute for a table grid and can provide Excel-specific capabilities.

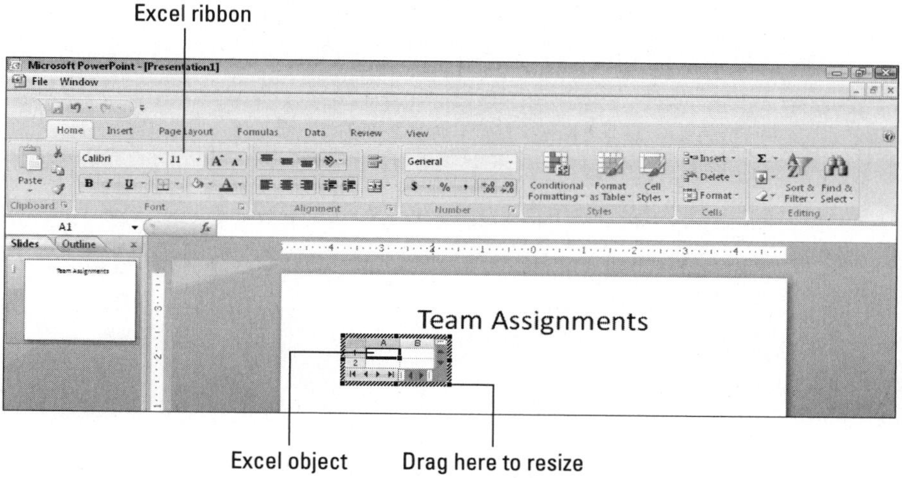

Excel ribbon

Excel object   Drag here to resize

> **NOTE** Don't worry that the object does not seem to be correctly aligned at the top and left. The cell row and column labels appear as you edit, and they disappear when you click away from the object.

4. If desired, enlarge the Excel object by doing the following:

   a. Click once on the Excel object's border to select it. Black selection handles appear around it.

   b. Drag a corner selection handle to enlarge the area of the object.

5. Create the table using Excel's tools and features.

6. (Optional) If there are unused cells, resize the object again (using its selection handles) so that they are not visible.

7. Click away from the object to deselect it and return to PowerPoint.

You've just created an embedded Excel object. It does not exist outside of this PowerPoint file; it's a mini-Excel spreadsheet that you use just for this one presentation. If you want to embed content from an existing Excel file, copy and paste it as in the earlier section on Word tables, or see Chapter 15 for more information about your options for linking and embedding content.

Summary

In this chapter, you learned the ins and outs of creating and formatting tables in PowerPoint including how to insert, draw, move and resize the various cells of a table as well as how to add fills, styles, and effects. You also learned now to integrate Excel cells into your PowerPoint slides. In the next chapter, you learn how to draw and format objects.

Part II

Using Graphics and Multimedia Content

Chapter 10

Drawing and Formatting Objects

Everything on a slide is a separate object. An *object* is anything that is in its own rectangular frame and can be moved, sized, and formatted independently. For example, each drawn shape is an object, as is each text box and each chart, diagram, and clip art image. So far in this book, you've learned about several types of objects that you can format with borders, shading, and other special effects, including text boxes, tables, and WordArt. In upcoming chapters, you learn about even more types of objects that you can format, such as SmartArt, charts, and clip art.

Most of the manipulation that you can apply to an object is the same, regardless of the object type. Rather than repeat the details for formatting each object type in individual chapters, almost everything you need to know about object formatting can be found in this chapter. You will practice these techniques on drawn lines and shapes, and in the process you will learn about the drawing tools. You can then apply these same techniques to text boxes and to virtually every type of graphic object that PowerPoint supports.

Working with the Drawing Tools

PowerPoint comes with a set of drawing tools that allow you to create simple lines and shapes on your slides. These used to be referred to as AutoShapes in earlier versions of the program, but in PowerPoint 2007, they are simply called *shapes*. (Lines are also called shapes, which seems counterintuitive, but there it is.)

About Vector Graphics

The drawing tools create simple, line-based vector graphics, each of which is a separate object on the slide. For example, if you make a drawing that consists of four rectangles, an oval, and several lines, you can move and resize each of these objects separately. You can stack them to create a more complex drawing, format each one individually, and even group them to create a single object that you can format, move, and resize as a single unit.

A *vector graphic* is one that is based on a mathematical formula, such as in geometry class. For example, if you draw a vector graphic line, PowerPoint stores the line start point, line end point, and line properties (width, color, and so on) as numeric values. When you move or resize the line, PowerPoint updates these numbers. Most clip-art images are also vector graphics. In contrast, a scanned image or a photo is a bitmap graphic, in which each individual colored pixel is represented by a separate numeric value. This is why bitmap files are so much larger than vector files—because there are more values to track.

The most important advantages of using vector graphics are:

- **Size.** Vector graphics files do not require much storage space because not every pixel of the image needs to be represented numerically.
- **Scalability.** When you resize a vector graphic, the math is recalculated and the shape is redrawn. This means that the picture is never distorted and its lines never become jagged the way bitmap graphics do.

The main drawback to vector graphics is their lack of realism. No matter how good an artist you are, a vector graphic will always have a flat, cartoonish quality to it.

NOTE 3-D graphics programs such as AutoCAD are also based on vector graphics. They start out with a wireframe image of a 3-D object (such as a cube), combine it with other wireframe images to make an object, and then use a rendering tool to cover the wireframe with a color, pattern, or texture that makes it look like a real object. Many popular video games, such as *The Sims*, also use vector graphics.

Drawing Lines and Shapes

The drawing tools in PowerPoint are the same as in other Office applications. For example, Word and Excel both have identical tool sets. The Shapes button appears on the Home tab, and you can click it to open a menu of the available shapes, as shown in Figure 10.1.

FIGURE 10.1

Select a shape from the Shapes list.

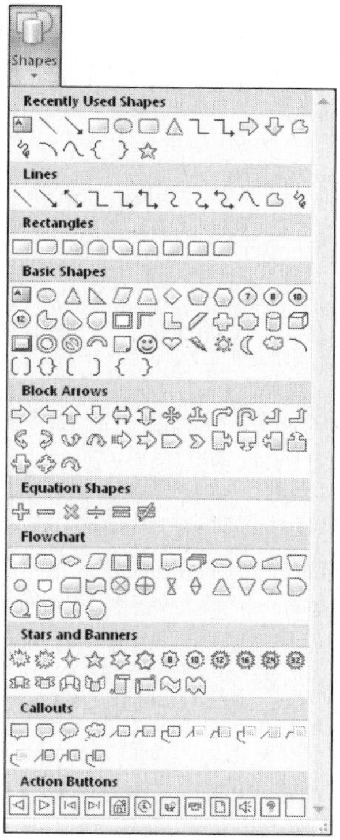

To draw a shape, follow these steps:

1. Select the desired shape from the Shapes palette (Figure 10.1).

2. (Optional) To constrain the dimensions of the shape — for example, to force a rectangle to be a square — hold down the Shift key.

3. Drag to draw the shape. A silhouette of the shape appears as you drag. Release the mouse button when you have the shape you want.

The preceding steps work well for most shapes, but there are a few special cases in which the drawing process works a little differently. The following sections explain these differences.

EXPERT TIP You can resize the Shapes menu by dragging its bottom-right corner.

EXPERT TIP More shapes are available through the Clip Organizer. When searching for clip-art images (see Chapter 12), use AutoShape as the keyword; you will see many more shapes, including ones that look like various types of office furniture and computers (which are useful in office plans).

EXPERT TIP To draw multiple objects of the same shape, you can lock the drawing tool on. Instead of clicking the shape to select it in the Shapes gallery, right-click it and choose Lock Shape. It then stays on until you press Esc to turn it off.

Straight or Curved Lines

The drawing tools include several types of lines, as shown in Figure 10.2. Here are some tips for using some of the line tools:

- **Straight line:** Click the start point and then click the end point. The line is now complete and the tool turns off. You can also draw lines with arrows at one or both ends.

- **Straight (elbow) connector:** Click and hold at the start point, and then drag to the end point. You can adjust the position of the elbow by dragging the yellow diamond in the center. If you click and release at the start point, a default size connector appears, which you can then move or resize. You can also draw lines with arrows at one or both ends.

- **Curved connector:** Click and hold at the start point, and then drag to the end point. Click a second time to complete the line. You can adjust the shape of the curve by dragging the yellow diamond in the center. If you click and release at the start point, a default size connector appears, which you can then move or resize. You can also draw lines with arrows at one or both ends.

- **Curve:** This is a freeform, multi-segment curve. Click the start point, click again to create a second point, and then click again to create more points. Between points, drag the mouse pointer to adjust the curve. When you are finished, double-click the mouse.

- **Scribble:** This is a freeform line. Hold down the mouse button and drag to draw; release the mouse button to finish.

FIGURE 10.2

Line tools.

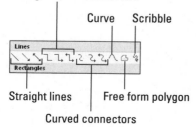

Straight elbow connectors

Curve   Scribble

Straight lines   Free form polygon

Curved connectors

Freeform Polygons

A *polygon* is a shape that consists of line segments. For example, stars, rectangles, triangles, and pentagons are all polygons. The lines do not need to be the same length or at any particular angle. The *Freeform Polygon* tool is in the Lines group (Figure 10.2), but it actually draws polygons. It enables you to draw each line segment one by one, with the mouse pointer functioning as a pencil. To use this tool, follow these steps:

1. Open the Shapes palette and click the Freeform button.

2. Click to place the start point, and then release the mouse button.

3. Click another location to place the next point. A line appears between the two points. Repeat this step as needed to create more points.

4. End the shape:

   ▪ For an open shape, double-click where you want to place the final point.

   ▪ For a closed shape, click the start point again as the final point.

You can fine-tune a freeform polygon by adjusting its points. You can also convert existing shapes to freeform polygons, which you can then adjust point by point.

CROSS-REF **See the section "Editing a Shape's Points" in this chapter for more information.**

Flow-Chart Connectors

Flow-chart shapes are just ordinary shapes that happen to correspond to those used in standard flow charts. Flow charts differ from other drawings, mainly in the way that connectors are used to join the shapes.

To experiment with flow-chart connectors, draw a couple of shapes (any closed shapes) and then draw a straight line between them. As you move the mouse pointer over the edge of a shape, certain selection handles glow red. If you click and drag from one of these handles to the other shape, the line becomes anchored to that shape. When you move the mouse to the second shape, once again, certain selection handles glow red. Click one of the red glowing handles to anchor the other end of the line there. Then delete the line and try an elbow connector; they work the same way. Figure 10.3 shows one.

When you select the line, both of the selection handles at the ends appear red, indicating that they are connected. If either end of the line is pale blue instead, this means that the end is not secured to a shape.

Connecting a line to a shape offers two advantages. One advantage is that you don't have to adjust the line exactly so that it touches the shape but does not overlap it. It lines up perfectly with the edge of the shape at all times. Another advantage is that if you move the shape, the line moves with it, changing its length and angle as needed so that the line remains anchored at both ends.

FIGURE 10.3

Flow-chart connectors have red balls on the ends when they are connected.

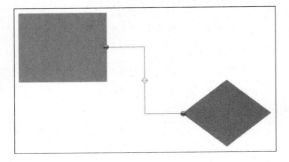

Callouts

A callout is a regular shape except it has a resizable point on it that can be dragged to point to other objects. Drag the yellow diamond on the callout shape to move its point.

Action Buttons

An action button is a type of drawing object that has an action associated with it. When users click the action button during the presentation, something happens. For example, perhaps a certain slide appears, an external program launches, or a sound plays.

The main difference between placing an action button and placing other types of drawing objects is that after you draw the action button, a dialog box appears, prompting you for the action.

CROSS-REF   You can learn how to use the action button dialog box in Chapter 21.

Choosing a Different Shape

If you chose the wrong shape to draw, it's easier to just delete the shape and start over if you have not applied any special formatting to it. However, if you have formatted the shape already, you might find it easier to change the shape rather than re-create it. To do so, follow these steps:

1. Click the shape to select it.
2. Click the Edit Shape button, and choose Change Shape from the menu. The same palette of shapes appears as when you initially created the shape, as shown in Figure 10.4.
3. Click the new shape that you want.

NOTE   Lines cannot be changed in this manner. You must right-click them to change their type.

FIGURE 10.4

Use the Change Shape option in the Edit Shape drop-down menu to reselect a shape.

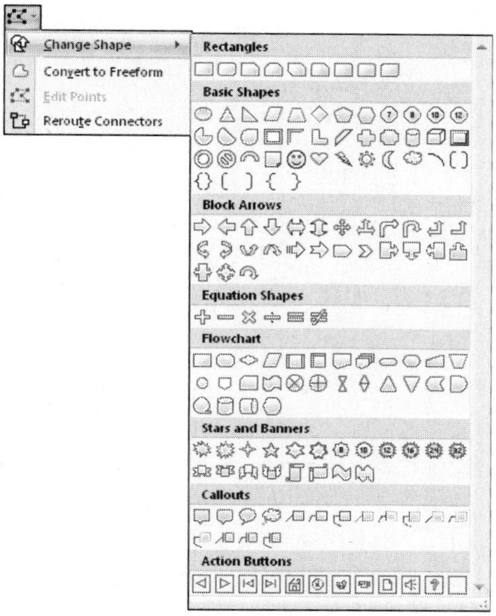

Editing a Shape's Points

Each shape consists of a series of points that are connected with straight or curved lines. On a freeform shape, you can adjust the positions of these points to change the shape of the object. First, you need to convert the shape to freeform:

1. Select the shape.

2. On the Format tab, open the Edit Shape drop-down menu (see Figure 10.4) and select Convert to Freeform.

3. Open the Edit Shape drop-down menu again and click Edit Points. Black selection handles (circles) appear around the shape, connected by red lines.

   You can also right-click the shape and choose Edit Points.

4. Drag one or more of the selection handles to change the shape.

5. Click away from the shape or press Esc.

FIGURE 10.5

Fine-tune a shape by converting it to freeform and adjusting its points.

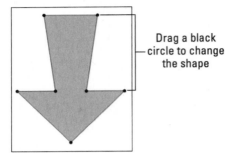

Drag a black
— circle to change
the shape

Adding Text to a Shape

You can use almost all of the closed shapes in PowerPoint as text boxes. PowerPoint recognizes a manually created text box as a variation on a rectangle with some text in it. As a result, you can just as easily place text in a shape of any other type. To add text to a shape, follow these steps:

1. Select the shape. (This is necessary to make the Format tab available.)

2. On the Format tab, in the Insert Shapes group, click the Text Box button.

3. Click inside the shape. A flashing insertion point appears inside the shape. Instead of steps 2 and 3, you can just click the shape and start typing if you prefer.

4. Type the desired text.

EXPERT TIP   You can also use the Text Box button to insert a new blank text box from the Format tab, independent of any existing shape. Instead of clicking inside a shape in step 3, click a blank area of the slide and begin typing to create a new text box. A text box is just a rectangular shape with no border or fill. You can change it to a different shape by selecting from the Edit Shape ⇨ Change Shape menu, as shown in the section "Choosing a Different Shape," earlier in this chapter. You can then apply a shape style, as explained in the section "Applying Shape or Picture Styles" later in this chapter, or apply a custom border or fill to it.

Text wraps within a shape automatically, in a rectangular area. If the shape is irregular, PowerPoint finds the largest available rectangular area within its center and confines the text to that area. If you have converted a shape to freeform and adjusted its points, the text wrapping inside the shape may not look right. For example, in Figure 10.6, the sides of the arrow have been pulled in a bit manually, but the original text area still applies, resulting in some overhang of the text. To correct this, you can manually insert line breaks where you want them by pressing Shift+Enter.

FIGURE 10.6

If the text overflows the shape (left), press Shift+Enter to insert line breaks where needed (right).

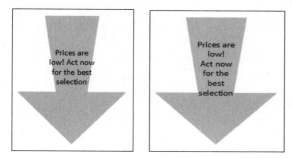

Selecting Objects

No matter what type of object you are dealing with, you can select it by clicking it with the mouse. Selection handles that look like pale blue circles appear around the object, as shown in Figure 10.7.

FIGURE 10.7

Selection handles appear around a selected object.

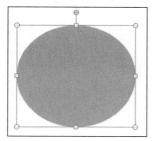

You have already learned that you can select a single object by clicking it. However, sometimes you might want to select multiple objects so that you can act upon them as a single unit. For example, suppose you have drawn several shapes, and you want to select them as a group so that you can move them or apply the same formatting to them.

To select more than one object, click the first one to select it, and then hold down the Shift key as you click additional objects. They all become selected.

EXPERT TIP Holding down the Ctrl key when you select multiple objects also does the same thing as Shift; however, if you hold down the Ctrl key and drag, it makes a copy of the original item. This is why it's better to use the Shift key than the Ctrl key for selecting multiple objects — so that you don't accidentally make copies by dragging the item.

If you can't easily click each object (perhaps because they are overlapping one another), an easy way to select a whole group is to drag the cursor around them. For example, if you wanted to select several stacked shapes, you would drag the cursor over them to select them all, as follows: Simply click and hold down the mouse button above and to the left of the objects, and drag down and to the right until you create a box around them. The box adds a light-blue shading over the top of the area, as shown in Figure 10. 8. Then, release the mouse button. All objects that were entirely inside the boundary that you drew are selected, as shown in Figure 10.9.

NOTE Dragging from the top-left to the bottom-right is just one way of selecting the group; for example, you can also drag from the lower-right to the upper-left if you prefer.

FIGURE 10.8

Hold down the mouse button and drag a box that includes all of the shapes that you want to select.

FIGURE 10.9

Each selected object displays its own selection handles.

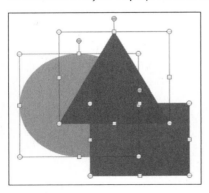

Another way to select objects is with the Selection and Visibility pane, which is a new feature in PowerPoint 2007. To display this pane, from the Home tab, choose Select ➪ Selection Pane. In the Selection and Visibility pane, you can click any object's name to select it, or hold down the Ctrl key and click multiple objects to select them. Figure 10.10 shows three selected objects.

The Selection and Visibility pane does more than just select objects. For example, you can use the Re-order arrow buttons at the bottom of the pane to change the stacking order of objects, which is covered later in this chapter. You can also click the eye icon next to an object to toggle its display on or off in the slide. This provides a way of temporarily hiding an object without affecting its presence or position on the slide.

EXPERT TIP   If you have more than one of a certain type of object, PowerPoint names them generically in the Selection and Visibility pane — for example, Oval 4, Rectangle 2, and so on. It is easier to keep track of which shape is which if you change their names to something more meaningful. To change the name of an object, click its name in the Selection and Visibility pane, and then click it again. The insertion point appears inside the name, and you can edit it. Having recognizable names for objects also helps when you are sequencing their animation.

FIGURE 10.10

The Selection and Visibility pane assists you in selecting objects.

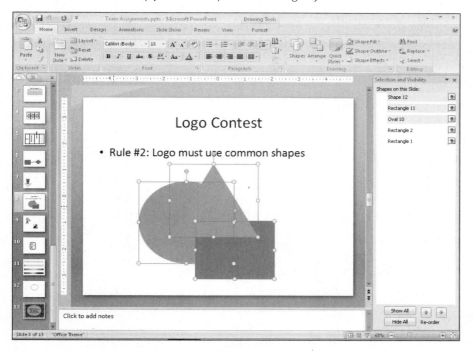

Deleting Objects

To delete an object, the easiest way is to select it and then press the Delete key on the keyboard. To delete more than one object at once, you can select multiple objects before pressing the Delete key.

You can also right-click the selected object or objects and choose Cut. When you cut an object, it is not the same as deleting it; the Cut command moves the object to the Clipboard, so that you can use the Paste command to place it somewhere else. However, if you cut something, and then never paste it, this is actually the same as deleting it.

Moving and Copying Objects

You can move or copy objects anywhere you like: within a single slide, from one slide to another, or from one presentation to another. You can even copy or move an object to a completely different program, such as Word or Excel.

Within a Slide

To move an object on a slide, you can simply drag it with the mouse. Just position the mouse pointer over any part of the object except for a handle. When the mouse pointer changes to a four-headed arrow, drag the object to a new location. A pale version of the original appears to show the object's new location, as shown in Figure 10.11.

EXPERT TIP Holding down the Shift key as you drag constrains the movement of the object, making it possible to drag it *only* horizontally or *only* vertically. Holding down the Ctrl key as you drag makes a copy of the original object.

FIGURE 10.11

Drag an object on the slide to reposition it.

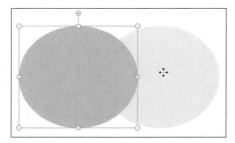

To copy an object on a slide, use the Copy command. Select the object and press Ctrl+C to copy it, or click the Copy button on the Home tab. Then, press Ctrl+V to paste the object, or click the Paste button on the Home tab. You can then drag the copy to wherever you want it on the slide.

NOTE Whenever you need to cut, copy, or paste, you have a variety of methods to choose from. There are the Cut, Copy, and Paste buttons on the Home tab, the Cut, Copy, and Paste commands on the right-click menu, and the shortcut key combinations, Cut (Ctrl+X), Copy (Ctrl+C), and Paste (Ctrl+V).

EXPERT TIP Ctrl+D works as a combination Copy-and-Paste command by automatically duplicating the object or objects that you have selected.

From One Slide to Another

To move an object to a different slide, cutting and pasting works best. Select the object and press Ctrl+X, or click Cut on the Home tab. Then display the slide on which you want the object to appear, and press Ctrl+V, or click Paste on the Home tab.

To copy an object to a different slide without removing it from the original slide, you can do the same thing, except that you need to use the Copy command (Ctrl+C or Copy button) instead of the Cut command.

NOTE If you want an object to appear in the same spot on every slide in the presentation, add the object to the slide master rather than trying to copy it onto every slide. See Chapter 5 for more information.

EXPERT TIP When you copy and paste an object onto the same slide, the copy is offset from the original to allow for easy selection. When you copy and paste an object onto a different slide, the copy appears in the same position as the original.

From One Presentation to Another

To move or copy from one presentation to another, use Cut, Copy, and Paste commands. First, select the object, and then cut or copy it. Display the destination slide (in normal view) in the other presentation, and then paste.

EXPERT TIP An object that you move or copy to a different presentation might change its color because the destination file is using a different color theme. This is because objects that have their colors defined by a color theme rather than by a fixed color will change colors when you apply a different theme or template.

To Another Program

You can also move and copy objects from PowerPoint into other programs. For example, suppose that you have created a table on a slide and you want to include it in a report in Word. You can move or copy it to a Word document by cutting and pasting. For more information on tables, see Chapter 9.

EXPERT TIP Depending on the object and the destination application, copying and pasting usually results in smaller file sizes than dragging and dropping.

Using the Office Clipboard

The Microsoft Office Clipboard lets you store more than one object at a time. You can copy or cut multiple objects to the Clipboard and then paste them all into the same or different locations afterwards. To use the Clipboard in multi-clip mode, click the dialog box launcher for the Clipboard group on the Home tab. The Clipboard pane appears, as shown in Figure 10.12.

FIGURE 10.12

Move or copy multiple items using the Clipboard pane.

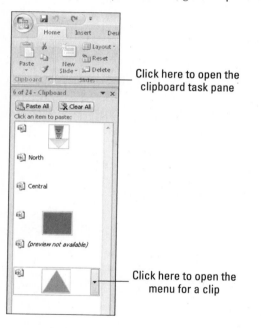

Click here to open the clipboard task pane

Click here to open the menu for a clip

As you copy or cut items, they appear on a list in the Clipboard pane. When you want to paste an item, display the slide on which you want to paste it — position the insertion point at the desired location if the item is text — and then click the item in the Clipboard pane. The Clipboard can hold up to 24 items. To remove an item, click the drop-down arrow next to it, and choose Delete, as shown in Figure 10.12.

EXPERT TIP Click the Options button at the bottom of the Clipboard pane to display a list of on/off toggles that you can set for Clipboard operation. For example, you can specify that the Clipboard pane appears automatically when you press Ctrl+C twice in a row, and whether it displays an icon at the bottom of the screen when it is active.

Understanding Object Formatting

Up until this point, we've considered all objects to be equal, but there are actually two major classes of objects that PowerPoint supports: those that you create from within PowerPoint, and those that you import from other sources. Each object type causes a different version of the Format tab to display when you select it.

For drawn shapes, charts, SmartArt, and text boxes, the Drawing Tools Format tab in Figure 10.13 appears. From here you can apply shape styles, as well as WordArt formatting, to the text within the object.

FIGURE 10.13

For drawn objects, charts, and text boxes, these formatting options are available.

> **NOTE** SmartArt has some formatting features in common with drawn shapes and charts, but it also has some special features and quirks of its own. For more information, see Chapter 11.

For photos and clip art, the Picture Tools Format tab in Figure 10.14 appears. It focuses on applying filters through which you view the image (such as brightness and contrast), and applying Picture Styles that affect the shape and border of the frame.

FIGURE 10.14

For photos and clip art, these formatting options are available.

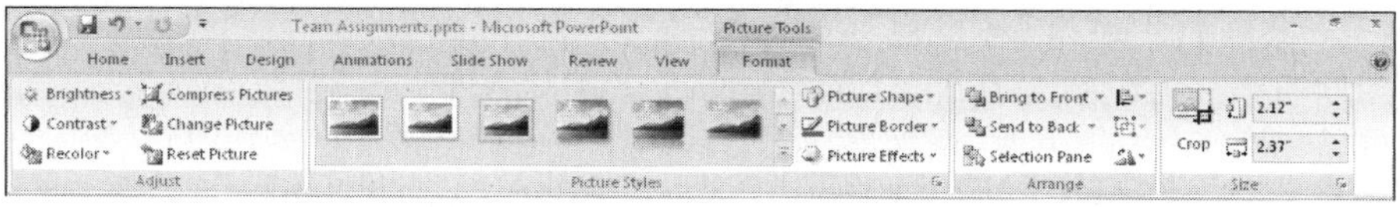

Both of these versions of the Format tab (Drawing Tools and Picture Tools) have Size and Arrange groups that work the same way.

In the following sections, I'll explain how to apply formatting to the two types of objects, by using the Drawing Tools Format tab or the Picture Tools Format tab. Some features are unique to one object type or the other; other features can be used for both types, although some features that do basically the same thing have different names, depending on the object type.

Resizing Objects

Let's start with something that all objects have in common: resizing. You can resize any object on a slide, either by dragging a selection handle on its border or by using the Size group in the Format tab.

In Chapter 4, you learned how to resize a text box; you can resize any object in this same way, simply by dragging a corner or side selection handle to change the object's size and shape. The mouse pointer changes to a double-headed arrow when you move it over a selection handle. As you resize the object, a faint shadow of the object appears to show its new size.

> **EXPERT TIP** Some objects, such as photos, maintain their aspect ratio by default when you resize them using a corner selection handle. In other words, the ratio of height to width does not change when you resize using the corner selection handles. If you want to distort the object by changing its aspect ratio, drag one of the side selection handles instead of a corner one. Other objects, such as drawn shapes, do not maintain the aspect ratio unless you hold down the Shift key as you drag a corner selection handle.

You can also size an object by incrementing the values in the Size group on the Format tab, or by typing numbers directly into these text boxes.

Alternatively, you can click the dialog box launcher for the Size group to open a Size and Position dialog box, from which you can enter a height and width, the same as you would in the Size group on the ribbon (see Figure 10.15). This same dialog box is available for all object types, although more of the options are available for photos than for drawn objects. Figure 10.15 shows the dialog box for a photo. For a drawn object, some of the Scale options are unavailable, as well as the Crop From and Original Size sections.

FIGURE 10.15

Adjust an object's size from the Size tab in the Size and Position dialog box.

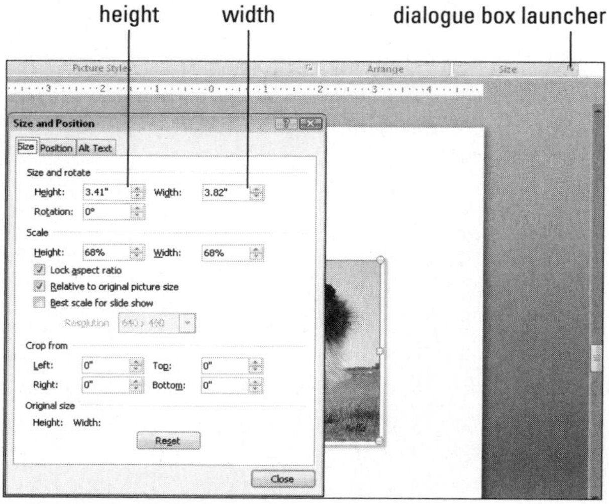

An advantage of using the dialog box is that you can adjust the scale of the object by a percentage. For example, you can shrink the object to 50 percent of its original size by changing its Height and Width values in the Scale section to 50 percent each (see Figure 10.15). This feature is more useful for photos than for drawn objects, but it works for all object types.

For imported objects only — such as pictures, clip art, and so on — you can also set these scale options:

- **Relative to Original Picture Size:** The measurements in the Scale section refer to the original picture size if you select this option; otherwise, they refer to the previous size of the picture.

- **Best Scale for Slide Show:** When you select this option, PowerPoint adjusts the picture size to match the resolution at which you show the presentation, as you have specified in the Resolution drop-down list.

CROSS-REF The Crop From options are available only for imported objects such as photos, and are covered in Chapter 13.

The Original Size section is also available only for imported objects. You can click the Reset button in this section to reset the object back to the size that it was when you initially placed it on the slide.

Arranging Objects

Arranging is another action that you can perform with all object types. For example, you can specify an object's position in relation to the slide or to other objects, change the stacking order, rotate the object, group it with other objects, and much more.

Rotating and Flipping Objects

Most objects display a green circle at the top when you select them; this is called the *rotation* handle. You can drag it to rotate the object, as shown in Figure 10.16. This action is called *free rotation* because there is no precise numeric measurement that is related to the amount of rotation, although, by holding down the Shift key while rotating, you can rotate the object by 15-degree increments.

You can also rotate an object by exactly 90 degrees. To do so, click the Rotate button on the Format tab and select Rotate Right 90° or Rotate Left 90°, as shown in Figure 10.17.

FIGURE 10.16

Rotate an object by dragging its rotation handle.

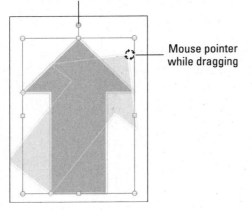

Rotation handle

Mouse pointer
while dragging

FIGURE 10.17

Rotate an object 90 degrees, or flip an object from the Rotate menu.

On this same menu, you can also flip an object either vertically or horizontally. Flipping is different from rotating in that it creates a mirror image of the object, not just a rotated version.

To set a precise amount of rotation for an object, use the Rotation text box in the Size and Position dialog box, shown in Figure 10.15. Use the increment buttons to increase or decrease the rotation amount, or enter a precise number of degrees.

Snapping Objects to a Grid

There is an invisible grid on every slide to which all objects snap. If you move an object and position it so that it doesn't quite align with the gridlines, when you release the object, it moves slightly to snap into alignment with the nearest gridlines. This feature is on by default.

To turn off snapping for an individual instance, hold down the Alt key as you drag the object. The object moves smoothly, unencumbered by the grid. To turn off snapping permanently, follow these steps:

1. On the Design tab, click Align and choose Grid Settings. The Grid and Guides dialog box opens.

   The Align button is also available on most contextual tabs, such as the Picture Tools Format tab.

2. Deselect the Snap Objects to Grid option, as shown in Figure 10.18.

3. Click OK.

Toggle the grid on and off in the Grid and Guides dialog box.

You can also turn a feature on or off that is called Snap Objects to Other Objects (see Figure 10.18). This feature is off by default. It helps you to precisely align shapes — for example, to draw complex pictures where one line must exactly meet another — by snapping shapes into position in relation to one another. You will not want to use this feature all of the time because it makes it harder to position objects precisely in those instances where you do *not* need one shape to align with another.

To display or hide the grid on the screen, select or deselect the Display Grid On Screen option. To change the grid spacing, enter the desired amount in the Spacing text box.

Nudging Objects

If you are one of those people who have a hard time positioning objects precisely when you drag them, you'll appreciate the Nudge command. It moves an object slightly in the direction that you want without altering it in the other plane. For example, suppose you have positioned a text box in exactly the spot you want vertically but a little bit too far to the right. If you drag it manually, you might accidentally change the vertical position. Instead, you can press an arrow key to move it. Hold down Ctrl to override snapping to the grid.

Nudging moves the object one space on the grid when you have enabled the Snap Objects to Grid option. (See the section, "Snapping Objects to a Grid" earlier in this chapter). When the Snap Objects to Grid option is turned off, you can nudge the object 1 pixel at a time.

EXPERT TIP   Certain objects, such as SmartArt, will sometimes refuse to be moved (including by nudging) after you have applied a 3-D Quick Style with a perspective view. To move such an object, click Edit in 2-D on the Format tab. You can then move the object. Afterward, you can click Edit in 2-D again to toggle it back to its regular 3-D appearance.

EXPERT TIP   Nudge buttons are not available on the ribbon in PowerPoint 2007. However, if you would like, you can add them to the Quick Access toolbar. See Appendix B for more details.

Aligning or Distributing Objects

You can align or distribute objects either in relation to the slide or in relation to other objects. Here are some examples:

- You can align an object to the top, bottom, left, right, or center of a slide.
- You can align two objects in relation to one another so that they are at the same vertical or horizontal position.
- You can distribute three or more objects so that the spacing between them is even.

You can perform all of these functions from the Align drop-down menu on the Format tab when you select one or more objects.

NOTE   The Align and Distribute features are not always available. To make them available, you must select Align to Slide from the Align drop-down menu, or you must select two or more objects (for aligning) or three or more objects (for distributing).

Aligning an Object in Relation to the Slide

To align a single object in relation to the slide, follow these steps:

1. Select the object.
2. On the Format tab, click Align, and make sure that Align to Slide is selected.
3. Click Align again and choose one of the horizontal alignment commands: Align Left, Align Center, or Align Right, as shown in Figure 10.19.
4. Click Align again and choose one of the vertical alignment commands: Align Top, Align Middle, or Align Bottom.

FIGURE 10.19

Choose an alignment for the object in relation to the slide.

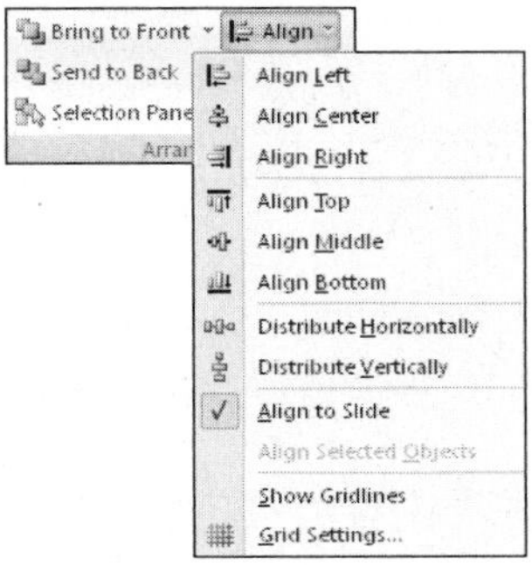

Aligning Two or More Objects with One Another

You can align two objects in relation to one another by assigning the same setting to both objects. For example, in the left illustration in Figure 10.20, the objects are in their starting positions. The right illustration shows what happens when you use the Align Top command to move the lower object to the same vertical position as the higher one. If you use Align Bottom, the higher object moves to match the lower one. If you use Align Center, both objects move to split the difference between their two positions.

FIGURE 10.20

The original positioning (left) and the positioning after you apply the Align Top command (right).

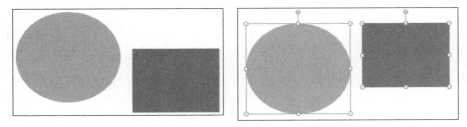

To align two or more objects with one another, follow these steps:

1. Select the objects.

2. On the Format tab, click Align, and make sure that Align Selected Objects is selected.

3. Click the Align button again to reopen the menu, and choose the desired alignment, either vertical or horizontal.

NOTE If you use the Align Top command and the objects move to the very top of the slide, you probably have selected the Align to Slide option. Undo (Ctrl+Z) the action and try again.

Distributing Objects

Distribution works only in relation to the slide or with three or more objects selected. When you distribute objects, you spread them evenly over a given space. For example, suppose you align three boxes vertically, and now you want to even out the space between each box, as shown in Figure 10.21. You can apply the Distribute Horizontally command to create the uniform spacing. To distribute objects, follow these steps:

1. Select the objects. To do so, hold down the Shift key while you click each one, or drag an outline that encircles all of the objects.
2. On the Format tab, click Align, and then click either Distribute Vertically or Distribute Horizontally.

If you have only two objects selected, you cannot distribute them unless you have already selected Align to Slide.

FIGURE 10.21

The original positioning (left) and the positioning after applying the Distribute Horizontally command (right).

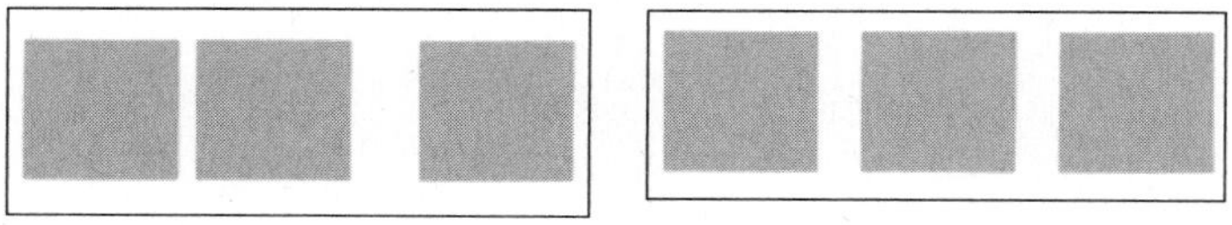

Layering Objects

You can stack objects on top of each other to create special effects. For example, you might create a logo by stacking a text box on top of an oval or a rectangle, as shown in Figure 10.22.

CROSS-REF To create a text box, see Chapter 4.

EXPERT TIP You can also type text directly into a drawn shape without using layering; simply right-click the shape and choose Edit Text; you can also just begin typing while the shape is selected.

FIGURE 10.22

You can create all kinds of logos, artwork, and other special effects by layering objects.

Text box in front

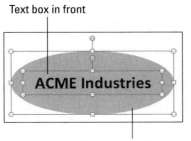

Drawn shape in back

By default, objects stack in the order in which you create them. For example, in Figure 10.22, the text box appears over the shape because the shape was created first, and so it is on the bottom of the stack. You can move the shape, but it will continue to be on the layer under the text box.

If you need to reorder the objects in a stack, follow these steps:

1. Click an object in the stack.

2. Use one of the buttons in the Arrange group on the Format tab:

   ▪ Click Bring to Front to bring that object to the top of the stack.

   ▪ Open the Bring to Front drop-down menu and choose Bring Forward to bring the object forward one position in the stack.

   ▪ Click Send to Back to send that object to the bottom of the stack.

   ▪ Open the Send to Back drop-down menu and choose Send Backward to send the object backward one position in the stack.

3. Repeat the steps to change the position of other objects in the stack as needed.

Another way to reorder object stacking is to use the Selection and Visibility pane:

1. On the Home tab, choose Select ➪ Selection Pane to display the Selection and Visibility pane.

2. Click an object's name on the list.

3. Click the Up or Down arrow buttons to move the object up or down in the stacking order.

Working with Object Groups

You have already learned how to select multiple objects and work with them as a single unit. For example, you might select several shapes together that collectively form a picture that you have drawn. If you intend to treat these objects as a single unit, you can save yourself some time by grouping them. When you group two or more objects, these objects become a single object for the purposes of moving and resizing. You can always ungroup them later if you need to work with the objects separately. To group two or more objects together, follow these steps:

1. Select all of the objects that you want to group.

2. On the Format tab, open the Group drop-down menu and click Group. (Alternatively you can press Ctrl+G.) The objects now form a group.

To ungroup a collection of objects, select the object group, open the Group drop-down menu, and choose Ungroup, or press Ctrl+Shift+G. After ungrouping, you can make changes to the objects separately. Then, if you want to regroup the same objects again, open the Group drop-down menu and choose Regroup.

EXPERT TIP   In PowerPoint 2007, you can make some changes to objects even when they are part of a group, so it is not as necessary to ungroup before editing or formatting an object. Try editing it first as part of the group, and if that doesn't work, resort to ungrouping.

Applying Shape or Picture Styles

Both the Drawing Tools Format tab and the Picture Tools Format tab (shown in Figures 10-13 and 10-14 respectively) have a style group from which you can apply preset formatting. For drawn objects and charts, it is called Shape Styles; for photos and clip art, it is called Picture Styles.

Using Shape Styles

Shape Styles are formatting presets that you can apply to drawn shapes, text boxes, and charts. Shape Styles make it easy to apply common border and fill combinations that use colors from the current theme. A Shape Style is a combination of three things:

- **Shape Fill:** The color and style of the inside

- **Shape Outline:** The color and style of the outer border

- **Shape Effects:** Special effects that are applied to the object, such as shadows, reflection, or beveled edges

Each of these can be separately applied, as you will learn later in this chapter. To apply a Shape Style, follow these steps:

1. Select the shape or shapes that you want to affect.

2. On the Format tab, open the Shape Styles gallery and click a style, as shown in Figure 10.23.

FIGURE 10.23

Apply a Shape Style as a shortcut to formatting a drawn object or a chart element.

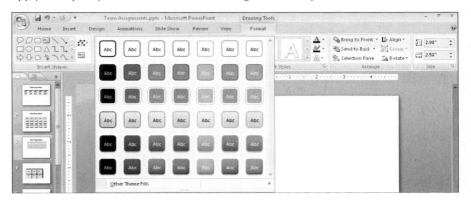

The styles that appear on the gallery menu are built into PowerPoint, and you cannot change them. Their colors change according to the color theme that is currently applied to the presentation.

EXPERT TIP The Other Theme Fills option at the bottom of the gallery menu opens an extra palette that contains several light and dark background fills that match the styles that display when you click Background Styles on the Design tab. See Chapter 5 for more about applying background styles. Filling a shape with the same color as the background makes it blend in with the background.

Applying Picture Styles

Picture Styles are like Shape Styles, except that they apply to photos, clip art, and media clips. A Picture Style applies different formatting than a Shape Style because pictures have different needs. For example, a picture does not need a fill color, because the picture is the fill. A Picture Style applies these things:

- **Picture Shape:** The shape of the frame in which the picture is placed
- **Picture Border:** The color and style of the outside of the picture frame
- **Picture Effects:** Special effects such as beveled edges and shadows

To apply a Picture Style, follow these steps:

1. Select the picture that you want to affect.
2. On the Format tab, open the Picture Styles gallery and click a style, as shown in Figure 10.24.

FIGURE 10.24

Apply a Picture Style to quickly format an imported graphic such as a photo.

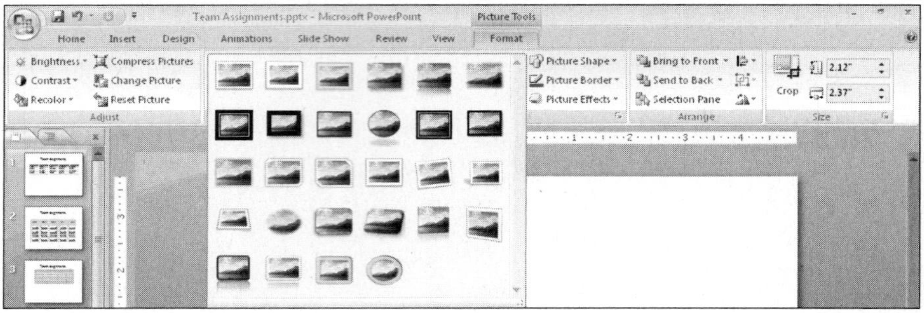

The styles that appear on the gallery menu are built into PowerPoint, and you cannot change them.

EXPERT TIP The formatting that you apply through Picture Styles is not dependent on the color theme, but some of the border formatting is partially dependent on the background that you have chosen. For the Picture Styles that include a border, the border color is either black or white, and it changes, depending on whether you are using a light or dark background. (You can choose a background from the Background Styles button on the Design tab.) If you want a different color border than the Picture Style provides, you can modify the border color after applying the style.

Understanding Color Selection

To apply a custom border or fill color to an object, you must know something about how PowerPoint uses and applies colors. Although this is covered in Chapter 5, here is a quick review.

PowerPoint uses a set of color placeholders for the bulk of its color formatting. Because each item's color is defined by a placeholder, and not as a fixed color, you can easily change the colors by switching to a different color theme. For example, if you decide that you want all of the slide titles to be blue rather than green, you can make the change once and PowerPoint applies it to all of the slides automatically.

A set of colors that is assigned to the preset positions is a *color theme*. You can apply both border (outline) and fill colors using *color pickers*. A color picker is a menu that shows the colors from the currently chosen color theme, along with tints (light versions) and shades (dark versions) of each of the theme colors. To stick with theme colors, which I recommend in most cases, choose one of the theme colors or one of its tints or shades, as shown in Figure 10.25. You also have the following options:

FIGURE 10.25

A color picker offers the current color theme's colors, and also some standard (fixed) colors.

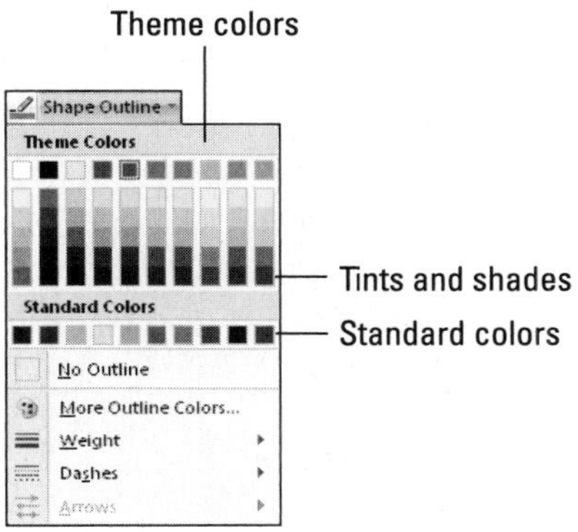

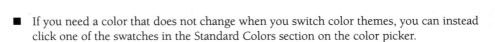

Theme colors

Tints and shades

Standard colors

- If you need a color that does not change when you switch color themes, you can instead click one of the swatches in the Standard Colors section on the color picker.

- If you need a color that is not represented in the Standard Colors section, you can choose More Colors. (The command name varies, depending on what you are coloring; in Figure 10-25, it is More Outline Colors.) This opens the Colors dialog box. The Standard tab in the Colors dialog box contains swatches for many common colors. Most people can find the color that they want on the Standard tab. Click the color that you want and click OK.

If you need a color that does not appear in the swatches, you may need to use the Custom tab, as shown in Figure 10.26. On this tab:

FIGURE 10.26

Use the Custom tab of the Colors dialog box to precisely define a color that you want to use.

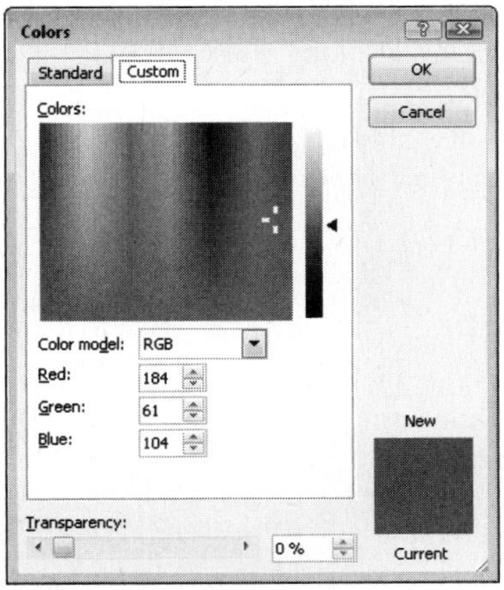

■ You can enter the precise numbers for a color; for example, you can match the exact color for a company logo.

■ You can define colors numerically using either the HSL (hue, saturation, and luminosity) or RGB (red, green, blue) color models. Choose the color model that you want from the Color Model drop-down list.

■ If you are using the HSL model, you can type the numbers into the Hue, Sat, and Lum fields on the Custom tab. The hue is the tint (that is, green versus blue versus red). A low number is a color at the red end of the spectrum, while a high number is a color at the violet end. Saturation refers to the vividness of the color, and luminosity is the lightness or darkness. A high luminosity mixes the color with white, while a low luminosity mixes the color with black.

■ An alternative way to define colors is by specifying numbers for red, green, and blue. Using this measurement, 0, 0, 0 is pure black and 255, 255, 255 is pure white. All other colors are some combination of the three colors. For example, pure blue is 0, 0, 255. A very pale blue would be 200, 200, 255. You can play around with the numbers in the fields on the Custom tab. The new color appears in the New area near the bottom of the dialog box. Click OK to accept your choice.

EXPERT TIP You can create an interesting see-through effect with the color by using the transparency slider. When this slider is used for a color, it creates an effect like a watercolor paint wash over an item, so that whatever is beneath it can partially show through.

Applying an Object Border

A border (outline) around an object can draw attention to it, as well as separate it from surrounding items.

When describing the buttons that create borders around an object, PowerPoint uses inconsistent terminology between the two versions of the Format tab. For drawn objects, the button that applies borders is called the Shape Outline button; for pictures it is called the Picture Border button. Both buttons open essentially the same menu — a standard color picker like the one shown in Figure 10-25.

NOTE The only difference between the Picture Border and the Shape Outline color pickers is that the latter has an Arrows command. This command is available only when the selected object is a line (not a closed shape); it applies arrowheads to one or both ends of the line.

Border Attributes

A border has three basic attributes: its color, its width (thickness), and its dash style (solid, dashed, dotted, etc.). You can set each of these basic attributes using the color picker, which contains fly-out menus at the bottom for Weight and Dashes. Each fly-out menu has presets that you can select.

To control the more advanced attributes of the line, or to make a selection other than a preset, choose More Lines from one of the fly-out submenus. This opens the Format Shape dialog box with Line Style attributes selected, as shown in Figure 10.27.

 **EXPERT TIP** You can also right-click and choose Format Picture to apply borders from the Format Picture dialog box.

FIGURE 10.27

Use the Format Shape dialog box to fine-tune the line style.

In the Line Style controls of the Format Shape dialog box, you can set the following:

- **Width:** The thickness of the line in points
- **Compound type:** The number of parallel lines that comprise the overall line, and their relative thicknesses
- **Dash type:** The style of line (solid, dashed, dotted)
- **Cap type:** The style for the ends of the line (applicable to lines only)
- **Join type:** The style for the corners of the shape
- **Arrow settings:** The types and sizes of the arrow heads (applicable to lines only)

NOTE For a gradient line, click Line in the Format Shape dialog box. From there, you can choose Gradient Line, and then choose a preset gradient or define your own. For more information about gradients, see the section, "Gradient Fills" later in this chapter.

Creating a Semi-Transparent Border

By default, a line is not transparent at all. To specify a level of transparency for it, you can click Line in the Format Shape dialog box and drag the Transparency slider to the right, or enter a transparency percentage in the text box provided.

> **NOTE** Some of the picture or shape effects also affect the border of the object. These are covered later in this chapter, in the section "Applying Object Effects."

Applying an Object Fill

An object can have no fill (that is, it can be transparent), or it can be filled with a solid color, a gradient, a texture, or a picture. Fills mostly apply to objects that you draw yourself, such as shapes, charts, and SmartArt. Although Fill commands are available for imported art such as pictures and clip art, these commands are not commonly applied to them. Because a picture takes up the entire frame that it is in, any fill that you might apply would not be visible anyway (unless the picture has a transparent color set for it). With clip art, you might occasionally want to apply a fill, because most clip art has a transparent background. By applying a fill to it, you make the clip art's background visible, so that it appears to be in a rectangular box rather than floating on the background.

Solid Fills

To apply a solid fill for a shape, or other type of object that uses the Drawing Tools Format tab (shown in Figure 10-13), you can choose a fill type from the color picker that you access through the Shape Fill button on the Format tab. You can use the following method.

To apply a solid fill for an object that uses the Picture Tools Format tab (shown in Figure 10.14), you must open the Format Shape dialog box for the object, and then click Fill. Follow these steps:

1. Right-click the object and choose Format Picture. The Format Picture dialog box opens.
2. Click Fill.
3. Click Solid Fill.
4. Click the Color button in the dialog box to open a color picker.
5. Select the desired color.

> **CROSS-REF** See the section "Understanding Color Selection" earlier in this chapter for more on selecting color.

6. (Optional) Drag the Transparency slider to set transparency.
7. Click Close.

Gradient Fills

When you watch a sunset, you can see how the red of the sun slowly fades into the blue-black of the evening sky. You may not have thought of it in this way before, but this is a gradient. Whenever one color turns gradually into another color, the transition is called a gradient. Gradients are often used on large shapes, on logos, and on backgrounds.

PowerPoint 2007 has much more powerful gradient capabilities than ever before; for example, you can now create gradients that consist of more than two colors, and you can specify the spot at which one color shifts to another.

Applying a One-Color Gradient Preset

For drawn shapes (and other objects that use the Drawing Tools Format tab), you can use the Shape Fill button to access preset gradients that blend one color with either black or white. These presets apply only to drawn objects, not to picture objects. Follow these steps to apply a one-color preset:

1. Apply a solid color fill to the object; use the color that you want to combine with black or white.
2. Select the object and display the Format tab.
3. Open the Shape Fill drop-down menu, select Gradient, and click the desired gradient style, as shown in Figure 10.28.

FIGURE 10.28

Apply a preset gradient from the Gradient submenu for a shape.

Applying a Custom Gradient

For more gradient options, use the Format Shape dialog box. This method works for all types of objects, regardless of the type of Format tab that they use. When setting up a custom gradient, you define stops. A *stop* is a position along the gradient that specifies a certain color. Each stop has three properties: color, stop position, and transparency. A gradient typically has as many stops as it has colors; however, you can use the same color for multiple stops. For a default, evenly spaced gradient, the stops are spaced out evenly in percentage. For example, if you defined three stops, they would be set at 0 percent, 50 percent, and 100 percent. You can also achieve different effects by spacing out the stops differently. Figure 10.29 shows some examples of various numbers and positions of stops.

FIGURE 10.29

Gradient stops define when and how the color will change.

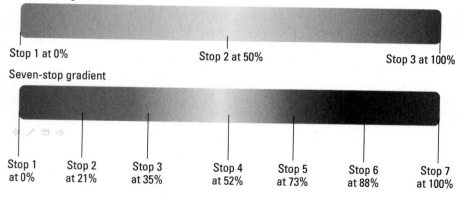

Two-color gradient

Stop 1 at 0% Stop 2 at 100%

Two-color gradient with non-standard stop position

Stop 1 at 0% Stop 2 at 10%

Three-color gradient

Stop 1 at 0% Stop 2 at 50% Stop 3 at 100%

Seven-stop gradient

Stop 1 at 0% Stop 2 at 21% Stop 3 at 35% Stop 4 at 52% Stop 5 at 73% Stop 6 at 88% Stop 7 at 100%

You can use the Fill controls in the Format Shape dialog box to define a gradient, as shown in Figure 10.30. The following list briefly explains the settings in the dialog box.

You can define gradient stops and settings in the Format Shape dialog box.

You can set gradients to the following types:

- **Linear:** A linear gradient, like the ones in Figure 10-29, travels from one point to another. You can set it to travel horizontally — as shown in Figure 10-29 — vertically, or diagonally, or you can set a specific angle.

- **Radial:** A radial gradient radiates out from a point. You can set it to radiate from the center of the object, or from any of its corners.

- **Rectangular:** This gradient is similar to Radial, except that it radiates as a rectangle, rather than as a curve.

- **Path:** This gradient follows the shape of the object. Try applying it to a starburst, for example; the color radiates out from the center of the star.

You can also define your own colors and stops for a gradient, or you can start with one of the Preset Colors settings. These are different from the single-color presets in the Format tab because they are color combinations with predefined stops. You can also start with one of these sets of combinations as a shortcut.

The Transparency setting adjusts the amount of transparency that is associated with that position in the gradient. You can use this setting to make certain areas of an object more transparent than others. For example, you could define the same color for all of the gradient stops, but set different levels of transparency for each stop, to make an object seem like it is fading away.

The Rotate with Shape option determines if the gradient rotates when you rotate a shape.

To create a custom gradient, follow these steps:

1. Right-click the object to be filled and choose Format Shape or Format Picture, depending on the object type. The Format Shape dialog box opens.

2. Click Fill, and then click the Gradient Fill button. Controls for creating a custom gradient appear, as shown in Figure 10-30.

3. (Optional) Select a preset from the Preset Colors drop-down list. If you select a preset, PowerPoint predefines two or more stops for you in the Gradient Stops section.

4. Open the Type drop-down list and select the type of gradient that you want: Linear, Radial, Rectangular, or Path.

5. If you chose Linear, Radial, or Rectangular, open the Direction drop-down list and choose a direction swatch.

6. If you chose Linear, increment the value in the Angle text box as needed to adjust the angle.

7. You can select or deselect the Rotate with Shape option.

8. Select Stop 1 in the Gradient Stops section.

9. Do the following to modify the stop:

   a. Open the Color drop-down list and select the color for that position.

   b. (Optional) Increment the Stop Position value, or drag its slider.

   c. (Optional) Increment the Transparency setting, or drag its slider. Zero percent is no transparency, while 100 percent is complete transparency.

10. Select Stop 2 in the Gradient Stops section, and repeat step 9.

11. (Optional) Add or remove stops:

    ▓ If you need to create more stops, click the Add button and then repeat step 9 for each new stop.

    ▓ If you need to delete a stop, select it and then click the Remove button.

12. Click Close to close the dialog box.

Texture and Picture Fills

A texture fill is actually a picture fill, but it is a special type of picture that, when tiled, looks like a surface texture such as wood, marble, or cloth. To apply a texture fill, select one from the Texture submenu on the Shape Fill drop-down menu (for an object that has the Drawing Tools Format tab). The More Textures option at the bottom of the palette of presets opens the Shape Fill dialog box (the same as the method in the following steps).

If you are filling an object that doesn't have a Shape Fill button on the Format tab, you can use the Format Shape dialog box instead. Follow these steps:

1. Right-click the object and choose Format Shape or Format Picture, depending on the object type. The Format Shape dialog box opens.

2. Click to select the Picture or Texture Fill option.

3. Click the Texture button and select a texture, as shown in Figure 10.31.

4. Click OK.

FIGURE 10.31

Select one of the preset textures from the Texture button's gallery.

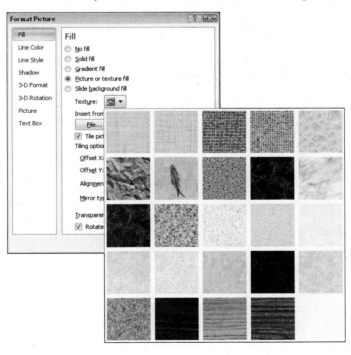

 You can also use your own pictures as textures. To do so, use the procedure for picture fills in the following section and make sure that you select the Tile Picture as Texture option.

You can also use a picture as an object fill. You can specify a picture from a file stored on your hard disk, from the contents of the Clipboard, or from the clip art that is available in your Office applications. Picture fills were discussed briefly at the end of Chapter 9 as they pertain to table cells, but you can fill almost any object with a picture, not just a text box or table cell.

EXPERT TIP You can fill a clip-art image that has a transparent background with another picture, creating a picture-on-picture effect.

In the Format Shape dialog box, when you select the Picture or Texture Fill option, shown in Figure 10-31, three buttons appear:

- **File:** Click this button to open an Insert Picture dialog box, and then select the picture that you want to use.

- **Clipboard:** Click this button to insert the contents of the Clipboard as the graphic to use. This technique works only with the last item that you placed on the Clipboard, not the full 24-item Office Clipboard.

- **ClipArt:** Click this button to open a Select Picture dialog box, which is a simplified version of the Clip Art pane. Search for a clip-art image by keyword, and then select and insert the clip art.

After you select the picture that you want to use, you can set any of the following options to control how it appears:

- **Tile Picture as Texture:** When you enable this option, the picture appears at its actual size as a background fill for the object. If the picture is smaller than the object that it is filling, then it tiles like a texture (where multiple copies are used). If the picture is larger than the object that it is filling, then a truncated copy appears.

- **Offsets:** This option controls how the picture fill adjusts within the object. An offset moves it in the specified direction.

EXPERT TIP Offsets are especially useful if you are using the Tile Picture as Texture option with a large picture; you can use offsets to position the desired part of the picture in the viewable area.

- **Transparency:** Drag the slider or enter a percentage if you want the picture fill to be semi-transparent; this works just the same as with colors and gradients.

- **Rotate with Shape:** Select or deselect this option to indicate whether the picture should rotate when the object is rotated. This is just the same as with gradients.

Background Fills

You can also apply the background as a fill for shapes and drawn objects. This is somewhat like setting the background fill to No Fill so that the background shows through, except that it hides any objects that are between the affected objected and the background. In the example in Figure 10.32, the oval has the background as its fill, and it is sitting on top of a text box. This is better than filling the oval with the same pattern, gradient, or texture as the background, because no matter where you move it on the slide, its background will continue to "match" with the slide's background. To apply a Background fill, choose the Background option from the Fill settings in the Format Shape dialog box.

FIGURE 10.32

A background fill allows the background to show through, but hides any intervening objects.

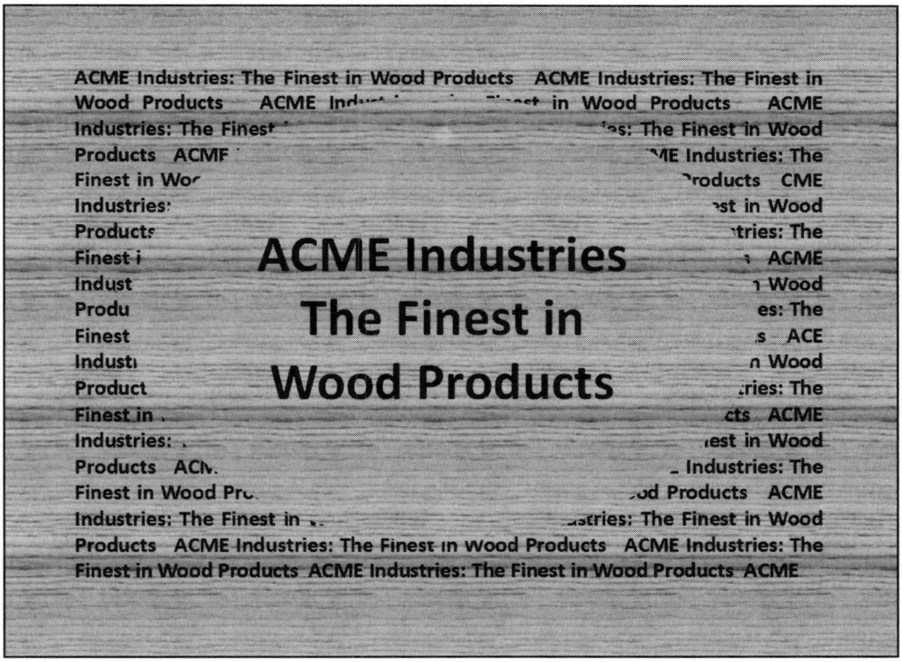

Applying Object Effects

Object effects are mostly new in PowerPoint 2007. Although a few effects, such as shadows and 3D effects, existed in a rudimentary form in earlier versions of PowerPoint, the capabilities of the new object effects far exceed those of the earlier ones. You can apply object effects from the Shape Effects or Picture Effects button on the Format tab, depending on the object type. The available effects are nearly identical for all types of objects, except for the different names of the buttons from which you select them. The following sections explain each effect.

Preset

Presets (in the context of object effects) are 3D effects. They include combinations of gradient fills and edge formatting (such as bevels) that make an object appear to have some depth. You can start with one of these presets as a shortcut to a more complex effect, or just use them as they are. Figure 10.33 shows some of the presets applied to a circle.

FIGURE 10.33

You can use presets to apply 3D object effects.

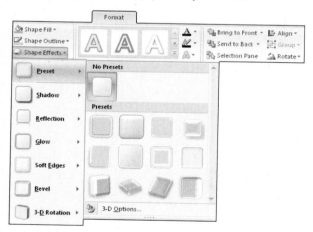

Shadow

Shadows were available in earlier versions of PowerPoint, but only as simple outer types. In PowerPoint 2007, you can create outer, inner, or perspective shadows, as shown in Figure 10.34.

FIGURE 10.34

Outer (left), inner (center), and perspective (right) shadows.

> **NOTE**   At first glance, an inner shadow might look the same as an outer one, but if you increase an inner shadow's size, you will notice that the increased size of the shadow decreases the size of the object — that is, the shadow cuts into the object, rather than appearing behind it as a separate element.

From the drop-down menu of the Shape Effects or Picture Effects button, select Shadow and then click one of the shadow presets, or click More Shadows to open Shadow controls in the Format Shape dialog box, as shown in Figure 10.35. To fine-tune the shadow, you can start with one of the presets from the Presets drop-down menu, customize it by choosing a color, and then drag the sliders for each of the shadow attributes: Transparency, Size, Blur, Angle, and Distance.

FIGURE 10.35

If none of the presets meets your needs, you can customize a shadow using the Format Shape dialog box.

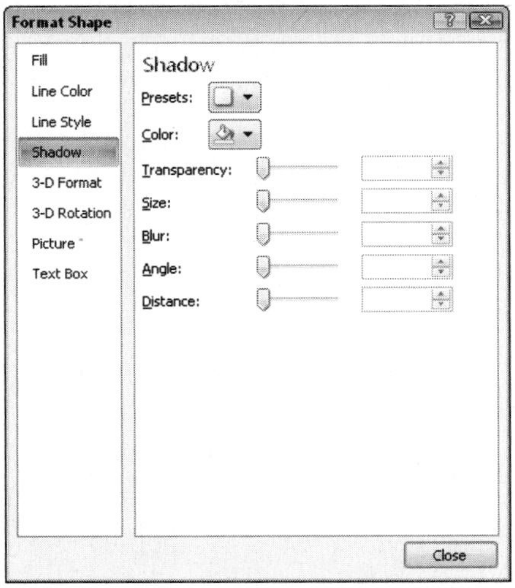

The shadow applies to either the object or its frame, depending on the object type and whether or not it has a transparent background. The following conditions create different results:

- **Text and drawn shapes:** The shadow clings directly to the object, regardless of the background fill.

NOTE If text is typed in a shape, the shadow applies only to the shape. If you want text typed in a shape to have a shadow, you must use Text Effects in the WordArt Styles.

- **Inserted pictures (such as scanned photos):** The shadow applies to the rectangular frame around the picture; if the picture is inserted in a shape, the shadow applies to the shape.

- **Clip art, text boxes, and charts:** If the background is set to No Fill, the shadow applies to the object inside the frame; if you have an applied fill, the shadow applies to the frame.

CAUTION If you change the shadow color, you should generally use a color that is darker than the object. Lighter-colored shadows do not look realistic. However, for black text, you should use a gray shadow.

Reflection

Reflection is a new effect in PowerPoint 2007. It creates a mirror image of the object, below the original. A reflection is affected by two factors: the amount of reflection — partial or full — and the offset, or distance between it and the original. The presets shown in Figure 10.36 use various combinations of these two factors. These factors are not customizable.

FIGURE 10.36

The reflection presets combine various amounts of reflection and offset.

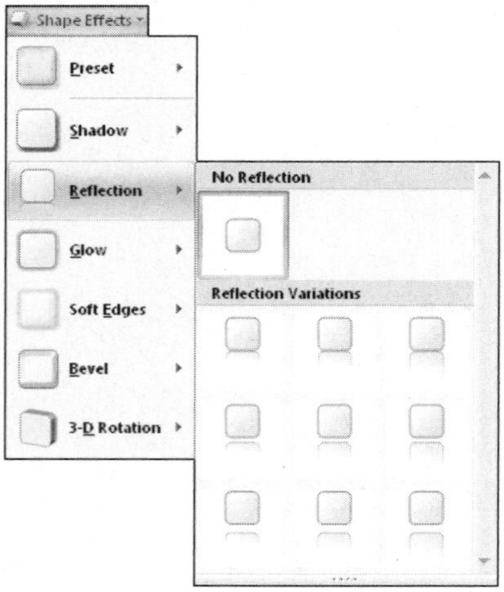

Glow and Soft Edges

Glow is a new effect that creates a colored "halo" around the object. You can choose the color either from the theme colors or from a fixed color that you specify. To select a different color, choose More Glow Colors and then choose a color from the Colors dialog box.

Soft Edges is similar to the Glow effect. Whereas Glow creates a fuzzy halo around the outside of an object, Soft Edges uses the same color as the object to create a fuzzy effect by cutting into the edges of the object. The difference between these two effects is similar to the difference between an outer and an inner shadow.

You cannot specify a custom amount for the Soft Edge effect, but you can choose from several presets on the Soft Edges submenu, ranging from 1 point to 50 points.

Bevels

A *bevel* is an effect that you apply to the edge of an object to make it look raised, sunken, or textured. You can apply beveling to flat shapes and other objects to give them a thick, three-dimensional appearance, or you can combine them with a real 3D rotation effect, as described in the following section. Figure 10.37 shows some examples of bevels that you can create using presets. You can access these presets through the Bevel submenu in either the Shape Effects or Picture Effects drop-down menu.

FIGURE 10.37

Beveled edges give a shape a three-dimensional appearance without tilting or rotating the object.

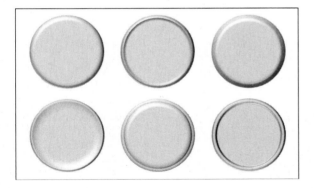

For more beveling choices, click the More 3-D Settings button in the Bevel submenu. This opens the Format Shape dialog box, as shown in Figure 10.38. You can also access this dialog box by right-clicking the object and choosing Format Shape (or Format Picture).

FIGURE 10.38

You can set bevels and other 3-D formatting effects in the 3-D Format section of the Format Shape dialog box.

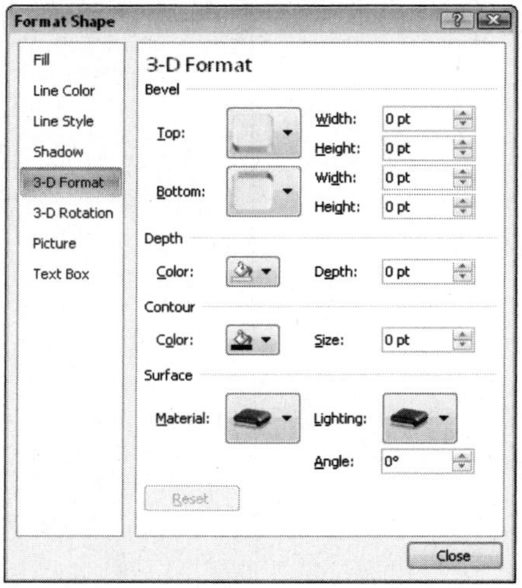

Beveling is a type of non-rotational 3-D effect — in other words, it is a 3-D format. You will learn about the other 3-D formatting options in the next section.

The Bottom bevel setting has no apparent effect unless you apply a 3-D rotation to the object, because you can't see the effect at zero rotation. As a result, we will only concern ourselves with the width and height settings for a top bevel:

- **Width:** Specifies how far the effect extends into the object
- **Height:** Specifies how dramatic the effect is vertically

You won't notice much height difference for a bevel unless you have applied a 3-D rotation to the object, but the width setting is immediately apparent for all objects.

3-D Rotation and 3-D Formatting

The 3-D rotation effect makes a two-dimensional object look three-dimensional by applying perspective to it. The 3-D rotation effect uses angle measurements for three dimensions: X, Y, and Z:

- **X rotation:** Rotation from side to side
- **Y rotation:** Rotation from top to bottom
- **Z rotation:** Pivoting around a center point

X and Y rotation actually change the shape of the object on the slide to simulate perspective; Z rotation simply spins the object, just as you would with a rotation handle.

You can combine 3-D rotation with 3-D formatting to create interesting effects, such as adding "sides" to a flat object and coloring these sides in a certain way. For example, you could combine these effects to turn a square into a cube. The 3-D formatting effect is formatting (colors, lengths, and textures) that affects an object's 3-D appearance. The 3-D formatting effect consists of the following aspects:

- **Bevel:** As discussed in the preceding section, this effect alters the edges of the object. You can set top and bottom bevels separately.

- **Depth:** This allows you to specify the size and color of the sides of the object. However, the sides are not visible unless the object is three-dimensionally rotated.

- **Contours:** This allows you to specify the color and size of outlines that mark the edges of the 3-D effect.

- **Surface:** This allows you to specify the material and lighting that the object should simulate.

Figure 10.39 shows several types of 3-D rotation and formatting. Beveling is also a type of 3-D formatting, and so some examples of it are included.

FIGURE 10.39

Some examples of 3D rotation and formatting.

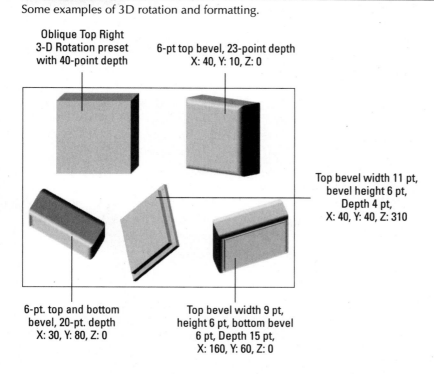

Oblique Top Right
3-D Rotation preset
with 40-point depth

6-pt top bevel, 23-point depth
X: 40, Y: 10, Z: 0

Top bevel width 11 pt,
bevel height 6 pt,
Depth 4 pt,
X: 40, Y: 40, Z: 310

6-pt. top and bottom
bevel, 20-pt. depth
X: 30, Y: 80, Z: 0

Top bevel width 9 pt,
height 6 pt, bottom bevel
6 pt, Depth 15 pt,
X: 160, Y: 60, Z: 0

Although you can use 3-D rotation and 3-D formatting together to create the effects shown in Figure 10-39, they are actually controlled separately in PowerPoint. Therefore, creating these effects is a two-step process.

Applying 3-D Rotation

To apply 3-D rotation, you can either use one of the 3-D Rotation presets, or you can enter rotation amounts directly into the Format Shape dialog box. To use a preset, Click the Shape Effects (or Picture Effects) button on the Format tab, select 3-D Rotation, and click a preset. The Oblique presets at the bottom of the menu are the most similar to the old PowerPoint 2003-style 3D effects.

> **CAUTION** If you have not yet added depth to the shape by using its 3-D Format settings, you won't see any effect from the Oblique presets because there are not yet any "sides" to the shape.

To rotate a precise amount, choose More 3-D Settings from the bottom of the presets menu, or right-click the object and choose Format Shape (or Format Picture) to open the Format Shape dialog box. Then click 3-D Rotation, as shown in Figure 10.40. You can start with one of the presets by selecting it from the Rotation Preset drop-down menu.

FIGURE 10.40

Set X, Y, and Z rotation for the object in the Format Shape dialog box.

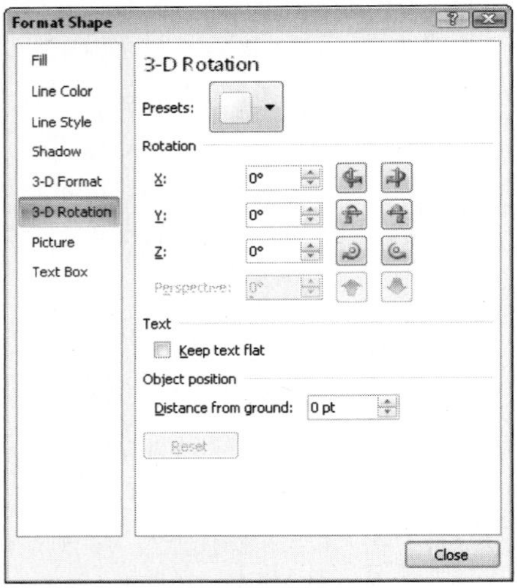

The other settings for rotation are:

- **Keep Text Flat:** This option prevents any text in the shape from rotating on the X- or Y-axis.

- **Distance from Ground:** This setting adds space between the object and the background. To see this effect more clearly, rotate the object.

- **Reset to 2-D:** You can press this button to remove all 3-D settings so that you can start fresh.

Applying 3-D Formatting

You can use 3-D formatting to control the colors and the amount of depth of the surfaces and sides of a 3-D rotated object. You control these settings from the 3-D Format section of the Format Shape dialog box, as shown in Figure 10..-38:

- The Depth of an object determines the length and color of its sides. In most cases, you want to keep the sides set to the default color setting, Match Shape Fill. This enables the sides to change colors when the shape changes colors. Although the sides are a darker shade of the object's color in order to create the illusion of depth, you can adjust their color through the application of surface material and lighting.

- Contours are similar to outlines, or borders, except that contours go around each side of a 3-D object. For example, if you have a square with sides (a cube), the color and size that you set for Contours creates a border around the front face as well as around each visible side surface.

- The surface material determines how shiny the surface appears, and how bright its color is on the front face compared to the sides. The Material button opens a palette that displays various materials such as Matte, Plastic, and Metal. The Lighting button opens a palette that displays various types of lighting that you can apply to the object, such as Harsh, Soft, Bright Room, and so on. To adjust the direction from which the light hits the object, you can change the Angle setting.

EXPERT TIP One unfortunate thing about the new 3-D settings in PowerPoint 2007 is that it is now harder to create a simple 3-D cube because it involves two steps: applying the Oblique preset, and then increasing the depth. If you often use a 3-D cube, consider creating a building block out of an existing one, so that you can easily insert cubes into your presentations.

Tips for Creating Common 3D Objects

The 3-D formatting and rotation settings in PowerPoint 2007 are a giant leap from the capabilities of earlier versions. As a result, they can seem a little overwhelming at first because of the variety of available options. Take your time in exploring them, and I think you'll be pleasantly surprised at what you can accomplish. Here are some things you can try:

To create a perfectly round sphere, which stays round no matter how you rotate it, follow these steps:

1. Draw an oval.

2. Select the oval and use the Size boxes on the Format tab to set its height and width to the same value, thus making it a perfect circle. For this experiment, use a whole number such as 1" or 2".

3. Right-click the circle and choose Format Shape.

4. In the 3-D Format settings, set the top and bottom bevel, both Height and Width, to 36 points for every 1" of diameter. For example, if your circle is 2" in diameter, use 72 points for each.

To create a four-sided pyramid, follow these steps:

1. Draw a rectangle.

2. Select the rectangle and use the Size boxes on the Format tab to set its height and width to the same value, making it a perfect square. For this experiment, use 1".

3. Right-click the square and choose Format Shape.

4. In the 3-D Format settings, for both the Top and Bottom bevel styles, choose Angle (the first preset on the second row).

5. Set the bevel settings as follows:

   a. Top Width: 36 points for every 1" of the square's size, plus 1 point. For example, for a 1" square, use 37 points; for a 2" square, use 73 points.

   b. Top Height: 72 points for every 1" of the square's size.

   c. Bottom (height and width): 0 points.

6. In the 3-D Rotation tab, rotate the object so that you can see it more clearly:

   - X: 30
   - Y: 300
   - Z: 325

EXPERT TIP To create pyramids with different numbers of sides, use different shapes than squares. To create a cone, use a circle.

Summary

In this chapter, you learned how to draw lines and shapes, and how to format almost any type of object. You'll use these skills as you go forward in the rest of the book learning about specific types of objects, including SmartArt, clip art, and so on. No matter what type of graphic you encounter, you'll be able to format it using these same techniques.

In the next chapter, you'll learn how to create and format SmartArt diagrams, which are new PowerPoint 2007 diagrams that combine the best of a bulleted list with the best of drawn objects to present text data in an interesting way.

Chapter 11

Creating SmartArt Diagrams

Just as charts and graphs can enliven a boring table of numbers, a SmartArt diagram can enliven a conceptual discussion. SmartArt helps the audience understand the interdependencies of objects or processes in a visual way, so they don't have to juggle that information mentally as you speak. Some potential uses include organizational charts, hierarchy diagrams, and flow charts.

Understanding SmartArt Types and Their Uses

SmartArt replaces the old Diagrams and Organization Chart features in earlier PowerPoint versions. SmartArt is a special class of vector graphic object that combines shapes, lines, and text placeholders. SmartArt is most often used to illustrate relationships between bits of text.

The SmartArt interface is similar regardless of the type of diagram you are creating. You can type directly into the placeholders on the diagram, or you can display a text pane to the side of the diagram and type into that, much as you would type into an outline pane to have text appear in a slide's text placeholder boxes. See Figure 11.1. You can also select some text, right-click it, and choose Convert to SmartArt.

FIGURE 11.1

A typical SmartArt diagram being constructed.

Toggle text pane on/off

Text pane

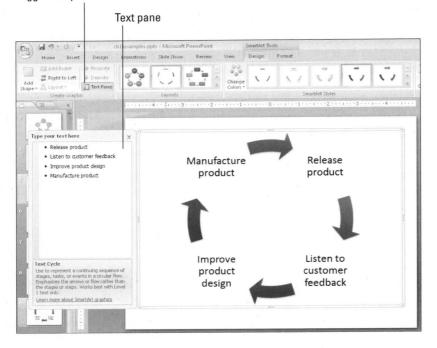

There are seven types of SmartArt diagrams in PowerPoint 2007, and each is uniquely suited for a certain type of data delivery.

List

A list diagram presents information in a fairly straightforward, text-based way, somewhat like a fancy outline. List diagrams are useful when information is not in any particular order, or when the process or progression between items is not important. The list can have multiple levels, and you can enclose each level in a shape or not. Figure 11.2 shows an example.

A list diagram deemphasizes any progression between items.

Process

A process diagram is similar to a list, but it has directional arrows or other connectors that represent the flow of one item to another. This adds an extra aspect of meaning to the diagram. For example, in Figure 11.3, the way the boxes are staggered and connected with arrows implies that the next step begins before the previous one ends.

FIGURE 11.3

A process diagram shows a flow from point A to point B.

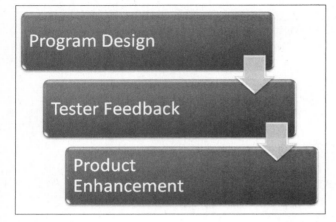

Cycle

A cycle diagram also illustrates a process, but a repeating or recursive one — usually a process in which there is no fixed beginning or end point. You can jump into the cycle at any point. In Figure 11.4, for example, the ongoing process of product development and improvement is illustrated.

FIGURE 11.4

A cycle diagram traces the steps of a repeating process.

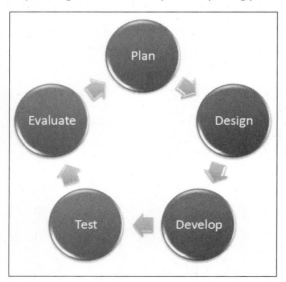

Hierarchy

A hierarchy chart is an organization chart. It shows structure and relationships between people or things in standardized levels. For example, it can show who reports to whom in a company's employment system. It is useful when describing how the organization functions and who is responsible for what. In Figure 11.5, for example, three organization levels are represented, with lines of reporting drawn between each level. Hierarchy diagrams can also run horizontally, for use in tournament rosters.

FIGURE 11.5

A hierarchy diagram, also called an organization chart, explains the structure of an organization.

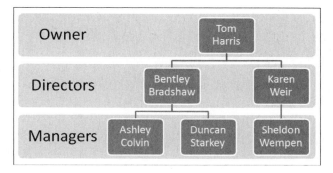

EXPERT TIP Should you include your company's organization chart in your presentation? That's a question that depends on your main message. If your speech is about the organization, you should. If not, show the organization structure only if it serves a purpose to advance your speech. Many presenters have found that an organization chart makes an excellent backup slide. You can prepare it and have it ready in case a question arises about the organization. Another useful strategy is to include a printed organization chart as part of the handouts you distribute to the audience, without including the slide in your main presentation.

Relationship

Relationship diagrams graphically illustrate how parts relate to a whole. One common type of relationship diagram is a Venn diagram, as in Figure 11.6, showing how categories of people or things overlap. Relationship diagrams can also break things into categories or show how parts contribute to a whole, as with a pie chart.

FIGURE 11.6

A relationship diagram shows how parts relate to a whole.

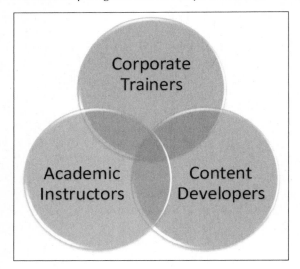

Matrix

A matrix also shows the relationship of parts to a whole, but it does so with the parts in orderly looking quadrants. You can use matrix diagrams when you do not need to show any particular relationship between items, but you want to make it clear that they make up a single unit. See Figure 11.7.

Pyramid

A pyramid diagram is just what the name sounds like — it's a striated triangle with text at various levels, representing not only the relationship between the items but also that the items at the smaller part of the triangle are less numerous or more important. For example, in Figure 11.8, the diagram shows that there are many more workers than there are executives.

FIGURE 11.7

A matrix diagram uses a grid to represent the contributions of parts to a whole.

FIGURE 11.8

A pyramid diagram represents the progression between less and more of something.

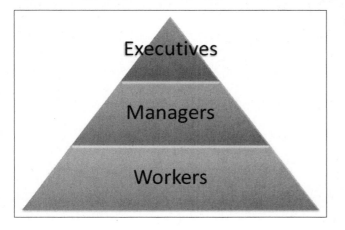

EXPERT TIP Notice in Figure 11.8 that the labels do not confine themselves to within the associated shape. If this is a problem, you might be able to make the labels fit with a combination of line breaks (Shift+Enter) and font changes.

Inserting a Diagram

All SmartArt diagrams start out the same way—you insert them on the slide as you can any other slide object. That means you can either use a diagram placeholder on a slide layout or you can insert the diagram manually.

To use a placeholder, start with a slide that contains a layout with a diagram placeholder in it, or change the current slide's layout to one that does. Then click the Insert SmartArt Graphic icon in the placeholder, as shown in Figure 11.9. To insert from scratch, click the SmartArt button on the Insert tab.

FIGURE 11.9

Click the SmartArt icon in the placeholder on a slide.

Insert SmartArt Graphic

Another way to start a new diagram is to select some text and then right-click the selection and choose Convert to SmartArt.

Any way you start it, the Choose a SmartArt Graphic dialog box opens, as shown in Figure 11.10. Select one of the seven SmartArt categories, click the desired SmartArt object, and click OK, and the diagram appears. From there it's just a matter of customizing.

> **NOTE**   Some diagrams appear in more than one category. To browse all of the categories at once, click All in Figure 11.10.

FIGURE 11.10

Select the diagram type you want to insert.

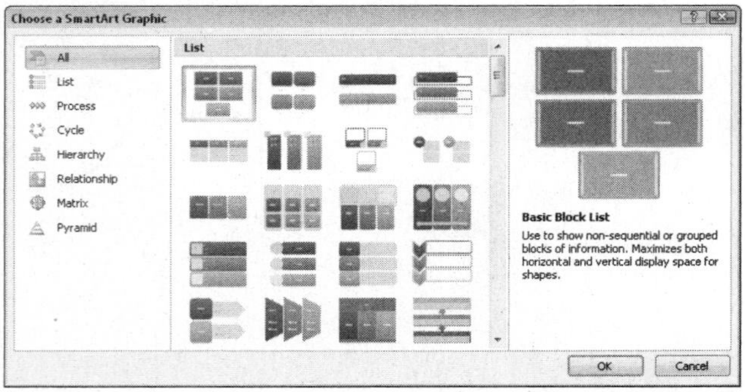

When you select a diagram, SmartArt Tools tabs become available (Design and Format). You will learn what each of the buttons on them does as this chapter progresses. The buttons change depending on the type of diagram.

Editing SmartArt Text

All SmartArt has text placeholders, which are basically text boxes. You simply click in one of them and type. Then use the normal text-formatting controls (Font, Font Size, Bold, Italic, and so on) on the Home tab to change the appearance of the text, or use the WordArt Styles group on the Format tab to apply WordArt formatting.

You can also display a text pane, as you saw in Figure 11.1, and type or edit the diagram's text there. The text pane serves the same purpose for a diagram that the Outline pane serves for the slide as a whole.

CAUTION The text in the outline pane is not always in the order you would expect it to be for the diagram because it forces text to appear in linear form from a diagram that is not necessarily linear. It does not matter how the text appears in the text pane because only you see that. What matters is how it looks in the actual diagram.

Here are some tips for working with diagram text:

- To leave a text box empty, just don't type anything in it. The *Click to add text* words do not show up in a printout or in Slide Show view.

- To promote a line of text, press Shift+Tab; to demote it, press Tab in the text pane.

- Text wraps automatically, but you can press Shift+Enter to insert a line break if needed.

- In most cases, the text size shrinks to fit the graphic in which it is located. There are some exceptions to that, though; for example, at the top of a pyramid, the text can overflow the tip of the pyramid.

- All of the text is the same size, so if you enter a really long string of text in one box, the text size in all of the related boxes shrinks too. You can manually format parts of the diagram to change this behavior, as you will learn later in the chapter.

- If you resize the diagram, its text resizes automatically.

NOTE In PowerPoint 2003, you could not move shapes around in a diagram by default because AutoLayout was enabled. You don't have that problem in PowerPoint 2007 with SmartArt, though; you can select and move individual parts of the diagram freely, as you would any shapes.

Modifying SmartArt Structure

The structure of the diagram includes how many boxes it has and where they are placed. Even though the diagram types are all very different, the way you add, remove, and reposition shapes in them is surprisingly similar across all types.

> **NOTE**   When you add a shape, you add both a graphical element (a circle, a bar, or other) and an associated text placeholder. The same applies to deletion; removing a shape also removes its associated text placeholder from the diagram.

Inserting and Deleting Shapes

To insert a shape in a diagram, follow these steps:

1. Click a shape that is adjacent to where you want the new shape to appear.
2. On the SmartArt Tools Design tab, click Add Shape.

You can either click the top part of the Add Shape button to add a shape of the same level and type as the selected one, or you can click the bottom part of the button to open a menu from which you can choose other variants. The choices on the menu depend on the diagram type and the type of shape selected. For example, in Figure 11.11, you can insert a shape into a diagram either before or after the current one (same outline level), or you can insert a shape that is subordinate (below) or superior to (above) the current one.

FIGURE 11.11

Add a shape to the diagram.

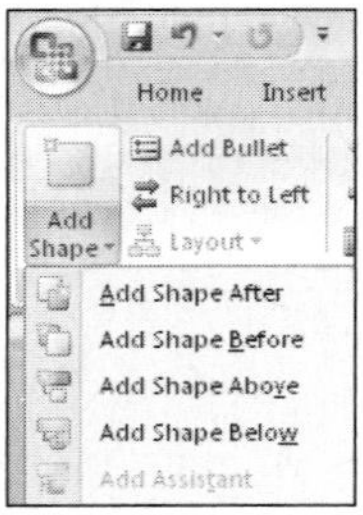

To delete a shape, click it to select it in the diagram, and then press the Delete key on the keyboard. You might need to delete subordinate shapes before you can delete the main shape.

> **NOTE**   Not all diagram types can accept different numbers of shapes. For example the four-square matrix diagram is fixed at four squares.

Adding Bullets

In addition to adding shapes to the diagram, you can add bullets — that is, subordinate text to a shape. To do so, click the Add Bullet button. Bullets appear indented under the shape's text in the text pane, as shown in Figure 11.12.

Create subordinate bullet points under a shape.

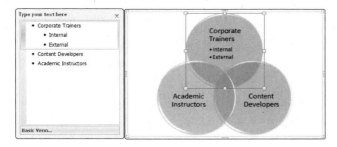

Promoting and Demoting Text

The difference between a shape and a bullet is primarily a matter of promotion and demotion in the Text Pane's outline. The text pane works just as the regular Outline pane does in this regard; you can promote with Shift+Tab or demote with Tab. You can also use the Promote and Demote buttons on the SmartArt Tools Design tab.

Changing the Flow Direction

Each diagram flows in a certain direction. A cycle diagram flows either clockwise or counterclockwise. A pyramid flows either up or down.

If you realize after typing all of the text that you should have made the SmartArt diagram flow in the other direction, you can change it by clicking the Right to Left button on the Design tab. It is a toggle; you can switch back and forth freely.

Reordering Shapes

Not only can you reverse the overall flow of the diagram, but you can also move around individual shapes. For example, suppose you have a diagram that illustrates five steps in a process and you realize that steps 3 and 4 are out of order. You can move one of them without having to retype all of the labels.

The best way to move a shape is to reorder the text in the text pane. Follow these steps:

1. Display the text pane if it does not already appear. You can either click the arrow button to the left of the diagram or click the Text Pane button on the SmartArt Tools Design tab.

2. Select some text to be moved in the text pane.

3. Press Ctrl+X to cut it to the Clipboard.

4. Click in the text pane at the beginning of the line above which it should appear.

5. Press Ctrl+V to paste.

NOTE PowerPoint 2003 diagrams had a Shape Forward and Shape Backward button for moving shapes, but SmartArt does not have that. The text pane's editing capabilities make up for it, though.

Repositioning Shapes

You can individually select and drag each shape to reposition it on the diagram. Any connectors between it and the other shapes are automatically resized and extended as needed. For example, in Figure 11.13, notice how the arrows that connect the circles in the cycle diagram have elongated as one of the circles has moved out.

FIGURE 11.13

When you move pieces of a diagram, connectors move and stretch as needed.

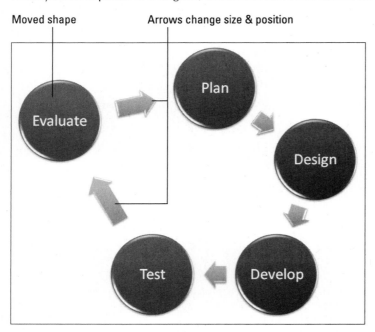

Resetting a Graphic

After making changes to a SmartArt diagram, you can return it to its default settings with the Reset Graphic button on the SmartArt Tools Design tab. This strips off everything, including any SmartArt styles and manual positioning, and makes it exactly as it was when you inserted it except it keeps the text that you've typed.

Changing to a Different Diagram Layout

The layouts are the diagram types. When you insert a SmartArt diagram you choose a type, and you can change that type at any time later.

To change the layout type, use the Layouts gallery on the Design tab, as shown in Figure 11.14. You can open the gallery and click the desired type, or click More Layouts at the bottom of its menu to redisplay the same dialog box as in Figure 11.10, from which you can choose any layout.

FIGURE 11.14

Switch to a different diagram layout.

Click here to open gallery

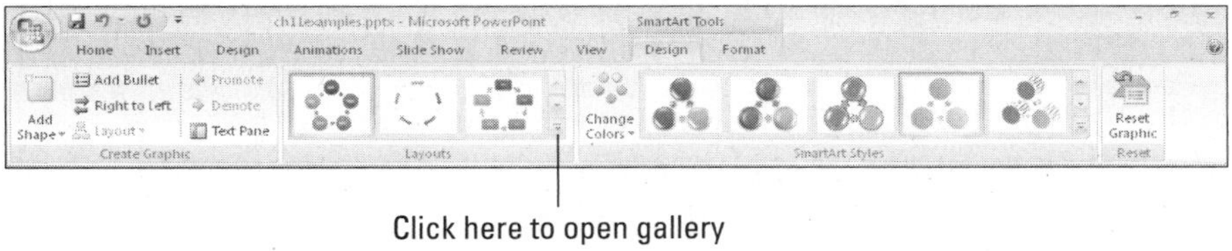

Modifying a Hierarchy Diagram Structure

Hierarchy diagrams (organization charts) show the structure of an organization. They have some different controls for changing their structure compared to other diagrams, so this chapter looks at them separately.

Inserting and Deleting Shapes

The main difference when inserting an organization chart shape (that is, a box into which you will type a name) is that you must specify which existing box the new one is related to and how it is related.

For example, suppose you have a supervisor already in the chart and you want to add some people to the chart who report to him. You would first select his box on the chart, and then insert the new shapes with the Add Shape button. For a box of the same level, or of the previously inserted level, click the top part of the button; for a subordinate or other relationship, open the button's menu. See Figure 11.15. The chart can have only one box at the top level, however, just as a company can have only one CEO.

FIGURE 11.15

Add more shapes to a hierarchy diagram.

Select the type of relationship to the selection

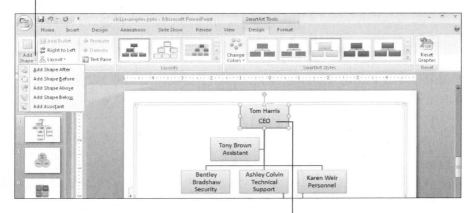

Select the box that the new box should be related to

When you insert a new shape in a hierarchy diagram, four of the options are the same as with any other diagram, and one is new: Add Shape After and Add Shape Before insert shapes of the same level as the selected one, and Add Shape Above and Add Shape Below insert a superior and subordinate level respectively. The new option, Add Assistant, adds a box that is neither subordinate nor superior, but a separate line of reporting, as shown in Figure 11.16.

FIGURE 11.16

An Assistant box in a hierarchy chart.

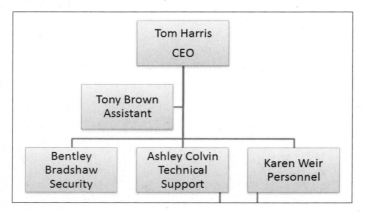

An *assistant* is a person whose job is to provide support to a certain person or office. An executive secretary is one example. In contrast, a *subordinate* is an employee who may report to a manager but whose job does not consist entirely of supporting that manager. Confused? Don't worry about it. You don't have to make a distinction in your organization chart. Everyone can be a subordinate (except the person at the top of the heap, of course).

To delete a shape, select it and press the Delete key, as with all of the other diagram types.

Changing a Person's Level in the Organization

As the organization changes, you might need to change your chart to show that people report to different supervisors. The easiest way to do that is to move the text in the text pane, the same way as you learned in the section "Reordering Shapes" earlier in this chapter.

For example, in Figure 11.16, suppose you want to promote Ashley Colvin to be at the same level as Karen Weir and Bentley Bradshaw. You could click Ashley Colvin in the text pane and press Shift+Tab to promote her. Furthermore, suppose you want Sheldon Wempen to report to her. You could select his name, press Ctrl+X to cut, click under Ashley Colvin, and then press Ctrl+V to paste.

Controlling Subordinate Layout Options

When subordinates report to a supervisor, you can list the subordinates beneath that supervisor in a variety of ways. In Standard layout, each subordinate appears horizontally beneath the supervisor. See Figure 11.17.

FIGURE 11.17

This is the standard layout for a branch of an organization chart.

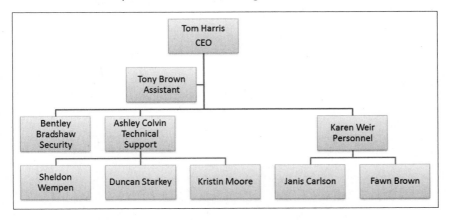

However, in a large or complex organization chart, the diagram can quickly become too wide with the Standard layout. Therefore, there are "hanging" alternatives that make the chart more vertically oriented. The alternatives are Both, Left Hanging, and Right Hanging. They are just what their names sound like. Figure 11-18 shows examples of Left Hanging (the people reporting to Ashley Colvin) and Right Hanging (the people reporting to Karen Weir).

FIGURE 11.18

Hanging layouts make the chart more vertically oriented.

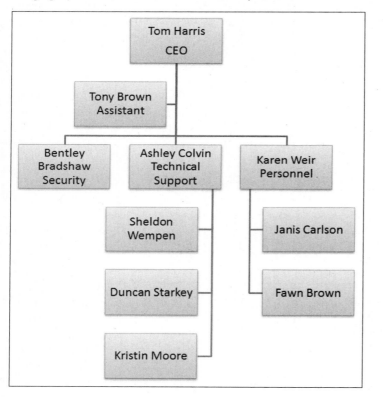

The layout is chosen for individual branches of the organization chart, so before selecting an alternative layout, you must click on the supervisor box whose subordinates you want to change. To change a layout, follow these steps:

1. Click the box for the supervisor whose layout you want to change.

2. On the Design tab, click Layouts. A menu of layout options appears.

3. Choose one of the layouts (Standard, Both, Left Hanging, or Right Hanging).

NOTE   If the Layout button's menu does not open, you do not have a box selected in a hierarchy diagram.

Formatting a Diagram

You can format a diagram either automatically or manually. Automatically is the default, and many PowerPoint users don't even realize that manual formatting is a possibility. The following sections cover both.

Applying a SmartArt Style

SmartArt Styles are preset formatting specs (border, fill, effects, shadows, and so on) that you can apply to an entire SmartArt diagram. They make it easy to apply surface texture effects that make the shapes look reflective or appear to have 3-D depth or perspective.

NOTE   SmartArt Styles do not include color changes. Those are separately controlled with the Change Colors button on the SmartArt Tools Design tab.

To apply a SmartArt style, follow these steps:

1. Select the diagram so that the SmartArt Tools Design tab becomes available.

2. On the SmartArt Tools Design tab, click one of the SmartArt Styles samples (see Figure 11.19), or open the gallery and select from a larger list (see Figure 11.20).

FIGURE 11.19

Select a SmartArt Style.

Click here to open the gallery

FIGURE 11.20

Open the SmartArt Style gallery for more choices.

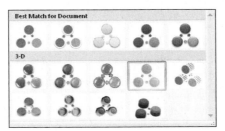

Changing SmartArt Colors

After you apply a SmartArt style, as in the preceding section, you might want to change the colors used in the diagram.

The easiest way to apply colors is to use the Change Colors button's menu on the Design tab. You can select from a gallery of color schemes. As shown in Figure 11.21, you can choose a Colorful scheme (one in which each shape has its own color), or you can choose a monochrome color scheme based on any of the current presentation color theme's color swatches.

FIGURE 11.21

Select a color scheme from the Change Colors button's menu.

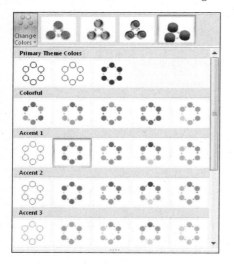

Manually Applying Colors and Effects to Individual Shapes

In addition to formatting the entire diagram with a SmartArt Style, you can also format individual shapes using Shape Styles, just as you did in Chapter 10 with drawn objects. Here's a quick review:

1. Select a shape in a SmartArt diagram.

2. On the SmartArt Tools Format tab, select a shape style from the Shape Styles gallery.

3. (Optional) Fine-tune the style by using the Shape Fill, Shape Outline, and/or Shape Effects buttons, and their associated menus.

FIGURE 11.22

Select a color scheme from the Change Colors button's menu.

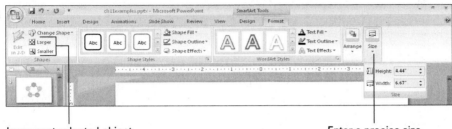

Increment selected object larger or smaller   Enter a precise size

Manually Formatting the Diagram Text

WordArt formatting works the same in a SmartArt diagram as it does everywhere else in PowerPoint. Use the WordArt Styles gallery and controls on the SmartArt Tools Format tab to apply text formatting to individual shapes, or select the entire diagram to apply the changes to all shapes at once. See Chapter 10 for more information about using WordArt Styles.

Making a Shape Larger or Smaller

In some diagram types, it is advantageous to make certain shapes larger or smaller than the others. For example, if you want to emphasize a certain step in a process, you can create a diagram where that step's shape is larger. Then you can repeat that same diagram on a series of slides, but with a different step in the process enlarged on each copy, to step through the process. There are several options for this:

- You can manually resize a shape by dragging its selection handles, the same as with any other object. However, this is imprecise, and can be a problem if you want multiple shapes to be enlarged because they won't be consistently so.

- You can set a precise size for the entire diagram using the Size group on the Format tab, a height and width measurement, as shown in Figure 11.22. However, if different shapes are already different sizes, and you want to resize them in proportion, this won't help.

- You can use the Larger or Smaller buttons on the Format tab to bump up or down the sizes of one or more shapes slightly with each successive click.

Resizing the Entire SmartArt Graphic Object

When you resize the entire SmartArt object as a whole, everything within its frame changes size proportionally. There are several ways to do this:

- Drag and drop a corner selection handle on the SmartArt graphic's outer frame.
- Use the Size controls on the SmartArt Tools Format tab to enter a precise height and width.

- Right-click the outer frame of the SmartArt and choose Size and Position. The Size and Position dialog box opens, as shown in Figure 11.23; on the Size tab, enter a height and width in inches, or scale it by a percentage in the Scale box. Mark the Lock Aspect Ratio check box if you want to maintain the proportions.

FIGURE 11.23

Right-click the graphic and choose Size and Position to open this dialog box.

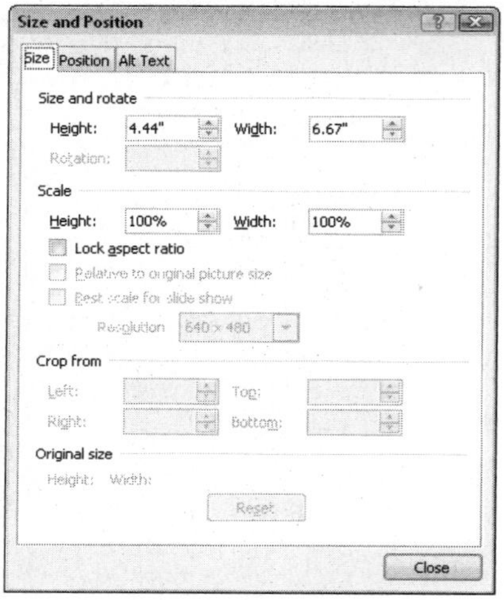

Editing in 2-D

If you choose one of the 3-D selections from the SmartArt Style gallery, the text might become a bit hard to read and edit when you are working with the diagram at a small zoom percentage. There are a couple of ways around this:

- Right-click a shape and choose Edit Text. The face of the shape appears in 2-D temporarily, making it easier to edit the text.

- Click the Edit in 2-D button on the SmartArt Tools Format tab. The entire diagram appears in 2-D temporarily.

CAUTION   Even though the face of the shape appears in 2-D, which you think would make it easier to read, in some diagram types and styles the text might still be fuzzy and hard to read. You might be better off editing it in the text pane.

Changing the Shapes Used in the Diagram

Each SmartArt layout has its own defaults that it uses for the shapes, but you can change these manually. On the SmartArt Tools Format tab, click Change Shape to open a palette of shapes, just like the ones you learned to work with in Chapter 10. Then click the desired shape to apply to the selected shape, as shown in Figure 11.24. You can also access this from the right-click menu.

Each shape is individually configurable. If you simply select the entire diagram, the Change Shape button is not available; you must select each shape you want to change. Hold down the Shift key as you click on each one to be selected.

Apply a different shape to a part of the diagram.

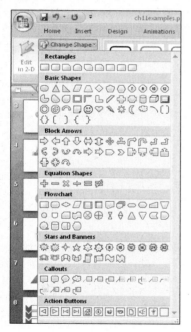

Saving a SmartArt Diagram as a Picture

SmartArt diagrams work only within Office applications, but you can easily export one for use in any other application. It is exported as a graphic (by default a .png file), which you can then import into any application that accepts graphics. To save a diagram as a picture, follow these steps:

1. Select the outer frame of the SmartArt graphic object.

2. Right-click the frame and choose Save as Picture. The Save as Picture dialog box opens.

3. (Optional) Open the Save as Type list and select a different file type if desired.

EXPERT TIP PowerPoint can save graphics in GIF, JPEG, TIFF, PNG, BMP, WMF, and EMF formats. Different formats have different qualities and advantages. EMF and WMF can be ungrouped, but not the other formats. EMF does not result in a quality loss when resized, but most of the others do. JPG doesn't use a transparent background, but PNG does.

Summary

In this chapter, you learned how to create SmartArt diagrams. You learned how to select a diagram type, how to rearrange shapes in a diagram, how to apply formatting, and how to export diagrams as artwork you can use in other programs. You will probably find lots of creative uses for diagrams now that you know they're available!

In the next chapter, you learn how to incorporate clip art, both from Microsoft and from other sources. You find out how to organize an artwork library using the Clip Organizer and how to import your own clips.

Chapter 12

Using and Organizing Clip Art

Clip art is pre-drawn art that comes with PowerPoint or that is available from other sources (such as through the Internet). There are thousands of images that you can use royalty-free in your work, without having to draw your own. For example, suppose you are creating a presentation about snow skiing equipment. Rather than hiring an artist to draw a picture of a skier, you can use one of PowerPoint's stock drawings of skiers and save yourself a bundle.

Being an owner of a Microsoft Office product entitles you to the use of the huge clip art collection that Microsoft maintains on its Web site, and if you are connected to the Internet while you are using PowerPoint, PowerPoint can automatically pull clips from that collection as easily as it can from your own hard drive. You can also use the Clip Organizer to catalog and organize artwork in a variety of other formats, including photos that you scan, photos that you take with your digital camera, and drawings and pictures that you acquire from the Internet and from other people.

In this chapter you learn how to select and insert clip art in your presentations, how to integrate photos and images from other sources into the Clip Organizer, and how to organize your clips for easy access.

Choosing Appropriate Clip Art

Don't just use any old image! You must never use clip art simply because you can; it must be a well-thought-out decision. Here are some reasons for using clip art, and ways to make it look good:

- If your message is very serious, or you are conveying bad news, don't use clip art. It looks frivolous in these situations.

- Use cartoonish images only if you specifically want to impart a lighthearted, fun feel to your presentation.

- The clip art included with Office has many styles of drawings, ranging from simple black-and-white shapes to very complex, shaded color drawings and photographs. Try to stick with one type of image rather than bouncing among several drawing styles.

- Use only one piece of clip art on each slide. Also, do not use clip art on every slide, or it becomes overpowering.

- Don't repeat the same clip art on more than one slide in the presentation unless you have a specific reason to do so.

- If you can't find clip art that is exactly right for the slide, then don't use any. It is better to have none than to have an inappropriate image.

- If clip art is important, and Office doesn't have what you want, you can buy more. Don't try to struggle along with the clips that come with Office if it isn't meeting your needs; impressive clip art collections are available at reasonable prices at your local computer store, as well as online.

About the Clip Organizer

The Clip Organizer is a Microsoft utility that you access from within an Office application such as PowerPoint. It organizes and catalogs artwork of various types. The primary type is clip art, but it can also hold sounds, videos, and photos. All of the Microsoft-provided clip art is automatically included in the Clip Organizer, including links to online Microsoft clip art; you can also add your own clips from your hard disk. Most of the Microsoft clip art is online, rather than stored locally, so you will need Internet access to use it.

The Clip Organizer has two main interfaces. When you use the Clip Art command on the Insert tab, you work with the Clip Art task pane, and clips that you select are inserted onto the active slide, as shown in the section "Inserting Clip Art on a Slide." When you use the Clip Organizer utility separately, you must copy and paste the clip art into the presentation using the Clipboard.

Depending on what you are inserting, you might also encounter other interfaces that access the Clip Organizer, such as interfaces for choosing custom bullet characters, which are also stored as clip art.

Inserting Clip Art on a Slide

You can insert clip art on a slide either with or without a content placeholder. If you use a content placeholder, PowerPoint inserts the clip art wherever the placeholder is; if you don't, PowerPoint inserts the clip art at the center of the slide. (You can move it afterwards, of course.)

Most clip art files in Microsoft Office applications have a .wmf extension, which stands for Windows Metafile. WMF is a *vector* graphic format, which means that it is composed of mathematical formulas rather than individual pixels. This allows you to resize it without distortion and keeps the file size very small. Some other clip art files are Enhanced Metafile (.emf) files, which are like WMF files but with some improvements. The Clip Organizer can also organize *bitmap* graphic files (that is, graphics composed of individual pixels of color), as you see later in this chapter. However, there are some editing activities through PowerPoint that you can perform only on WMF and EMF files.

To find and insert a piece of clip art, follow these steps:

1. *(Recommended)* If you want to include Web collections when searching for clip art, make sure that you are connected to the Internet. Otherwise, you are limited to the clip art on your local hard disk.

2. On the Insert tab, click Clip Art. The Clip Art pane appears. Alternatively, you can click the Clip Art icon in a content placeholder.

3. In the Search For text box, type the subject keyword that you want to search for.

4. *(Optional)* Narrow down where you want to search, using the Search In list, and the types of results that you want, using the Results Should Be list.

5. Click Go. The matching clip art appears, as shown in Figure 12.1.

FIGURE 12.1

The clip art that matches your search specifications appears in the task pane.

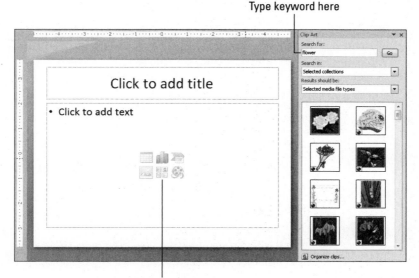

Type keyword here

Clip Art placeholder icon

6. Click the clip art that you want to insert. It appears on the slide.

7. Edit the image, for example, by resizing or moving it, as explained later in this chapter.

Clip Art Search Methods

Now that you've seen the basic process for searching for a clip by keyword, let's look at some ways to fine-tune those results so that you can more easily find what you want.

Using Multiple Keywords

If you enter multiple keywords in the Search For text box of the Clip Art pane, only clips that contain all of the entered keywords appear in the search results. You can simply type the words separated by spaces; you do not have to use any special symbols or punctuation in order to use multiple keywords.

Specify Which Collections to Search

Clip art is stored in *collections*, which are logical groupings of artwork arranged by subject or location. There are three main collections:

- **Office Collections**: These are the clips that came with Microsoft Office 2007.

- **My Collections**: These include any clips that you have marked as favorites, as well as any uncategorized clips. They also include any clips that you have added through the Clip Organizer, any downloaded clips, and any clips shared from a network drive.

- **Web Collections**: These are clip collections that are available online via Microsoft. This is by far the largest collection, but you must be connected to the Internet in order to access it. All of the clips from this collection appear with a little globe icon in the corner when you preview them in the task pane.

Within each of these large collections are multiple smaller collections (like subfolders within folders) that are based on subject. For example, Office Collections has sub-collections for Academic, Agriculture, Animals, and so on.

NOTE The physical location of the Office Collections clips is `Program Files\Microsoft Office\MEDIA\CAGCAT10`. However, users don't normally need to know this because PowerPoint manages the locations of the clip art automatically.

When you search for clips that contain certain keywords using the Clip Art pane, you have the option to specify which collections you want to look in. If you are working on a PC that uses a dial-up connection, or that has sporadic or no Web access, you might want to exclude the Web Collections from the search to avoid the delay while PowerPoint looks for and fails to find the Internet connection. You can also exclude certain categories to avoid having too many results to wade through.

To narrow the list of collections in which to search, follow these steps:

1. From the Clip Art pane, open the Search In drop-down list. A list of collections appears.

2. Deselect the check box for any collection that you want to exclude. You can also click the plus sign next to the collection to see its individual sub-collections, and then deselect the check box for one or more of these sub-collections, as shown in Figure 12.2.

3. Continue the clip search as you normally would.

FIGURE 12.2

Narrow the search for a clip to certain collections by deselecting the check boxes for unwanted collections.

Specify Which Media File Types to Find

Besides true clip art (WMF and EMF files), you can also find movies, sounds, and pictures using the Clip Art pane. You can learn more about each of these media types in later chapters, but let's take a quick look here at how to include them in searches. To filter results by media type (or to enable additional media types), follow these steps:

1. From the Clip Art pane, open the Results Should Be drop-down list. A list of media types appears.

2. Select or deselect check boxes for media types that you want to include or exclude, respectively. You can also click the plus sign next to a media type to see its individual subtypes, and then deselect the check box for one or more of these subtypes, as shown in Figure 12.3.

FIGURE 12.3

Narrow the search for a clip to certain file types by only selecting check boxes for the media types that you want.

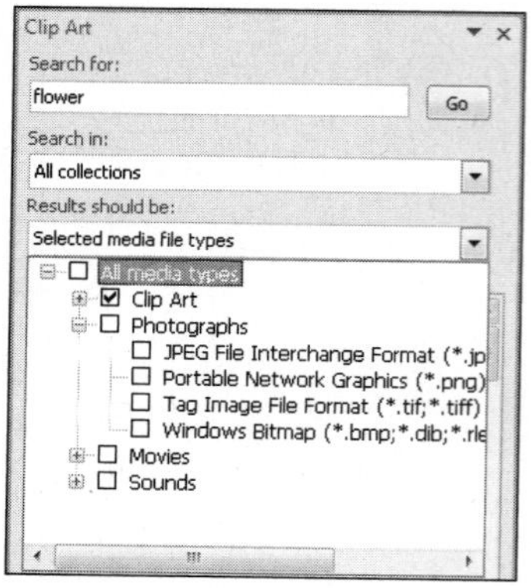

NOTE Notice in Figure 12.3 that the Clip Art pane is wider than in Figure 12.2. It is widened to show that you can view more of the descriptions of each file type. To widen this pane, click-and-drag its left edge to the left.

Working with Clip Art Collections

The Clip Organizer is a utility that manages the clips from various collections. You can use the Clip Organizer to browse entire clip collections by subject, regardless of keyword. It also manages clips of other types, including bitmap images (such as scanned photos), sounds, and video clips. In the following sections, you learn how to browse, categorize, and organize clips in the Clip Organizer, as well as how to add clips to it.

Opening and Browsing the Clip Organizer

To open the Clip Organizer, click the Organize Clips link at the bottom of the Clip Art pane. The Collection List pane lists the three default groups: My Collections, Office Collections, and Web Collections. Within each of these collections are nested folders, or sub-collections, containing clips. To expand or collapse a folder, double-click it, or click the plus or minus sign to its left, as shown in Figure 12.4.

FIGURE 12.4

You can browse clip art by collection, as well as by category within a collection.

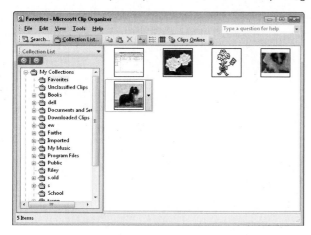

The My Collections group contains two collections by default:

- **Favorites**: This is where clips are placed when you make them available offline. (This is covered in the section "Making Clips Available Offline.")
- **Unclassified Clips**: This is where clips are placed when they are manually added to the Clip Organizer. (This is covered in the section "Working with Clip Keywords and Information.")

You can add more collections to the My Collections group, as well as more clips. It is the only group that you can modify. The Office Collections group contains collections that Microsoft provides and stores on your hard disk. The Web Collections group contains collections that you access through the Internet.

Using the Clip Organizer to Insert Clip Art

As you saw at the beginning of this chapter, when you insert clip art from the Clip Art pane, you cannot browse for it. You can only search based on keywords. If you would rather peruse the available clip art in a more leisurely fashion, you can open the Clip Organizer to do so.

The Clip Organizer is not really designed for easy insertion of clips into a presentation, but it is possible to do this using the Clipboard. To select a clip from the Clip Organizer for insertion in your presentation, do the following:

1. From the Clip Art pane, click Organize Clips. The Clip Organizer window opens.
2. Make sure that Collection List, and not Search, is selected on the toolbar. Click Collection List, if necessary.

3. Click the collection that you want to browse. The Clip Organizer displays the available clips. When you find the clip that you want to insert, right-click it and choose Copy.

4. Close or minimize the Clip Organizer. Display the slide in PowerPoint on which you want to place the clip, and then right-click and choose Paste. Alternatively, you can drag and drop clips from the Clip Organizer window onto a PowerPoint slide.

Creating and Deleting Folders

Each folder in the Clip Organizer represents a collection (or a sub-collection within a collection). The folders that you create are placed in the My Collections group, and you can place clips into a collection or sub-collection by dragging and dropping them into the desired folder. To create a folder in the Clip Organizer, follow these steps:

1. Choose File ⇨ New Collection. The New Collection dialog box opens, as shown in Figure 12.5.

2. In the Name text box, type a name for the new collection.

3. To create a top-level collection, click My Collections. To create a folder within a collection, click that collection within My Collections.

4. Click OK. The Clip Organizer creates the new folder.

To delete a folder, right-click it and choose Delete *foldername*, where *foldername* is the name of the folder.

FIGURE 12.5

You can create new collection folders.

Moving Clips between Collections

A clip can exist in multiple collections simultaneously; only one copy actually exists on your hard disk, but pointers to it can appear in multiple places. When you drag a clip from one collection to another, you are actually making a copy of its pointer to the new location. The shortcut to the clip is not removed from the original collection. You can delete a clip from a collection by right-clicking it and choosing Delete, or pressing the Delete key.

Cataloging Clips

There are probably images elsewhere on your PC that you would like to use in PowerPoint besides the Microsoft Office clip art collection. For example, perhaps you have some scanned photos or some clip art that you have downloaded from a Web site that offers free clips. If you need to use this downloaded clip art only once or twice, you can simply insert it with the Picture button on the Insert tab. However, if you want to use the clip art more often, you can add it to your Clip Organizer.

You can include images in all image formats in the Clip Organizer, not just the default format that PowerPoint's clip art uses. The image formats that PowerPoint supports are shown in Table 12.1.

TABLE 12.1

PowerPoint Image Formats

BMP	EPS	PCX
CDR	FPX	PNG
CGM	GIF	RLE
DIB	JPG/JPEG/JPE/JFIF	TGA
DRW	MIX	TIF/TIFF
DXF	PCD	WMF
EMF	PCT/PICT	WPG

The Clip Organizer is not only for clip art, but also for scanned and digital camera photos, video clips, and sound clips. It can accept many sound and video formats.

CROSS-REF You will work with the clip organizer further in Chapters 16 and 17, which deal with sound and video.

Adding a clip to the Clip Organizer does not physically move the clip; it simply creates a link to it in the Clip Organizer so that the clip is included when you search or browse for clips.

> **NOTE** Any clips that you add are placed in My Collections; you cannot add clips to the Office Collections or Web Collections categories. This is the case whether you add them automatically or manually.

Adding Clips Automatically to the Clip Organizer

The quickest way to catalog the clips on your hard disk is to allow the Clip Organizer to import the clips automatically. To automatically catalog your clips, follow these steps:

1. From the Clip Organizer, choose File ⇨ Add Clips to Organizer ⇨ Automatically.

2. *(Optional)* In the dialog box that appears, click the Options button to open the Auto Import Settings dialog box. You can then select or deselect check boxes for various locations that you want to include in the automatic cataloging, as shown in Figure 12.6. The first time you open this dialog box, the utility scans the hard disk for clips, and you must wait for a minute or so while it does this.

FIGURE 12.6

You can specify the locations that you want the Clip Organizer to catalog.

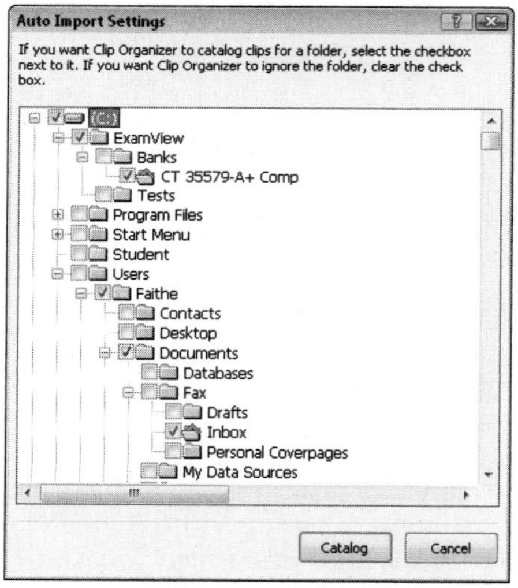

3. If you performed step 2, click Catalog to perform the search for clips. If you did not perform step 2, click OK to perform the search.

4. Wait for the Clip Organizer to catalog the clips. This process takes several minutes and includes several steps, including creating the collections, adding the clips, and adding keywords to them.

Adding Clips Manually to the Clip Organizer

Not all clips are picked up automatically during the cataloging process, and so you might need to manually add some clips. For example, the automatic cataloging process only looks for clips on your local hard disks, and you might want to catalog some clips in a network location.

> **CAUTION** Some earlier versions of Office stored the local collection of clip art in a different place. For example, Office XP stored this collection in `Program Files\Common Files\ Microsoft Shared\Clipart\Catcat50`. By default, the clip art in this old location does not appear in the collections for Office 2003 or 2007 applications. In addition, it is not detected by the automatic cataloging process. The only way to import it into the Clip Organizer is by manually cataloging it, as described here.

To manually add one or more clips, do the following:

1. From the Clip Organizer window, choose File ➪ Add Clips to Organizer ➪ On My Own. The Add Clips to Organizer window appears.

2. Navigate to the clips that you want to add. They can be in a local, network, or Internet location.

3. Select the clips. To select more than one clip, hold down the Shift key to select a contiguous group or the Ctrl key to select a non-contiguous group.

4. Click the Add To button. A list of the existing collections in the Clip Organizer appears, as shown in Figure 12.7.

FIGURE 12.7

You can specify the location to which you want to add the clips.

5. Select the collection in which you want to place the new clips, and click OK. If you would rather create a new clip collection, click My Collections and then click New. Type a name for the new collection and click OK. Then select the new folder on the list and click OK.

6. Click the Add button. The Clip Organizer adds the clips to the specified collection.

Working with CIL or MPF Files

Occasionally, you might encounter a file that claims to be clip art but that has a .cil or .mpf extension. Both of these are clip art "package" formats that Microsoft has used to bundle and transfer clip art at one time or another. MPF is the newer format, for Office XP and higher; CIL is the older format, for Office 97 and 2000.

These packages are executable, which means that executing them copies the art to the Clip Organizer. When you find one of these files, you can choose to run it rather than save it to immediately extract its clips, or you can download the file and then double-click it to extract the clip art from it later.

Deleting Clips from the Clip Organizer

After the automatic cataloging process (and possibly after the manual one), you might end up with some clip collections within My Collections that you don't want. The automatic cataloging process sometimes identifies files that are not really useful as clip art — for example, little graphics that are part of some other application's operation.

To remove a graphic — or even an entire folder — from your Clip Organizer, right-click it and choose Delete. Figure 12.8 shows a situation where the Clip Organizer has cataloged the clips from of a folder labeled i386; this folder is actually used for installing Windows. In the example, you can right-click the i386 folder in the folder tree and choose Delete "i386" to get rid of it. This does not delete the pictures or the folder from the hard disk; it simply removes its reference from the Clip Organizer. You can also delete individual clips in the same way.

FIGURE 12.8

You can remove a clip or a category from the Clip Organizer by right-clicking it and choosing Delete.

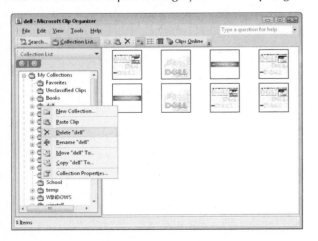

Inserting an Image from a Scanner

If you have a scanner or digital camera, you can use it from within the Clip Organizer to scan a picture and store it there. In PowerPoint 2007, this is the only way of accessing the Scanner and Camera Wizard, because that functionality is no longer in the main PowerPoint application. To scan a picture into the Clip Organizer, do the following:

1. Make sure your scanner is ready. Place the picture that you want to scan on the scanner glass.

2. From the Clip Organizer, choose File ⇨ Add Clips to Organizer ⇨ From Scanner or Camera.

3. Select the scanner from the Device list.

4. Choose a quality, such as Web quality (low) or Print quality (high).

5. To scan using default settings, click Insert. To adjust the settings further, click Custom Insert, change the settings, and then click Scan.

The scanned clip appears in the My Collections collection, in a folder with the same name as the device (in this case, the scanner's make and model). From there, you can assign keywords to the clip to make it easier to find, as explained in the next section.

EXPERT TIP On a Windows Vista system, the scanned file is located in the `Pictures\Microsoft Clip Organizer` folder on your hard disk, in case you want to use it in some other application that does not support the Clip Organizer. It is assigned a filename that begins with `mso` (for example, `mso414611`), and it is saved in JPEG format. Under Windows XP, it is located in `My Pictures\Microsoft Clip Organizer`.

CAUTION Good-quality scanners can scan at 300 dpi or more, but for use in PowerPoint, an image needs to have a resolution no higher than 96 dpi, the resolution of a monitor. Excessive resolution when scanning is one reason why graphics take up so much space. If you want to use an image in PowerPoint that has already been scanned and has a high resolution, consider opening it in a graphics program and reducing its resolution before importing it into PowerPoint.

Making Clips Available Offline

Most of the clips that appear in the Clip Organizer are not on your local hard disk; they are online. This means that you do not have access to them when you are not connected to the Internet. If you find some clip art in the Clip Organizer that you want to have available offline, you can add the clip to your local hard disk, as follows:

1. In the Clip Organizer or the Clip Art pane, open the menu of the clip that you want (the arrow to its right) and choose Make Available Offline. The Copy to Collection dialog box opens.

    If the Make Available Offline command is not present, it means that this clip is already on your local hard disk.

2. Select the collection in which you want to place the clip. (You can also click New to create a new collection.) Then click OK.

Strategies for Organizing Your Clips

To use the Clip Organizer most effectively, you need to put some thought into how you want to structure your collections. When you select File ➪ Add Clips to Organizer ➪ Automatically, the Clip Organizer automatically generates collections that are great for initially populating the organizer. However, you will probably want to arrange these files afterwards. There are several ways to organize the My Collections group, and each method has its pros and cons:

- **By location**: This is how the automatic cataloging sets up your collection. Pros: you can browse all of the clips in a location at once. Cons: the clips are not grouped logically according to content.

- **By topic**: You can create folders for various subjects, such as agriculture, animals, business, and so on, similar to the Office Collections and Web Collections. Pros: it is easy to find clips for a certain subject. Cons: there is no differentiation between media types.

- **By media type**: You can create folders for various media types, such as clip art, pictures, sounds, and videos. Pros: you do not have to wade through a lot of clips of the wrong file type to find what you want. For example, you do not have to look through clip art to find sounds, and vice versa. Cons: when creating a presentation, you usually have a topic in mind before a media type.

EXPERT TIP Perhaps the best solution if you have a lot of clips is to combine the topic and media-type methods. You can organize first by topic, and then within topic into separate folders by media type, or you can organize first by media type and then by topic within those folders.

To change the organization method of your Clip Organizer window from location-based to topic- or type-based, you can create new folders and then drag clips into the new folders. The Clip Organizer only copies the shortcuts there — it does not move them there — and so they remain in their location-based folders, as well. You can either leave these location-based folders in place for extra flexibility, or you can delete them.

Working with Clip Keywords and Information

After creating an automatic catalog, you will probably end up with a lot of clips in the Unclassified Clips collection. You can delete any you don't want. The remaining ones must be assigned keywords so they will show up when you do a search by keyword in the Clip Art pane.

You can edit the keywords and information only for clips stored on your own hard disk, not for clips stored online. That's because the online collection is shared by all Office users. If you want to re-keyword an online clip, copy it to your hard disk first and then work with that copy.

Automatically cataloged clips have several keywords pre-assigned, based on their filename and location. For example, suppose that the clip `Blue Hills.jpg` is cataloged from the `Documents and Settings\All Users\Documents\My Pictures\Sample Pictures` folder. (This is where Windows XP stores its sample pictures, and that picture came with Windows XP.) It will have the following keywords pre-assigned: Blue Hills, Documents and Settings, All Users,

Documents, My Pictures, and Sample Pictures. However, these keywords are not very helpful when you want to locate the clip by subject, and so you will want to add some content-based keywords, as well.

Changing the Keywords for an Individual Clip

To modify a clip's keywords and information, do the following:

1. From the Clip Organizer, right-click the clip (or click the down arrow to its right) and choose Edit Keywords.

2. The default caption for the clip is the filename. You can change it to a more meaningful caption in the Caption text box. This caption will appear in some views as well as anywhere that an application automatically pulls a caption.

3. To add a keyword for the clip, type the new keywords in the Keyword text box and click Add, as shown in Figure 12.9.

4. To remove a keyword, click the keyword on the list and click Delete.

5. When you finish changing the clip's keywords and caption, click OK to close the dialog box, or click the Previous or Next button to move to a different clip in the same folder.

FIGURE 12.9

You can add or delete keywords for a clip.

Changing the Keywords for Multiple Clips at Once

You can modify multiple clips at once by selecting multiple clips before you right-click (step 1 in the preceding steps). When you select multiple clips, the All Clips at Once tab becomes available in the Keywords dialog box. From there, you can add keywords that apply to all of the selected clips. For example, in Figure 12.10, you can add the keyword "landscapes" to all of the selected clips.

FIGURE 12.10

You can add or delete keywords for multiple clips at once on the All Clips at Once tab.

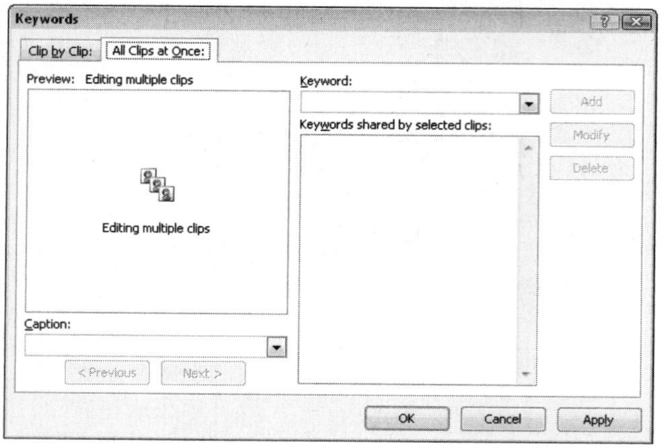

Browsing for More Clips on Office Online

When you browse for clip art while connected to the Internet, the Office Online clip art automatically appears. However, you can also visit the Office Online Web site to browse the clip art directly.

To open a Web browser window for the Office Online clip art gallery, do one of the following:

- From the Clip Art pane, click the Clip art on Office Online link.
- From the Clip Organizer window, click the Clips Online toolbar button.

Either way, the same Web page displays (provided you have Internet access). It contains information about clip art, links to art collections, featured clips, and more. It is constantly changing, but Figure 12.11 shows how it looked on the day I visited.

If you have a full-time Internet connection, there is little reason to download clips to your hard disk from the Office Online Web site because your clip art search by keyword will always include this Web site. However, if your Internet connection is not always active, you might want to download the clips you need in advance so that they will be available when you need them.

FIGURE 12.11

Visit the Office Online clip art Web page for more information and more clip art.

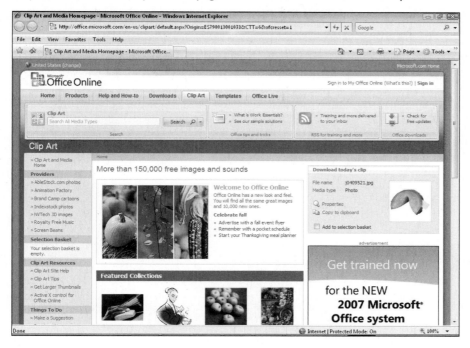

To copy clips from the Office Online Web site to your hard disk for later use, follow these steps:

1. From the Office Online clip art Web page, scroll down to the Browse Clip Art and Media Categories list and click a category to display it.

2. In the list of clips, select the check boxes for the clips that you want, as shown in Figure 12.12. You may find multiple pages of clips in that category; click the Next arrow to go to the next page.

3. When you finish making selections, click the Download hyperlink at the left. For example, in Figure 12-12, the link is labeled "Download 5 items" because I have chosen five items.

4. If this is the first time that you have used the service, a Terms of Use screen appears. Scroll down to the bottom and click Accept to continue.

FIGURE 12.12

You can download clips from Office Online for future use.

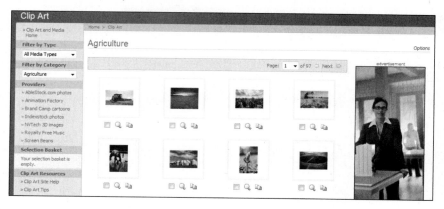

5. Click Download Now.

6. A dialog box appears, saying that it is downloading the file Clipart.mpf, and asking whether you want to save or open it. Choose Open.

NOTE   MPF stands for Media Package File. When downloading one of these files, you should choose to open it rather than save it, because opening it integrates its content automatically with the Clip Organizer. Saving the file stores it somewhere on your hard disk without adding the clips to the Clip Organizer. However, you might need to do this if you download clips that you want to use on another PC; in this case, you can transfer the MPF file to the other PC before double-clicking to open it.

CAUTION   When an MPF file unpacks, it uses the Temporary Internet File folder to do so. If this folder is too full (indicating that there is insufficient space remaining on the hard disk), the clips may not import into Clip Organizer.

The selected clips appear in the Clip Organizer, in the Downloaded Clips folder under My Collections. They are now ready for you to use.

Modifying Clip Art

Most of the modifications that you will learn about in Chapter 13 apply to both photographs and clip art. For example, you can increase or decrease brightness and contrast, crop, rotate, and so on. However, there are also some special modifications that apply only to clip art and other vector images.

Recoloring a Clip

One of the top complaints about clip art is that the colors are wrong. For example, you may have the perfect drawing, but its colors clash with your presentation design. In earlier versions of PowerPoint, you could change an individual color within a clip art image. PowerPoint 2007 doesn't offer this capability, but you can recolor individual parts of a clip by changing it to a Microsoft Drawing object and then selecting and coloring individual lines or shapes. For more information, see the section "Deconstructing and Editing a Clip," later in this chapter.

On a more basic level, PowerPoint 2007 provides a Recolor option that enables you to apply a single-color wash to the image, based on any of the theme's colors or any fixed color. To apply a color wash to a clip, follow these steps:

1. Select the clip that you want to recolor. The Format tab becomes available.
2. On the Format tab, click Recolor to open the menu shown in Figure 12.13.
3. Click the color wash that you want to apply, or click More Variations to choose another color.

FIGURE 12.13

Select a color wash to apply to the clip.

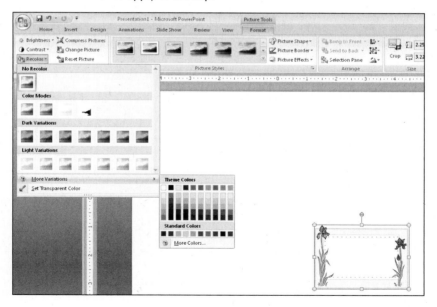

The colors on the Recolor menu are grouped as follows:

- **Color Modes**: These are like the color modes from PowerPoint 2003 and earlier: Grayscale, Washout, and Black-and-White, plus one addition: Sepia.
- **Dark Variations**: These are deep color washes of the theme colors.
- **Light Variations**: These are light color washes of the theme colors.
- **More Variations**: This opens a Theme Colors palette, from which you can select light and dark tints of the themes or standard (fixed) colors. You can also choose More Colors to open a Color dialog box for more fixed colors.

Setting a Transparent Color

Some clips enable you to redefine one of the colors as see-through, so that anything behind it shows through. This doesn't work on all clips because most clips already have a color defined as transparent: the background. This is why a clip art image appears to float directly on a colored background rather than being locked into a rectangle. However, for clips that do not have a transparent color already defined, you can define one.

CAUTION Setting a transparent color works best on clip art; in a photograph, an area that looks at first glance like a single color is often actually dozens of different shades of the same overall tint, and setting the transparent color sets only one of those many shades to be transparent.

To set a transparent color, open the Recolor menu, as in the preceding section (Figure 12.13). Then choose Set Transparent Color, and click a color in the image.

Deconstructing and Editing a Clip

Have you ever wished that you could open a clip art image in an image-editing program and make some small change to it? Well, you can. And what's more, you can do it without leaving PowerPoint.

Because clip art is composed of vector-graphic lines and fills, you can literally take it apart piece by piece. Not only can you apply certain colors (as in the preceding section), but you can also choose individual lines and shapes from it to recolor, move, and otherwise modify.

To deconstruct a piece of clip art, follow these steps:

1. Right-click the clip and choose Edit Picture. A message appears, telling you that it is an imported picture, and asking whether you want to convert it to a Microsoft Office drawing object.

CAUTION Ungrouping a recolored clip resets the color adjustments you have made.

2. Click Yes. Each individual shape and line in the clip is now a separate object that you can select individually.

To recolor an individual line or shape, follow these steps:

1. Select the line or shape. Selection handles appear around it.

2. On the Format tab, click Shape Fill and select a fill color.

3. Click Shape Outline and select an outline color.

To move the pieces of the clip around, follow these steps:

1. Right-click the clip and choose Group ➪ Ungroup. All of the individual shapes show their own separate selection handles, as shown in Figure 12.14.

NOTE In some cases you do not have to ungroup in order to move an individual piece; you can try moving a piece without performing step 1 and see if that works for you.

2. Click away from the selected shapes to deselect them all, and then click the individual shape that you want to move. Hold down the Ctrl key and click multiple shapes, if needed.

3. Drag the shape where you want it.

FIGURE 12.14

You can break apart a clip art image into separate shapes.

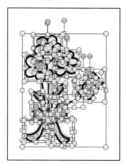

Summary

In this chapter, you learned how to insert and manage clip art and how to modify it in PowerPoint. You learned how to organize your clips in the Clip Organizer and how to find more clips online. You learned how to recolor a clip, and even how to break it down into individual pieces and modify each piece. In the next chapter, you learn how to work with photographic images, which present their own set of challenges in terms of file size, resolution, cropping, and more.

Chapter 13

Working with Photographic Images

Whether you're putting together a slide show to display your vacation photos or adding photos of industrial products to a business presentation, PowerPoint has the tools and capabilities you need. And with the new Picture Styles feature in PowerPoint 2007, it has never been easier to give those photos professional-looking frames, shadows, and other effects.

In this chapter you'll learn the ins and outs of using photographs in a PowerPoint presentation, including tips and tricks for preparing them beforehand, compressing them so they take up less disk space, and exporting pictures out of PowerPoint so you can save them separately.

Understanding Raster Graphics

There are two kinds of graphics in the computer world: *vector* and *raster*. As you learned earlier in the book, vector graphics (clip art, drawn lines and shapes, and so on) are created with mathematical formulas. Some of the advantages of vector graphics are their small file size and the fact that they can be resized without losing any quality. The main disadvantage of a vector graphic is that it doesn't look "real." Even when an expert artist draws a vector graphic, you can still tell that it's a drawing, not a photograph. For example, perhaps you've seen the game *The Sims*? Those characters and objects are 3-D vector graphics. They look pretty good but there's no way you would mistake them for real people and objects.

In this chapter, you'll be working with raster graphics. A raster graphic is made up of a very fine grid of individual colored *pixels* (dots). The grid is sometimes called a *bitmap*. Each pixel has a unique numeric value representing its color. Figure 13.1 shows a close-up of a raster image. You can create raster graphics from scratch with a "paint" program on a computer, but a more common way to acquire a raster graphic is by using a scanner or digital camera as an input device.

FIGURE 13.1

A raster graphic, normal size (right) and zoomed in to show individual pixels (left).

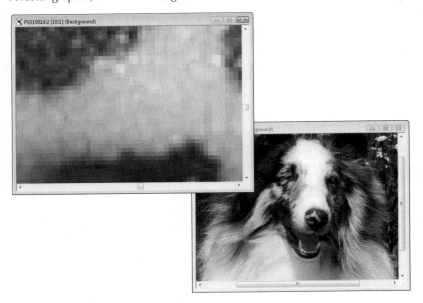

NOTE The term *bitmap* is sometimes used to refer generically to any raster graphic, but it is also a specific file format for raster graphics, with a BMP extension. This is the default format for the Paint program that comes with Windows XP and Windows XP desktop wallpaper.

Because there are so many individual pixels and each one must be represented numerically, raster graphics are much larger than vector graphics. They take longer to load into the PC's memory, take up more space when you store them as separate files on disk, and make your PowerPoint presentation file much larger. You can compress a raster graphic so that it takes up less space on disk, but the quality may suffer. Therefore, it's best to use vector graphics when you want simple lines, shapes, or cartoons and reserve raster graphics for situations where you need photographic quality.

The following sections explain some of the technical specifications behind raster graphics; you'll need this information to make the right decisions about the way you capture the images with your scanner or digital camera, and the way you use them in PowerPoint.

Resolution

The term *resolution* has two subtly different meanings. One is the size of an image, expressed in the number of pixels of width and height, such as 800x600. The other meaning is the number of pixels per inch when the image is printed, such as 100 dots per inch (dpi). The former meaning is used mostly when referring to images of fixed physical size, such as the display resolution of a monitor. In this book, the later meaning is mostly used.

If you know the resolution of the picture (that is, the number of pixels in it), and the resolution of the printer on which you will print it (for example, 300 dpi), you can figure out how large the picture will be in inches when you print it at its native size. Suppose you have a picture that is 900 pixels square, and you print it on a 300 dpi printer. This makes it 3 inches square on the printout.

Resolution on Preexisting Graphics Files

When you acquire an image file from an outside source, such as downloading it from a Web site or getting it from a CD of artwork, its resolution has already been determined. Whoever created the file originally made that decision. For example, if the image was originally scanned on a scanner, whoever scanned it chose the scan resolution — that is, the dpi setting. That determined how many individual pixels each inch of the original picture would be carved up into. At a 100 dpi scan, each inch of the picture is represented by 100 pixels vertically and horizontally. At 300 dpi, each inch of the picture is broken down into three times that many.

If you want to make a graphic take up less disk space, you can use an image-editing program to change the image size, and/or you can crop off one or more sides of the image.

CAUTION If you crop or decrease the size of an image in an image-editing program, save the changes under a different filename. Maintain the original image in case you ever need it for some other purpose. Decreasing the image resolution decreases its dpi setting, which decreases its quality. You might not notice any quality degradation on-screen, but you will probably notice a difference when you are printing the image at a large size. That's because the average monitor displays only 96 dpi, but the average printer prints at 600 dpi or higher.

PowerPoint slides do not usually need to be printed at a professional-quality resolution, so image quality on a PowerPoint printout is not usually an issue. However, if you use the picture for something else later, such as printing it as a full-page color image on photo paper, then a high dpi file can make a difference.

Resolution on Graphics You Scan Yourself

When you create an image file yourself by using a scanner, *you* choose the resolution, expressed in dpi, through the scanner software. For example, suppose you scan a 4-inch by 6-inch photo at 100 dpi. The scanner will break down each 1-inch section of the photo horizontally and vertically into 100 separate pieces and decide on a numeric value that best represents the color of each piece. The result is a total number of pixels of 4 x 100 x 6 x 100, or 240,000 pixels. Assuming each pixel requires 3 bytes of storage, the fill becomes approximately 720KB in size. The actual size varies slightly depending on the file format.

Now, suppose you scan the same photo at 200 dpi. The scanner breaks down each 1-inch section of the photo into 200 pieces, so that the result is 4 x 200 x 6 x 200, or 960,000 pixels. Assuming again that 1 pixel required 3 bytes for storage (24 bits), the file will be approximately 2.9MB in size. That's a big difference.

The higher the resolution in which you scan, the larger the file becomes, but the details of the scan also become finer. However, unless you are zooming in on the photo, you cannot tell a difference between 100 dpi and a higher resolution. That's because most computer monitors display at 96 dpi, so any resolution higher than that does not improve the output.

Let's look at an example. In Figure 13.2 you can see two copies of an image open in a graphics program. The same photo was scanned at 75 dpi (left) and 150 dpi (right). However, the difference between them is not significant when the two images are placed on a PowerPoint slide, as shown in Figure 13.3. The lower resolution image is at the top left, but there is no observable difference in the size at which they are being used.

FIGURE 13.2

At high magnification, the difference in dpi for a scan is apparent.

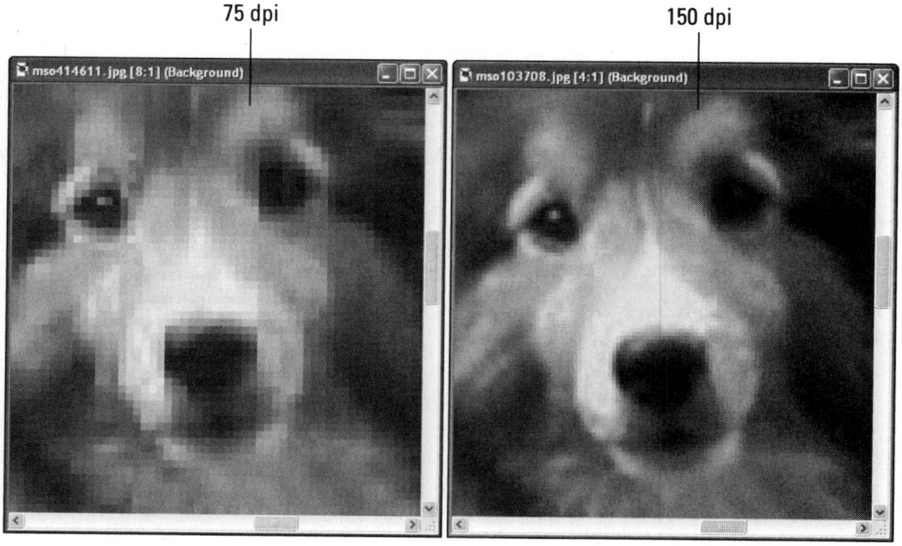

FIGURE 13.3

When the image is used at a normal size, there is virtually no difference between a high-dpi and low-dpi scan.

75 dpi

150 dpi

Resolution on Digital Camera Photos

Top-quality digital cameras today take very high resolution pictures, and are much higher than you will need for an on-screen PowerPoint presentation. At a typical size and magnification, a high-resolution graphic file is overkill; it wastes disk space needlessly. Therefore, you may want to adjust the camera's image size so that it takes lower-resolution pictures for your PowerPoint show.

If you think you might want to use those same pictures for some other purpose in the future, such as printing them in a magazine or newsletter, then go ahead and take them with the camera's highest setting, but you should compress them in PowerPoint or resize them in a third-party image editing program. See the section "Compressing Images" later in this chapter to learn how.

Color Depth

Color depth is the number of bits required to describe the color of a single pixel in the image. For example, in 1-bit color, a single binary digit represents each pixel. Each pixel is either black (1) or white (0). In 4-bit color, there are 16 possible colors because there are 16 combinations of 1s and 0s in a four-digit binary number. In 8-bit color there are 256 combinations.

Scanners and Color Depth

If you are shopping for a scanner, you will probably notice that they're advertised with higher numbers of bits than the graphics formats support. This is for error correction. If there are extra bits, it can throw out the bad bits to account for "noise" and still end up with a full set of good bits. Error correction in a scan is a rather complicated process, but fortunately your scanner driver software takes care of it for you.

For most file formats, the highest number of colors you can have in an image is 16.7 million colors, which is 24-bit color (also called *true color*). It uses 8 bits each for Red, Green, and Blue.

There is also 32-bit color, which has the same number of colors as 24-bit, but adds 8 more bits for an Alpha channel. The Alpha channel describes the amount of transparency for each pixel. This is not so much an issue for single-layer graphics, but in multi-layer graphics, such as the ones you can create in high-end graphics programs like Photoshop, the extent to which a lower layer shows through an upper one is important.

EXPERT TIP   For a great article on alpha channel usage in PowerPoint by Geetesh Bajaj, go to www.indezine.com/products/powerpoint/ppalpha.html.

A color depth of 48-bit is fairly new, and it's just like 24-bit color except it uses 16 rather than 8 bits to define each of the three channels: Red, Green, and Blue. It does not have an Alpha channel bit. Forty-eight-bit color depth is not really necessary, because the human eye cannot detect the small differences it introduces. Of the graphics formats that PowerPoint supports, only PNG and TIFF support 48-bit color depth.

Normally, you should not decrease the color depth of a photo to less than 24-bit unless there is a major issue with lack of disk space that you cannot resolve any other way. To decrease the color depth, you would need to open the graphic file in a third-party image-editing program, and use the command in that program for decreasing the number of colors. Before going through that, try compressing the images in the presentation (see the section "Compressing Images" later in the chapter) to see if that solves the problem.

File Format

Many scanners scan in JPEG format by default, but most also support TIF, and some also support other formats. Images you acquire from a digital camera are almost always JPEG. Images from other sources may be any of dozens of graphics formats, including PCX, BMP, GIF, or PNG.

Different graphic formats can vary tremendously in the size and quality of the image they produce. The main differentiators between formats are the color depth they support and the type of compression they use (which determines the file size).

Remember earlier how I explained that each pixel in a 24-bit image requires 3 bytes? (That's derived by dividing 24 by 8 because there are 8 bits in a byte.) Then you multiply that by the height, and then by the width, to determine the image size. Well, that formula was not completely accurate because it does not include compression. *Compression* is an algorithm (basically a math formula) that decreases the amount of space that the file takes up on the disk by storing the data about the pixels more compactly. A file format will have one of these three states in regard to compression:

- **No compression:** The image is not compressed.
- **Lossless compression:** The image is compressed, but the algorithm for doing so does not throw out any pixels so there is no loss of image quality when you resize the image.
- **Lossy compression:** The image is compressed by recording less data about the pixels, so that when you resize the image there may be a loss of image quality.

Table 13.1 provides a brief guide to some of the most common graphics formats. Generally speaking, for most on-screen presentations JPEG should be your preferred choice for graphics because it is compact and Web-accessible (although PNG is also a good choice and uses lossless compression).

TABLE 13.1

Popular Graphics Formats

Extension	Pronunciation	Compression	Notes
JPEG or JPG	"Jay-peg"	Yes	Stands for Joint Photographic Experts Group. Very small image size. Uses lossy compression. Common on the Web. Up to 24-bit.
GIF	"gif" or "jif"	Yes	Stands for Graphic Interchange Format. Limited to 8-bit (256 color). Uses proprietary compression algorithm. Allows animated graphics, which are useful on the web. Color depth limitation makes this format unsuitable for photos.
PNG	"ping"	Yes	Stands for Portable Network Graphic. An improvement on GIF. Up to 48-bit color depth. Lossless compression, but smaller file sizes than TIF. Public domain format.
BMP	"B-M-P" or "bump" or "bitmap"	No	Default image type for Windows XP. Up to 24-bit color. Used for some Windows wallpaper and other Windows graphics.
PCX	"P-C-X"	Yes	There are three versions: 0, 2, and 5. Use version 5 for 24-bit support. Originally introduced by a company called ZSoft; sometimes called ZSoft Paintbrush format.
TIF or TIFF	"tiff"	Optional	Stands for Tagged Image Format. Supported by most scanners and some digital cameras. Up to 48-bit color. Uses lossless compression. Large file size but high quality.

EXPERT TIP   If you are not sure what format you will eventually use for an image, scan it in TIF format and keep the TIF copy on your hard disk. You can always save a copy in JPEG or
other formats when you need them for specific projects. The TIF format's compression is lossless, so it
results in a high-quality image.

Importing Image Files into PowerPoint

Most of the choices you make regarding a raster image's resolution, color depth, and file type are
done outside of PowerPoint. Consequently, by the time you're ready to put them into PowerPoint,
the hard part is over.

Assuming you have already acquired the image, use the following steps to insert it into
PowerPoint.

1. Display the slide on which you want to place the image.

2. If the slide has a content placeholder for Insert Picture from File, as in Figure 13.4, click
   it. Otherwise, click Picture on the Insert tab. The Insert Picture dialog box opens.

FIGURE 13.4

You can insert a picture by using the Insert Picture from File content placeholder icon.

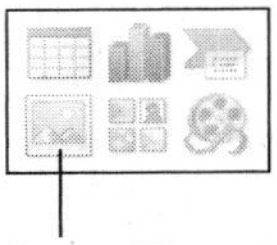

Insert Picture From File

3. Select the picture to import. See Figure 13.5. You can switch the view by using the View
   (or Views) button in the dialog box to see thumbnails or details if either is effective in
   helping you determine which file is which.

4. Click Insert. The picture is inserted.

FIGURE 13.5

Select the picture to be inserted.

EXPERT TIP If you have a lot of graphics in different formats, consider narrowing down the list that appears by selecting a specific file type from the file type list. By default it is set to All Pictures, as in Figure 13.5.

Linking to a Graphic File

If you have a sharp eye, you may have noticed that the Insert button in Figure 13.5 has a drop-down list associated with it. That list has these choices:

- **Insert:** The default, inserts the graphic but maintains no connection.

- **Link to File:** Creates an OLE link to the file, but does not maintain a local copy of it in PowerPoint.

- **Insert and Link:** Creates a link to the file, and also inserts a local copy of its current state, so if the linked copy is not available in the future, the local copy will still appear.

Use Link to File whenever you want to insert a pointer rather than the original. When the presentation opens, it pulls in the graphic from the disk. If the graphic is not available, it displays an empty frame with a red X in the corner in the graphic's place. Using Link to File keeps the size of the original PowerPoint file very small because it doesn't actually contain the graphics — only links to them. However, if you move or delete the graphic, PowerPoint won't be able to find it anymore.

The important thing to know about this link in the Link to File feature is that it is not the same thing as an OLE link. This is not a dynamic link that you can manage. It is a much simpler link and much less flexible. You can't change the file location to which it is linked, for example; if the location of the graphic changes, you must delete it from PowerPoint and reinsert it.

EXPERT TIP   If you are building a graphic-heavy presentation on an older computer, you might find that it takes a long time to move between slides and for each graphic to appear. You can take some of the hassle away by using Link to File instead of inserting the graphics. Then temporarily move the graphic files to a subfolder so PowerPoint can't find them. It displays the placeholders for the graphics on the appropriate slides, and the presentation file is much faster to page through and edit. Then when you are ready to finish up, close PowerPoint and move the graphics files back to their original locations so PowerPoint can find them again when you reopen the presentation file.

Acquiring Images from a Scanner

If you have a compatible scanner attached to your PC, you can scan a picture directly into the Clip Organizer (which you learned about in Chapter 12), and from there import it into PowerPoint. You can also use the scanner's interface from outside of PowerPoint (and outside of the Clip Organizer).

NOTE   Earlier versions of PowerPoint had direct access to the Scanner and Camera Wizard in Windows from the Insert menu, but PowerPoint 2007 does not have this. The only way to access the Scanner and Camera Wizard in Office 2007 applications is via the Clip Organizer.

To scan an image from the Clip Organizer, follow these steps:

1. On the Insert tab, click Clip Art. The Clip Art task pane opens.
2. Click Organize Clips. The Clip Organizer window opens.
3. Choose File ➪ Add Clips to Organizer ➪ From Scanner or Camera. The Insert Picture from Scanner or Camera dialog box opens.
4. Choose the scanner from the Device list, as shown in Figure 13.6.

FIGURE 13.6

Select the device and the basic properties.

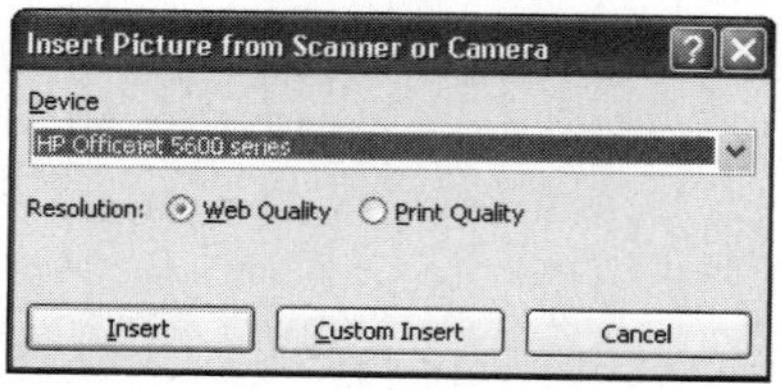

5. Choose a resolution: Web (low) or Print (high). Lower resolution means smaller file size and fewer pixels overall comprising the image. Low resolution is the best choice for on-screen presentations.

6. Click Insert to scan with the default settings, or click Custom Insert, make changes to the settings, and click Scan.

The Custom Insert option opens the full controls for the scanner. They vary a bit depending on the model; the box for an HP scanner is shown in Figure 13.7.

FIGURE 13.7

Custom insert options are available when scanning into the Clip Organizer.

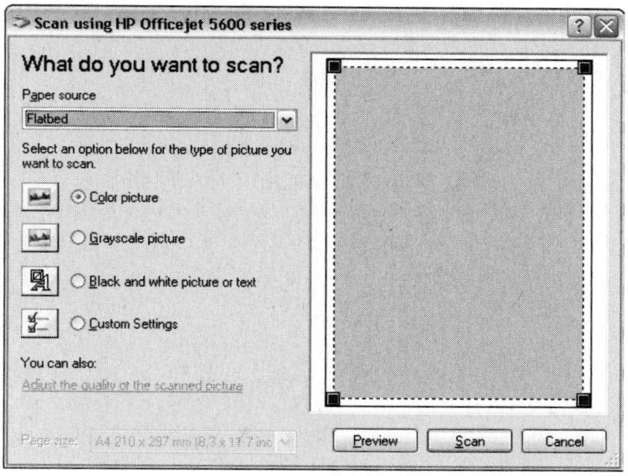

Here are some of the things you can do here:

- **Choose a scanning mode:** Color Picture, Grayscale Picture, or Black and White Picture or Text. This option determines the color depth. Color is full 24-bit color. Grayscale is 256 shades of gray (8-bit, single color). Black and white is single-bit scanning that produces an extremely small file similar to a fax.

- **Preview the scan:** Click the Preview button to do a test scan and then drag the black squares in the preview area to adjust what portion of the image is saved when you do the "real scan" by clicking the Scan button.

- **Choose a paper source:** If your scanner has a document feeder, you have that choice on the Paper Source drop-down list in addition to Flatbed (the default).

- **Adjust the resolution, brightness, and contrast:** Click the Adjust the Quality of the Scanned Picture hyperlink to open an Advanced Properties dialog box. From there you can drag the Brightness and Contrast sliders and choose a resolution setting (dots per inch). The default is 150 dpi.

EXPERT TIP   The default setting of 150 dpi is appropriate in most cases where you are using the image at approximately the same size as the original, but if you are concerned about file size, you can reduce this to 100 dpi without a noticeable loss of image quality on-screen. If you plan on using the image at a large size, like full screen, and the image was originally a very small hard copy, then scan at a higher resolution.

Acquiring Images from a Digital Camera

There are a lot of ways to transfer images from a digital camera in Windows XP or Windows Vista. You can connect most cameras to the PC via a USB port and treat them as a removable drive, from which you can drag and drop pictures into a folder on your hard disk. You can also remove the memory card from the camera and use a card reader, and in some cases you can even insert a memory card into a printer and print the images directly.

With all of these methods available, inserting directly from the camera into the Clip Organizer is probably not your first choice. However, if you want to try it, use the same method as with the scanner. Then just follow the prompts to select and insert the picture.

NOTE   When you hear digital cameras referred to in *megapixel* that means a million pixels in total — the height multiplied by the width. For example, a 1,152 by 864-pixel image is approximately 1 megapixel (995,328 pixels, to be exact). High-end cameras are in the 8-megapixel or more range these days, which is overkill for use in a PowerPoint show. Such cameras have settings you can change that control the image size, though, so you can reduce the image size on the camera itself.

Sizing and Cropping Photos

After placing a photo on a slide, you will probably need to adjust its size, and/or crop it, to make it fit in the allotted space the way you want it. The following sections explain these techniques.

Sizing a Photo

Sizing a photo is just like sizing any other object. Drag its selection handles. Drag a corner to maintain the aspect ratio, or drag a side to distort it. (Distorting a photo is seldom a good idea, though, unless you're after some weird funhouse effect.)

You can also specify an exact size for a photo the same as with drawn objects. Right-click the photo and choose Size and Position to set a size in the Size and Position dialog box (see Figure 13.8). Alternatively, you can display the Format tab, and then use the Height and Width boxes in the Size group.

Size a photo via either the dialog box or the Format tab.

The most straightforward way to specify the size is in inches in the Height and Width boxes, either in the dialog box or on the tab. These measurements correspond to the markers on the on-screen ruler in Normal view. The size of a slide varies depending on how you have it set up (by using the Page Setup tab), but an average slide size is 10 inches wide by 7.5 inches tall. You can also size the photo using the Scale controls in the Size and Position dialog box, in which you adjust the size based on a percentage of the original size.

NOTE   The Scale is based on the original size, not the current size. So, for example, if you set the Height and Width to 50%, close the dialog box, and then reopen it and set them each to 75%, the net result will be 75% of the original, not 75% of the 50%. You can override this by deselecting the Relative to Original Picture Size check box, however (see Figure 13-8).

If you are setting up a presentation for the primary purpose of showing full-screen graphics, you can use the Best Scale for Slide Show check box (see Figure 13.8). This enables you to choose a screen resolution, such as 640x480 or 800x600, and size the pictures so that they will show to the best advantage in that resolution. Choose the resolution that corresponds to the display setting on the PC on which you will show the presentation. To determine what the resolution is on the PC, right-click the Windows desktop, choose Properties, and then look up the resolution under Settings.

EXPERT TIP   When possible, develop your presentation at the same Windows screen resolution as the PC on which you present the show. Many digital projectors display at 1024 x 768.

Cropping a Photo

Cropping is for those times when you want only a part of the image. For example, you might have a great photo of a person or animal, but there is extraneous detail around it, as shown in Figure 13.9. You can crop away all but the important object in the image with a cropping tool.

FIGURE 13.9

This picture can benefit from cropping.

Crop button

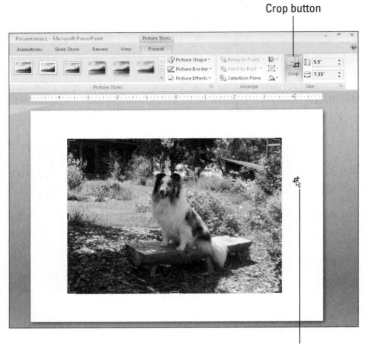

Mouse pointer

EXPERT TIP   Here's something important to know: Cropping and sizing a picture in PowerPoint does not reduce the overall size of the PowerPoint presentation file. When you insert a picture, PowerPoint stores the whole thing at its original size and continues to store it that way regardless of any manipulations you perform on it within PowerPoint. That's why it's recommended throughout this chapter that you do any editing of the photo in a third-party image program before you import it into PowerPoint. However, there's a work-around. If you use the Compress Pictures option (covered later in this chapter), it discards any cropped portions of the images. That means the file size decreases with the cropping, and that you can't reverse the cropping later.

You can crop two sides at once by cropping at the corner of the image, or crop each side individually by cropping at the sides. To crop an image, do the following:

1. Select the image, so the Picture Tools Format tab becomes available.

2. Click the Crop button on the Picture Tools Format tab. Your mouse pointer changes to a cropping tool and crop marks appear on the picture (see Figure 13.9).

3. Position the pointer over a side handle of the image frame, on a side where you want to cut some of the image off.

4. Drag the handle inward toward the center of the image until only the part of the image you want to keep is inside the thin line.

5. Repeat steps 3 and 4 for each side. Then click the Crop button again, or press Esc, to turn cropping off.

Figure 13.10 shows the result of cropping the image from Figure 13.9.

FIGURE 13.10

The picture has been improved by cropping and resizing it.

To undo a crop, reenter cropping mode by clicking the Crop button again, and then drag the side(s) back outward again. Or you can simply reset the photo, as described in the following section.

You can also crop "by the numbers" with the Crop settings in the Size and Position dialog box (see Figure 13.8).

CAUTION **You cannot uncrop after compressing the picture (assuming you use the default compression options that include deleting cropped areas of pictures). By default, saving compresses and makes crops permanent, so be sure to undo any unwanted cropping before you save.**

Resetting a Photo

Once the picture is in PowerPoint, any manipulations you do to it are strictly on the surface. It changes how the picture appears on the slide, but it doesn't change how the picture is stored in

PowerPoint. Consequently you can reset the picture back to its original settings at any time (provided you have not compressed the picture). This resetting also clears any changes you make to the image's size, contrast, and brightness (which are discussed in the next section).

Resetting a photo is different depending on what aspects of it you want to reset:

■ If you want to reset its cropping and sizing, on the Picture Tools Format tab, click the dialog box launcher in the Size group and click the Reset button in the Size and Position dialog box.

■ If you want to reset its formatting, on the Picture Tools Format tab, click the Reset Picture button in the Adjust group.

Adjusting Photo Contrast and Brightness

PowerPoint is not a very sophisticated photo editor, but it can do some very elementary things like increase or decrease a picture's brightness and contrast. The easiest way to access those controls is through the Brightness and Contrast drop-down lists on the Format tab. For example, Figure 13.11 shows the Brightness settings. To choose a value other than the ones listed, click Picture Corrections Options to open the Format Picture dialog box, also shown in Figure 13.11. From there you can enter an exact percentage or drag the Brightness and/or Contrast sliders.

FIGURE 13.11

Adjust the brightness or contrast for the selected picture.

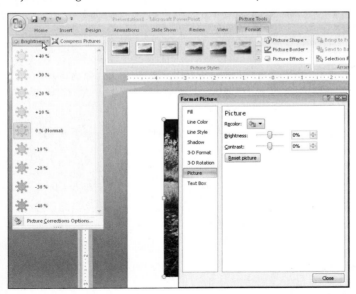

Setting a Transparent Color

The Transparent Color feature can be really useful, but not all pictures support it. It's available for bitmap images (including scans) and for some but not all clip art. For example, suppose you have a scanned photo of your CEO and you want to make the background transparent so it looks like his head is sitting right on the slide. This feature could help you out with that.

Why some clip art images but not others? An image can have only one color set to be transparent, and some clip art images already have their backgrounds set to be transparent. That's why those clips won't work with the Set Transparent Color feature. To check it out, first insert the picture on a slide. Then select the picture, and open the Recolor menu. If the Set Transparent Color option is available, you can set the transparent color by clicking that command, and then clicking the color that you want to make transparent on the picture. If the results are not what you expected, press Ctrl+Z or click the Undo button on the Quick Access Toolbar to choose a different color to be transparent.

If you set a color to transparent in PowerPoint, every instance of that color in that picture will become transparent. So if you have a picture of a man with a white shirt on a white background and choose to make white the transparent color (because you want to drop out the background), the man's shirt becomes transparent, too. Conversely, what looks like one color in a photo is not usually just one color. Think of a blue sky, for example. It probably consists of at least two dozen different shades of blue. If you try to make one of those shades of blue transparent using PowerPoint's transparency tool, you'll probably just end up with splotches of transparent areas.

So what's the solution? The best way to go is to use Alpha channels in a third-party image-editing program to create true transparency and save the image as TIF or PNG. (JPEG format does not support Alpha channels.)

Recoloring a Picture

Recoloring a picture is just like recoloring clip art, which is covered in Chapter 12. Here's a review.

Recoloring options are available from the Recolor button's drop-down list on the Format tab. There are four basic image modes (besides the default No Recolor), shown in the Color Modes section of Figure 13.12.

- **Grayscale:** Converts the image to a 256-color grayscale.
- **Sepia:** Same as grayscale except it's browns, not blacks.
- **Washout:** Sets the Brightness to 70% increase and the Contrast to 70% decrease. You can manually adjust those percentages from the Format Picture dialog box.
- **Black and White:** Converts all colors to either black or white, whichever they are closest to.

FIGURE 13.12

Set an image mode from the Recolor button's menu.

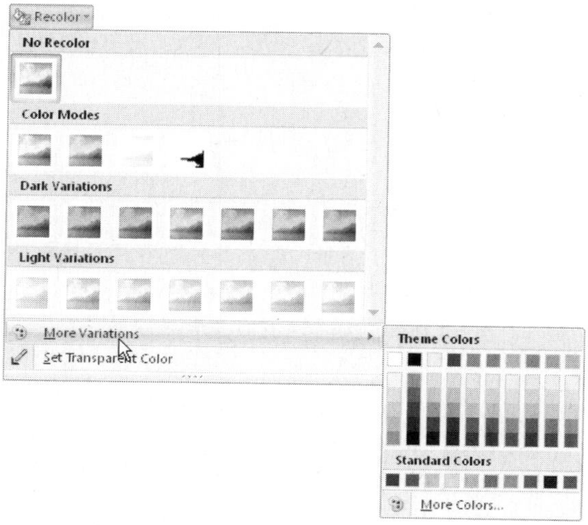

In addition to those basic modes, the following options that are new in PowerPoint 2007 apply a solid-color wash to the picture (such as Grayscale or Sepia but with the chosen color):

- **Dark Variations:** These are deep color washes of the theme colors.

- **Light Variations:** These are light color washes of the theme colors.

- **More Variations:** This opens a Theme Colors palette, from which you can select light and dark tints of the themes or standard (fixed) colors. You can also choose More Colors to open a full Color dialog box for more fixed colors.

Compressing Images

Having an image that is too large (that is, too high a dpi) is not a problem quality-wise. You can resize it in PowerPoint to make it as small as you like; just drag its selection handles. There will be no loss of quality as it gets smaller. However, as mentioned earlier in the chapter, having a picture that is much larger than necessary can increase the overall size of the PowerPoint file, which can become problematic if you plan to distribute the presentation on floppy disk or over the Internet.

To avoid problems with overly large graphic files, you can compress the images to reduce their resolution and remove any cropped portions. You can do this from within PowerPoint or with a third-party utility.

Reducing Resolution and Compressing Images in PowerPoint

PowerPoint offers an image compression utility that compresses all of the pictures in the presentation in a single step and reduces their resolution to the amount needed for the type of output you specify (e-mail, Screen, or Print). To reduce resolution and compress images, do the following:

1. Click a picture, so that the Format tab appears.

2. Click the Compress Pictures button. The Compress Pictures dialog box appears, as shown in Figure 13.13.

FIGURE 13.13

Click OK to compress with the default settings or click Options to fine-tune.

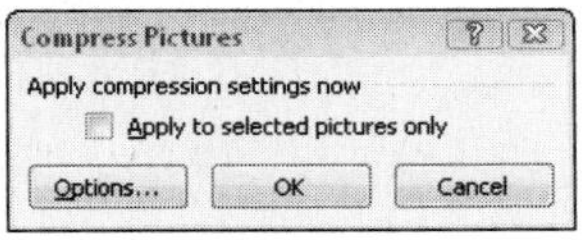

3. (Optional) If you do not want to compress all of the pictures, mark the Apply to Selected Pictures Only check box.

4. (Optional) Click the Options button to display the Compression Settings dialog box, as shown in Figure 13.14, and then change any of these options and click OK.

   ■ **Automatically Perform Basic Compression on Save:** This automatically compresses any images in your file when you save the file.

   ■ **Delete Cropped Areas of Pictures:** This makes any cropping you've done permanent.

   ■ **Target Output:** Choose a resolution to which you want to reduce the picture(s): Print, Screen, or E-mail.

5. Click OK to perform the compression.

FIGURE 13.14

Adjust compression settings here.

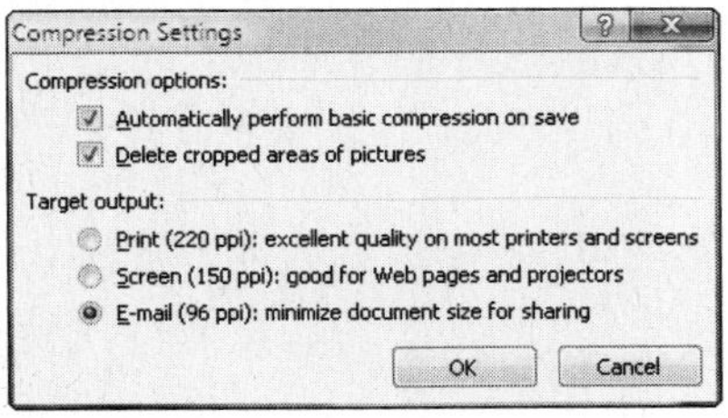

Reducing Resolution with a Third-Party Utility

Working with resolution reduction from an image-editing program is somewhat of a trial-and-error process, and you must do each image separately.

You can approximate the correct resolution by simply "doing the math." For example, suppose you have a 10" x 7.5" slide. Your desktop display is set to 800 x 600. So your image needs to be 800 pixels wide to fill the slide. Your image is a 5" x 3" image, so if you set it to 200 dpi, that gives you 1,000 pixels, which is a little larger than you need but in the ballpark.

Exporting a Photo from PowerPoint to a Separate File

What goes in must come out, right? Suppose you have a picture that exists only in PowerPoint, for whatever reason. Perhaps it was scanned directly into PowerPoint in an earlier version, for example, and you no longer have access to the original file.

There are two ways to get a graphic out of PowerPoint and make it a separate file again: You can use the Save As Picture feature in PowerPoint, or you can simply use the Windows Clipboard to copy and paste a graphic into an image-editing program.

- **Exporting a Graphic with Save As Picture**:

  To save a picture separately from PowerPoint, do the following:

  1. Right-click the picture in PowerPoint and choose Save as Picture.

  2. In the Save as Picture dialog box, display the location where you want to save the file.

  3. Open the Save As Type list and choose the graphic format you want. You can choose TIF, JPEG, or a variety of others. See the discussion of file formats earlier in this chapter for guidance.

  4. Enter a name in the File Name box.

  5. Click Save.

- **Exporting a Graphic with the Clipboard:** Copy-and-paste is a fast and simple way of transferring a graphic from PowerPoint into an image-editing program, and from there you can save it in any supported format. Select a graphic in PowerPoint, copy it (Ctrl+C), open the graphics program, and paste it (Ctrl+V).

- **Exporting Entire PowerPoint Slides as Graphics:** You can save entire slides — or all slides in the whole presentation — as images by simply choosing a graphic file format when doing an Office ⇨ Save As. If you save the whole presentation as graphics, the files are placed in a folder.

EXPERT TIP   You could also save the presentation in HTML format. This will generate an HTML file and a folder full of support files, and each graphic will be in there as a separate file.

Picture Shapes, Styles, and Effects

By default, a picture appears in a rectangular frame. You can place a picture in any shape you like, though, to create special effects. (This is especially useful in a photo album, covered later in this chapter.)

To place a picture in a shape, follow these steps:

1. Select the picture. The Picture Tools Format tab appears.
2. Open the Picture Shape button's menu and click the desired shape. See Figure 13.15.

FIGURE 13.15

Choose a shape in which the selected picture should appear.

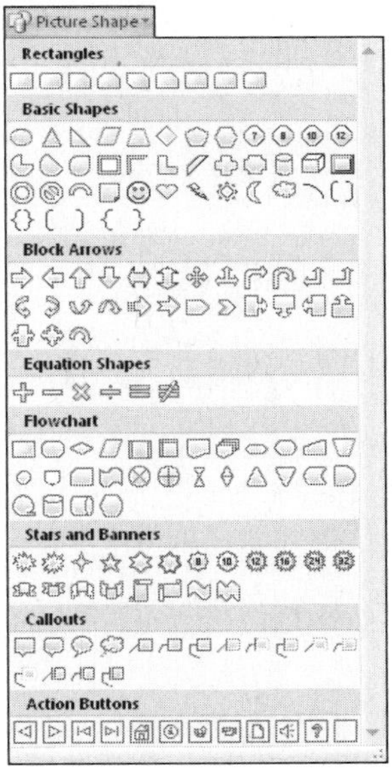

Picture styles are new in PowerPoint 2007. They consist of formatting presets you can quickly apply to pictures such as shadows, reflections, borders, and 3-D effects. Most of these are similar to the effects you learned how to apply to shapes in Chapter 10.

To apply a picture style, select one from the Picture Styles group on the Picture Tools Format tab. Figure 13.16 shows the Picture Styles gallery open.

FIGURE 13.16

Select a picture style from the Picture Styles gallery.

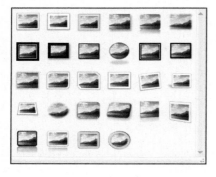

CROSS-REF The Picture Border button works just like the Object Border controls. To apply an object border or to use the Picture Effects button to apply object effects, see Chapter 10 for details.

Creating a Photo Album Layout

Most presentations in PowerPoint are text-based, with accompanying photographs. The default Blank Presentation template is biased in favor of text. Graphics, as you have seen in this chapter, require some extra effort.

The *Photo Albums* feature in PowerPoint creates a new presentation that is specifically designed as a carrier of pictures. It is useful when you need to create a presentation that is very heavy on graphics, with little or no text except picture captions.

Creating a New Photo Album

When you create a new photo album, it starts a new presentation for you. Any other presentations that you may have open are not disturbed, and you can switch back to them at any time with the View tab. The new presentation has a title slide, as well as slides for the photos you place in the album.

To start a new photo album, follow these steps:

1. On the Insert tab, click Photo Album. The Photo Album dialog box opens.

2. To add a photo from a file, click the File/Disk button. The Insert New Pictures dialog box opens.

3. Select one or more pictures, and then click Insert. (To select multiple pictures, hold down Ctrl or Shift as you click on the ones you want.) The photos appear in the Photo Album dialog box as shown in Figure 13.17.

FIGURE 13.17

Specify graphics to appear in the photo album, a page layout, and a style of photo frame.

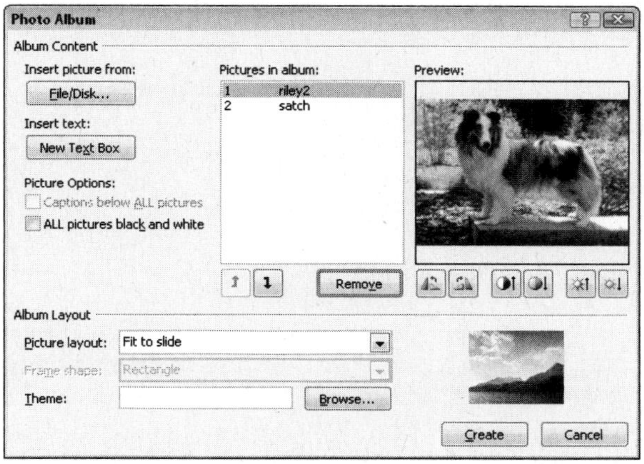

4. Repeat steps 2 and 3 as needed to insert all the photos from disk that you want.

5. For each image on the Pictures in Album list, select the picture and then apply any correction needed with the buttons beneath the Preview pane. You can rotate right or left, increase or decrease the contrast, and increase or decrease the brightness.

6. Use the arrows to move an image up or down in the order.

7. In the Album Layout section, open the Picture Layout box and choose the layout for the presentation slides. For example, in Figure 13.17, 1 Picture has been chosen.

8. If available, choose a frame shape from the Frame Shape list. Some choices from step 7 do not permit a frame shape to be chosen.

EXPERT TIP You can create themes specifically for photo albums, and then use them here by clicking the Browse button to browse for a theme. You might also want to experiment with the photo album themes in the dialog box when you create the photo album initially.

9. (Optional) To add caption boxes for each picture, mark the Captions Below ALL Pictures check box.

10. (Optional) To show the pictures in black and white, mark the ALL Pictures Black and White check box.

11. Click Create. PowerPoint creates the new presentation containing the photos and the layout you specified.

12. Save the photo album (Office ⇨ Save) as a presentation. Or, to save it in Web format, use Office ⇨ Save as ⇨ Other Formats and then choose Web Page as the file type.

Modifying a Photo Album

You can reopen the dialog box from Figure 13.15 by clicking the down arrow beneath the Photo Album button on the Insert tab and choosing Edit Photo Album.

You can also modify the slides in the presentation individually. These are just regular, editable slides, and you can add anything to them that you like, including text boxes, clip art, and so on. Think of it as an on-screen scrapbook! And new in PowerPoint 2007, you can also crop the photos inserted via the photo album as well.

Summary

In this chapter, you learned about the technical specs for graphics that determine their file size, quality, and flexibility, and you learned how to insert them into your presentations. You learned how to format a photo, and how to color, crop, and manipulate photos to create special effects.

In the next chapter, you'll learn how to work with charts. The charting tool in PowerPoint 2007 is much improved from earlier PowerPoint versions, and you'll find out how to take advantage of its new graphics-like capabilities for structuring and formatting numeric data in chart format.

Chapter 14

Working with Charts

Many times when you include a chart in PowerPoint, this chart already exists in some other application. For example, you might have an Excel workbook that contains some charts that you want to use in PowerPoint. If this is the case, you can simply copy-and-paste them into PowerPoint, or link or embed them, as you will learn in Chapter 15.

However, when you need to create a quick chart that has no external source, PowerPoint's charting tool is perfect for this purpose. The new PowerPoint 2007 charting interface is based upon the one in Excel, and so you don't have to leave PowerPoint to create, modify, and format professional-looking charts.

NOTE What's the difference between a chart and a graph? Some purists will tell you that a chart is either a table or a pie chart, whereas a graph is a chart that plots data points on two axes, such as a bar chart. However, Microsoft does not make this distinction, and neither do I in this book. I use the term "chart" in this book for either kind.

Understanding Charts

PowerPoint 2007's charting feature is based upon the same Escher 2.0 graphics engine as is used for drawn objects. Consequently, most of what you have learned about formatting objects in earlier chapters (especially Chapter 10) also applies to charts. For example, you can apply shape styles to the individual elements of a chart, and apply WordArt styles to chart text. However, there are also many chart-specific formatting and layout options, as you will see throughout this chapter.

Parts of a Chart

The sample chart shown in Figure 14.1 contains these elements:

- **Data series:** Each different bar color represents a different series: Q1, Q2, and Q3.
- **Legend:** Colored squares in the Legend box describe the correlation of each color to a data series.
- **Categories:** The North, South, East, and West labels along the bottom of the chart are the categories.
- **Category axis:** The horizontal line running across the bottom of the chart is the category axis, also called the horizontal axis.
- **Value axis:** The vertical line running up the left side of the chart, with the numbers on it, is the value axis, also called the vertical axis.
- **Data points:** Each individual bar is a data point. The numeric value for that data point corresponds to the height of the bar, measured against the value axis.
- **Walls:** The walls are the areas behind the data points. On a 3D chart, as shown in Figure 14.1, there are both back and side walls. On a 2D chart, there is only a back wall.
- **Floor:** The floor is the area on which the data points sit. A floor appears only in a 3D chart.

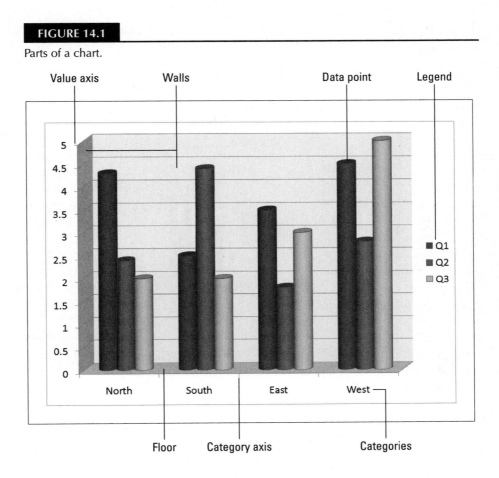

FIGURE 14.1

Parts of a chart.

PowerPoint 2007 versus Legacy Charts

When you are working with a chart in PowerPoint 2007 format, you have access to three Chart Tools tabs — Design, Layout, and Format — and also to a separate Excel window for entering and editing your data. Because the PowerPoint 2007 charting engine uses Excel as its basis, there is no longer a big advantage to creating charts in Excel and then copying them over to PowerPoint. Figure 14.2 shows the PowerPoint 2007 charting interface, along with the Layout tab.

FIGURE 14.2

The PowerPoint 2007 charting interface.

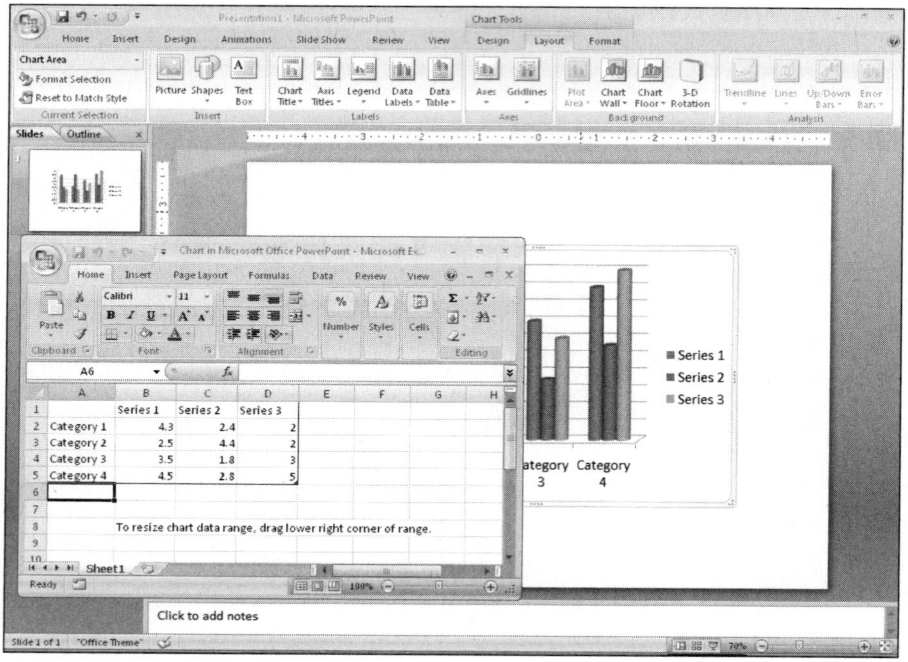

If you later save the file as a PowerPoint 97-2003 presentation, it does not take away your ability to access the PowerPoint 2007 charting interface when working in PowerPoint 2007. The chart is still saved as a PowerPoint 2007 object in the 2003 file, but it also contains a 2003 version of itself, for backward compatibility. When you open the presentation in PowerPoint 2003, it initially looks like a PowerPoint 2007 style chart, but if you double-click it to edit it (or enter editing mode for it in some other way), it switches to a 97-to-2003-style chart and loses its 2007-style appearance.

If you want to make sure that the chart appears exactly as you created it in PowerPoint 2003, even if it is edited there, then you should insert the chart initially using Microsoft Graph, rather than the PowerPoint 2007 charting tools. To do this, insert a Microsoft Graph object by following these steps:

1. On the Insert tab, click Object. The Object dialog box opens.

2. Click Create New.

3. On the Object Type list, click Microsoft Graph Chart.

4. Click OK. The Microsoft Graph window opens within PowerPoint, complete with a 2003-style menu bar from which you can access all of the same controls that were available in PowerPoint 2003's charting interface. The Microsoft Graph window is shown in Figure 14.3.

FIGURE 14.3

Microsoft Graph from within PowerPoint 2007.

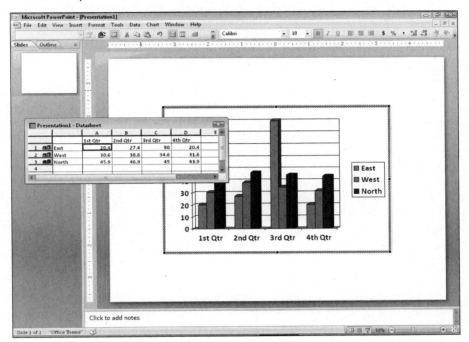

EXPERT TIP When you double-click to edit a Microsoft Graph chart within a PowerPoint 2007 presentation file, a message appears asking whether you want to Convert, Convert All, or Edit Existing. If you choose to convert (this chart or all charts) to 2007 format, you can use the new charting tools. If you choose Edit Exiting, MS Graph opens.

Starting a New Chart

The main difficulty with creating a chart in a non-spreadsheet application such as PowerPoint is that there is no data table from which to pull the numbers. Therefore, PowerPoint creates charts using data that you have entered in an Excel window. By default, it contains sample data, which you can replace with your own data.

You can place a new chart on a slide in two ways: you can either use a chart placeholder from a layout, or you can place one manually.

If you are using a placeholder, click the Insert Chart icon. If you are placing a chart manually, follow these steps:

1. On the Insert tab, click Chart. The Insert Chart dialog box opens, as shown in Figure 14.4.

Select the desired chart type.

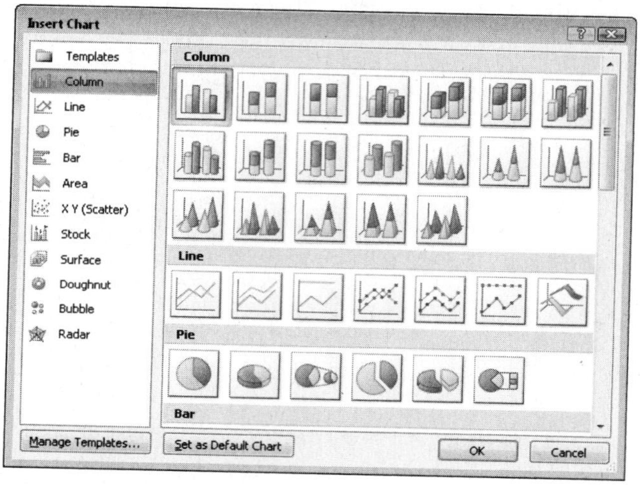

2. Click the desired chart type. See Table 14.1 for an explanation of the chart types. Figures 14.5 and 14.6 show examples of some of the chart types.
3. Click OK. The chart appears on the slide, and an Excel datasheet opens with sample data.
4. Modify the sample data as needed. To change the range of cells that appear in the chart, see the section "Redefining the Data Range," later in this chapter. If you want, you can then close the Excel window to move it out of the way.

NOTE   After you have closed the Excel window, you can open it again by clicking Edit Data on the Chart Tools Design tab.

FIGURE 14.5

Examples of chart types, from top left, clockwise: column, line, bar, and pie.

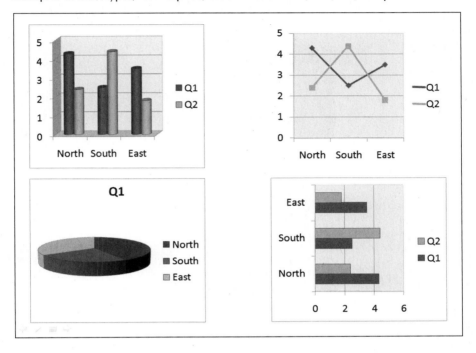

FIGURE 14.6

Examples of chart types, from top left, clockwise: area, scatter, donut, and surface.

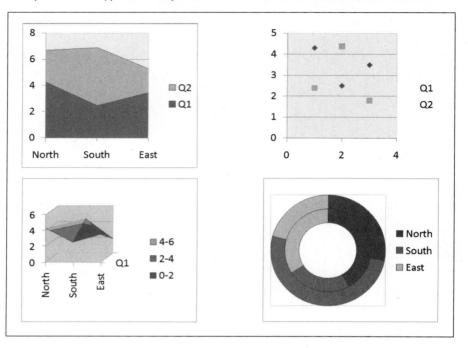

TABLE 14.1

Chart Types in PowerPoint 2007's Charting Tool

Type	Description
Column	Vertical bars, optionally with multiple data series. Bars can be clustered, stacked, or based on a percentage, and either 2-D or 3-D.
Line	Shows values as points, and connects the points with a line. Different series use different colors and/or line styles.
Pie	A circle broken into wedges to show how parts contribute to a whole. This de-emphasizes the actual numeric values. In most cases, this type is a single-series only.
Bar	Just like a column chart, but horizontal.
Area	Just like a column chart, but with the spaces filled in between the bars.

Type	Description
XY (Scatter)	Shows values as points on both axes, but does not connect them with a line. However, you can add trend lines.
Stock	A special type of chart that is used to show stock prices.
Surface	A 3-D sheet that is used to illustrate the highest and lowest points of the data set.
Doughnut	Similar to a pie chart, but with multiple concentric rings, so that multiple series can be illustrated.
Bubble	Similar to a scatter chart, but instead of fixed-size data points, bubbles of varying sizes are used to represent a third data variable.
Radar	Shows changes of data frequency in relation to a center point.

NOTE At any point, you can return to your PowerPoint presentation by clicking anywhere outside of the chart on the slide. To edit the chart again, you can click the chart to redisplay the chart-specific tabs.

EXPERT TIP If you delete a column or row by selecting individual cells and pressing Delete to clear them, the empty space that these cells occupied remains in the chart. To completely remove a row or column from the data range, select the row or column by clicking its header (letter for column; number for row) and click Delete on the Home tab in Excel.

Working with Chart Data

After you create a chart, you might want to change the data range on which it is based, or how this data is plotted. The following sections explain how you can do this.

Plotting by Rows versus by Columns

By default, the columns of the datasheet form the data series. However, if you want, you can switch the data around so that the rows form the series. Figures 14.7 and 14.8 show the same chart plotted both ways so that you can see the difference.

NOTE What does the term *data series* mean? Take a look at Figures 14.7 and 14.8. Notice that there is a legend next to each chart that shows what each color (or shade of gray) represents. Each of these colors, and the label associated with it, is a series. The other variable (the one that is not the series) is plotted on the chart's horizontal axis.

FIGURE 14.7

A chart with the columns representing the series.

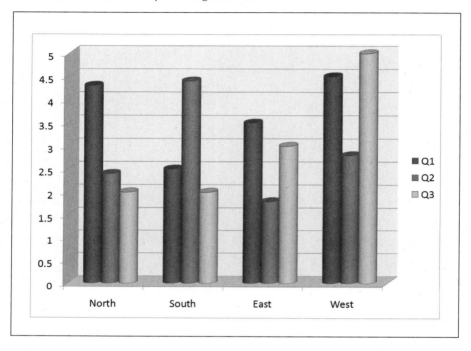

To switch back and forth between plotting by rows and by columns, click the Switch Row/Column button on the Chart Tools Design tab.

EXPERT TIP   A chart can carry a very different message when you arrange it by rows versus by columns. For example, in Figure 14.7, the chart compares the quarters. The message here is about improvement — or lack thereof — over time. Contrast this to Figure 14.8, where the series are the regions. Here, you can compare one region to another. The overriding message here is about competition — which division performed the best in each quarter? It's easy to see how the same data can convey very different messages; make sure that you pick the arrangement that tells the story that you want to tell in your presentation.

FIGURE 14.8

A chart with the rows representing the series.

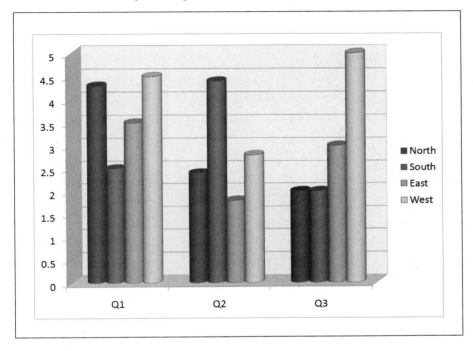

Redefining the Data Range

After you have created your chart, you may decide that you need to use more or less data. Perhaps you want to exclude a month or quarter of data, or to add another region or salesperson. To add or remove a data series, you can simply edit the datasheet. To do so, follow these steps:

1. On the Chart Tools Design tab, click Edit Data. The Excel datasheet appears. A blue outline appears around the range that is to be plotted.

2. (Optional) To change the data range to be plotted, drag the bottom-right corner of the blue outline. For example, in Figure 14.9, the West division is being excluded.

   You can also enlarge the data range by expanding the blue outline. For example, you could enter another series in column E in Figure 14.9 and then extend the outline to encompass column E.

FIGURE 14.9

You can redefine the range for the chart by dragging the blue outline on the datasheet.

Drag the corner of the blue outline to change your range.

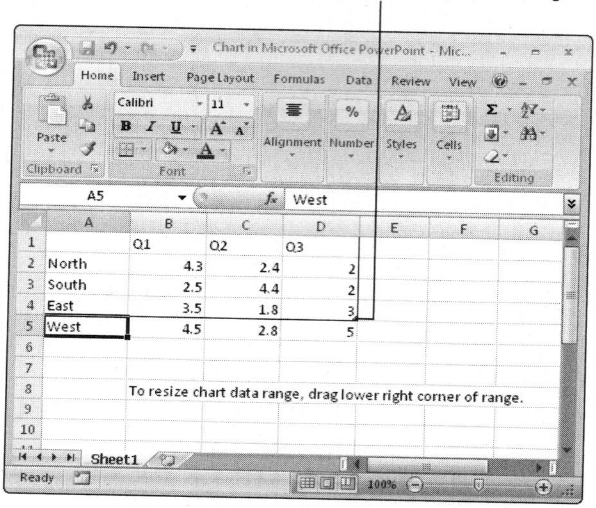

The preceding steps work well if the range that you want to include is contiguous, but what if you wanted to exclude a row or column that is in the middle of the range? To define the range more precisely, follow these steps:

1. On the Chart Tools Design tab, click Select Data. The Select Data Source dialog box opens, along with the Excel datasheet, as shown in Figure 14.10.

2. Do any of the following:

   ▪ To remove a series, select it from the Legend Entries (Series) list and click Remove.

   ▪ To add a series, click Add, and then drag across the range on the datasheet to enter it into the Edit Series dialog box; then click OK to accept it.

   ▪ To edit a series, select it in the Legend Entries (Series) list and click Edit. Then drag across the range or make a change in the Edit Series dialog box, and click OK.

FIGURE 14.10

To fine-tune the data ranges, you can use the Select Data Source dialog box.

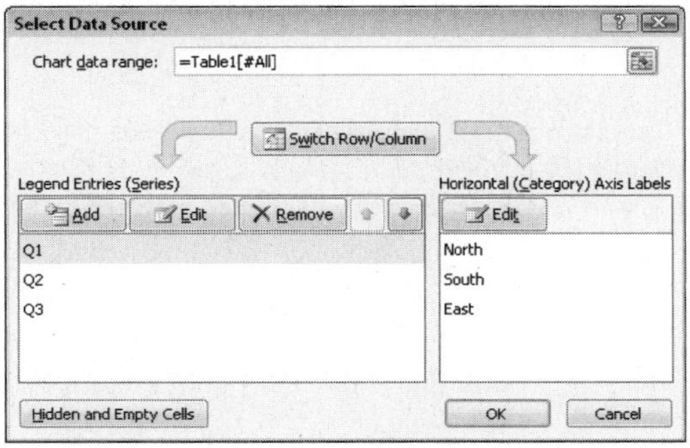

3. (Optional) To redefine the range from which to pull the horizontal axis labels, click the Edit button in the Horizontal (Category) Axis Labels section. A dotted outline appears around the current range; drag to redefine that range and click OK.

4. (Optional) To redefine how empty or hidden cells should be treated, click the Hidden and Empty Cells button. In the Hidden and Empty Cell Settings dialog box that appears, choose whether to show data in hidden rows and columns, and whether to define empty cells as gaps in the chart or as zero values. Then click OK. The Hidden and Empty Cells Settings dialog box is shown in Figure 14.11.

FIGURE 14.11

Specify what should happen when the data range contains blank or hidden cells.

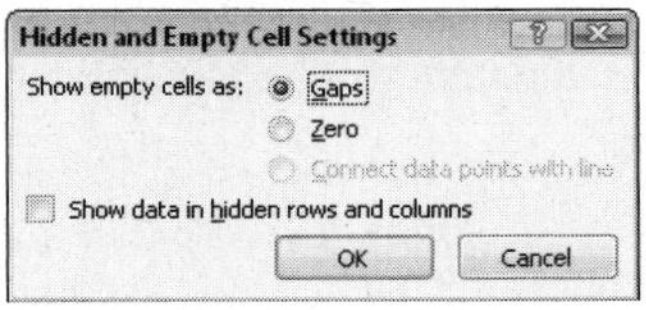

5. When you are finished editing the settings for the data ranges, click OK to close the Select Data Source dialog box.

6. (Optional) Close the Excel datasheet window, or leave it open for later reference.

Chart Types and Chart Layout Presets

The default chart is a column chart. However, there are a lot of alternative chart types to choose from. Not all of them will be appropriate for your data, of course, but you may be surprised at the different spin on the message that a different chart type presents.

> **CAUTION** Many chart types come in both 2-D and 3-D models, and you can choose which chart type looks most appropriate for your presentation. However, try to be consistent. For example, it looks nicer to stay with all 2-D or all 3-D charts rather than mixing the types in a presentation.

You can revisit your choice of chart type at any time by following these steps:

1. Select the chart, if needed, so that the Chart Tools Design tab becomes available.

2. On the Design tab, click Change Chart Type.

3. Select the desired type, just as you did when you originally created the chart. Figure 14.4 shows the chart types.

4. Click OK.

This is the basic procedure for the overall chart type selection, but there are also many options for fine-tuning the layout. The following sections explain these options.

> **EXPERT TIP** To change the default chart type, after selecting a chart from the Change Chart Type dialog box, click the Set as Default Chart button.

PowerPoint provides a limited number of preset chart layouts for each chart type. You can choose these presets from the Chart Layouts group in the Chart Tools Design tab. They are good starting points for creating your own layouts, which you will learn about in this chapter.

To choose a layout, click the down arrow in the Chart Layouts group and select one from the gallery, as shown in Figure 14.12. Although you cannot add your own layouts to these presets, you can create chart templates, which are basically the same thing with additional formatting settings. This chapter also covers chart template creation.

FIGURE 14.12

You can choose one of the preset layouts that fits your needs.

Working with Labels

On the Chart Tools Layout tab, the Labels group provides buttons for controlling which labels appear on the chart. Figure 14.13 points out the various labels that you can use.

FIGURE 14.13

Labels help to make it clear to the audience what the chart represents.

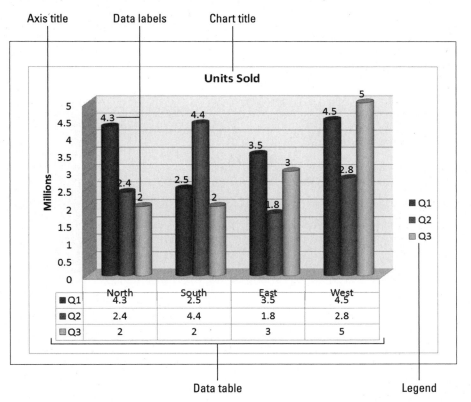

Each of these label types has a button on the Layout tab that opens a drop-down list that contains some presets. The drop-down list also contains a "More" command for opening a dialog box that contains additional options. For example, the drop-down list for the Chart Title button contains a "More Title Options" command, as shown in Figure 14.14.

Each type of label has its own button that displays a drop-down list.

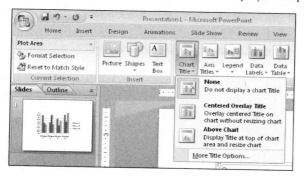

EXPERT TIP New in PowerPoint 2007, you can add data labels by right-clicking a series and choosing Add Data Labels. You can also format label text from the mini bar, which may be easier than using the Home tab's controls.

You can format the label text, just as you can format any other text. To do this, select the text and then use the Font group on the Home tab. This allows you to choose a font, size, color, alignment, and so on.

You can also format the label box by right-clicking it and choosing Format *name*, where *name* is the type of label that the box contains. In some cases, the dialog box that appears contains only standard formatting controls that you would find for any object, such as Fill, Border Color, Border Styles, Shadow, 3-D Format, and Alignment. These controls should already be very familiar to you from Chapter 9. In other cases, in addition to the standard formatting types, there is also a unique section that contains extra options that are specific to the content type. For example, for the Legend, there is a Legend Options section in which you can set the position of a legend.

The following sections look at each of the label types more closely. These sections will not dwell on the formatting that you can apply to them (fonts, sizes, borders, fills, and so on) because this formatting is the same for all of them, as it is with any other object. Instead, they concentrate on the options that make each label different.

Working with Chart Titles

A chart title is text that typically appears above the chart — and sometimes overlapping it — that indicates what the chart represents. Although you would usually want either a chart title *or* a slide title, but not both, this could vary if you have multiple charts or different content on the same slide.

You can select a basic chart title, either above the chart or overlapping it, from the Chart Title drop-down list, as shown in Figure 14.14. You can also drag the chart title around after placing it. For more options, you can choose More Title Options to open the Format Chart Title dialog box.

However, in this dialog box there is nothing that specifically relates to chart titles; the available options are for formatting (Fill, Border Color, and so on), as for any text box.

Working with Axis Titles

An axis title is text that defines the category or the unit of measurement on an axis. For example, in Figure 14.13, the vertical axis title is Millions.

Axis titles are defined separately for the vertical and the horizontal axes. Click the Axis Titles button on the Layout tab, and then select either Primary Horizontal Axis Title or Primary Vertical Axis Title to display a submenu that is specific to that axis. When you turn on an axis title, a text box appears containing default placeholder text, "Axis Title." Click in this text box and type your own label to replace it, as shown in Figure 14.15. If you've plotted any data on a secondary axis, you'll see Secondary Horizontal and Secondary Vertical Axis Title options as well.

EXPERT TIP You can easily select all of the placeholder text by clicking in the text box and pressing Ctrl+A.

FIGURE 14.15

An axis title describes what is being measured on the axis; you can edit the placeholder text in the title.

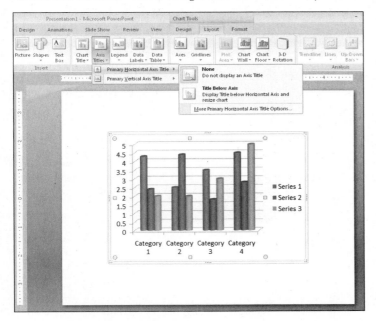

For the horizontal axis title, the options are simple: either None or Title Below Axis, as shown in Figure 14.15. You can choose More Primary Horizontal Axis Title Options, but again, as with the regular title options, there are no unique settings in the dialog box—just general formatting controls.

For the vertical axis title, you can choose from among the following options, as shown in Figure 14.16.

- **Rotated Title:** The title appears vertically along the vertical axis, with the letters rotated 90 degrees (so that their bases run along the axis).

- **Vertical Title:** The title appears vertically along the vertical axis, but each letter remains unrotated, so that the letters are stacked one on top of the other.

- **Horizontal Title:** The title appears horizontally, like regular text, to the left of the vertical axis.

FIGURE 14.16

You can select these vertical axis titles, from left to right: Rotated Title, Vertical Title, and Horizontal Title.

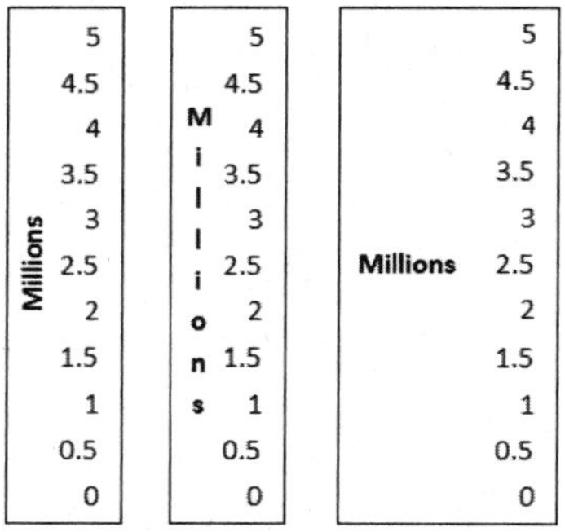

Each type of vertical axis shrinks the chart somewhat when you activate it, but the Horizontal Title format shrinks the chart more than the others because it requires more space to the left of the chart.

CAUTION   If you turn off an axis title by setting it to None and then turn it back on again, you will need to retype the axis title; it returns to the generic placeholder text.

If the chart does not resize itself automatically when you turn on the vertical axis title, you might need to adjust the chart size manually. Click the chart, so that selection handles appear around the inner part of the chart (the *plot area*), as shown in Figure 14.17. Then drag the left side-selection handle inward to decrease the width of the chart to make room for the vertical axis label.

FIGURE 14.17

You can adjust the size of the plot area to make more room for the vertical axis title.

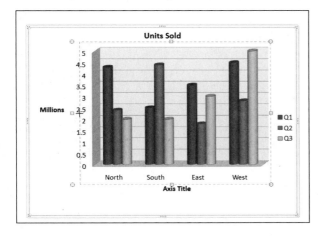

Working with Legends

The *legend* is the little box that appears next to the chart (or sometimes above or below it). It provides the key that describes what the different colors or patterns mean. For some chart types and labels, you may not find the legend to be useful. If it is not useful for the chart that you are working on, you can turn it off by clicking the Legend button on the Layout tab and then clicking None. You can also just click it and press Delete. Turning off the legend makes more room for the chart, which grows to fill the available space. To turn the legend back on, click the Legend button again and select the position that you want for it, as shown in Figure 14.18.

FIGURE 14.18

You can select a legend position, or turn the legend off altogether.

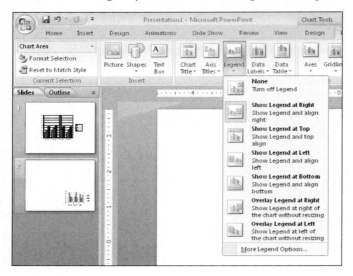

> **CAUTION** Hiding the legend is not a good idea if you have more than one series in your chart, because the legend helps people to distinguish which series is which. However, if you have only one series, a legend might not be useful.

To resize a legend box, you can drag one of its selection handles. The text and keys inside the box do not change in size.

When you right-click the legend and choose Format Legend, or when you choose More Legend Options from the Legend drop-down list on the Layout tab, the Format Legend dialog box opens with the Legend Options displayed, as shown in Figure 14.19. From here, you can choose the legend's position in relation to the chart and whether or not it should overlap the chart. If it does not overlap the chart, the plot area will be automatically reduced to accommodate the legend.

> **NOTE** The controls on the Legend Options tab refer to the legend's position in relation to the chart, not to the position of the legend text within the legend box. You can drag the legend wherever you want it on the chart after placing it.

FIGURE 14.19

You can set legend options in the Format Legend dialog box.

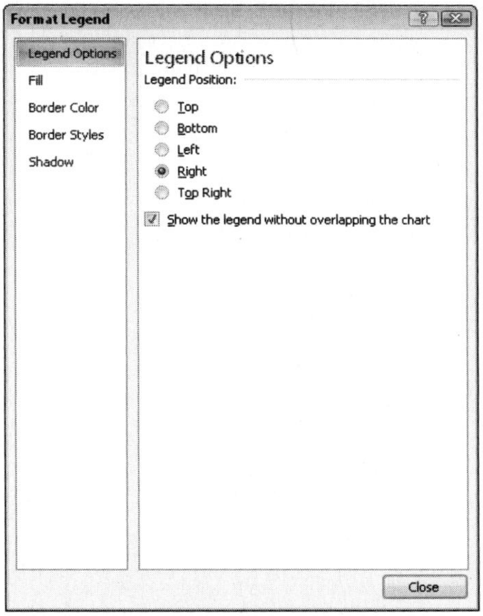

Adding Data Labels

Data labels show the numeric values (or other information) that are represented by each bar or other shape on the chart. These labels are useful when the exact numbers are important or where the chart is so small that it is not clear from the axes what the data points represent.

To turn on data labels for the chart, click the Data Labels button on the Layout tab. The options available depend on whether it's a 2-D or 3-D chart. Figure 14.20 shows the options for 2-D charting; for a 3-D chart your only choices are Show and None.

FIGURE 14.20

You can display or hide data labels using the Data labels button.

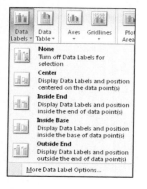

Data labels show the values by default, but you can also set them to display the series name and the category name, or any combination of the three. The data labels can also include the legend key, which is a colored square. To set these options, choose More Data Label Options from the Data Labels drop-down menu, to access the Format Data Labels dialog box, as shown in Figure 14.21. For a 3-D chart, the Label Position section does not appear.

FIGURE 14.21

You can set data label options using the Format Data Labels dialog box.

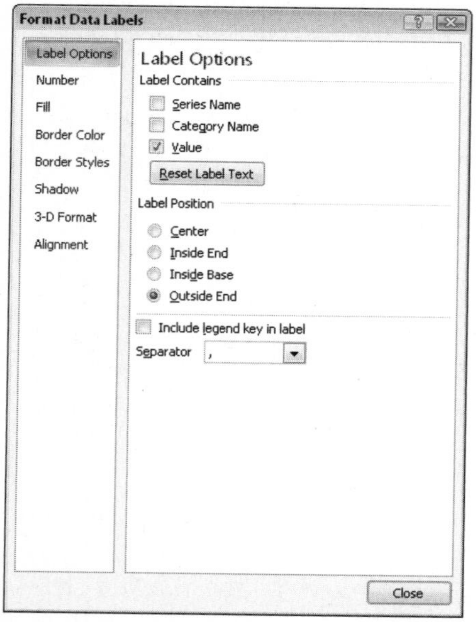

EXPERT TIP To turn the data labels on or off for a particular data point or data series, select it and then select the None or Show option in the Data Labels drop-down menu. This is useful when you want to highlight a particular value or set of values.

Adding a Data Table

Sometimes the chart tells the full story that you want to tell, but other times the audience may benefit from seeing the actual numbers on which you have built the chart. In these cases, it is a good idea to include the data table with the chart. A data table contains the same information that appears on the datasheet.

To display the data table with a chart, click the Data Table button on the Layout tab, as shown in Figure 14.22, and choose to include a data table either with or without a legend key.

FIGURE 14.22

Use a data table to show the audience the numbers on which the chart is based.

To format the data table, choose More Data Table Options from the Data Table drop-down menu. From the Format Data Table dialog box that appears, you can set data table border options, as shown in Figure 14.23. For example, you can display or hide the horizontal, vertical, and outline borders for the table from here.

FIGURE 14.23

Use the Data Table Options to specify which borders should appear in the data table.

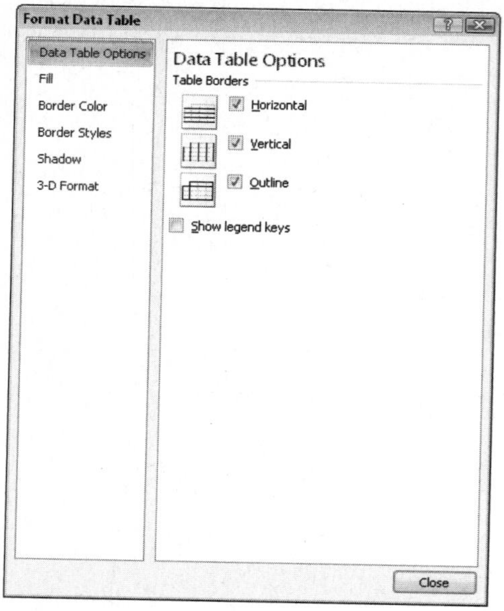

Controlling the Axes

No, axes are not the tools that chop down trees. *Axes* is the plural of *axis*, and an axis is the side of the chart containing the measurements against which your data is plotted.

You can change the various axes in a chart in several ways. For example, you can make an axis run in a different direction (such as from top-to-bottom instead of bottom-to-top for a vertical axis), and you can turn the text on or off for the axis and change the axis scale.

Using Axis Presets

You can select some of the most popular axis presets using the Axes button on the Layout tab. As with the axis titles that you learned about earlier in this chapter, there are separate submenus for horizontal and vertical axes. Figure 14.24 shows the options for horizontal axes, and Figure 14.25 shows those for vertical axes.

FIGURE 14.24

Presets for horizontal axes.

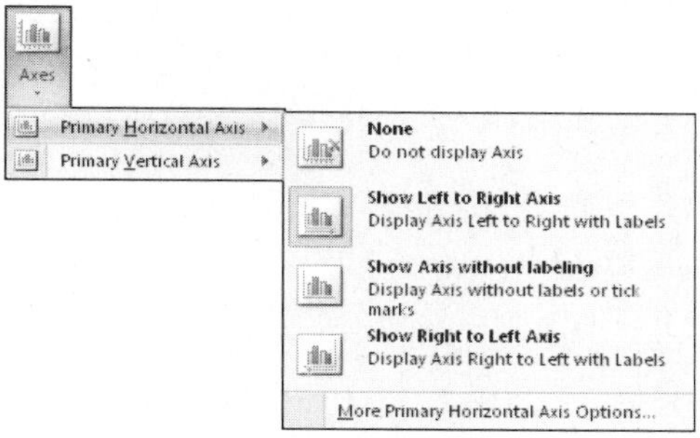

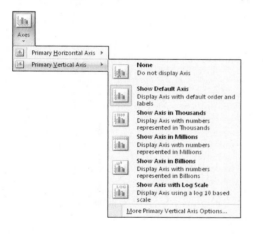

FIGURE 14.25

Presets for vertical axes.

Setting Axis Scale Options

The *scale* determines which numbers will form the start and endpoints of the axis line. For example, take a look at the chart in Figure 14.26. The bars are so close to one another in value that it is difficult to see the difference between them. Compare this chart to one showing the same data in Figure 14.27, but with an adjusted scale. Because the scale is smaller, the differences now appear more dramatic.

FIGURE 14.26

This chart does not show the differences between the values very well.

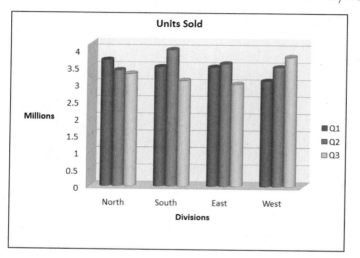

FIGURE 14.27

A change to the values of the axis scale makes it easier to see the differences between values.

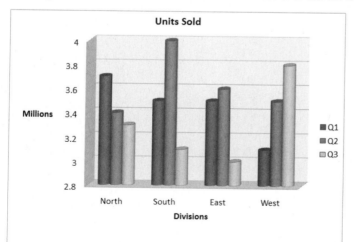

You will probably never run into a case as dramatic as the difference between Figures 14.26 and 14.27 because PowerPoint's charting feature has an automatic setting for the scale that is turned on by default. However, you may sometimes want to override this setting for a different effect, such as to minimize or enhance the difference between data series. This is a good example of "making the data say what you want." For example, if you wanted to make the point that the differences between three months were insignificant, then you would use a larger scale. If you wanted to highlight the importance of the differences, then you would use a smaller scale.

To set the scale for an axis, follow these steps:

1. On the Layout tab, choose Axes ➪ Primary Vertical Axis ➪ More Primary Vertical Axis Options. The Format Axis dialog box opens, displaying the Axis Options, as shown in Figure 14.28.

FIGURE 14.28

You can set axis options in the Format Axis dialog box, including the axis scale.

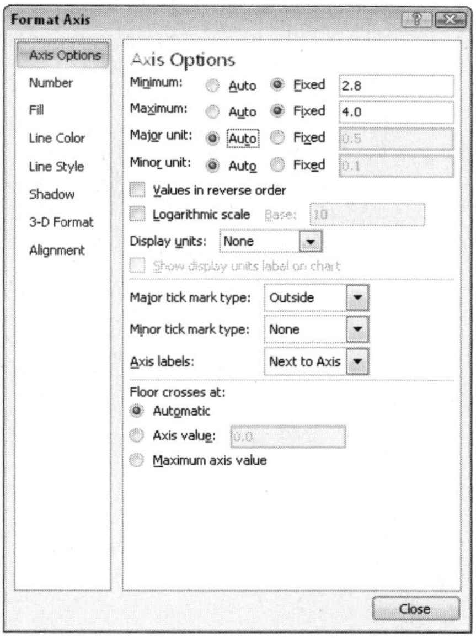

2. Drag the Format Axis dialog box to the side so that you can see the results on the chart.

3. If you do not want the automatic value for one of the measurements, click Fixed and enter a different number in its text box.

   ▪ **Minimum** is the starting number. The usual setting is 0, as shown in Figure 1.26, although in Figure 14.27, it is set to 2.8.

   ▪ **Maximum** is the top number. This number is 4 in both Figure 14-26 and Figure 14.27.

- **Major unit** determines the axis text. It is also the unit by which gridlines stretch out across the back wall of the chart. In Figure 14-26, gridlines appear at increments of 0.5 million units; in Figure 14.27, they appear by 0.2 million units.

- **Minor unit** is the interval of smaller gridlines between the major ones. Most charts look better without minor units, because these units can make a chart look cluttered. You should leave this setting at Auto. You can also use this feature to place tick marks on the axes between the labels of the major units.

4. *(Optional)* If you want to activate any of these special features, select their check boxes. Each of these check boxes recalculates the numbers in the Minimum, Maximum, Major Unit, and Minor Unit text boxes.

  - **Values in reverse order.** This check box turns the scale backwards so that the greater values appear at the bottom or left.

  - **Logarithmic scale.** Rarely used by ordinary folks, this check box recalculates the Minimum, Maximum, Major Unit, and Minor Unit according to a power of 10 for the value axis, based on the range of data. (If this explanation doesn't make any sense to you, then you're not the target audience for this feature.)

  - **Floor crosses at.** When you select this feature, you can enter a value indicating where the axes should cross. You can specify an axis value of a particular number, or use Maximum axis value.

5. (Optional) You can set a display unit to simplify large numbers. For example, if you set display units to Thousands, then the number 1000 appears as "1" on the chart. If you then select the Show Display Units Label on Chart check box, an axis label will appear as "Thousands."

6. (Optional) You can set tick-mark types for major and minor marks. These marks appear as little lines on the axis to indicate the units. You can use tick marks either with or without gridlines. (To set gridlines, use the Gridlines button's menu on the Chart Tools Layout tab.)

7. If you are happy with the results, click Close.

Setting a Number Format

You can apply a number format to axes and data labels that show numeric data. This is similar to the number format that is used for Excel cells; you can choose a category, such as Currency or Percentage, and then fine-tune this format by choosing a number of decimal places, a method of handling negative numbers, and so on.

To set a number format, follow these steps:

1. Right-click the axis and choose Format Axis.

2. In the Format Axis dialog box that appears, click Number. A list of number formats appears.

3. (Optional) You can select the number format in two ways: the first way is to select the Linked to Source check box if you want the number format to be taken from the number format that is applied to the datasheet in Excel. The second way is to click the desired number format in the Category list. Options appear that are specific to the format that you selected. For example, Figure 14.29 shows the options for the Number type of format, which is a generic format.

FIGURE 14.29

You can set a number format in the Format Axis dialog box.

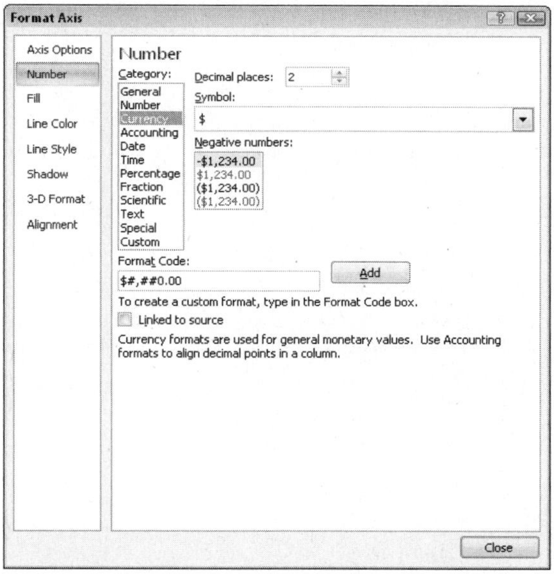

4. (Optional) You can fine-tune the numbering format by changing the code in the Format Code text box. The number signs (#) represent optional digits, while the zeroes represent required digits.

5. Click Close to close the dialog box.

NOTE To see some examples of custom number formats that you might use in the Format Code text box, choose Custom as the number format.

Formatting a Chart

In the following sections, you learn about chart formatting. There is so much that you can do to a chart that this subject could easily take up its own chapter! For example, just like any other object, you can resize a chart. You can also change the fonts, change the colors and shading of bars, lines, or pie slices, use different background colors, change the 3-D angle, and much more.

EXPERT TIP   The Format dialog box can remain open while you format various parts of the chart. Just click a different part of the chart behind the open dialog box (drag it off to the side if needed); the controls in the dialog box change to reflect the part that you have selected.

Clearing Manually Applied Formatting

PowerPoint uses Format dialog boxes that are related to the various parts of the chart. These dialog boxes are *nonmodal*, which means that they can stay open indefinitely, that their changes are applied immediately, and that you don't have to close the dialog box to continue working on the document. Although this is handy, it is all too easy to make an unintended formatting change.

To clear the formatting that is applied to a chart element, select it and then, on the Format tab, click Reset to Match Style. This strips off the manually applied formatting from that element, returning it to whatever appearance is specified by the chart style that you have applied.

Formatting Titles and Labels

Once you add a title or label to your chart, you can change its size, attributes, colors, and font. Just right-click the title that you want to format and choose Format Chart Title (or whatever kind of title it is; for example, an axis label is called Axis Title). The Format Chart Title (or Format Axis Title) dialog box appears.

NOTE   The formatting covered in this section applies to the text box, not to the text within it. If you need to format the fill, outline, or typeface, use the mini toolbar (right-click to open it) or use the font tools on the Home tab.

The categories in this dialog box vary, depending on the type of text that you are formatting, but the following categories are generally available:

- **Fill:** You can choose No Fill, Solid Fill, Gradient Fill, Picture or Text Fill, or Automatic. When you select Automatic, the color changes to contrast with the background color specified by the theme.

- **Border Color:** You can choose No Line, Solid Line, or Automatic. When you select Automatic, the color changes to contrast with the background color specified by the theme.

- **Border Styles:** You can set a width, a compound type (that is, a line made up of multiple lines), and a dash type.

- **Shadow:** You can apply a preset shadow in any color you want, or you can fine-tune the shadow in terms of transparency, size, angle, and so on. You might need to apply a fill to the box in order for the shadow to appear. This shadow is for the text box, not for the text within it; use the Font group on the Home tab to apply the text shadow, or the shadows available for WordArt.

- **3-D Format:** You can define 3-D settings for the text box, such as Bevel, Depth, Contour, and Surface.

- **Alignment:** You can set vertical and horizontal alignment, angle, and text direction, as well as control AutoFit settings for some types of text.

NOTE Alignment is usually not relevant in a short label or title text box. The text box is usually exactly the right size to hold the text, and so there is no other way for the text to be aligned. Therefore, no matter what alignment you choose, the text looks very much the same.

From the Home tab or the mini toolbar, you can also choose all of the text effects that you learned about earlier in this book, such as font, size, font style, underline, color, alignment, and so on.

Applying Chart Styles

Chart styles are presets that you can apply to charts in order to add colors, backgrounds, and fill styles. The Chart Styles gallery, shown in Figure 14.30, is located on the Chart Tools Design tab, which appears when you select a chart.

FIGURE 14.30

You can apply a chart style using the Chart Styles gallery.

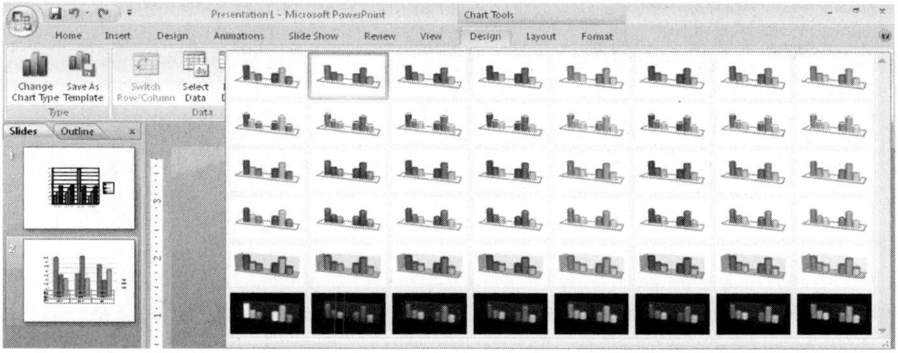

Chart styles are based on the themes and color schemes in the PowerPoint Design tab. When you change the theme or the colors, the chart style choices also change.

NOTE You cannot add to the presets in the Chart Styles gallery, but you can save a group of settings as a template. To do this, use the Save As Template command on the Chart Tools Design tab.

Formatting the Chart Area

Your next task is to format the big picture: the *chart area*. The chart area is the big frame that contains the chart and all of its elements: the legend, the data series, the data table, the titles, and so on.

The Format Chart Area dialog box has many of the same categories as for text boxes — such as fill, border color, border styles, shadow, and 3-D format — and it also adds 3-D rotation if you are working with a 3-D chart. You can choose to rotate and tilt the entire chart, just as you did with drawn shapes earlier in this book.

Formatting the Legend

When you use a multi-series chart, the value of the legend is obvious — it tells you which colors represent which series. Without the legend, your audience will not know what the various bars or lines mean. You can do all of the same formatting for a legend that you can for other chart elements. Just right-click the legend, choose Format Legend from the shortcut menu, and then use the tabs in the Format Legend dialog box to make your modifications. The available categories are Fill, Border Color, Border Styles, and Shadow, as well as the Legend options mentioned earlier in this chapter.

EXPERT TIP If you select one of the individual keys in the legend and change its color, the color on the data series in the chart changes to match. This is especially useful with stacked charts, where it is sometimes difficult to select the data series that you want.

Formatting Gridlines and Walls

Gridlines help the reader's eyes move across the chart. Gridlines are related to the axes, which you learned about earlier in this chapter. Although both vertical and horizontal gridlines are available, most people use only horizontal ones. *Walls* are nothing more than the space between the gridlines, formatted in a different color than the plot area. You can set the Walls fill to None to hide them. (Don't you wish tearing down walls was always that easy?) You can also use the Chart Wall and Chart Floor buttons on the Layout tab.

NOTE You can only format walls on 3-D charts; 2-D charts do not have them. To change the background behind a 2-D chart, you must format the plot area.

In most cases, the default gridlines that PowerPoint adds work well. However, you may want to make the lines thicker or a different color, or turn them off altogether.

Gridline presets are available from the Gridlines drop-down menu on the Layout tab. There are separate submenus for vertical and horizontal gridlines, as shown in Figure 14. 31. You can also choose the More command for either of the gridlines submenus for additional options.

FIGURE 14.31

You can apply gridline presets from the Gridlines drop-down menu.

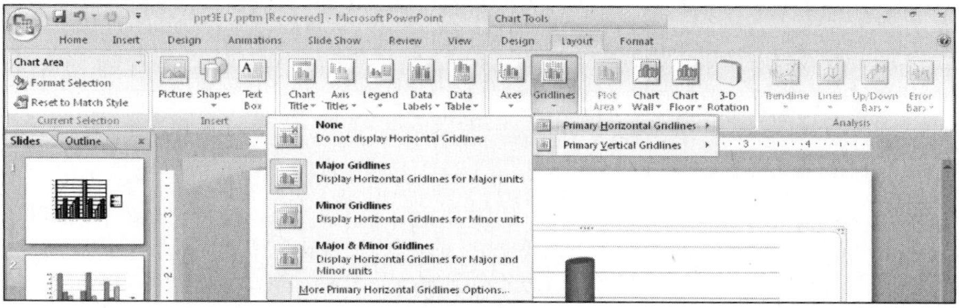

To change the gridline formatting, right-click a gridline and choose Format Major Gridlines. You can then adjust the line color, line style, and shadow from the Format Major Gridlines dialog box, as shown in Figure 14.32.

FIGURE 14.32

You can set gridline colors, styles, and shadows in the Format Major Gridlines dialog box.

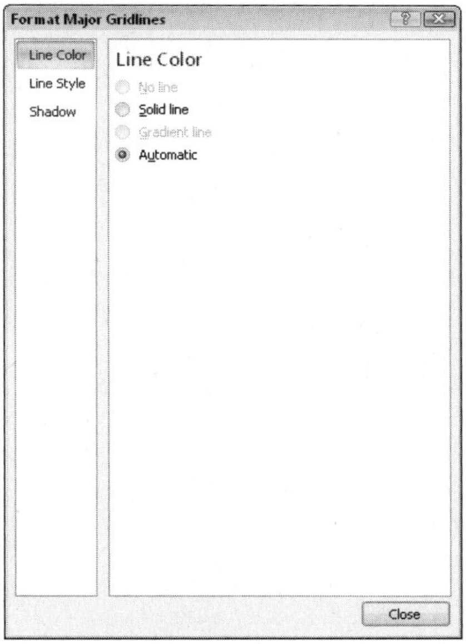

NOTE Gridline spacing is based on the major and minor units that you have set in the Format Axis dialog box (vertical or horizontal). To set this spacing, see the section, "Setting Axis Scale Options," earlier in this chapter.

Formatting the Data Series

To format a data series, just right-click the bar, slice, or chart element, and choose Format Data Series from the shortcut menu. Then, depending on your chart type, different tabs appear that you can use to modify the series appearance. Here are the ones for bar and column charts, for example:

- **Series Options:** This tab contains options that are specific to the selected chart type. For example, when working with a 3-D bar or column chart, the series options include Gap Depth and Gap Width, which determine the thickness and depth of the bars. For a pie chart, you can set the rotation angle for the first slice, as well as whether a slice is "exploded" or not.

- **Shape:** For charts involving bars and columns, you can choose a shape option such as Box, Full Pyramid, Partial Pyramid, Cylinder, Full Cone, or Partial Cone. The partial options truncate the top part of the shape when it is less than the largest value in the chart.

- **Fill:** You can choose a fill, including solid, gradient, or picture/texture.

- **Border Color:** The border is the line around the shape. You can set it to a solid line, no line, or Automatic (that is, based on the theme).

- **Border Styles:** The only option available on this tab for most chart types is Width, which controls the thickness of the border. For line charts, you can set arrow options and other line attributes.

- **Shadow:** You can add shadows to the data series bars or other shapes, just as you would add shadows to anything else.

- **3-D Format:** These settings control the contours, surfaces, and beveling for 3D data series.

Other chart types have very different categories available. For example, a line chart has Marker Options, Marker Fill, Line Color, Line Style, Marker Line Color, and Marker Line Style, in addition to the generic Series Options, Shadow, and 3-D Format categories.

Rotating a 3-D Chart

Three-dimensional charts have a 3-D Rotation option in the Format Chart Area dialog box. This feature works just the same as with other 3-D objects, where you can rotate the chart on the X-, Y-, and Z-axis. In addition, there are some extra chart-specific options, as shown in Figure 14.33. For example, you can set the chart to AutoScale, control its depth, and reset it to the default rotation.

FIGURE 14.33

You can adjust the 3-D rotation of a chart.

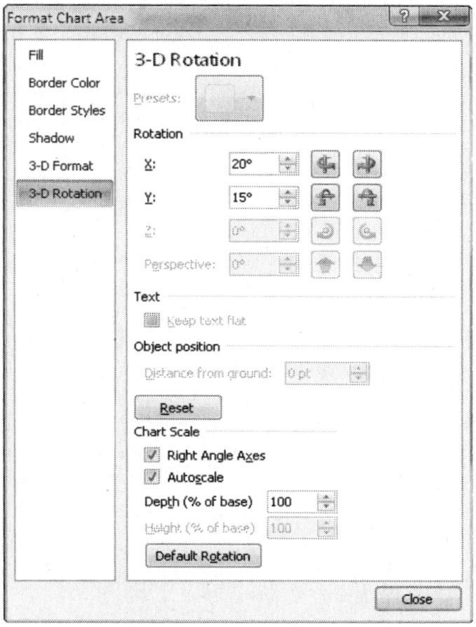

Working with Chart Templates

After you have formatted a chart the way you want it, you can save it as a template. You can then apply these same formatting options to other charts at a later time.

Creating a Chart Template

To create a chart template, follow these steps:

1. Select a chart that is formatted exactly the way you want the template to be. If you want the template to use theme colors, use them in the chart; if you want the template to use fixed colors, apply them instead.

2. On the Chart Tools Design tab, click Save As Template. The Chart Template dialog box opens.

3. Type a name for the template.

NOTE By default, under Windows Vista, templates are stored in Users\username\AppData\ Roaming\Microsoft\Template\Charts, with a .crtx (Chart Template) extension. In Windows XP, it's \Documents and Settings\username\Application Data\Microsoft\Templates\Charts. You can copy templates from another PC and store them in that location and they will show up on your list of chart templates on the current PC.

4. Click Save.

Applying a Chart Template

To apply a chart template to an existing chart, follow these steps:

1. Select the chart, and on the Chart Tools Design tab, click Change Chart Type.

   You can also right-click the chart and choose Change Chart Type.

2. At the top of the list of categories, click Templates. PowerPoint displays all of the custom templates that you have created.

3. Click the template that you want to use.

4. Click OK.

To apply a chart template to a new chart as you are creating it, after choosing Insert ➪ Chart, click Templates folder and select the desired template.

Managing Template Files

Chart template files remain on your hard disk until you delete them. If you want to get rid of a chart template, or rename it, you can do so by opening the folder location that contains these templates. Although you can manually browse to the location (Users\username\AppData\Roaming\Microsoft\Template\Charts), this is an easier way:

1. On the Insert tab, click Chart.

2. In the Insert Chart dialog box, click Manage Templates. The folder location opens in an Explorer window. From here, you can rename or delete files.

Summary

In this chapter, you learned how to create and format charts using PowerPoint. You learned how to create charts, change their type and their data range, and use optional text elements on them such as titles, data labels, and so on. You also learned how to format charts and how to save formatting in chart templates. In the next chapter, you learn how to incorporate data from other sources, including programs that do not necessarily have anything to do with PowerPoint or Office.

Chapter 15

Incorporating Data from Other Programs

As you have already seen, PowerPoint contains an assortment of tools for creating various types of objects: charts, WordArt, SmartArt diagrams, clip art, and so on. You have also learned how to place graphics into PowerPoint from a saved file, how to embed Excel charts on slides, and how to borrow slides from other PowerPoint presentations and outlines from Word or other text editors.

However, a lot of other objects don't fall into any of these categories, so PowerPoint doesn't have a special command for bringing in exactly that type of object. Examples include a flow chart from a program like Microsoft Visio, a slide from a different presentation application, some records from a database, or a map from a mapping program.

This chapter looks at the various ways to import and create content from other applications in PowerPoint, as well as how to export PowerPoint objects for use in other programs.

Working with External Content: An Overview

There are several ways to bring content from other programs into your presentation. The method you choose depends on how you want the content to behave once it arrives. You can make the inserted content a full citizen of the presentation — that is, with no ties to its native application or data file — or you can help it retain a connection to its original application (called *embedding*) or to its original data file (called *linking*).

The simplest way to import content into PowerPoint is to use the Copy and Paste commands. For text-type data from most applications, this results in the incoming data integrating itself with PowerPoint without retaining any connection to the source. For example, you can select some cells from an Excel worksheet, and then click Copy on the Home tab to copy them to the Clipboard. Then in PowerPoint you can paste them by clicking Paste, and the Excel cells become a PowerPoint table. You can also do the same thing with drag-and-drop from one application to the other.

> **CAUTION** Not all data types exhibit the behavior described here. With some source data types, especially types that are more graphical than text-based, copy-and-paste results in an embedded object that will open its native application for editing. For example, when you copy and paste a chart from Excel, it is by default linked.

Another choice is to *embed* the data. You can do this for existing or new data. Embedding it maintains the relationship between that data and its native application, so that you can double-click it to edit it with that native application later. To embed existing data, you copy the data to the Clipboard, use the Paste button's menu to select Paste Special, and then choose the appropriate data type from the list. For example, suppose you want to be able to edit the pasted cells in Excel later. You can use Paste Special and choose Microsoft Excel Worksheet Object as the type. (More on this shortly.)

To embed new data, you use the Object button on the Insert tab, and then choose to create a new embedded object of the desired type. (More on this shortly too.) For example, suppose you have a favorite program for creating organization charts. You can start a new embedded organization chart on a PowerPoint slide instead of using PowerPoint's own SmartArt hierarchy chart. That organization chart is then stored only within your PowerPoint file, not separately.

Yet another choice is to link the data from its original source file. When you do this, PowerPoint maintains information about the name and location of the original, and each time you open the presentation file it rechecks the original to see if any changes have been made to the original data file. If so, PowerPoint updates its copy of the object to the latest version. For example, suppose you want to include data from an Excel workbook that a coworker is creating. He warns you that his data is not final yet, but you want to create the presentation anyway. By creating a link to his data, rather than pasting a static copy of it, you ensure that you will always have the latest data no matter how many times he changes it.

You can create a link to an entire file or to a specific part of a file. For example, you can link to the entire Excel workbook, or just to a certain range of cells on a certain sheet. The procedures are different — for the entire file you use Object (Insert tab), but for a portion of the file you use Paste Special (Home tab). Both methods create a link to the entire Excel workbook, but Object automatically displays the entire first sheet of the workbook in your PowerPoint file, whereas Paste Special displays only the cells that you've selected.

Copying Content from Other Programs

Let's assume for the moment that you don't need any special linking or embedding. You just want the content from some other program to be placed on a PowerPoint slide. You have two choices: Use the Clipboard, or use drag-and-drop.

Using the Clipboard

The easiest way to place something into PowerPoint is to use the Windows Clipboard. Because almost all Windows-based programs employ the Clipboard, you can move data from any program to almost any other with a minimum of fuss. Follow these steps:

1. Create the data in its native program or open a file that contains it.

2. Select the data you want, and click Copy on the Home tab, or if it is not an Office program, open the Edit menu and choose Copy.

NOTE   Ctrl+C always works to copy to the Clipboard, so use that if you can't find the copy command in the application.

3. Switch to PowerPoint, and display the slide on which you want to place the content.

4. Click Paste on the Home tab. The content appears on the slide. PowerPoint makes its best guess as to the correct formatting. For example, if you paste Excel worksheet cells, it attempts to convert them to a table because that's the closest match among the native PowerPoint layouts.

5. Move or resize the new content as necessary on the slide.

NOTE   Don't forget that there are many alternative methods for using the Copy and Paste commands. The shortcut keys are among the fastest: Ctrl+C for copy and Ctrl+V for paste.

PowerPoint, like all Office 2007 applications, has an enhanced version of the Clipboard that is available when both the source and destination locations are Microsoft Office applications. It enables you to copy more than one item at a time to the Clipboard, and then choose among them when pasting. When pasting to a non-Office application, however, only the last item copied to the Clipboard is available.

When you copy twice in a row without pasting while in an Office application, the Clipboard task pane appears, with each copied clip separately listed. You can also open this Clipboard task pane by clicking the dialog box launcher in the Clipboard group on the Home tab.

EXPERT TIP   If pressing Ctrl+C twice doesn't open the clipboard, open the task pane the other way (by clicking the dialog box launcher in the Clipboard group on the Home tab) and then click the Options button and click Show Office Clipboard When Ctrl+C Pressed Twice.

You can then open the destination and click the clip you want to paste. Or you can click the down arrow next to a clip and choose Delete to delete it. See Figure 15.1.

Using the Office 2007 Clipboard task pane enables you to copy more than one clip to the Clipboard.

Click here to display the Clipboard

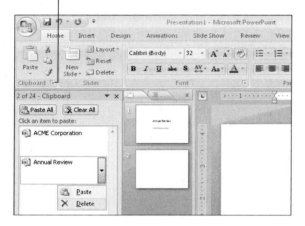

EXPERT TIP Fine-tune the way the Clipboard works in Office 2007 applications by clicking the Options button at the bottom of the Clipboard task pane. This opens a menu from which you can specify when and how the Clipboard task pane appears. For example, you can set it to show a Clipboard icon in the taskbar.

As mentioned earlier, when you are copying and pasting some types of content, especially graphical types, PowerPoint embeds the content by default rather than simply pasting it.

Embedding the content tends to increase the size of the PowerPoint presentation file, so avoid doing it unless you think you will need that capability. (More on embedding later in the chapter.) You can tell whether content has been embedded by double-clicking it. If it's embedded, its native application will open within PowerPoint (or in a separate window). If it's not embedded, a PowerPoint dialog box will open for the content. To avoid embedding content that PowerPoint wants to embed by default, follow these steps:

1. Copy the data to the Clipboard in its native application.
2. In PowerPoint, on the Home tab, open the Paste button's menu and click Paste Special.
3. Choose a different format for the paste, such as Bitmap. Do not choose the format that ends with "Object" or you will get an embedded copy.
4. Click OK.

Using Drag and Drop

In some cases, you can also use drag and drop to move an object from some other application (or from a file management window) to PowerPoint. Not all Windows programs support this feature though. If you're not sure whether a program supports it, try it and see. Here's how to drag and drop something:

1. Create the object in its native program or open the file that contains it. The object can be a single unit such as an entire graphic, or it can be a small piece of a larger document or image such as a few cells selected from a large worksheet.

2. Open PowerPoint and display the slide on which you want to place the data.

3. Resize both applications' windows so that both the data and its destination are visible on-screen.

4. Select the data in its native program.

5. If you want to copy, rather than move, hold down the Ctrl key.

6. Drag the content to the PowerPoint slide. See Figure 15.2. An outline appears on the PowerPoint slide showing where the data will go.

7. Release the mouse button. The data is moved or copied.

FIGURE 15.2

You can drag data from one application to another. Hold down the Ctrl key to copy rather than move.

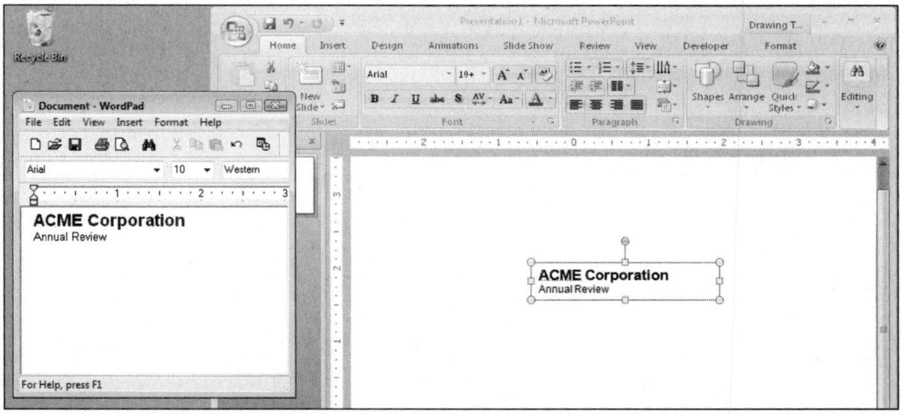

CAUTION When dragging-and-dropping from Excel, data arrives in PowerPoint in a plain text box, with columns and rows separated by spaces. If you want to retain the original tabular format from Excel, use Copy and Paste, not drag and drop.

As with copying and pasting, not all content gets the "plain paste" treatment when you drag and drop. Generally speaking, text-based data will drag without embedding, but graphic-based data will usually embed. (There are exceptions.) Use the Paste Special method described earlier rather than drag and drop if you run into this situation.

Inserting Graphics from a File

When you use copy-and-paste or drag and drop to insert content from a graphics-based application, as mentioned in the preceding section, PowerPoint embeds by default. This makes the file size larger than necessary for the PowerPoint presentation, however, so it's better to use the Picture button (Insert tab) when you insert graphics. This inserts a plain-old copy of the picture, without embedding, and keeps the PowerPoint file size more manageable.

Introducing OLE

The abbreviation OLE stands for *Object Linking and Embedding*. It enables Windows-based applications that support it to share information dynamically. That means that the object remembers where it came from and has special abilities based on that memory. Even though the name OLE is a little scary (it ranks right up there with SQL in my book!), the concept is very elementary, and anyone can understand and use it.

You already understand the term *object* in the PowerPoint sense, and the term is similar to that in the case of OLE. An object is any bit of data (or a whole file) that you want to use in another program. You can paste it in with no connection to its source, or you can link or embed it.

Two actions are involved in OLE: linking and embedding. Here are quick definitions of each:

- Linking creates a connection between the original file and the copy in your presentation, so that the copy is always updated.

- Embedding creates a connection between the object in the presentation and the application that originally created it, so that you can edit the object in that original application at any time from within PowerPoint.

The key difference is that linking connects to the source *data file*, whereas embedding connects to the source *application*.

For a link to be updatable, linked objects must already exist independently of the PowerPoint presentation. For example, if you want to link an Excel chart, you must first create that chart in Excel and save your work in an Excel file. That way, PowerPoint has a filename to refer to when updating the link.

CAUTION Links can slow down your presentation's loading and editing performance. Therefore, you should create links last, after you have finished adding content and polishing the formatting.

Linking and embedding are not appropriate for every insertion. If you want to use content (such as cells from an Excel worksheet or a picture from a graphics program) that will not change, it's best to copy it normally. For the Excel data cells or text from a Word document, use regular Copy/Paste; for the graphic image, use Picture (on the Insert tab). Reserve linking for objects that will change and that you will always need the most recent version of. Reserve embedding for objects that you plan to edit later and require the native applications editing tools to do so.

Here are some ideas of when linking or embedding might be useful:

- If you have to give the same presentation every month that shows the monthly sales statistics, *link* to your Excel worksheet where you track them during the month. Your presentation will always contain the most current data.

- If you want to draw a picture in Paint (a program that comes with Windows) or some other graphics program, *embed* the picture in PowerPoint. That way, you don't have to open Paint (or the other program) separately every time you want to work on the picture while you're fine-tuning your presentation. You can just double-click the picture in PowerPoint. You can always break the link when you finalize the presentation if you want to cut down on the file size.

- If you know that a coworker is still finalizing a chart or drawing, *link* to her working file on the network. Then whenever changes are made to it, your copy will also be updated. (Beware, however, that once you take your presentation away from the computer that has network access, you can no longer update the link.)

Linking and/or Embedding Part of a File

As I mentioned earlier, you can link or embed either a part of an existing file or the whole file. If you need only a part of an existing file, such as a few cells from a worksheet, an individual chart, or a few paragraphs of text, you use the following procedure:

1. In its native application, create or open the file containing the data you want to copy.
2. If you have just created the file, save it. The file should have a name before you go any further if you are linking; this is not necessary for embedding, but it won't hurt anything.
3. Select the data you want.
4. On the Home tab, click Copy, or press Ctrl+C.
5. Switch to PowerPoint and display the slide on which you want to paste the data.
6. On the Home tab, open the Paste button's menu and click Paste Special. The Paste Special dialog box opens. See Figure 15.3.

Use the Paste Special dialog box to link or embed a piece of a data file from another program.

7. If you want to embed, leave Paste selected. If you want to link, click Paste Link.

8. Choose the format from the As list. Because you want to link or embed, choose a type that ends with the word *object*.

9. If you want the pasted object to appear as an icon instead of as itself, mark the Display as Icon check box. This check box might be unavailable if the object type you chose in step 8 does not support it.

10. Click OK. The object is placed in your presentation.

If you link the object, each time you open your PowerPoint presentation, PowerPoint checks the source file for an updated version. If you embed the object, you can double-click it at any time to open it in its native application for editing.

Perhaps you are wondering about the other data types. If you chose Paste in step 7 (rather than Paste Link), you will see other formats on the list. All of these are non-linkable, non-embeddable formats. The choices depend on the type of data, but include some of the following:

- **Formatted Text (RTF).** This data type formats text as it is formatted in the original file. For example, if the text is formatted as underlined in the original file, it is pasted as underlined text in PowerPoint.

- **Unformatted Text.** This option ignores the formatting from the native file and formats the text as the default PowerPoint font you've specified.

- **Picture (Windows Metafile).** The object appears as a 16-bit WMF-format graphic.

- **Picture (Enhanced Metafile).** The object appears as a 32-bit EMF-format graphic.

- **Device Independent Bitmap.** The object comes in as a bitmap picture, like a Windows Paint image.

EXPERT TIP Enhanced Metafile is, as the name implies, an updated and improved file format from Windows Metafile. It is a 32-bit format, whereas Windows Metafile is a 16-bit format. Enhanced metafile graphics cannot be used in MS-DOS or 16-bit Windows applications. If that backward-compatibility is important to use, use Windows Metafile. You can get more information about Windows metafiles at `multivac.fatburen.org/localdoc/libwmf/caolan/ora-wmf.html`.

Embedding an Entire File

Sometimes you might want to place an entire file on a PowerPoint slide — for example, if the file is small and contains only the object that you want to display, like a picture. To create this connection, you use the Object button (on the Insert tab), which is handier than the procedure you just learned because you do not have to open the other application.

1. In PowerPoint, display the slide on which you want to place the file.
2. On the Insert tab, click Object. The Insert Object dialog box opens.
3. Click the Create from File button. The controls change to those shown in Figure 15.4.
4. Click Browse, and use the Browse dialog box to locate the file you want. Then click OK to accept the filename.
5. (Optional) If you want to link instead of embed the file, mark the Link check box.

CAUTION Do not link to a file housed on a disk that might not always be available during your presentation. For example, don't link to a floppy unless you are also storing the presentation file on the same floppy. And don't link to a network drive unless you know the network will be available at show time from the computer on which you will present.

6. Click OK. The file is inserted on your PowerPoint slide.

FIGURE 15.4

Enter the filename or browse for it with the Browse button.

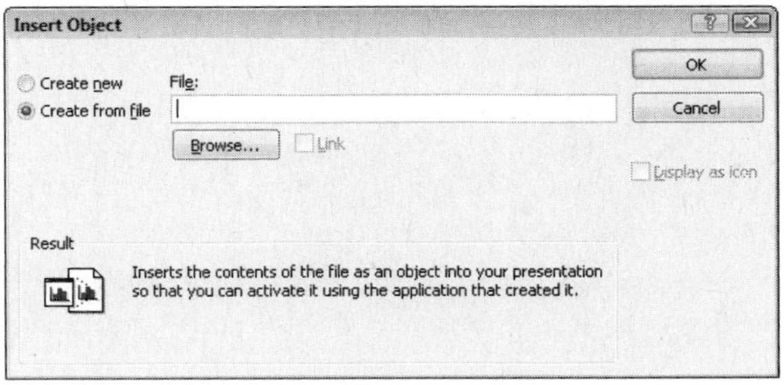

You can tell that the file is embedded, rather than simply copied, because when you double-click it, it opens in its native application. In contrast, when you double-click an item that is copied without embedding, its Properties box or some other PowerPoint-specific dialog box opens in PowerPoint. If you choose to link the object, you need to edit it in the native application.

Embedding a New File

If you want to embed a foreign object, but you haven't created that object yet, a really easy way to do so is to embed it on the fly. When you do this, the controls for the program open within PowerPoint (or in a separate application window, depending on the application) and you can create your object. Then, your work is saved within PowerPoint rather than as a separate file.

1. Open PowerPoint and display the slide on which you want to put the new object.

2. Choose Insert ➪ Object. The Insert Object dialog box appears.

3. Click Create New. A list of available object types appears. See Figure 15.5.

FIGURE 15.5

Choose the object type you want to create. The object types listed come from the OLE-compliant programs installed on your PC.

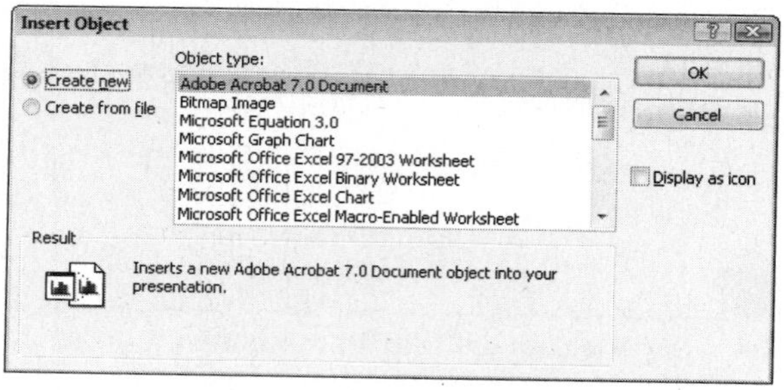

4. Click the object type you want and then click OK. The application opens.

5. Depending on the application, additional dialog boxes might appear. For example, if you are creating a new graphic object, a box might appear asking you about the size and color depth. Respond to any dialog boxes that appear for creating the new object.

6. Create the object using the program's controls. The program might be in a separate window from PowerPoint, or it might be contained within the PowerPoint window as in Figure 15.6.

FIGURE 15.6

The embedded program's controls appear, with PowerPoint in the background.

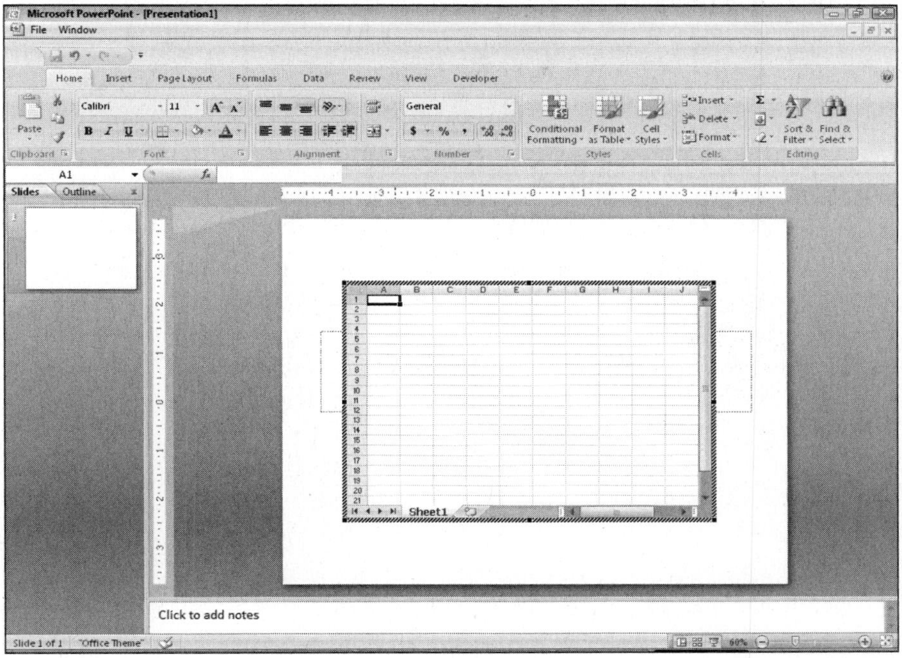

7. When you are finished, if the program was opened within PowerPoint, click anywhere on the slide outside of that object's frame. Or, if the application was in a separate window, choose File ➪ Exit and Return to *Filename* (where *Filename* is the name of your PowerPoint file). If you are prompted to save the file, choose No.

EXPERT TIP If you are prompted to save the object in a file and you choose Yes, the application creates a copy of the object that exists outside of PowerPoint. The copy is not linked to PowerPoint.

If you are asked whether you want to update the object in *filename* before proceeding, you should choose Yes. This prompt occurs in many of the applications that open in separate windows.

8. Resize and move the object on the slide as necessary.

Because you are creating a file that doesn't have a name or saved location separate from the PowerPoint presentation, there is no need to link it to anything. Embedding is the only option.

Working with Linked and Embedded Objects

Now that you have a linked or embedded object, what can you do with it? Many things. You can edit an embedded object by double-clicking it, of course. And you can update, change, and even break the links associated with a linked object. The following sections provide some details.

Opening and Converting Embedded Objects

When you select an embedded object in PowerPoint and then right-click the object, you can choose *datatype* Object where *datatype* is the object type. (Its exact name depends on the object type, for example, Worksheet Object.) From the submenu you can choose:

- **Edit:** Opens the object for editing within PowerPoint (if possible). Some applications can work from within PowerPoint, such as the Excel example in Figure 15.6. If the object is related to an application that can't do this, the object opens for editing in a separate window for that application.

- **Open:** Opens the object for editing in a separate window for the application with which it is associated.

- **Convert:** Opens a dialog box that enables you to convert the object to some other type (if possible). This sounds great in theory, but in practice there are usually very few alternatives to choose from.

EXPERT TIP Although convert options also appear for linked objects, you cannot convert them; you must break the link first. That's because a linked object must have a certain object type to maintain its link. Even after breaking a link, there might not be any viable choices for converting it to other formats.

Editing a Linked or Embedded Object

To edit a linked or embedded object, follow these steps:

1. Display the slide containing the linked or embedded object.

2. Double-click the object. The object's program's controls appear. They might be integrated into the PowerPoint window, like the ones for Excel that you saw in Figure 15.6, or they might appear in a separate window.

3. Edit the object as needed.

4. Return to PowerPoint by doing one of the following:

   - If the object is embedded (not linked), click the slide behind the object to return to PowerPoint.

   - If the object is linked, choose File ➪ Exit (or Office ➪ Exit if it's an Office 2007 program). Remember, the menu system that appears is for the embedded application, not for PowerPoint. When you are asked to save your changes, click Yes.

You can also edit a linked object directly in its original application, independently from PowerPoint. Close your PowerPoint presentation and open the original application. Do your editing, and save your work. Then, reopen your PowerPoint presentation and the object will reflect the changes.

Changing How Links Update

OLE links are automatically updated each time you open your PowerPoint file. However, updating these links slows down the file opening considerably, so if you open and close the file frequently, you might want to set the link updating to Manual. That way, the links are updated only when you issue a command to update them. To set a link to update manually, follow these steps:

1. Open the PowerPoint presentation that contains the linked object(s).
2. Choose Office ➪ Prepare ➪ Edit Links to Files. The Links dialog box appears as shown in Figure 15.7.

NOTE   If you don't see Edit Links to Files, scroll down on the Prepare submenu. Click the down arrow at the bottom of it to move down.

FIGURE 15.7

You can change the update setting for the links in your presentation here.

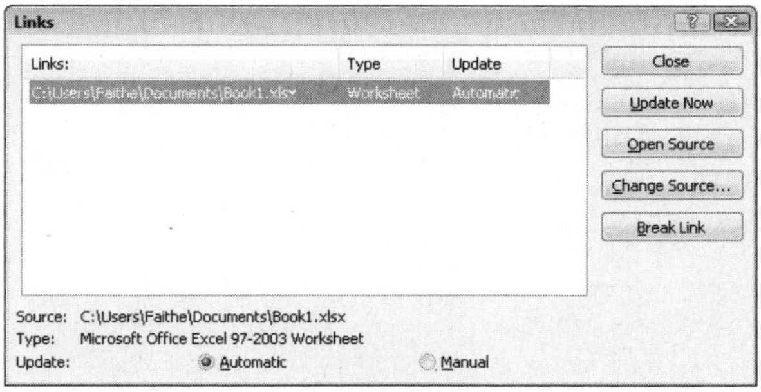

3. Click the link that you want to change.
4. Click the Manual button.
5. If you want to change any other links, repeat steps 3 and 4. You can also use the Shift and Ctrl keys to select more than one link at once.
6. If you want to update a link now, select it and click the Update Now button.
7. Click OK.
8. Choose Office ➪ Save to save the presentation changes (including the changes to the link settings).

When you set a link to manual, you have to open the Links dialog box and click Update Now, as in step 6, each time you want to update it. Or, you can right-click the object and choose Update Link from its shortcut menu.

Breaking a Link

When you break a link, the object remains in the presentation, but it becomes an ordinary object, just like any other picture or other object you might have placed there. You can't double-click it to edit it anymore, and it doesn't update when the source changes. To break a link, reopen the Links dialog box shown in Figure 15-7 (Office ⇨ Prepare ⇨ Edit Links to Files), click the link to break, and then click Break Link. If a warning box appears, click OK.

When you break a link, embedding information disappears, too. For example, if you have a linked Excel chart and you break the link, the result is a simple pasted image of the chart with no ties to the Excel application. To reestablish a link, simply recreate it as you did originally.

Changing the Referenced Location of a Link

If you move files around on your hard disk, or move them to other disks, you might need to change the link location reference. For example, perhaps you are moving the presentation file to a floppy disk and you want to place all of the linked files needed for the presentation in a separate folder on the floppy disk. To change a link reference, do the following:

1. Copy or move the files where you want them. For example, if you want to transfer the presentation and linked files to a floppy, do that first.

2. Open the PowerPoint presentation that contains the linked object(s) to change. If you copied the presentation to some new location, make sure you open the copy that you want to change.

3. Choose Office ⇨ Prepare ⇨ Edit Links to Files. The Links dialog box opens, as shown in Figure 15.7.

4. Click the link you want to change.

5. Click Change Source. A Change Source dialog box opens. It is just like the normal Open dialog boxes you have worked with many times.

6. Select the file to be linked from its new location, and click Open. The link is updated.

7. In the Links dialog box, click Close.

> **CAUTION**   If you change the location of a link to a different file, depending on the object type, the link may change to refer to the entire file, as if you had inserted it with Insert ⇨ Object. If you used Edit ⇨ Paste Special, Paste Link to insert only a part of the original file, that aspect might be lost and the entire file might appear as the object in the presentation. In such situations, it is better to delete the object and recreate the link from scratch.

Exporting PowerPoint Objects to Other Programs

You can copy any object in your PowerPoint presentation to another program, either linked or unlinked. For example, perhaps you created a chart using the PowerPoint charting tools for one of your PowerPoint slides, and now you want to use that chart in a Microsoft Word document. To use a PowerPoint object in another program, you do the same basic things that you've learned in this chapter, but you start with PowerPoint. Here are some examples:

- To copy an object from PowerPoint, select it in PowerPoint and copy it to the Clipboard (Ctrl+C). Then switch to the other program and Paste (Ctrl+V).

- To embed (or optionally link) an object from a PowerPoint presentation into another program's document, choose it in PowerPoint and copy it (Ctrl+C). Then, switch to the other program and use Paste Special. (In programs other than Office 2007, the command is usually Edit ➪ Paste Special.)

- To embed or link an entire PowerPoint presentation in another program's document, use the Object command in that other program (probably on an Insert tab or menu), and choose your PowerPoint file as the source.

You can also save individual slides as various types of graphics with the Office ➪ Save As command, as you learned to do in Chapter 3.

Summary

In this chapter, you learned the mysteries of OLE, a term you have probably heard bandied about but were never quite sure what it meant. You can now use objects freely between PowerPoint and other programs, and include links and embedding for them whenever appropriate.

In the next chapter, you learn how to add sound effects, music, and soundtracks to a presentation.

Chapter 16

Adding Sound Effects, Music, and Soundtracks

Whether it's a simple sound effect or a complete musical soundtrack, sounds in a PowerPoint presentation can make a big difference in the audience's perception of your message. In this chapter, you will learn when and how to use sounds, how to place them in the presentation, and how to manage their playback.

When Are Sounds Appropriate?

Sounds should serve the purpose of the presentation; you should never use them simply because you can. If you add a lot of sounds purely for the fun of it, then your audience may lose respect for the seriousness of your message. That being said, there are many legitimate reasons to use sounds in a presentation. Just make sure that you are clear on what your reasons are before you start working with them. Here are some ideas:

- You can assign a recognizable sound, such as a beep or a bell, to each slide, so that when your audience hears the sound, they know to look up and read the new slide.

- You can record a short voice-over message from a CEO or some other important person who could not be there in person.

- You can punctuate important points with sounds, or use sounds to add occasional humorous touches.

However, if you are trying to pack a lot of information into a short presentation, you should avoid sounds because they take up time when you play them. You should also avoid sounds and other whimsical touches if you are delivering very serious news. You may also want to avoid sounds if you

IN THIS CHAPTER

When are sounds appropriate?

Sound file formats

Where to find sounds

Inserting a sound file as an icon

Fine-tuning sound play settings

Assigning a sound to an object

Adding a CD audio soundtrack

Using the advanced timeline to fine-tune sound events

Recording sounds

intend to present on a very old and slow computer because any kind of media clip—whether sound or video—will slow the system down even more, both when you load the presentation and when you present it.

There are several ways that you can include a sound in a presentation:

- **Insert a sound file.** The sound plays during the presentation whenever anyone points to or clicks the sound icon, depending on the settings that you specify. This is useful in an interactive presentation because it gives the audience a choice of whether to play the sound.

- **Associate a sound with an object** (such as a graphic), so that the sound plays when anyone points to or clicks that object. This is another good technique for interactive presentations.

- **Associate a sound with an animation effect** (such as a series appearing in a graph), so that the sound plays when the animation effect occurs. For example, you might have some text "drive in" onto a slide and associate the sound of an engine revving with that action.

- **Associate a sound with a slide transition** (a move from one slide to the next), so that the sound plays when the next slide appears. For example, you may assign a shutter-click sound, such as the sound that a slide projector makes when it changes slides, to the transitions between slides.

- **Insert a sound that plays automatically in the background.** This is useful for unattended (kiosk-style) presentations.

CROSS-REF   In this chapter, you learn about the first two of these techniques: inserting files as icons and associating them with objects. Chapter 18 covers transition and animation sounds.

Sound File Formats

Computer sound files come in several formats, but they can be divided into two broad categories: WAV and MIDI.

- **WAV:** This can refer to a specific file format that has a `.wav` extension, but it can also refer generically to any sound file that has an analog origin. For example, when you record sound using a microphone, the resulting file is a WAV file in a generic sense of the word because it was originally a "sound wave" that the microphone captured. The tracks on an audio CD can also be considered WAV files because at some point, presumably, a person went to a recording studio and made music with their voice or with instruments that were recorded. Similarly, the very popular MP3 music format is a WAV format. Other WAV formats include `RMI`, `AU`, `AIF`, and `AIFC`. WAV files sound very realistic because they are recordings of real-life sounds. The drawback is that the file size is typically large. MP3 is a relatively compact format, but even MP3 files require about 1MB per minute of recording.

■ **MIDI:** MIDI stands for multi-instrument digital interface, and refers to the interface between a computer and a digital instrument such as an electronic keyboard. When you make a MIDI recording, there is no analog source — it is purely digital. For example, you press a key on an electronic keyboard, and that key press is translated into instructions that are written to a computer file. No microphone, and no sound waves in the air. What is the sound of one key pressing? It is completely up to the software. It could sound like a piano, a saxophone, or a harpsichord — whatever instrument it is set up to "be" at the moment. MIDI files (usually identified by a .mid extension) are smaller in size than WAV files, and several minutes of recording typically take up much less than 1MB of space. The drawback to MIDI music is that it can sound rather artificial and cold. After all, a computer emulating a saxophone is not the same thing as a real saxophone.

You need to understand the difference between these sound formats so that you can choose the correct format when recording sounds for your presentation, or when choosing recorded music. Keep in mind that whenever you use a WAV file in a presentation, you will add considerably to the presentation's file size. But also keep in mind that when you choose MIDI over WAV for your music, you get a different type of music, one that sounds more artificial.

CAUTION The sounds that come with Microsoft Office are royalty-free, which means that you can use them freely in your presentation without paying an extra fee. However, if you download sounds from the Internet or acquire them from other sources, you must be careful not to violate any copyright laws. Sounds recorded from television, radio, or compact discs are protected by copyright law, and you or your company might face serious legal action if you use them in a presentation without the permission of the copyright holder.

To hear the difference, do the following exercise as an experiment:

1. In Windows, use the Search feature to locate the sample MIDI files that came with Windows. To do so, search for *.mid.

NOTE Windows Vista does not come with any sample sounds. However, if you have Windows XP, or if you upgraded from Windows XP to Windows Vista, then you will have some sample sounds.

2. Double-click one of the files to play it.

3. Use Search (or Find) to locate some sample WAV files that came with Windows. To do so, search for *.wav.

4. Double-click one of the files to play it.

Can you hear the difference?

Where to Find Sounds

There are sound collections available all over the Internet, just as there are clip art collections. You can also buy sound collections on CD. If you find yourself putting together a lot of presentations, or searching the Internet for hours to find specific sounds for this or that purpose, then you might find it more cost-effective to simply buy a good collection of sounds.

Here are some Web sites where you can find some sounds:

- **A1 Free Sound Effects** (`www.a1freesoundeffects.com/noflash.htm`): This Web site offers a lot of free sounds for non-commercial use. You can also buy them quite cheaply for commercial use.
- **Microsoft** (`office.microsoft.com/downloads/2002/Sounds.aspx`): Microsoft offers a nice collection of free sounds to work with Office versions 2000 and higher. You can also check out `http://office.microsoft.com`.
- **Partners in Rhyme** (`www.sound-effect.com`): This Web site offers sound and music collections for sale, as well as some free files for download. Their background music clips are cool because they are set up for perfect looping — that is, continuous play without a noticeable break between the end and the beginning.
- **Wav Central** (`wavcentral.com`): This is a big repository of all kinds of free sounds in WAV format. (Beware of possible copyright violations, though; some of the clips here appear to be from movies, TV shows, and so on.)

PowerPoint offers a selection of sounds, and you can find out how to access them within the program later in this chapter.

The Microsoft Clip Organizer can help you find sounds in Microsoft's collection of clips. Although the collection of sounds is not as extensive as what you would find in clip art, you may be able to find something of use.

CROSS-REF   This chapter does not specifically address the Clip Organizer because it was covered quite thoroughly in Chapter 12.

Now that you know where to find sounds, and how to make intelligent decisions about their use, let's start using them in your presentations.

Inserting a Sound File as an Icon

The most elementary way to use a sound file in a presentation is to place the sound clip directly on a slide as an object. An icon appears on the slide, and you can click the icon during the presentation to play the sound. This method works well if you want to play the sound at exactly the right moment in the presentation.

EXPERT TIP To "hide" the sound icon, drag it off the edge of the slide. The sound still works, but the audience cannot see the icon.

You can place a sound file on a slide in either of two ways: by selecting a sound from the Clip Organizer, or by selecting a sound from a file on your computer or network. The following sections cover each method.

EXPERT TIP You can also assign the sound to another object on the slide instead, as explained in the section "Assigning a Sound to an Object," later in this chapter. When you do this, the object to which you attach the sound serves the same function as an icon; you click the object to play the sound.

Choosing a Sound from the Clip Organizer

You learned about the Clip Organizer in Chapter 12. Its primary function is to help you insert clip art (graphics), but it also manages sounds and movie files. The Clip Organizer is a good place to start if you are not sure which sound files are available or what kind of sound you want.

Follow these steps to choose a sound from the Clip Organizer:

1. Establish your Internet connection, if possible. This will make a much wider variety of clips available.

2. On the Insert tab, click the down arrow beneath the Sound button, and click Sound from Clip Organizer. The Clip Organizer appears with icons for the available clips.

EXPERT TIP If you are getting a lot of music files in the task pane that you don't want to wade through, open the Results Should Be list, click the plus sign next to Sounds, and deselect the check boxes for MP3 Format and Windows Media Audio.

3. (Optional) To narrow down the list of clips to only those with certain keywords, type the keyword in the Search For text box and press Enter.

4. (Optional) To preview the clip, do the following:

   a. Right-click a clip and choose Preview/Properties from the shortcut menu. A Preview/Properties dialog box opens, and the sound plays.

   b. If you want to play the sound again, click the Play button (right-pointing triangle), as shown in Figure 16.1.

   c. (Optional) To preview another clip, click the Next (≥) or Previous (≤) buttons.

   d. To close the dialog box, click Close.

FIGURE 16.1

You can preview a clip in the Preview/Properties dialog box.

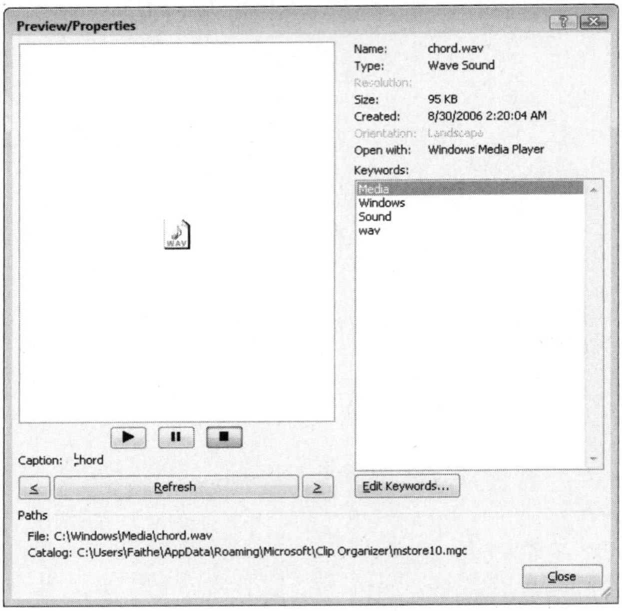

EXPERT TIP The Preview/Properties dialog box also enables you to change or add keywords to the clip, as you did with the clip art in Chapter 12. Click the Edit Keywords button to expand the dialog box to include controls for editing the keyword list.

5. Click the clip that you want to insert. A box appears, asking how you want it to play: Automatically or When Clicked. Choose one of these options. An icon for the sound appears in the center of the slide.

6. Reposition and resize the icon if necessary. For example, in Figure 16.2, the icon has been moved off to the corner where it is less noticeable. You can even drag it completely off the slide and it still works (but it does not appear on-screen).

CAUTION If you set a sound clip to play only when clicked, don't drag it off the edge of the slide or you won't have any way of playing it during the show.

FIGURE 16.2

The sound clip appears as a small speaker icon on the slide.

Relax at Sycamore Knoll!

Looking for that
special getaway
for the weekend?

Sound icon

7. If you want to insert another sound clip, repeat steps 3 to 6. If you are finished with the Clip Organizer for now, close it by clicking its Close (X) button.

Once the Sound icon is on the slide, you can move and resize it as you would any other object. You can also specify when the sound will play: when the mouse pointer moves over it, when you click it, or automatically. See the section "Fine-Tuning Sound Play Settings," later in this chapter for more details.

Choosing a Sound from a File

If the sound that you want is not accessible from the Clip Organizer, you can either add it to the Clip Organizer, as you learned in Chapter 12, or you can simply import it from a file. The former technique is better if you plan to use the clip a lot; the latter makes more sense if you are using the clip only once or expect to use it only infrequently.

NOTE If you installed PowerPoint or Office using the default options, then there are many sound files available in the Windows\Media folder on your hard disk. You can use one of these files if you want to practice the following steps.

Follow these steps to insert a sound from a file:

1. On the Insert tab, click the Sound button (or open its list and click Sound from File). The Insert Sound dialog box opens.

2. Navigate to the drive and folder that contain the sound that you want. If you do not know which location to use, try the Windows\Media folder on the hard disk where Windows is installed.

3. Click the sound file that you want to use, as shown in Figure 16.3, and then click OK.

4. A dialog box appears, asking how you want the file to play in the slide show. Choose Automatically or When Clicked. A Speaker icon appears on the slide, as shown in Figure 16.2.

FIGURE 16.3

Choose a sound file from your hard disk or other location (such as your company's network).

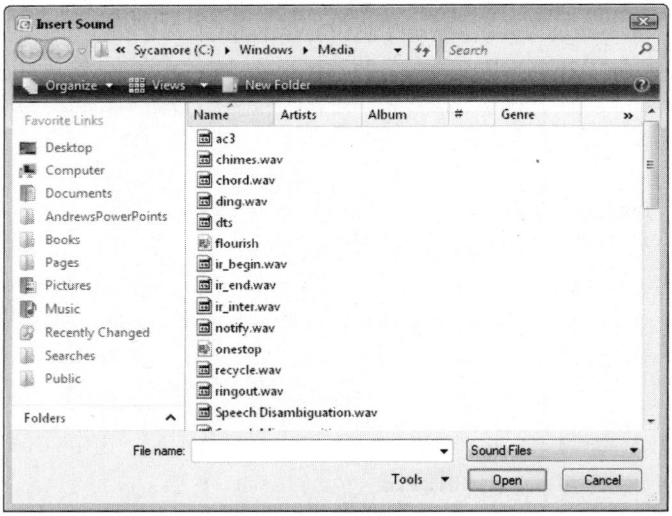

EXPERT TIP When sound (WAV) files are smaller than the size specified in PowerPoint's options, they are embedded; sound files that are larger than the specified size are linked. To adjust the size limit, choose Office ➪ PowerPoint Options, click Advanced, and specify a value in the Link Sounds with File Size Greater Than _____ KB text box. If you want a sound file to be linked, then place it in the same folder as the PowerPoint presentation file before you insert it. This ensures a relative reference in the link, so that when you move the files to another location, the link retains its integrity.

Fine-Tuning Sound Play Settings

When you insert a sound, you can choose the options, Automatically or When Clicked. Automatically makes the sound play when the icon appears. If you don't have any animation set up for the slide, the sound icon appears at the same time as everything else on the slide, and so the sound plays when the slide appears. (See Chapter 18 to learn about animation that can make different items on a slide appear at different times.) The When Clicked option makes the sound play only when a user clicks the icon.

If you want to more precisely define when a sound will play, or change the volume for the sound, try the following method.

Playing on a Mouse Click or Mouseover

As you insert a sound, PowerPoint prompts you to choose whether it is played when clicked or automatically. You can change this behavior later by adding or changing the action setting.

CAUTION   When you set a sound to play when clicked as you are inserting it, PowerPoint sets up both an Action setting and a custom animation for it, both of which play when clicked. If you turn off the action setting, the custom animation trigger will still be there, and it will still play when clicked. Vice versa applies too; if you delete the custom animation trigger, the action setting will still be there.

CAUTION   If you set up a sound to play automatically and also allow it to play on a mouse-click or mouseover, then you may end up with two copies playing, and they may not be synchronized.

To play a sound when the mouse either clicks it (mouse-click) or moves over it (mouseover), or to modify the Action settings, do the following:

1. Click the icon to select it. Selection handles appear around it.

2. On the Insert tab, click Action. The Action Settings dialog box appears.

3. Click the Mouse Click or Mouse Over tab. Figure 16.4 shows the Mouse Click tab.

EXPERT TIP   You can have separate settings for the mouse-click and mouseover actions, and one does not preclude the other. For example, if you have already specified that the sound should play on mouse-click, and you set it up to play on mouseover, this does not change the mouse-click setting.

4. To make the sound play on mouse-click (or mouseover, depending on the tab that you selected), select the Object Action option. Then make sure that Play is selected from the Object Action drop-down list. To prevent the sound from playing on mouse-click (or mouseover), you can select the None option. (This doesn't take away any custom animation trigger, though.)

5. Click OK.

FIGURE 16.4

To make a sound play when the mouse pointer is over its icon, you can set it up on the Mouse Over tab. You can use the Mouse Click tab to make the sound play when you click it.

Adjusting the Sound Play Settings for Custom Animation

When you choose Automatically as the setting when you first place a sound, PowerPoint sets it up to play at the exact moment that the sound icon appears on-screen, with no delay. You can change this default so that there is a delay, or you can turn it off so that the sound does not play automatically.

To access a sound's animation settings, click Custom Animation on the Animations tab. The Custom Animation pane appears, with a clip at the top of the list. A clock icon next to the clip indicates that the clip has a Start After Previous designation; this means that the clip is set up to play automatically. A clip that is set up to play on mouse click or mouseover appears with a mouse icon. Both icon types appear in Figure 16.5.

Clips that you insert from the Clip Organizer have generic names, such as "Media 3." Clips that you insert manually with the Sound from File command have names that match the filename, such as chord.wav. You can rename them in the Selection and Visibility task pane (accessed from the Home tab), and the new name will appear in the Custom Animation pane.

FIGURE 16.5

Custom animation settings allow you to specify when a sound plays.

Clip will play automatically after previous event.

Clip will play when clicked

> **NOTE** The following sections give a brief overview of the animation settings in PowerPoint; for a fuller discussion, see Chapter 18.

Turning Automatic Play On or Off

To turn the automatic play on or off for a clip, do the following:

1. On the Animations tab, click Custom Animation to open the Custom Animation pane if it does not already appear.

2. Select the icon for the sound. A gray box appears around its name in the pane.

3. Move your cursor over the sound on the pane, so that a drop-down arrow appears to its right. Click the arrow to open the menu, as shown in Figure 16.6.

4. If you want the sound to play automatically, choose Start With Previous or Start After Previous. Otherwise, choose Start On Click.

EXPERT TIP   Specifying Start On Click in the Custom Animation pane starts the sound file when a user clicks the mouse anywhere on the slide, even if they do not click the sound icon itself. However, you can mimic the on-mouse-click action settings by clicking the arrow to the right of the sound name in the Custom Animation pane and clicking Timing to open the Timing tab. You can then click the Triggers button, and select the sound in the Start Effect on Click of box.

FIGURE 16.6

You can choose whether the sound should play automatically or only when a user clicks it.

Delaying or Repeating a Sound

Depending on the situation, it may be useful to have a sound play after a short delay, or to repeat the sound more than once. In Chapter 18, you can learn more about setting animation options. However, here are some quick instructions for customizing a sound:

1. On the Animations tab, click Custom Animation to open the Custom Animation pane if it does not already appear.

2. Select the icon for the sound. A gray box appears around its name in the pane.

3. Open the menu for the sound clip, as shown in Figure 16.6, and choose Timing. The Play Sound dialog box opens with the Timing tab displayed, as shown in Figure 16.7.

FIGURE 16.7

You can use the Timing controls to set a delay for when the sound will play.

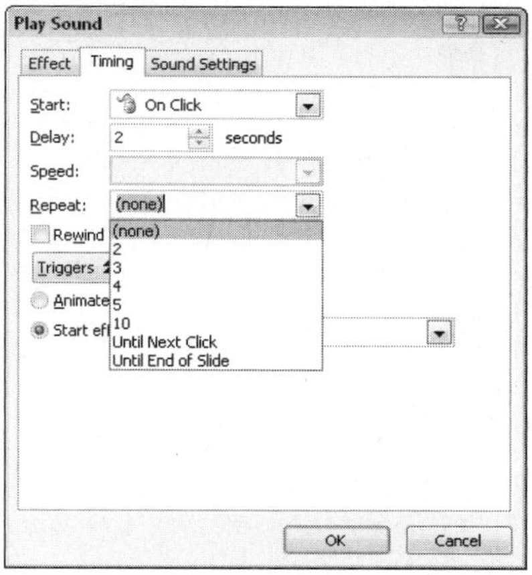

4. Enter a number of seconds in the Delay text box. The delay occurs between when the previous event happens (in this case, the event is the initial appearance of the slide on-screen) and when the sound begins.

5. Open the Repeat drop-down list and choose the number of times that the sound should repeat. You can choose 2, 3, 4, 5, or 10 times, as well as Until Next Click, and Until Next Slide. You can also type in your own number (up to 9999).

6. Click OK.

Choosing the Starting Point for a Sound Clip

There might be times when you want to start the clip from some point other than the beginning. For example, you may have a really good sound clip, except that the first 5 seconds are garbled or it may contain content that you do not want to use; or you may want to play just the first 15 seconds of the clip. To control the point at which a clip starts, do the following:

1. On the Animations tab, click Custom Animation to open the Custom Animation pane if it does not already appear.

2. Select the icon for the sound. A gray box appears around its name in the pane.

3. Open the menu for the sound clip and choose Effect Options. The Play Sound dialog box opens with the Effect tab displayed, as shown in Figure 16.8.

FIGURE 16.8

You can specify that a clip plays at a different time than the beginning, or set it to restart playing from wherever it left off if you stop it.

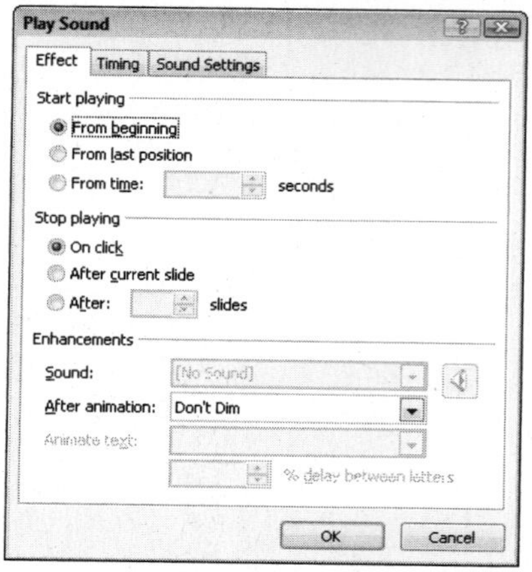

4. In the Start Playing area, choose one of these options:

   ■ **From the beginning**, which is the default play mode.

   ■ **From the last position** if you want it to pick up where it left off when you stopped it.

   ■ **From a specific time**, and then enter the number of seconds into the clip that it should begin playing.

5. Click OK.

Choosing When the Sound Clip Will Stop

Normally a clip will stop playing after it has played once (or however many times you have set it up to play), or until a mouse-click. However, there may be times when you want it to stop earlier. For example, you may want a particular song to play while a certain slide is on-screen, but to stop when you move to the next slide. You may also want it to continue for the next two slides, and then stop.

To control when a sound clip stops, you can use the Effect tab of the Play Sound dialog box, as shown in Figure 16.8:

1. Perform steps 1 to 4 of the preceding section.

2. In the Stop Playing area, choose one of these options:

   ▪ **On Click** to use the default play mode.

   ▪ **After Current Slide** to stop the audio when you move to the next slide, or when the clip has finished playing, whichever comes first.

   ▪ **After ____ Slides**, and then enter a number of slides; the audio will continue until the specified number of additional slides have passed.

3. Click OK.

EXPERT TIP If you want to play more than one sound back-to-back throughout your presentation (as a background track), type **999** in the After ____ Slides text box. PowerPoint will stop the first sound when it starts the second one. If you simply put the number of slides that you expect PowerPoint to play the sound, it will not work the way that you expect. For more information, go to this article: www.rdpslides.com/pptfaq/FAQ00047.htm. You can also use the Play Across Slides option in the Play Sound dialog box for this.

Specifying the Sound Volume

When you give your presentation, you can specify an overall volume using the computer's volume controls in Windows. However, sometimes you might want the volume of one sound to be different than others. To set the volume for a specific sound, follow these steps:

1. On the Animations tab, click Custom Animation to open the Custom Animation pane if it does not already appear.

2. Select the icon for the sound. A gray box appears around its name in the pane.

3. Open the drop-down menu for the sound clip and choose Effect Options. The Play Sound dialog box opens with the Effect tab displayed.

4. Click the Sound Settings tab.

5. Click the Sound Volume button to display a volume slider. Drag the slider up or down to adjust the volume, as shown in Figure 16.9.

6. Click OK to close the Play Sound dialog box.

FIGURE 16.9

You can set the volume for an individual sound in comparison to the overall volume for the entire presentation.

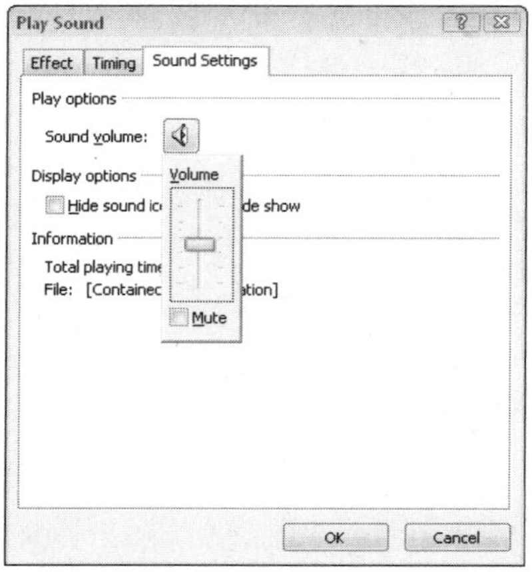

EXPERT TIP The sound will play at a consistent volume throughout the duration of the clip. If you need the volume to change partway through, you can use a sound-editing program to change the clip volume before inserting it.

Setting Sound Options from the Ribbon

You can control some sound options from the Options tab, which appears when you select a sound clip. This tab allows you to quickly change some settings so that you do not have to open the full dialog boxes, For example, you can adjust the slide show volume, set a sound to play when clicked or automatically, set the sound's icon size, and so on. See Figure 16.10.

FIGURE 16.10

The Options tab allows you to adjust some sound settings.

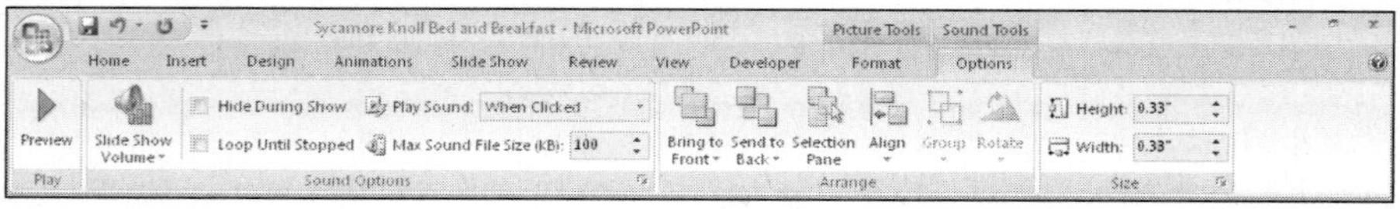

Assigning a Sound to an Object

Many presenters believe that sound icons are distracting and unprofessional , and so they prefer to assign sound files to clip art or to other objects that they place in the presentation. This way, they still have precise control over when a sound plays (for example, when they click the clip art), but the control mechanism is hidden.

Although you can assign a sound to any object, many people assign their sounds to graphics. For example, you might attach a sound file of a greeting from your CEO to the CEO's picture.

Follow these steps to assign a sound to an object:

1. Insert the object that you want to associate with the sound. For example, the object can be a graphic, chart, or text box.

2. Select the object, and on the Insert tab, click Action. The Action Settings dialog box appears.

3. Click either the Mouse Click tab or the Mouse Over tab, depending on which action you want. For example, mouse-click plays the sound when you click the object, while mouse over plays the sound when you move your mouse pointer over the object.

4. Select the Play Sound check box. Then open the drop-down list and choose a sound, as shown in Figure 16.11. You can choose from a variety of sounds that are stored in C:\Windows\Media, or you can choose Other Sound to open the Add Sound dialog box and pick a sound from any location. You can only use WAV sounds for this, though.

5. Click OK. The object now has the sound associated with it so that when you click it or move the mouse over it during the presentation, the sound plays.

FIGURE 16.11

You can choose the sound that you want to assign to the object.

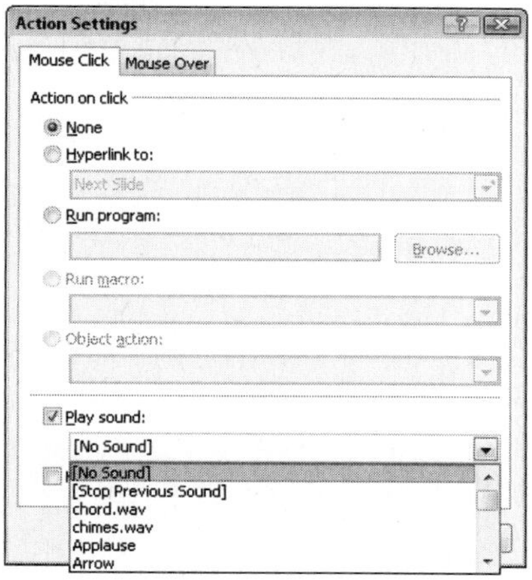

> **NOTE** Chapter 18 is devoted entirely to transitions and animation effects, and so this chapter does not describe them in detail. In Chapter 18, you can learn how to assign sounds to the transition between slides, or to the movement (animation) of any object on any slide.

Adding a CD Audio Soundtrack

A lot of great music is available on CD these days, and most computers contain a CD-ROM drive that reads not only computer CDs but also plays audio CDs. PowerPoint takes advantage of this feature by letting you play tracks from an audio CD during your presentation.

Adding a CD audio clip to a slide is much like adding a regular sound clip. You place the clip on the slide and a little CD icon appears to allow you to activate the clip. You can then set properties for the clip to make it play exactly the way you want. However, the difference is that the audio track is not stored with the presentation file. Therefore, the audio CD must be in the CD drive of the computer that you are using to present the show. You cannot use CD audio tracks in presentations that you plan to distribute as self-running presentations on a data CD or over the Internet, because the computers on which it will run will not have access to the CD.

> **EXPERT TIP** If you need to include audio from a CD in a presentation that will be shown on a PC that does not have access to the original audio CD, you can record a part of the CD track as a WAV file. To do this, you can use the Windows Sound Recorder program or another audio-recording utility. However, keep in mind that WAV files can be extremely large and can take up many megabytes for less than a minute of sound. To keep the file size smaller, consider using an MP3 or an ASF file instead of a WAV file. As always, make sure that you are not violating any copyright laws.

Placing a CD Soundtrack Icon on a Slide

To play a CD track for a slide, you must place an icon for it on the slide. You can actually place a range of tracks, such as multiple tracks from a CD, using a single icon. To do so, follow these steps:

1. Insert the CD in your PC.

2. On the Insert tab, click the Sound drop-down arrow and then click Play Audio CD Track. The Insert CD Audio dialog box appears.

3. Specify the starting track number in the Start at Track text box in the Clip selection section, as shown in Figure 16.12.

4. Specify the ending track number in the End at Track text box. If you want to play only a single track, the Start at Track and End at Track numbers should be the same. The start or end time changes only after you click one of the up- or down-arrows next to the time. For example, if you want to play tracks 1, 2, and 3, you should select track 1 as the start track and track 3 as the end track (as opposed to track 4).

5. If you want to begin the starting track at a particular spot (other than the beginning), enter this start time in the Time text box for that track. For example, to start the track 50 seconds into the song, you would type **00:50**.

FIGURE 16.12

You can specify a starting and ending track, as well as a time within those tracks.

6. By default, PowerPoint plays an entire track. If you want to stop the ending track at a particular spot, enter this end time in the Time text box for that track. For example, in Figure 16-12, track 1 is the starting track, and track 4 is the ending track, at 2:57 seconds long. If you want to end track 4 ten seconds early, you can change the Time setting under End to 2:47. You can see the total playing time at the bottom of the dialog box.

7. (Optional) You can adjust the volume with the Sound Volume button.

8. Click OK. A message appears, asking whether you want the sound to play Automatically or When Clicked. Make your selection. Depending on your choice, the CD track activates either when the slide appears (Automatically) or when you click its icon during the presentation (When Clicked).

9. The CD icon now appears in the center of the slide. You can drag it off the edge of the slide if it interferes with your slide content. You can also resize it if you want, just like any other object.

10. In the Custom Animation pane, open the menu for the CD icon and select Effect Options. Type a number in the Stop Playing After ____ Slides text box. Keep in mind that, in this context, PowerPoint considers each transition (whether backward or forward) a "slide," and so typing **999** in this text box ensures that your soundtrack will play throughout the entire presentation. (You can also do this by setting the Play Track setting on the Options tab to Play Across Slides.)

EXPERT TIP You can play any number of tracks from a single CD using a single icon, as long as they are contiguous and you play them in their default order. If you need non-contiguous tracks from the CD, or in a different order, or you just want certain segments of some of the clips, then you must place each clip individually on the slide, and then control their order in Custom Animation. See Chapter 18 for details. If you do not want the icons to appear on the slide, then drag them off the slide's edge.

The CD track is now an animated object on your slide. By animated, I mean that it is an object that has some action associated with it.

EXPERT TIP To play CD tracks across multiple slides, you must use custom animation, and you must set the sound to stop playing after 999 slides. Chapter 18 covers custom animation in more detail, but this is briefly how it works: Suppose you have a 30-slide presentation, and you want to play tracks 2, 4, and 6 from your CD, each for 10 slides. On slide 1, you would insert track 2, and set its custom animation to stop playing after 999 slides. Then you would do the same for track 4 on slide 11, and track 6 on slide 21.

Editing the CD Track Start and End Times

To specify which track you want to play and where you want to start it, do the following:

1. Click the CD icon on the slide.

2. Display the CD Audio Tools Options tab, and set new values in the Start Playing and Stop Playing text boxes, as shown in Figure 16.13. This is an alternative to opening the Play Audio CD dialog box again (from the CD clip's menu in the Custom Animation pane).

FIGURE 16.13

You can adjust the CD track times from the Options tab.

Controlling When a CD Track Plays

You can set many of the same properties for a CD track on a slide that you can for a sound file icon. You can also use the Custom Animation controls to specify precisely when and how a track will play. To do this, follow these steps:

1. Display the Custom Animation pane from the Animations tab.

2. Select the CD icon on the slide. A gray box appears around its name in the Custom Animation pane.

3. Open the drop-down menu for the selected clip and choose Effect Options. This opens the Play CD Audio dialog box.

From this point, the options are exactly the same as those for regular sound files that you have learned about earlier in this chapter. Refer back to the "Fine-tuning Sound Play Settings" section earlier in this chapter for details. All of the same tabs are available, including Effect, Timing, and Sound Settings.

Using the Advanced Timeline to Fine-Tune Sound Events

The Advanced Timeline is turned off by default. When you turn it on, a timeline appears at the bottom of the Custom Animation pane, and indicators appear next to each clip to show how long it will take to play and at what point it starts. This is useful when you are trying to coordinate several sound and/or video clips to play sequentially with a certain amount of space between them. It also saves you from having to calculate their starting and ending times in relation to the initial appearance of the slide.

To turn the Advanced Timeline on, do the following:

1. If the Custom Animation pane does not already appear, click Custom Animation on the Animations tab.

2. Open the drop-down menu for any of the items in the pane and choose Show Advanced Timeline. The timeline appears.

3. *(Optional)* Widen the pane by dragging its left border toward the center of the slide, so that you have more working room.

4. *(Optional)* Click the word *Seconds* at the bottom of the pane. This opens a menu where you can choose Zoom In or Zoom Out to change the zoom on the timeline.

5. Click a clip to select it on the Custom Animation list. A red, right-pointing arrow appears next to the clip. The arrow position corresponds to the place on the timeline where the clip is currently set to begin. For example, Figure 16.14 shows two clips, with each clip beginning at a different point.

6. Open the clip's drop-down menu and choose either With Previous or After Previous, depending on how you want it to relate to the earlier clip.

CAUTION If there is more than one sound clip set to After Previous, a vertical line appears where the first clip will finish. If a clip is set to After Previous, it cannot start before the clip that precedes it. Therefore, any delay that you set up for a subsequent clip will be in relation to the end of the preceding clip. If the clip is set to With Previous, the two can overlap.

7. *(Optional)* To reorder the clips on the list, click a clip and then click the up or down Re-Order arrow at the bottom of the pane.

FIGURE 16.14

You can use a timeline to graphically set the timing between clips on a slide.

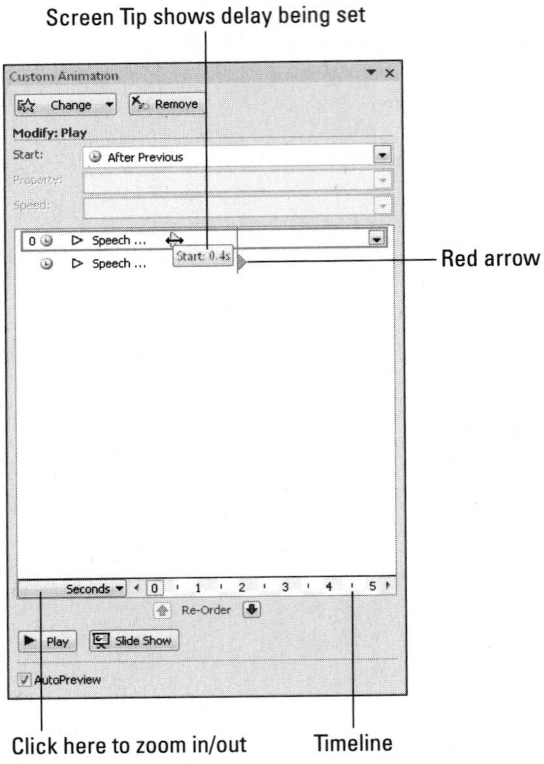

Screen Tip shows delay being set

Red arrow

Click here to zoom in/out   Timeline

8. To change the amount of delay that is assigned to a clip, drag the red arrow next to the clip to the right or left. This is the same as changing the number in the Delay text box in the clip's properties.

EXPERT TIP   You can use custom animation to create complex systems of sounds that play, pause, and stop in relation to other animated objects on the slide. Although Chapter 18 contains full details, here is a quick explanation of how to use custom animation: add a sound to the Custom Animation pane by clicking Add Effect, then choose Sound Actions, and then select Play, Pause, or Stop. In this way, you can create separate actions for the same clip to start, pause, or stop at various points.

Recording Sounds

Most PCs have a microphone jack on the sound card where you can plug in a small microphone. You can then record your own sounds to include in the presentation. In this case, I am referring to simple, short sounds. If you want to record a full-blown voice-over narration, see Chapter 16. To record a sound, follow these steps:

1. Display the slide on which you want to place the sound clip.

2. On the Insert tab, open the Sound drop-down menu and choose Record Sound. The Sound Recorder dialog box appears, as shown in Figure 16.15.

FIGURE 16.15

You can record your own sounds using your PC's microphone.

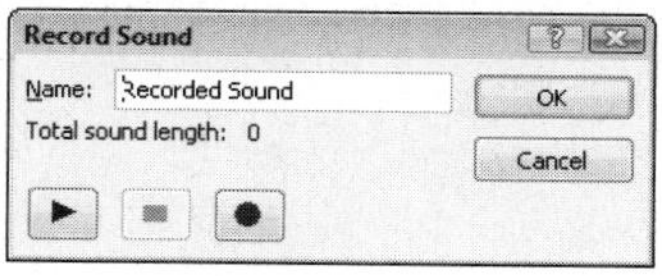

3. Click the Start Recording button.

4. Record the sound. When you are finished, click the Stop Recording button (the black square).

5. (Optional) To play back the sound, click the Play button (the black triangle).

6. Click OK to place the sound on the slide. A sound icon appears on the slide.

7. Use the controls that you learned about earlier in this chapter to specify when and how the sound plays.

Summary

In this chapter, you learned about the many ways that you can use sound in your presentation. You learned how to place a sound object on a slide, how to associate sounds with other objects, how to use a CD soundtrack, and how to record your own sounds. The next chapter continues to discuss multimedia by looking at how you can place video clips on slides.

Chapter 17

Incorporating Motion Video

PowerPoint creates complete multimedia presentations, which means that not only can you include pictures and sounds but also movies and animations. In this chapter, you'll learn how to select the appropriate video type, how to insert clips, and how to control when they will play.

Understanding Video Types

Let's begin at an obvious starting point: figuring out how you are going to get a hold of the videos you need. Not all videos are live-action recordings; some are digitally created cartoons (either 2-D or 3-D). PowerPoint can show both kinds. The difference is not that important once you get clips into PowerPoint, but when you are determining how you will acquire them, it is helpful to make the distinction. The following sections discuss the types of videos that PowerPoint supports.

Animated GIFs

When is a video not *really* a video? When it's an animated GIF.

As you may already know, GIF is a file format for static graphics files. One of the advantages of it over other graphic file formats is that you can create animated versions. These are not really videos in the traditional sense; they are a collection of still graphics stored in a single file under one name. When the file is displayed — on a presentation slide, a Web page, or some other place — it cycles through the still graphics at a certain speed, making a very rudimentary animation. You cannot control the animation of an animated GIF through PowerPoint, nor can you set it up to repeat a certain number of

IN THIS CHAPTER

Placing a video on a slide

Specifying when a movie will play

Configuring the movie clip size on the slide

Locating movie clips to use in your presentations

Troubleshooting movie problems

times. That information is contained within the GIF file itself. PowerPoint simply reads that information and plays the GIF accordingly.

PowerPoint's Clip Organizer comes with many animated GIFs that have simple conceptual plots, such as time passing, gears turning, and computers passing data between them. They are more like animated clip art than real movies or real animated clips, but they do add an active element to an otherwise static slide.

EXPERT TIP   It is possible to convert an animated GIF to a "true" video format such as AVI. However, you can't do it using PowerPoint alone; you need a conversion utility. Corel Animation Shop will do this (www.corel.com), as will many GIF-editing programs.

Live-Action Videos

Now you get to learn about the "real videos." Recorded videos have a live origin. Someone went out with a video camera and pointed at something in the world. You can get live-action videos from the Internet, but in most cases for business presentations you will want to record it yourself with a camera to suit your purpose. You might use recorded video to present a message from someone who could not be present in person, show how a product functions, or provide a tour of a facility, for example.

There are two kinds of video cameras: digital and non-digital. It is important to know which kind you have because they hook up to the PC differently to transfer the video. A digital video camera hooks up directly to the PC via USB or FireWire port, whereas a regular (analog) video camera requires a conversion box or an adapter card that converts analog to digital.

If you are not sure what type of video camera you have, look at how it stores the video. If it stores it on VHS or some other kind of tape, it's analog. If it stores it on a disk or cartridge that says "digital" on it, it's digital. Also look at its interfaces. If it's digital, it will have either a USB or FireWire plug that fits into your PC; the end of the cable that fits into the video camera will be smaller and more square.

You don't usually import videos directly from the camera into PowerPoint because they are too rough and may contain extraneous footage, unwanted sounds, or awkward jerks or transitions. Instead you want to polish up your videos in a video-editing program. Windows Movie Maker, which comes with Windows XP and Vista, is a decent low-end choice. If you bought an analog-to-digital video converter box or card, it may have come with video-editing software as well. Video editing can be very time-consuming, so allow plenty of time to do this work before assembling your presentation in PowerPoint.

EXPERT TIP   Don't assume that you have to record every bit of live-action footage with your own camera. As long as you are diligent about obeying copyright restrictions, you can safely download tons of great footage from the Internet. For example, the Internet Archive at www.archive.org contains links to huge repositories of footage on all subjects, mostly pre-1964 material on which the copyright has expired. Warning — you can easily get sucked in here and waste several days browsing!

Digital Animation

Digital animation does not have a live origin—it's a simulation of life. Simple animations appear cartoonish, but there are animation applications that, in the right hands, can create extremely realistic 3-D simulations. Digital animation is useful when you are showing things that either don't exist yet or are unavailable for live filming. For example, you could show how a planned product will be manufactured or how it will work. Simple cartoons can also add a whimsical touch or lighten the mood.

To create your own animations, turn to a separate animation application; PowerPoint doesn't have any capability for doing it. If you want high-end, high-quality 3-D animations, use a professional-quality application like Adobe After Effects.

Video File Formats

The video capture and video-editing program you use to create or acquire your video clips will determine the file's format and specs. PowerPoint can accept videos with the following file formats:

- Motion Picture Experts Group (.mpg, .mpeg, .m1v, .mp2, .mpa, and .mpe)
- Microsoft streaming format (.asf and .asx)
- Microsoft Windows Media Video (.wmv)
- Audio Video Interleave (.avi)
- QuickTime (.mov or .qt) versions 1 and 2.x

CAUTION Versions of QuickTime 3 and higher will not work as an inserted movie in PowerPoint. You would need to either insert a later-format QuickTime file as an object (Object button on the Insert tab) or convert it to a supported format such as AVI using a third-party utility.

You may not have a choice in the settings used for the recording of live video or the file format. If you do have a choice, AVI is among the best formats for use in PowerPoint because of its near-universal compatibility. There may be compatibility issues with video in some MPEG variants, such as MPEG-2 and MPEG-4, such that you might need to install a separate DVD-playing utility or a specific codec to handle those formats.

CROSS-REF See the "Troubleshooting Movies That Won't Play" section later in this chapter for more information on MPEG variants.

On the theory that Microsoft-to-Microsoft always works, the Windows Media Video format (.wmv) is also a good choice. Because Windows Movie Maker creates its movies in this format by default, it's a good bet that they will work well in PowerPoint.

If you have a choice in quality, you should balance file size against quality. This is usually measured either in frames per second (fps), which is anywhere from 15 (low) to 30 (high), or in kilobits per second, which is anywhere from 38 kbps to 2.1 mbps. You might experiment with different settings to find one with acceptable quality for the task at hand with the minimum of file size. For example, with Windows Movie Maker, a wide variety of quality settings are available.

 What's the difference between a movie and a video? There really isn't any. PowerPoint uses the terms interchangeably.

Locating Sources of Movie Clips

Not sure where to find video clips? Here are some places to start:

- **Your own video camera.** You can connect a digital video camera directly to your PC, or connect an analog video camera to an adapter board that digitizes its input.

- **The Clip Organizer.** When you're connected to the Internet, you get the whole collection as you browse.

- **The Internet in general.** There are millions of interesting video clips on every imaginable subject. Use the search term video clips plus a few keywords that describe the type of clips you are looking for. Yahoo! is a good place to start looking (www.yahoo.com). Some clips are copyrighted or have usage limitations, but others can be used freely; check the usage information provided with the clip.

> **CAUTION** Whenever you get a video clip from the Internet, make sure you carefully read any restrictions or usage agreements to avoid copyright violations. If you create a presentation using copyrighted material in an unauthorized way, you or your company could potentially get sued.

- **Commercial collections of video clips and animated GIFs.** Many of these companies advertise on the Internet and provide free samples for downloading. Several such companies have included samples on the CD that accompanies this book.

- **The Internet Archive.** (www.archive.org). This site contains links to huge repositories of public domain footage on all subjects, mostly pre-1964 material on which the copyright has expired. Warning—you can easily get sucked in here and waste several days browsing!

Placing a Movie on a Slide

Your first step is to place the movie on the slide. After that, you can worry about position, size, and playing options. Just as with audio clips, you can place a video clip on a slide using the Clip Organizer, or do so directly by inserting from a file or pasting from another application.

> **CAUTION** Video clips are linked, not embedded, in the presentation. If you move the presentation file to another location, make sure you move the movie clips too. For this reason, inserting videos from the Clip Organizer may not be a good idea; it's linked from the original location and difficult to move. You can get around this by using the Office ➪ Publish ➪ Package for CD command, which gathers and packages all the needed files.

Inserting a Movie from the Clip Organizer

Just as with sounds and graphics, you can organize movie files with the Clip Organizer. I don't go into it in detail here, because the Clip Organizer is discussed in detail in Chapter 12. Most of the clips that come with the Clip Organizer are animations rather than recorded videos. To select a movie from the Clip Organizer, follow these steps:

1. Make sure your Internet connection is established (for the best selection of clips).

2. Display the slide on which you want to place the movie.

3. On the Insert tab, click the down arrow on the Movie button, and choose Movie from Clip Organizer. The Clip Organizer task pane appears, showing the available movie clips. Thumbnails of each clip appear, showing the first frame of the clip. You can tell that each is an animation or movie rather than a static graphic because of the little star icon in the bottom-right corner of each thumbnail image. See Figure 17.1.

FIGURE 17.1

Inserting a video clip from the Clip Organizer.

Video clip inserted

Animation icon

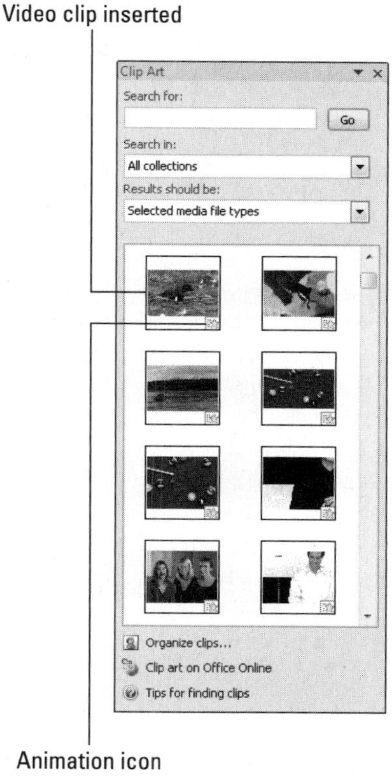

> **NOTE**   The Clip Organizer shows real movies mixed together with animated GIFs in the search results. Check a clip's properties if you're in doubt as to its type.

4. (Optional) If you want to preview the clip, open its menu (the down arrow to its right) and choose Preview/Properties. The clip plays in a dialog box; when you're done watching it, click Close.

5. Click the clip you want to insert. A box may appear asking when you want it to play. (This box won't appear when you insert an animated GIF, because they play automatically.)

6. Click either Automatically or When Clicked. The clip appears on the slide.

7. Close the Clip Organizer, and then move the clip as needed. It won't play in Normal view, but you can switch to Slide Show view to test it if desired.

> **CAUTION**   Be careful when resizing the video, because it can compromise quality; it's usually better to resize the video in your video-editing software.

To test the movie, enter Slide Show view and click it to play it (if it does not play automatically). You can control when and how the clip plays; you learn to do that later in this chapter.

> **EXPERT TIP**   Many interesting clips are available through the Clip Organizer if you are connected to the Internet so you can access the Microsoft site. Unlike with artwork, it is not obvious what a clip does just by looking at its name and the first frame (which is what appears as its thumbnail image). Take some time to insert a lot of clips and try them out to see what you have to choose from.

Remember that you can add your own video clips to the Clip Organizer, as you learned in Chapter 12, and you can categorize them, add keywords, and everything else that you can do to artwork.

Making Clip Organizer Content Available Offline

If you find some video clips in the Clip Organizer that you want to have available later, you can add them to the local collection of clips on your hard disk. That way, if your Internet connection is not available later, you can still access them. To make a clip available offline, do the following:

1. Make sure your Internet connection is established.

2. On the Insert tab, click the down arrow on the Movie button and choose Movie from Clip Organizer. The Clip Organizer task pane appears, showing the available movie clips. The clips that are on the Web have a little globe icon in their bottom-left corner.

3. Open the menu of the clip that you want (the arrow to its right) and choose Make Available Offline. The Copy to Collection dialog box opens as shown in Figure 17.2. If the Make Available Offline command is not present, it means that this clip is already on your local hard disk.

4. Select the collection in which you want to place the clip. (Or click New to create a new collection.) Then click OK.

FIGURE 17.2

Making a clip available offline involves copying it to one of your local clip collections.

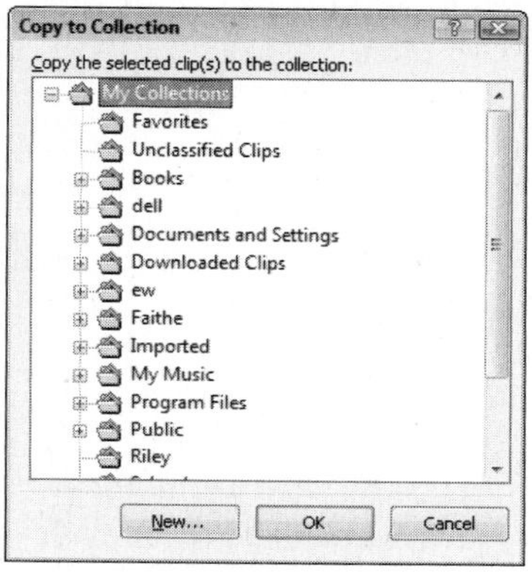

Inserting a Movie from a File

If the movie that you want is not in the Clip Organizer (and you don't want to bother with placing it there), you can place it directly on the slide, just like any other object. For example, you might have video of your CEO's last speech saved on your hard drive.

CAUTION If you plan on moving the presentation to another location later, place the movie clip in the same folder as the presentation itself before you insert the movie clip into the presentation. That way the path to it stored in the presentation file will be relative, and the link will still work after you move the presentation and movie clip.

To insert a video clip from a file, follow these steps:

1. Display the slide on which the movie should appear.

2. On the Insert tab, click Movie. You don't need to open the button's menu because the option that you want, Movie from File, is the default.

3. In the Insert Movie dialog box, locate the clip you want. Select the clip and click OK.

4. A box appears asking when you want it to play. Choose Automatically or When Clicked. The movie clip appears on the slide.

5. Move the clip as desired. Again, be careful when resizing the clip.

Setting Movie Options

Video clips are a lot like sounds in terms of what you can do with them. You can specify that they should play when you point at them or click them, or you can make them play automatically at a certain time.

> **CAUTION** If you are using an animated GIF, it plays the number of times specified in its header. That could be infinite looping (0), or it could be a specified number of times. You can't set it to do otherwise. (You can, however, delay its appearance with custom animation. See Chapter 18 for details.) Other movies, such as your own recorded video clips (AVI, WMV, and MPEG format), have more settings you can control.

Playing on Mouse Click or Mouse Over

The default setting for a video clip is to play when you click it with the mouse. To set it to play when you point to it, or not to play in response to the mouse, follow these steps:

1. Select the clip, and then on the Insert tab, click Action. The Action Settings dialog box opens. See Figure 17.3.

2. On the Mouse Click and Mouse Over tabs, click the None button if you want no action, or click the Object Action button if you want it to play in either case.

3. Click OK.

FIGURE 17.3

Set the Object Action to Play on the Mouse Click and Mouse Over tabs.

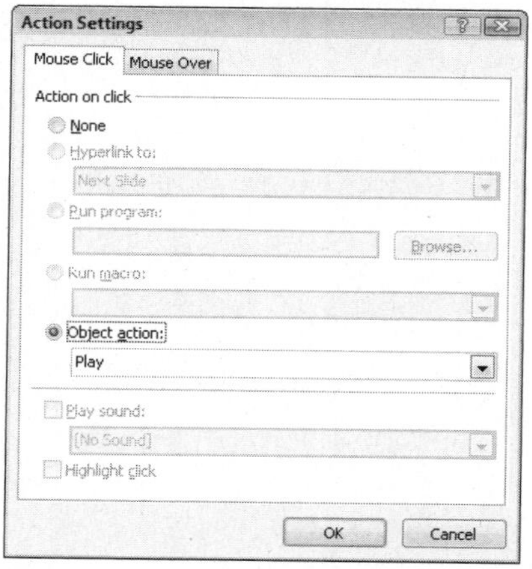

Controlling the Volume and Appearance

If you are working with a real video clip (not an animated GIF), you can also edit the Movie object's controls. These controls enable you to specify whether the video plays in a continuous loop or not, and which frame of the movie remains on the screen when it is finished (the first or the last). You can also control whether any clip controls appear on the slide. Chapter 16 goes into clip controls for sounds, but they are even more appropriate here for videos because you are more likely to want to pause, rewind, and fast-forward a video clip.

There are two ways to set the clip's volume and appearance; you can do so using the Movie Tools Options tab (Figure 17.4), or you can click the dialog box launcher in the Movie Options group there and set the same options up via a dialog box similar to the one from PowerPoint 2003 (shown in Figure 17.5) that controls those features. There is only one difference between the two methods, and it is minor — the volume for the clip, when set from the Options tab, has only four settings: Low, Medium, High, or Mute. When set via the dialog box, a continuously variable slider is available. Table 17.1 lists the available settings and the controls for each one using the Options tab and dialog box methods.

FIGURE 17.4

The Movie Options group controls movie playback directly from the Options tab.

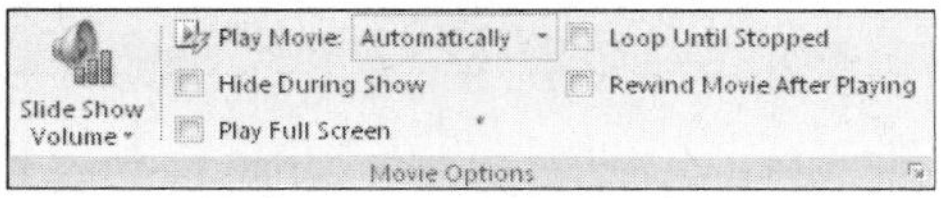

FIGURE 17.5

The Movie Options dialog box offers many of the same options as the Options tab.

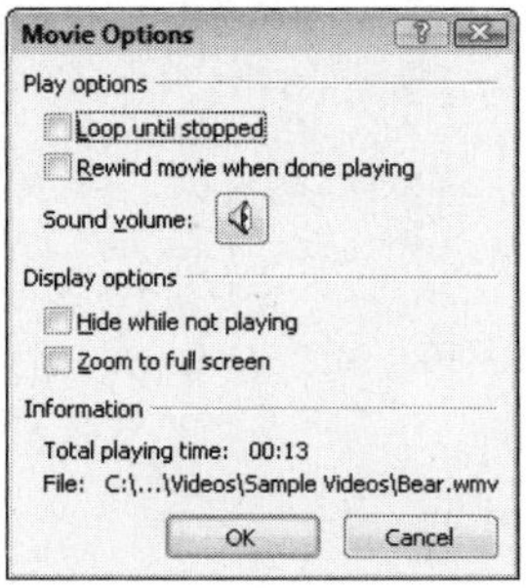

EXPERT TIP Some of the same controls in the Movie Options dialog box (see Figure 17.4) are also accessible while you are working on Custom Animation (covered in the following section). From the Custom Animation task pane, open the menu for the clip and choose Effect Options; then click the Movie Settings tab.

TABLE 17.1

Setting Sound and Appearance Options via Options Tab or Movie Options Dialog Box

Action	Movie Tools Options Tab	Movie Options Dialog Box
Play movie when clicked or automatically	Play Movie drop-down list	n/a
Hide the clip when it is not playing	Hide During Show check box	Hide While Not Playing check box
Play the clip full-screen, temporarily obscuring the rest of the slide	Play Full Screen check box	Zoom to Full Screen check box
Repeat the clip until another animation event stops it or until the next slide appears	Loop Until Stopped check box	Loop Until Stopped check box
Return the movie to its first frame after playing	Rewind Movie After Playing check box	Rewind Movie When Done Playing check box
Adjust sound volume for clip in relation to overall volume for presentation	Slide Show Volume drop-down list	Sound Volume button (opens slider)

Understanding the Custom Animation Task Pane Entries

When you place a movie clip on a slide, an entry for it is created on the Custom Animation task pane, as shown in Figure 17.6.

CAUTION   If you choose to set the clip to play automatically when you insert the clip initially, two entries appear in the Custom Animation task pane: one for Play and one for Pause. If you choose to set the clip to play on click, only the Pause entry appears. Changing the behavior later does not affect the presence/absence of the Play entry, and you need the Play entry to do some of the things in the upcoming sections. If you inserted it to play On Click initially, you might want to delete it and reinsert it and choose Automatically so you get both of those custom animation entries. That way you can more easily follow along in the next section.

FIGURE 17.6

If you set the clip to play automatically, separate entries for Pause and Play appear in the Custom Animation task pane.

Clip starts automatically

Play symbol

Pause symbol

Clip pauses on click

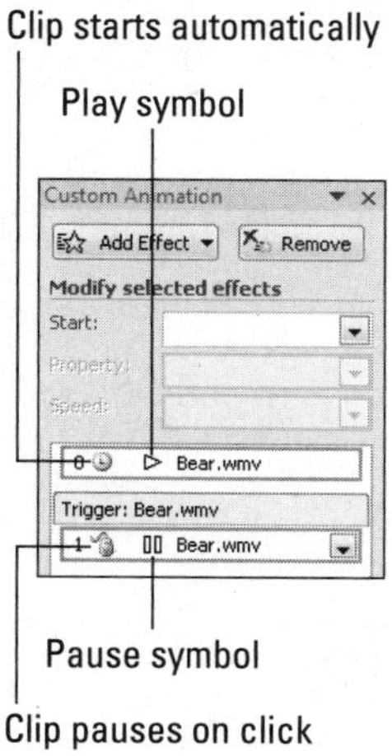

Controlling When the Video Will Play

You can control the play timing for real video clips (not animated GIFs) through the Custom Animation task pane and the Options tab. These settings enable you to specify whether the video should play automatically when the slide appears and whether there should be a delay before it.

To set this up, you need to display the Start and Delay controls for the clip. Be careful, though, because different dialog boxes appear — with different options — depending on what you select before you issue the command to open the dialog box. For example, in Figure 17.5, you saw that a single clip can have two entries in the Custom Animation task pane: Pause (triggered on click) and Play (occurring automatically). If you open the menu for the Pause entry and choose Timing, you get a Pause Movie dialog box. In this dialog box, a trigger has been set to start the effect on click of the movie. If you open the menu for Play and choose Timing, you get a Play Movie dialog box. And if you select the clip on the slide directly, and then right-click either the pause or the play entry and choose Timing, you get an entirely different dialog box called Effect Options. Figures 17.7 through 17-9 shows these dialog boxes, respectively, so that you can see how they are different.

FIGURE 17.7

Timing options for pausing the movie.

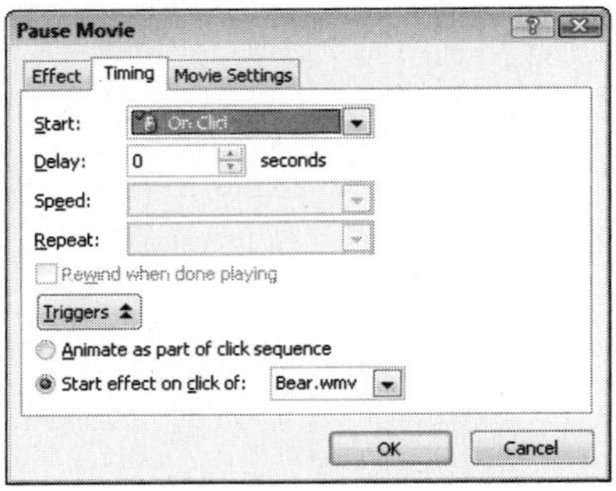

FIGURE 17.8

Timing options for playing the movie. Notice that Repeat and Rewind are available (unlike in Figure 17.7).

FIGURE 17.9

Timing options for the clip in general.

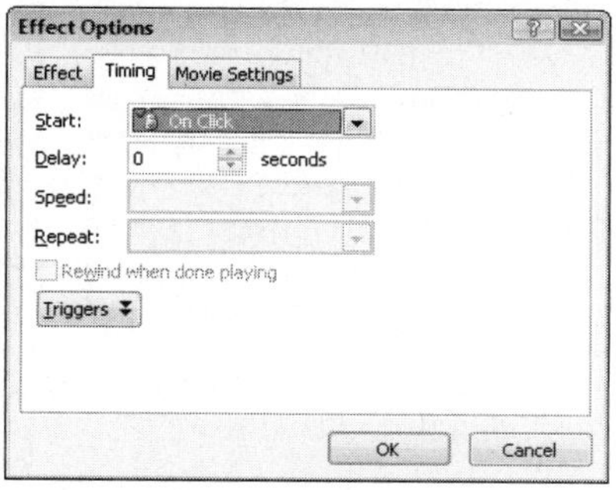

Follow these steps to control the clip timing:

1. From the Animations tab, click Custom Animation to display the Custom Animation task pane if needed.

2. Open the menu for the video clip (either the clip as a whole or just the Pause or Play animation) and choose Timing. A dialog box opens.

 Instead of opening the menu, you can just double-click the desired animation effect in the task pane and the dialog box opens. Then you can click the tab you want (in this case, Timing).

3. Set the timing options (as available in the dialog boxes that appear in Figures 17.7 through 17.9):

   - **Start:** Your choices are On Click, With Previous, or After Previous. These are movie actions that can also be added via custom animation.

   - **Delay:** This is the delay in seconds between the previous animation event and this one.

   - **Speed:** For animation effects, this controls the speed; for a movie clip, it is unavailable because you cannot change the speed at which the movie plays.

   - **Repeat:** Choose how many times you want the clip to repeat before it stops. This is available only for Play Movie (see Figure 17.8).

   - **Rewind When Done Playing:** If you want the last frame of the movie to remain on-screen after it completes, leave this check box unmarked. If you want the first frame to reappear, mark this check box. This is available only for Play Movie (see Figure 17.8).

4. Click OK.

Triggering Play by Clicking Another Object

All three dialog boxes (see Figures 17.7 through 17.9) have a Triggers button that displays or hides the extra triggers options, shown in Figure 17.10. *Triggers* specify when the action should occur. They enable you to trigger an event as a result of clicking the event object or something other than the event object. For example, you can place a sound icon on a slide, but then have it triggered to start playing when someone clicks on a graphic. In the case of a video, the default setting for the Pause Movie animation event is triggered when you click the clip itself. For example, you can potentially have the Play triggered by one button on your slide and the Pause triggered by another.

FIGURE 17.10

Set up optional triggers that make the clip play when you click something other than the clip.

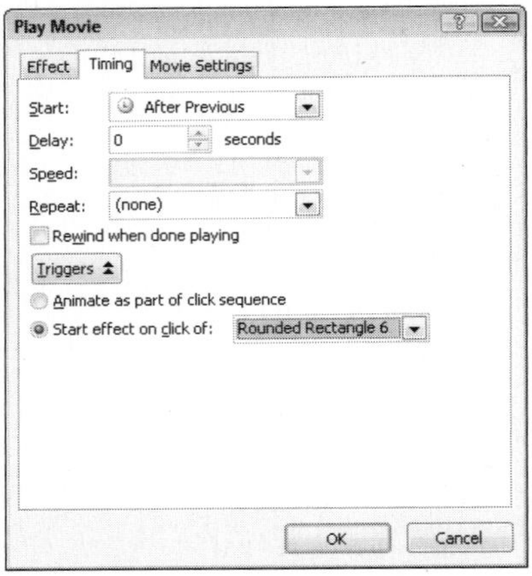

Setting the Start Point for a Clip

Just like with sounds, you can set up a video clip to play from some point other than the beginning, and continue through a certain number of slides and then stop. Because you probably do not want a clip to continue to play after you have moved past its slide, the stopping portion is less useful for videos than for sounds. However, the Start feature can be very helpful in trimming off any portion of the beginning of the clip that you don't want.

NOTE To set the start point for the clip, you must have the Play portion of the custom animation selected — not the Pause portion or the clip as a whole. If you don't have a Play animation for the clip, the easiest way to get one is to reinsert the clip and choose **Automatically** when you are asked when it should play. You can also create a new Play Movie animation, as you learn in Chapter 18.

To set the start and stop points for a movie clip, follow these steps:

1. In the Custom Animation task pane, click the animation event for the clip that represents Play (with the Play triangle to the left of the name), so that only that item is selected.

2. Open the clip's menu and choose Effect Options. The Play Movie dialog box opens with the Effect tab on top as shown in Figure 17.11.

CAUTION   If you get the Effect Options dialog box or the Pause Movie dialog box in step 2, you have selected the wrong option; click Cancel and go back to step 1 to try again.

FIGURE 17.11

Specify from what point the clip should begin playing and when it should stop.

3. In the Start Playing section, choose the desired start point:

   ▪ **From Beginning:** Starts the clip from its beginning (default setting).

   ▪ **From Last Position:** Starts from whatever point the clip was paused or stopped earlier. If it was not paused or stopped earlier, this is the beginning.

   ▪ **From Time:** Starts at a certain number of seconds into the clip. (Then specify the number of seconds in the Seconds drop-down list.)

4. (Optional) In the Stop Playing section, if desired, set up the video to stop on click, after the current slide, or after a specified number of slides.

5. Click OK.

Choosing the Size of the Video Clip Window

You can resize a video clip's window just like any other object. Simply drag its selection handles. Be careful, however, that you do not distort the image by resizing in only one dimension. Make sure you drag a corner selection handle, not one on a single side of the object.

Also be aware that when you enlarge a video clip's window, the quality of the clip suffers. If you make the clip large and are unhappy with its quality, you can reset it to its original size by following these steps:

1. Right-click the clip and choose Size and Position.
2. Click Reset.
3. Click Close.

Inserting Shockwave or Director Content

Shockwave Flash is an animation format by a company called Macromedia. PowerPoint and this format do not naturally go together smoothly, but you can insert Shockwave content on a slide as an ActiveX control in a pinch. Similarly Macromedia Director content (another multimedia format by the same company) can also be inserted via ActiveX.

CAUTION   Shockwave and Director content will not play using the PowerPoint Viewer because the viewer does not support ActiveX content.

To insert Shockwave or Director content, first turn on the Developer tab (Office ⇨ PowerPoint Options, click Popular, and mark the Show Developer Tab in the Ribbon check box). Then follow these steps:

1. On the Developer tab, in the Controls group, click More Controls. (It's the icon that looks like a hammer and wrench.) The More Controls dialog box opens.
2. Select Shockwave Flash Object (for Shockwave) or Shockwave ActiveX Control (for Director). The mouse pointer turns into a crosshair.

NOTE   If you do not have those formats listed in the More Controls dialog box, you'll need to exit PowerPoint and then open up Internet Explorer to install the ActiveX control. You can do so by going to www.adobe.com/shockwave/download/index.cgi?.

3. Drag on the slide to create a boxed area where the content should appear.
4. With the new box selected, click the Properties button on the Developer tab. A Properties box appears for the object.

5. Do one of the following:

  ▢ For Shockwave content: Click Custom (the top row). A button with an ellipsis on it (...) appears to the right of that row. Click the ellipsis button to open the Property Pages dialog box. In the Movie URL box, type the path or URL to the file. Mark the Embed Movie check box, and click OK.

  ▢ For Director content: Click the SRC line, and type the Director file's name (and path if it is not in the same folder as the presentation itself). Director files are not embedded (but rather, linked), so it's a good idea to put them in the same folder as the presentation file itself before adding them.

6. Close all open dialog boxes.

EXPERT TIP A tutorial and more information about inserting Director content are available at `www.indezine.com/products/powerpoint/ppdirector.html`. This information was written for earlier versions of PowerPoint, but most of it still applies except for the step-by-step walkthrough.

Troubleshooting Movie Problems

PowerPoint's handling of movie files is not always optimal because it uses the antiquated MCI Media player to play video. For more information about PowerPoint and video, see `http://www.pfcmedia.com/multimediatutorial.htm`. There are some workarounds available for most of the common problems, however, and the following sections explain some of them.

Troubleshooting Movies That Won't Play

For problems with movies that won't play, explore one or more of these possible fixes:

■ **Play it in Windows Media Player:** If your movie won't play in PowerPoint, try Media Player. (Go to `www.microsoft.com` and download the latest version of Media Player if you don't have it.) If it plays there, you can insert the clip as an object with the Insert tab's Object button, as you learned in Chapter 15. You can't set any of the normal PowerPoint options for the clip; you play it through Windows Media Player instead during the presentation.

■ **Download a codec:** If your movie won't play anywhere, not in PowerPoint or in any of your players, perhaps your system does not have the needed *codec*, which is a compression/decompression driver; different formats need different ones. When you play a video clip in Windows Media Player for which you do not have the proper codec, it tries to connect to Microsoft's servers to download one automatically. If that fails, you can try manually searching the Web for suitable codecs for that file format. You can also try downloading the latest official set of codecs for Windows Media Player from `www.microsoft.com/windows/windowsmedia/format/codecdownload.aspx`.

- **Still doesn't work? Try a different player:** Windows Media Player does not support all video formats, but you can find a different player that will. If you do, you can install it, and then embed the movie as an object associated with that program, as you embedded objects in Chapter 15. To do this, you need to set the new program as the default for handling that file extension. In Windows XP, choose Tools ➪ Folder Options ➪ File Types in a Windows file-management window to change extension associations. In Windows Vista, from the Control Panel, click Programs, and under Default Programs, click Make a File Type Always Open in a Specific Program.

- **Troubles with DVDs:** DVD movie clips are a special case. Windows Media Player may attempt to play them but fail, and you get an unhelpful generic error message. This is usually caused by not having a DVD hardware or software-based encoder/decoder. If your PC plays DVD movies, then you already have one. If not, there are many good ones. See if your PC originally came with a DVD movie player application, and if so, reinstall it — that's the cheap option. Otherwise, you can try WinDVD; a free trial is available at www.intervideo.com. You can then use the Object button on the Insert tab to insert the clip and let it play with WinDVD or whatever player you are using.

- **Convert to WMV format:** PowerPoint easily handles Windows Media Video (WMV) format clips. You can import a video clip into Windows Movie Maker (free with Windows XP and Windows Vista) and then export it to WMV format from there.

- **Use a third-party utility:** PlaysForCertain (PFC) is a utility that converts and prepares video files to work within PowerPoint. A free 14-day trial is available from www.pfcmedia.com. You might find it easier to simply get this utility than to spend a lot of time messing with various file formats.

EXPERT TIP If you record video with your own video camera, and it won't play in PowerPoint, it's probably because your camera uses a proprietary codec. Use the software that comes with the camera to re-render it using a more common codec. Some of the most popular standard codecs are Cinepak and Indeo Video Codec. A utility called gspot, available at www.headbands.com/gspot, can identify what codecs are being used in your video files.

EXPERT TIP This may seem hard to believe, but it works. If you get an error message when you try to drag and drop an AVI video clip into your presentation or if you try to insert it and PowerPoint simply ignores you, try renaming the file extension from .avi to .mpg. This often will fix it.

Troubleshooting Poor Playback Quality

Be aware that slower, older computers, especially those with a meager amount of RAM, may not present your video clip to its best advantage. The sound may not match the video, the video may be jerky, and a host of other little annoying performance glitches may occur. On such PCs, it is best to limit the live-action video that you use and rely more on animated GIFs, simple WMV animations, and other less system-taxing video clips.

When you are constructing a presentation, keep in mind that you may be showing it on a lesser computer than the one on which you are creating it, and therefore performance problems may crop up during the presentation that you did not anticipate. Here are some ideas for at least partially remediating the situation:

- Make sure you test the presentation on the actual computer on which you are going to show it, especially if you need a nonstandard codec.

- Copy the entire presentation and all of its support files to the fastest hard disk on the system instead of running it from a CD. Hard disks have much faster access time. Use Package for CD to collect the needed files instead of manually copying them through Windows, to ensure that you get all of the files and properly resolve their links.

- Run the entire presentation on the playback PC from start to finish beforehand. If there are delays, jerks, and lack of synchronization, just let it play itself out. Then try the whole presentation again, and it will usually be much better the second time. This happens because the system caches some of the data, and it's faster to read it from the cache than from the disk.

- Make sure the playback PC is in the best shape it can be in. If feasible, upgrade its RAM. Run Disk Defragmenter and Disk Cleanup on it, and make sure its video driver is up to date.

- Work with the original media clips to decrease their complexity, and then reimport them into PowerPoint. For example, use video-editing software to lower the frames per second of video clips, and use image-editing software to lower the dots per inch of any large graphics.

- If possible, spread out the more complex slides in the presentation so that they are not adjacent to one another. Have an intervening slide that is just simple text.

- If all else fails, transfer the presentation to videotape or digital video from the original PC (where presumably it plays correctly). This is covered later in the chapter.

Balancing Video Impact with File Size and Performance

When you are recording your own video clips with a video camera or other device, it is easy to overshoot. Video clips take up a huge amount of disk space.

Movie files are linked to the PowerPoint file, rather than embedded, so they do not dramatically increase the size of the PowerPoint file. However, because the linked movie file is required when you show the presentation, having a movie does greatly increase the amount of disk space required for storing the whole presentation package.

Depending on the amount of space available on your computer's hard disk, and whether you need to transfer your PowerPoint file to another PC, you may want to keep the number of seconds of recorded video to a minimum to ensure that the file size stays manageable. On the other hand, if you have a powerful computer with plenty of hard disk space and a lot of cool video clips to show, go for it!

EXPERT TIP Place the movie clip in the same folder as the presentation file before inserting the movie clip. This creates a relative reference to the clip within the PowerPoint link to it, so that when you move both items to another location the link's integrity remains.

Transferring a Presentation to Videotape

While not normally considered an optimal presentation method, sometimes VHS video is the only format that will do for a presentation, for one reason or another.

If you have a video card with TV/Video out capability, the process is very straightforward. Hook the video card to the VCR with a compatible cable (S-video if possible because it's the highest quality), press Record on the VCR, and start the presentation on the PC. It doesn't get much easier than that.

If you don't have a video card like that, consider buying one; they're not that expensive and you will save yourself a tremendous amount of grief and headache. Otherwise you will need to buy a scan converter, which is an external box that converts between PC and TV/VCR, and a decent one of these will cost more than the video card with TV/Video out.

NOTE If you are determined *not* to buy a video card with TV/Video out, see the tutorial produced by Austin Myers at `www.soniacoleman.com/Tutorials/PowerPoint/ recordvhs.htm`, which provides much more thorough coverage of the topic.

But wait — you'll want to do some testing before recording your presentation to VHS in its entirety. TV screens, especially the old-time picture tube types (not so much with the newer plasma ones), show colors and shapes differently than PC monitors do, and what looks good on a PC may not look so good on a TV. Before doing the final recording, hook up a TV to the VCR and do a test recording. You might decide you need to adjust some colors or change the slide dimensions.

Summary

In this chapter, you learned how to place video clips on your slides and how to set them up to play when you want them to. You learned about the differences between various video formats, and how to set up clips to play when you display the slide and/or when you click them. You learned how to set a clip's volume and appearance, and how to make it play at different starting points and stop at different ending points. Finally, you learned how to incorporate Shockwave and Director content and how to output a presentation to videotape.

In the next chapter, you learn about transitions and object animation. With a transition, you can create special effects for the movement from one slide to another. With object animation, you can control the entry and exit of individual objects on a slide. You can make them fly in with special effects or build them dramatically one paragraph, bar, or shape at a time.

Chapter 18

Creating Animation Effects and Transitions

So far in this book, you have learned about several types of moving objects on a slide. One object type is a movie, or video clip, that has been created in an animation program or recorded with a video camera. Another type is an animated GIF, which is essentially a graphic that has some special properties that enable it to play a short animation sequence over and over.

However, neither of these types is what PowerPoint means by animation. In PowerPoint, *animation* is the way that individual objects enter or exit a slide. On a slide with no animation, all of the objects on the slide simply appear at the same time when you display it. (Boring, eh?) However, you can apply animation to the slide so that the bullet points fly in from the left, one at a time, and the graphic drops down from the top afterward.

A *transition* is another kind of animation. A transition refers to the entry or exit of the entire slide, rather than of an individual object on the slide.

Here are some ideas for using animation effectively in your presentations:

- Animate parts of a chart so that the data appears one series at a time. This technique works well if you want to talk about each series separately.

- Set up questions and answers on a slide so that the question appears first, and then, when you click the question, the answer appears.

- Dim each bullet point when the next one comes into view, so that you are, in effect, highlighting the current one.

IN THIS CHAPTER

Assigning transitions to slides

Using an animation preset

Using custom animation

Layering animated objects

- Make an object appear and then disappear. For example, you might have an image of a lightning bolt that flashes on the slide for one second and then disappears, or a picture of a racecar that drives onto the slide from the left and then immediately drives out of sight to the right.

- Rearrange the order in which objects appear on the slide. For example, you could make numbered points appear from the bottom up for a Top Ten list.

Assigning Transitions to Slides

Transitions determine how you get from slide A to slide B. Back in the old slide projector days, there was only one transition: the old slide was pushed out, and the new slide dropped into place. However, with a computerized presentation, you can choose from all kinds of fun transitions, including wipes, blinds, fly-ins, and much more. These transitions are almost exactly like the animations, except that they apply to the whole slide (or at least the background — the base part of the slide — if the slide's objects are separately animated).

> **NOTE**   The transition effect for a slide refers to how the slide enters, and not how it exits. As a result, if you want to assign a particular transition while moving from slide 1 to slide 2, you would assign the transition effect to slide 2.

The individual transitions are hard to describe in words; it is best if you just view them on-screen to understand what each one does. You should try out several transitions before making your final selection.

Automatic versus Manual Transitions

Generally speaking, if there is a live person controlling and presenting the show, transitions should be manual. With manual transitions, the presenter must click the mouse to move to the next slide, just like clicking the advance button on a 35mm slide projector. This might sound distracting, but it helps the speaker to maintain control of the show. If someone in the audience asks a question or wants to make a comment, the show does not continue on blindly, but pauses to accommodate the delay.

However, if you are preparing a self-running presentation, such as for a kiosk, automatic transitions are a virtual necessity. You learned in Chapter 16 how to record narration and set timings for a presentation, and these timings represent the length of time between one slide and the next. You can also set automatic timings for slides without recording any narration.

Setting up Automatic Transition Timings

By default, PowerPoint uses manual transitions, and so you must specifically set up automatic timings if you want them. For automatic timings, you can either assign the same transition time to all slides, or individual times for each slide. The most effective method of assigning individual times for each slide is to rehearse the timings. This is covered in the next section.

CAUTION You will probably want to assign automatic transitions to either all or none of the slides in the presentation, but not a mixture of the two. This is because mixed transition times can cause confusion, when some of the slides automatically advance and others do not. However, there may be situations where you need to assign different timings and effects to the various slides' transitions.

To assign an automatic transition to an individual slide, follow these steps:

1. View or select the slide in Normal or Slide Sorter view. If you use Slide Sorter view, you can more easily select multiple slides to which you can apply the transition.

2. On the Animations tab, in the Transition to This Slide group, select the Automatically After check box.

3. In the Automatically After text box, type a transition time, in seconds, to replace the default time, as shown in Figure 18.1.

FIGURE 18.1

You can specify automatic transition times on the Animations tab.

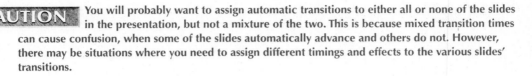

4. (Optional) To apply this setting to all slides in the presentation, click Apply to All.

It is perfectly okay to leave the On Mouse Click check box selected, even if you choose automatic transitions — in fact, this is a good idea. There may be times when you want to manually advance to the next slide before the automatic transition time has elapsed, and leaving this option selected allows you to do so.

NOTE It does not matter what transition you select. Even if you select No Transition, transitions will still occur — that is, one slide will change to another. There will simply be no special effect.

Transition timings appear beneath each slide in Slide Sorter view, as shown in Figure 18.2.

FIGURE 18.2

You can view slide timings in Slide Sorter view.

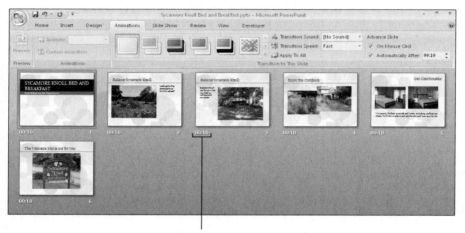

Slide timing

Rehearsing and Recording Timings

The trouble with setting the same automatic timings for all slides is that not all slides deserve or need equal time on-screen. For example, some slides may have more text than others, or more complex concepts to grasp. To allow for the differences, you can manually set the timings for each slide, as described in the preceding section. However, another way is to use the Rehearse Timings feature to run through your presentation in real time, and then to allow PowerPoint to set the timings for you, based on that rehearsal.

NOTE   When you set timings with the Rehearse Timings feature, PowerPoint ignores any hidden slides. If you later unhide these slides, they are set to advance automatically. You need to individually assign them an Automatically After transition time, as described in the preceding section.

To set transition timings with the Rehearse Timings feature, follow these steps:

1. On the Slide Show tab, click Rehearse Timings. The slide show starts with the Rehearsal toolbar in the upper-left corner, as shown in Figure 18.3.

FIGURE 18.3

Use the Rehearsal toolbar to set timings for automatic transitions.

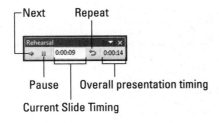

2. Click through the presentation, displaying each slide for as long as you want it to appear in the actual show. To move to the next slide, you can click the slide, click the Next button in the Rehearsal toolbar (right-pointing arrow), or press Page Down.

When setting timings, it may help to read the text on the slide, slowly and out loud, to simulate how an audience member who reads slowly would proceed. When you have read all of the text on the slide, pause for one or two more seconds and then advance. If you need to pause the rehearsal at any time, click the Pause button. When you are ready to resume, click the Pause button again.

If you make a mistake on the timing for a slide, click the Repeat button to begin timing this slide again from 00:00.

EXPERT TIP If you want a slide to display for a fairly long time, such as 30 seconds or more, you might find it faster to enter the desired time in the Current Slide Timing text box on the Rehearsal toolbar, rather than waiting the full amount of time before advancing. To do this, click in the text box, type the desired time, and press Tab. You must press the Tab key after entering the time — do not click the Next button — or PowerPoint will not apply your change.

3. When you reach the final slide, a dialog box appears, asking whether you want to keep the new slide timings. Click Yes.

EXPERT TIP If you want to temporarily discard the rehearsed timings, deselect the Use Rehearsed Timings check box on the Slide Show tab. This turns off all automatic timings and allows the show to advance through mouse-clicks only.

Choosing Transition Effects

Transitions occur from slide to slide, even if you select No Transition as the effect. With the No Transition effect, the previous slide disappears and the next one appears. If you want a different transition, you must specify it from the Transition to This Slide group in the Animations tab. A gallery of transition effects appears, where you can select an effect, as shown in Figure 18.4. You can also select a sound and change the transition speed.

FIGURE 18.4

Select a transition effect.

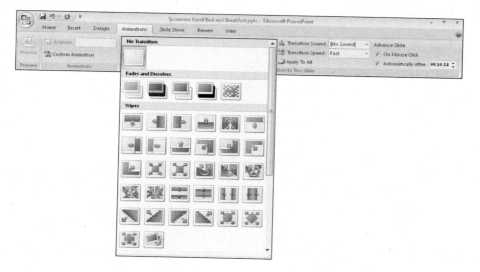

To apply a transition effect to a slide, follow these steps:

1. Select and display the slide or slides that you want to affect.

2. On the Animations tab, open the gallery of effects in the Transition to This Slide group and click the one that you want, or click No Transition to turn off any existing transition effect. The gallery of effects is shown in Figure 18-4.

3. (Optional) Open the Transition Speed drop-down list and select a transition speed.

4. (Optional) Open the Transition Sound drop-down list and select a transition sound.

5. (Optional) Click Apply to All to make the same transition apply to all slides in the presentation, and not just the selected slides.

Although you learned about sounds in Chapter 16, the transition sounds have different controls. In the Transition Sound menu, shown in Figure 18.5, you can choose from among PowerPoint's default sound collection, or you can choose any of the following:

- **No Sound:** Does not assign a sound to the transition.

- **Stop Previous Sound:** Stops any sound that is already playing. This usually applies where the previous sound was very long and was not finished when you moved on to the next slide, or in cases where you used the Loop Until Next Sound transition (see below).

- **Other Sound:** Opens a dialog box from which you can select another sound file stored on your system.

- **Loop Until Next Sound:** An on/off toggle that sets whatever sound you select to loop continuously either until another sound is triggered or until a slide appears that has Stop Previous Sound set for its transition.

FIGURE 18.5

You can select a transition sound.

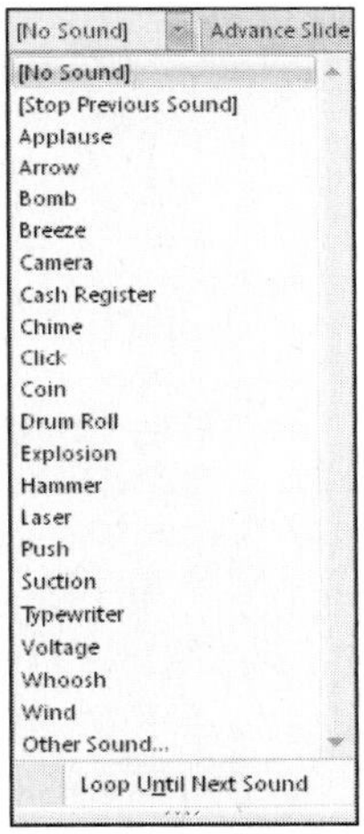

Using an Animation Preset

PowerPoint 2007 has very few animation presets compared to earlier versions. In fact, there are just three: Fade, Wipe, and Fly In. Each preset has two options: for the text to enter the slide all at once or by paragraphs. These presets provide quick and convenient shortcuts to common effects. To apply an animation preset, follow these steps:

1. Select the text box or other object to which you want the animation preset to apply.

2. On the Animations tab, open the Animate drop-down list and select a preset, as shown in Figure 18.6.

FIGURE 18.6

You can select an animation preset.

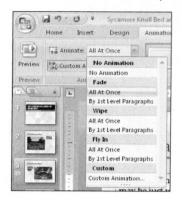

Using Custom Animation

Custom animation gives you full control over how the objects on your slides are animated. You can not only choose from the full range of animation effects for each object, but you can also specify in what order the objects appear and what sound is associated with their appearance.

Custom Animation: A First Look

A good way to learn about custom animation is to start with an animation preset and analyze it in the Custom Animation pane to see how it works. The following example looks at one of the By First Level Paragraphs presets:

1. Select a slide that contains a title and at least two bullet points.

2. Open the Animate drop-down list on the Animations tab and choose By 1st Level Paragraphs under any of the headings.

3. Click the Custom Animation button on the Animations tab to display the Custom Animation pane, as shown in Figure 18.7.

FIGURE 18.7

You can view an animation in the Custom Animation pane.

Animation effects are numbered on slide | Click here to expand list | Selected animation | Description of effect for selected animation

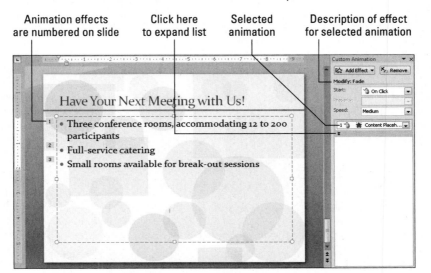

In Figure 18.7, each of the animated items on the slide is numbered in the order in which they will be animated. This animation uses a top-down order; however, you can use the Re-Order arrow buttons at the bottom of the pane to move items around.

In Figure 18.7, the 1 animation is selected in the Custom Animation pane; this represents the first bullet point. From the pane, you can gather the following information:

- The effect is currently set to Modify: Fade.
- The effect will start when you click (On Click). You can tell this both from the value in the Start text box and also from the mouse icon that appears next to it on the list.
- The animation speed is set to Medium.
- There are more animations for the additional bullet points beneath this one, as shown by the double-down arrow in the bar below it.

You can click this double-down arrow to expand the list, as shown in Figure 18.8. Notice that each of the other bullet points has identical animation settings to the first one (because they are all first-level bullet points). To change these settings for only one of the bullet points, leave the list expanded. If you want to change these settings for all of the bullet points, then you must collapse the list first.

FIGURE 18.8

You can expand the animations list to show the animations for bullet points 1, 2, and 3 individually.

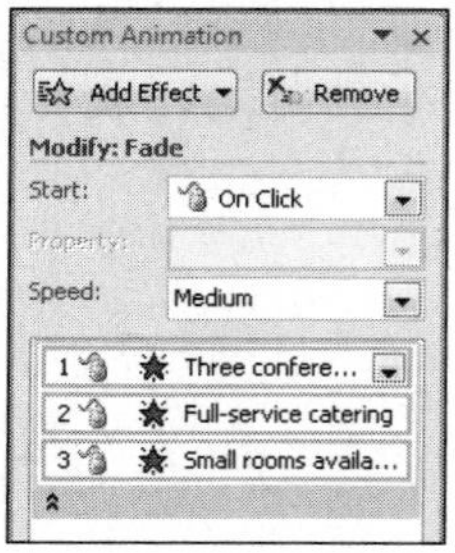

Applying a Custom Animation Effect

Now that you have seen an example of some custom animation, we can assign some animation to a regular slide. You can first create a new slide with a title and a few bullets, or you can remove the animation from an existing slide. The easiest way to remove all of the animation from a slide is to select everything in the Custom Animation task pane and press the Delete key.

Follow these steps to create a new custom animation:

1. Display a slide that currently has no animation.

2. On the Animations tab, click Custom Animation to open the Custom Animation pane.

3. Click the object that you want to animate. This can be the title, a text box containing a bulleted list, a graphic, or any object that you can select.

4. In the pane, click Add Effect. A menu appears, containing four categories of effects: Entrance, Emphasis, Exit, or Motion Paths. This example uses an Entrance effect.

5. A submenu appears, containing effects for that category. Select one of these effects, as shown in Figure 18. 9, and then skip to step 7.

    OR

    Choose More Effects to open the Add Effect dialog box, as shown in Figure 18-10. The exact name of the dialog box depends on the category that you choose. In Figure 18-10, the selected category is Add Entrance Effect.

NOTE   The menus shown in Figure 18.9 are usage-sensitive; they remember what you chose. If you choose an effect from the dialog box in Figure 18.10, the next time you open the menu in Figure 18.9, the selected effect will appear on the list.

FIGURE 18.9

You can apply an effect from the Add Effect drop-down menu.

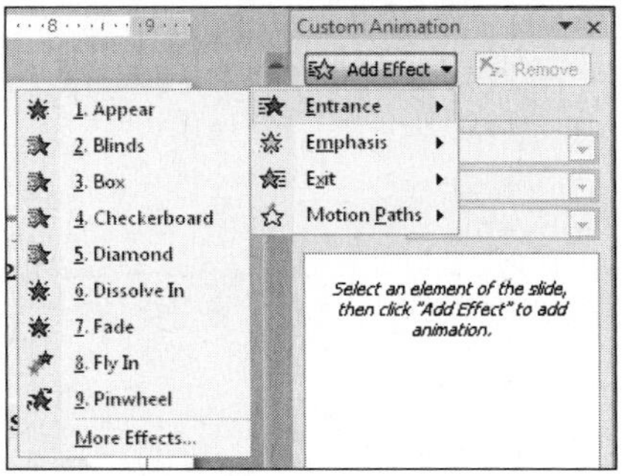

FIGURE 18.10

When you choose More Effects from the Add Effects submenu in Figure 18.9, the Add Effects dialog box appears, displaying additional choices.

6. If you opened the dialog box in step 5, then make your selection and click OK. The effects are divided into categories according to how dramatic they are, and these categories range from Basic to Exciting. If you select the Preview Effect check box in the dialog box, the effect appears on the slide behind the dialog box.

7. In the Custom Animation pane, open the Start drop-down list and choose when you want the animation to start, as shown in Figure 18.11. You can select one of the following start settings:

- **With Previous:** Runs the animation simultaneously with any previous animations on the slide. For example, you can set up two different objects to animate at the same time by setting the second of the two objects to With Previous.

FIGURE 18.11

Use the Custom Animation pane's drop-down lists to fine-tune the selected animation.

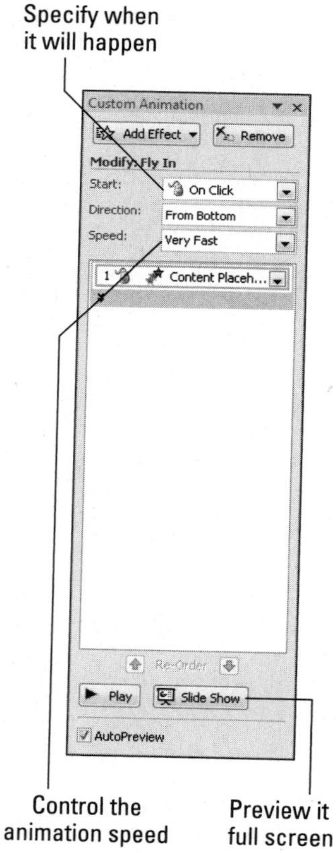

Specify when it will happen

Control the animation speed

Preview it full screen

- **After Previous:** Runs the animation immediately after the previous animation that is on the slide ends. If there is no previous animation, PowerPoint treats the appearance of the slide as the previous event and runs the animation immediately after the slide appears.

- **With Previous:** Runs the animation concurrently with the previous animation, or if there is no previous animation, concurrently with the slide's initial appearance.

- **On Click:** Runs the animation when a user clicks the mouse. This is useful when you want to build a slide item-by-item with each click, or for an exit effect.

8. Some animation effects have extra properties that you can set. If the effect that you choose has an extra property, this property appears directly beneath the Start text box. For example, in Figure 18.11, the property is Direction. Make a selection here, if appropriate. If no properties are available, then the Property box is grayed out.

9. Open the Speed drop-down list and choose a speed for the animation.

These steps showed you how to create a simple custom animation. If you want to, feel free to experiment with the custom settings on your own. However, if you still need some more help and ideas, keep reading.

Types of Custom Animation

As mentioned in the preceding steps, there are four categories of custom animation effects. Each effect has a specific purpose, as well as a different icon color:

- **Entrance (green):** The item's appearance on the slide is animated. Either it does not appear right away when the rest of the slide appears, or it appears in some unusual way (such as flying or fading), or both.

- **Emphasis (yellow):** The item is already on the slide, and is modified in some way. For example, it may shrink, grow, wiggle, or change color.

- **Exit (red):** The item disappears from the slide before the slide itself disappears, and you can specify that it does so in some unusual way.

- **Motion Paths (gray):** The item moves on the slide according to a preset path. Motion paths are discussed later in the chapter.

Within each of these broad categories are a multitude of animations. Although the appearance of the icons may vary, the colors always match the category. For example, Figure 18.10 shows some of the different icons for Entrance effects.

Other effect categories have other choices. For example, the Emphasis category, in addition to motion effects, also has effects that change the color, background, or other attributes of the object. Figure 18.12 shows some of these choices. You may want to try some of them on your own to find out what they do.

FIGURE 18.12

Emphasis effects have some choices that do not involve motion.

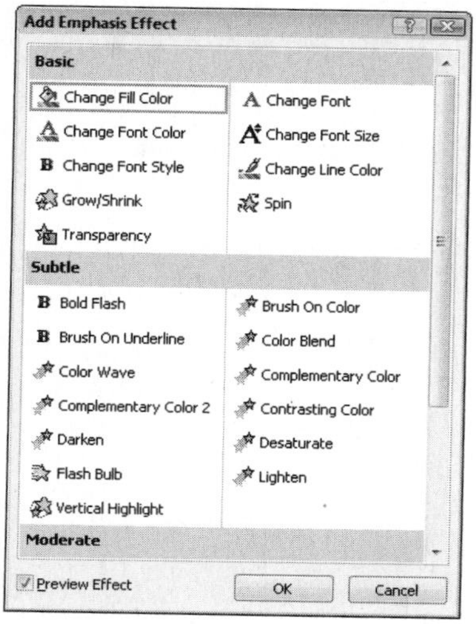

Changing to a Different Animation Effect

If you change your mind about an animation for an object, you do not have to remove the animation and reapply it; you can simply change it. To change to a different animation for an object, do the following:

1. Display the Custom Animation pane.
2. Select the animation effect from the pane — not on the slide — and then click the Change button. The same menus appear as when you originally applied the effect.
3. Select a different animation. You can either choose from the menus or select More Effects to display the dialog box that contains the full selection of effects.

Besides choosing a different animation effect, you can also fine-tune its settings at any time, such as changing its speed or other properties.

Removing an Animation Effect

You can remove the animation for a specific object, or remove all of the animation for the entire slide. When an object is not animated, it simply appears when the slide appears, with no delay. For example, if the title is not animated, the slide background and the title appear first, after which any animation executes for the remaining objects. To remove animation from a specific object, do the following:

1. Display the Custom Animation pane.

2. If the object is part of a group, such as a bulleted list, then expand or collapse the list, depending on the effect that you want to remove. For example, to remove an effect from an entire text box, you must first collapse the list. To remove an effect from only a single paragraph, such as a bulleted item, you must first expand the list.

3. Select the animation effect from the pane, and then click the Remove button or right-click and choose Remove. PowerPoint removes the animation and then renumbers any remaining animation effects.

Assigning Multiple Animation Effects to a Single Object

Some objects might need more than one animation effect. For example, you may want an object to have an Entrance and an Exit effect, or you may want a bulleted list to enter one way and then emphasize each point in a different way.

To assign a new animation effect to an object that is already animated, do the following:

1. On the slide, click the object to which you want to assign the animation. The Custom Animation pane should contain an Add Effect button. If it shows a Change button instead, or if the Add Effect button is unavailable, this means that you have not clicked the object on the slide.

2. Click Add Effect, and then create the new effect just as you did earlier in the section "Applying a Custom Animation Effect."

NOTE Keep in mind that the numbers that appear next to the objects on the slides in Custom Animation do not refer to the objects themselves — they refer to the animations. If an object does not have any animation assigned to it, then it does not have a number. Conversely, if an object has more than one animation effect assigned to it, then it has two or more numbers.

Reordering Animation Effects

By default, animation effects are numbered in the order that you created them. To change this order, do the following:

1. On the Custom Animation pane, click the effect whose position you want to change.

2. Click the Re-Order up- or down-arrow buttons at the bottom of the pane to move the position of the animation in the list.

You can also drag-and-drop items in the animations list to rearrange them. Position the mouse pointer over an object, so that the pointer turns into a double-headed up or down arrow, and then drag the object up or down in the list.

Figure 18.13 shows the same slide as before, but now the bullets are set to animate in reverse order — from the bottom up.

FIGURE 18.13

You can rearrange animations on the animations list in the Custom Animation pane by dragging them or by using the Re-Order arrow buttons.

Animations set for bottom to top order

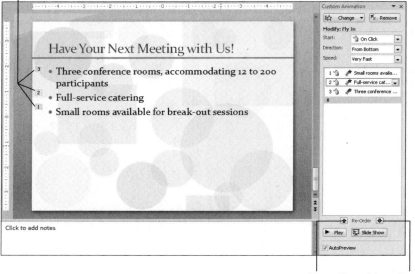

Move Up   Move Down

Special Animation Options for Text

When you are animating the text in a text box, some extra options become available. For example, in the preceding section, you saw one way to animate the text in reverse — from the bottom up. However, there is a special Reverse option that you can set for a text box that will do this automatically.

You can also choose the grouping that you want to animate. For example, suppose that you have three levels of bullets in the text box, and you want them to be animated with each second-level bullet appearing separately. You can specify the second level as the animation grouping, so that all third-level bullets appear as a group, along with their associated second-level bullet.

To access the text options for an animation effect, do the following:

1. From the Custom Animation pane, click the animation that you want to work with. A down arrow appears to the right of the animation.

2. Click the down arrow and choose Effect Options. A dialog box appears with the name of the animation. For example, Figure 18.14 shows the Fly In dialog box.

3. Click the Text Animation tab. The Text Animation controls appear, as shown in Figure 18.14.

4. Open the Group Text drop-down list and choose how you want to group the animation. The default setting is By 1st Level Paragraphs.

5. (Optional) If you want the bullet and its associated bullets to appear automatically, without having to click the mouse again, select the Automatically After check box and then type a delay time in seconds.

6. (Optional) Select the In Reverse Order check box if you want PowerPoint to build the list from the bottom up.

7. Click OK.

FIGURE 18.14

You can control how text in a text box is animated.

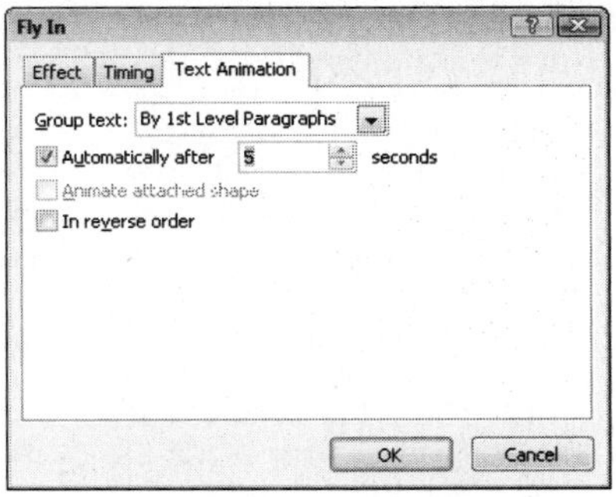

Setting Animation Timing

You can adjust the timing settings for an animation. Timing refers to the speed of the effect, the delay before it starts, and how many times it should repeat, if any.

To set timing for a custom animation effect, do the following:

1. On the Custom Animation pane, click the effect whose timing you want to set. A down arrow appears to the right of the effect.

2. Click the down arrow and choose Timing. A dialog box appears, with the Timing tab displayed, as shown in Figure 18.15.

FIGURE 18.15

You can control the timing of an animation effect in the Timing tab.

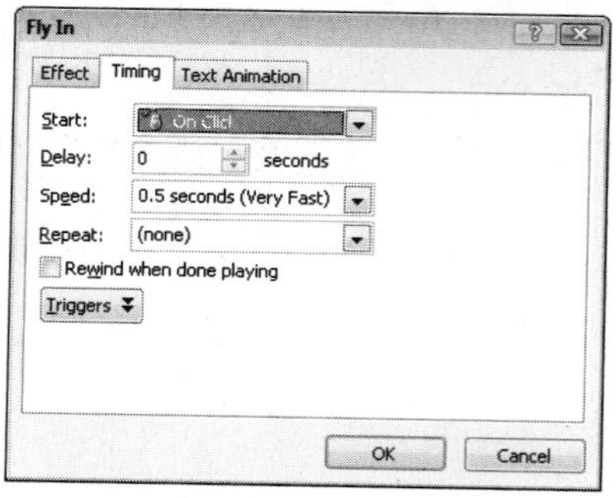

3. You can choose from the following settings to control the animation timing:

- **Start** is the same as the Start setting in the Custom Animation pane.

- **Delay** refers to the amount of delay between the beginning or end of the previous animation and the start of the current animation. For example, if you set the animation effect to After Previous, the delay is the number of seconds between the *end* of the previous event and the beginning of the animation. If you set the animation effect to With Previous, the delay is the number of seconds between the *beginning* of the previous event and the beginning of the animation. By default, the delay is set to zero.

- **Speed** is the overall speed of the animation. This is the same setting as in the Speed drop-down list in the Custom Animation pane. The choices range from Very Fast (0.5 seconds) to Very Slow (5 seconds). Unlike in the Custom Animation pane, the number of seconds associated with each choice appears on the Timing tab, as shown in Figure 18-15.

- **Repeat** is the number of times that the animation should repeat. The default setting is None. You would rarely set a text animation to repeat because this makes it harder for the audience to read (although this effect is useful when you want a graphic to flash until the end of the slide).

EXPERT TIP You can type any number you want into the Delay, Speed, and Repeat boxes in the dialog box. This is one advantage of using the dialog box rather than the task pane.

■ **Rewind when done playing** pertains mostly to video clips; this setting is available for animation effects, but you will not see much difference between the on and off settings.

■ **Triggers** enables you to set up an animation to occur when the user clicks a particular object. This object does not necessarily have to be the object that is being animated. Triggers are discussed in the next section.

4. Click OK when you are done. Then test the new animation settings by clicking Play or Slide Show in the Custom Animation pane.

Setting Animation Event Triggers

Animation event triggers tell PowerPoint when to execute an animation. By default, an animation occurs as part of the normal animation sequence, using whatever settings you have assigned to it, such as On Click, With Previous, or After Previous.

When you set an animation to On Click, the click being referred to is *any* click. The mouse does not need to be pointing at anything in particular. In fact, pressing a key on the keyboard can serve the same purpose.

If you want an animation effect to occur only when you click something in particular, you can use a trigger to specify this condition. For example, you may have three bullet points on a list, and three photos. If you want each bullet point to appear when you click its corresponding photo, you can animate each bullet point with the graphic object as its trigger.

CAUTION   There is a small complication in the preceding example: you can have only one trigger for each object, and in this case, object means the entire text placeholder. Therefore, if you want to animate bullet points separately with separate triggers, then you need to place each of them in a separate text box.

To set up a trigger, do the following:

1. On the Custom Animation pane, click the effect whose timing you want to set. A down arrow appears to the right of the effect name.

2. Open the menu for this effect, as you did in the preceding steps, and choose Timing. The Timing tab appears.

3. Click the Triggers button. The controls for setting up a trigger appear on the Timing tab, as shown in Figure 18.16.

4. Select the Start Effect on Click Of option, and then open the drop-down list and select an object. All of the objects on the slide appear in this list.

5. Click OK.

CAUTION Do not trigger the entrance of an object on click of itself, or there will be no way to make it appear.

FIGURE 18.16

You can set a trigger for an animation.

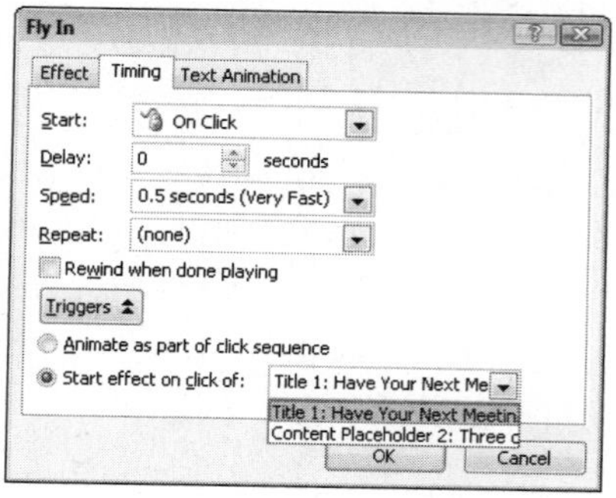

Associating Sounds with Animations

You learned about sounds in Chapter 16, including how to associate a sound with an object. However, associating a sound with an animation effect is different because the sound plays when the animation occurs, not necessarily when the object appears or is clicked. By default, animation effects do not have sounds assigned, but you can assign a sound by doing the following:

1. In the Custom Animation pane, select the animation effect to which you want to assign a sound. Then open the drop-down list for the effect, and choose Effect Options.

2. On the Effect tab (Figure 18-17), open the Sound drop-down list and choose a sound. You can choose any of the sounds in the list, or you can choose Other Sound to select a sound file from another location.

   OR

   To make a previously playing sound stop when this animation occurs, choose Stop Previous Sound from the Sound drop-down list.

CAUTION The Volume button next to the Sound list appears to let you set a volume for the sound, but it does not work with WAV files, the only type of sound that can be added in this manner, so it is essentially useless. See http://support.microsoft.com/kb/818226/en-us for more information.

FIGURE 18.17

You can adjust the volume for an animation in relation to the general volume of the presentation.

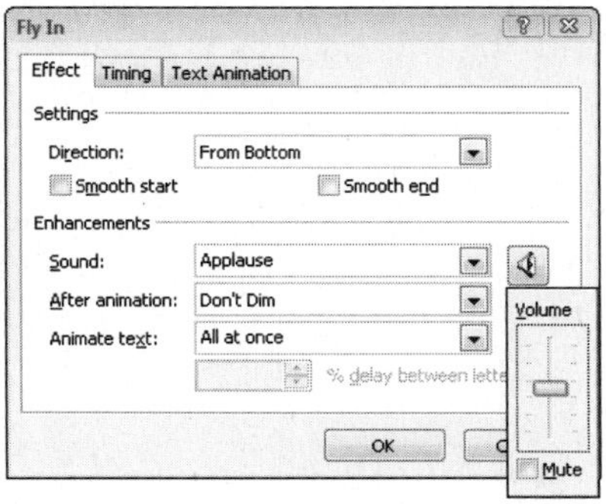

3. *(Optional)* If you want the object to change color or to hide after its animation, then open the After Animation drop-down list and choose one of the following options, as shown in Figure 18.18:

- **A scheme color:** You can choose one of the colored squares, which represent each of the current scheme colors.

- **More Colors:** Click here to choose a specific color, just as you would for any object. For example, you can set text to gray to make it appear dimmed.

- **Don't Dim:** This is the default setting; it specifies that PowerPoint should do nothing to the object after animation.

- **Hide After Animation:** This setting makes the object disappear immediately after the animation finishes.

- **Hide on Next Mouse Click:** This setting makes the object disappear when you click the mouse after the animation has completed. For example, this is useful for showing and then hiding individual bullet points.

FIGURE 18.18

You can choose a color for the object after animation, or specify that it should be hidden afterwards.

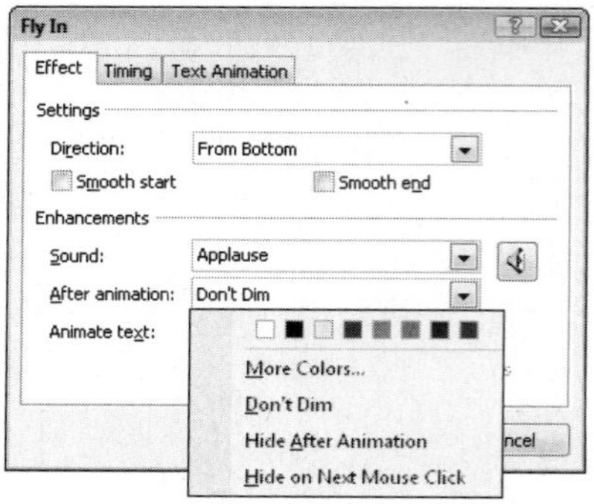

4. If the object contains text, set the Animate Text setting to indicate how the text should be animated. The default setting is All at Once, which makes each paragraph appear as a whole. The alternatives are By Letter or By Word.

> **NOTE** The Animate Text setting in step 4 is *not* the setting that allows you to specify which bullet points should appear separately on the slide and which should appear as a group. To do this, you can use the Text Animation tab, which is discussed earlier in "Special Animation Options for Text."

5. If you chose By Letter or By Word in step 4, an additional text box appears beneath the first text box. You can type a percentage delay between letters or words. The higher the percentage, the more time between words or letters.

6. Click OK.

Working with Motion Paths

Motion paths enable you to make an object fly onto or off of the slide, and also make it fly *around* on the slide in a particular motion path! For example, suppose you are showing a map on a slide, and you want to graphically illustrate the route that you took when traveling in that country. You could create a little square, circle, or other AutoShape to represent yourself, and then set up a custom motion path for the shape that traces your route on the map.

Using a Preset Motion Path

PowerPoint comes with dozens of motion paths, in every shape that you can imagine. To choose one of them for an object, follow these steps:

1. Display the Custom Animation pane.

2. Click the object that you want to animate, and then click the Add Effect button. On the menu that appears, choose Motion Path, and then either click one of the paths on the list or choose More Motion Paths.

3. If you choose More Motion Paths, the Add Motion Path dialog box appears, as shown in Figure 18.19. Click the path that you want.

   If you select the Preview Effect check box, the effect previews on the slide behind the dialog box; you can drag the dialog box to the side to see the preview more clearly.

FIGURE 18.19

You can select a motion path.

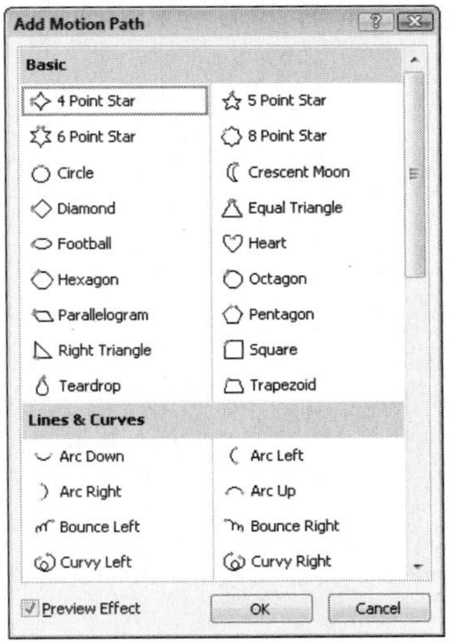

4. Click OK. The motion path appears on the slide, adjacent to the object. A green arrow shows where the object will begin, and a dotted line shows the path that it will take, as shown in Figure 18.20. A red arrow shows where the path ends. If it's a closed path you will only see the green arrow.

FIGURE 18.20

The motion path appears on the slide.

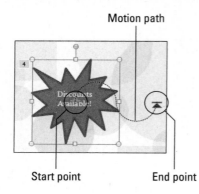

5. *(Optional)* To change the starting point for the motion path, drag the green arrow. To change the ending point, drag the red arrow.

6. *(Optional)* You can change any of the settings for the motion path, just as you would for any other custom animation:

   ▪ Change the Speed setting. The default is Medium.

   ▪ Change the Start setting. The default is On Click.

   ▪ Change the path's timing or effects.

7. *(Optional)* Open the Path drop-down list on the Custom Animation pane and choose any of the following options:

   ▪ **Unlocked/Locked:** If the path is unlocked and you move the animated object on the slide, the path repositions itself with the object; if the path is locked, then it stays in the same place, even when you move the object on the slide. You can toggle these two options.

   ▪ **Edit Points:** This option enables you to change the motion path, and is discussed in the next section, Editing a Motion Path.

   ▪ **Reverse Path Direction:** This option does just what it says: it makes the animation run in the opposite direction.

8. *(Optional)* Resize or reshape the motion path by dragging its selection handles (the circles around its frame); this is just like resizing any other object.

9. *(Optional)* Rotate the motion path by dragging the green circle at the top of the path; this is just like rotating any other object.

10. (Optional) Move the motion path by dragging it, or by nudging it with the arrow keys, as you would any object.

Editing a Motion Path

A motion path consists of anchor points with straight lines or curves between them. These points are normally invisible, but you can also display them and change them. To edit a motion path, follow these steps:

1. Select the motion path on the slide (not the object itself).

2. In the Custom Animation pane, open the Path drop-down list and choose Edit Points. (You can also right-click and choose Edit Points.) Small black squares appear around the path.

3. Click one of the black squares; a slightly larger white square appears near it. A line with white squares on either end of the segment is a curve. These white squares are handles that you can drag to modify the point. You can also drag the black square itself; either way will work, although each method affects the path differently. For example, dragging the black square moves the point itself, whereas dragging the handle repositions the curve and leaves the point in place.

4. Drag a square to change the path, as in Figure 18.21.

5. When you are finished editing the path, open the Path drop-down list and choose Edit Points again to turn the editing feature off.

FIGURE 18.21

You can edit a motion path by dragging the black or white squares that represent its anchor points.

Drawing a Custom Motion Path

If none of the motion paths suit your needs, or if you cannot easily edit them to the way you want, you can create your own motion path. A motion path can be a straight line, a curve, a closed loop, or a freeform scribble.

To draw a custom motion path for an object, follow these steps:

1. With the Custom Animation pane displayed, select the object that you want to move on the slide.

2. Choose Add Effect ➪ Motion Paths ➪ Draw Custom Path, and then choose the type of path that you want: Line, Curve, Freeform, or Scribble.

3. Drag to draw the path on the slide. Here are some hints:

   - **For a Line**, drag from the start point to the end point. The start point will have a green arrow, and the end point will have a red one.

   - **For a Curve**, click at the beginning of the line, and then move the mouse a little and click again to anchor the next point. Keep creating points like this until you have completely defined the curve. Don't draw the entire curve before you click — you need to create interim anchor points along the way. Double-click when you are finished.

   - **For a Freeform path**, click for each anchor point that you want; straight lines will appear between the anchor points. You can also click and drag to create non-straight lines too. Double-click when you are finished.

   - **For a Scribble**, the pointer changes to a pencil. Draw on the slide with the mouse button held down. Double-click when you are finished.

4. After drawing the path, edit and fine-tune it as you would any other motion path.

Animating Parts of a Chart

If you create a chart using PowerPoint's charting tool, then you can display the chart all at once or apply a custom animation effect to it. For example, you can make the chart appear by series (divided by legend entries), by category (divided by X-axis points), or by individual element in a series or category. Figures 18.22 and 18.23 show progressions based on series and category.

FIGURE 18.22

In this progression, the chart is appearing by series.

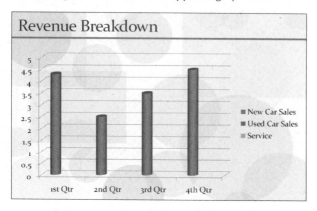

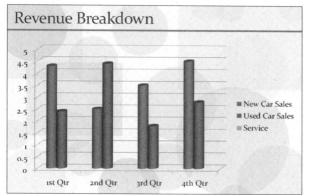

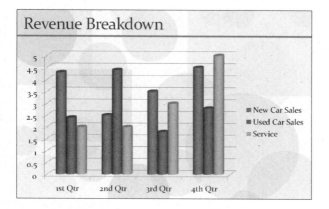

FIGURE 18.23

Here, the chart is appearing by category.

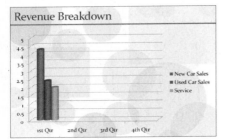

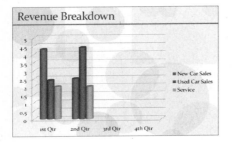

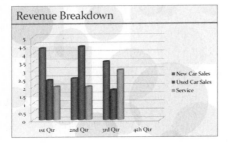

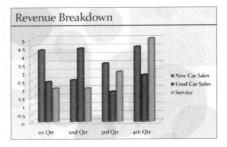

Along with making various parts of the chart appear at different times, you can also make them appear using any of the animated techniques that you have already learned, such as flying in, dropping in, fading in, and so on. You can also associate sounds with the parts, and dim them or change them to various colors when the animation is finished.

NOTE When you add an animation effect to a chart, you might notice that a new category appears on the Add Effect menu: Object Actions. Ignore it for the moment and choose a normal animation, such as an Entrance effect. I will explain Object Actions in the section "Layering Animated Objects."

To animate a chart, you must first set up the entire chart to be animated, just as you would any other object on a slide. Then, to set up the chart so that different parts of it are animated separately, do the following:

1. In the Custom Animation pane, select the animation that you want for the chart, and open its menu. Choose Effect Options from the menu.

2. Click the Chart Animation tab. Then open the Group Chart drop-down list and choose an animation option: As One Object, By Series, By Category, By Element in Series, or By Element in Category. An *element* is an individual data point such as a data bar or slice, as shown in Figure 18.24. Depending on the type of chart and animation effect that you are working with, you may not have all of these options available.

FIGURE 18.24

You can animate the chart by series, by category, or by individual data points.

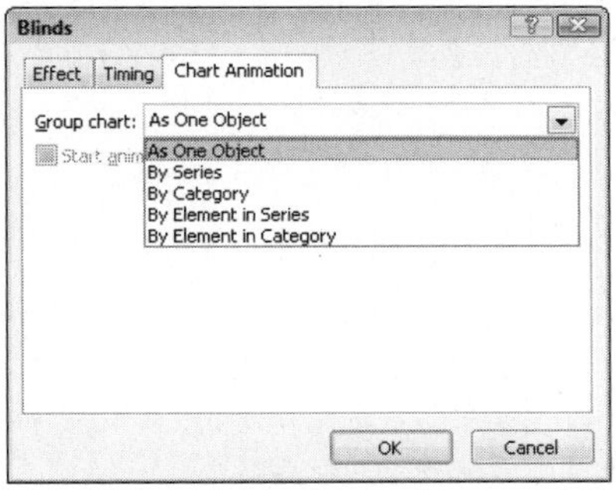

3. *(Optional)* If you also want to animate the grid and legend, select the Start Animation by Drawing the Chart Background check box. If you do not select this option, these items will appear immediately on the slide, and the data bars, slices, or other chart elements will appear separately from them.

4. Click OK to accept the settings. You can then test them.

EXPERT TIP You do not have to use the same animation effect for each category or each series of the chart. After you set up the chart to animate each piece individually, individual entries appear for each piece on the list in the Custom Animation pane. You can expand this list and then apply individual settings to each piece. For example, you could have some data bars on a chart fly in from one direction, and other data bars fly in from another direction. You can also reorder the pieces so that the data points build in a different order from the default order.

Controlling Animation Timing with the Advanced Timeline

The animation timeline is a graphical representation of how animated content will appear on the slide. The timeline is covered in Chapter 16, in the discussion about sounds and soundtracks. To turn on the timeline, open the menu for any animation in the Custom Animation pane and choose Show Advanced Timeline. For example, Figure 18.25 shows a timeline for a chart that is animated by category. The timeline is useful because it can tell you the total time involved in all of the animations that you have set up, including any delays that you have built in.

FIGURE 18.25

The advanced timeline shows how much time is allotted to each animated element on the slide.

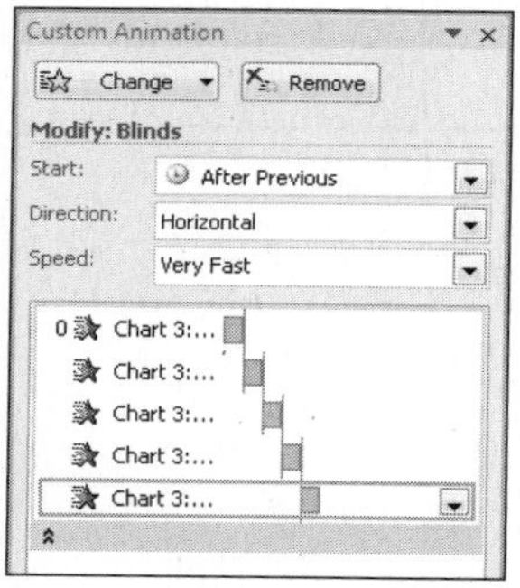

You can also use the timeline to create delays between animations and to increase the duration of individual animations. To increase the duration of an item, drag the right side of the red bar representing its length in the Custom Animation pane, as shown in Figure 18.26. Drag the left side of the bar to create a delay between animations. When you drag the bar for an item that is set to After Previous, the other bars also move. However, when you drag the bar for an item that is set to With Previous, PowerPoint allows an overlap.

FIGURE 18.26

Drag a bar on the timeline to increase or decrease the duration of an individual animation.

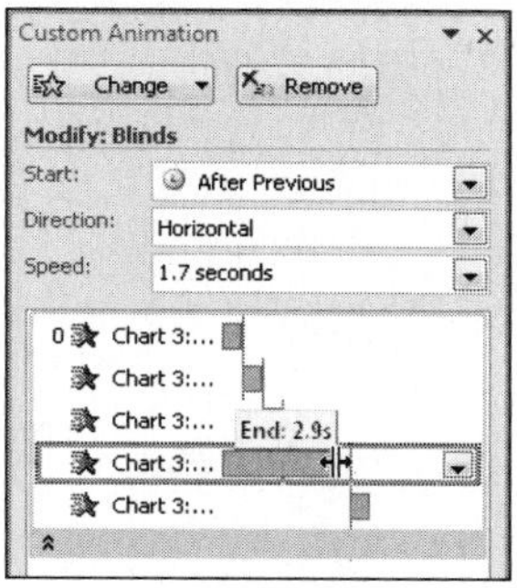

Animation Tips

Here are some tips for using animation in your own work:

- Try to use the same animation effect for each slide in a related series of slides. If you want to differentiate one section of the presentation from another, use a different animation effect for the text in each different section.

- If you want to discuss only one bullet point at a time on a slide, set the others to dim or change to a lighter color after animation.

- If you want to obscure an element but you cannot make the animation settings do it the way you want, consider using an AutoShape that is set to the same color fill as your background color and that has no outside border. This shape will appear "invisible" but will obscure whatever is behind it.

- Animate a chart based on the way you want to lead your audience through the data. For example, if each series on your chart shows the sales for a different division and you want to compare one division to another, you can animate by series. If you want to talk about the results of that chart over time rather than by division, you can animate by category, instead.

- If you want to create your own moving graphic but you do not have access to a program that creates animated GIFs, you can build a very simple animation on a slide. Simply create the frames of the animation — three or more drawings that you want to progress through in quick succession. Then, lay them one on top of another on the slide and set the timings so that they play in order. You can adjust the delays and repeats as needed.

Layering Animated Objects

Part of the challenge of custom animation is in deciding which objects should appear and disappear and in what order. Theoretically, you could layer all of the objects for every slide in the entire presentation on a single slide and use custom animation to make them appear and disappear on cue.

CAUTION   If you are thinking about creating complex layers of animation where some objects disappear and are replaced by other objects on the same slide, step back and consider whether it would be easier to simply use two or more separate slides. When there is no delay or animation defined in the transition between two slides (if their content is identical or very similar), the effect is virtually identical to that of layered, animated objects—with much less time and effort required to set them up.

You can use layering when you want part of a slide to change while the rest of it remains static. For example, you could create your own animated series of illustrations by stacking several photos and then animating them so that the bottom one appears, followed by the next one on top of it, and so on. This can provide a rough simulation of motion video from stills, much like flipping through illustrations in the corners of a stack of pages. You can set the animation speeds and delays between clips as needed to achieve the effect you want.

When you stack objects, the new object that is placed on top of the old object obscures it, so that it is not necessary to include an exit action for the old object. However, if the item being placed on top is smaller than the one beneath, then you need to set up an exit effect for the object beneath and have it occur concurrently (that is, With Previous) with the entrance of the new one. For example, suppose that you want to place a photo on the right side of a slide, and some explanatory text for it on the left, and then you want to replace these elements with a different photo and different text, as shown in Figure 18.27.

FIGURE 18.27

Although these figures look like two separate slides, they are actually a single slide at two different points in the animation sequence.

To set up this animation to occur on the same slide, you would first place the content that should appear first, and then apply exit effects to this content. For example, set the initial photo to On Click for its exit trigger, which will make it disappear when you click the mouse. Set its associated text box to With Previous and have it animate immediately after this photo, so that the text box disappears at the same time as the photo.

Next, place the other text box and other picture over the top of the first items. In Normal view, it looks like each spot has both a picture and a text box. You must now animate the new text box and the new picture with entrance effects that are set to With Previous, so that both will appear at the same time that the other two items are exiting. They all have the same animation number because they all occur simultaneously.

It is always a good idea to preview animation effects in Slide Show view after creating them. To do this, click the Slide Show View icon in the Custom Animation pane. When you have finished checking the effects, press Esc to return to PowerPoint.

Summary

In this chapter, you learned how to animate the objects on your slides to create some great special effects, and how to create animated transitions from slide to slide. You learned how to specify sounds, speeds, and timing for effects, and how to layer effects to occur sequentially or simultaneously. Use this newfound knowledge for good, not evil! In other words, do not apply so many animations that your audience focuses more on the effects than on your message. If you would like more practice with these effects, work through Lab 2 at the end of this book.

In the next chapter, you'll learn how to create support materials for a presentation, such as handouts and speaker notes, and how to format and fine-tune their formatting.

Part III

Interfacing with Your Audience

Chapter 19

Creating Support Materials

I f you are presenting a live show, the centerpiece of your presentation is your slides. Whether you show them using a computer screen, a slide projector, or an overhead projector, the slides — combined with your own dazzling personality — make the biggest impact. But if you rely on your audience to remember everything you say, you may be disappointed. With handouts, the audience members can follow along with you during the show and even take their own notes. They can then take the handouts home with them to review the information again later.

You probably want a different set of support materials for yourself than you want for the audience. Support materials designed for the speaker's use are called speaker notes. In addition to small printouts of the slides, the speaker notes contain any extra notes or background information that you think you may need to jog your memory as you speak. Some people get very nervous when they speak in front of a crowd; speaker notes can remind you of the joke you wanted to open with or the exact figures behind a particular pie chart.

The When and How of Handouts

Presentation professionals are divided about how and when to use handouts most effectively. Here are some of the many conflicting viewpoints. I can't say who is right or wrong, but each of these statements brings up issues that you should consider. The bottom line is that each of them is an opinion on how much power and credit to give to the audience; your answer may vary depending on the audience you are addressing.

- **You should give handouts at the beginning of the presentation. The audience can absorb the information better if they can follow along on paper.**

This approach makes a lot of sense. Research has proven that people absorb more facts if presented with them in more than one medium. This approach also gives your audience free will; they can listen to you or not, and they still have the information. It's their choice, and this can be extremely scary for less-confident speakers. It's not just a speaker confidence issue in some cases, however. If you plan to give a lot of extra information in your speech that's not on the handouts, people might miss it if you distribute the handouts at the beginning because they're reading ahead.

- **You shouldn't give the audience handouts because they won't pay as close attention to your speech if they know that the information is already written down for them.**

This philosophy falls at the other end of the spectrum. It gives the audience the least power and shows the least confidence in their ability to pay attention to you in the presence of a distraction (handouts). If you truly don't trust your audience to be professional and listen, this approach may be your best option. However, don't let insecurity as a speaker drive you prematurely to this conclusion. The fact is that people won't take away as much knowledge about the topic without handouts as they would if you provide handouts. So, ask yourself if your ultimate goal is to fill the audience with knowledge or to make them pay attention to you.

- **You should give handouts at the end of the presentation so that people will have the information to take home but not be distracted during the speech.**

This approach attempts to solve the dilemma with compromise. The trouble with it, as with all compromises, is that it does an incomplete job from both angles. Because audience members can't follow along on the handouts during the presentation, they miss the opportunity to jot notes on the handouts. And because the audience knows that handouts are coming, they might nod off and miss something important. The other problem is that if you don't clearly tell people that handouts are coming later, some people spend the entire presentation frantically copying down each slide on their own notepaper.

Creating Handouts

To create handouts, you simply decide on a layout (a number of slides per page) and then choose that layout from the Print dialog box as you print. No muss, no fuss! If you want to get more involved, you can edit the layout in Handout Master view before printing.

Choosing a Layout

Assuming you have decided that handouts are appropriate for your speech, you must decide on the format for them. You have a choice of one, two, three, four, six, or nine slides per page.

- **1:** Places a single slide vertically and horizontally "centered" on the page.

■ **2:** Prints two big slides on each page. This layout is good for slides that have a lot of fine print and small details or for situations where you are not confident that the reproduction quality will be good. There is nothing more frustrating for an audience than not being able to read the handouts!

■ **3:** Makes the slides much smaller — less than one-half the size of the ones in the two-slide layout. But you get a nice bonus with this layout: lines to the side of each slide for note-taking. This layout works well for presentations where the slides are big and simple, and the speaker is providing a lot of extra information that isn't on the slides. The audience members can write the extra information in the note-taking space provided.

■ **4:** Uses the same size slides as the three-slide layout, but they are spaced out two-by-two without note-taking lines. However, there is still plenty of room above and below each slide, so the audience members still have lots of room to take notes.

■ **6:** Uses slides the same size as the three-slide and four-slide layouts, but crams more slides on the page at the expense of note-taking space. This layout is good for presentation with big, simple slides where the audience does not need to take notes. If you are not sure if the audience will benefit at all from handouts being distributed, consider whether this layout would be a good compromise. This format also saves paper, which might be an issue if you need to make hundreds of copies.

■ **9:** Makes the slides very tiny, almost like a Slide Sorter view, so that you can see nine at a time. This layout makes them very hard to read unless the slide text is extremely simple. I don't recommend this layout in most cases, because the audience really won't get much out of such handouts.

EXPERT TIP One good use for the nine-slides model is as an index or table of contents for a large presentation. You can include a nine-slides-per-page version of the handouts at the beginning of the packet that you give to the audience members, and then follow it up with a two-slides-per-page version that they can refer to if they want a closer look at one of the slides.

Finally, there is an Outline handout layout, which prints an outline of all of the text in your presentation — that is, all of the text that is part of placeholders in slide layouts; any text in extra text boxes you have added manually is excluded. It is not considered a handout when you are printing, but it is included with the handout layouts in the Handout Master. More on this type of handout later in the chapter.

Printing Handouts

When you have decided which layout is appropriate for your needs, print your handouts as follows:

1. (Optional) If you want to print only one particular slide, or a group of slides, select the ones you want in either Slide Sorter view or in the slide thumbnails task pane on the left.

2. Select Office ➪ Print. The Print dialog box appears.

3. Set options for your printer or choose a different printer. See the "Setting Printer-Specific Options" section later in this chapter for help with this.

4. In the Print Range area, choose one of the following:

   ■ **All** to print the entire presentation.

   ■ **Current Slide** to print whatever slide you selected before you issued the Print command.

   ■ **Selection** to print multiple slides you selected before you issued the Print command. It is not available if you did not select any slides beforehand.

   ■ **Custom Show** to print a certain custom show you have set up. It is not available if you do not have any custom shows.

   ■ **Slides** to print the slide numbers that you type in the accompanying text box. Indicate a contiguous range with a dash. For example, to print slides 1 through 9, type **1-9**. Indicate noncontiguous slides with commas. For example, to print slides, 2, 4, and 6, type **2, 4, 6**. Or to print slides 2 plus 6 through 10, type **2, 6-10**. To print them in reverse order, type the order that way, such as **10-6, 2**.

5. Enter a number of copies in the Number of Copies text box. The default is 1. If you want the copies collated (applicable to multipage printouts only), make sure you mark the Collate check box.

6. Open the Print What drop-down list and choose Handouts. The Handouts section of the box becomes available, as shown in Figure 19.1.

FIGURE 19.1

Choose Handouts to print and specify which handout layout you want.

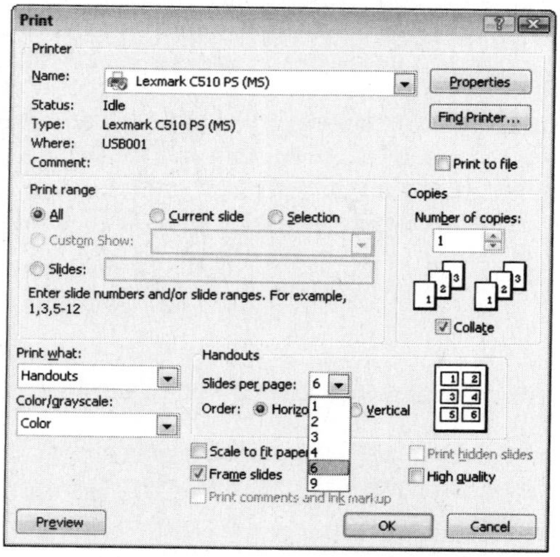

 If you want to print an outline, choose Outline View instead of Handouts in step 6, and then skip steps 7–9. An outline can be a useful handout for an audience in certain situations.

7. Open the Slides Per Page drop-down list and choose the number of slides per page you want.

8. If available, choose an Order: Horizontal or Vertical. Not all number-of-slide choices (from step 7) support an Order choice.

 Order in step 8 refers to the order in which the slides are placed on the page. Horizontal places them by rows, and Vertical places them by columns. This ordering has nothing to do with the orientation of the paper (Portrait or Landscape). You set the paper orientation in the Page Setup dialog box (Design ➪ Page Setup).

9. Open the Color/Grayscale drop-down list and select the color setting for the printouts:

- **Color:** Sends the data to the printer assuming that color will be used. When you use this setting with a black-and-white printer, it results in slides with grayscale or black backgrounds. Use this setting if you want the handouts to look as much as possible like the on-screen slides.

- **Grayscale:** Sends the data to the printer assuming that color will not be used. Colored backgrounds are removed, and if text is normally a light color on a dark background, that is reversed. Use this setting if you want PowerPoint to optimize the printout for viewing on white paper.

- **Pure Black and White:** This format hides most shadows and patterns, as described in Table 19.1. It's good for faxes and overhead transparencies.

TABLE 19.1

Differences Between Grayscale and Pure Black and White

Object	Grayscale	Pure Black and White
Text	Black	Black
Text Shadows	Grayscale	Black
Fill	Grayscale	Grayscale
Lines	Black	Black
Object Shadows	Grayscale	Black
Bitmaps	Grayscale	Grayscale
Clip Art	Grayscale	Grayscale
Slide Backgrounds	White	White
Charts	Grayscale	White

EXPERT TIP To see what your presentation will look like when printed to a black-and-white printer, on the View tab click Grayscale or Pure Black and White. If you see an object that is not displaying the way you want, right-click it and choose Grayscale or Black and White. One of the options there may help you achieve the look you're after.

10. Mark any desired check boxes at the bottom of the dialog box:

■ **Scale to Fit Paper:** Enlarges the slides to the maximum size they can be and still fit on the layout (as defined in the Handout Master, covered later in this chapter).

■ **Frame Slides:** Draws a black border around each slide image. Useful for slides being printed with white backgrounds.

■ **Print Comments:** Prints any comments that you have inserted with the Comments feature in PowerPoint (covered in Chapter 23).

■ **Print Hidden Slides:** Includes hidden slides in the printout. This option is not available if you don't have any hidden slides in your presentation.

■ **High Quality:** Optimizes the appearance of the printout in small ways, such as allowing text shadows to print.

11. (Optional) Click the Preview button to see a preview of your handouts; then click the Print button to return to the Print dialog box.

12. Click OK. The handouts print, and you're ready to roll!

CAUTION Beware of the cost of printer supplies. If you are planning to distribute copies of the presentation to a lot of people, it may be tempting to print all of the copies on your printer. But the cost per page of printing is fairly high, especially if you have an inkjet printer. You will quickly run out of ink in your ink cartridge and have to spend $20 or more for a replacement. Consider whether it might be cheaper to print one original and take it to a copy shop.

Setting Printer-Specific Options

In addition to the controls in the Print dialog box in PowerPoint, there are controls you can set that affect the printer you have chosen. In the Printer section of the Print dialog box, you can open the Name drop-down list and choose the printer you want to use to print the job, as shown in Figure 19.2. Most home users have only one printer, but business users may have more than one to choose from, especially on a network.

NOTE Some of the "printers" listed are not really physical printers but drivers that create other types of files. For example, Microsoft XPS Document Writer saves a file in XPS format, which is Microsoft's version of a PostScript-type format.

After choosing a printer, you can click the Properties button to display its Properties dialog box. The properties shown are different for different kinds of printers. Figure 19.2 shows the box for my Lexmark Optra S 1855 printer, a color laser printer. Notice that there are six tabs: Layout, Paper/Quality, Output Options, Watermark, Profiles, and About. The tabs may be different for your printer.

FIGURE 19.2

Select a printer if you have more than one.

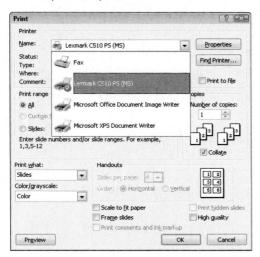

FIGURE 19.3

Each printer's options are slightly different, but the same types of settings are available on most printers.

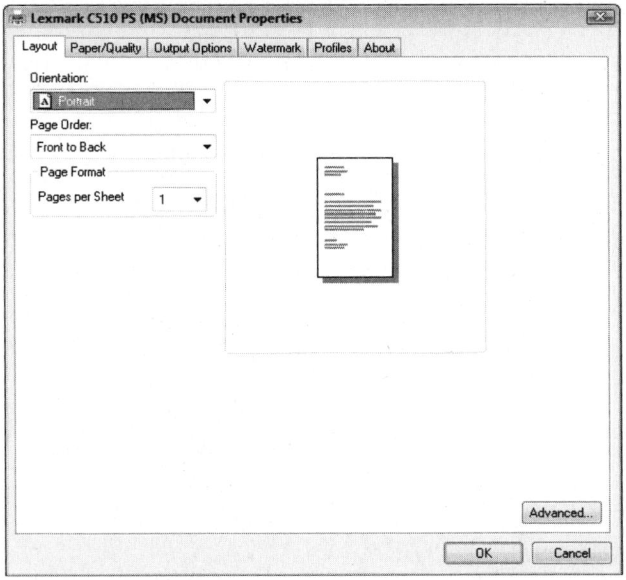

These settings affect how the printer behaves in all Windows-based programs, not just in PowerPoint, so you need to be careful not to change anything that you don't want globally changed. Here are some of the settings you may be able to change on your printer:

- **Orientation:** You can choose between Portrait and Landscape. It's not recommended that you change this setting here, though; make such changes in the Page Setup dialog box in PowerPoint instead. Otherwise, you may get the wrong orientation on a printout in other programs.

- **Page Order:** You can choose Front to Back or Back to Front. This determines the order the pages print.

- **Pages Per Sheet:** The default is 1, but you can print smaller versions of several pages on a single sheet. This option is usually only available on PostScript printers.

- **Paper Size:** The default is Letter, but you can change to Legal, A4, or any of several other sizes.

- **Paper Source:** If your printer has more than one paper tray, you may be able to select Upper or Lower.

- **Copies:** This sets the default number of copies that should print. Be careful; this number is a multiplier. If you set two copies here, and then set two copies in the Print dialog box in PowerPoint, you end up with four copies.

- **Graphics Resolution:** If your printer has a range of resolutions available, you may be able to choose the resolution you want. My printer lets me choose between 300 and 600 dots per inch (dpi); on an inkjet printer, choices are usually 360, 720, and 1,440 dpi. Achieving a resolution of 1,440 on an inkjet printer usually requires special glossy paper.

- **Graphic Dithering:** On some printers, you can set the type of dithering that makes up images. *Dithering* is a method of creating shadows (shades of gray) from black ink by using tiny crosshatch patterns. You may be able to choose between Coarse, Fine, and None.

- **Image Intensity:** On some printers, you can control the image appearance with a light/dark slide bar.

Some printers, notably inkjets, come with their own print-management software. If that's the case, you may have to run that print-management software separately from outside of PowerPoint for full control over the printer's settings. You can usually access such software from the Windows Start menu.

Using the Handout Master

Just as the Slide Master controls your slide layout, the Handout Master controls your handout layout. To view the Handout Master, on the View tab click Handout Master, as shown in Figure 19.4. Unlike the Slide Master and Title Master, you can have only one Handout Master layout per presentation.

FIGURE 19.4

The Handout Master lets you define the handout layout to be printed.

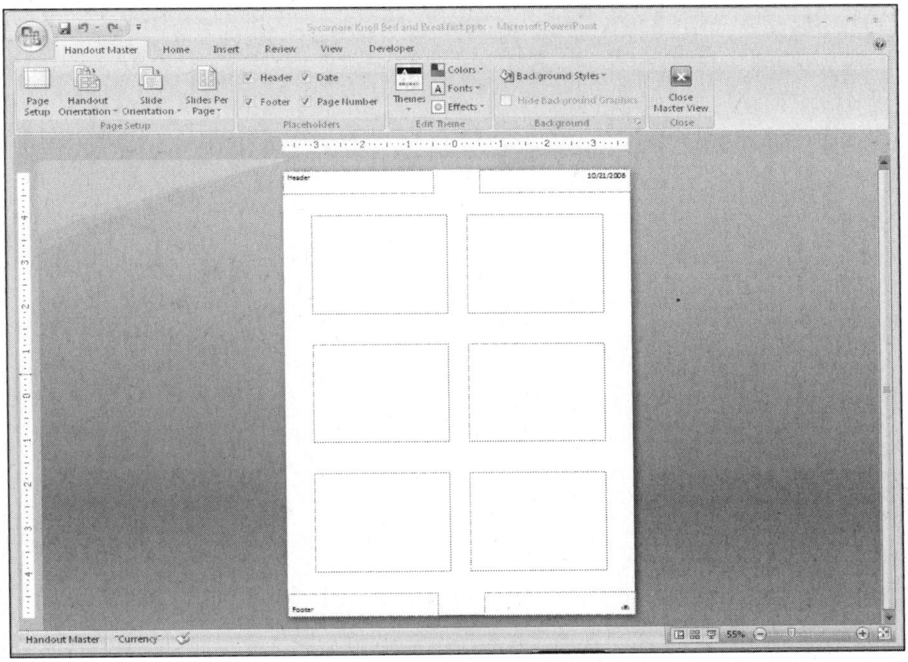

You can do almost exactly the same things with the Handout Master that you can with the Slide Master. The following sections describe some of the common activities.

Setting the Number of Slides Per Page

You can view the Handout Master with various numbers of slides per page to help you see how the layout will look when you print it. However, the settings are not different for each number of slides per page; for example, if you apply a header or footer, or page background, for a three-slides-per-page layout, it also applies to all the others as well. To choose the number of slides per page to display as you work with the Handout Master, click the Slides Per Page button and then make your selection from its menu. See Figure 19.5.

FIGURE 19.5

Choose a number of slides per page.

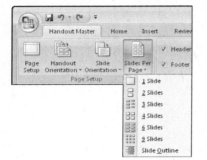

Using and Positioning Placeholders

The Handout Master has four placeholders by default: Header, Footer, Date, and Page Number, in the four corners of the handout respectively:

- **Header:** Appears in the upper-left corner, and is a blank box into which you can type fixed text that will appear on each page of the printout.
- **Footer:** Same thing as Header but appears in the lower-left corner.
- **Date:** Appears in the upper-right corner, and shows today's date by default.
- **Page Number:** Appears in lower-right corner and shows a code for a page number <#>. This will be replaced by an actual page number when you print.

In each placeholder box, you can type text (replacing, if desired, the Date and Page codes already there in those). You can also drag the placeholder boxes around on the layout.

There are two ways to remove the default placeholders from the layout. You select the placeholder box and press Delete, or you can clear the check box for that element on the Handout Master tab as shown in Figure 19.6.

FIGURE 19.6

Turn on/off placeholder elements from the Handout Master tab.

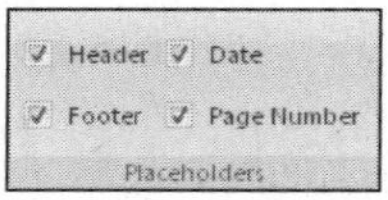

Because the header and footer are blank by default, there is no advantage to deleting these placeholders unless they have something in them you want to dispose of; having a blank box and having no box at all have the same result.

EXPERT TIP You can't move or resize the *slide* placeholder boxes on the Handout Master, nor can you change its margins. If you want to change the size of the slide boxes on the handout or change the margins of the page, consider exporting the handouts to Word and working on them there. See the section "Exporting Handouts or Notes Pages to Word" at the end of this chapter for more information.

Setting Handout and Slide Orientation

Orientation refers to the direction on the page the material runs. If the top of the paper is one of the narrow edges, it's called Portrait; if the top of the paper is a wide edge, it's Landscape. Figure 19.7 shows the difference in handout orientation.

FIGURE 19.7

Portrait (left) and Landscape (right) handout orientation.

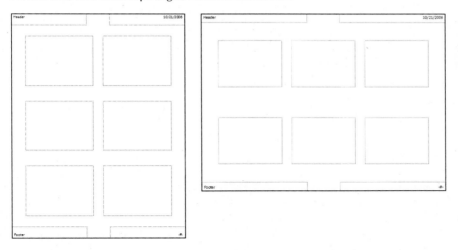

You can also set an orientation for the slides themselves on the handouts. This is a separate setting that does not affect the handout page in terms of the placement of the header, footer, and other repeated elements. Figure 19.8 shows the difference between portrait and landscape slide orientation on a portrait handout.

FIGURE 19.8

Landscape (left) and Portrait (right) slide orientation.

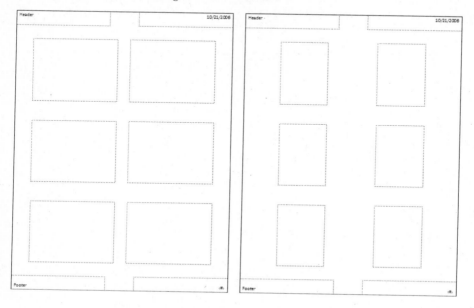

To set either of these orientations, use their respective drop-down lists on the Handout Master tab, in the Page Setup group. See Figure 19.9.

FIGURE 19.9

Set orientation from the Page Setup group.

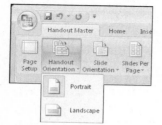

Formatting Handouts

You can manually format any text on a handout layout using the formatting controls on the Home tab, the same as with any other text. Such formatting affects only the text you select, and only on the layout you're working with. You can also select the entire placeholder box and apply formatting.

You can also apply Colors, Fonts, and/or Effects themes from the Edit Theme group, as shown in Figure 19.10, much like you can do for the presentation as a whole. The main difference is that you cannot select an overall theme from the Themes button; all the themes are unavailable from the list while in Handout Master view. The settings you apply here affect only the handouts, not the presentation as a whole.

NOTE You probably won't have much occasion to apply an Effects theme to a handout layout because handouts do not usually have objects that use effects (i.e., drawn shapes, charts, or SmartArt diagrams).

FIGURE 19.10

Apply color, font, and/or effect themes from the Edit Theme group.

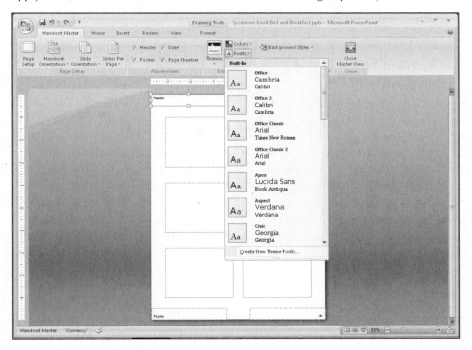

Creating Speaker Notes

Speaker notes are like handouts, but for you. Only one printout format is available for them: the Notes Pages layout. It consists of the slide on the top half (the same size as in the two-slides-per-page handout) with the blank space below it for your notes to yourself.

Speaker notes printed in PowerPoint are better than traditional note cards for several reasons. For one thing, you can type your notes right into the computer and print them out on regular paper. There's no need to jam a note card into a typewriter and use messy correction fluid or erasers to make changes. The other benefit is that each note page contains a picture of the slide, so it's not as easy to lose your place while speaking.

Typing Speaker Notes

You can type your notes for a slide in Normal view (in the notes pane), or in Notes Page view. The latter shows the page more or less as it will look when you print your notes pages; this can help if you need to gauge how much text will fit on the printed page.

To switch to Notes Page view, on the View tab click Notes Page as shown in Figure 19.11. Unlike some of the other views, there is no shortcut button for this view in the bottom-right corner of the PowerPoint window. Once you're in Notes Page view, you can zoom and scroll just like in any other view to see more or less of the page at once. You can scroll further to move from slide to slide, or you can move from slide to slide in the traditional ways (the Page Up and Page Down keys on the keyboard or the Next Slide or Previous Slide buttons on-screen).

> **NOTE** Use the Zoom control to zoom in or out until you find the optimal view so that the text you type is large enough to be clear, but small enough so that you can see across the entire width of the note area. I find that 66 to 85 percent works well on my screen at 800x600 resolution, but yours may vary.

Just type your notes in the Notes area, the same as you would type any text box in PowerPoint. The lines in the paragraph wrap automatically. Press Enter to start a new paragraph. When you're done, move to the next slide.

FIGURE 19.11

Notes Page view is one of the best ways to work with your speaker notes.

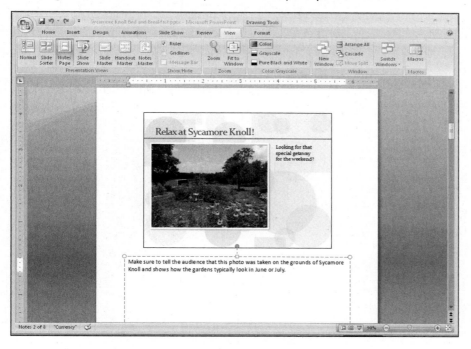

Changing the Notes Page Layout

Just as you can edit your handout layouts, you can also edit your notes page layout. Just switch to its Master and make your changes. Follow these steps:

1. On the View tab, click Notes Master.

2. Edit the layout, as you have learned to edit other masters. See Figure 19.12. This can include:

   - Moving placeholders for the slide, the notes, or any of the header or footer elements.

   - Changing the font used for the text in any of those areas.

   - Resizing the placeholder for the slide graphic.

   - Resizing the Notes pane.

   - Adding clip art or other graphics to the background.

   - Adding a colored, textured, or patterned background to the notes page.

3. When you are finished, click the Close Master View button to return to Normal view.

FIGURE 19.12

You can edit the layout of the notes pages in Notes Master view.

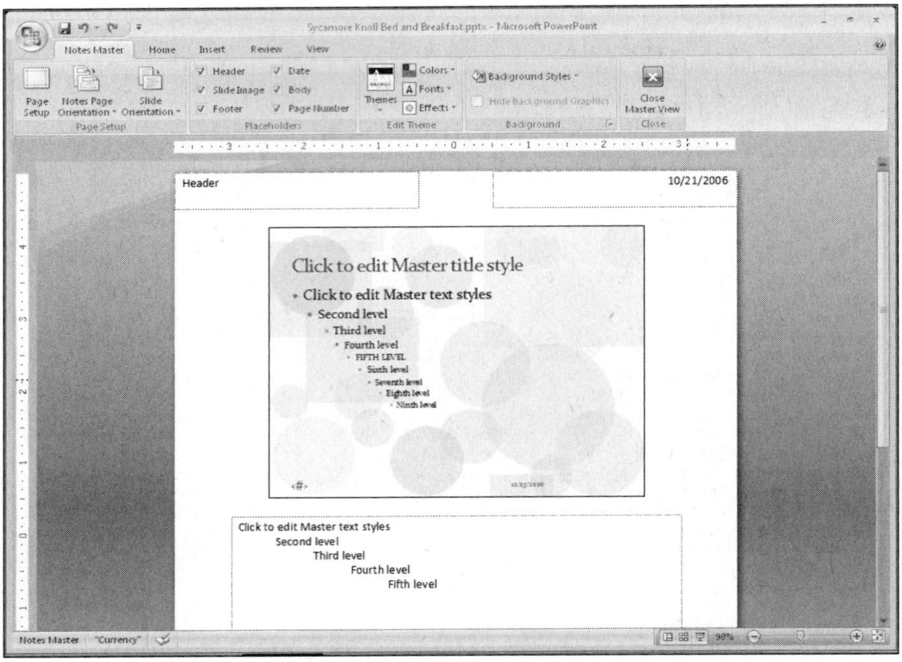

Printing Notes Pages

When you're ready to print your notes pages, follow these steps:

1. Choose Office ➪ Print. The Print dialog box opens.

2. Open the Print What drop-down list and choose Notes Pages.

3. Set any other options, just as you did when printing handouts earlier in the chapter. (If you need to choose which printer to use or to set the options for that printer, see the "Setting Printer-Specific Options" section earlier in this chapter.) There are no special options for notes pages.

4. Click OK. The notes pages print.

CAUTION If you print notes pages for hidden slides, you may want to arrange your stack after they're printed so that the hidden slides are at the bottom. That way you won't get confused when giving the presentation.

Printing an Outline

If text is the main part of your presentation, you might prefer to print an outline instead of mini-slides. You can use the outline for speaker notes, audience handouts, or both. To print the text from Outline view, follow these steps:

1. View the outline in Normal or Outline view.
2. Choose Office ➪ Print. The Print dialog box opens.
3. Open the Print What drop-down list and choose Outline View.
4. Set any other print options, as you learned in the "Printing Handouts" section earlier in the chapter.
5. Click OK.

Be aware, however, that the outline will not contain text that you've typed in manually placed text boxes or any other non-text information, such as tables, charts, and so on.

Exporting Handouts or Notes Pages to Word

One of the drawbacks to PowerPoint is that the notes and handouts pages are not fully formattable. There's a lot you can't do with them — such as set margins, or change the sizes of the slide images for handouts. To get around this, you might want to create your handouts in Microsoft Word. To send your presentation to Word, follow these steps:

1. Choose Office ➪ Publish ➪ Create Handouts in Microsoft Office Word. The Send to Microsoft Office Word dialog box appears as shown in Figure 19.13.

FIGURE 19.13

Choose a format for sending the presentation to Word.

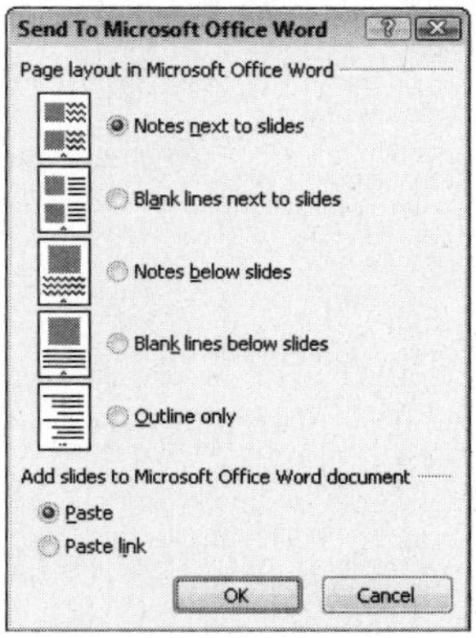

2. Choose one of the formats shown in Figure 19.13. You can send to Word in a variety of formats. Some formats are more appropriate for handouts, others for speaker notes. Here are some suggestions:

For Handouts	For Speaker Notes
Blank Lines Next to Slides	Notes Next to Slides
Blank Lines Below Slides	Notes Below Slides
Outline Only	Outline Only

3. (Optional) If you want to maintain a link between the PowerPoint file and the Word file, choose Paste Link. Otherwise, leave Paste selected. If you maintain a link, then the changes you make to the PowerPoint file are reflected in the Word file.

4. Click OK. Word opens and the slides appear in the format you chose. See Figure 19.14.

5. Modify the formatting as desired, and then print from Word.

6. (Optional) Save your work in Word if you want to print the same pages again later. (You may choose to resend to Word later, after making changes in PowerPoint instead.)

FIGURE 19.14

With the notes pages or handouts in Word, you can change the margins and other settings.

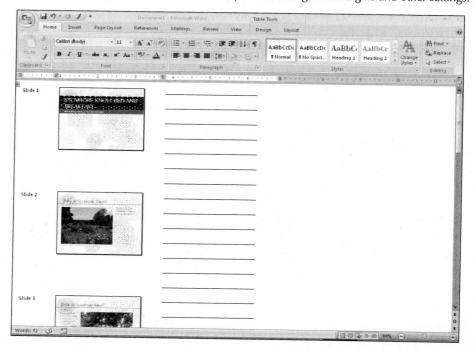

NOTE The slides appear in Word in a table (if you chose a Next to Slides option), but without visible gridlines showing. You can resize (or even delete) the columns for each element by dragging the column dividers, just like you do in a table in PowerPoint.

Changing the Margins in Word

One benefit of exporting handouts to Word is being able to change the margins. In Word, on the Page Layout tab, click the Margins button, and choose a margin preset or choose Custom Margins.

However, note that changing the page margins does not resize the table. If you change the left margin, the table may start at a different place in relation to the left margin (because the table is left-aligned), but if you want to increase the margins so that you can increase the table width, those are two separate activities.

You can also set internal margins in the cells in a table. To do so, on the Table Tools Layout tab, click Cell Margins.

Change the Table Alignment

The table itself has a default alignment in relationship to the page: Top left. If you prefer the look of a centered table, you may want to switch this:

■ To make the table horizontally centered on the page, select the table as a whole. To do this, click the square above and to the left of the table with the four-headed arrow in it. Then use the Center button on the Home tab (Paragraph group) to center it. Note that this does not center the text within the cells; this refers only to the table.

■ To vertically center the table on the page, you need to set the vertical alignment for the document. To do so, on the Page Layout tab in Word, click the dialog box launcher in the Page Setup group, and on the Layout tab in the Page Setup dialog box, set the vertical alignment to Center.

Change Alignment Within a Cell

To center the content within a cell horizontally, click in that cell and then on the Table Tools Layout tab, click the Middle Center button (or any of the other buttons that are combinations of vertical and horizontal alignment) as shown in Figure 19.15.

FIGURE 19.15

Set table alignment from the Table Tools Layout tab.

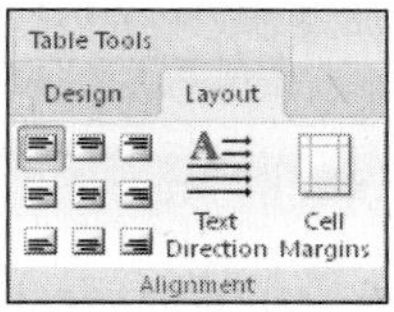

Resize Rows and Columns

To resize a column, drag the border between that column and the one to its right. When the mouse pointer is over a column border, it changes to a double-headed arrow with a line between the arrows. Alternatively you can specify an exact size by clicking in the column, and then on the Table Tools Layout tab, set a value in the Cell Size group. Do the same for row heights. For a better look at the gridlines, on the Table Tools Format tab, enable View Gridlines. These appear only on-screen; they will not print.

NOTE   You cannot resize a row or column to the point that its text content no longer fits. (And the lines for the audience to write on are comprised of underline characters, which are considered text.) Therefore, you may need to resize the content or even delete some of it. For example, if you use a layout that includes blank lines, you'll get several blank lines in some of the cells. To make these cells narrower, you need to decrease the length of the lines first. To make these cells shorter, you may need to delete one or more of the lines.

Turn On/Off Cell Borders

By default, all borders are turned off for all cells in the table. You can turn them on in a variety of ways, but perhaps the easiest is to select one or more cells, and then use the Borders button on the Table Tools Design tab. Choose the button that has no borders (all dotted lines) to turn all borders off again.

FIGURE 19.16

The Borders button has a drop-down list of border sides to turn on/off.

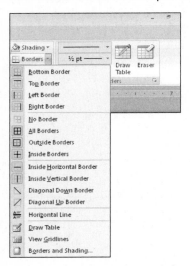

NOTE   One thing to note about these borders is that whatever you choose applies to the selected range, not to the individual cells. For example, suppose you choose a range of cells that contains three rows and you apply a bottom border. The border would be applied only to the bottom of the bottom row of cells.

Apply a Background

To apply a background to the entire page, use the Page Color button on the Page Layout tab in Word. A palette of colors appears. The choices are much the same as in PowerPoint.

EXPERT TIP   Word 2007 uses the same themes as PowerPoint. You can apply a theme to the document in Word to make it match the formatting of the presentation in PowerPoint.

To apply a background to only certain cells, select the cells and then on the Table Tools Design tab, click the Shading button and select a color. This is a lot like applying a fill color in PowerPoint.

Resize the Graphics

Resizing the slide images is one of the most common reasons why people export PowerPoint handouts to Word. Each image is resizable individually, so they need not necessarily be the same size (although it usually looks better if they are).

If you want to make the slides larger, you can first increase the column width for the column in which they reside. Then drag the selection handles on the slide thumbnail to resize.

NOTE   If you want to resize all of the slide images and you want them all to be the same size, set the table column width to the width you want for the images and then resize each picture as large as it can be while still fitting in that column. Unfortunately you cannot resize multiple images as a batch.

Summary

In this chapter, you learned how to create hard copy to support your presentation. You can now create a variety of handouts, and write and print out speaker notes for yourself. You also learned how to export handouts, notes pages, and outlines to Word, where you can use the full power of Word's formatting tools to create exactly the look you want.

In the next chapter, you take a look at the controls that PowerPoint offers for preparing for a live presentation. You learn how to create custom shows, work with hidden slides, and navigate through a presentation in Slide Show view.

Preparing for a Live Presentation

I t's show time! Well, actually I hope for your sake that it is *not* time for the show this very instant, because things will go much more smoothly if you can practice using PowerPoint's slide-show controls before you have to go live.

Presenting the show can be as simple or as complex as you make it. At the most basic level, you can start the show, move through it slide-by-slide with simple mouse-clicks or key presses, and then end the show. However, to take advantage of PowerPoint's extra slide-show features, you should spend a little time studying the following sections.

> **NOTE** The first part of this chapter assumes that you are showing your presentation on a PC that has PowerPoint 2007 installed; sections later in this chapter discuss other situations.

Starting and Ending a Show

To start a show, do any of the following:

- Click the Slide Show View button in the bottom-right corner of the screen.
- On the View tab, click Slide Show.
- Press F5.
- Press Shift+F5

These methods are not all exactly alike. For example, if you click the Slide Show View button in the bottom-right corner, or press Shift+F5, the first slide to appear is the currently selected one in PowerPoint. If you click the Slide Show button on the View tab or press F5, it starts with the first slide in the presentation, regardless of which slide was selected.

Once the show is underway, you can control the movement from slide to slide as described in the section, "Moving from Slide to Slide."

To end the show, do any of the following:

- Right-click and choose End Show.
- Press Esc, - (minus), or Ctrl+Break.

If you want to temporarily pause the show while you have a discussion, you can blank the screen by pressing W or , (comma) for a white screen, or B or . (period) for a black screen. To resume the show, press any key.

EXPERT TIP **If you set up the slide transitions to occur automatically at a certain time, you can stop or restart the show by pressing S or + (plus sign). However, this is more of an issue for self-running shows, which are discussed in Chapter 21.**

Using the On-screen Show Controls

When you display a slide show, the mouse pointer and show controls are hidden. To make them appear, you can move the mouse. When you do this, very faint buttons appear in the bottom-left corner of the slide show, as shown in Figure 20.1, and the mouse pointer also appears. You can toggle the pointer and these buttons on and off by pressing A or = (equals). Ctrl+H hides the pointer and buttons. When you toggle this feature on, the following buttons appear:

FIGURE 20.1

Buttons appear in the bottom-left corner of a slide in Slide Show view. The third button opens a menu that controls navigation between slides.

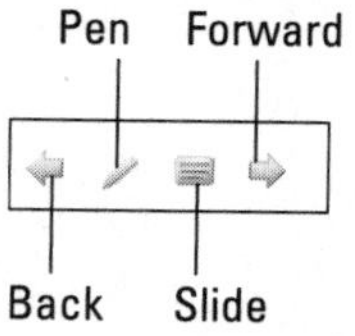

- **Back**, the leftmost button, takes you back to the previous slide, or to the previous animation event if the present slide contains animation.

- **Pen**, next to Back, opens a menu for controlling the appearance of the pen or pointer. (I discuss this feature later in this chapter.)

- **Slide**, which displays a box icon, opens a menu for navigating between slides. You can also open the navigation menu, shown in Figure 20.2, by right-clicking anywhere on the slide.

EXPERT TIP You can set up your show to move backwards when you click the right-mouse button. Choose Office ✪ PowerPoint Options, click Advanced, and in the Slide Show section deselect the Show Menu on Right Mouse Click check box. If you do that, you can't right-click to open the navigation menu, though.

FIGURE 20.2

Click the Slide button or right-click on the slide to open this menu.

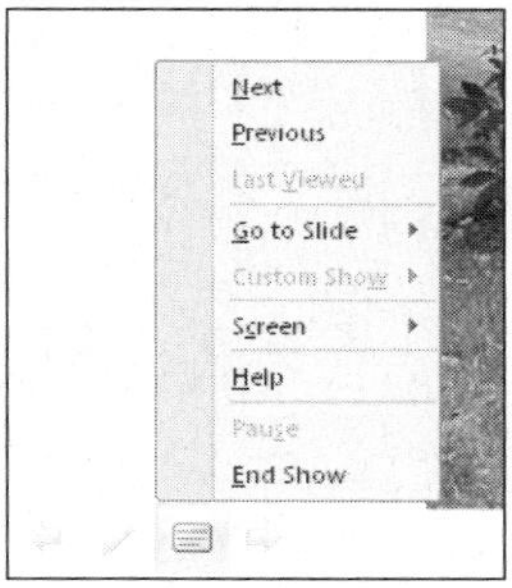

- **Forward**, the rightmost button, moves you to the next slide. Normally, you can just click to go to the next slide, but if you are using the pen (covered later in this chapter), then clicking it causes it to draw, rather than advance the presentation. In this situation, you can use the Forward button.

NOTE Because the slide navigation menu that appears is identical whether you click the Slide button or right-click anywhere on the slide, this chapter only mentions the right-click method whenever you need to choose something from this menu. However, keep in mind that you can also click the Slide button if you prefer.

There are a lot of shortcut keys to remember when working in Slide Show view, and so PowerPoint provides a handy summary of these keys. To see them, right-click and choose Help, or press F1. The Slide Show Help dialog box appears, as shown in Figure 20.3. Click OK to close this dialog box when you are done.

FIGURE 20.3

The Slide Show Help dialog box provides a quick summary of the shortcut keys that are available during a presentation.

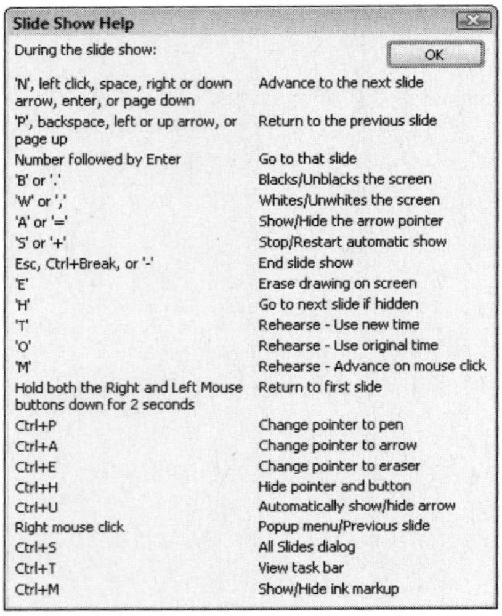

Slide Show Help	
During the slide show:	OK
'N', left click, space, right or down arrow, enter, or page down	Advance to the next slide
'P', backspace, left or up arrow, or page up	Return to the previous slide
Number followed by Enter	Go to that slide
'B' or '.'	Blacks/Unblacks the screen
'W' or ','	Whites/Unwhites the screen
'A' or '='	Show/Hide the arrow pointer
'S' or '+'	Stop/Restart automatic show
Esc, Ctrl+Break, or '-'	End slide show
'E'	Erase drawing on screen
'H'	Go to next slide if hidden
'T'	Rehearse - Use new time
'O'	Rehearse - Use original time
'M'	Rehearse - Advance on mouse click
Hold both the Right and Left Mouse buttons down for 2 seconds	Return to first slide
Ctrl+P	Change pointer to pen
Ctrl+A	Change pointer to arrow
Ctrl+E	Change pointer to eraser
Ctrl+H	Hide pointer and button
Ctrl+U	Automatically show/hide arrow
Right mouse click	Popup menu/Previous slide
Ctrl+S	All Slides dialog
Ctrl+T	View task bar
Ctrl+M	Show/Hide ink markup

Moving from Slide to Slide

The simplest way to move through a presentation is to move to the next slide. To do so, you can use any of these methods:

- Press any of these keys: N, Spacebar, right arrow, down arrow, Enter, or Page Down.
- Click the left-mouse button.
- Right-click and then choose Next.
- Click the right-pointing arrow button in the bottom-left corner of the slide.

If you have animated any elements on a slide, these methods advance the animation, and do not necessarily move to the next slide. For example, if you have animated your bulleted list so that the bullets appear one at a time, then any of the actions in this list make the next bullet appear, rather than making the next slide appear. Only after all of the objects on the current slide have displayed does PowerPoint advance to the next slide. If you need to immediately advance to the next slide, you can use the instructions in the section, "Jumping to Specific Slides," later in this chapter.

To back up to the previous slide, use any of these methods:

- Press any of these keys: P, Backspace, left arrow, up arrow, or Page Up.
- Click the left-pointing arrow button on the bottom-left corner of the slide.
- Right-click and then choose Previous.

You can also go back to the last slide that you viewed. To do this, right-click and choose Last Viewed. Although you would think that the last slide viewed would be the same as the previous slide, this is not always the case. For example, if you jump around in the slide show — such as to a hidden slide — then the last slide viewed is not the previous slide in the show but the hidden slide that you have just viewed.

Jumping to Specific Slides

There are several ways to jump to a particular slide. One of the easiest ways is to select the slide by its title. To do so, follow these steps:

1. During the slide show, right-click to display the shortcut menu.

2. Select Go to Slide. A submenu appears, listing the titles of all of the slides in the presentation, as shown in Figure 20.4. Parentheses around the slide numbers indicate hidden slides.

3. Click the slide title to which you want to jump.

EXPERT TIP The slide titles in this list come from title placeholders. If you want to show text on the list here but you don't want it to appear on the slide, type it in a title placeholder and then drag the placeholder off the edge of the slide, so it doesn't show in Slide Show view.

FIGURE 20.4

You can go to a specific slide using the Go to Slide command on the menu.

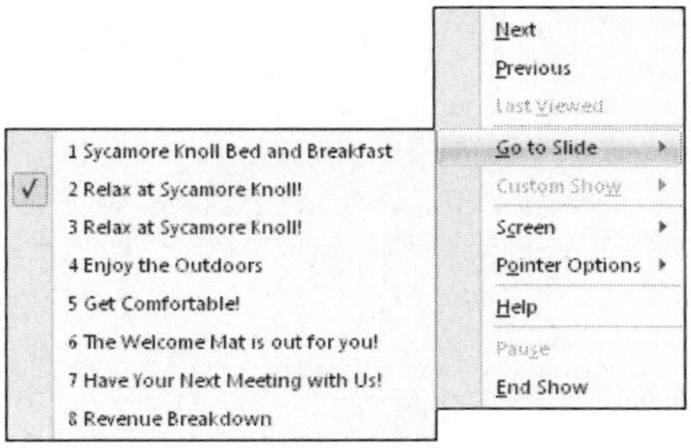

You can also jump to a certain slide number by typing this number and pressing Enter. For example, to go to the third slide, you would type **3** and then press Enter. Another way is to press Ctrl+S to open an All Slides dialog box listing the titles of all of the slides in the presentation. You can click a slide to select it and then click Go To, as shown in Figure 20.5.

To jump back to the first slide in the presentation, hold down both the left- and right-mouse buttons for two seconds (or type **1** and press Enter).

FIGURE 20.5

The All Slides dialog box lists the titles of all of the slides so that you can select the one that you want to go to.

Blanking the Screen

Sometimes during a live presentation there may be a delay. Whether it is a chatty audience member with a complicated question, a fire drill, or just an intermission, you will want to pause the show.

If you have the slides set for manual transition, then whichever slide you stopped on remains on the screen until you resume. However, you may not want this. For example, it may be distracting to the audience, especially if the pause is to allow someone to get up and speak in front of the screen. A solution is to turn the screen into a blank expanse of black or white. To do so, type W or a comma (for white), or B or a period (for black). To return to the presentation, you can press the same key, or press any key on the keyboard.

EXPERT TIP   While the screen is completely black or white, you can draw on it with the Pen tool so that it becomes a convenient "scratch pad." Any annotations that you make with the pen on the blank screen are not saved; when you resume the presentation, they are gone forever.

Using the On-screen Pen

Have you ever seen a coach in a locker room drawing out football plays on a chalkboard? Well, you can do the same thing in PowerPoint. You can have impromptu discussions of concepts that are illustrated on slides, and punctuate the discussion with your own circles, arrows, and lines. Perhaps during the discussion portion of your presentation, you may decide that one point on the slide is not important. In this case, you can use the pen to cross it out. Conversely, a certain point may become really important during a discussion so that you want to emphasize it. In this case, you can circle it or underline it with the pen cursor.

You can choose your pen color as follows:

1. Move the mouse or press A to make the buttons appear.
2. Click the Pointers button (the one that looks like a pen). A menu appears.
3. Select Ink Color and then click the color you want, as shown in Figure 20-6.

FIGURE 20.6

You can select a pen type and an ink color for it.

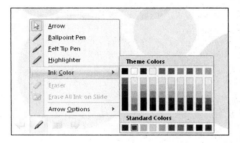

EXPERT TIP To change the default pen color for the show, so that you do not always have to manually select the color you want, click Set Up Show on the Slide Show tab. Then, in the Pen Color drop-down list, choose the color you want.

You can turn on the type of pen that you want, as follows:

1. Click the Pointers button again.
2. Click the type of pen that you want:

    Ballpoint: A thin line

    Felt Tip Pen: A thicker line

    Highlighter: A thick, semi-transparent line

NOTE The on-screen buttons in the slide show continue to work while you have a pen enabled, but you have to click them twice to activate them—once to tell PowerPoint to temporarily switch out of the Pen mode, and then again to open the menu.

You can also turn on the default pen type (Felt Tip) by pressing Ctrl+P, and then return to the arrow again by pressing Ctrl+A or Esc.

After enabling a pen, just drag-and-draw on the slide to make your mark. You should practice drawing lines, arrows, and other shapes because it takes a while to master. Figure 20.7 shows an example of using the pen.

FIGURE 20.7

You can draw on the slide with the pen tools.

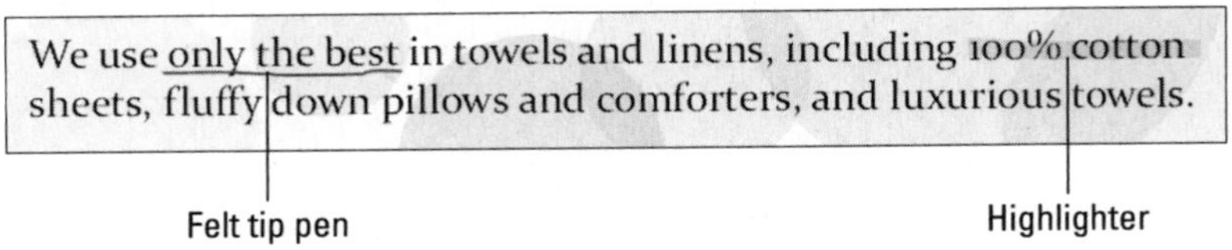

We use <u>only the best</u> in towels and linens, including 100% cotton sheets, fluffy down pillows and comforters, and luxurious towels.

Felt tip pen   Highlighter

> **CAUTION**
> As you can see from Figure 20.7, the on-screen pen is not very attractive. If you know in advance that you are going to emphasize certain points, then you may prefer to build the emphasis into the presentation by making these points larger, bolder, or in different colors. You can also circle the points using an oval shape with a 1-spoke wheel animation.

To erase your lines and try again, press E (for Erase), or open the Pointer menu and choose Erase All Ink On Slide. To erase just a part of the ink, open the Pointer menu, choose Eraser, and then use the mouse pointer to erase individual lines.

> **NOTE**
> Unlike in some earlier versions of PowerPoint, drawings stay with a slide, even when you move to another slide.

When you exit Slide Show view after drawing on slides, a dialog box appears, asking whether you want to keep or discard your annotations. If you choose Keep, the annotations become drawn objects on the slides, which you can then move or delete, similar to an AutoShape.

To change the pen back to a pointer again, open the Pointer menu and choose Arrow, press Ctrl+A, or press Esc. The pen remains a pen when you advance from slide to slide. In earlier versions of PowerPoint, it reverted back to an arrow automatically when you changed slides.

Hiding Slides for Backup Use

You may not always want to show every slide that you have prepared. Sometimes it pays to prepare extra data in anticipation of a question that you think someone might ask, or to hold back certain data unless someone specifically requests it.

By hiding a slide, you keep it filed in reserve, without making it a part of the main slide show. Then, at any time during the presentation when (or if) it becomes appropriate, you can display that slide. Hiding refers only to whether the slide is a part of the main presentation's flow; it has no effect in any other view.

> **EXPERT TIP**
> If you have only a handful of slides to hide, go ahead and hide them. However, if you have a large group of related slides to hide, consider creating a custom show for them instead.

Hiding and Unhiding Slides

A good way to hide and unhide slides is in Slide Sorter view because an indicator appears below each slide to show whether it is hidden. This way, you can easily determine which slides are part of the main presentation. In the slide thumbnail pane in Normal view, hidden slides appear ghosted out.

Follow these steps to hide a slide:

1. Switch to Slide Sorter view.

2. Select the slide or slides that you want to hide. Remember, to select more than one slide, hold down the Ctrl key as you click the ones that you want.

3. Click the Hide Slide button on the Slide Show toolbar. A gray box appears around the slide number and a diagonal line crosses through it, indicating that it is hidden.

To unhide a slide, select the slide and click the Hide Slide button again. The slide's number returns to normal. You can also right-click a slide and choose Hide Slide or Unhide Slide to toggle the hidden attribute on and off.

EXPERT TIP To quickly unhide all slides, select all of the slides (press Ctrl+A) and then click the Hide Slides button twice. The first click hides all of the remaining slides that were not already hidden, and the second click unhides them all.

Showing a Hidden Slide During a Presentation

When you advance from one slide to the next during a show, hidden slides do not appear. (This is what being hidden is about, after all.) If you need to display one of the hidden slides, follow these steps:

1. In Slide Show view, open the Screen menu, either by clicking the Screen icon or by right-clicking anywhere in the screen.

2. Choose Go to Slide, and then choose the slide to which you want to jump. Hidden slides show their slide numbers in parentheses, but you can access them like any other slide, as shown in Figure 20.8.

EXPERT TIP If you already know the number of the hidden slide, then you can simply type the number on the keyboard and press Enter to display it. This also works with slides that are not hidden.

Once you display a hidden slide, you can easily return to it later. When you move backwards through the presentation (using the Backspace key, the left- or up-arrow key, or the on-screen Back button), any hidden slides that you displayed previously are included in the slides that PowerPoint scrolls back through. However, when you move forward through the presentation, the hidden slide does not reappear, regardless of when you viewed it previously. You can always jump back to it again using the preceding steps.

FIGURE 20.8

You can jump to a hidden slide just as you would to any other slide.

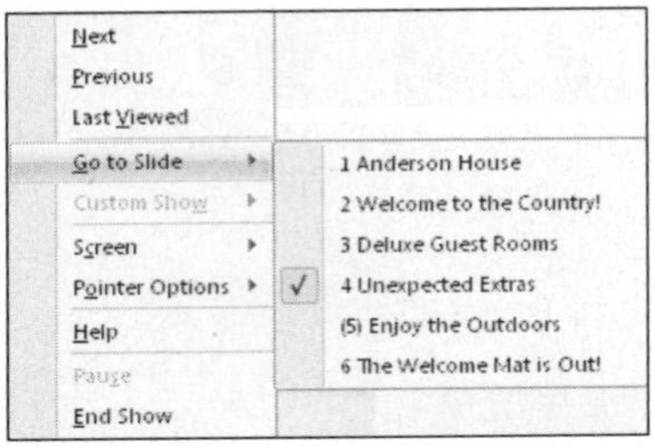

Next	
Previous	
Last Viewed	
Go to Slide ▶	1 Anderson House
Custom Show ▶	2 Welcome to the Country!
Screen ▶	3 Deluxe Guest Rooms
Pointer Options ▶	√ 4 Unexpected Extras
Help	(5) Enjoy the Outdoors
Pause	6 The Welcome Mat is Out!
End Show	

Using Custom Shows

Many slide shows have a linear flow: First you show slide one, and then slide two, and so on, until you have completed the entire presentation. This format is suitable for situations where you are presenting clear-cut information with few variables, such as a presentation about a new insurance plan for a group of employees. However, when the situation becomes more complex, a single-path slide show may not suffice. This is especially true when you are presenting a persuasive message to decision-makers; you want to anticipate their questions and needs for more information and have many backup slides, or even entire backup slide shows that are prepared in case questions arise. Figure 20.9 shows a flow chart for this kind of presentation.

NOTE If you simply want to hide a few slides for backup use, then you do not need to create a custom show. Instead, you can just hide the slides.

Another great use for custom shows is to set aside a group of slides for a specific audience. For example, you might need to present essentially the same information to employees at two different sites. In this case, you could create two custom shows within the main show, where each show includes slides that they both have in common, as well as slides that are appropriate for only one audience or the other. Figure 20.10 shows a flow chart for this kind of presentation.

FIGURE 20.9

You can use custom shows to hide related groups of backup slides.

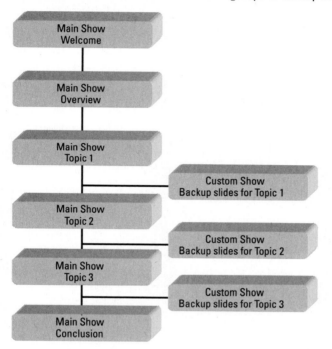

Notice in Figure 20.10 that although some of the slides in the two custom shows are the same, they repeat in each custom show rather than jumping back to the main presentation. This is because it is much easier to jump to the custom show once and stay there, than it is to keep jumping into and out of the show.

Slides in a custom show remain a part of the main presentation. Placing a slide in a custom show does not exclude it from the regular presentation flow. However, you may decide that you no longer want to show the main presentation in its present form; you may just want to use it as a resource pool from which you can select slides for other custom shows. To learn how to set up PowerPoint so that a custom show starts rather than the main presentation when you enter Slide Show view, see the section, "Using a Custom Show as the Main Presentation," later in this chapter.

FIGURE 20.10

You can create custom shows that allow you to use the same presentation for multiple audiences.

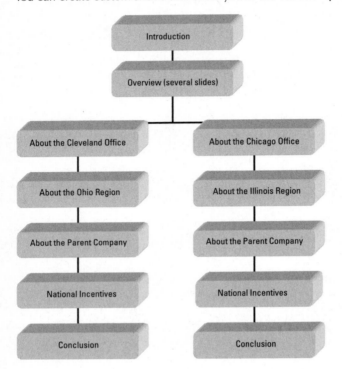

Ideas for Using Custom Shows

Here are some ideas to start you thinking about how and why you might want to include some custom shows in your presentation files:

- **Avoiding duplication:** If you have several shows that use about 50 percent of the same slides and 50 percent different ones, then you can create all of the shows as custom shows within a single presentation file. This way, the presentations can share the 50 percent of the slides that they have in common.

- **Managing change:** By creating a single presentation file with custom shows, you make it easy to manage changes. If any changes occur in your company that affect any of the common slides, then making the change once in your presentation file makes the change to each of the custom shows immediately.

- **Overcoming objections:** You can anticipate client objections to your sales pitch and prepare several custom shows, each of which addresses a particular objection. Then, whatever reason your potential customer gives for not buying your product, you have a counteractive argument at hand.

- **Covering your backside:** If you think that you may be asked for specific figures or other information during a speech, you can have this information ready in a custom show (or on a few simple hidden slides, if there is not a lot of information) to display if needed. No more going through the embarrassment of having to say, "I'm not sure, but let me get back to you on that."

Creating Custom Shows

To create a custom show, first create all of the slides that should go into it. Start with all of the slides in the main presentation. Then follow these steps:

1. On the Slide Show tab, click Custom Slide Show, and then click Custom Shows. The Custom Shows dialog box opens.

NOTE If no custom shows are defined yet, the Custom Shows command is the only item that appears on this menu. Otherwise, your existing custom shows appear on the menu, and you can run them from here.

2. Click New. The Define Custom Show dialog box opens.

3. Type a name for your custom show in the Slide Show Name text box, replacing the default name.

4. In the Slides in Presentation pane, click the first slide that you want to appear in the custom show.

EXPERT TIP You can select multiple slides in step 4 by holding down the Ctrl key as you click each one. However, be aware that if you do this, the slides move to the Slides in Custom Show pane in the order that they originally appeared. If you want them in a different order, copy each slide over separately, in the order that you want, or rearrange the order as described in step 7.

5. Click Add to copy the slide to the Slides in Custom Show pane, as shown in Figure 20.11.

6. Repeat steps 4 and 5 for each slide that you want to include in the custom show.

FIGURE 20.11

Use the Add button to copy slides from the main presentation into the custom show.

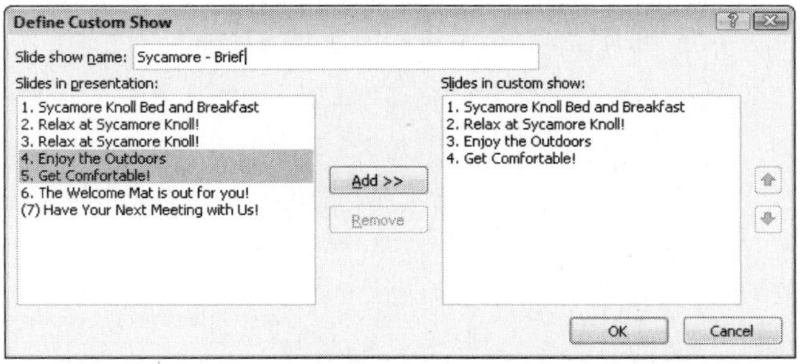

7. If you need to rearrange the slides in the custom show, click the slide that you want to move in the Slides in Custom Show pane and then click the up- or down-arrow button to change its position.

8. When you are finished building your custom show, click OK. The new show appears in the Custom Shows dialog box.

9. (Optional.) To test your custom show, click the Show button. Otherwise, click Close to close the Custom Shows dialog box.

Editing Custom Shows

You can manage your custom shows from the Custom Shows dialog box, the same place in which you created them. This includes editing, deleting, or making a copy of a show. To change which slides appear in a custom show, and in what order, follow these steps:

1. On the Slide Show tab, click Custom Slide Show and then click Custom Shows. The Custom Shows dialog box appears, as shown in Figure 20.12.

FIGURE 20.12

You can select a custom show to edit, copy, or delete, and then click the appropriate button.

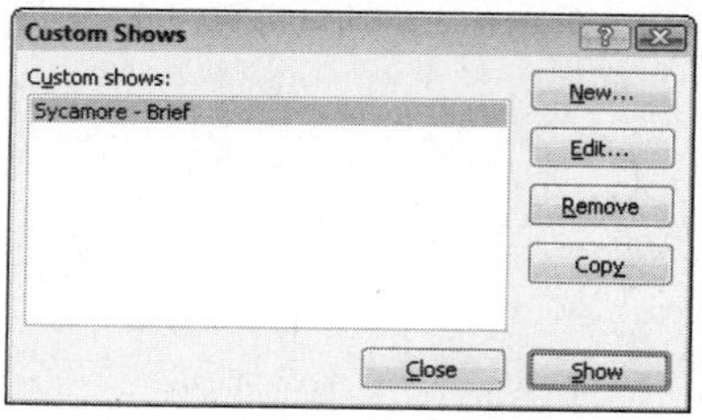

2. If you have more than one custom show, then click the one that you want to edit.

3. Click Edit. The Define Custom Show dialog box reappears, as shown in Figure 20.11.

4. Add or remove slides, as needed. To add a slide, select it in the left pane and click Add. To remove a slide, select it in the right pane and click Remove.

NOTE Removing a slide from a custom show does not remove it from the overall presentation.

5. Rearrange slides as needed with the up- and down-arrow buttons.

6. (Optional). You can change the custom show's name in the Slide Show Name text box.

7. Click OK. PowerPoint saves your changes.

8. Click Close to close the Custom Shows dialog box.

Copying Custom Shows

A good way to create several similar custom shows is to create the first one and then copy it. You can then make small changes to the copies as necessary. To copy a custom show, follow these steps:

1. On the Slide Show tab, click Custom Slide Show and then click Custom Shows. The Custom Shows dialog box appears, as shown in Figure 20.12.

2. If you have more than one custom show, then select the show that you want to copy.

3. Click Copy. A copy of the show appears in the dialog box. The filename includes the words *Copy of* so that you can distinguish it from the original.

4. Edit the copy, as explained in the preceding section, to change its name and content.

5. When you are finished, click Close to close the Custom Shows dialog box.

Deleting Custom Shows

It is not necessary to delete a custom show when you do not want it anymore; it does not do any harm remaining in your presentation. Because custom shows do not display unless you call for them, you can simply choose not to display it. However, if you want to make your presentation more orderly, you can delete a custom show that you no longer want. Follow these steps:

1. On the Slide Show tab, click Custom Slide Show and then click Custom Shows. The Custom Shows dialog box appears, as shown in Figure 20.12.

2. Select the show that you want to delete.

3. Click Remove. The show disappears from the list.

4. Click Close to close the Custom Shows dialog box.

Displaying a Custom Show

To start your presentation with a custom show, on the Slide Show tab, click Custom Slide Show and then click the name of the custom show on the drop-down menu. The custom show runs.

You can also call up the custom show at any time during your main presentation. There are two ways to do this: you can navigate to the custom show with PowerPoint's regular presentation controls, or you can create a hyperlink to the custom show on your slide.

Navigating to a Custom Show

During a presentation, you can jump to any of your custom shows by following these steps:

1. Open the shortcut menu in Slide Show view by right-clicking or by clicking the navigation button.

2. Choose Custom Show and then select the custom show that you want, as shown in Figure 20.13. The custom show starts.

FIGURE 20.13

Choose the custom show that you want to jump to.

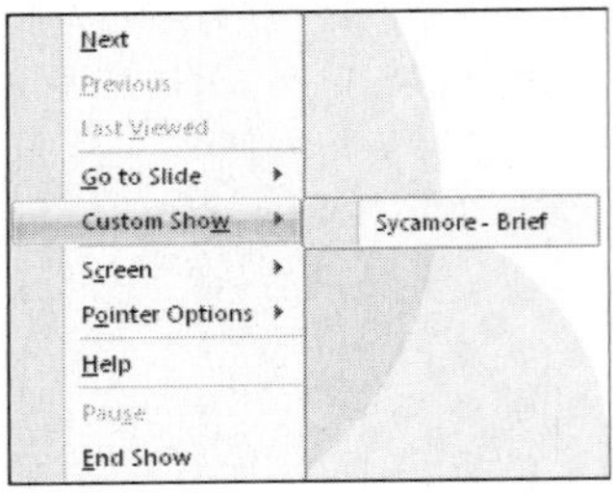

When you start a custom show, you are no longer in the main presentation. To verify this, open the shortcut menu again, choose Go to Slide, and check out the list of slides. This list shows only the slides that belong to the custom show.

Navigating Back to the Main Show

To return to the main show, follow these steps:

1. Press Ctrl+S to open the All Slides dialog box.

2. Open the Show drop-down list and choose All Slides.

3. Select the slide that you want to go to. You can choose from all of the slides in the entire presentation, as shown in Figure 20.14.

4. Click Go To.

EXPERT TIP   To avoid having to click Ctrl+S to return to the main show, you can create a hyperlink or action button for a specific slide in your main show.

FIGURE 20.14

You can return to the full presentation from the All Slides dialog box.

Creating a Hyperlink to a Custom Show

Although you learn a lot about hyperlinks in upcoming chapters, here is a preview. Hyperlinks are hot links that you place on your slides. When you click a hyperlink, you jump the display to some other location. This is why they are called *hot*. A hyperlink can jump to an Internet location, a different spot in your presentation, an external file (such as a Word document), or just about anywhere else.

One way to gain quick access to your custom shows in a presentation is to create hyperlinks for them on certain key slides that act as jumping-points. You can insert a text hyperlink into any text box, and its text becomes the marker that you click. For example, if you insert a hyperlink for a custom show called Radio Spots, then the hyperlink text could read *Radio Spots*. If you want to get fancier, you can select some existing text or an existing graphic object, and then attach the hyperlink to it. For example, in Figure 20.15, I have inserted a clip-art image of a radio and set it up to be a hyperlink to the custom show that provides details about the radio spots.

FIGURE 20.15

You can create hyperlinks on slides that display custom shows.

Radio Plan

▸ Will develop three 30-second radio spots to be aired on the following stations:
- 98.1 WIUQ Adult Contemporary
- 97.3 WAZZ Classic Rock
- 91.0 WSOL Contemporary Country

Click the radio to learn more about these spots

Text box with instructions   Hyperlink to custom show

Follow these steps:

1. If you are attaching the hyperlink to another object (such as the radio in Figure 20.15) or some text, then select the object or text.

2. On the Insert tab, click Hyperlink. The Insert Hyperlink dialog box appears.

3. Click the Place in This Document icon along the left side of the screen.

4. In the Select a Place in This Document pane, scroll down to the Custom Shows list.

5. Click the custom show that you want to jump to with this hyperlink, as shown in Figure 20-16.

6. (Optional) . If you want to return to the same spot that you left in the main presentation after viewing this custom show, then select the Show and Return check box. If you do not select this option, the presentation will simply end when the custom show ends.

7. (Optional) If you want to specify a ScreenTip for the hyperlink, click the ScreenTip button to create one.

8. Click OK.

FIGURE 20.16

Choose one of your custom shows as the place to jump to when the user clicks the hyperlink.

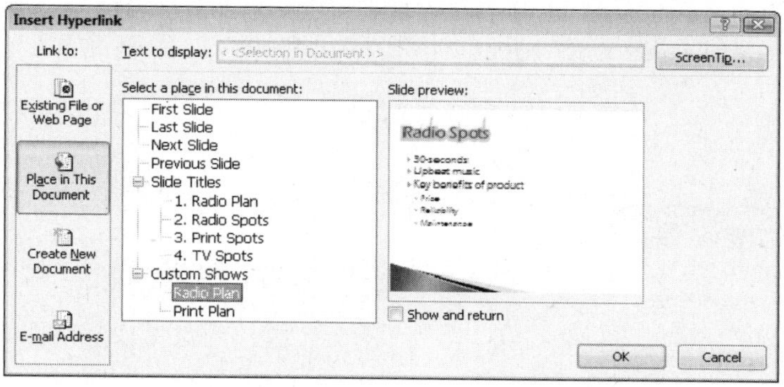

If you are using text for the hyperlink, the text now appears underlined and in a different color. This color is controlled by the color theme of your presentation (specifically the Hyperlink and Followed Hyperlink colors). If you are using a graphic, its appearance does not change. However, when you are in Slide Show view and you move the mouse pointer over the object, the pointer changes to a pointing hand, indicating that the object is a hyperlink.

EXPERT TIP If you do not want your linked text to be underlined or to change colors upon return, you can put an AutoShape rectangle with no line and no fill over the top of the text and link to the AutoShape instead. Because this shape is on top of the text, you click it instead of the text. Keep in mind that you should probably create your link before changing the line and fill to no color!

Another way to use hyperlinks for custom shows is to set up the first few slides generically for all audiences, and then to branch off into one custom show or another, based on user input. The diagram in Figure 20-9 is an example of this type of presentation. After the first two slides, you could set up a "decision" slide that contains two hyperlinks — one for Digital Products and one for Audio Products. The user would then click the hyperlink they want.

EXPERT TIP You can also create hyperlinks to custom shows by using action buttons. Action buttons are a special type of AutoShape that is designed specifically for creating hyperlinks within a presentation.

Using a Custom Show as the Main Presentation

If you have a complete show contained in one of your custom shows, you may sometimes want to show it as the default presentation. To do this, you must tell PowerPoint that you want to bypass the main presentation and start with the custom show.

The easiest way to show a custom show is to select it from the Custom Slide Show drop-down menu on the Slide Show tab. However, you can also set up a custom show to be the default show for the presentation by following these steps:

1. On the Slide Show tab, click Set Up Slide Show. The Set Up Show dialog box appears.

2. Open the Custom Show drop-down list and choose the show that you want to use, as shown in Figure 20.17.

3. Click OK. Now, when you start the show, the custom show runs.

FIGURE 20.17

Use the Set Up Show dialog box to control which of your custom shows runs when you start the show.

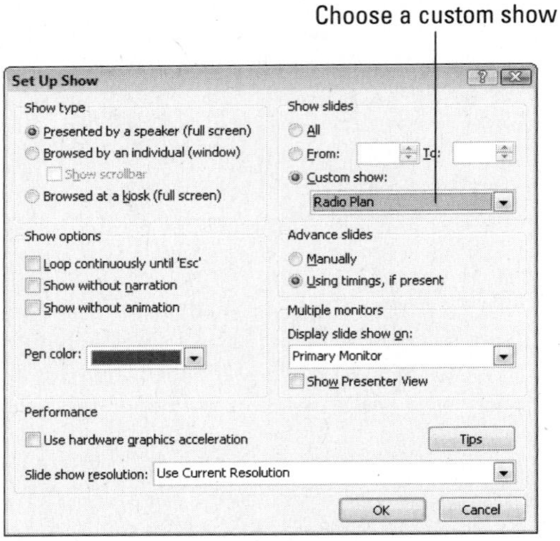

Choose a custom show

Set Up Show
Show type
● Presented by a speaker (full screen)
○ Browsed by an individual (window)
☐ Show scrollbar
○ Browsed at a kiosk (full screen)
Show options
☐ Loop continuously until 'Esc'
☐ Show without narration
☐ Show without animation
Pen color:
Performance
☐ Use hardware graphics acceleration
Slide show resolution: Use Current Resolution

Show slides: ○ All; ○ From: __ To: __; ● Custom show: Radio Plan
Advance slides: ○ Manually; ● Using timings, if present
Multiple monitors — Display slide show on: Primary Monitor; ☐ Show Presenter View
Tips   OK   Cancel

EXPERT TIP
You do not have to set up a custom show to narrow down the list of slides that appear when you run your presentation. You can choose which slides you want to show by using the From and To text boxes in the Show Slides section, as shown in Figure 20.17. For example, to show slides 5 to 10, you would type 5 in the From text box and 10 in the To text box.

Giving a Presentation on a Different Computer

The computer on which you create a presentation is usually not the same computer that you will use to show it. For example, you may be doing the bulk of your work on your desktop computer in your office in Los Angeles, but you need to use your laptop computer to give the presentation in Phoenix.

One way to transfer a presentation to another computer is simply to copy the PowerPoint file (the file with the .pptx extension) using a floppy disk or other removable media. However, this method is imperfect because it assumes that the other computer has all of the fonts, sounds, and other elements that you need for every part of the show. This can be a dangerous assumption. For example, suppose that your presentation contains a link to some Excel data. If you do not also copy the Excel file, then you cannot update the data when you are on the road.

A better way to ensure that you are taking everything you need while traveling is to use the Package for CD feature in PowerPoint. This feature reads all of the linked files and associated objects and ensures that they are transferred along with the main presentation. You do not actually need to copy the presentation to a writeable CD, and you do not need a CD-R or CD-RW drive to use this feature. You can copy the presentation to anywhere you want, such as to a ZIP drive or a network location.

Copying a Presentation to CD

If you have a CD-R or CD-RW drive, then copying the presentation to CD is an attractive choice. It produces a self-running disc that contains a PowerPoint Viewer application, the presentation file, and any linked files.

By default, a packaged CD includes the PowerPoint Viewer, and the presentation file is in PowerPoint 2003 format. PowerPoint automatically saves 2007-version files back to 2003 format before it burns them to CD. However, you can override this behavior, as you will see later in this chapter in "Setting Copy Options."

EXPERT TIP You can copy many presentation files onto a single CD, not just the currently active one. The only limit is the size of the disc (usually 650MB to 700MB). By default, the currently active presentation is included, although the following steps show you how to add other presentations. You can also set up these presentations to run automatically one after another, or you can specify that a menu appears so that the user can choose the presentation that they want to view.

Here is the basic procedure, which is elaborated on in the following sections:

1. Place a blank CD-R or CD-RW disc in your writeable CD drive.

2. Finalize the presentation in PowerPoint. If you are using a CD-R disc, keep in mind that this disc type is not rewriteable, and so you should ensure that the presentation is exactly as you want it.

3. Choose Office ➪ Publish ➪ Package for CD.

4. A warning appears about updating file formats; click OK. The Package for CD dialog box opens, as shown in Figure 20.18.

Use the Package for CD feature to place all of the necessary files for the presentation on a CD.

5. Type a name for the CD; this is similar to adding a volume label for the disc.

6. *(Optional)* . Add more files to the CD if you want. See the next section, "Creating a CD Containing Multiple Presentation Files," for more details.

7. *(Optional)*. Set any options that you want. See the section, "Setting Copy Options," later in this chapter, for more details.

8. Click Copy to CD. The CD-writing process may take several minutes, depending on the writing speed of your CD drive and the size of the presentation files that you are placing on it.

9. A message appears when the files are successfully copied to the CD, asking whether you want to copy the same files to another CD. Click Yes or No. If you choose No, then you must also click Close to close the Package for CD dialog box.

The resulting CD automatically plays the presentations when you insert it in any computer. You can also browse the CD's contents to open the PowerPoint Viewer separately and use it to play specific presentations.

CAUTION   File corruption can occur on a CD drive during the writing process. After burning a CD, test it thoroughly by running the complete presentation from CD before you rely on the CD copy as the version that you take with you while traveling.

Creating a CD Containing Multiple Presentation Files

By default, the active presentation is included on the CD, but you can also add others, up to the capacity of your disc. For example, if you have several versions of the same presentation for different audiences, then a single CD can contain all of them. As you are preparing to copy the files using the Package for CD dialog box, shown in Figure 20/18, follow these steps to add more files:

1. Click Add Files. An Add dialog box opens, similar to the Open dialog box that you use to open PowerPoint files.

2. Select the additional files that you want to include, and click Add to return to the Package for CD dialog box. The list of files now appears as shown in Figure 20/19, with extra controls.

NOTE You can select multiple files from the same location by holding down the Ctrl key as you click the ones you want. To include multiple files from different locations, repeat steps 1 and 2 for each location.

FIGURE 20.19

When you specify multiple files for a CD, you can specify the order in which they should play.

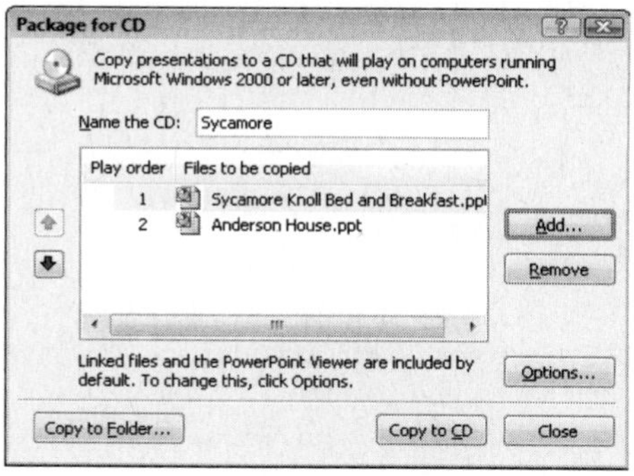

3. If you set up the CD to play the presentations automatically (as shown in the next section), the order in which they appear on the list becomes significant. You can rearrange the list by clicking a presentation and then clicking the Up- or Down-arrow buttons to the left of the list.

4. If you need to remove a presentation from the list, click it and then click Remove.

5. Continue making the CD as you normally would.

Setting Copy Options

The default copy options are suitable in most situations. However, you may sometimes want to modify them. To do this, open the Package for CD dialog box, and follow these steps:

1. Click Options. The Options dialog box open, as shown in Figure 20.20.

2. Select a package type. You can choose Viewer Package, which includes the PowerPoint Viewer and saves the file in 2003 format, or you can choose Archive Package, which does not update the file format and does not include the viewer on the CD.

You can set options for copying the presentations to CD.

3. The Linked Files check box is selected by default; this option tells PowerPoint to include the full copies of all linked files. You can deselect this option if you want; a static copy of the linked data will remain in the presentation, but the link will not work. You should leave this option selected if you have sounds or multimedia files in your presentation, because these files are always linked (with the exception of some WAV files).

4. The Embedded TrueType Fonts check box is deselected by default. If you think that the destination computer may not contain all of the fonts that are used in the presentation, then select this option. This makes the presentation file slightly larger. Remember, not all fonts can be embedded; this depends on the level of embedding allowed by the font's manufacturer.

5. If you want to add passwords for the presentations, do so in the Enhance Security and Privacy section. There are separate text boxes for open and modify passwords.

6. If you want to check the presentation for private information, such as your name or any comments, select the Inspect Presentations for Inappropriate or Private Information check box.

7. Click OK, and then write the CD as you normally would.

> **NOTE** If you select the check box in step 6, as part of the process, the Document Inspector window opens, and you can use it to check the document for selected types of content. Inspect it and click Inspect.

Copying a Presentation to Other Locations

Although it is not well known, you can also use the Package for CD feature to copy presentation files and their associated support files to any location you want. For example, you can transfer files to another computer on a network, or place them on a floppy or ZIP disc. To do so, follow these steps:

1. In the Package for CD dialog box, set up the package exactly the way you want it, including all of the presentation files and options. See the preceding sections for more information.
2. Click Copy to Folder. A Copy to Folder dialog box appears.
3. Type a name for the new folder to be created in the Name the Folder text box.
4. Type a path for the folder in the Choose Location text box, as shown in Figure 20.21.
5. Click OK.
6. If a warning appears about linked files, then click Yes or No as appropriate. PowerPoint copies the files to that location.
7. If a warning appears about comments or ink annotations, click Continue.
8. Click Close to close the Package for CD dialog box.

FIGURE 20.21

You can copy presentation files and support files anywhere, not just to a CD.

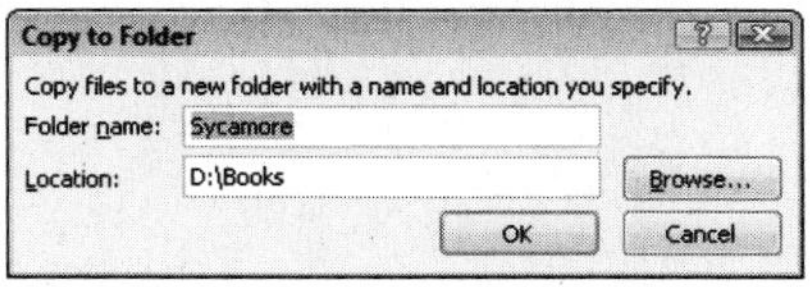

Using a Presentation CD with the PowerPoint Viewer

To use a self-running presentation CD, just insert it in the CD drive. The presentation starts automatically. You can then move through the presentation as described later in this chapter.

If you have placed multiple presentations on the CD and have specified that a menu should appear for them, then this menu appears when you insert the CD. Select the presentation that you want, and click Open to start it. When the presentation has finished, this menu will reappear.

Working with Audio-visual Equipment

The first part of this chapter assumed that you were using a computer with a single monitor to show your presentation, but this may not always be the case. This section looks at the entire range of audio-visual options from which you can choose. There are many models of projection equipment in conference rooms all across the world, but most of them fall into one of these categories:

- **Noncomputerized equipment:** This can include an overhead transparency viewer, a 35mm slide projector, or other older technology. You face two challenges if you need to work with this category of equipment: one is figuring out how the equipment works because every model is different, and the other is producing attractive versions of your slides to work with them. There are companies that can produce 35mm slides from your PowerPoint files, or you can invest in a slide-making machine yourself. For transparencies, you simply print your slides on transparency film that is designed for your type of printer.

- **Single computer with a single monitor:** If there is a computer with a monitor in the meeting room, then you can run your presentation on that computer. You can do this with the Publish to CD feature that is discussed in the preceding sections, and then run the presentation directly from the CD.

- **Single computer with a dual-monitor system:** On systems with dual monitors, one monitor is shown to the audience and the other is for your own use. This is useful when you want to display your speaker notes on the monitor that the audience does not see. However, you might need to set up multi-monitor support in Windows so that you can view different displays on each monitor.

- **Projection system (LCD) or large monitor without a computer:** If the meeting room has a large monitor but no computer, you will need to bring your own laptop computer and connect it to the monitor. Most of these systems use a standard VGA plug and cable.

The following sections look at some of these options in more detail.

Presenting with Two Screens

If you have two monitors — either your laptop computer screen and an external monitor, or two external monitors hooked up to the same computer — you can display the presentation on one of them and your own notes on the other one. This is a very handy setup!

CAUTION To use two screens, you need the full version of PowerPoint on your laptop, not just the PowerPoint Viewer. You also need compatible hardware. For example, your laptop must have an external VGA port and a built-in video card that supports DualView in your version of Windows. If you have a desktop computer, you must have two separate video cards or a video card with two separate video ports.

Configuring Display Hardware for Multi-screen Viewing

First, you need to prepare your hardware. On a laptop computer, this means enabling both the built-in and the external monitor ports and connecting an external monitor. Some laptops toggle between internal, external, and dual monitors with an Fn key combination; refer to your laptop's documentation.

On a desktop computer, install a second video card and monitor, and then do the following to set them up in Windows:

1. When Windows restarts after you install the second video card, right-click the desktop and choose Personalize (Windows Vista) or Properties (Windows XP).

2. Click Display Settings (Windows Vista), or click the Settings tab (Windows XP).

3. A sample area displays two monitors, as shown in Figure 20.22.

FIGURE 20.22

You must set up the second monitor in Windows before setting it up in PowerPoint.

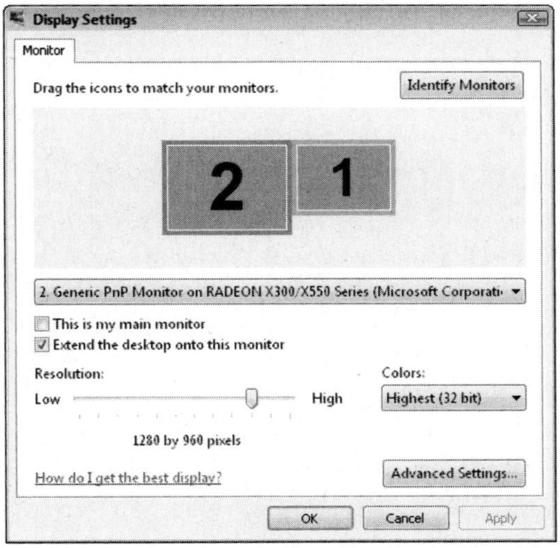

4. The monitor that you use most of the time should be monitor 1, and the other one should be monitor 2. To determine which is which, click Identify Monitors (or the Identify button if you are using Windows XP); large numbers appear briefly on each screen.

5. If you need to swap the numbering of the monitors, click the one that should be the primary monitor and then select the This is My Main Monitor check box (Windows Vista) or the Use This Device as the Primary Monitor check box (Windows XP). This option will be unavailable if the currently selected monitor is already set to be the primary one.

6. Select the secondary monitor, and then select the Extend my Desktop onto This Monitor check box (Windows Vista) or Extend the Desktop Onto This Monitor check box (Windows XP).

7. *(Optional)* If the monitors are not arranged in the sample area in the way that they are physically positioned on your desk, you can drag the icons for the monitors to where you want them.

8. *(Optional)* You can click a monitor in the sample area to adjust its display settings.

EXPERT TIP   You can also adjust the refresh rate for each monitor. To do this, make sure that you have selected the video card to which the monitor is attached, and then click the Advanced Settings button (Windows Vista) or the Advanced button (Windows XP). On the Monitor tab in the dialog box that appears, change the refresh rate. A higher refresh rate reduces screen flicker, but if you exceed the monitor's maximum supported rate, the display may appear distorted and the screen may be damaged.

9. Click OK. You are now ready to work with the two monitors in PowerPoint.

You can now drag items from your primary monitor to your secondary one! This can also be useful outside of PowerPoint as well. For example, you can have two applications open at once, each in its own monitor window.

Setting Up a Presentation for Two Screens

If you have two monitors available, and configured as described in the preceding section, you can use the following steps to help PowerPoint recognize and take advantage of these monitors:

1. Open the presentation in PowerPoint.

2. On the Slide Show tab, click Set Up Slide Show. The Set Up Show dialog box opens, as shown in Figure 20.23.

3. In the Multiple Monitors section, open the Display Slide Show On drop-down list and choose the monitor that the audience will see.

4. Select the Show Presenter View check box. This will give you a separate, very useful control panel on the other monitor during the show, as described in the next section.

5. Click OK. You are now ready to show the presentation using two separate displays — one for you and one for the audience.

FIGURE 20.23

You can set up the show for multiple monitors in the Set Up Show dialog box.

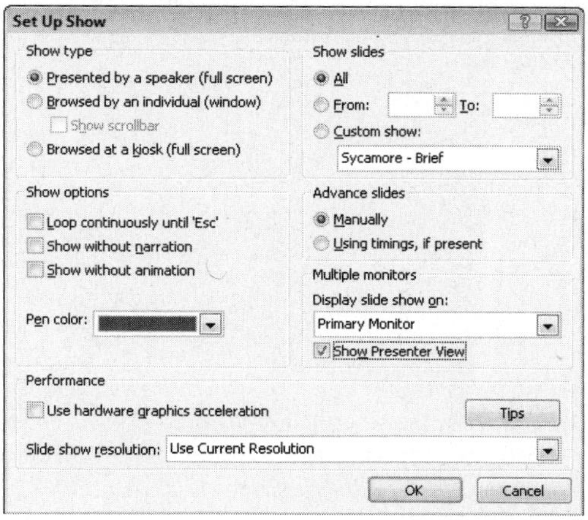

Presenting with Two Screens Using Presenter View

Presenter View is a special view of the presentation that is available only on systems with more than one monitor, and only where you have selected the Show Presenter View check box in the Set Up Show dialog box, as described in the preceding section. This view provides many useful tools for managing the show behind-the-scenes, as shown in Figure 20.24. It appears automatically on the non-audience monitor when you enter Slide Show view, and includes the following features:

- At the bottom of the screen is a pane containing thumbnail images of each slide. You can jump to a slide by selecting it here. You can also move between slides by using the large left- and right-arrow buttons.

- The speaker notes for each slide appear in the right pane. You cannot edit them from here, however. Zoom buttons appear below the speaker notes pane, so you can zoom in and out on the notes.

- A Time and Duration display appears below the current slide. It tells you the current time and how long you have been talking.

- The panes are adjustable by dragging the dividers between them, so you can have larger thumbnails, a smaller slide display, more or less room for notes, and so on.

Presenter View does not have all of the features that you have learned about so far in Slide Show view. However, keep in mind that the audience's monitor is still active and available for your use! Because you extended the desktop onto the second monitor, you can simply move the mouse pointer onto the audience's display and then use the buttons in the corner (or the right-click menu) as you normally would.

FIGURE 20.24

Presenter View provides tools for helping you manage your slideshow from a second monitor.

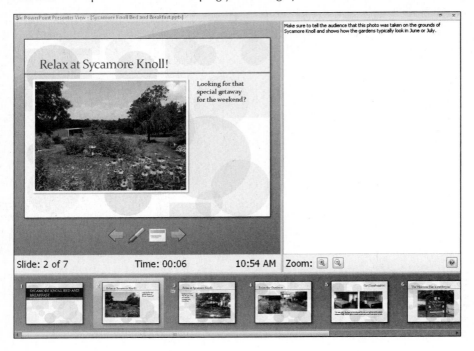

Summary

In this chapter, you learned how to prepare for a big presentation. You now know how to package a presentation and move it to another computer, how to set up single and multi-screen audio-visual equipment to work with your laptop, and how to control a presentation on-screen using your computer. You also know how to jump to different slides, how to take notes during a meeting, and how to assign action items. You're all set! All you need now is a nice starched shirt and a shoeshine.

In the next chapter, you learn about designing presentations that are user-interactive or self-running. You can do this by creating easy-to-use action buttons for situations where you cannot be there to press the buttons yourself.

Chapter 21

Designing User-Interactive or Self-Running Presentations

In the last few chapters, you've been learning how to build and present slide shows that support you as you speak to your audience directly. When you build such presentations, you design each slide to *assist* you, not duplicate your efforts. Slides designed for a live presentation typically do not contain a lot of detail; they function as pointers and reminders for the much more detailed live discussion or lecture taking place in the foreground.

When you build a self-running or user-interactive presentation, the focus is exactly the opposite. The slides are going out there all alone and must be capable of projecting the entire message all by themselves. Therefore, you want to create slides that contain much more information.

Another consideration is audience interest. When you speak to your audience live, the primary focus is on you and your words. The slides assist you, but the audience watches and listens primarily to you. Therefore, to keep the audience interested, you have to be interesting. If the slides are interesting, that's a nice bonus. With a self-running or user-interactive presentation, on the other hand, each slide must be fascinating. The animations and transitions that you learned about in Chapter 18 come in very handy in creating interest, as do sounds and videos, discussed in Chapters 16 and 17.

IN THIS CHAPTER

Understanding user interactivity

Using navigational control

Creating text hyperlinks

Creating action buttons

Creating other graphical hyperlinks

Creating self-running presentations

> **NOTE** Another name for a self-running presentation is a *kiosk* presentation. This name comes from the fact that many self-running informational presentations are located in little buildings, or kiosks, in public areas such as malls and convention centers.

Understanding User Interactivity

Letting the audience take control can be scary. If you aren't forcing people to go at a certain pace and view all the slides, what's to guarantee that they don't skim through quickly or quit halfway through?

Well, there are no guarantees. Even in a show with a live speaker, though, you can't control whether people pay attention. The best you can do is put together a compelling presentation and hope that people want to view it. The same applies to a user-interactive presentation. People are either going to watch and absorb it or they're not. There's no point in treating the audience like children. On the contrary, they will likely respond much better if you give them the options and let them decide what content they need.

Navigational controls are the main thing that separates user-interactive presentations from normal ones. You have to provide an idiot-proof way for people to move from slide to slide. Okay, technically yes, they could use the same navigational controls that you use when presenting a show (see Chapter 20), but those controls aren't always obvious. Moving forward is a no-brainer (click the mouse), but what about moving backward? Would you have guessed "P" for Previous if you hadn't already known? Probably not. And what if they want to end the show early? The first half of this chapter shows you various techniques for creating navigational controls.

Here are some ideas for ways to use navigational controls:

- **Web resource listings.** Include a slide that lists Web page addresses that users can visit for more information about various topics covered in your presentation. You can also include Web cross-references throughout the presentation at the bottom of pertinent slides.

- **Product information.** Create a basic presentation that describes your products, with For More Information buttons for each product. Then create hidden slides with the detailed information about each product and hyperlink those slides to the For More Information buttons. Don't forget to put a Return button on each hidden slide so that users can easily return to the main presentation.

- **Access to custom shows.** If you have created custom shows, set up action buttons or hyperlinks that jump the users to them on request.

- **Quizzes.** Create a presentation with a series of multiple-choice questions. Create custom action buttons for each answer. Depending on which answer the user clicks, set it up to jump to either a "Congratulations, you're right!" slide or a "Sorry, try again" slide. From each, include a Return button to go on with the quiz.

- **Troubleshooting information.** Ask the user a series of questions and include action buttons or hyperlinks for the answers. Set them up to jump to the slides that further narrow down the problem based on their answers until they finally arrive at a slide that explains the exact problem and proposes a solution.

- **Directories.** Include a company directory with e-mail hyperlinks for various people or departments so that anyone reading the presentation can easily make contact.

Besides navigational controls, the other big consideration with a user-interactive show is distribution. How will you distribute the presentation to your audience? Some of the methods you've already learned about in this book will serve you well here, such as packaging a presentation on CD (Chapter 20). Or you may choose instead to set up a user kiosk in a public location, e-mail the presentation file to others, or make it available on the Web.

Navigational Control Basics

All navigational controls that you create on slides are, at their core, hyperlinks. You're probably familiar with these already from using the Web; they're underlined bits of text or specially enabled graphics that take you to a different site or page that you clicked. In the case of your PowerPoint presentation, the hyperlinks take users to the next or previous slide, a hidden slide, a custom slide show, or perhaps some external source such as a Web site or data file.

Types of Navigational Controls

Even though they are all hyperlinks (so they all work the same underneath), the various types of navigational controls can look very different on the surface. You can have "bare" hyperlinks where the actual address appears, hyperlinks where the text is different from the address, action button graphics, or graphics you create or import yourself. In addition, a navigational control can have pop-up helper text in a ScreenTip. Figure 21.1 shows several types of navigational controls on a sample slide.

> **NOTE** Most people associate the word hyperlink with the Internet. However, a hyperlink is simply a link to somewhere else; it does not necessarily refer to an Internet location. You can hyperlink to another slide in the same presentation, for example, or to a different presentation, or even to some unrelated data file in another application like Word or Excel.

Notice the directions at the bottom of Figure 21.1. This is necessary because it's not obvious that the graphic is a hyperlink, and users would not normally think to try clicking on it. Notice also the ScreenTip associated with the second text hyperlink. This is useful because the text itself does not provide the address, and the user may want to know the address before clicking the hyperlink. For example, if the PC does not have Internet access, the user would not want to click a hyperlink that points to a Web page.

The action buttons in the bottom-right corner in Figure 21.1 are typical of the action buttons that PowerPoint creates. They are just AutoShapes with pre-assigned action settings for On Click. You can create your own, but the preset ones are awfully handy.

FIGURE 21.1

A sampler of the various navigational control types available in PowerPoint.

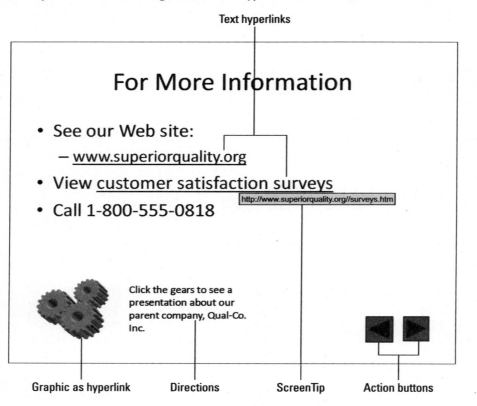

Evaluating Your Audience's Needs

Before you dive into building an interactive presentation, you must decide how the audience will navigate from slide to slide. There is no one best way; the right decision depends on the audience's comfort level with computers and hyperlinks.

Consider these points:

- Is the audience technically savvy enough to know that they should press a key or click the mouse to advance the slide, or do you need to provide that instruction?

- Does your audience understand that the arrow action buttons mean Forward and Back, or do you need to explain that?

- Does your audience understand hyperlinks and Web addresses? If they see underlined text, will they know that they can click it to jump elsewhere?

- Is it enough to include some instructions on a slide at the beginning of the show, or do you need to repeat the instructions on every slide?

Think about your audience's needs and come up with a plan. Here are some sample plans:

- For a beginner level audience: Begin the presentation with an instructional slide explaining how to navigate. Place action buttons in the same place on each slide (using the Slide Master) to help them move backward and forward and include a Help button that they can click to get more detailed instructions.

- For an intermediate level audience: Place action buttons on the same place on each slide, along with a brief note on the first slide explaining their presence.

- For an advanced audience: Include other action buttons on the slide that allow the user to jump around freely in the presentation — go to the beginning, to the end, to a certain section, and so on. Advanced users understand and can take advantage of a more sophisticated navigation system.

In the next few sections, I show you how to create all of the types of navigational controls shown in Figure 21.1.

Creating Text Hyperlinks

Now that you know that hyperlinks are the key to user interactivity, you will want to add some to your presentation. You can start with text-based hyperlinks because they're the easiest. You can add them either bare or with explanatory text.

Typing a Bare Hyperlink

The most basic kind of hyperlink is an Internet address, typed directly into a text box. When you enter text in any of the following formats, PowerPoint automatically converts it to a hyperlink:

- **Web addresses:** Anything that begins with `http://` or `www.`.
- **E-mail addresses:** Any string of characters with no spaces and an @ sign in the middle somewhere.
- **FTP addresses:** Anything that begins with `ftp://`.

You do not have to do anything special to create these hyperlinks; when you type them and press Enter or the space bar, PowerPoint converts them to hyperlinks. You know the conversion has taken place because the text becomes underlined and a different color. (The exact color depends on the color scheme in use.)

Figure 21.2 shows some examples of these bare hyperlinks. I call them bare because you see what's underneath them — the actual address — right there on the surface. There is no friendly "click here" text that the link hides behind. For example, the text support@microsoft.com is a hyperlink that sends e-mail to that address. In contrast, a link that reads "Click here to send e-mail to me" and contains the same hyperlink address is *not* bare, because you do not see the address directly.

> **NOTE** If PowerPoint does not automatically create hyperlinks, the feature may be disabled. Choose Office ➪ PowerPoint Options. Click Proofing, and then click AutoCorrect Options. Click the AutoFormat As You Type tab, and make sure the Internet and network paths with hyperlinks check box is marked.

> **NOTE** FTP stands for File Transfer Protocol. It's a method of transferring files via the Internet. Up until a few years ago, FTP was a totally separate system from the Web, but nowadays, most Web browsers have FTP download capabilities built-in, so anyone who has a Web browser can receive files via FTP. However, to *send* files via FTP, the user must have a separate FTP program.

FIGURE 21.2

Some examples of bare Internet hyperlinks.

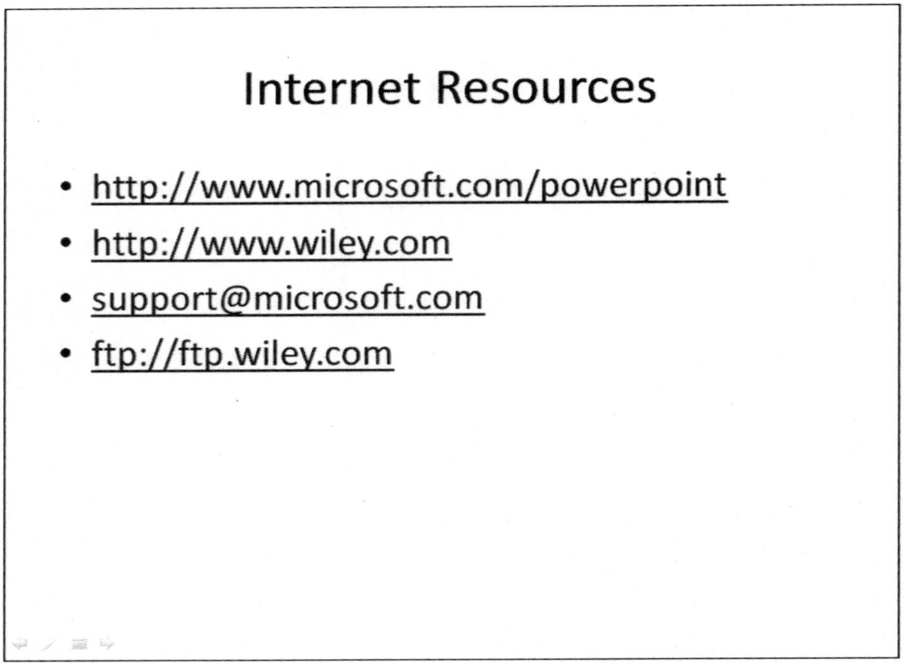

Internet Resources

- http://www.microsoft.com/powerpoint
- http://www.wiley.com
- support@microsoft.com
- ftp://ftp.wiley.com

Creating a Friendly Text Hyperlink

A "friendly" hyperlink is a hyperlink comprising text but not just the bare address. For example, in Figure 21.1, "Customer Satisfaction Surveys" is a text hyperlink. ("Friendly" is not an industry-standard technical term; it's just one I find convenient for discussion in this book.)

You can select already-entered text and make it a hyperlink, or you can enter new text. Either way, follow these steps:

NOTE These steps take you through the process generically; see the sections in "Choosing the Hyperlink Address" later in the chapter for specific information about various kinds of hyperlinks you can create.

1. To use existing text, select the text or its text box. Otherwise, just position the insertion point where you want the hyperlink.

2. On the Insert tab, click Hyperlink, or press Ctrl+K. The Insert Hyperlink dialog box opens as shown in Figure 21.3.

FIGURE 21.3

Insert a hyperlink by typing the text to display and choosing the address of the slide or other location to jump to.

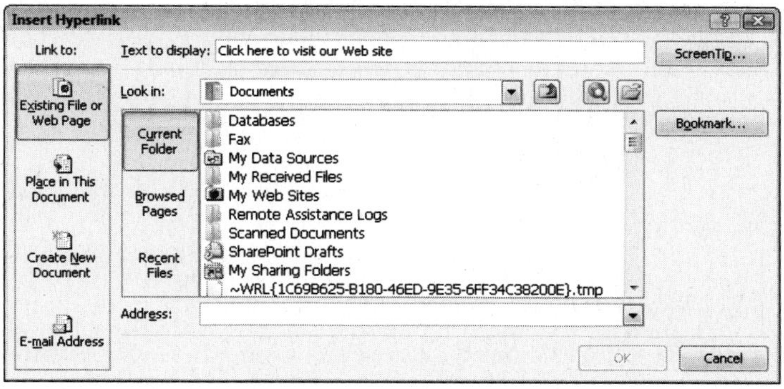

3. In the Text to Display field, type or edit the hyperlink text. This text is what appears underlined on the slide. Any text you've selected appears in this field by default; changing the text here changes it on your slide as well.

4. Enter the hyperlink or select it from one of the available lists. (See the following section, "Choosing the Hyperlink Address," to learn about your options in this regard.)

5. (Optional) The default ScreenTip for a hyperlink is its address (URL) or the file path if it is a file stored on a local disk. If you want the ScreenTip to show something different when the user points the mouse at the hyperlink, click the ScreenTip button and enter the text for the ScreenTip. See Figure 21.4.

FIGURE 21.4

Enter a custom ScreenTip if desired.

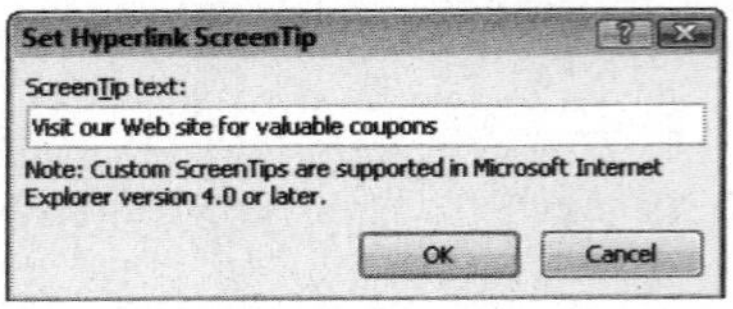

> **CAUTION**   Internet Explorer supports ScreenTips (in version 4.0 and higher), but other browsers may not. This is not an issue if you plan to distribute the presentation in PowerPoint format, but if you plan to convert it to Web pages (see Chapter 22), it might make a difference.

6. Click OK to close the Set Hyperlink ScreenTip dialog box.
7. Click OK to accept the newly created hyperlink.

> **EXPERT TIP**   Ideally the combination of the hyperlink text and the ScreenTip should provide both the actual address and some friendly explanation of it. If the bare address appears as the hyperlink text, use friendly text describing the link location as the ScreenTip. If the friendly text appears as the hyperlink text, use the actual address as the ScreenTip.

The options in step 4 for selecting the address were purposely glossed over because this is a rather complex topic. The various options are shown in the next section.

Choosing the Hyperlink Address

You can use the Insert Hyperlink dialog box to create a hyperlink to any address that's accessible via the computer where the presentation will run. Although many people think of a hyperlink as an Internet address, it can actually be a link to any file, application, Internet location, or slide.

> **CAUTION**   A hyperlink will not work if the person viewing the presentation does not have access to the needed files and programs or does not have the needed Internet or network connectivity. A hyperlink that works fine on your own PC might not work after the presentation has been transferred to the user's PC.

Possible addresses to hyperlink include the following:

■ Other slides in the current presentation

■ Slides in other presentations (if you provide access to those presentations)

■ Documents created in other applications (if the user has those applications installed and those document files are available)

■ Graphic files (if the user has access to an application that can display them)

■ Internet Web pages (if the user has an Internet connection and a Web browser)

■ E-mail addresses (if the user has an Internet connection and an e-mail program)

■ FTP site addresses (if the user has an Internet connection and a Web browser or an FTP program)

Creating a Link to a Slide in This Presentation

The most common kind of link is to another slide in the same presentation. There are many uses for this link type; for example, you can hide several backup slides that contain extra information. You can then create hyperlinks on certain key slides that allow the users to jump to one of those hidden slides to peruse the extra facts. To create a hyperlink to another slide:

1. Start the hyperlink normally (on the Insert tab, click Hyperlink).

2. In the Insert Hyperlink dialog box, click Place in This Document. The dialog box controls change to show a list of the slides in the presentation (see Figure 21.5).

FIGURE 21.5

Select the slide that the hyperlink should refer to.

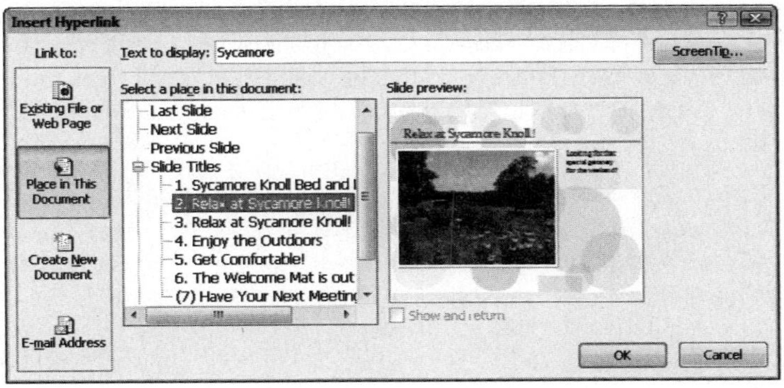

3. Select the slide or custom show that you want.

4. Click OK.

EXPERT TIP If you are choosing a custom show and you want the presentation to continue from the original spot after showing this custom show, mark the Show and Return check box (see Figure 21-5). This check box is not available for individual slides. For an individual slide, put a Return action button on it to return to the previously viewed slide. See the section "Creating Your Own Action Buttons" later in this chapter.

Creating a Link to a Web or FTP Site

If you want to link to a Web or FTP site, as you learned earlier in the chapter, you can simply type the address directly into any text box. Alternatively, you can use the Insert Hyperlink command to create the link.

When the Insert Hyperlink dialog box is open, if you don't know the address you want to refer to, you can browse for it. Here's how:

1. Leaving the Insert Hyperlink dialog box open, switch out of PowerPoint and back to Windows.

2. Open a Web browser and navigate to the page to which you want to refer.

3. Switch back to PowerPoint. The address is filled in for you in the Address box.

4. Continue creating the hyperlink normally.

EXPERT TIP   You can also copy and paste a URL into the Address box, or choose a page from the Browsed Pages list.

Creating a Link to a File on Your Hard Disk or LAN

You can also create a hyperlink to any file available on your PC's hard disk or on your local area network. This can be a PowerPoint file or a data file for any other program, such as a Word document or an Excel spreadsheet. Or, if you don't want to open a particular data file, you can hyperlink to the program file itself, so that the other application simply opens.

For example, perhaps you have some detailed documentation for your product in Adobe Acrobat format (PDF). This type of document requires the Adobe Acrobat Reader. So you can create a hyperlink with the text "Click here to read the documentation" and link to the appropriate PDF file. When your audience member clicks that link, Adobe Acrobat Reader opens and the documentation displays.

CAUTION   Remember that not everyone has the same applications installed that you do. For example, although Adobe Acrobat Reader is free, many people don't have it installed yet. You might want to add another hyperlink or button to your slide that users can click to download a free viewer for that application's data from the Web if needed.

To link to a data file, start the hyperlink normally (on the Insert tab, click Hyperlink) and click Existing File or Web Page if that is not already selected. Then do one of the following:

- Click Current Folder to display a file management interface from which you can select any folder or drive on your system. You can open the Look In list and choose Computer to start from the top level of your drives/folders structure, and then navigate to the location containing the file and select it. See Figure 21.6.

- Click Recent Files to display a list of the files you have recently opened on your PC (all types), and click the file you want from the list.

FIGURE 21.6

You can browse files on your hard disk by choosing Current Folder, and then setting Look In to Computer.

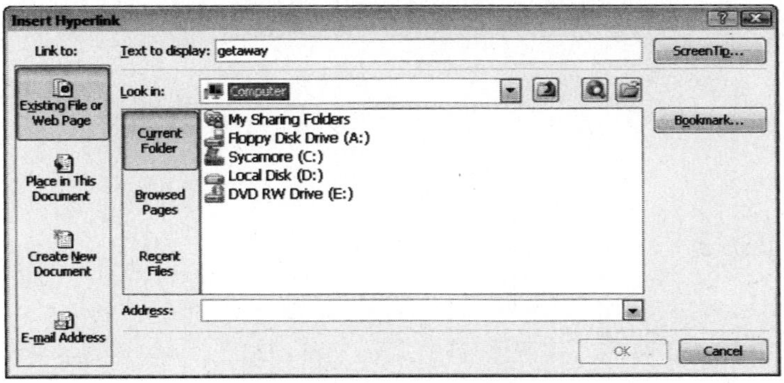

Complete the hyperlink normally from that point. You are not limited to only the folder on your local drives if you choose Current Folder; you can open the Look In list and choose My Network Places to browse the network. However, make sure that the PC on which the presentation will be displayed will also have access to this same location.

Creating a Link to an Application for Creating a New Document

Perhaps you want the audience to be able to create a new document by clicking a hyperlink. For example, perhaps you would like them to be able to provide information about their experience with your Customer Service department. One way to do this is to let them create a new document using a program that they have on their system, such as a word processor.

CAUTION Keep in mind that not everyone will have the same applications you do. A new document hyperlink will not work if the user does not have an appropriate application for creating that file type.

To create a link to a new document, start the hyperlink normally. Click the Create New Document button, and the controls in the Insert Hyperlink dialog box change to those shown in Figure 21.7.

Enter the name of the new document that you want to create. The type of document created depends on the extension you include. For example, to create a Word document, use the .doc extension. See Table 21.1 for other extensions. If the path where it should be stored is not correct in the Full Path area, click the Change button. Navigate to the desired location, and click OK to return. Then click Edit the New Document Later and finish up normally.

CAUTION If you provide this presentation to multiple users, each one will use the same filename for the new document. This can be a problem because one file may overwrite another. It might be easier to collect information from multiple users using an e-mail address hyperlink (discussed later in this chapter).

You can create a new document with a hyperlink.

The most important part about adding a link to create a new file is to make sure that you use an extension that corresponds to a program that users have on the PCs where they will be viewing the presentation. When a program is installed, it registers its extension (the usually-three-character code after the period in a file's name) in the Windows Registry, so that any data files with that extension are associated with that program. For example, when you install Microsoft Word, it registers the extension .doc for itself, and PowerPoint registers .ppt for its own use. Table 21.1 lists some of the more common file types and their registered extensions on most PCs. Also make sure that the location you specify for the Full Path will always be accessible whenever the presentation is run.

EXPERT TIP   If you need to hyperlink to an executable file, but you do *not* need a new document (for example, to link to a program like Calculator), do not use Hyperlink on the Insert tab. Instead use an Action Setting and choose Run Program as the action. For the program to run, use the full path to the application, in quotation marks. Because you must enter the full paths to each of these, the link will probably not work when the presentation is run on a different computer.

TABLE 21.1

Commonly Used Extensions for Popular Programs

Extension	Associated Program
DOCX, DOCM, or DOC	Microsoft Word, or WordPad if Word is not installed. Use for documents if you are not sure whether your audience has Word, but you are sure they at least have Windows 95. DOCX is the Word 2007 format, and DOCM is the macro-enabled version of that. DOC is the Word 2003 and earlier format.

Extension	Associated Program
WRI	Write, the predecessor to WordPad. WordPad and Word also open these if Write is not installed. Safest to use for documents if you do not know which version of Windows your audience uses.
TXT	Notepad, a plain text editor. Creates text files without any formatting. Not the first choice for documents unless you specifically need them to be without formatting.
WPD	WordPerfect, a competitor to Word.
BMP	Microsoft Paint (which comes free with Windows), or some other more sophisticated graphics program if one is installed.
MDB	Microsoft Access, a database program.
MPP	Microsoft Project, a project management program.
PPTX or PPT	Microsoft PowerPoint (you know what that is!). PPTX is the 2007 version; PPT is the 2003 and earlier.
XLSX, XLSM, or XLS	Microsoft Excel, a spreadsheet program. XLSX and XLSM are the 2007 versions (non-macro-enabled and macro-enabled, respectively) and XLS is the 2003 and earlier version.

Creating a Link to an E-Mail Address

You can also create a link that opens the user's e-mail program and addresses an e-mail to a certain recipient. For example, perhaps you want the user to e-mail feedback to you about how he liked your presentation or send you requests for more information about your product.

CAUTION For an e-mail hyperlink to work, the person viewing the presentation must have an e-mail application installed on his or her PC and at least one e-mail account configured for sending e-mail. This isn't always a given, but it's probably more likely than betting that they have a certain application installed (as in the preceding section).

To create an e-mail hyperlink, either type the e-mail address directly into the text box on the slide (for a bare hyperlink) or start a hyperlink normally with the Hyperlink button on the Insert tab. Then click the E-mail Address button in the dialog box and fill in the e-mail address and an optional subject line. PowerPoint will automatically add `mailto:` in front of the address. Then complete the hyperlink normally. See Figure 21.8.

You can use a hyperlink to send e-mail.

Editing or Removing Hyperlink

If you need to change the displayed text for the hyperlink, simply edit it just as you do any text on a slide. Move the insertion point into it and press Backspace or Delete to remove characters, and then retype new ones.

If you need to change the address, or the ScreenTip, right-click the hyperlink and choose Edit Hyperlink. The Edit Hyperlink dialog box appears, which is identical to the Add Hyperlink dialog box except for the name. From there you can change any properties of the link, just like you did when you created it initially.

To remove a hyperlink, you can either delete the text completely (select it and press Delete), or just remove the hyperlink leaving the text intact. To do the latter, right-click the hyperlink and choose Remove Hyperlink.

Creating Graphical Hyperlinks

There are two ways to create a graphics-based hyperlink. Both involve skills that you have already learned in this chapter. Both work equally well, but you may find that you prefer one to the other. The Action Settings method is a little bit simpler, but the Insert Hyperlink method allows you to browse for Web addresses more easily.

Creating a Graphical Hyperlink with Action Settings

A graphics-based hyperlink is really no more than a graphic with an action setting attached to it. You set it up just as you do with the action buttons (which you will learn more about later in this chapter).

1. Place the graphic that you want to use for a hyperlink.
2. Click the graphic and then on the Insert tab, click Action. The Action Settings dialog box opens.
3. Choose Hyperlink To.
4. Open the Hyperlink To drop-down list and choose URL. The Hyperlink to URL dialog box opens.
5. Type the URL to link to and click OK as shown in Figure 21. 9.

CAUTION If you are using an e-mail address, type mailto: in front of the address you enter in step 5. If you do not, PowerPoint will automatically add http:// in front of it and the link will not work.

6. Click OK.

FIGURE 21.9

You can create a hyperlink via an action setting.

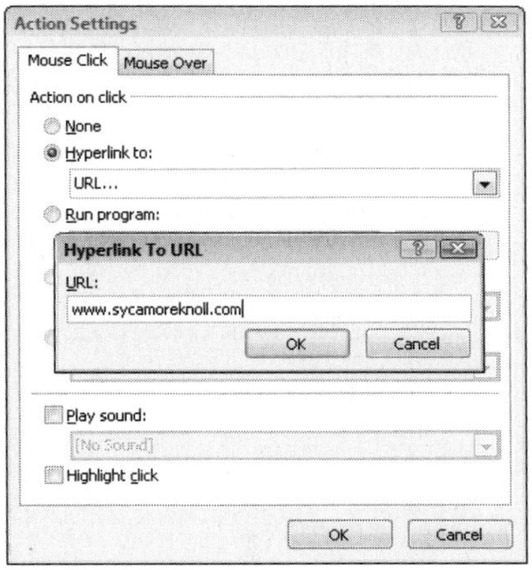

Now the graphic functions just like an action button in the presentation; the audience can click it to jump to the specified location.

Creating a Graphical Hyperlink with Insert Hyperlink

If you would like to take advantage of the superior address-browsing capabilities of the Insert Hyperlink dialog box when setting up a graphical hyperlink, follow these steps instead of the preceding ones:

1. Place the graphic that you want to use for a hyperlink.
2. Right-click it and choose Hyperlink. The Insert Hyperlink dialog box appears.

3. Choose the location, as you learned earlier in this chapter for text-based hyperlinks. The only difference is that the Text to Display box is unavailable because there is no text. If you typed the text in a graphic, Text to Display is available.

4. Click OK.

Using Action Buttons

Action buttons, which you saw in Figure 21.1, enable your audience members to move from slide to slide in the presentation with a minimum of fuss. PowerPoint provides many preset action buttons that already have hyperlinks assigned to them, so all you have to do is place them on your slides.

The action buttons that come with PowerPoint are shown in Table 21.2, along with their preset hyperlinks. As you can see, some of them are all ready to go; others require you to specify to where they jump. Most of the buttons have a default action assigned to them, but you can change any of these as needed.

EXPERT TIP At first glance, there seems little reason to use action buttons that simply move the slide show forward and backward. After all, isn't it just as easy to use the keyboard's Page Up and Page Down keys, or to click the left mouse button to advance to the next slide? Well, yes, but if you use Kiosk mode, described in the later in the chapter, you cannot move from slide to slide using any of the conventional keyboard or mouse methods. The only thing the mouse can do is click on action buttons and hyperlinks.

TABLE 21.2

Action Buttons

Button	Name	Hyperlinks to
◁	Back or Previous	Previous slide in the presentation (not necessarily the last slide viewed; compare to Return).
▷	Forward or Next	Next slide in the presentation.
◁|	Beginning	First slide in the presentation.
▷|	End	Last slide in the presentation.
🏠	Home	First slide in the presentation. (Home is where you get started and it's a picture of a house, get it?)
ⓘ	Information	Nothing, by default, but you can point it to a slide or document containing information.

Button	Name	Hyperlinks to
	Return	Last slide viewed, regardless of normal order. This is useful to place on a hidden slide that the audience will jump to with another link (such as Help), to help them return to the main presentation when they are finished.
	Movie	Nothing, by default, but you can set it to play a movie that you specify.
	Document	Nothing, by default, but you can set it to open a file that you specify.
	Sound	Plays a sound that you specify. If you don't choose a sound, it plays the first sound on PowerPoint's list of standard sounds (Applause).
	Help	Nothing, by default, but you can point it toward a slide containing help or a Help file from an application (usually has a .hlp extension but could also have a .chm or .html extension).
	None	Nothing, by default. You can add text or fills to the button to create custom buttons.

Placing an Action Button on a Slide

To place an action button, follow these steps:

1. If you want to place the button on the Slide Master, display it (on the View tab, click Slide Master). If you want to place the button on all layouts, click the top slide (the slide master itself). If you want only a certain layout to receive the buttons, click it.

EXPERT TIP Some action buttons are best placed on the Slide Master, such as Next and Previous; others, such as Return, are special-use buttons that are best placed on individual slides such as hidden slides.

2. On the Insert or Home tab, click Shapes. A palette of shapes appears; at the bottom of the palette are the action buttons. See Figure 21.10.

3. Click the button that you want to place. Your mouse pointer turns into a crosshair.

4. To create a button of a specific size, drag on the slide (or Slide Master) where you want it to go. Or, to create a button of a default size, simply click once where you want to place it. You can resize the button at any time later, the same as you can any object.

EXPERT TIP If you want to place several buttons, and you want them all to be the same size, place them at the default size to begin with. Then select them all, and resize them as a group. That way they will all be exactly the same size.

5. The Action Settings dialog box appears. Make sure the Mouse Click tab is on top. See Figure 21.11.

FIGURE 21.10

Action buttons are shapes, inserted from the Shapes palette.

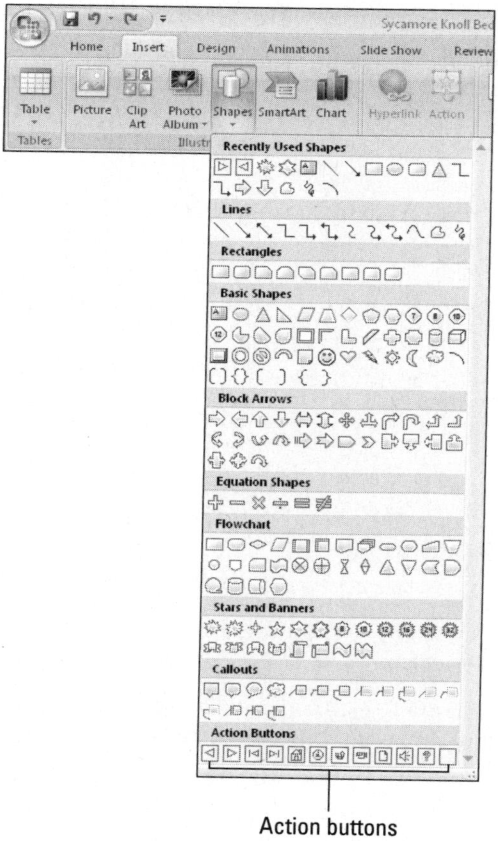

Action buttons

6. Confirm or change the hyperlink set up there:

- **If the action button should take the reader to a specific location**, make sure the correct slide appears in the Hyperlink To box. Refer to Table 21.2 to see the default setting for each action button. Table 21.3 lists the choices you can make and what they do.

- **If the action button should run a program**, choose Run program and enter the program's name and path, or click Browse to locate it. For example, you could open the Calculator application from an action button. The executable file that runs it is calc.exe.

- **If the action button should play a sound**, make sure the Play Sound check box is marked, and choose the correct sound from the Play Sound drop-down list (or pick a different sound file by choosing Other Sound).

FIGURE 21.11

Specify what should happen when you click the action button.

7. Click OK. The button has been assigned the action you specified.

8. Add more action buttons as desired by repeating these steps.

9. If you are working in Slide Master view, exit it by clicking the Close Master View button.

10. Test your action buttons in Slide Show view to make sure they jump where you want them to.

To edit a button's action, right-click it and choose Hyperlink to reopen this dialog box at any time.

TABLE 21.3

Hyperlink to Choices in the Action Settings Dialog Box

Drop-Down Menu Choice	Result
Previous Slide Next Slide First Slide Last Slide Last Slide Viewed	These choices do just what their names say. These are the default actions assigned to certain buttons you learned about in Table 21.2.
End Show	Sets the button to stop the show when clicked.
Custom Show . . .	Opens a Link to Custom Show dialog box, where you can choose a custom show to jump to when the button is clicked.

continued

TABLE 21.3	*(continued)*
Drop-Down Menu Choice	**Result**
Slide . . .	Opens a Hyperlink to Slide dialog box, where you can choose any slide in the current presentation to jump to when the button is clicked.
URL . . .	Opens a Hyperlink to URL dialog box, where you can enter a Web address to jump to when the button is clicked.
Other PowerPoint Presentation . . .	Opens a Hyperlink to Other PowerPoint Presentation dialog box, where you can choose another PowerPoint presentation to display when the button is clicked.
Other File . . .	Opens a Hyperlink to Other File dialog box, where you can choose any file to open when the button is clicked. If the file requires a certain application, that application will open when needed. (To run another application without opening a specific file in it, use the Run Program option in the Action Settings dialog box instead of Hyperlink To.)

Adding Text to a Blank Action Button

The blank action button you saw in Table 21.2 can be very useful. You can place several of them on a slide and type text into them, creating your own set of buttons. To type text into a blank button, follow these steps:

1. Place a blank action button on the slide (from the Shapes gallery).

2. Right-click the action button and choose Edit Text. An insertion point appears in it. (You can also select the button and simply start typing.)

3. Type your text, and then click away from the button when you are finished. If you need to edit the text later, simply click the text to move the insertion point back into it, just as you do with any text box.

Formatting and Changing the Shape of an Action Button

You can format action buttons just like other shapes, as you learned to do in Chapter 10. You can apply borders, fills and effects to them, and apply Shape Style presets. You can also use WordArt styles or individual text formatting controls to format the text on them.

To make action buttons of different shapes, you can use the Change Shape button, as in the following steps:

1. Select the action button(s) to change.

2. On the Drawing Tools Format tab, click Edit Shape ⇨ Change Shape.

3. Click a different shape. See Figure 21.12.

FIGURE 21.12

Change the shape of an action button as you would any other shape.

Figure 21.13 shows some examples of custom buttons you can create with your own text and some shape formatting.

FIGURE 21.13

You can create any of these sets of action buttons by typing and formatting text on blank buttons.

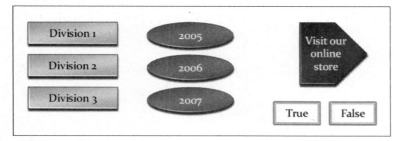

Creating Your Own Action Buttons

You can create an action button out of any object on your slide: a drawn shape, a piece of clip art, a photograph, a text box — anything. To do so, just from the Insert tab click Action. Then, set the On Click action to Hyperlink To, Run Program, or Play Sound, just as you did for the action buttons in the preceding sections.

Make sure you clearly label the object that you are using as an action button so that the users will know what they are getting when they click it. You can add text to the object directly (for example, with an AutoShape), or you can add a text box next to the button that explains its function. If you want to use a ScreenTip to label the item, use a hyperlink rather than an action setting.

Creating Self-Running Presentations

Self-running presentations are not exactly user-interactive because the user does not participate in their running. The show runs at its own pace and the user sits (or stands) passively and observes it.

Not sure when you might use a self-running presentation in your daily life? Here are some ideas:

- **Trade shows:** A self-running presentation outlining your product or service can run continuously in your booth on equipment as simple as a laptop and an external monitor. People who might not feel comfortable talking to a salesperson may stop a few moments to watch a colorful, multimedia slide show.

- **Conventions:** Trying to provide hundreds of convention-goers with some basic information, such as session starting times or cocktail party locations? Set up an information booth in the convention center lobby to provide this information. The slide show can loop endlessly through three or four slides that contain meeting room locations, schedules, and other critical data.

- **In-store sales:** Retail stores can increase sales by strategically placing PC monitors in areas of the store where customers gather. For example, if there is a line where customers stand waiting for the next available register or clerk, you can show those waiting customers a few slides that describe the benefits of extended warranties or that detail the special sales of the week.

- **Waiting areas:** Auto repair shops and other places where customers wait for something to be done provide excellent sales opportunities. The customers don't have anything to do except sit and wait, so they will watch just about anything — including a slide presentation informing them of the other services that your shop provides.

The most important aspect of a self-running show is that it loops continuously until you stop it. This is important because there won't be anyone there to restart it each time it ends.

To set up the show to do just that, follow these steps:

1. On the Slide Show tab, click Set Up Slide Show. The Set Up Show dialog box opens.

2. Mark the Loop Continuously Until 'Esc' check box. See Figure 21.14. Notice that the Loop Continuously until Esc check box is set permanently to On whenever Browsed at a Kiosk is selected.

3. In the Advance Slides area, make sure the Using Timings, if Present option is selected.

4. Click OK.

FIGURE 21.14

Tell PowerPoint that this show should loop continuously.

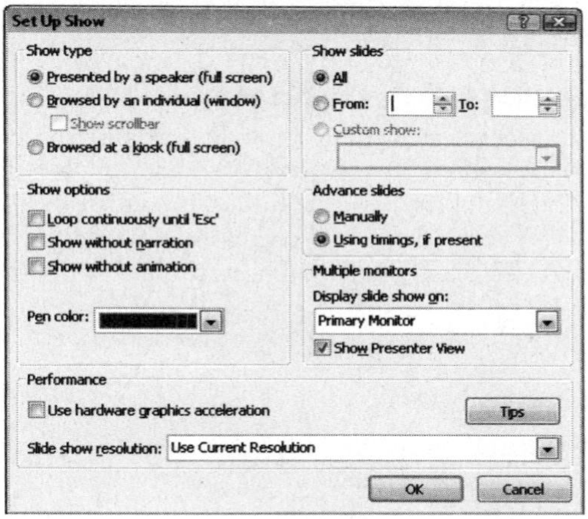

CROSS-REF Timings refers to transition timings, which you learned about in Chapter 18, in the section "Assigning Transitions to Slides." Self-running presentations are good candidates for recorded voice-over narration, which you learned how to set up in Chapter 16.

Using Kiosk Mode

A kiosk is a self-serve booth or workstation where people can view something without supervision. You have probably seen information kiosks at malls, for example, where users can click or touch buttons on-screen to get information.

When providing a computer to operate unattended to the public, one major concern is that some prankster will come along and tamper with the system. You will learn about some ways to thwart that kind of tampering in the next section, "Setting Up a Secure System," but first let's look at one really basic thing you can do: enable Kiosk mode.

When Kiosk mode is enabled, keyboard navigation is not possible (except for pressing Esc to exit Slide Show view), so users must employ the action buttons and hyperlinks on the slides for navigation. If you place a presentation in Kiosk mode and then hide the keyboard, users will only be able to view the content to which you have linked.

To enable Kiosk mode, follow these steps:

1. On the Slide Show tab, click Set Up Slide Show. The Set Up Show dialog box opens (Figure 21.14).

2. In the Show Type area, click Browsed at a Kiosk (Full Screen).

3. Click OK.

Setting Up a Secure System

Security is a definite concern in self-running presentations. Any time you leave a computer unattended with the public, you run the risk of tampering and theft. At the very least, some guru geek will come along and experiment with your PC to see what you've got and whether he or she can do anything clever with it. At the worst, your entire computer setup could disappear entirely.

There are two levels of security involved in unattended presentation situations:

- The security of the physical hardware
- The security that the presentation will continue to run

Securing Your Hardware

For the most foolproof hardware security, get it out of sight. Hide everything except the monitor in a locked drawer, cabinet, or panel of the kiosk you are using, if possible. If you are at a trade show or convention where you don't have the luxury of a lockable system, at least put everything except the monitor under a table, and try to make sure that someone is attending the booth at all times.

> **CAUTION** Don't drape running computers with cloth or any other material that inhibits the airflow around them; doing so increases the risk of overheating.

In an unattended setting, the best way to protect your monitor from walking off is to place it behind a Plexiglas panel where nobody can touch it. Without such a barrier, you run the risk of some jokester turning off its power or turning down its contrast, and anyone who knows something about computers could walk right up and disconnect it and carry it away.

You can also buy various locking cables at computer stores and office supply centers. These cables lock down computer equipment to prevent it from being removed. They include steel cables with padlocks, metal locking brackets, and electronically controlled magnetic locks.

Making Sure the Presentation Continues to Run

I admit that I am guilty of disrupting other people's presentations. When I walk up to an unattended computer in a store, the first thing I do is abort whatever program is running and restart the system to check out its diagnostics and find out what kind of computer it is. It's a geek thing, but all geeks do it.

You will doubtless encounter such geeks wherever you set up your presentation, but especially at trade shows and conventions. (We geeks love trade shows and conventions.) Your mission is to prevent them from stopping your presentation.

The best way to prevent someone from tinkering with your presentation is to get the input devices out of sight. Hide the CPU (the main box of the computer), the keyboard, and the mouse. You can't disconnect the keyboard and mouse from the PC, or an error message will appear, but you can hide them. Again, don't cover them with anything that might restrict the airflow, or you might end up with an overheated PC. You can also set up the following security measures in your presentation file:

- On the Slide Show tab, click Set Up Slide Show and make sure you have chosen Browsed at a Kiosk. This disables the mouse while the slide show is running. The only way to stop the show will be to use the keyboard. This works best for self-running shows where the slides advance automatically.

EXPERT TIP If you make the keyboard available for user navigation, the Esc key will also be available for stopping the program. A utility is available that disables the Esc key at www.mvps.org/skp/noesc.htm.

- Show the presentation using the PowerPoint Viewer program rather than PowerPoint itself. That way nobody can access PowerPoint and create a new presentation to show. For further security, remove the PowerPoint application completely from the PC on which the presentation is showing.

- Set a startup password for your PC so that if people manage to reboot it, they won't get into your PC to tamper with its settings. This is usually set through the BIOS setup program. If you can't do that, set a Windows startup password for each of the user accounts. (Do that through the User Accounts in the Control Panel in Windows.)

- Assign a password to a PowerPoint file, as you learned in Chapter 3, to prevent it from being opened, modified, or both. Although this will not prevent a running presentation from being stopped, it will at least prevent it from being altered or deleted. However, if it is already open, hackers will have full access to it, and if you set it to have a password only for modifications, a hacker could save it under a different name, make changes, and then run the changed version.

Summary

In this chapter, you learned the ins and outs of preparing a presentation that users can run interactively or that can run unattended without user interaction. You learned how to create action buttons, and how to set up kiosk mode and to create a secure presentation system that can be left unattended. You can probably think of some uses for such shows, and even more may occur to you later. In the next chapter, you learn how to prepare a presentation — either a user-interactive one or a self-running one — for mass distribution on CD or over the Web.

Chapter 22

Preparing a Presentation for Mass Distribution

When preparing a presentation that you will send out into the world, whether through e-mail, on CD, or on the Web, you never know what will happen to it or how people will end up viewing or even changing it. This can be a little unnerving!

In this chapter, you will learn how to protect your privacy by removing personal information from a PowerPoint file. You will also learn how to decide on a file format for distribution and how to ensure that the presentation contains nothing that will be incompatible with an earlier version of PowerPoint. You will also learn how to distribute a presentation on CD, and how to publish one in HTML format on the Web.

Working with File Properties

The properties of a file include fixed attributes such as its creation date and size, as well as properties that you can edit, such as the author name, keywords, subject, and comments. Some of these variable properties are also referred to as *metadata* — literally, "data about data."

PowerPoint automatically saves some properties for you, such as the author name, and provides opportunities for you to save additional properties. Properties can be helpful when you are searching for a certain file or maintaining a presentation library, as discussed in Chapter 23. However, when you are distributing a presentation widely, you might prefer to remove some or all of its properties to preserve your privacy.

Changing a File's Properties

To add or change a file's properties, choose Office ➪ Prepare ➪ Properties to display a Document Properties window along the top of the presentation window. You can then add, delete, or change the properties, as shown in Figure 22.1. To close the Document Properties window, click the X in its upper-right corner.

FIGURE 22.1

Use the Document Properties window that appears at the top of the presentation window to assign or change document metadata.

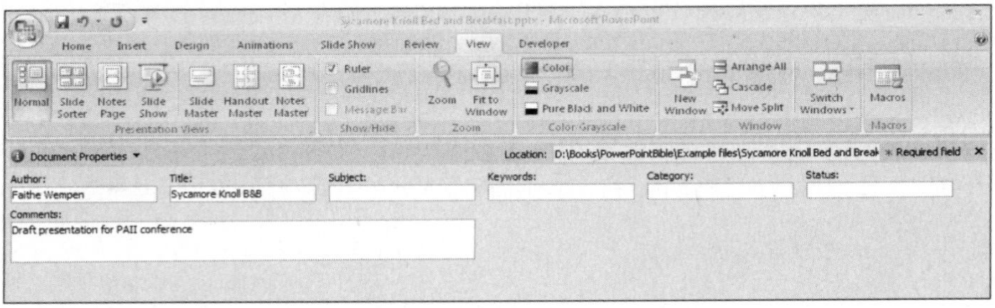

The properties that you can find in the Document Properties window include:

- **Author:** Filled in automatically from the username that you specified when you installed Office.

- **Title:** Used mostly when creating a Web page. The title text appears in the title bar of the Web browser when the page displays. By default, the title is the first line of the document.

- **Subject, Keywords, Category, and Status:** By default, these fields are empty, but you can specify your own information and settings.

NOTE The author's name is automatically added to each file that you create in PowerPoint, based on the username that you specified when you installed Office. To change this name, choose Office ➪ PowerPoint Options, click Popular, and then change the entry in the User Name text box.

You can also display a Properties dialog box for the file, in which you can set advanced properties. To do this, click the down arrow next to Document Properties in the Document Properties window, as shown in Figure 22.1. Then, from the menu that appears, click Advanced Properties.

The Document Properties dialog box is the same dialog box that you would see if you right-clicked the file and then clicked Properties from outside of PowerPoint (that is, from Windows Explorer or any file management window). This dialog box contains the following tabs:

- **General:** Uneditable data about the file, such as its type, location, size, and operating system attributes — for example, read-only and hidden.
- **Summary:** A continuation of the Document Properties window, with additional properties that you can specify or change, as shown in Figure 22.2.

FIGURE 22.2

The Summary tab of the Properties dialog box contains additional property fields.

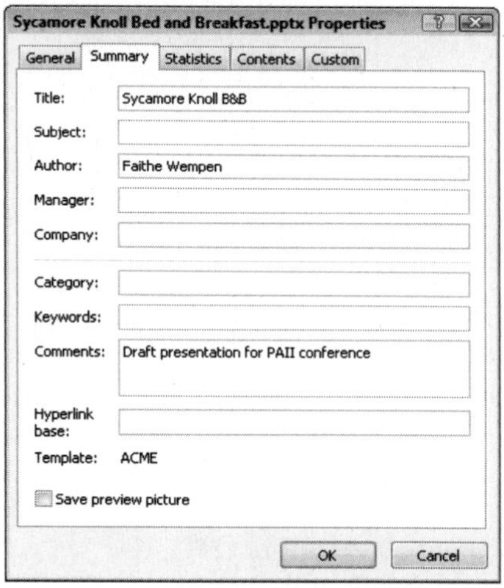

- **Statistics:** Another page of uneditable data, this one relating to statistical analysis of the presentation, such as number of slides, number of words, number of revisions, and total editing time.
- **Contents:** Still more uneditable data. This data includes the fonts that are used, the theme, and the titles of the slides.
- **Custom:** A tab where you can set some of the less-common properties for the file.

You can define custom properties in the Custom tab. Custom properties are special-purpose fields that you can add when you need them. To set a custom property, follow these steps:

1. In the Custom tab, click the property from the Name list that you want to use.
2. Open the Type drop-down list and select the type of data that it should hold. The default is Text, which accepts any input.
3. In the Value field, type the desired value for this property.
4. Click Add to add the property, type, and value to the Properties list, as shown in Figure 22.3.

FIGURE 22.3

You can set a custom property in the Custom tab.

5. Repeat steps 1 to 4 to add more custom properties, if needed; then click OK.

Removing Personal Information from a File

Before you distribute a PowerPoint file, you might want to remove some of the properties from it that contain sensitive information. For example, if you have entered confidential information about a client in the Comments property, then you may not want the client or others to see it.

If you can remember all of the properties that you set for the file, then you can go back in and remove them manually, as you learned in the preceding section. However, it is much easier to use the new Document Inspector feature in PowerPoint 2007 to remove personal information from the file. Follow these steps:

1. Choose Office ➪ Prepare ➪ Inspect Document. The Document Inspector dialog box opens, as shown in Figure 22.4.

2. Select or deselect the check boxes for the various types of information that you want to look for. The personal information contained in properties falls under the Document Properties and Personal Information category.

3. Click Inspect.

4. Review the inspection results. Categories in which items have been found display their findings; categories in which no items have been found appear with check marks, as shown in Figure 22.5.

FIGURE 22.4

You can inspect the presentation for information that you might want to remove.

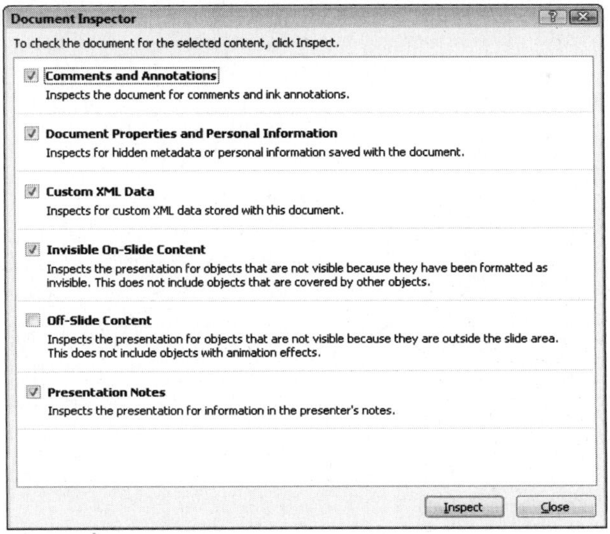

FIGURE 22.5

You can view the inspection results.

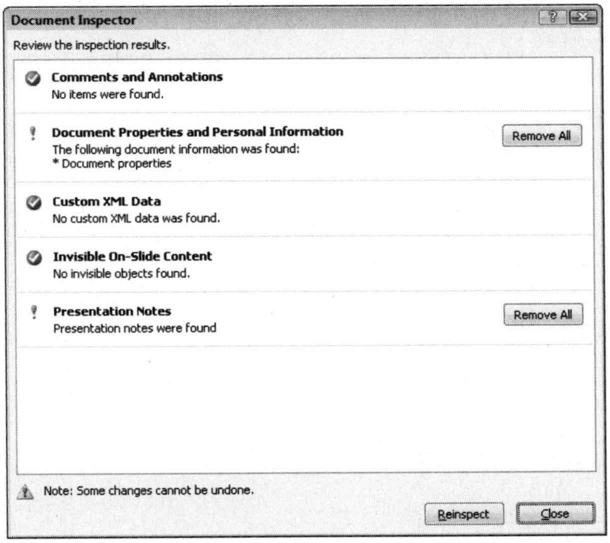

5. For each category that you want to clear, click Remove All.

6. When you are finished, click Reinspect to check the document again, or click Close to end the process.

> **CAUTION** Be careful that you don't remove hidden object you want to keep, or strip all the speaker notes out of a presentation unintentionally. One way to ensure that you don't do this is to perform the inspection on a copy of the presentation, not the original.

Finalizing a Presentation

When the presentation is completely finished, you may want to mark it as finalized. This prevents users from inadvertently making additional changes to it, and so it gives you some measure of protection against unexpected modifications that can distort your message.

> **CAUTION** Finalizing a presentation has no measure of security in it. Anyone who has PowerPoint 2007 and knows about the Mark as Final command will be able to un-finalize it and make changes to it.

To mark a presentation as final, follow these steps:

1. Choose Office ➪ Prepare ➪ Mark as Final. A message appears that the presentation will be marked as final and then saved.

2. Click OK. A message appears, explaining that the presentation has been marked as final, and that editing has been turned off for it, as shown in Figure 22.6.

FIGURE 22.6

This message appears after you mark a document as final.

Microsoft Office PowerPoint

This document has been marked as final to indicate that editing is complete and that this is the final version of the document.

When a document is marked as final, the status property is set to "Final" and typing, editing commands, and proofing marks are turned off.
You can recognize that a document is marked as final when the Mark As Final icon displays in the status bar.

☐ Don't show this message again

[OK]

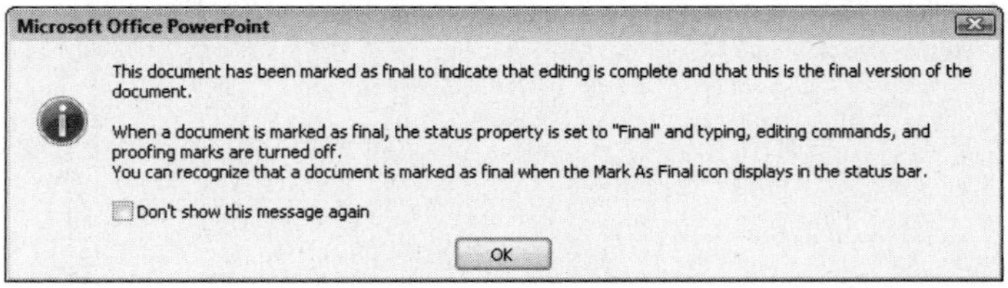

When you mark a document as final, an icon appears in the status bar to indicate that it is final, and the presentation becomes uneditable. If you change your mind about the presentation and need to edit it, you can easily turn off this attribute and edit it again. Just choose Office ➪ Prepare ➪ Mark as Final again to toggle off the Finalized status.

Checking for Prior-version Compatibility

If you plan to share your presentation with people who have earlier versions of PowerPoint, you need to send it to them in a format that they can display and edit. The "display" part is actually easier than the "edit" part because, generally speaking, when you convert a PowerPoint 2007 file to 2003 format, it retains most of its original appearance, from a Slide Show View perspective. However, editing some of the content in the presentation is a different matter. When a 2007-only object, such as a SmartArt diagram or chart, is saved in 97-2003 format, PowerPoint converts it to a graphic. It looks the same as it always did, but you cannot edit the object in an earlier version as the type of content that it actually is.

If you plan to share a presentation file with someone who will need to edit it, it is a good idea to run the Compatibility Checker to find out exactly which parts of the presentation may cause a problem. To run the Compatibility Checker, follow these steps:

1. Choose Office ➪ Prepare ➪ Run Compatibility Checker. The Microsoft Office PowerPoint Compatibility Checker dialog box appears, as shown in Figure 22.7.

FIGURE 22.7

You can find out about potential problems that may occur when sharing the file in 97-2003 format.

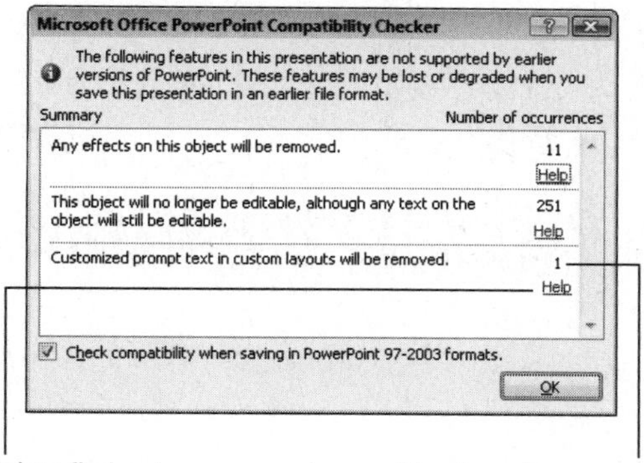

Click to find out
more about the error

Number of occurences
of this problem

2. Read the summary information that appears. If you do not understand one of the messages, click its Help link to open a Help document that explains it.

3. (Optional) To specify whether this check runs automatically when you save in PowerPoint 97-2003 format, select or deselect the Check Compatibility When Saving in PowerPoint 97-2003 Formats check box.

4. Click OK.

Encrypting a File with a Password

You can prevent unauthorized access to a PowerPoint file by assigning a password to it. Without the password, nobody can open the file. To assign a password, follow these steps:

1. Choose Office ➪ Prepare ➪ Encrypt Document. The Encrypt Document dialog box opens.

2. Type a password in the Password text box, as shown in Figure 22.8.

FIGURE 22.8

You can add a password to a presentation file.

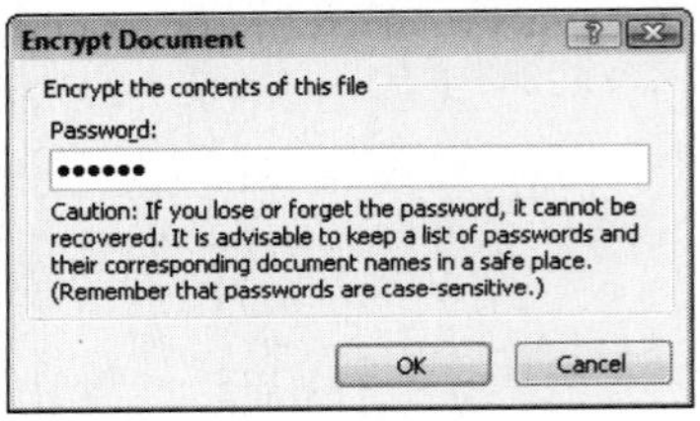

3. Click OK. A Confirm Password dialog box appears.

4. Retype the same password that you typed in step 2.

5. Click OK.

When anyone attempts to open the file in the future, a password prompt will appear. They must enter the password and click OK to continue.

To remove a password, returning the document to its original unencrypted status, follow these steps:

1. Choose Office ➪ Prepare ➪ Encrypt Document. The Encrypt Document dialog box opens.

2. Delete the contents of the Password text box.

3. Click OK.

NOTE   Another way to assign a password is to choose File ➪ Save As, click Tools ➪ General, and enter a password in the dialog box that appears. This method is the same as it was in PowerPoint 2003.

Publishing a Presentation on a CD or DVD

Often the computer that you use to create a presentation is not the same one that you use to show it, especially if it is a desktop computer. This is an issue whether you are showing the presentation "live," distributing it as a self-running presentation through e-mail or the Web, or creating a kiosk. As a result, the issue of transferring files from one computer to another is a very common concern.

One way to transfer a PowerPoint presentation to another computer is simply to copy the PowerPoint file using a floppy disk, writeable CD or DVD, network, or other medium. However, this method is imperfect because it assumes that the other computer has PowerPoint or the PowerPoint Viewer, as well as all of the necessary fonts, sounds, graphics (if any are linked), music files, and other elements that are needed for every part of the show. This can be a dangerous assumption.

A better way to transfer the presentation is to use the Package for CD feature in PowerPoint. This feature reads all of the linked files and associated objects, and ensures that they are transferred along with the main presentation. You can create a CD or DVD that you can then copy and mass-distribute to a wide audience, or you can send the package to any folder on any drive and then compress, or ZIP, the folder and send it to others through e-mail.

NOTE   *Zipping* consists of creating a compressed archive file with a .zip extension. You do this by selecting files in Windows Explorer, right-clicking the selection, and choosing Send To ⇨ Compressed (zipped) Folder.

CAUTION   Packaged versions of presentations do not include comments, revisions, or ink annotations. If you want a version that includes these items, then you need to manually copy the files to the CD or DVD.

If you have a CD or DVD drive that writes to blank discs, copying the presentation to a CD or DVD is an attractive choice. This produces a self-running disc that contains the PowerPoint Viewer application, the presentation file, and any linked files that you need for the show.

You can copy many presentation files to a single CD or DVD, not just the currently active presentation. The only limit is the capacity of the disc. Further, you can set the presentations up to run automatically one after the other, or you can specify that a menu appears so that the user can choose the presentation that runs each time they insert the CD or DVD.

NOTE   The DVDs referred to in this chapter contain data files, not the type of DVD movies you could put in a DVD player hooked up to your TV.

When you copy to CD using the default settings, the file is saved in PowerPoint 97-2003 format so that it can be played with the PowerPoint Viewer that is packaged on the CD. If you do not want to include the viewer, then you can set the copy options, as described later in this chapter, to copy the presentation file as-is and omit the viewer from the disk.

NOTE CD-R stands for Compact Disc Recordable; it is a standard for writeable CDs that you can write to only once. CD-RW is Compact Disc ReWriteable, the standard for write-able CDs that you can write to multiple times. Modern drives support both CD types, and some drives also support various types of writeable DVDs.

To package the presentation on a CD or DVD — assuming that you have a CD or DVD drive that writes — follow these steps:

1. Place a blank disc in your writeable CD or DVD drive.

2. Open the presentation in PowerPoint to review it and make sure that it is exactly the way you want it. CD-R, DVD+R, and DVD-R discs are not rewritable, and so if you make a mistake, you will have wasted a disc. For this reason, it is often better to package to a folder and then burn these files to a CD after testing.

3. Choose Office ➪ Publish ➪ Package for CD. The Package for CD dialog box opens, as shown in Figure 22.9.

FIGURE 22.9

You can use the Package for CD feature to place all of the necessary files for the presentation on a CD, or in another location.

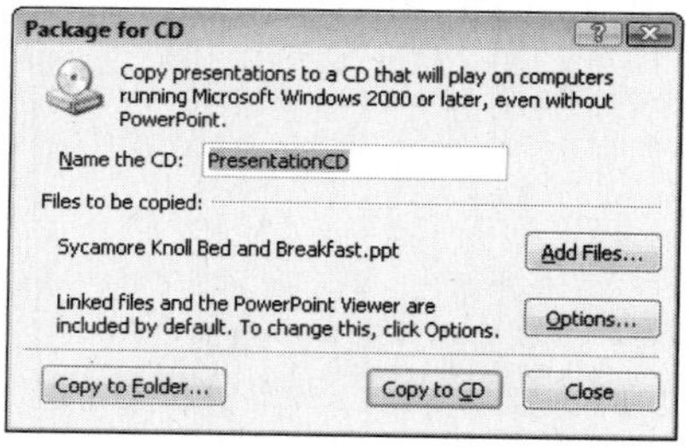

4. Type a name for the CD; this name is similar to a volume label for the disc.

5. (Optional) You can add more files to the disc layout. See the section, Including Multiple Presentations, later in this chapter, for more details.

6. (Optional) You can set other options, as shown in the section, Setting Copy Options, later in this chapter.

7. Click Copy to CD.

8. If a message appears asking whether you want to package linked files, click Yes.

9. The CD drive writes the files to the CD or DVD. It may take several minutes, depending on the size of the files, the speed of your computer, and the writing speed of the CD drive.

10. A message appears when the files are successfully written to the disc, asking whether you want to copy the same files to another disc. Click Yes or No. If you choose No, then click Close to close the Package for CD dialog box.

> **NOTE** If you are packaging a presentation that PowerPoint originally saved in the Web format, PowerPoint converts it back to native PowerPoint format when it copies the presentation to CD. However, standard Web files that PowerPoint did not create itself will remain MHT files.

Copying to Other Locations

If you do not have a CD or DVD writer, then you cannot directly write to a CD as shown in the preceding section. Instead, you need to package the presentation to a folder on a drive that can be accessed by a computer with a CD or DVD burner. You can then create the CD using either a third-party disc-burning program or the writing software in Windows.

> **NOTE** If you are burning a CD using a third-party application, you should include on that CD only the contents of the folder in which you packaged the presentation, not the folder itself.

To change the package location from the CD to another location, in the Package for CD dialog box, click the Copy to Folder button. A Copy to Folder dialog box appears, as shown in Figure 22.10. Type a name for the new folder to be created, and type a path for this folder in the Location text box. When you click OK, PowerPoint automatically packages the presentation to this location.

FIGURE 22.10

You can package the presentation files to another location.

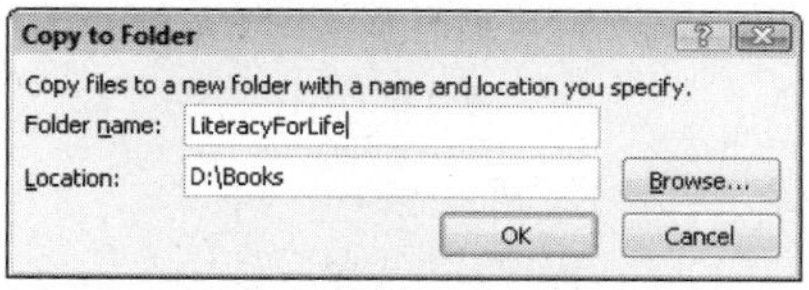

> **CAUTION** When you use the Copy to Folder feature to specify a location, PowerPoint immediately copies the presentation there; it does not wait for you to click OK in the Package for CD dialog box. Therefore, if you need to add files or set options, as described in the following sections, you should do these things *first*.

Including Multiple Presentations

By default, PowerPoint includes the active presentation on the CD, but you can also add other presentations, up to the capacity of the disc. For example, if you have several versions of the same presentation for different audiences, you can place all of them on a single CD.

As you prepare to copy using the Package for CD dialog box, click the Add Files button. An Add Files dialog box opens. Select the additional files that you want to include by holding down the Ctrl key and selecting the files you want. Then click Open to return to the Package for CD dialog box. The list of files appears, as shown in Figure 22.11, with extra controls.

FIGURE 22.11

You can select multiple presentations to include on the CD, and set the order in which they should play.

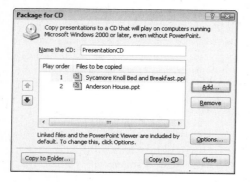

If you set up the CD to play the presentations automatically (which is one of the options that is covered in the next section), the order in which they appear on the list becomes significant. Rearrange the list by clicking the Up- or Down-arrow buttons to the left of the list, and use the Remove button to remove any files that you do not need. You can then continue packaging the presentation.

EXPERT TIP   If you make a mistake in the presentation order, or you want to include more or fewer presentations, then you are out of luck if you write directly to a disc. However, if you write to a hard-disk folder, then you can manually edit the playlist.txt file using Notepad, to modify the list of presentations that will play and the order in which they will run. Playlist.txt is a plain-text file that contains a simple list of presentation files, each one on a separate line. You can remove or rearrange these presentations, and you can add other presentations to the list. However, if you do this, you must also manually copy these presentations to the folder, along with any necessary support files. You cannot repackage to the same folder if you want to repackage the presentations through PowerPoint; you must repackage to a different folder name.

Setting Copy Options

From the Package for CD dialog box, you can click the Options button to display the Options dialog box, as shown in Figure 22.12. This dialog box contains the following options:

FIGURE 22.12

You can set options for copying your presentations to disc.

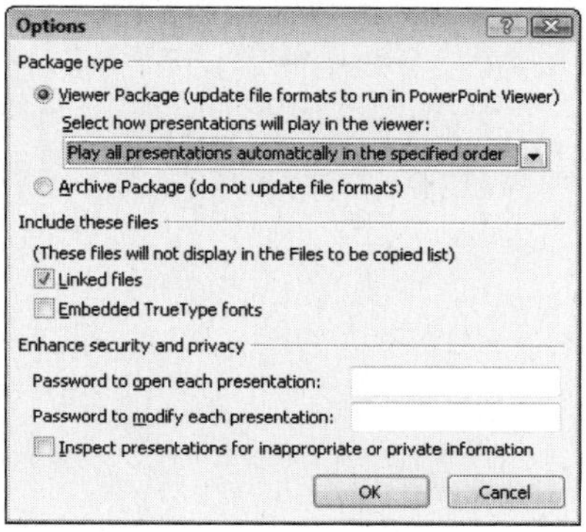

- **Setting the Package Type:** You can choose whether to include the PowerPoint Viewer on the disc. This viewer does not play PowerPoint 2007 files, and so if you include it, your presentation files are saved as in PowerPoint 97-2003 format. If the computer on which you will show the presentations already has PowerPoint 2007, then you do not need the PowerPoint Viewer, and so you can package the presentations in their original file format. To do this, choose Archive Package as the package type.

- **Selecting How the Presentations Will Play:** If you choose Viewer Package in the preceding section, then you can choose from the following play methods in the drop-down list beneath Viewer Package:

  - **Play all presentations automatically in the specified order.** If you choose this method, the order in which the presentations appear on the list becomes significant. (See the section "Including Multiple Presentations," earlier in this chapter.)

  - **Play only the first presentation automatically.** Again, this method makes the order significant. By default, the first presentation is the one that was active when you opened the dialog box to begin the packaging process.

  - **Let the user select which presentation to view.** This method shows a menu when the user inserts the CD. It is a nice feature if you want the user to be able to select the presentation that they want to view each time.

CAUTION   If you are going to allow the user to make the selection, then make sure that the filenames are descriptive enough so that the user can tell what they are.

  - **Don't play the CD automatically.** This method completely turns off the autorun feature for the disc.

- **Specifying Support Files to Include:** In the Include These Files section of the dialog box, you can use the check boxes to include linked files and/or embedded TrueType fonts. Linked files are any files, such as sounds or movies, that are not embedded in the main presentation file. You would generally want to include these files. Embedded TrueType fonts are font files that are needed to display the presentation. If the computer on which the presentation will play does not have the fonts that are used in the presentation, it will try to substitute fonts, and the presentation may not look exactly the same. Embedding fonts takes up only a little space and can save you the inconvenience of missing a font.

- **Setting Security and Privacy Options:** You can assign passwords to open and modify the presentations. To do this, you enter passwords in the Password to Open Each Presentation and Password to Modify Each Presentation text boxes, as shown in Figure 22-14.

> **CAUTION** These passwords apply to all presentations on the CD or DVD, and so you cannot set passwords individually through this interface. If you need individual passwords, you should use the Office ➪ Save As ➪ Tools ➪ General command instead and specify passwords for each file.

- **Inspect Presentations for Inappropriate or Private Information:** You can also select this check box, which causes the Document Inspector to run before the files are written to CD.

Working with the PowerPoint Viewer

The PowerPoint Viewer is a utility that shows PowerPoint presentations but cannot edit them. It is similar to being permanently in Slide Show view. If the computer on which you will show the presentation does not have PowerPoint installed, you will need the PowerPoint Viewer to view the presentation.

> **NOTE** The PowerPoint Viewer that comes with PowerPoint 2007 does not show PowerPoint 2007 files — only PowerPoint 97-2003 format files. Therefore, when you create a CD with the Package for CD feature, as shown in the preceding section, PowerPoint converts the files to the 97-2003 format.

Playing a Presentation with the PowerPoint Viewer

To use a self-running presentation CD that was created with the Package for CD feature, just insert the CD into your computer. If the computer has AutoPlay set up for the CD drive, the presentation starts automatically. If it does not, double-click the CD icon in the Computer window.

If you have placed multiple presentations on the CD and specified that a selection menu should appear for them, then a menu — actually a modified Open dialog box — appears when you insert the CD. Select the presentation that you want and click Open. This dialog box reappears when the presentation has completed; click the Cancel button in the menu when you are finished.

You can also play presentations with the PowerPoint Viewer independently from any package. Simply double-click the executable file for the viewer (pptview.exe); a dialog box prompts you to choose the presentation that you want to open.

Making the PowerPoint Viewer Available Separately

The PowerPoint Viewer must be packaged with a set of dynamic link library, or DLL, files in order to work. When you use the Package for CD feature, it automatically includes these support files.

Here are the files that you need to keep together when you distribute the PowerPoint Viewer:

- Autorun.inf
- Intldate.dll
- Microsoft.vs80.crt.manifest
- Msvcm80.dll
- Msvcp80.dll
- Msvcr80.dll
- Ogl.dll
- Pptview.exe
- Pptviewexe.manifest
- Ppvwintl.dll
- Saext.dll

The following steps describe an easy way to make a disc or folder that contains the necessary files:

1. Create a blank presentation and save it as Deleteme.ppt. Then package this presentation for CD, but package it to a folder on your hard disk rather than to a CD.

2. Open the folder in a file management window and delete the following files: Deleteme.ppt, Autorun.inf, Playlist.txt, and Play.bat. You can keep the pvreadme.htm file if you want.

3. (Optional) If you want to make the set of files available to others through e-mail or the Web, use a compression program (or right-click and select Send To ➪ Compressed [zipped] Folder) to create a ZIP file containing the files.

Publishing a Presentation to the Web

A presentation delivered on the Web has the same overall goal as any other presentation: you want the audience to see it, appreciate it, and accept it. However, the means for accomplishing this over the Web are slightly different. A successful presentation over the Web should meet the following requirements:

- **Universally accessible to the intended audience.** You must know your audience and their Web browser versions, so that you can save your presentation in the most appropriate format to their needs. This chapter discusses this issue in detail.

- **Friendly and user-interactive.** This means that you should include directions, hyperlinks, and action buttons to help the users navigate through the presentation, as you learned in Chapter 21.

- **Quick to download.** This means that you should keep the file size as small as possible without sacrificing important features. For example, do not use unnecessary sounds, graphics, videos, or photos, because these items all contribute to the file size.

- **Quick to view.** You should skip complex animation and transition effects in a Web show. Web users like to get right to the point of each slide. Although long-lasting animation effects may be great for a speaker-led presentation, they are usually just annoying to Web users.

- **Does not rely heavily on sound.** Do not make sound an integral part of your presentation, because you cannot assume that everyone who views it will have a computer with sound support. For example, library computers usually do not. Further, consider making the sounds that you do include optional, perhaps by including a button on the slide that they can click to hear the sound. A lot of people object to Web pages that play sounds or music automatically.

You may find that you have to partially sacrifice one of these goals to meet another. For example, PowerPoint offers a way to ensure compatibility with multiple browsers when saving in Web format, but this results in larger file sizes. I will discuss these dilemmas as the chapter progresses and let you come up with your own solutions.

Deciding on a File Format for Web Distribution

You can begin by deciding which file format you want to use. This can be a rather complex question because of the wide array of choices. You first need to decide whether you want to publish in Web format or in native PowerPoint format. If you decide to publish in Web format, you then need to decide whether to create a single-page Web file or a traditional HTML file. You must then decide which browsers you want to support.

Native PowerPoint Format versus Web Format

First, you must decide whether to upload the presentation to a Web server in its native PowerPoint format or to publish it in Web format. Both formats have pros and cons:

- **PowerPoint format.** You can make the PowerPoint presentation file available for download from your Web site, just as you can make any other file type available, such as a graphic or an application.

  - **Pros:** The audience sees the presentation exactly as you created it, including any embedded sounds, movies, transitions, and animation.

  - **Cons:** Only people who own a copy of PowerPoint or who have downloaded the PowerPoint Viewer program can see it.

- **Web format.** You can convert your PowerPoint presentation to Web format.

  - **Pros:** Anyone with a Web browser can view the presentation without any special software. This makes your work widely accessible.

  - **Cons:** Certain special effects in your presentation might not be visible to all users, depending on the effects that you used and the Web browsers that the audience members use.

If you choose Web format, there are a few PowerPoint features that will not work correctly. It is good to know about these features so that you can avoid using them in a presentation that is destined for the Web. Here are some examples:

- If you set a sound or music clip to continue to play for a certain number of slides, it will stop when you advance past the initial slide.

EXPERT TIP   If you need to make a music clip play through multiple slides, then you might be interested in this article: www.onppt.com/ppt/article1018.html.

You can also edit the HTML file itself in a text editor. Open the fullscreen.html file and add the following line between the `<html>` and the `<head>` tags at the top (where `yoursong` is the name of the music clip and the actual file extension of that clip type is substituted for `wma`):

```
<bgsound src="yoursong.wma" loop=infinite>
```

- If you set up the text on a shape to have a different animation than its shape, it loses the special animation and is animated together with the shape.

- If the presentation is set up for automatic transitions between slides, all mouse-click animations behave as automatic animations.

- Sounds attached to objects that are hyperlinks (for example, action buttons) do not play.

- If a hyperlink on the Slide Master is covered by a placeholder, even if that placeholder is transparent, the hyperlink is unavailable on the individual slides.

- Shadow text effects are not supported; the text appears as normal text.

You may also find other features that will not work correctly on Web page presentations, such as certain animation effects.

CAUTION   Do not assume that the presentation will look the same in all Web browsers. At a minimum, run the presentation in both Internet Explorer and Firefox, and note any differences.

Single-Page Web File versus Traditional HTML File

If you decide to go with the Web format, you have a second decision: should you use a single-page Web file or a traditional HTML file? Here is the difference:

- **Single-page Web file.** This creates a single file with an .mht extension that contains everything that you need for the entire Web presentation. No support folder is needed.

Pros: Great convenience. The entire presentation is encapsulated in a single file, so that you can e-mail this file, upload it, or do anything else with it as a single unit.

Cons: The file size is slightly larger than the combined file size of the traditional HTML file and all of its support files. Also, some older Web browsers do not support the use of MHT files, and so some audience members may be excluded.

■ **Traditional HTML file.** This creates a single text-based HTML file and a support folder containing all of the graphics and helper files necessary to turn it into a Web presentation.

Pros: You can import this page into a larger Web site (for example, in FrontPage), and you can edit the HTML file in any application that supports text editing. You do not have to go back to PowerPoint every time you need to make a change.

Cons: Working with a support folder is somewhat unwieldy. For example, you might forget to copy the folder when you are moving the page to a server.

An HTML presentation consists of many files. PowerPoint creates a home page (an entry point) with the same name as the original presentation. This is the file that you name when you save the presentation. For example, if the presentation file is named Rondo.ppt, the home page is named Rondo.htm. Then, PowerPoint creates a folder named *presentation name* Files (for example, Rondo Files) that contains all of the HTML, graphics, and other support files needed to display the complete presentation.

CAUTION   If you are transferring the HTML presentation to another computer (which is very likely if you are going to make it available on the Internet through your company's server), then you must be careful to transfer both the HTML home page and the entire associated folder.

Browser-Compatibility File Formats

The third and final format decision is based on which Web browsers you want to support. This is applicable both to HTML and MHT formats.

The higher the Web browser version that you support, the more of PowerPoint's features you can transfer to the Web version, and the better the quality of the multimedia content. You can export a better show using the higher version support.

However, by choosing higher version support, you may exclude a portion of your audience. Anyone who does not have this version or higher either cannot see the show at all or cannot see it as you intended, depending on the version. As a result, the lower version support results in greater compatibility.

The version support that you select also affects the file size — in general, the lower the version, the smaller the file size. An exception to this is the option to save for multi-browser compatibility (which I discuss later in this chapter); choosing this option accomplishes both near-universal support and inclusion of all of the features, but at the expense of a much greater file size.

The default Web browser support is Internet Explorer 4.0 or later, and this works well in most cases. If you decide to support Microsoft Internet Explorer 3.0 and Netscape Navigator 3.0 or later, you will run into the following problems:

- Animation and transitions will not be supported.
- Animated GIFs will not play if you save the presentation with a screen size of 640x480 or less.
- Sounds and movies will not be supported.
- Some graphics will appear degraded in quality.
- The slide will not be scaled to fit the Web browser window. It will run at a fixed size, based on the screen size setting that you select when you publish the presentation.
- You will not be able to view the presentation in full screen.
- You will not be able to open or close frames.
- The active slide will not appear highlighted in the outline pane.
- You will not be able to use the mouse to highlight elements in the outline pane.

If you save the presentation to support Internet Explorer 4.0 or later, but someone tries to view the presentation with an earlier version or with Netscape Navigator, then they will still be able to see the presentation, but the following problems will occur:

- The presentation outline will appear permanently expanded.
- No notes or additional frames will appear.
- Hyperlinks will not work.
- Clicking a slide title in the outline pane will not take you to that slide.
- The default Web browser colors will be used to display the presentation text color and background color. An exception is that the colors will appear correctly in Internet Explorer 3.0.
- Sounds and movies will not play.

As you will learn in the section, Browser Options, you can also fine-tune the version number by choosing compatibility for Internet Explorer 5.0 or 6.0. If you choose either of these versions, PowerPoint will use Vector Markup Language, or VML, for graphics, in order to reduce loading time. However, earlier Web browser versions will not be able to view the graphics.

If you choose Internet Explorer 6.0 compatibility, PowerPoint allows the use of PNG graphics (a graphic format that is an improved version of GIF) in the presentation. Earlier Web browser versions cannot see these graphics.

Now that you know the pros and cons of the different options, we can start with saving your presentation as a Web page.

Saving the Presentation as a Web Page

If you use the default settings, saving a presentation as a Web page is almost as easy as saving it normally. You simply issue a command and provide a name; PowerPoint does the rest.

CAUTION When you save your presentation as a Web page, the resulting HTML or MHT presentation remains open and on-screen. If you make additional edits, these edits do not apply to the original PowerPoint presentation file on which the Web version is based. After saving your work on the Web version, make sure that you also use Office ⇨ Save As to re-save your work in PowerPoint format if you want all of the copies to remain updated.

Follow these steps to perform a basic save in Web format without setting any special options.

1. Choose File ⇨ Save As. The Save As dialog box appears.

2. Open the Save As Type drop-down list and select either the Web Page format or the Single File Web Page format. The Save As dialog box changes to show a Publish button and a Change Title button, as shown in Figure 22.13.

FIGURE 22.13

The Save As dialog box appears different when you are saving in a Web format.

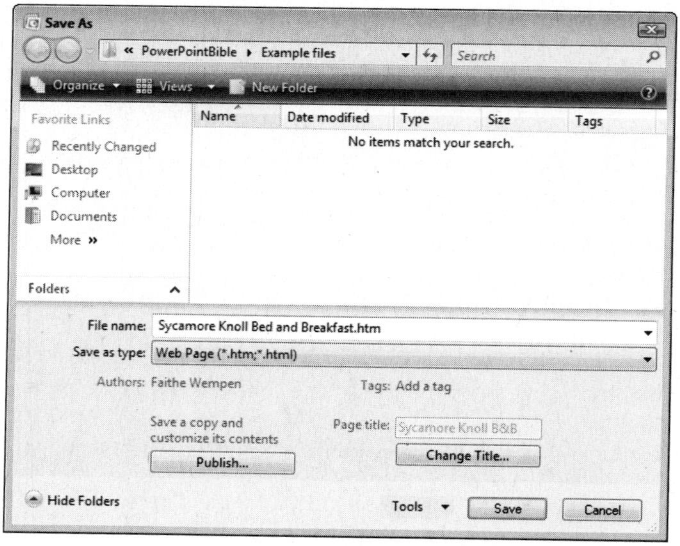

3. The default name is the presentation name. If you want a different name, type it in the File Name text box.

4. PowerPoint takes the default Page title from the title of the first slide. This title appears in the Web browser title bar when the page displays. If you want a different title, click Change Title, type a new title, and click OK.

5. If you want to save the presentation in a different location, navigate to the drive or folder that you want.

6. Click Save. PowerPoint saves the presentation in the format that you chose.

You will probably want to check your work by opening the file in your Web browser and making sure that all of the slides appear as you intended. To do so, browse to the location where you saved the presentation and double-click the file to open it. Figure 22.14 shows an example of a presentation in Web page format.

NOTE When you view a Web presentation in the default view, as shown in Figure 22.16, many of the animations, transitions, and other features do not work. To take full advantage of these features, you must switch to Slide Show view by clicking the Slide Show button.

FIGURE 22.14

This is a PowerPoint presentation that was saved in Web page format.

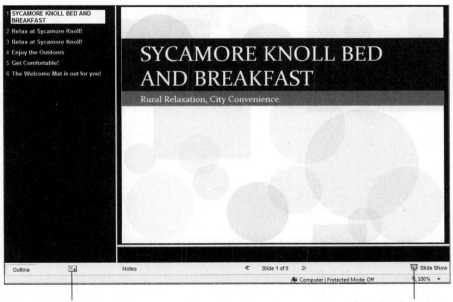

Expand or collapse outline   Switch to full screen

Setting Web Publishing Options

When you save using the steps in the preceding section, you have very little control over how PowerPoint translates your presentation. For more control, click the Publish button in the Save As dialog box. The Publish As Web Page dialog box appears, as shown in Figure 22.15.

FIGURE 22.15

You can use this dialog box to provide more input on how PowerPoint converts your presentation to Web format.

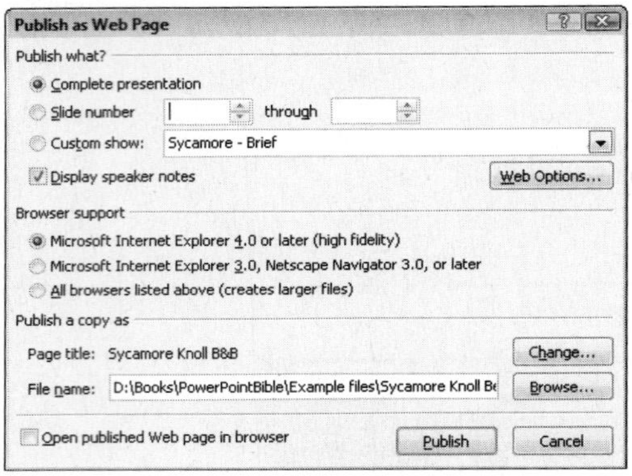

Use the Publish As Web Page dialog box as a replacement for the Save As dialog box, and set any of these options:

- **Publish What?** The default setting is Complete Presentation, but you can choose a range of slides or a custom show.

- **Display Speaker Notes.** This check box is selected by default, so that an icon on each page enables your readers to jump to the notes for that page.

- **Browser Support.** The default setting is Microsoft Internet Explorer 4.0 or later (High Fidelity). This format takes advantage of the capability of these Web browser versions to process certain codes and run certain mini-applications. If you think that some of your audience may not have this Web browser version, you can choose one of the other options instead.

  - **Microsoft Internet Explorer 3.0, Netscape Navigator 3.0, or Later.** This option results in many of the animated features of the presentation not being saved, but it also makes for a smaller file size and greater compatibility with a wide variety of Web browsers.

  - **All Browsers Listed Above (Creates Larger Files).** This option offers you maximum compatibility. It essentially saves two versions of the presentation in the same file — one for Internet Explorer 4.0 and higher, and the other for everything else. This way, you do not have to sacrifice features in order to ensure compatibility.

- **Publish a Copy As.** These are the same controls as the ones in the Save As dialog box. You can change the page title with the Change button, or type a different name and location in the File Name text box.

- **Open Published Web Page in Browser.** If you leave this check box selected, PowerPoint opens Internet Explorer and displays your presentation's first page automatically. This is a good way to check your work.

But wait! There's more! Notice the Web Options button in Figure 22.15. You can click it to display the Web Options dialog box, shown in Figure 22.16, where you can change even more conversion options. The following sections cover these options.

General Options

On the General tab, shown in Figure 22.16, you can change the following options:

FIGURE 22.16

You can fine-tune the Web export settings of your presentation even more precisely with these options.

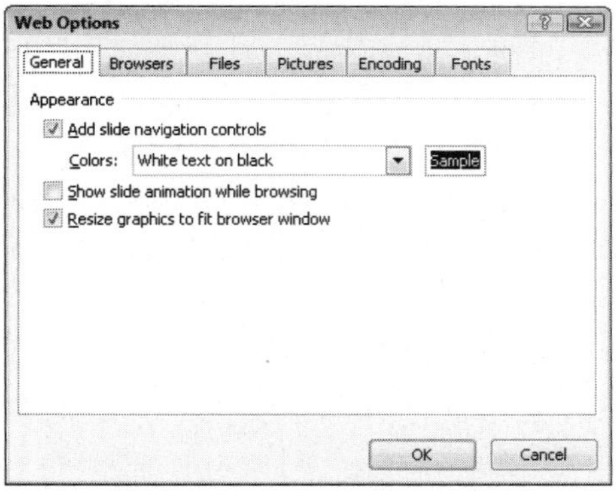

- **Add Slide Navigation Controls.** When you leave this option selected, a pane on the left side of the Web browser window displays the names of the slides. Users can click a slide's name to jump to it.

- **Colors.** Notice in Figure 22-16 that the aforementioned navigation area is black with white lettering. You can choose a different color scheme for this area from the Colors drop-down list. Choices include Browser Colors (whatever default colors are set in the user's Web browser), Presentation Colors taken from the presentation (text color or accent color), or Black Text on White.

- **Show Slide Animation While Browsing.** If you have set any slide animations, as discussed in Chapter 18, and you want to include them in the Web presentation, then select this check box. It is deselected by default because Web users may find animations annoying, rather than clever, due to slow Internet connection speeds.

■ **Resize Graphics to Fit Browser Window.** This option is selected by default. As a result, if users are running their Web browsers at less that full-screen size or if they are using a different screen resolution, then your content will not be cut off, but rather resized to fit their screen.

Browser Options

The features that PowerPoint makes available to your audience depend on the different Web browser versions and compatibility settings that you select. You can find these settings on the Browsers tab, as shown in Figure 22.17.

FIGURE 22.17

You can customize how you save your presentation for a specific Web browser version.

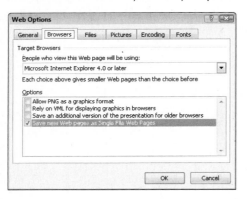

Choose a Web browser version from the Target Browsers drop-down list; the check boxes in the Options section are automatically selected or deselected for that version based on its capabilities. You can also manually select or deselect any of these check boxes. The lower the version you choose, the fewer features that are used, and the smaller the files become. The four check boxes are:

■ **Allow PNG as a Graphics Format.** PNG is an improved version of the GIF format. Internet Explorer 6.0 fully supports this format, while earlier versions may not. If your presentation contains PNG files and this option is not selected, then they will be converted to a supported file format when you save the presentation.

■ **Rely on VML for Displaying Graphics in Browsers.** Vector Markup Language, or VML, enables graphics to appear more quickly in Web pages. You must have at least Internet Explorer 5.0 to see graphics that rely on VML; people with older Web browsers cannot see the graphics.

■ **Save an Additional Version of the Presentation for Older Browsers.** This check box is deselected by default, regardless of the version that you select. Selecting this option will insert the needed codes for backward compatibility with older Web browsers (all the way back to Internet Explorer 3.0); however, this will also increase the file size.

- **Save New Web Pages as Single File Web Pages.** This option either enables or disables the use of the MHT format, which was discussed earlier in this chapter. To view a Single File Web Page, users must have at least Internet Explorer 4.0.

File Options

On the Files tab, shown in Figure 22.18, you can set the following options to control how your files are saved, named, organized, and updated:

FIGURE 22.18

All of these file options are enabled by default; you can deselect the ones that you do not want.

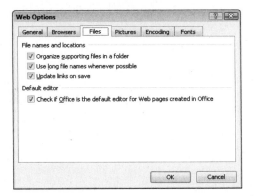

- **Organize Supporting Files in a Folder.** This option is the default setting. PowerPoint saves the needed files in a folder with the same name as the presentation home page. If you deselect this option, all of the supporting files are saved in the same folder as the home page.

- **Use Long File Names Whenever Possible.** This option preserves the long filenames of Windows 95 and higher, which are usually more descriptive than the shorter eight-character names in DOS and Windows 3.1. If you need to transfer the presentation to a server that does not support long filenames, deselect this option.

- **Update Links on Save.** With this option selected, every time you save your PowerPoint presentation in Web format, all of the links are also updated.

- **Check if Office Is the Default Editor for Web Pages Created in Office.** Deselect this option if you want to use a third-party editing program as the default program for editing Web pages. This prevents the appearance of a warning message each time you open the file in the third-party program.

Pictures Options

There is only one control on the Pictures tab: Target Monitor. In most cases, the default setting of 800x600 is the right choice.

The presentation can run at several screen resolutions, with the smallest being 640x480. These numbers refer to the number of pixels, or individual dots, that make up the display. Most people run Windows at 800x600 or higher, but people with older, smaller monitors may still be using 640x480. If you choose a higher setting for the presentation than users have on their screens, then they will have to scroll in Internet Explorer to see the complete slides.

Encoding Options

The Encoding tab contains a few settings that only multilingual offices will use:

- **Save This Document As.** Choose a language character set here. The default for United States usage is US-ASCII, which is acceptable in most cases. A more general setting for any English-speaking country or for languages that use the same alphabet as English is Western European (ISO).

- **Always Save Web Pages in the Default Encoding.** If you want PowerPoint to always rely on Windows' information about what kind of alphabet you are using, select this check box; you will never have to worry about the character set again.

Fonts Options

The Fonts tab enables you to select a character set to encode with the Web presentation. This is mostly an issue when you are creating a presentation in a non-English language. The default setting is English/Western European/Other Latin Script, as shown in Figure 22.19.

FIGURE 22.19

You can choose default fonts.

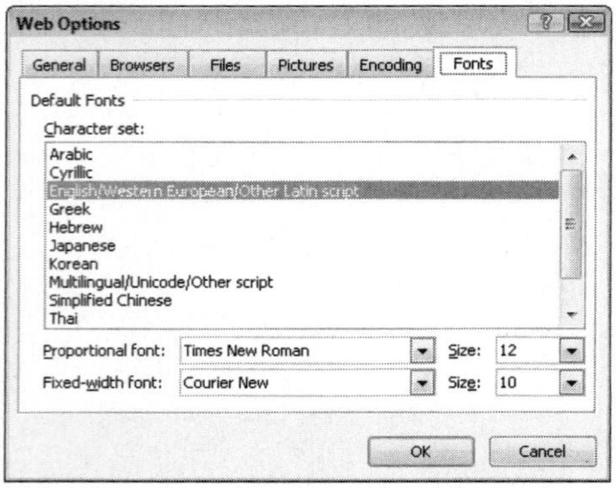

What's all this about character sets? To see a demonstration, open Microsoft Word and choose Insert ⇨ Symbol. Then open the Subset drop-down list. Notice all of the different subsets within this font? Each of these is a character set. Each character has a unique four-digit hexadecimal code — that's over 65,000 possible codes. As a result, there is much more flexibility to a given font than just the few characters that you can generate by typing on your keyboard.

You can also select a font for any text in the Web presentation that does not have a specific font assigned to it. Actually, you select two fonts: one proportional and the other fixed-width, or monospace. Leaving these fonts at their default settings is a good idea because the defaults (Times New Roman and Courier New) are available on almost every computer.

Navigating a Presentation in a Web Browser

To test the Web version of your presentation, you need to use a Web browser. Internet Explorer works very well for this purpose, and it is probably already installed on your computer. Other Web browsers, such as Firefox, are also acceptable. To test your work, follow these steps:

1. Open your Web browser, and type the URL of the presentation (this is the address where you stored it). Then press Enter.

2. The first page appears. Use any of the navigation methods in the following list to move to each slide, making sure that there are no errors.

   - Move to the next slide by clicking the greater-than (>) button at the bottom of the window.
   - Click the Speaker button to pause or play the narration.
   - Click the Slide Show button to switch to a full-screen view of the slide, similar to Slide Show view in PowerPoint. To return to the Web page view, press Esc.
   - To jump to a specific slide, click its name in the left pane (the outline). To hide the outline, click the Outline button.
   - To expand or collapse the outline, click the Expand/Collapse Outline button.

3. To end the show, close the Web browser or navigate to a different Web site.

Making Native PowerPoint Presentations Available Online

If you plan to distribute the presentation as a regular PowerPoint presentation, you must do some extra work. You cannot assume that every member of your intended audience owns a copy of PowerPoint, and so you should make the PowerPoint Viewer available to them. If you are distributing your presentation internally (that is, only to people in your company), then you can make the PowerPoint Viewer program available on your LAN. However, if the presentation will be available to the entire Internet, then you should create a Web page from which the audience can download both the viewer and your presentation file.

EXPERT TIP   If you are providing the presentation in PowerPoint format, you might want to save it as a PowerPoint Show rather than a regular PowerPoint file. A PowerPoint Show is the same as a normal PowerPoint file, except that it opens in Slide Show View instead of normal editing mode.

Creating a Viewer Distribution Package

You first need to package the presentation for distribution. You can do this with the Package for CD feature, except that you save it to a folder instead of a CD. You can then make the contents of this folder available to users.

Use Package for CD to copy the presentation and all of its support files to a folder on your hard disk, as you learned earlier in this chapter. Next, you need to compress, or "ZIP," the contents of the packaged-for-CD folder so that you can make this file available for download on the Web. It is easy to compress files in Windows Vista and Windows XP because they both include built-in support for the ZIP format. To compress your packaged files, follow these steps:

1. In Windows, open the folder where you have copied the packaged files.

2. Select all of the files (Ctrl+A).

3. *(Optional)* .If you want to make the presentation file available separately from the PowerPoint Viewer files, deselect it. To do this, hold down the Ctrl key and click the file.

4. Right-click the selected files and choose Send To ➪ Compressed (Zipped) Folder. A compressed folder is created with the same name as the first file in the group.

5. Give the compressed file a more meaningful name, such as pptviewer.zip. To do this, right-click it, choose Rename, type a name, and then press Enter.

NOTE   Should you type an extension when renaming the ZIP file? This depends on whether or not you have Windows set up to show the file extensions for known file types. If the file that you are renaming appears with a .zip extension on-screen, then type .zip at the end when renaming it. If the extension does not appear, then do not type an extension.

EXPERT TIP   If you want to make many different presentations available online, then you may want to ZIP only the PowerPoint Viewer and its support files, separate from the presentation file. You can then make each presentation file a separate download from the PowerPoint Viewer. To do this, after selecting all of the files in step 2, hold down Ctrl and click the presentation files that you want to deselect.

Creating the Starting Web Page

You can use any Web page creation program to create a simple start page from which to make your presentation available. For example, you can use PowerPoint (which has the advantage of being familiar to you already), FrontPage (Expression Web Designer), Publisher, or Microsoft Word. In this section, I show you how to create a start page with PowerPoint.

To create a single Web page in PowerPoint, start a new presentation that contains a single slide. Then, create instructions and hyperlinks on the slide to access the PowerPoint Viewer and your PowerPoint presentation. Follow these steps:

1. Start a new presentation. It can either be blank or based on a design template.

2. Change the layout of the slide to Title and Content.

3. Add some text to the Title placeholder.

4. Click in the body area, and then click the Bullet List button on the Formatting toolbar to turn off the bullets.

5. Type the instructions, as shown in Figure 22.20.

6. Create the hyperlinks to the files that you have placed on the server. Make sure the links refer to the file copies on your server, not on your hard disk.

7. Save the presentation to the server.

FIGURE 22.20

An instruction page such as this one provides links to the downloadable PowerPoint file, as well as to the PowerPoint Viewer program.

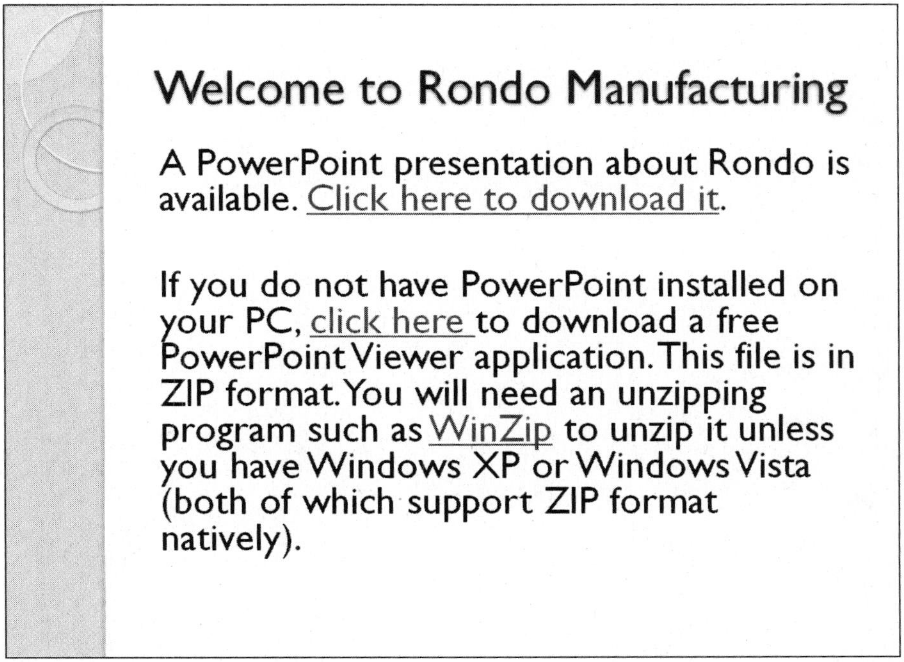

Welcome to Rondo Manufacturing

A PowerPoint presentation about Rondo is available. Click here to download it.

If you do not have PowerPoint installed on your PC, click here to download a free PowerPoint Viewer application. This file is in ZIP format. You will need an unzipping program such as WinZip to unzip it unless you have Windows XP or Windows Vista (both of which support ZIP format natively).

Summary

In this chapter, you learned how to prepare a presentation for mass distribution through CD, e-mail, or the Internet, and how to prepare a presentation for these distribution methods by removing personal information and setting properties. This process involves not only designing the presentation thoughtfully with Internet users in mind, but also saving the file in HTML or MHT format, or providing the audience with a PowerPoint Viewer. You can now save presentations as Web pages, transfer them to Internet servers online, and prepare introductory Web pages that contain links to presentations.

Chapter 23

Sharing and Collaborating

I n many organizations, creating an important presentation is a collaborative project, with several people providing input on a draft. There are several ways to share a draft presentation with others; you can post a presentation to a server, distribute one via e-mail, or post a draft on a document management server. If you have access to a Microsoft Office SharePoint Server (MOSS), you can also create a Slide Library and make individual slides available for reuse.

In this chapter, you'll learn how to use PowerPoint's collaborative tools, such as comments, and how to share and distribute presentations and individual slides in a variety of ways.

Working with Comments

Comments are like sticky notes that you can attach to various spots in a presentation, just as you would attach notes to a paper copy. With comments, multiple reviewers can offer suggestions without changing the actual presentation.

Adding Comments

As you review a presentation, you can insert comments pertaining to a slide as a whole or to an individual object on that slide. To add a comment, follow these steps:

1. Display the slide on which you want to place the comment. If you want to attach the comment to a specific object, select it.

2. On the Review tab, click New Comment. A new comment appears. If you did not choose a specific object in step 1, the comment is placed in the top-left corner of the slide.

3. Type the comment into the box provided, as shown in Figure 23.1.

4. Click away from the comment box to close it.

A small box with your initials and the comment number remain visible on the slide.

To view the comment at any time, click the box containing your initials. To edit the comment, double-click that box, or click it once and then click Edit Comment on the Review tab.

FIGURE 23.1

Type a comment in the box.

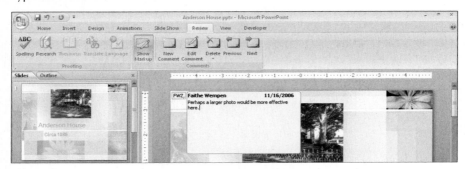

> **NOTE**   Comments are numbered in the order you add them to your presentation, not the slide order. If you add a comment to a slide earlier in your presentation, the numbers for comments later in the presentation do not change. Comments that you add to notes are considered to have been added to the slide itself.

The only places you can't add comments are to the slide masters and layouts. If you want to mark something up for a master or layout, you need to build a slide from that master or layout, and then add the comment.

Printing Comments

To print comments, mark the Print Comments and Ink Markup check box in the Print dialog box, as shown in Figure 23.2. The comments print on a separate page.

FIGURE 23.2

Mark the Print Comments and Ink Markup box to see the comments in print.

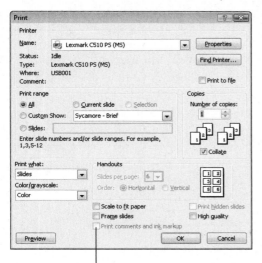

The Print comments and
ink markup checkbox

Reviewing and Deleting Comments

After everyone has had a chance to comment on a draft presentation, you will want to review those comments, and probably delete some or all of them.

EXPERT TIP You do not have to delete the comments to hide them. Instead, you can click the Show Markup button on the Review tab to toggle the comments on/off. Comments do not show in Slide Show view, though.

To move from one comment to the next in the presentation, use the Previous and Next buttons on the Review tab. The comments appear open (so that you can read them) but they are uneditable. To edit a comment, double-click it.

To delete a comment, do any of the following:

- To delete an individual comment, select its box and press the Delete key or click Delete on the Review tab.

- To delete all of the comments on the current slide, click the down arrow below the Delete button on the Review tab and click Delete All Markup on the Current Slide.

- To delete all of the comments in the entire presentation, click the down arrow beneath the Delete button and click Delete All Markup in This Presentation.

Sharing Your Presentation File on a LAN

If your PC is on a network, you can share a presentation file with others by placing it in a location that other network users can access. You can save it to a centrally accessible network drive, such as a file server, or you can make a folder on your own hard disk network-accessible.

To save to a network drive that others also have access to, navigate to that location in the Save As dialog box. In Windows Vista, start by choosing Network; in Windows XP, use the My Network Places shortcut in the Places bar.

To share one of your own local folders on the LAN, follow these steps:

In Windows Vista:

1. From any file management window, right-click the folder or drive to be shared and choose Share.

2. Do any of the following:

   ▪ To share with a particular user who has a user account and password, enter that user's name and click Add.

   ▪ To share with everyone, type **Everyone** and click Add, as shown in Figure 23.3.

FIGURE 23.3

In Windows Vista, you can choose to share with Everyone to provide wide access to the folder location.

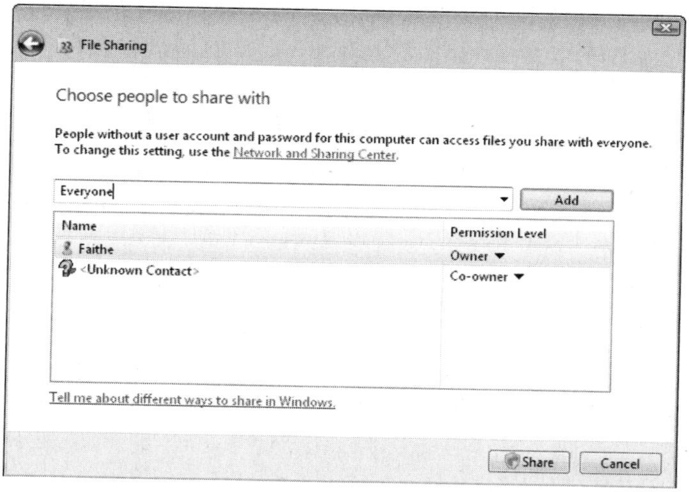

3. The default permission level is Reader, which offers read-only access. To grant write access (so that users can change the presentation), click the down arrow next to the current permission level and click Co-Owner. See Figure 23.4.

You can allow others to make changes to the presentation file by setting the permission level for the Everyone group (or for a specific user) to Co-Owner.

Choosing Co-owner enables
others to change the files.

4. Click the Share button to begin sharing with everyone.

In Windows XP, sharing a folder location is simpler. Follow these steps:

1. From any file management window, right-click the folder or drive to be shared and choose Sharing and Security.

2. On the Sharing tab, mark the Share This Folder on the Network check box. See Figure 23.5.

3. (Optional) To allow others to make changes, mark the Allow Network Users to Change My Files check box.

4. Click OK.

FIGURE 23.5

In Windows XP, you can grant read-only or write permission to the folder.

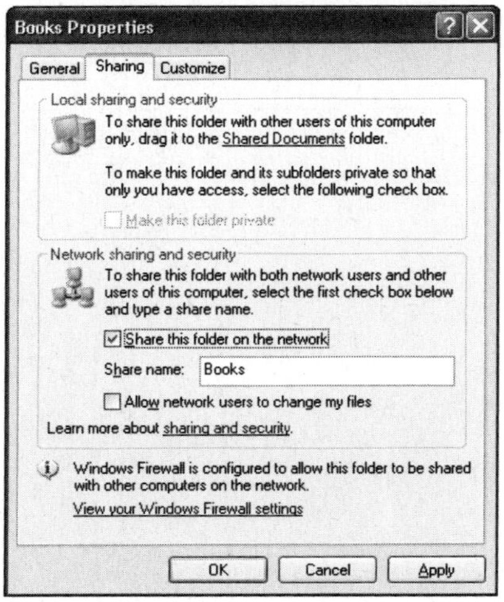

CAUTION When you are editing a presentation stored on a network drive, save it to your hard disk first, and then edit the copy there. Working with an open copy from the network drive can generate a lot of traffic across the network and could cause your document to have problems later.

Sending a Presentation via E-mail

You can e-mail a presentation file to others directly from within PowerPoint using your default e-mail program, such as Outlook, Windows Mail, or Outlook Express. Recipients get the presentation as an e-mail attachment, which they can then open in their own copies of PowerPoint.

To e-mail a presentation from within PowerPoint, follow these steps:

1. From an open presentation, choose Office ➪ Send ➪ E-mail. A new e-mail message opens in your default e-mail application with the presentation set as an attachment as shown in Figure 23.6.

FIGURE 23.6

PowerPoint helps you e-mail presentations easily.

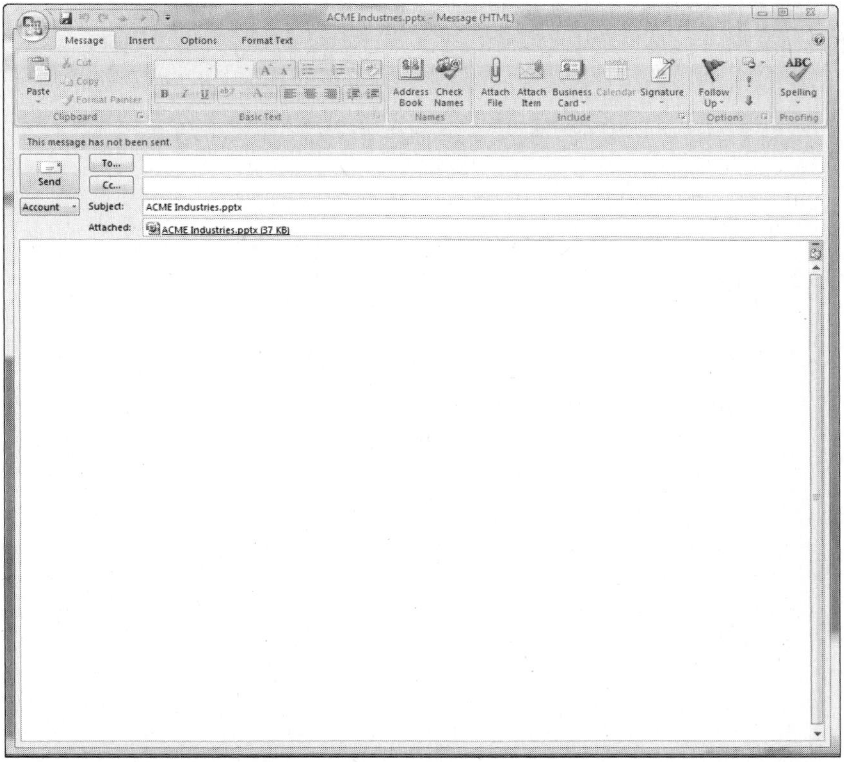

2. Type or select the e-mail addresses for the recipients. The exact procedure depends on the e-mail application you are using.

3. The default Subject is the PowerPoint file's name; change it if desired.

4. If desired, in the body section of the e-mail, type a note telling the recipients what you have attached and what you want them to do with the presentation.

5. Click Send.

Sharing Presentations via Document Libraries and Workspaces

If you have access to a SharePoint server, you can save your presentations on the server in a document library. A *document library* organizes presentation files and manages their availability to other users. Users can check a presentation file out of a document library for editing, and then check it back in when finished. While a presentation is "out," other users can check out read-only copies but cannot upload any changes. This ensures that two people do not try to make changes at the same time to the same file; there is always one current version, and only one person can edit it at a time.

> **NOTE** Document libraries share entire presentations (or other files); *slide libraries,* on the other hand, share individual slides. You learn about slide libraries later in this chapter.

There are several advantages to having your presentation files saved in a document library:

- **Controlled Access:** Access to documents in a document library is controlled by a system administrator, who grants access to users as needed. Individual users and groups of users can have different permissions, such as creating, editing, deleting, and reading.

- **Controlled Processing:** A document library helps manage the approval process when multiple people need to sign off on a draft. You can have SharePoint send notification e-mails, and require signatures prior to accepting new or changed documents.

- **Multiple Access, Single Edit:** With a document library, users can check out a document for either viewing or editing. Multiple people can have a document checked out for viewing, but only one person can have it checked out for editing. Because only one person at a time can have the document checked out for editing, you don't have to worry about merging changes back together or overwriting changes made by different people.

- **Document History:** Because all changes to the file must be checked in via the document library, there is a written history of who had the document and made changes to it. The library can even be set up to require a description of the changes prior to sign off via the approval process.

A SharePoint site can have one or more document libraries and workspaces. A document library typically holds multiple documents, and serves as a more-or-less permanent repository for files. A *document workspace*, on the other hand, is usually temporary and is created specifically for a certain project. Figure 23.7 shows a document workspace with a single document (a presentation) in it.

FIGURE 23.7

A SharePoint document workspace.

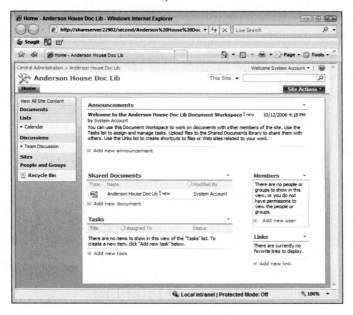

Creating a Document Workspace

To create a document workspace, follow these steps:

1. From an open presentation, choose Office ➪ Publish ➪ Create Document Workspace. The Document Management task pane appears.

2. In the Document Workspace Name box, type the name for the workspace. By default it is the same as the presentation name, but you might want to make it more generic if this workspace will be used to hold multiple files.

3. In the Location for New Workspace box, type the path to the SharePoint server. See Figure 23.8.

FIGURE 23.8

Create a Document Workspace.

Document Management ▾ ✕

Document Workspace

Create a Document Workspace site if you want to share a copy of this document with others. Your local copy of the document will be synchronized with the server so that you can see your changes and work on the document with others. When you click Create, a new site is created automatically.

ⓘ Tell me more...

Document Workspace name:

Anderson Presentations

Location for new workspace:

http://shareserver:22902/A ▾

Create

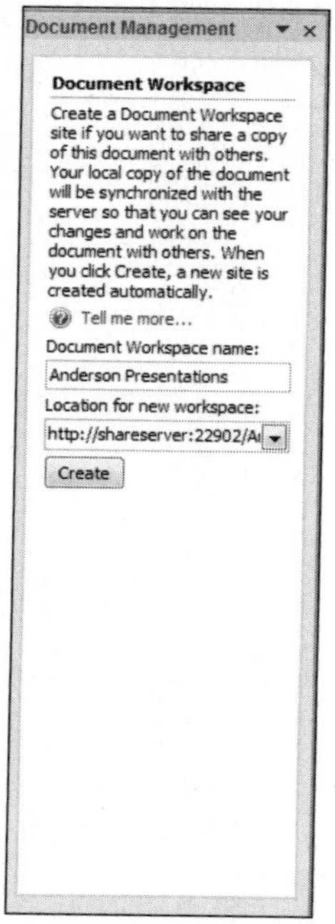

4. Click Create.

5. If prompted, enter your username and password to access the SharePoint site.

   Once you save the presentation file to the workspace, the task pane will change as shown in Figure 23.9.

The task pane displays the status of the document in the workspace.

Across the top of the task pane in Figure 23.10 are five tabs:

- **Status:** Reports whether the document is currently up to date with the copy in the document workspace. (At this point it is because no changes have been made yet.)

- **Members:** Shows who else has access to the presentation in the workspace and what level of access they have. You can click the Add New Members link at the bottom of the pane to allow others to have access.

- **Tasks:** Displays tasks to be done with this presentation and sign offs needed for approval of this document. Examples of tasks you might create include: Submitted for Sign-off, Submitted for Review, Presented, Updated, and so on. You can create tasks by clicking Add New Task at the bottom of that pane.

- **Documents:** This tab shows the documents that are currently open in this workspace. It also allows you to get updates to any of the documents that you have opened from there. And you can click Add New Document at the bottom of the pane to add more documents to the workspace from within PowerPoint.

- **Links:** If any hyperlinks are associated with the workspace, you can access them here.

Once a presentation has been saved to a document workspace, PowerPoint prompts you to synchronize it with the server every time you open or close it. You can choose to Update Workspace Copy or Don't Update, as shown in Figure 23.10.

FIGURE 23.10

You can choose to update the document workspace's copy of the presentation with any changes you make to it.

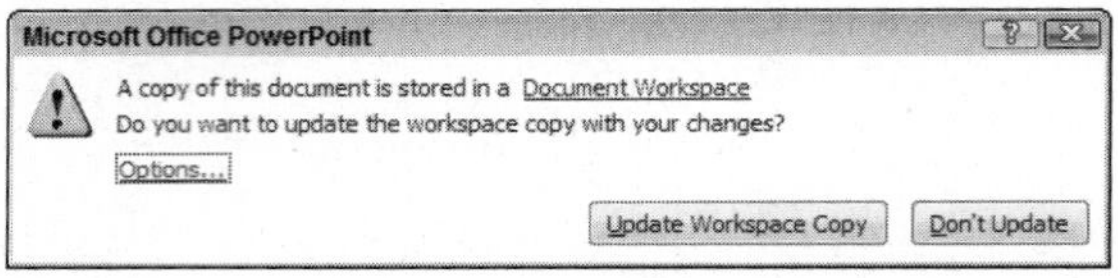

Setting Document Workspace Options

You can fine-tune the way document workspaces operate within PowerPoint by configuring the workspace options. To do so, follow these steps:

1. Choose Office ➪ PowerPoint Options.

2. Click Advanced.

3. Scroll down to the bottom of the window and click Service Options. The Service Options dialog box opens. See Figure 23.11.

4. In the Document Management Pane section, mark or clear either of the check boxes to determine when the Document Management pane will appear:

    The document is part of a workspace or SharePoint site.

    There is important status information regarding the document.

5. Set when update should be retrieved (Always, Sometimes, or Never).

6. Set a time interval for updates in the Get Updates Every ___ Minutes box.

7. Set when a document should be updated on the workspace (Always, Sometimes, or Never).

8. Click OK.

FIGURE 23.11

Set workspace management options here.

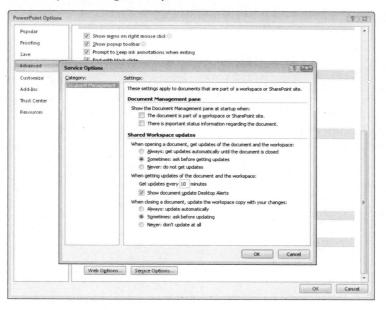

Working with the Server Menu

When you are working with documents that have been saved to a SharePoint server, a Server menu command appears on the Office menu. When you click Server, a menu appears containing commands for working with the document's information stored on the server:

- **View Version History:** Version History information tells you who has checked in and out this document and worked with it. You can use this list to find out who made changes to the presentation since you last accessed it.

- **View Workflow Tasks:** Workflow tasks are the things that you need to do with this presentation. They also appear on the Tasks tab in the Document Management task pane.

- **Document Management Information:** This option opens the Document Management task pane.

- **Check Out:** This option checks the document out of the workspace, so you have exclusive rights to edit it, as described in the next section.

EXPERT TIP An alternative way to save the path to your presentation to a document management server is to choose Office ➪ Publish ➪ Document Management Server. This option opens a Save As box, with the default location being your network shortcuts. If you have placed a shortcut to your SharePoint server here, you can use that to save your presentations to the server. If you haven't, you will need to fill in the full path at the top of the dialog. This is really the hard way around everything you just learned.

Checking a Presentation Out and In

If multiple people have permission to edit a presentation, it is important that only one person edit it at a time to ensure that everyone's changes get made. Therefore you should check the presentation out of the workspace to edit it.

To check out the presentation file, from the Document Management pane, do one of the following:

- Click the drop-down arrow next to the name of the document and select Check Out from the list.
- Choose Office ➪ Server ➪ Check Out.
- If you are browsing the SharePoint site via the Web, hover over the name of a presentation so that an arrow appears, and then click the arrow and click Check Out.

Whatever method you go with, you are prompted to check out the presentation as shown in Figure 23.12.

FIGURE 23.12

Check a file out of the document library or workspace.

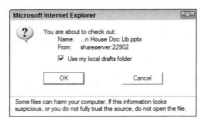

When a presentation file has been checked out, every time you save your changes, you are prompted to check the changed document back into the workspace. If you are ready for those changes to become permanent — that is, a part of the master copy stored in the workspace — choose Yes. If you are still experimenting on the local copy and don't want to save your changes to the workspace, click No.

If you choose Yes to check the document back in, a prompt asks you to add a comment describing the changes you made. Be sure to describe what you did in enough detail so that others can understand. You can also mark the Keep the Document Checked Out After Checking in This Version check box so that you can continue to retain the editing rights to the document. This helps keep the copy on the server up to date without relinquishing your editing rights.

Creating a SharePoint Slide Library

Often people who work at the same company can benefit from sharing slides with one another. For example, a product manager might have slides that describe his product, and a sales or marketing person in the company could save a great deal of time by copying such slides instead of recreating them from scratch. However, it can be time-consuming to wade through large presentations to find a single slide that could be of benefit.

A *slide library* is a specialized type of document library that stores individual slides rather than entire presentations. A slide library enables users to publish individual slides that they think might be of interest to others in their organization. For example, with a slide library, product managers could post two or three slides about their products, and an executive or salesperson could easily browse these and choose the ones needed for a presentation to a particular client.

CAUTION If a slide contains links to other content, such as videos or sounds, that linked content is not included in the slide library.

Just as with a document library, you can check out slides from a slide library and attach an approval process and tasks to them. In addition, you can tag each slide in several ways, and search the slide libraries for just the slides you need.

CAUTION Slide libraries are possible only if the SharePoint server has Microsoft Office SharePoint Server (MOSS) extensions installed and enabled. Not all SharePoint sites have this. If you are not able to access slide libraries, check with your SharePoint administrator.

You might need to activate the Slide Library feature on your SharePoint site before you can use slide libraries. To do so, follow these steps:

1. In your browser, navigate to your SharePoint site.

2. Click the Site Actions button on the upper right of your home page. From the menu that appears, select Site Settings.

3. In the Site Administration column, click Site Features.

4. On the list of site features, click the Activate button for the slide libraries.

Creating a Slide Library

Before you can create a slide library, your SharePoint administrator must give you permission to create slide libraries on your particular site. Once you have access to build a slide library on your SharePoint site, you can add the slide library you want. You must build the slide library from the Web-based interface to your SharePoint site, not directly from within PowerPoint.

Follow these steps to create a slide library:

1. In your browser, navigate to your SharePoint site.

2. Click the Site Actions button and click Create. If you don't have a Create option, you don't have access to create a slide library. Contact your SharePoint administrator and have them give you the access.

3. In the first column of site options, click Slide Library to create a new slide library. The New dialog box opens, as shown in Figure 23.13.

FIGURE 23.13

Create a slide library.

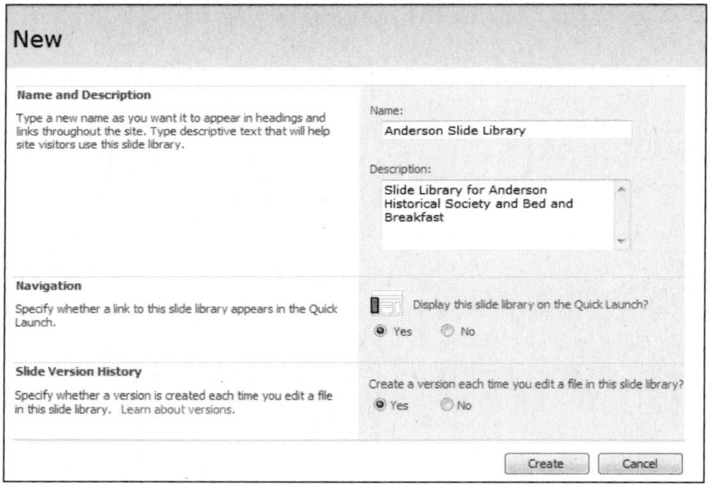

4. Fill in your library name and description.

5. Change the slide version history from No to Yes.

NOTE Creating a versioned library allows you to track when slides are changed, who changed them, and what was changed. In addition, it allows you to keep the old versions of the slides in your library in case you need to refer to them again. It takes more disk space on the server, but it can save you some hassles later when you need to look at the old version of a slide.

6. Click Create.

When you return to the home page of your site, you see your new slide library in the left column of the home page. To access it, click the library name. You can also access the library by clicking the View All Site Content link at the top of that list. Once you view the site content, the slide library shows under Document Libraries.

Now that you have a slide library, it is time to put slides into it. You can add slides from either PowerPoint or the Web interface.

Placing Slides in a Slide Library from PowerPoint

If the presentation is already open in PowerPoint, it's a natural next step to publish slides directly from within PowerPoint to the slide library. To store slides in a Slide Library from within PowerPoint, follow these steps:

1. Open your presentation and choose Office ➪ Publish ➪ Publish Slides. The Publish Slides dialog box opens as shown in Figure 23.14.

FIGURE 23.14

Publish slides to a slide library from within PowerPoint.

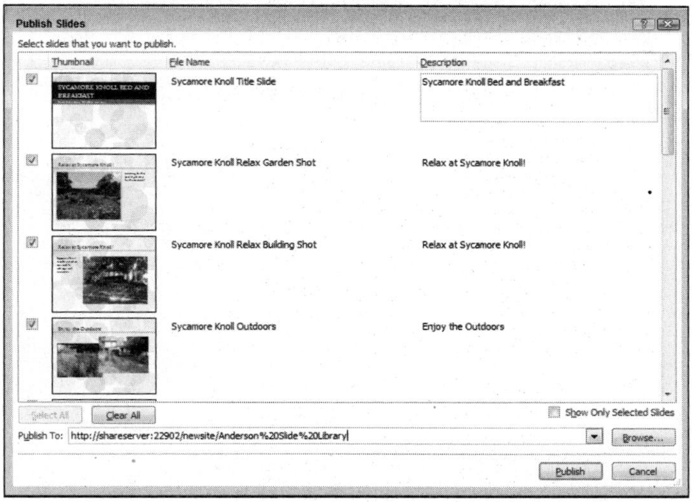

2. Mark the check box for each slide that you want to publish, or click the Select All button to add all of the slides to the library.

   Can't see all of the slides? Use the scroll bar on the right to move down through the slides.

3. (Optional) Change the filename and/or description for a slide if desired.

4. Type the path to your slide library in the Publish To field. The easiest way to get the path to your slide library is to go to it in your browser. Select the beginning of the path. (Don't select from the /Forms part on.)

5. Click the Publish button to publish the slides to the library. (You may be prompted for a username and password for the server.)

   As the slides are prepared for the library, you see status updates in the green status bar, found at the bottom of your presentation, which grows as each slide publishes. When PowerPoint finishes publishing the slides, it returns you to the regular interface.

6. To see the published slides, return to the browser window and refresh the display (press the F5 key). See Figure 23.15.

FIGURE 23.15

The list of published slides in the library.

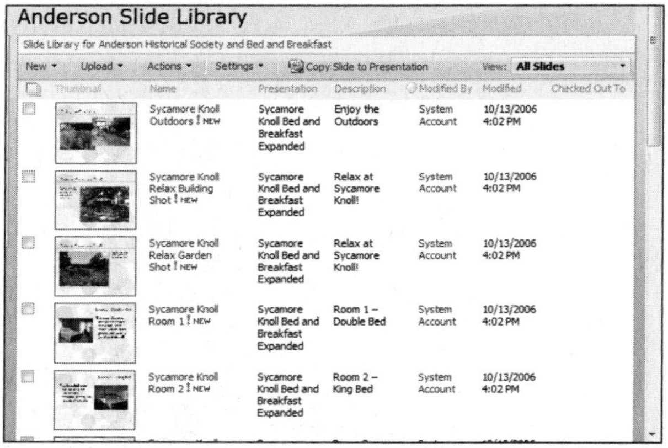

Placing Slides in a Slide Library from the SharePoint Web Interface

You can place slides in a slide library directly from the SharePoint site if you prefer. This method opens PowerPoint, so you must have PowerPoint installed on the PC to do this.

To publish slides starting from the Web interface, follow these steps:

1. View your slide library in a browser window.

2. From the Upload drop-down list, select Publish Slides. Your view switches to PowerPoint. If it wasn't opened, it will open, and a Browse dialog box appears.

3. Browse to the presentation you want to add to your slide library, select it and click Open.

From here, the process is the same as it was in PowerPoint. Select the slides, make any changes to the files or the descriptions, and then click publish. When PowerPoint finishes publishing, it remains open but no presentations are shown.

Once you have published slides to a library, the library shows up in the drop-down list of available libraries on the Publish Slides dialog box. The most recently used library will show in the Publish To field.

Managing Slides in a Slide Library

Once your slides are in the library, you can browse them, delete them, and reorganize them in SharePoint. For example, you might want to create additional folders into which to save slides, or create views that sort by a certain attribute, such as author.

By default, the slides in the library are shown in alphabetical order by filename. To change the sort order, click the title of the column and select the correct sort order from the drop-down menu. Notice that you can't sort the view on the thumbnails.

You can work with the whole library of slides by using any of the first four buttons in the blue bar shown in Figure 23.16. These buttons are discussed in detail in the following sections.

The first four buttons on the blue bar are drop-down menus for managing the slide library.

The New and Upload Buttons

The New button allows you to create folders within your library to help organize your slides. To create a new folder, simply click New, select New Folder, give the new folder a descriptive name, and click OK. The new folder appears at the top of your list. You can publish slides to the new folder from within PowerPoint, or you can open the folder on the SharePoint site and choose Upload ➪ Publish Slides, but you cannot move existing slides from the main library to the folder.

The Upload button allows you to upload new slides.

CROSS-REF For more on uploading new slides, see the section "Placing Slides in a Slide Library from the SharePoint Web Interface" earlier in the chapter.

The Actions Button

The Actions button's menu provides commands for working with the slide library, as follows:

- **Delete Slides:** Enables you to remove one or more slides from the library by selecting the slides, and then choosing Delete Slides. Be aware that deleting a slide deletes its history as well.

- **Edit in Datasheet:** Opens a datatsheet from which you can make bulk changes to certain slide properties.

- **Open with Windows Explorer:** Opens the library in a Windows Explorer view instead of the browser view

- **Connect to Outlook:** Enables you to synchronize the slides in the library using Outlook 2007 when you are not connected to the SharePoint server.

- **View RSS Feed and Alert Me:** These two options notify you when slides in this library have changed. Alert Me sends the notification by e-mail; RSS Feed sends the same notification, but through RSS. If you are using Outlook 2007, use the RSS Feed — it is simpler to understand and easier to work with.

The Settings Button

The first two elements on this menu change how you view the slides in your library. You can create columns that show additional information about the slides, create new views, and more.

Create a Column

Creating a column enables you to add information to slides that you can search for, sort, or filter. By creating your own custom columns of data (and keeping that data current), you can find what you need quickly and easily.

To create columns, follow these steps:

1. Click Settings and select Create Column. A page appears to help you create the column as shown in Figure 23.17.
2. Type a name in the column.
3. Select the type of information for the column. This example selects the Choice option to limit the answers that can be provided for any given slide.
4. Describe the new column and complete the column specific information. This information will change for each type of column you select.
5. Set up the other fields as needed for your column type.
6. Click OK

The new column appears to the right of the other columns. Even though it is a required column, it is blank. This is because the slides that are already in the library were added before this column. When you work with the details and properties of each slide, you are prompted to add this value.

FIGURE 23.17

Set up a new column for slide type.

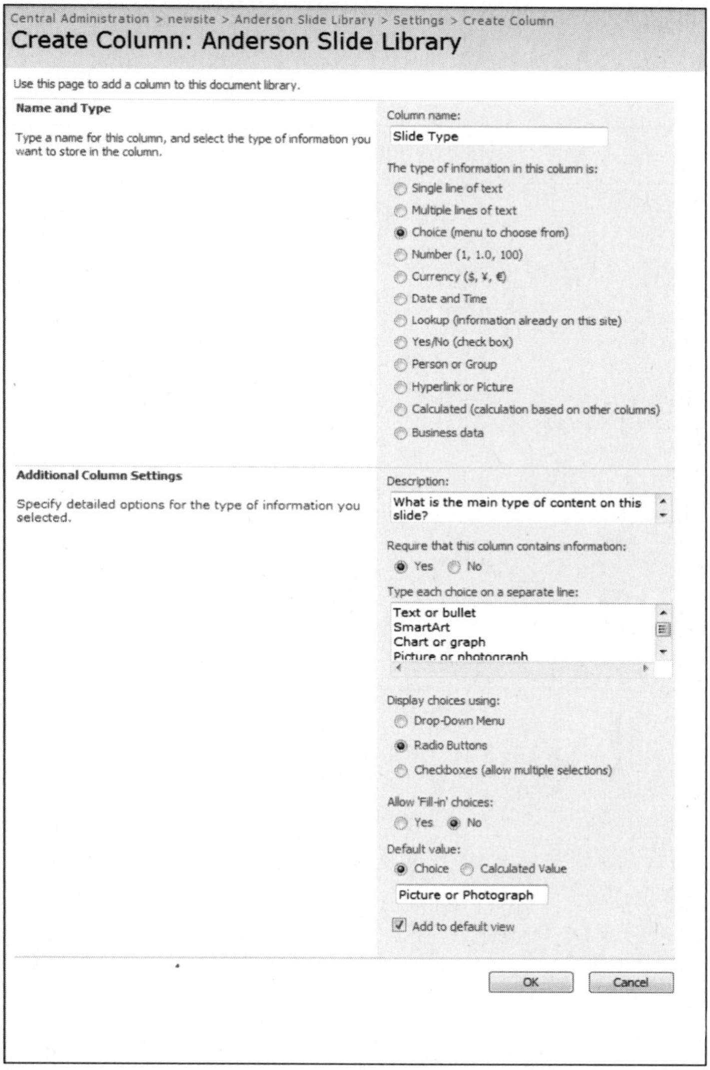

Create a View

A view is a viewing specification applied to a slide library that enables you to see just the slides and details that you are interested in. For example, Figure 23.18 shows a view that omits the presentation name but includes the Slide Type column created in the preceding section.

FIGURE 23.18

This alternate view of the slide library contains columns that are different from the default.

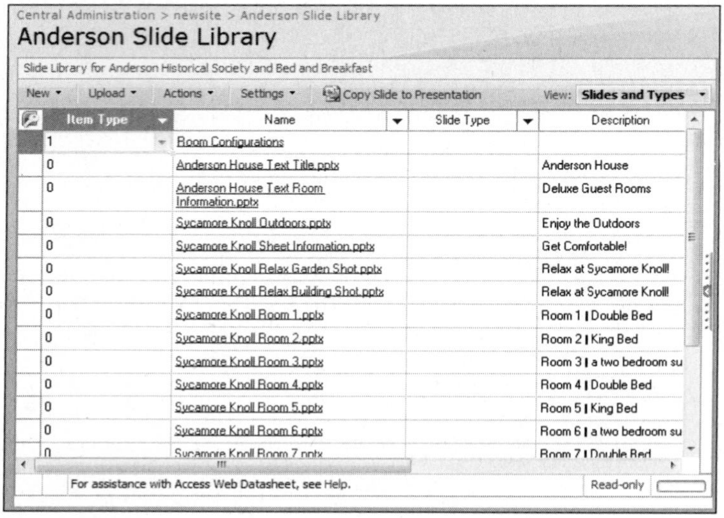

To create a view, follow these steps:

1. Click Settings and select Create View.

2. From the list of view types, select the view you want to make. For example, you might start with the Standard View.

3. Type a name for the view in the Name box.

4. Mark or clear check boxes for the desired columns, and choose their positions from the left. See Figure 23.19.

5. In the Sort section, choose the columns by which to sort, and in what order.

6. (Optional) Set up any filtering or grouping you want from the Filter or Group By section, respectively. For filtering, you can choose Show Items Only When the Following is True, and then set up one or more criteria.

   For grouping, you can choose to group by a certain column's value.

7. Click OK

FIGURE 23.19

Mark or clear check boxes for the desired columns and set their positions.

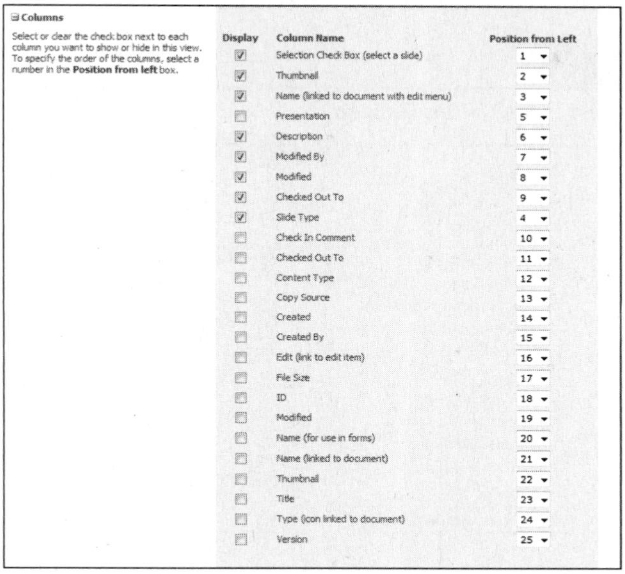

Display	Column Name	Position from Left
☑	Selection Check Box (select a slide)	1 ▾
☑	Thumbnail	2 ▾
☑	Name (linked to document with edit menu)	3 ▾
☐	Presentation	5 ▾
☑	Description	6 ▾
☑	Modified By	7 ▾
☑	Modified	8 ▾
☑	Checked Out To	9 ▾
☑	Slide Type	4 ▾
☐	Check In Comment	10 ▾
☐	Checked Out To	11 ▾
☐	Content Type	12 ▾
☐	Copy Source	13 ▾
☐	Created	14 ▾
☐	Created By	15 ▾
☐	Edit (link to edit item)	16 ▾
☐	File Size	17 ▾
☐	ID	18 ▾
☐	Modified	19 ▾
☐	Name (for use in forms)	20 ▾
☐	Name (linked to document)	21 ▾
☐	Thumbnail	22 ▾
☐	Title	23 ▾
☐	Type (icon linked to document)	24 ▾
☐	Version	25 ▾

*☐ Columns — Select or clear the check box next to each column you want to show or hide in this view. To specify the order of the columns, select a number in the **Position from left** box.*

Manage Library Settings

The Document Library Settings option enables the owner of a slide library to specify who can view and change its slides, who can create new views, and how views are used. These skills are beyond the scope of this chapter; see your SharePoint administrator for help with them.

Working with Slide Properties

Adding slide properties to each slide in your library helps you find the slides you need more easily. As long as you are diligent about keeping the slide properties up to date, you will find that they are an easy way to sort, organize, and find just the slides you need.

Setting Properties for Multiple Slides at Once

As you learned earlier in the chapter, you can create a new column and add it to a view to store additional information about the slides. You can easily populate the new column with values by using Datasheet view, as in the following steps:

 You learned how to add a column in the section called "The Settings Button."

1. From the Action menu, click Edit in Datasheet. The Datasheet view appears as shown in Figure 23.20. This sheet lets you change properties for each slide by working down the column for the property you want to change.

FIGURE 23.20

Anderson Slide Library datasheet view.

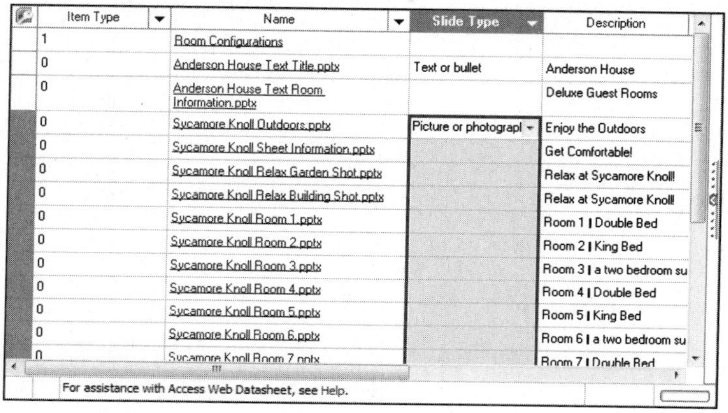

CAUTION **Notice the 1 in the Item Type for Room Configurations? It means that Room Configurations is a folder, not a slide. You can't change properties for a folder, only for slides in that folder.**

2. Click in the Slide Type column for the first slide and select a slide type using the drop-down list at its right. This sets the property for the first slide.
3. Click in the Slide Type cell for the first slide in a group and select a slide type. In Figure 23-20, that is Sycamore Knoll Outdoors.pptx. So, from the drop-down list at its right, you would select Picture or photograph.
4. Click and drag in the Slide Type field to select the field for the slide that you just set and for the other slides in the group.
5. Right-click the selected cells and select Fill ➪ Fill Down to fill that value into the cells below it.

Setting Properties for a Single Slide

In addition to setting the properties of slides in bulk through Datasheet view, you can work with the properties of individual slides. To do so, hover over the slide name, so that an arrow appears, and then click the arrow to open a menu. Then choose Edit Properties. The properties for that slide appear, as shown in Figure 23.21. Make any changes as desired, and click OK to save them.

FIGURE 23.21

Change slide properties on a single slide, and then click OK.

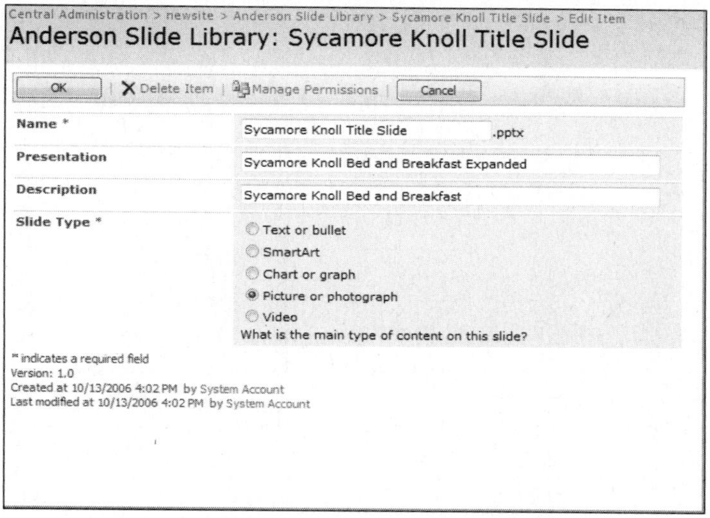

Central Administration > newsite > Anderson Slide Library > Sycamore Knoll Title Slide > Edit Item

Anderson Slide Library: Sycamore Knoll Title Slide

| OK | ✕ Delete Item | 🖳 Manage Permissions | Cancel |

Name *	Sycamore Knoll Title Slide .pptx
Presentation	Sycamore Knoll Bed and Breakfast Expanded
Description	Sycamore Knoll Bed and Breakfast
Slide Type *	○ Text or bullet ○ SmartArt ○ Chart or graph ◉ Picture or photograph ○ Video What is the main type of content on this slide?

* indicates a required field
Version: 1.0
Created at 10/13/2006 4:02 PM by System Account
Last modified at 10/13/2006 4:02 PM by System Account

Pulling Slides from the Library to PowerPoint

Once you have slides in your library, you will work with them primarily from within PowerPoint. You can quickly pull slides into presentations using the following steps:

1. Open the presentation into which you want to insert one or more slides.

2. On the Home tab, click the down arrow under the New Slides button and click Reuse Slides.

3. In the task pane that appears, click Open a Slide Library.

4. In the Folder Name box, type or paste the URL for your library. If you paste it from your browser, remove everything after the slide library name.

EXPERT TIP To best see all of the slides, you might want to widen and/or undock the task pane. To undock it, click the blue bar at the top of the task pane and drag it toward the middle of the screen. Drag the edge of the task pane to widen it.

5. (Optional) To keep the source formatting for the slide(s), mark the Keep Source Formatting check box.

6. (Optional) Mark the check box for Tell Me When the Slide Changes. This ensures that if someone else changes this slide and checks it into the library, you will be notified.

7. Click a slide to add it to the presentation.

EXPERT TIP If your library is very large and you want to search for slides that match a certain criteria, type criteria in the Search box. This works only if your server supports Search.

8. Close the task pane.

Summary

In this chapter, you learned how to share both your presentations and your slides with other users. You learned about sharing full presentation files using a LAN drive, e-mail, and a basic SharePoint document library. As you read about each method of sharing full presentations, you learned good practices for keeping information current. You can use the Slide Libraries, a special SharePoint library, to store individual slides for access later. You can customize the Library by changing document properties and views. You can also pull information from the Libraries to your presentations and keep the presentation content current. Finally, you learned about using comments to share information with other users of your presentation.

Part IV

Project Labs

Lab 1

Presenting Content Without Bulleted Lists

In this lab, you have the opportunity to practice several ways of serving up content that's free from the traditional bulleted-list structure.

You are creating slides for a computer technology teacher to use in a class on PC hardware. The lecture she is preparing for involves safety issues when working on a PC.

Lab 1A: Using Shapes as Text Boxes

In this lab session, you create a set of starbursts and use them as text boxes.

Level of difficulty: Moderate

Time to complete: 10 to 20 minutes

1. **Open the file Lab1A.pptx from the Labs folder (from the CD) and save it as MyLab1A.pptx.**

2. **Insert a new slide that uses the Title Only layout.**

   a. On the Home tab, click the down arrow below New Slide.

   b. Click Title Only.

   c. In the title box, type Protect Yourself from Hazards.

2A

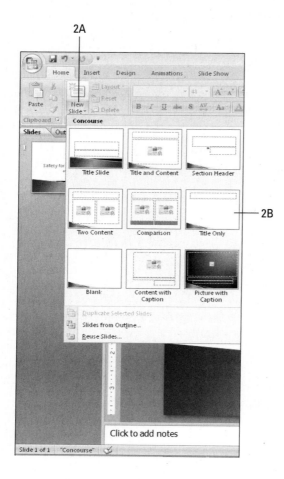

2B

3. **Draw an Explosion shape on the slide.**

   a. On the Insert tab, open the Shapes gallery and choose Explosion 1 from the Stars and Banners section.

   b. Drag on the slide to create the shape (any size).

3A

4. **Apply an orange and white Path gradient to the shape and remove the outline.**

   a. Click the shape to select it.

   b. On the Drawing Tools Format tab, open the Shape Fill button's menu and select Gradient ⇨ More Gradients.

   c. Click Fill, and then click Gradient Fill.

   d. Set the Type to Path.

   e. In the Gradient Stops section, open the Color button's menu and choose white.

   f. Open the Gradient Stops list and choose Stop 2.

   g. Open the Color button's menu and choose the bright orange Standard color.

   h. Drag the Stop Position slider to 75%.

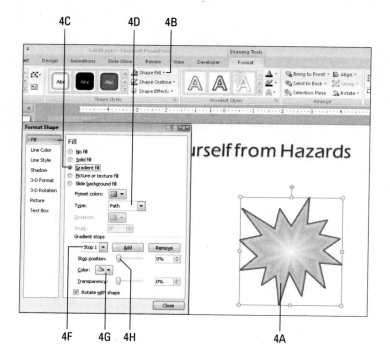

i. Click the Line Color category at the left.

j. Click No Line.

k. Click Close.

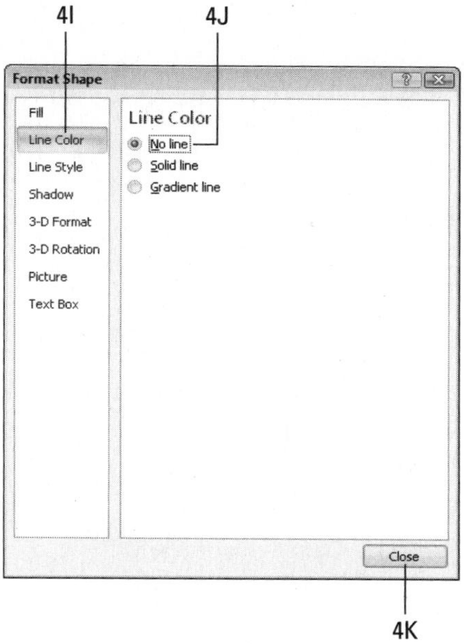

4I **4J**

Format Shape

Fill
Line Color
Line Style
Shadow
3-D Format
3-D Rotation
Picture
Text Box

Line Color

○ No line
○ Solid line
○ Gradient line

Close

4K

5. **Size the shape to 3" × 3" and position it below the word Hazards.**

   a. Click the shape to select it.

   b. On the Drawing Tools Format tab, in the Size group, set the Height and Width values to 3" each.

   c. Drag the shape so that it is about ½ inch below the word Hazards and centered beneath it horizontally.

6. **Create a copy of the shape, and flip it horizontally.**

   a. Hold down the Ctrl key and drag the shape to the left, creating a copy next to the original.

   b. On the Drawing Tools Format tab, click Rotate, and click Flip Horizontal.

7. **Modify the gradient for the copy so that it uses bright red instead of orange.**
   a. Select the copy you just made.
   b. Open the Shape Fill button's menu and choose Gradient ⇨ More Gradients.
   c. Open the Gradient Stops menu and choose Stop 2.
   d. Open the Color button's menu and choose the bright red Standard color.
   e. Click Close.

7B

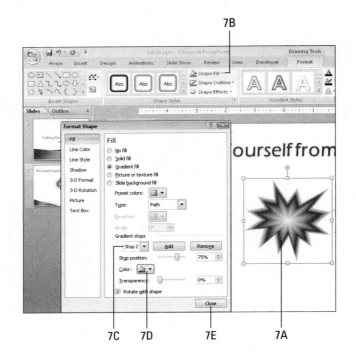

7C   7D   7E   7A

8. **Create a copy of the orange shape, and place it to the left of the red shape.**

   a. Hold down the Ctrl key and drag the shape to the left of the red shape.

9. **Modify the gradient for the new shape so that it uses bright yellow instead of orange.**

   a. Select the shape.

   b. Open the Shape Fill button's menu and choose Gradient ➪ More Gradients.

   c. Open the Gradient Stops menu and choose Stop 2.

   d. Open the Color button's menu and choose the bright yellow Standard color.

   e. Click Close.

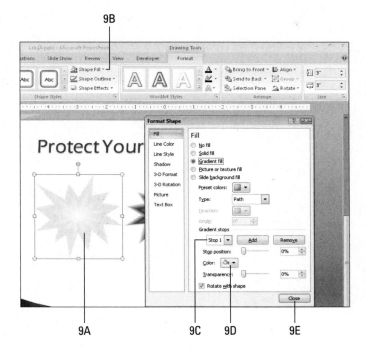

10. **In the yellow shape, type Watch for protruding wires and change the text color to black.**

   a. Click the yellow shape.

   b. Type **Watch for protruding wires**. The text appears in white.

   c. Select the text you just typed.

   d. On the Drawing Tools Format tab, in the WordArt Styles group, click Text Fill and change the text to the black swatch in the color theme.

10D

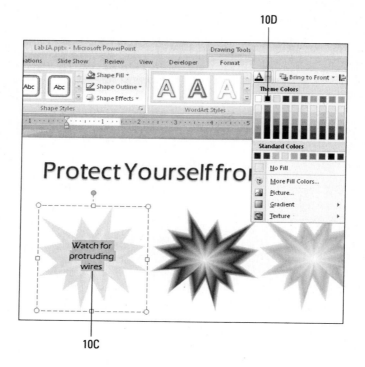

10C

11. In the red shape (center), type "Don't wear dangling jewelry" and change the text color to black.

12. In the orange shape (right), type "Inner edges of cases may be sharp" and change the text color to black.

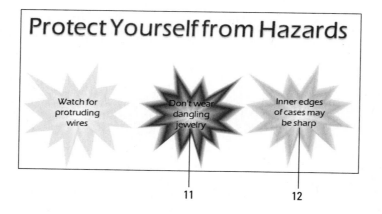

11   12

13. Apply custom animation so that each shape pinwheels in individually when you click the mouse.

   a. Select the yellow shape.

   b. On the Animations tab, click Custom Animation.

   c. Click Add Effect.

   d. Click Entrance.

   e. Click More Effects.

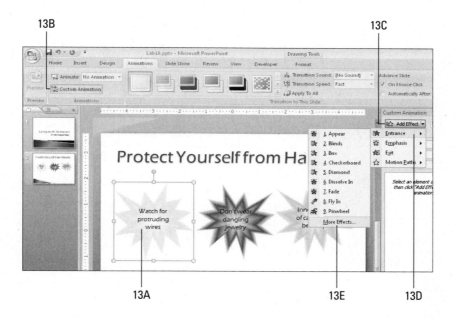

   f. In the Add Entrance Effect dialog box, choose Pinwheel.

   g. Click OK.

13F   13G

14. **Apply the same pinwheel entrance effect to the red and orange shapes (individually).**

   a. Select the red shape.

   b. Click Add Effect.

   c. Click Entrance.

   d. Click More Effects.

   e. Choose Pinwheel.

   f. Repeat steps 14a through 14e for the orange shape.

15. **Check the animation in Slide Show view.**

   a. Click the Slide Show View button in the status bar.

   b. Click the mouse and watch the first shape appear. Repeat for each shape.

   c. Press Esc to return to Normal view.

16. **Save your work and close the presentation file.**

   You should have saved the file in step 1 as MyLab1A.pptx, so you can simply resave with the Save button on the Quick Access Toolbar.

Lab 1B: Converting Bullets to SmartArt

If a presentation is already set up using bulleted lists, you might not want to take the time to retype them in shapes. You can easily convert a bulleted list to SmartArt in PowerPoint 2007, making the list appear more graphical and interesting. In this exercise, you create a bulleted list and then convert it to SmartArt.

Level of difficulty: Easy

Time to complete: 5 to 10 minutes

1. **Open the file Lab1B.pptx from the Labs folder (from the CD) and save it as MyLab1B.pptx.**

2. **Convert the content on slide #2 to SmartArt.**

   a. Display slide #2 (Electrostatic Discharge).

   b. Right-click the slide content and choose Convert to SmartArt.

   c. Click the Vertical Bullet List type (leftmost on the top row).

      The list is converted to a SmartArt diagram.

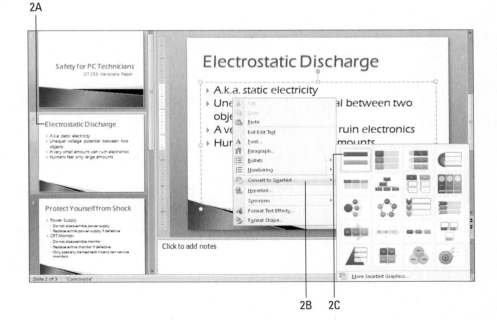

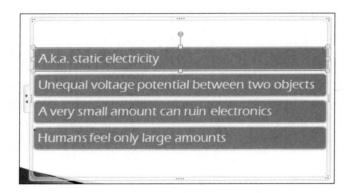

3. **Convert the content on slide #3 to SmartArt.**

   a. Display slide #3 (Protect Yourself from Shock).

   b. Right-click the slide content and choose Convert to SmartArt.

   c. Click the Vertical Block List type (second from the left on the top row).

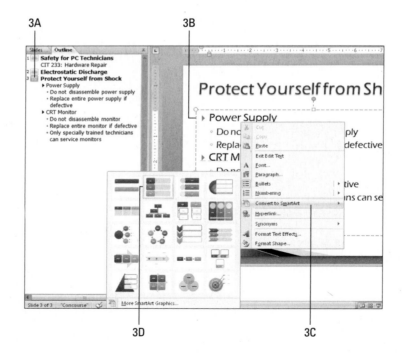

4. Apply a Quick Style to the SmartArt on slide #3.

   a. On the SmartArt Tools Design tab, open the SmartArt Styles gallery and click the second 3-D style.

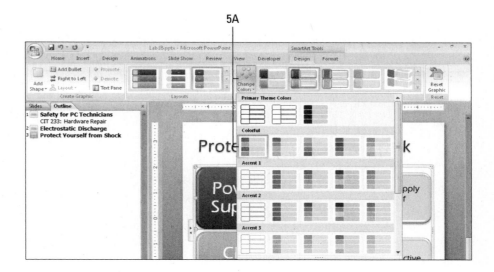

5. Change the colors for the SmartArt on slide #3 to Colorful – Accent Colors.

   a. On the SmartArt Tools Design tab, click Change Colors and click the first color set in the Colorful section.

6. Save your work and close the presentation file.

   You should have saved the file in step 1 as MyLab1B.pptx, so you can simply resave with the Save button on the Quick Access Toolbar.

Lab 2

Project Lab: Adding Sound and Movement to a Presentation

In an ideal world, you'd have great video equipment to create live-action movies for your audiences, but that's not always the case. Often you're stuck with a bunch of static images, and you need to make them as lively and animated as possible within the confines of PowerPoint.

In this lab, you animate a presentation for Spice Meadow Shelties, a small kennel that breeds purebred Shetland Sheepdogs. The graphics and text are already in place. Your job is to apply animations and transitions to make the presentation more interesting and appealing.

IN THIS LAB

Applying custom animations

Assigning transitions to slides

Adding a musical soundtrack from a file

Lab 2A: Fading Text and Graphics In and Out

In this lab session, you add some text to a slide. You then animate it and the photos so that the first set fades in and out, and then the other set fades in. Even though the text and pictures seem to overlap in Normal view, they appear at different times in Slide Show view so there is no conflict.

Level of difficulty: Moderate

Time to complete: 15 to 30 minutes

1. Open the file Lab2A.pptx from the Labs folder (from the CD accompanying the book) and save it as MyLab2A.pptx.

2. **On slide #2, set up the Champion Sires text box to appear by fading in when the slide first appears.**

   a. On the Animations tab, click Custom Animation. The Custom Animation task pane appears.

   b. Select the text box on the left (Champion Sires).

   c. Choose Add Effect ➪ Entrance ➪ More Effects.

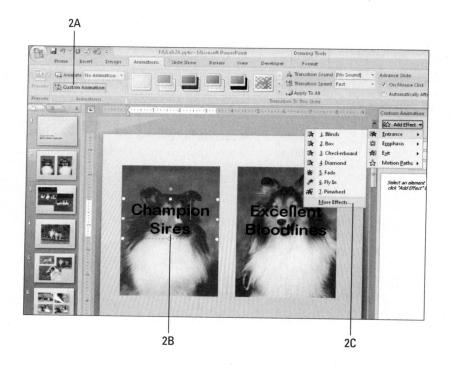

   d. In the Add Entrance Effect dialog box, choose Fade.

   e. Click OK.

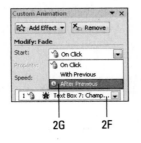

2E   2D

f. In the Custom Animation pane, select the new animation.

g. Open the Start drop-down list and choose After Previous.

2G   2F

3. **Set up the picture on the right to appear by fading in simultaneously with the text that you animated in step 2.**

   a. Select the picture on the right.

   b. Choose Add Effect ⇨ Entrance ⇨ Fade. (Notice that Fade is on the top-level list because you recently used it. It might have already been in step 2 but it was good to learn the other technique.)

3A

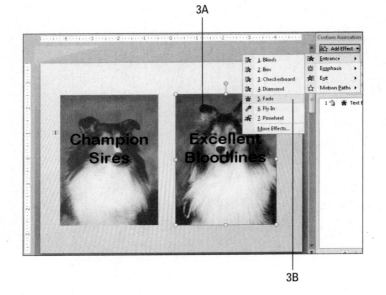

3B

c. Click the new animation in the Custom Animation pane.

d. Open the Start drop-down list and choose With Previous.

3C   3D

4. **Repeat steps 2 and 3, but this time set up exit effects instead of entrance effects.**

a. Create an exit effect for the left text box set to occur After Previous.

b. Create an exit effect for the right picture set to occur With Previous.

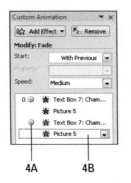

4A   4B

5. **Create a delay of five seconds between the text box's entrance and its exit.**

a. Select the exit animation for the text box in the Custom Animation pane.

b. Open its menu and choose Timing.

5B   5A

c. Enter 5 in the Delay box.

d. Click OK.

5C   5D

6. Repeat step 5 for the exit animation for the right picture.

7. Create a Fade entrance effect for the opposite text box (the one on the right) that occurs After Previous.

   Refer to step 2.

8. Create a Fade entrance effect for the opposite picture (the one on the left) that occurs With Previous.

   Refer to step 3.

9. Preview the slide's animation and check your work.

   a. Click the Slide Show View button.

   b. If you did the animation correctly, the Champion Sires text and the right photo will appear first, fading in.

   c. They will pause for five seconds, fade out, and then the opposite text and picture will fade in. They will remain on the screen until you click to move to the next slide.

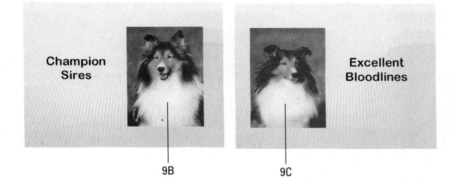

                      9B   9C

10. Press Esc to exit Slide Show view.

11. Save your work.

Lab 2B: Replacing One Picture with Another

In this lab session, you place one photo on top of another, and animate the top one so that it disappears, revealing the one underneath, after a delay.

Level of difficulty: Moderate

Time to complete: 10 to 15 minutes

1. **Open the presentation file if it is not already open.**

   Start in your completed file from the previous project (MyLab2A.pptx), or open Lab2B.pptx from the Labs folder if you did not do the previous lab.

2. **Save the file as MyLab2B.pptx.**

3. **Display slide #3, and arrange the pictures so that they are stacked one on top of the other.**

   a. Click slide #3 in the Slides pane.

   b. Drag the pictures so that they are both in the same spot in the center of the slide. Only the top one (where all three dogs are sitting up) should be visible.

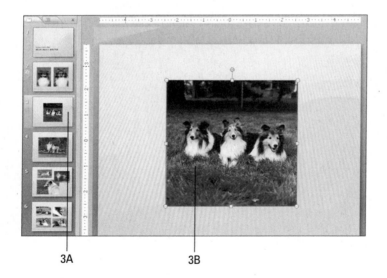

3A   3B

4. Add a Checkerboard exit animation to the top picture so that it goes away after being displayed for six seconds.

    a. If it does not already appear, display the Custom Animation task pane by clicking Custom Animation on the Animations tab.

    b. Click the top picture to select it.

    c. Choose Add Effect ⇨ Exit ⇨ More Effects.

    d. In the Add Exit Effect dialog box, choose Checkerboard.

    e. Click OK.

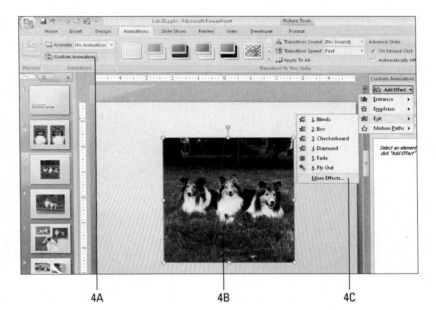

4D

4E

f. Select the animation in the Custom Animation pane and open its menu.

g. Choose Timing.

4G   4F

h. In the Checkerboard dialog box, open the Start drop-down list and choose After Previous.

i. Type **6** in the Delay box.

j. Open the Speed drop-down list and choose 2 Seconds (Medium).

k. Click OK.

5. Preview the slide's animation and check your work.

a. Click the Slide Show View button. If you did the animation correctly, the top picture will appear, and after six seconds, it will checkerboard into the picture beneath it.

b. Press Esc to return to PowerPoint.

6. Save your work.

Lab 2C: Zooming In on a Picture

In this lab session, you make a picture grow so that it looks like the camera is zooming in on it.

Level of difficulty: Easy

Time to complete: 5 minutes

1. Open the presentation file if it is not already open.

Start in your completed file from the previous project (MyLab2B.pptx), or open Lab2C.pptx from the Labs folder if you did not do the previous lab.

2. Save the file as MyLab2C.pptx.

3. **On slide #4, set an emphasis animation for the picture to Grow.**

   a. If it does not already appear, display the Custom Animation task pane by clicking Custom Animation on the Animations tab.

   b. Click the picture to select it.

   c. Choose Add Effect ➪ Emphasis ➪ Grow/Shrink.

4. **Set the animation to occur after five seconds.**

   a. Select the animation in the Custom Animation pane and open its menu.

   b. Click Timing on the menu that appears.

   c. In the Grow/Shrink dialog box, set the Start value to After Previous.

   d. Set the Delay to 2 Seconds.

   e. Set the Speed to 5 Seconds (Very Slow).

   f. Click OK.

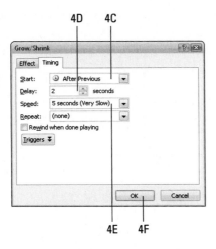

5. **Preview the slide's animation and check your work.**

   a. Click the Slide Show View button. If you did the animation correctly, the picture will begin a slow zoom in after two seconds.

   b. Press Esc to return to PowerPoint.

6. **Save your work.**

Lab 2D: More Animation Practice

In this lab session, you complete the animations for the rest of the presentation. This project is more challenging, not because of the animations per se, but because less detailed instructions are provided here. You will need to determine how to accomplish each animation on your own.

Level of difficulty: Challenging

Time to complete: 15 to 30 minutes

1. **Open the presentation file if it is not already open, and save it as MyLab2D.pptx.**

   Start in your completed file from the previous project (MyLab2C.pptx), or open Lab2D.pptx from the Labs folder if you did not do the previous lab.

2. Add a text box to slide #4, near the bottom of the picture, with the following text: **Puppies raised with adult dogs are better socialized.**

   Make the text center-aligned, Arial Rounded Bold MT font, 24 point, and white.

3. Animate the text box you just added so that it appears after the picture's Grow effect has taken place, and two seconds later it changes color to bright yellow with a Brush-On Color effect.

   (Hint: Apply two separate animations to the text: an entrance with an Appear effect, and an emphasis with a Brush-On Color effect.)

4. On slide #5, animate each of the pictures to appear using the Dissolve In animation, one after the other, with a two-second delay between them. Set the animation speed for each of them to Fast.

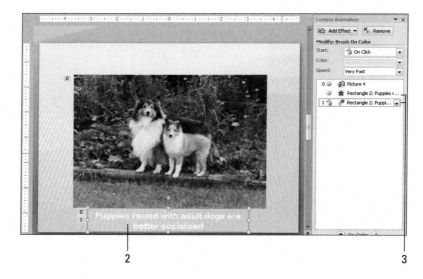

First

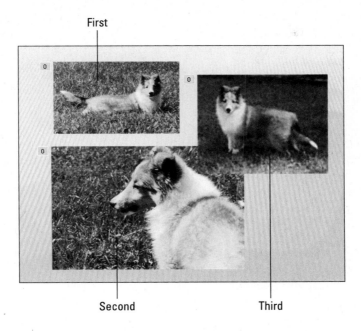

Second   Third

5. **On slide #6, use the Align commands to more precisely align all four pictures.**

To do this, first align the top two pictures at their tops, and then align the two bottom pictures at their tops.

Next align the two left pictures at the left side, and then the two right pictures at the right side, if they are not already aligned.

6. Animate the pictures on slide #6 so that the top-left and bottom-right pictures appear (simultaneously) first using the Diamond entrance effect, and then a three-second delay. The other two pictures then appear simultaneously using the same effect.

7. On slide #7, make the top-left picture fade out after six seconds, and at the same time as it is fading out, make the bottom-right picture fade in.

8. View the entire presentation in Slide Show view to check your work.

9. Return to PowerPoint and save your work.

First, these two

...then these two

This one appears for six seconds...

...then this one fades in as the other fades out

Lab 2E: Using Transitions and Soundtracks

In this project, you set up each slide to automatically advance after 15 seconds, and you specify a transition effect. You also add a MIDI-based soundtrack to the presentation that will loop continuously as long as the presentation is playing.

Level of difficulty: Easy

Time to complete: 5 to 10 minutes

1. **Open the presentation file if it is not already open, and save it as MyLab2E.pptx.**

   Start in your completed file from the previous project (MyLab2D.pptx), or open Lab2E.pptx from the Labs folder if you did not do the previous lab.

2. **Set all slides to the Fade Smoothly transition automatically after 15 seconds.**

   a. On the Animations tab, in the Transition to This Slide group, click Fade Smoothly.

   b. Open the Transition Speed drop-down list and choose Slow.

   c. Mark the Automatically After check box and enter 00:15 for it.

   d. Click Apply to All.

3. **Locate a MIDI, WMA, or MP3 music clip.**

   There are many sources of free music on the Internet. Use whatever music you think would be appropriate for this presentation. If possible, try to find something without lyrics so that a speaker will be audible while the presentation is showing in the background.

   If you do not want to take the time to find one for this lab, search your computer for sound files (Start ➪ Search). Sample sounds may be available in the My Music folder, depending on the Windows version.

4. Insert the music clip on slide #1, and set it up to play automatically when the slide appears and to continue playing until the presentation is over (or until the clip ends).

 a. Display slide #1.

 b. On the Insert tab, choose Sound ⇨ Sound from File.

4B

 c. In the Insert Sound dialog box, navigate to and select the sound clip.

 d. Click OK.

4C   4D

e. In the dialog box that appears, click Automatically.

A speaker icon appears on the slide.

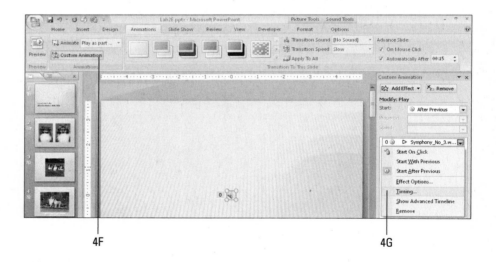

4E

f. On the Animations tab, click Custom Animation to display the Custom Animation task pane if it is not already visible.

g. In the Custom Animation task pane, open the object's menu and choose Timing.

4F   4G

h. Click the Effect tab.

i. In the Stop Playing section, click the After button, and then enter **999** in its text box. This makes it play continuously, looping back through if needed.

j. Click OK.

k. Drag the sound icon off the edge of the slide so that it doesn't show in the presentation.

4H   4I   4J

5. Watch the entire presentation in Slide Show view, without clicking, to check the transitions, animation, and music. Then adjust any transition timings that might seem awkward to you.

6. Save your work.

Lab 3

Creating a Menu-Based Navigation System

When you create user-interactive presentations that contain many slides, it is considered courteous to provide your audience with a navigation system so that they can browse through the presentation without having to view every single slide. Menu systems can be as simple or as complex as you like and can be integrated into the slide design.

IN THIS LAB
Making room for a navigation bar
Creating a navigation bar
Creating a graphical navigation system

The Scenario

In this project lab, you learn how to create a navigation system in a presentation that is designed to teach computer technicians about safety issues for working on PCs. You modify the presentation's layout and design to make room for a menu system, and then you create navigational hyperlinks on the Slide Master.

Lab 3A: Making Room for a Navigation Bar

In this lab session, you start with a plain-looking presentation and modify its Slide Master to make room for a menu system on the left side of the slide.

This lab session includes some cleanup work on a "messy" PowerPoint file that is missing a layout needed for some of the slides. This session simulates the type of cleanup situations you might run into in everyday work on older presentation files.

Level of difficulty: Moderate

Time to complete: 15 to 30 minutes

1. **Open the file Lab03A.pptx from the Labs folder (from the CD accompanying the book) and save it as MyLab03A.pptx.**

2. **Display the Slide Master.** On the View tab, click Slide Master.

3. **On the top-level Slide Master, draw a rectangle that covers the entire slide vertically and stops at the 3" mark on the ruler.**

   a. Click the Insert tab.

   b. Click Shapes.

   c. Click a rectangle.

3A 3B 3C

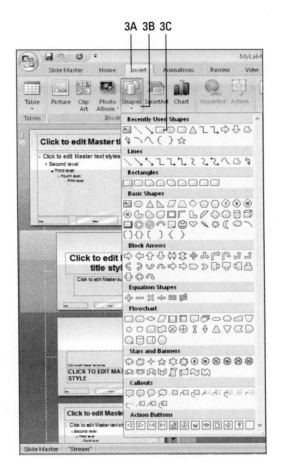

d. Draw a rectangle that covers 2" at the left of the slide.

3D

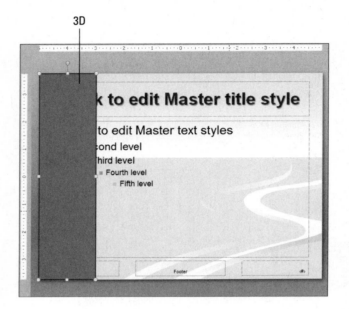

4. **Bring the text boxes to the front so that the rectangle overlaps.**

   a. Click the Title placeholder box.

   b. Hold down the Shift key and click the Content placeholder box.

   c. Hold down the Shift key and click the Date placeholder box.

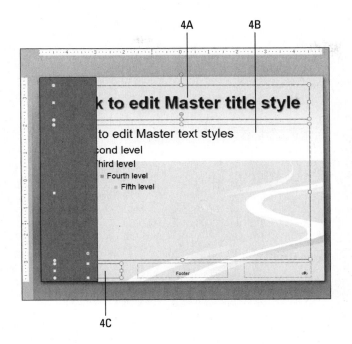

d. Click the Drawing Tools Format tab.

e. Click Bring to Front.

5. Change the color of the rectangle to a dark blue shade from the second column of the color palette.

a. Select the rectangle.

b. On the Drawing Tools Format tab, click Shape Fill.

c. Click the second square from the bottom in the second column in the Theme Colors section.

5C   5B

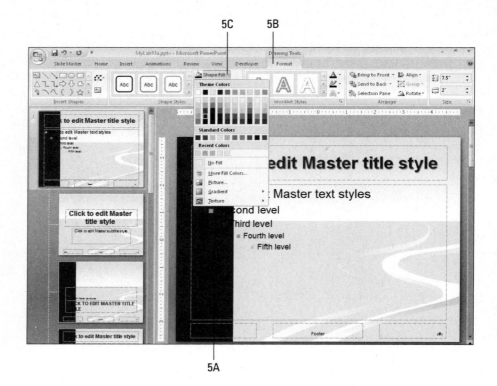

5A

6. **Move the left borders of the title and content placeholder boxes to the right so that they do not overlap the rectangle.**

    a. Select the main Slide Master (top slide).

    b. Click the title placeholder.

    c. Hold down the Shift key and click the content placeholder.

    d. Drag the left border of the content placeholder to align with the 3 ¼" mark on the horizontal ruler.

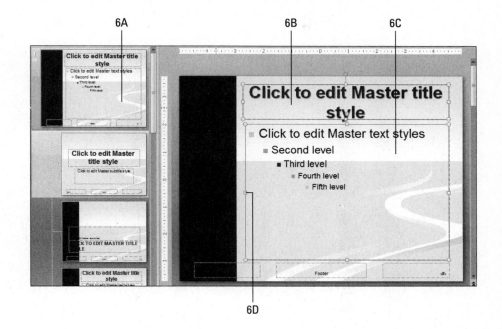

7. **Repeat step 6 for the individual slide layouts that were not affected by step 6.**

   a. Select the Section Header Layout master (the second slide layout in the list).

   b. Select the title and text placeholders.

   c. Drag the left border to the right to the 3 ¼" mark on the horizontal ruler.

7A   7B

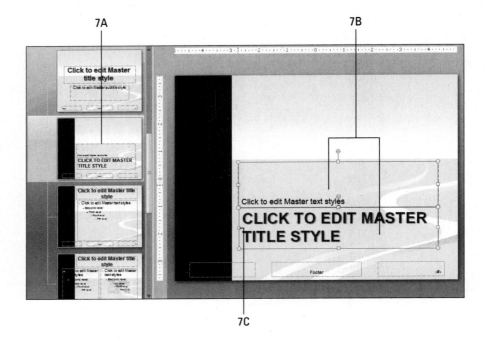

7C

d. Select the Title, Text, and Content layout (bottom slide layout).

e. Select the left content placeholder.

f. Drag the left border to the right to the 3 ¼" mark on the horizontal ruler.

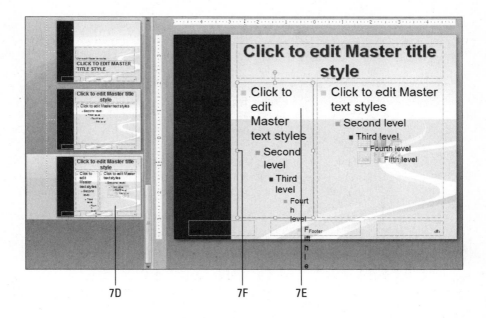

7D   7F   7E

8. Exit from Slide Master view and clean up the presentation so that all slides use valid layouts and no content overflows or overlaps.

 a. Click Close Master View.

8A

 b. On slide #2, click inside the text box and then click the AutoFit Options button.

 c. Click AutoFit Text to Placeholder.

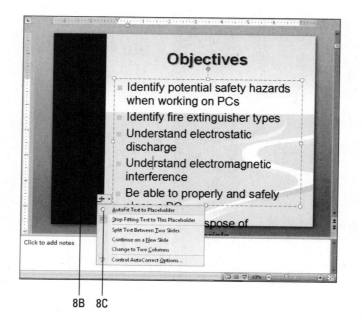

8B   8C

d. Select slides 4 and 5.

e. On the Home tab, click Layout.

f. Click Title and Text.

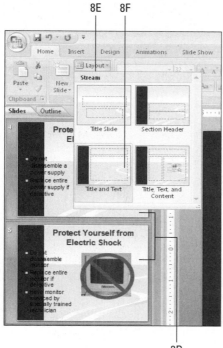

8E   8F

8D

g. Resize and reposition the graphics so that they do not overlap with the text.

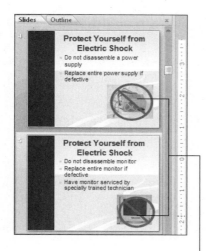

8G

h. Repeat steps 8e through 8g for slides 11, 21, 23, 25, 27, and 29, and repeat steps 8b and 8c for slide 22.

> **NOTE**   Slide #25 has an unusual layout. Only the first bullet is in a placeholder box; the other one is in a manual text box. Adjust as needed.

9. **Save your work.**

Lab 3B: Creating a Navigation Bar

In this lab session, you start with a presentation that has an area cleared for a navigation bar (from Lab 3A) and you create hyperlinks on the Slide Master that link to the section titles within the presentation.

Level of difficulty: Moderate

Time to complete: 15 to 20 minutes

1. **Open the presentation file if it is not already open.** Start in your completed file from the previous project (MyLab3A.pptx), or open Lab3B.pptx from the Labs folder if you did not do the previous lab.

2. **Save the file as MyLab3B.pptx.**

3. **Display the Slide Master and create a text box on top of the blue rectangle.**

   a. On the View tab, click Slide Master.

   b. Click the top-level slide master.

   c. On the Insert tab, click Text Box.

   d. Drag to create a text box near the top of the blue rectangle.

3D 3C

3B

4. **Type the names of the section titles in white, from the presentation into the new text box.**

   a. Click in the new text box.

   If the insertion point does not appear, right-click the text box and choose Edit Text to make it appear there.

   b. On the Home tab, open the Font Color list and click the white square in the Theme Colors section.

4B

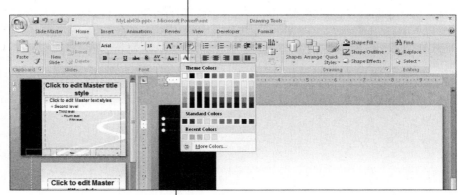

4A

c. Type the following list into the text box:

Protect Yourself

Avoid ESD

Avoid EMI

Protect the PC

Clean the PC

Work Safely with Hazardous Materials

d. With the insertion point inside the text box, press Ctrl+A to select all of the text in it.

e. Click the dialog box launcher in the Paragraph group on the Home tab. The Paragraph dialog box appears.

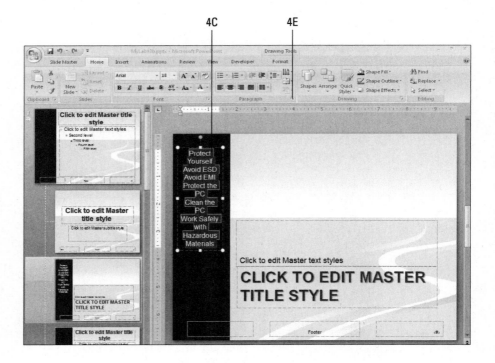

f. In the Spacing section, set the Before value to 12 pt.

g. Click OK.

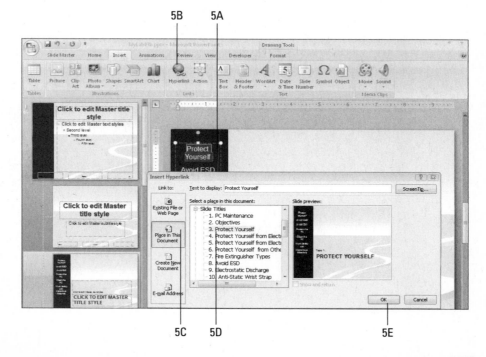

5. Hyperlink each of the paragraphs you just typed to the corresponding slide.

   a. In the text box, select Protect Yourself.

   b. On the Insert tab, click Hyperlink. The Insert Hyperlink dialog box appears.

   c. Click Place in This Document.

   d. On the Slide Titles list, click Protect Yourself (slide #3).

   e. Click OK.

f. Repeat steps 5a through 5e for each of the other section title slides:

Avoid ESD: Slide #8

Avoid EMI: Slide #13

Protect the PC: Slide #16

Clean the PC: Slide #19

Work Safely with Hazardous Materials: Slide #28

6. **Exit from Slide Master view.** On the Slide Master tab, click Close Master View.

7. Try out the presentation in Slide Show view and click each of the links to make sure they work.

8. Save your work.

Lab 3C: Creating a Graphical Navigation System

In this lab session, you learn how to create a navigation bar similar to the one in Lab 3B except you use shapes for buttons instead of text-based hyperlinks.

Level of difficulty: Moderate

Time to complete: 20 minutes

1. **Open the presentation file if it is not already open.** Start in your completed file from the previous project (MyLab3B.pptx), or open Lab3C.pptx from the Labs folder if you did not do the previous lab.

2. **Save the file as MyLab3C.pptx.**

3. **Display the Slide Master.**

    a. On the View tab, click Slide Master.

    b. Click the slide master (topmost slide).

4. **Replace the text Protect Yourself with a rectangle containing that text.**

    a. Move the text box down ½" to make room above it for the rectangle.

    b. On the Insert tab, click Shapes, and click a rectangle.

4B

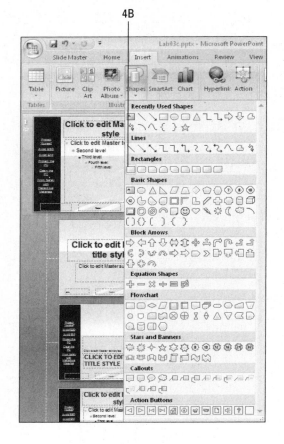

c. Draw a rectangle above the text box.

d. Select the Protect Yourself text in the text box and press Ctrl+X to cut it to the Clipboard.

4C   4D

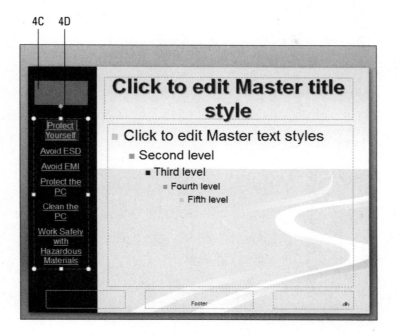

e. Click the rectangle and press Ctrl+V to paste the text into it.

4E

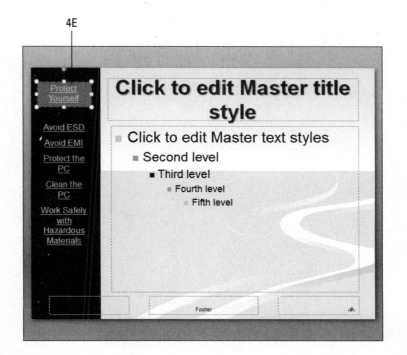

5. **Repeat step 4 for each of the other text hyperlinks, to create the rest of the buttons.**

    a. Move the text box off of the blue rectangle as needed to make room for the buttons.

> **NOTE** To duplicate the size of the original rectangle, you can copy and paste it or you can Ctrl+drag it instead of drawing new ones each time. Alternatively you can draw them, and then use the Size group on the Drawing Tools Format tab to standardize the size.

    b. You might need to change the size of the button(s) to make all of the text fit.

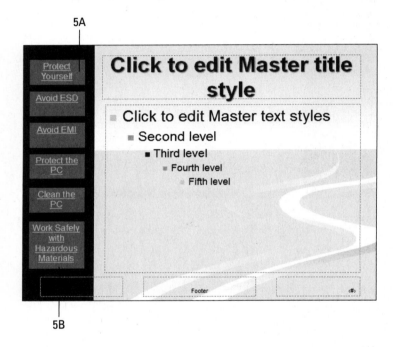

6. **Format the buttons to make them more attractive.**

    a. Select all of the buttons. Hold down the Shift key as you click each one.

    b. On the Drawing Tools Format tab, open the Shape Effects menu, click Shadow, and click the first Shadow setting (top left).

6B

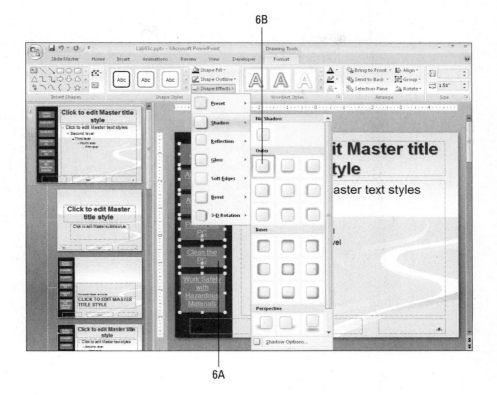

6A

c. Open the Shape Effects menu, click Bevel, and click the first bevel style (top left).

6C

7. Save your work.

EXPERT TIP If you prefer buttons that do not have the text underlined, you can set them up differently. Instead of using the existing hyperlink text, you remove the hyperlink from the
text to make it ordinary text typed in a shape, and then set the button as a graphical hyperlink.

Lab 4

Creating a Classroom Game

PowerPoint's ability to hyperlink between slides and hide slides until they are needed makes it a natural choice for creating multiple-choice quizzes and games. You can create a slide with a question on it, and then create hidden slides for each of the possible answers. Then depending on which answer the user clicks, a different hidden slide appears indicating whether the answer was right or wrong.

The Scenario

In this project lab, you learn how to create a simple game to use in a classroom setting that tests students' understanding of the informational presentation you worked with in Lab 3.

Lab 4A: Making the Game Board

In this lab session, you will create the basic game board by drawing a set of shapes and arranging them in relation to one another.

Level of difficulty: Moderate

Time to complete: 15 to 30 minutes

1. **Start a new blank presentation and save it as MyLab04A.pptx.**
2. **Change the layout of the slide to Blank.**
   a. On the Home tab, click Layout.
   b. Click Blank.

2A

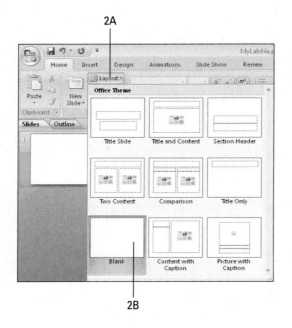

2B

3. **Draw a rounded rectangle on the slide that is 0.75" high and 2" wide.**

   a. On the Insert tab (or Home tab), click Shapes, and click the rounded rectangle.

3A

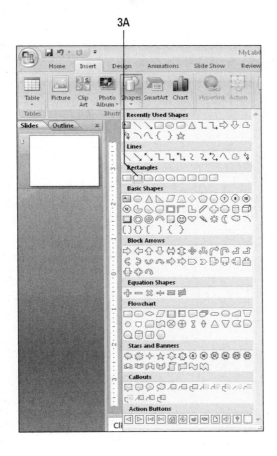

b. Drag on the slide, near the top-left corner, to create the shape.

c. On the Drawing Tools Format tab, click in the Shape Height box and type **0.75**".

d. Click in the Shape Width box and type **2**".

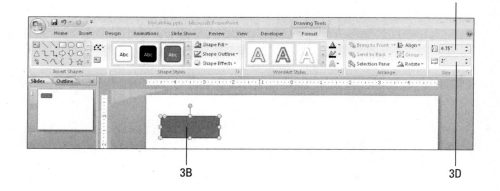

4. **Apply a dark purple Shape Style to the shape.** On the Drawing Tools Format tab, open the Shape Styles gallery and click the bottommost dark purple style.

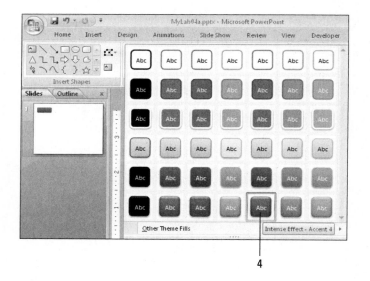

5. **Copy the shape, and paste it three times. Then arrange the copies side-by-side horizontally across the top of the slide and distribute them evenly.**

   a. Select the purple shape.

   b. Hold down Shift+Ctrl and drag it to the right to create a copy. Repeat two more times so that you have a total of four shapes.

   c. Select all four shapes by holding down the Shift key and clicking each one.

d. On the Drawing Tools Format tab, click Align.

e. Click Distribute Horizontally.

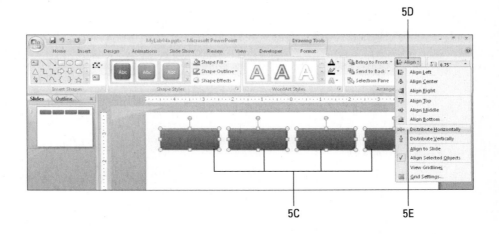

6. **Copy the four shapes four times, and place the copies under the originals to form columns.**

   a. Select all four purple shapes if they are not already selected.

   b. Hold down Shift+Ctrl and drag downward to create a copy below the originals.

   c. Repeat 6B three more times to create three more rows of buttons.

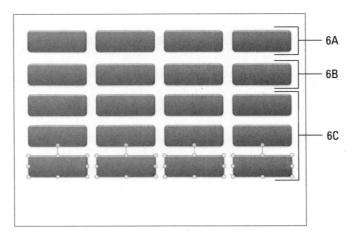

7. **Use Align and Distribute to make sure the grid of buttons is evenly spaced.**

   a. Select all of the shapes in the first column.

   b. On the Drawing Tools Format tab, click Align

   c. Click Distribute Vertically.

   d. Repeat steps 7a through 7c for each column.

8. **Change the color of all of the rows except the first one to turquoise blue.**

   a. Select all of the shapes in each row except the first one.

   b. On the Drawing Tools Format tab, open the Shape Styles gallery and click the turquoise blue sample in the bottom row.

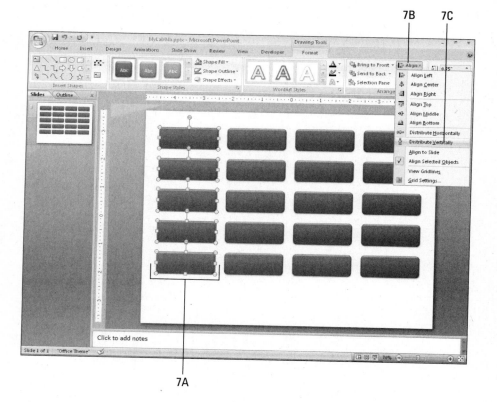

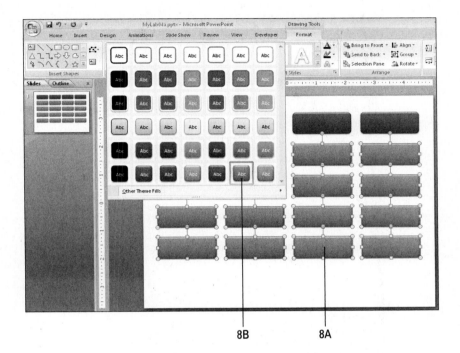

8B   8A

9. **Type the following text into the top row of shapes.**

   a. Select the leftmost purple shape and type **Safety**.

   b. Select the second purple shape and type **ESD**.

   c. Select the third purple shape and type **EMI**.

   d. Select the fourth purple shape and type **Cleaning**.

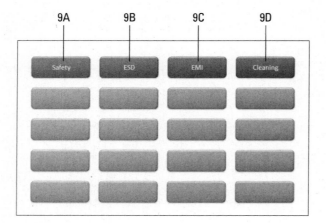

10. **Type 10, 20, 30, and 40 in each column.**

    a. In the topmost leftmost turquoise shape, type **10**.

    b. Select the 10 you just typed and press Ctrl+C to copy it.

    c. Select the next shape in that row and press Ctrl+V. Repeat two more times so that all of the shapes in the first turquoise row have 10 in them.

    d. Repeat the process to put **20** in the next row, **30** in the next, and then **40** in the bottom row.

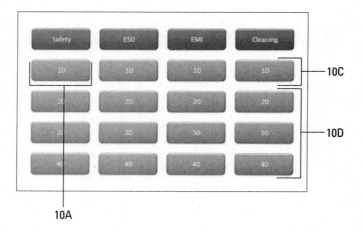

11. Save your work.

Lab 4B: Creating the Question Slides

In this lab session, you generate slides containing the questions that the game board, created in Lab 4A, will link to. Because the game board is large, you'll do just one slide step-by-step here, and then you can create the rest of the slides on your own.

Level of difficulty: Easy

Time to complete: 15 to 20 minutes

1. **Open the presentation file if it is not already open.** Start in your completed file from the previous project (MyLab04A.pptx), or open Lab04B.pptx from the Labs folder (from the CD accompanying the book) if you did not do the previous lab.

2. **Save the file as MyLab04B.pptx.**

3. **Create a new blank slide using the Title and Content layout after the first one.**

   a. On the Home tab, click the text below the New Slide button.

   b. Click Title and Content.

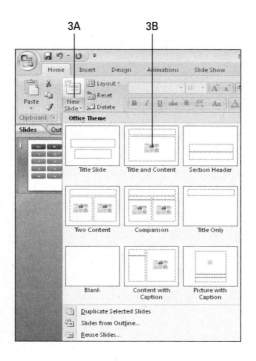

4. For the new slide's title, type the following:

Safety for 10 Points

5. For the new slide's body, type the following:

True or false: you should wear long sleeves when working on a PC.

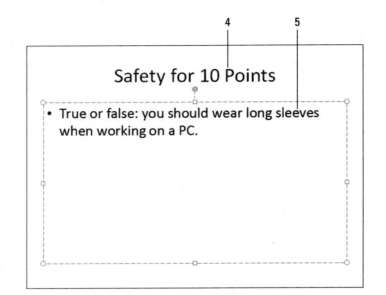

6. Add True and False buttons below the question.

a. Display slide #1, and select any of the turquoise shapes.

b. Press Ctrl+C to copy the shape.

c. Display slide #2.

d. Press Ctrl+V to paste the shape.

e. Edit the text on the shape to read **True**.

f. Hold down the Ctrl key and drag the True shape to create a copy of it.

g. Edit the text on the new shape to read **False**.

h. Arrange the shapes side-by-side under the question text.

6A

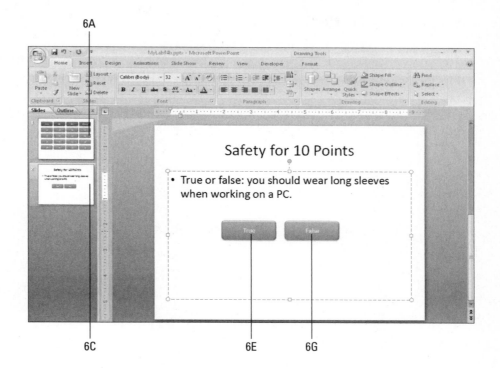

6C 6E 6G

7. **Create additional slides for the other questions by copying the slide you just created and modifying its text.** Refer to the following table for the question text to use. (If you do not want to do all of that typing, see the solution file MyLab04B.pptx provided on the CD accompanying the book.)

Question Number	Question Text
Safety 20	True or false: you should replace the entire power supply if it is defective, not try to repair it.
Safety 30	True or false: monitors must be serviced by specially trained technicians.
Safety 40	True or false: a Class A fire extinguisher is best for electrical fires.
ESD 10	True or false: ESD stands for Electrostatic Discharge.
ESD 20	True or false: A circuit board can be ruined by ESD that is too weak for a human to feel.
ESD 30	True or false: to minimize ESD, work in a room with very low humidity (0% to 30%).
ESD 40	True or false: rubber-soled shoes are best for avoiding ESD.
EMI 10	True or false: EMI stands for Electrostatic Issues.

continued

Question Number	Question Text
EMI 20	True or false: EMI is a magnetic field generated by electricity passing through a cable.
EMI 30	True or false: shielded cables can prevent problems caused by EMI.
EM 40	True or false: longer cables are more susceptible to EMI.
Cleaning 10	True or false: you should not use regular glass cleaner on a monitor screen.
Cleaning 20	True or false: the best way to clean a circuit board is with soapy water.
Cleaning 30	True or false: to clean the print heads on an inkjet printer, run the printer's self-cleaning utility.
Cleaning 40	True or false: you should use alcohol to clean the corona wires in a laser printer.

8. **Hide all of the slides except the game board.**

   a. From Slide Sorter view, select all slides except slide #1.

   b. On the Slide Show tab, click Hide Slide.

8B

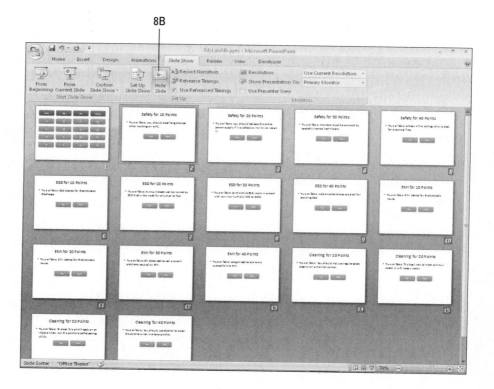

9. **Save your work.**

Lab 4C: Creating the Answer Slides

In this lab session, you create slides that tell the players whether or not their answers are correct, and you will link each of the True and False buttons from Lab 4B to one of those slides or the other.

Level of difficulty: Moderate

Time to complete: 20 minutes

1. **Open the presentation file if it is not already open.** Start in your completed file from the previous project (MyLab04B.pptx), or open Lab4C.pptx from the Labs folder if you did not do the previous lab.

2. **Save the file as MyLab04C.pptx.**

3. **Create a slide to display when the player answers correctly.**

   a. Create a new slide with the Title and Content layout after the existing slides in the presentation.

   b. For the slide title, type **You Are Correct!**

   c. For the slide body text, type **Congratulations, that is the correct answer.**

   d. Remove the bullet from the body text.

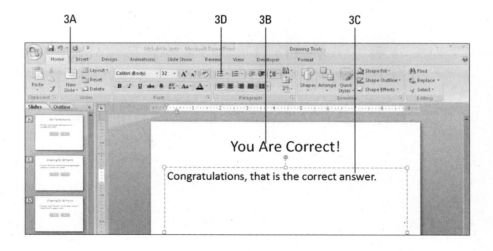

4. **Add a Return button at the bottom of the slide, and set it to return to the game board.**

   a. Copy and paste any turquoise button from any existing slide onto the bottom of the You Are Correct slide.

   b. Edit the text on the button to read **Return**.

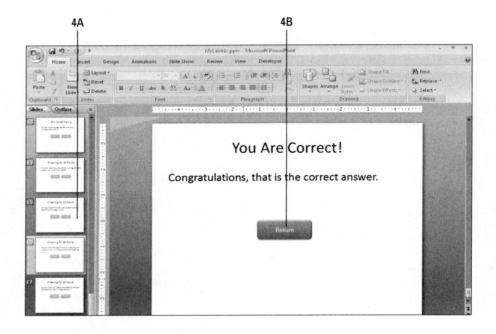

   c. Select the Return button.

   d. On the Insert tab click Action.

   e. Click Hyperlink To

   f. Open the drop-down list and choose First Slide.

   g. Click OK.

4E　4F　4D

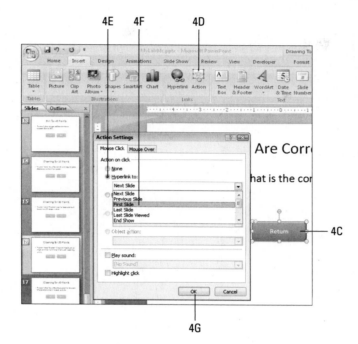

4C

4G

5. **Copy the You Are Correct slide**. In the Slides pane, right-click the You Are Correct slide and choose Duplicate Slide.

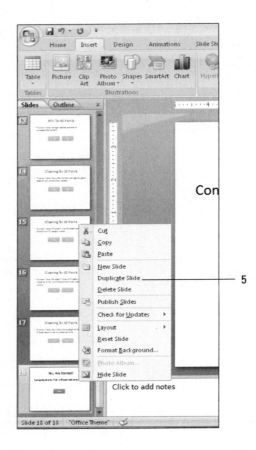

6. Change the text on the copy of the You Are Correct slide to reflect that the player has answered incorrectly.

   a. Change the slide title text to **You Are Incorrect**.

   b. Change the slide body text to **Sorry, you answered incorrectly.**

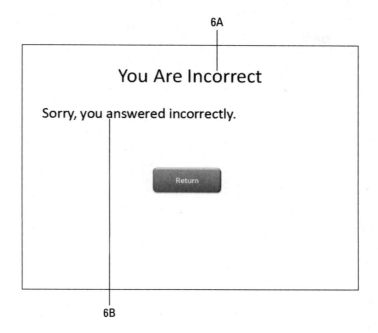

7. Save your work.

Lab 4D: Linking Up the Game Board

In this lab session, you finish the game board built in Labs 4A through 4C by creating hyperlinks from the game board to the question slides, and from the True and False buttons on each question slide to the result slides you created in Lab 4C.

Level of difficulty: Moderate

Time to complete: 30 minutes or more

1. **Open the presentation file if it is not already open.** Start in your completed file from the previous project (MyLab04C.pptx), or open Lab04D.pptx from the Labs folder if you did not do the previous lab.

2. **Save the file as MyLab04D.pptx.**

3. **Create a hyperlink between the leftmost 10 button on the game board to the Safety for 10 Points slide.**

   a. On the game board, select the 10 button in the Safety column. (Select the button itself, not the text on the button.)

   b. On the Insert tab, click Hyperlink.

   c. Click Place in This Document.

   d. Click Safety for 10 Points.

   e. Click OK.

4. **Repeat the process in step 3 to create links from each of the other buttons on the game board to its corresponding question.**

5. **Hide the You Are Correct and You Are Incorrect slides.**

   a. From the Slides pane, select slide #18 (You Are Correct) and slide #19 (You Are Incorrect).

   b. On the Slide Show tab, click Hide Slide.

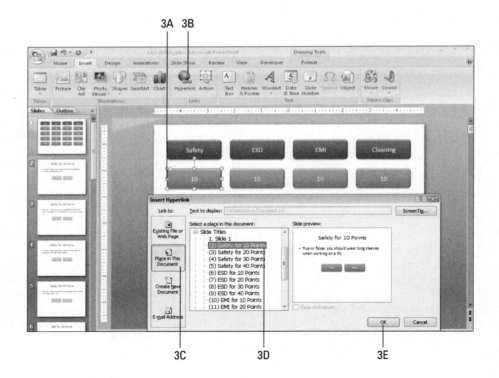

5B

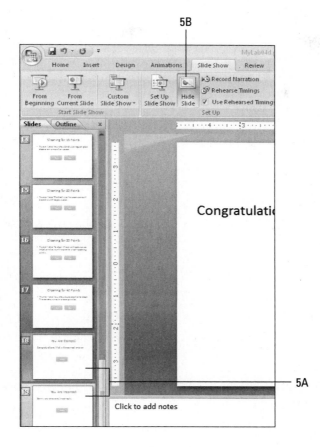

5A

6. On slide #2 (Safety for 10 points), hyperlink from the True button to the You Are Incorrect slide.

   a. On slide #2, select the True button.

   b. On the Insert tab, click Hyperlink.

   c. Click Place in This Document.

   d. Click slide #19, You Are Incorrect.

   e. Click OK.

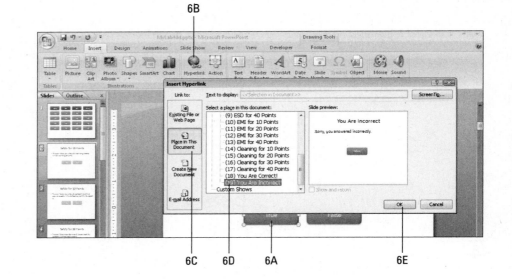

7. **Repeat step 6 for the False button, linking it to the You Are Correct slide.**

8. Assign hyperlinks to the True and False buttons on all of the other question slides the same way. Refer to the following table for the correct answers.

Question Number	Correct Answer
Safety 20	True
Safety 30	True
Safety 40	False
ESD 10	True
ESD 20	True
ESD 30	False
ESD 40	True
EMI 10	False
EMI 20	True

Question Number	Correct Answer
EMI 30	True
EM 40	False
Cleaning 10	True
Cleaning 20	False
Cleaning 30	True
Cleaning 40	True

9. Display the game board in Slide Show view and try out the game to make sure that all of the buttons have been programmed correctly.

10. Save your work.

EXPERT TIP If you were going to set this game up on a self-running kiosk, you would want to put it into Kiosk mode so that clicking on the slide itself does not advance the presentation. To do so, on the Slide Show tab, click Set Up Slide Show and choose Browsed at a Kiosk (Full Screen).

Part V

Appendixes

Feature Finder: 2003 to 2007

The new Ribbon-based command structure in PowerPoint 2007 is a radical departure from the old-style menu and toolbar commands from previous versions of the program. Upgraders might find that they need a little help in locating certain features. This appendix helps you to find many of the most popular commands.

Getting Help in the Help System

The PowerPoint 2007 Help system provides several tools for finding where a particular feature has moved. In the main Help window (F1), the What's New section contains an article called Reference: Locations of PowerPoint 2003 Commands in PowerPoint 2007. This appendix is based upon that article, and so you can look there if you need to find a command that this appendix does not cover.

An interactive lookup tool is also available. Search the Help system for Interactive Locations, to locate an article called Interactive: PowerPoint 2003 to PowerPoint 2007 Command Reference Guide. This article is actually not an article, but an ASP application. It presents a dummy version of PowerPoint 2003's menu system; roll your mouse over a menu to open it, and then select a command to see a ScreenTip explaining where to find this command in PowerPoint 2007, as shown in Figure A.1.

The interactive PowerPoint lookup tool tells you where to find commands in PowerPoint 2007.

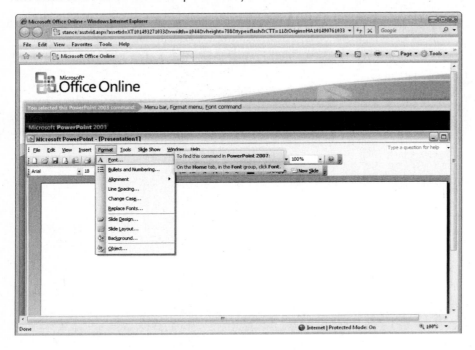

Menus

The following tables cross-reference the default menu system in PowerPoint 2003 with the PowerPoint 2007 application.

File Menu

PowerPoint 2003	PowerPoint 2007	Notes
New	Office, New	
Open	Office, Open	
Close	Office, Close	

PowerPoint 2003	PowerPoint 2007	Notes
Save	Office, Save	This feature is also available on the Quick Access toolbar.
Save As	Office, Save As	
Save as Web Page	Not available	You can access the same function by choosing a Web-based format from the regular Save As dialog box.
File Search	Not available	You can search from Windows using the Search command on the Start menu; if you have Windows Vista, a Search text box appears in the upper-right corner of the Open dialog box.
Package for CD	Office, Publish, Package for CD	
Web Page Preview	Not available by default	You can add a Web Page Preview button to the Quick Access toolbar.
Page Setup	Design tab, Page Setup group	
Print Preview	Office, Print, Print Preview	
Print	Office, Print	
Send, Mail Recipient (for Review)	Not available	E-mail routing is no longer available.
Send, Mail Recipient (as Attachment)	Office, Send, Email	
Send, Exchange Folder	Not available by default	You can add this command to the Quick Access toolbar.
Send, Online Meeting Participant	Not available by default	You can add this command to the Quick Access toolbar.
Send, Recipient Using Internet Fax Service	Office, Send, Internet Fax	
Send, Microsoft Office Word	Office, Publish, Create Handouts in Microsoft Office Word	
Properties	Office, Prepare, Properties	

Edit Menu

PowerPoint 2003	PowerPoint 2007	Notes
Undo	Quick Access Toolbar	
Redo	Quick Access Toolbar	
Repeat	Quick Access Toolbar	
Cut	Home tab, Clipboard group, Cut button	
Copy	Home tab, Clipboard group, Copy button	
Office Clipboard	Home tab, Clipboard group, Dialog box launcher	
Paste	Home tab, Clipboard group, Paste button	
Paste Special	Home tab, Clipboard group, Paste button	Use the drop-down arrow at the bottom of the Paste button to open a menu and select Paste Special.
Paste as Hyperlink	Home tab, Clipboard group, Paste button	Use the drop-down arrow at the bottom of the Paste button to open a menu and select Paste as Hyperlink.
Clear	Not available by default	You can add this button to the Quick Access toolbar.
Select All	Home tab, Editing group, Select, Select All	
Duplicate	Home tab, Clipboard group, Paste button	Use the drop-down arrow at the bottom of the Paste button to open a menu and select Duplicate.
Delete Slide	Home tab, Slides group, Delete	You can also press the Delete key on the keyboard.
Find	Home tab, Editing group, Find	
Replace	Home tab, Editing group, Replace	
Go to Property	Not available by default	You can add this button to the Quick Access toolbar.
Links	Office, Prepare, Edit Links to Files	This feature is available only if there are linked objects in the file.
Object	Not available	When you select the object, tabs specific to the object appear in the Ribbon as needed.

View Menu

PowerPoint 2003	PowerPoint 2007	Notes
Normal Slide Sorter Slide Show Notes Page	View tab, Presentation Views group	You can also use the view buttons in the bottom-right corner of the window.
Master (Slide Master, Handout Master, Notes Master)	View tab, Presentation Views group	
Color/Grayscale (Color, Grayscale, Pure Black and White)	View tab, Color/Grayscale group	
Task Pane	Not available	Task panes have generally been replaced by contextual tabs in the Ribbon.
Toolbars	Not available	Toolbars have been replaced by the Ribbon.
Ruler	View tab, Show/Hide group, Ruler	
Grids and Guides	To change settings: Home tab, Drawing group, Arrange, Align, Grid Settings	
	To toggle gridlines: View tab, Show/Hide group, Gridlines	
Header and Footer	Insert tab, Text group, Header & Footer	
Markup	Review tab, Comments group, Show Markup	
Zoom	View tab, Zoom group, or slider in bottom right corner of screen	

Insert Menu

PowerPoint 2003	PowerPoint 2007	Notes
New Slide	Home tab, Slides group, New Slide	
Duplicate Slide	Home tab, Slides group, New Slide, Duplicate Selected Slides	Click the drop-down arrow below the New Slide button to open its menu.

continued

PowerPoint 2003	PowerPoint 2007	Notes
Slide Number	Insert tab, Text group, Slide Number	
Date and Time	Insert tab, Text group, Date & Time	
Symbol	Insert tab, Text group, Symbol	
Comment	Review tab, Comments group, New Comment	
Slides from Files	Home tab, Slides group, New Slide, Reuse Slides	Click the drop-down arrow below the New Slide button to open its menu.
Slides from Outline	Home tab, Slides group, New Slide, Slides from Outline	Click the drop-down arrow below the New Slide button to open its menu.
Picture, Clip Art	Insert tab, Illustrations group, Clip Art	
Picture, From File	Insert tab, Illustrations group, Picture	
Picture, From Scanner or Camera	Not available	The Scanner and Camera Wizard is still available through the Clip Organizer. Choose Clip Art, click Organize Clips, and in the Clip Organizer window, choose File, Add Clips to Organizer, From Scanner or Camera.
Picture, New Photo Album	Insert tab, Illustrations group, Photo Album	
Picture, AutoShapes	Insert tab, Illustrations group, Shapes	
Picture, WordArt	Insert tab, Text group, WordArt	You can no longer insert WordArt as a graphical element; instead, you type regular text and then apply WordArt styles and formatting to it. It is also available from some contextual tabs.
Picture, Organization Chart	Insert tab, Illustrations group, SmartArt, Hierarchy	
Diagram	Insert tab, Illustrations group, SmartArt	
Text Box	Insert tab, Text group, Text Box	
	Insert tab, Illustrations group, Shapes gallery, Text Box	
	Home tab, Drawing group, Shapes gallery, Text Box	
Movies and Sounds, Movie from Clip Organizer	Insert tab, Media Clips group, Movie, Movie from Clip Organizer	
Movies and Sounds, Movie from File	Insert tab, Media Clips group, Movie, Movie from File	

PowerPoint 2003	PowerPoint 2007	Notes
Movies and Sounds, Sound from Clip Organizer	Insert tab, Media Clips group, Sound, Sound from Clip Organizer	
Movies and Sounds, Sound from File	Insert tab, Media Clips group, Sound, Sound from File	
Movies and Sounds, Play CD Audio Track	Insert tab, Media Clips group, Sound, Play CD Audio Track	
Movies and Sounds, Record Sound	Insert tab, Media Clips group, Sound, Record Sound	
Chart	Insert tab, Illustrations group, Chart	
Table	Insert tab, Tables group, Table	
Object	Insert tab, Text group, Object	
Hyperlink	Insert tab, Links group, Hyperlink	

Format Menu

PowerPoint 2003	PowerPoint 2007	Notes
Font	Home tab, Font group	Also available on the Mini Bar.
Bullets and Numbering	Home tab, Paragraph group, Bullets OR Home tab, Paragraph group, Numbering	Also available on the Mini Bar.
Alignment	Home tab, Paragraph group, alignment buttons (Left, Center, Right, Justified)	Also available on the Mini Bar.
Line Spacing	Home tab, Paragraph group, Line Spacing	
Change Case	Home tab, Font group, Change Case	
Replace Fonts	Home tab, Editing group, Replace, Replace Fonts	
Slide Design	Design tab, Themes group	
Slide Layout	Home tab, Slides group, Layout	
Background	Design tab, Background group, Background Styles	Also right-click the slide, format background.
Object	Not available	Commands for working with objects appear on contextual tabs and right-click menus when you select the object.

Tools Menu

PowerPoint 2003	PowerPoint 2007	Notes
Spelling	Review tab, Proofing group, Spelling	
Research	Review tab, Proofing group, Research	
Thesaurus	Review tab, Proofing group, Thesaurus	
Language	Review tab, Proofing group, Language	
Shared Workspace	Office, Publish, Create Document Workspace	
Compare and Merge Presentations	Not available	This feature has been removed.
Online Collaboration, Meet Now	Not available by default	You can add this command to the Quick Access toolbar.
Online Collaboration, Schedule Meeting	Not available by default	You can add this command to the Quick Access toolbar.
Online Collaboration, Web Discussions	Not available	This feature has been removed.
Macro, Macros	View tab, Macros group, Macros OR Developer tab, Code group, Macros	This lets you access existing macros, but you cannot record new ones in PowerPoint 2007.
Macro, Record New Macros	Not available	This feature has been removed. You cannot record new macros in PowerPoint 2007.
Macro, Security	Developer tab, Code group, Macro Security	
Macro, Visual Basic Editor	Developer tab, Code group, Visual Basic	
Macro, Microsoft Script Editor	Not available	This feature has been removed.
Add-Ins	Office, PowerPoint Options, Add-Ins, PowerPoint Add-Ins.	
AutoCorrect Options	Office, PowerPoint Options, Proofing, AutoCorrect Options	
Customize	Office, PowerPoint Options, Customize	Customization is different than in earlier versions; you can add and remove commands only from the Quick Access toolbar.
Options	Office, PowerPoint Options	

Slide Show Menu

PowerPoint 2003	PowerPoint 2007	Notes
View Show	View tab, Presentation Views group, Slide Show OR Slide Show tab, Start Slide Show group, From Beginning	
Set Up Show	Slide Show tab, Set Up group, Set Up Slide Show	
Rehearse Timings	Slide Show tab, Set Up group, Rehearse Timings	
Record Narration	Slide Show tab, Set Up group, Record Narration	
Action Buttons	Insert tab, Shapes group	
Action Settings	Insert tab, Links group, Action	
Animation Schemes	Not available	There are no animation schemes per se in PowerPoint 2007. However, there are a few preset animations available on the Animations tab in the Animations group from the Animate drop-down list.
Custom Animation	Animations tab, Animations group, Custom Animation	
Slide Transitions	Animations tab, Transitions to This Slide group	
Hide Slide	Slide Show tab, Set Up group, Hide Slide	
Custom Shows	Slide Show tab, Start Slide Show group, Custom Slide Show	

Window Menu

PowerPoint 2003	PowerPoint 2007	Notes
New Window	View tab, Window group, New Window	
Arrange All	View tab, Window group, Arrange All	
Cascade	View tab, Window group, Cascade	

continued

PowerPoint 2003	PowerPoint 2007	Notes
Next Pane	Not available by default	You can add this command to the Quick Access toolbar.
List of Windows	View tab, Window group, Switch Windows	

Help Menu

PowerPoint 2003	PowerPoint 2007	Notes
Microsoft PowerPoint Help	Click the question mark icon in the top-right corner	
Show the Office Assistant	Not available	This feature has been removed.
Microsoft Office Online	Office, PowerPoint Options, Resources, Go Online	
Contact Us	Office, PowerPoint Options, Resources, Contact Us	
Check for Updates	Office, PowerPoint Options, Resources, Check for Updates	
Detect and Repair	Office, PowerPoint Options, Resources, Diagnose	
Activate Product	Office, PowerPoint Options, Resources, Activate	
Customer Feedback Options	Office, PowerPoint Options, Resources, Trust Center, Trust Center Settings, Privacy Options, Sign up for the Customer Experience Improvement Program	Various dialogs ask, "Was this helpful?" If you click, you can submit feedback.
About Microsoft Office PowerPoint	Office, PowerPoint Options, Resources, About	

Toolbars

The following sections cross-reference the buttons on the default toolbars from PowerPoint 2003 (Standard, Formatting, and Drawing) with PowerPoint 2007 features.

Standard Toolbar

PowerPoint 2003	PowerPoint 2007	Notes
New	Office, New	
Open	Office, Open	
Save	Office, Save	
Send Email	Office, Send, Email	
Print (Quick Print)	Office, Print, Quick Print	
Print Preview	Office, Print, Print Preview	
Spelling	Review tab, Proofing group, Spelling	
Research	Review tab, Proofing group, Research	
Cut	Home tab, Clipboard group, Cut	
Copy	Home tab, Clipboard group, Copy	
Paste	Home tab, Clipboard group, Paste	
Format Painter	Home tab, Clipboard group, Format Painter	
Undo	Quick Access Toolbar	
Redo	Quick Access Toolbar	
Ink Annotations	Review tab, Inking, Start Inking	This feature appears only on Tablet PCs.
Chart	Insert tab, Illustrations group, Chart	
Insert Table	Insert tab, Tables group, Table	
Tables and Borders Toolbar	Not available	This feature was replaced by the Tables tab.
Hyperlink	Insert tab, Links group, Hyperlink	
Expand All	Not available by default	You can add this command to the Quick Access toolbar.
Show Formatting	Not available by default	You can add this command to the Quick Access toolbar.
Show/Hide Grid	View tab, Show/Hide group, Gridlines	Also available with Arrange/Align tools.
Color/Grayscale	View tab, Color/Grayscale group	
Zoom	Status bar Zoom controls OR View tab, Zoom group	
Help	Help button (?) in upper-right corner	

Formatting Toolbar

PowerPoint 2003	PowerPoint 2007	Notes
Font	Home tab, Font group, Font	Also available on Mini Toolbar.
Font Size	Home tab, Font group, Font Size	Also available on Mini Toolbar.
Bold	Home tab, Font group, Bold	Also available on Mini Toolbar.
Italic	Home tab, Font group, Italic	Also available on Mini Toolbar.
Underline	Home tab, Font group, Underline	
Shadow	Home tab, Font group, Shadow	
Align Left	Home tab, Paragraph group, Align Left OR Layout tab (with table selected), Alignment group, Align Left	Also available on Mini Toolbar.
Center	Home tab, Paragraph group, Center OR Layout tab (with table selected), Alignment group, Center	Also available on Mini Toolbar.
Align Right	Home tab, Paragraph group, Align Right OR Layout tab (with table selected), Alignment group, Align Right	Also available on Mini Toolbar.
Change Text Direction	Home tab, Paragraph Group, Text Direction OR Tools tab (with table selected), Alignment group, Text Direction	
Numbering	Home tab, Paragraph group, Numbering	Also available on Mini Toolbar.
Bullets	Home tab, Paragraph group, Bullets	Also available on Mini Toolbar.
Decrease Font Size	Home tab, Font group, Decrease Font Size	Also available on Mini Toolbar.
Increase Font Size	Home tab, Font group, Increase Font Size	Also available on Mini Toolbar.
Decrease Indent	Home tab, Paragraph group, Decrease Indent	Also available on Mini Toolbar.
Increase Indent	Home tab, Paragraph group, Increase Indent	Also available on Mini Toolbar.

PowerPoint 2003	PowerPoint 2007	Notes
Font Color	Home tab, Font group, Font Color	Also available on Mini Toolbar.
Design	Design tab, Themes group	
New Slide	Home tab, Slides group, New Slides	

Drawing Toolbar

PowerPoint 2003	PowerPoint 2007	Notes
Draw, Group	Home tab (or Format tab), Arrange group, Group	
Draw, Ungroup	Home tab (or Format tab), Arrange group, Ungroup	
Draw, Regroup	Home tab (or Format tab), Arrange group, Regroup	
Draw, Order, Bring to Front	Home tab (or Format tab), Arrange, Bring to Front	
Draw, Order, Send to Back	Home tab (or Format tab), Arrange, Send to Back	
Draw, Order, Bring Forward	Home tab (or Format tab), Arrange, Bring Forward	
Draw, Order, Send Backward	Home tab (or Format tab), Arrange, Send Backward	
Draw, Grid and Guides	Home tab (or Format tab), Arrange group, Align, Grid Settings	
Draw, Nudge (Up, Down, Left, Right)	Not available by default	You can add this command to the Quick Access toolbar, or use the arrow keys on the keyboard.
Draw, Align or Distribute	Home tab (or Format tab), Arrange group, Align	The options to align or distribute relative to slide, canvas, organization chart, or diagram have been removed.
Draw, Rotate or Flip, Free Rotate	Use the rotation handle on the object.	
Draw, Rotate or Flip, Rotate Left 90°	Home tab (or Format tab), Arrange group, Rotate, Rotate Left 90°	
Draw, Rotate or Flip, Rotate Right 90°	Home tab (or Format tab), Arrange group, Rotate, Rotate Right 90°	

continued

PowerPoint 2003	PowerPoint 2007	Notes
Draw, Rotate or Flip, Flip Horizontal	Home tab (or Format tab), Arrange group, Rotate, Flip Horizontal	
Draw, Rotate or Flip, Flip Vertical	Home tab (or Format tab), Arrange group, Rotate, Flip Vertical	
Draw, Reroute Connectors	Drawing Tools Format tab, Insert Shapes group, Edit Shape, Reroute Connectors	
Draw, Edit Points	Drawing Tools Format tab, Insert Shapes group, Edit Shape, Edit Points	
Draw, Change AutoShape	Drawing Tools Format tab, Insert Shapes group, Edit Shape, Change Shape	
Draw, Set AutoShape Defaults	Right-click and choose Set as Default Shape.	You can also add this command to the Quick Access toolbar.
Select Objects	Home tab, Editing group, Select, Select Objects	This feature is also available in Slide Master view and when working with Ink Tools.
AutoShapes	Home tab, Drawing group, Shapes gallery OR Insert tab, Illustrations group, Shapes	
Line	Insert tab, Shapes group	
Arrow	Insert tab, Shapes group	
Rectangle	Insert tab, Shapes group	
Oval	Insert tab, Shapes group	
Text Box	Home tab, Drawing group, Shapes gallery OR Insert tab, Text group, Text Box	
WordArt	Insert tab, Text group, WordArt	You can apply WordArt to regular text.
Diagram	Insert tab, Illustrations group, SmartArt	
Clip Art	Insert tab, Illustrations group, Clip Art	
Picture	Insert tab, Illustrations group, Picture	
Ink Drawing and Writing	Review tab, Ink group, Start Inking	This feature is only available on a Tablet PC.
Fill Color	Format tab, Shape Styles group, Shape Fill	The tab, group, and button name depends on the object type.

PowerPoint 2003	PowerPoint 2007	Notes
Line Color	Format tab, Shape Styles group, Shape Outline OR Format tab, Picture Styles group, Picture Border	The tab, group, and button name depends on the object type.
Font Color	Format tab, WordArt Quick Styles group, Font Color OR Home tab, Font group, Font Color	The tab, group, and button name depends on the object type.
Line Style	Format tab, Shape Styles group, Shape Outline, Weight OR Format tab, Picture Styles group, Picture Border, Weight	The tab, group, and button name depends on the object type.
Dash Style	Format tab, Shape Styles group, Shape Outline, Dashes OR Format tab, Picture Styles group, Picture Border, Dashes	The tab, group, and button name depends on the object type.
Arrow Style	Format tab, Shape Styles group, Shape Outline, Arrows	This feature is only available for drawn lines and connectors.
Shadow Style	Format tab, Shape Styles group, Shape Effects, Shadow	
3-D Style	Format tab, Shape Styles group, Shape Effects, 3-D Rotation	

Appendix B

Customizing PowerPoint

Although PowerPoint works great right out of the box, it can work even better for you with a few tweaks. In this appendix you will learn about the customizations that you can apply to PowerPoint 2007 to make it work better for you.

What You *Can't* Do

If there is one way in which PowerPoint 2007 is actually a step *backwards* from earlier versions, it is in the area of customization, so don't get your hopes up too high. For example, in earlier versions of PowerPoint, you could create your own custom menus and toolbars. Menus and toolbars technically do not exist anymore in PowerPoint 2007, but you might expect that you could customize the Ribbon and perhaps create your own tabs.

Not so. Or at least, not so easily anymore. A Ribbon customization utility called RibbonX is available from Microsoft, but it is not for end users. To use it, you need to know something about XML, and you need to be able to hack the data files or templates to implement your custom code. Third-party utilities are available to make this process easier, but they are still trying to do something that Microsoft does not want you to do, and so the whole process is awkward. As a result, you are better off not trying to customize the Ribbon.

EXPERT TIP Patrick Schmid's Office 2007 RibbonCustomizer utility, available from `pschmid.net/office2007/ribboncustomizer/`, is one attempt to make it easier for end users to customize their Ribbon.

So what can you do, then? Well, you can add and remove buttons from the Quick Access toolbar, and you can move the Quick Access toolbar above or below the Ribbon. When the Quick Access toolbar is below the Ribbon, it can run the full length of the PowerPoint window, and so there is plenty of room for all of the buttons that you may need. You can also make changes to PowerPoint's settings, from file locations to macro security. There are actually quite a lot of available program settings; you can try them out to make it easier to use some of your favorite PowerPoint features.

Customizing the Quick Access Toolbar

The Quick Access Toolbar, or QAT, is the row of buttons to the right of the Office button, in the upper-left corner of the PowerPoint window. It contains a few buttons by default, such as Save and Print, and you can add others to it. For example, I use Format Painter a lot, but every time I need it, I don't want to have to click the Home tab. By adding Format Painter to the QAT, I make it available all of the time, without having to remember which tab it is on.

Adding Already-Available Commands to the QAT

If the command is already available on a tab or menu, then adding it to the QAT is easy. Just right-click it and choose Add to Quick Access Toolbar. You can use this method to combine all of your most-used commands and buttons in a single location, so that you do not have to switch among the tabs as frequently.

However, in order to use this method, the command already has to be available somewhere within PowerPoint's Ribbon or Office menu. As a result, you cannot use this method to add capabilities to PowerPoint that it does not already have by default.

Removing Commands from the QAT

To remove a command from the QAT, right-click it on the QAT and choose Remove from Quick Access Toolbar. If you want to add it again later, you can use the method in the preceding section if the command exists on a tab or menu. You can use the method in the following section if it does not, or if you cannot seem to find it on any of the tabs or menus.

Adding Other Commands to the QAT

Besides the standard set of commands, PowerPoint also contains a secret list of extra commands and capabilities. Most of these are old features from previous versions of PowerPoint that Microsoft is phasing out, or for which there was no room on the Ribbon. For example, one very useful command, Send to Microsoft Word, is available only if you add it to the QAT in PowerPoint 2007. This command exports your notes pages to Word so that you can adjust their layout.

The list from which you can select commands for placement on the QAT is known as the *command well*. To add a command from the command well to the QAT, follow these steps:

1. Choose Office ⇨ PowerPoint Options. The PowerPoint Options dialog box opens.

2. Click Customization.

3. Open the Customize Quick Access Toolbar drop-down list, and choose For All Documents or choose a particular presentation name from the list. You can only customize for either one presentation or for all presentations.

4. Open the Choose Commands From drop-down list and select a category. There are categories for every tab, as well as some extra ones at the bottom of the list:

   ■ **Macros**: Any macros stored in the current presentation or template appear here.

   ■ **Commands Not in the Ribbon**: The collection of commands that do not have Ribbon or Office menu equivalents; this is where you will find the hidden goodies.

   ■ **All Commands**: A complete list of all commands; use this list when you think a command is already available on a tab but you do not know which one.

5. Select a command from the list, and click the Add>> button to move it to the Customize Quick Access Toolbar list, as shown in Figure B.1.

FIGURE B.1

You can add commands to the Quick Access toolbar from the Customization section of the PowerPoint Options dialog box.

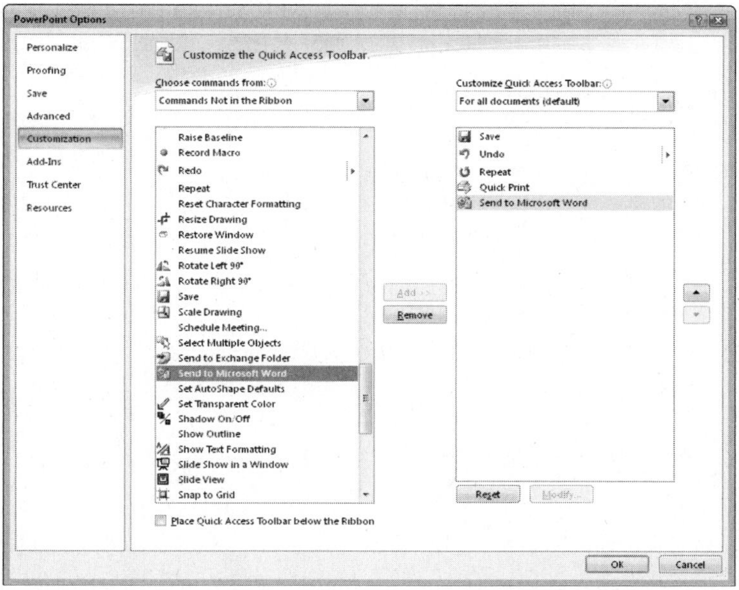

6. Add any other commands that you want.

7. (Optional) Perform any of the following tasks, if necessary:

    ▪ To reset the QAT, click Reset.

    ▪ To modify a macro after adding it to the QAT, select it and click Modify.

    ▪ To change the order in which buttons appear on the QAT, select a button and click the Up- or Down-arrow button to the right of the listing.

8. Click OK to accept the changes.

Changing PowerPoint's Program Options

PowerPoint contains a large assortment of customizable program settings. Some of these settings make purely cosmetic changes to the interface, whereas others enable or disable timesaving or safety features. You can access most options by selecting Office ➪ PowerPoint Options and working in the PowerPoint Options dialog box, as you saw in Figure B-1. Click a category in the PowerPoint Options dialog box along the left side, and then set the options that you want. Table B.1 lists all of the options, divided by category (or most of them, anyway; depending on the language, you may have a few extra options or be missing a few).

TABLE B.1

PowerPoint Options

Section	Option	Description
Category: Personalize		
Top Options for Working with PowerPoint	Show Mini Toolbar on Selection	Shows or hides the floating mini toolbar when you select text.
	ScreenTip Scheme	Determines how detailed the ScreenTips are when you hover the mouse pointer over a command or button.
	Enable Live Preview	Shows a preview of a setting when you move your mouse pointer over it in a gallery. For example, if you hover over a different theme on the Design tab, the slide shows it in the background, behind the open menu.
	Show Developer Tab in the Ribbon	Turns the Developer tab on or off, from which you can access commands for macros and ActiveX controls.
	Color Scheme	Enables you to apply different color schemes to PowerPoint (and all Office programs), independently from your color scheme in Windows.

Section	Option	Description
Personalize Your Copy of Office	User Name	Your name appears here; changing this name affects the username that is associated with comments and file properties.
	Initials	Same as the username, except that it uses only your initials; for example, your initials appear on comments.
	Choose the Languages You Want to Use with Office	Installs additional language-editing packs, so that you can use spell-checkers and research tools in other languages than your default language.
Category: Proofing		
AutoCorrect Options	Change how PowerPoint Corrects and Formats Text as You Type	Click the AutoCorrect Options button here to access and configure AutoCorrect, as described in Chapter 8, Correcting and Improving Text.
When Correcting Spelling in Office Programs	Ignore words in UPPERCASE Ignore words that contain numbers Ignore Internet and file addresses Flag repeated words Enforce accented uppercase in French Suggest from main dictionary only Custom Dictionaries French modes	Use these check boxes to adjust the spelling check, as described in Chapter 8. The options here affect all Office applications.
When Correcting Spelling in PowerPoint	Check spelling as you type Use contextual spelling Hide spelling errors	Use these check boxes to adjust the spelling check, as described in Chapter 8. The options here affect only PowerPoint.
Category: Save		
Save presentations	Save files in this format	Sets the default file format for new presentations.
	Save AutoRecover information every XX minutes	Enables PowerPoint to AutoSave your changes, so that PowerPoint may be able to restore them in the event of a system crash.
	Default file location	Sets the location that appears by default in the Save As dialog box.
Offline editing options for document management server files	Save checked-out files to	When you check out a file from a document server, this option allows you to specify whether the draft is stored locally or back to the Web.

continued

TABLE B.1   *(continued)*

Section	Option	Description
	Server drafts location	When you check out a file from a document server, and you choose to save a local copy, this option determines the location of that local copy.
Preserve fidelity when sharing this presentation	Embed fonts in the file	Packages the fonts with the presentation file so that when the presentation is shown on a computer that does not have these fonts, it still displays correctly.

Category: Advanced

Section	Option	Description
Editing Options	When selecting, automatically select entire word	Extends the selection to entire words when you drag to select.
	Allow text to be dragged and dropped	Enables drag-and-drop moving and copying.
	Maximum number of undos	Sets the number of undo operations.
Cut, copy, and paste	Use smart cut and paste	Automatically adjusts sentence and word spacing, table formatting, and table formatting, as well as other formatting details.
	Show Paste Options buttons	If this option is enabled, then when you paste, an icon appears that opens a menu where you can specify paste options.
Display	Number of documents in the Recent Documents list	Controls the number of documents that appear on the right side of the Office menu.
	Show all windows in the taskbar	Uses a separate icon for each presentation in the taskbar.
	Show shortcut keys in ScreenTips	Includes shortcut keys when you move your mouse over a command or button.
	Show vertical ruler	Includes the vertical ruler when the Ruler is enabled (from the View tab).
	Open all documents using this view	Chooses the default view with which to open presentations.
Slide Show	Show menu on right-mouse click	Enables the right-click menu in Slide Show view.
	Show popup toolbar	Enables the pop-up toolbar in Slide Show view.

Section	Option	Description
	Prompt to keep ink annotations when exiting	When exiting from Slide Show view after using ink annotations, this option asks whether you want to save them.
	End with black slide	Displays a black screen after the final slide (otherwise, it returns to Normal view).
Print	Print in background	Enables print spooling, so that PowerPoint is freed up faster to continue working.
	Print TrueType fonts as graphics	Sends TrueType fonts to the printer as graphics rather than as fonts.
	Print inserted objects at printer resolution	When an object has a different resolution than the printer, this changes the object to match the printer resolution.
	High quality	Enables high-quality printing, including minor improvements such as printing text shadows.
When Printing This Document	Use the most recently used print settings OR Use the following print settings	Selects whether to remember print settings or to use settings that you specify.
Save	Link sounds with file size greater than	Sets a threshold over which a sound file will not be embedded in the PowerPoint file.
General	Provide feedback with sound	Enables sound with visual notifications, such as alerts when a process is complete.
	Show add-in user interface errors	Turns on RibboxX-related error messages.
	Web Options	Opens a dialog box where you can adjust settings for saving in HTML format.
	Service Options	Opens a dialog box for setting customer feedback options.
Category: Customization		
Customization	Customize the Quick Access Toolbar	Customizes the QAT, as described earlier in this Appendix

continued

TABLE B.1   *(continued)*

Section	Option	Description
Category: Add-Ins		
Add-Ins	(List)	Displays the installed add-ins.
	Manage	Selects an add-in category. You can then click Go to manage this category.
Category: Trust Center		
Protecting Your Privacy	Show the Microsoft Office PowerPoint privacy statement Microsoft Office Online privacy statement Customer Experience Improvement Program	Hyperlinks to information, regarding how Microsoft collects information from you as you use the product
Security & More	Microsoft Windows Security Center Microsoft Trustworthy Computing	Hyperlinks to information about security on Office Online
Microsoft Office PowerPoint Trust Center	Trust Center Settings	Opens a dialog box in which you can configure the Trust Center, as described later in this Appendix
Category: Resources		
N/A	Check for Updates	Connects to Microsoft Office Online to look for program updates, and offers to install any that it finds.
	Diagnose	Checks your Office installation for problems, and offers to repair them.
	Contact Us	Displays information about how to contact Microsoft for free or for-pay technical support.
	Activate	Connects to the activation server to activate your copy of Office. You are periodically reminded to connect to the server until you do it, and a certain number of uses, Office will not work until you do it.
	Go Online	Opens the Microsoft Office Online Web site in your default browser.
	About	Displays information about your copy of PowerPoint, including serial number, version number, and registered owner.

Configuring the Trust Center

The Trust Center is a separate dialog box from the main PowerPoint options; it contains categories for controlling the permissions that users, programs, and Internet sites have to access your computer through PowerPoint. After clicking the Trust Center category in the PowerPoint Options dialog box, you can click the Trust Center Settings button to access it.

Setting Up Trusted Locations

A *trusted location* is a location that you verify to be threat-free. When a presentation file is stored in a trusted location, PowerPoint allows macros to run without the usual safeguards (discussed later in this Appendix). To allow free access to your macros in a presentation file, you should store it in a trusted location.

The following folders are trusted by default:

Program Files\Microsoft Office\Document Themes 12

Program Files\Microsoft Office\Templates

Users*username*\Application Data\Microsoft\Addins

Users*username*\Application Data\Microsoft\Templates

You can also add more trusted locations. For example, you may want to trust a folder in which you store your presentation files for a certain client.

To add a trusted location, follow these steps:

1. Choose Office ➪ PowerPoint Options.
2. Click Trust Center, and click the Trust Center Settings button.
3. Click Trusted Locations. A list of currently trusted locations appears, as shown in Figure B.2.
4. Click Add New Location.
5. Click the Browse button, browse to the location you want, and then click OK.
6. (Optional) If you want, you can select the Subfolders of This Location Are Also Trusted check box.
7. Click OK.

You can set up new trusted locations in the Trust Center dialog box.

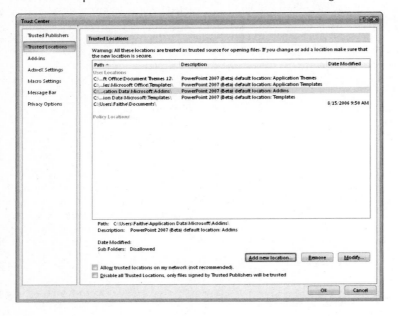

Figure B.2 shows other settings and buttons that you can also select:

■ **Allow trusted locations on my network**: Enables you to add trusted locations that exist other than on your local computer.

■ **Disable all Trusted Locations, only files signed by Trusted Publishers will be trusted**: This setting does just what its name says. You will learn more about trusted publishers later in this Appendix.

■ **Remove**: Removes a trusted location from the list. (There is no confirmation; it is removed immediately.)

■ **Modify**: Opens the Trusted Location dialog box for a location, so that you can change its path or options.

Working with Trusted Publishers

Another way to trust a macro is to verify that it comes from a trusted publisher. The Macro Settings (covered in the next section) enable you to specify what should happen when a macro from a trusted publisher wants to run outside of a trusted location.

When you open a presentation that includes one or more signed macros, PowerPoint prompts you, asking whether or not you want to trust macros from that signer. Information about the signer's certificate appears, including the name, the issuing authority, and the valid dates. If you choose Yes, then this signer is added to your Trusted Publishers list. If you have not yet added a signer to the Trusted Publishers list, then the list will be blank in the Trust Center dialog box.

If you have a trusted publisher on your list, you can select it and then click View to view its information, or click Remove to remove it from the Trusted Publishers list.

Macro Settings

Macro settings apply only to macros that are stored in presentations that are not in trusted locations. These settings determine whether or not the macro should run, and whether you should receive notification, as shown in Figure B.3.

FIGURE B.3

You can specify what should happen when a presentation outside a trusted location tries to run a macro.

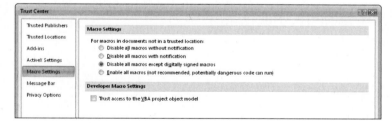

ActiveX Settings

ActiveX controls are somewhat like macros in that they contain code to be executed. Programmers write them to extend the capabilities of an application. These controls have their own set of behaviors that you can configure when they run from outside a trusted location, as shown in Figure B.4.

FIGURE B.4

You can specify what should happen when a presentation outside a trusted location tries to run an ActiveX control.

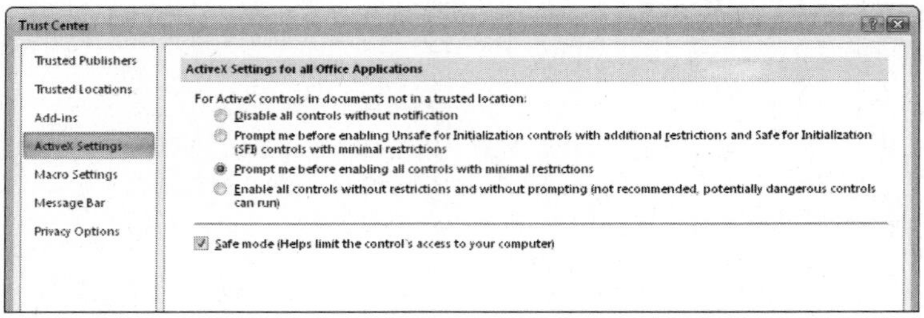

Add-Ins

An add-in is like a super macro. Add-ins can often dramatically extend the capabilities of an application, by adding new tabs on the Ribbon, new buttons, and more. Because they connect with the application at a fairly low level, they can be devastating if they contain viruses. (It is not common for add-is to contain viruses, but you never know what could happen.) You can specify that add-ins must be signed by a trusted publisher, or you can disable all add-ins from running.

Message Bar

By default, when content is blocked, a message bar appears between the Ribbon and the presentation to let you know what has happened. You can enable or disable the appearance of this message bar.

Privacy Options

It is usually safe to connect to the Internet to download content such as clip art and templates, and to send feedback to Microsoft about errors and usage. However, some people are concerned about security, and prefer to control their computer's connection to outside sources such as the Internet. (Yes, I know, just because you are paranoid does not mean that someone is not out to get you.) In the Privacy Options category, you can find a set of check boxes where you can decide what connectivity to allow.

Customizing the Status Bar

The status bar is the bar across the bottom of the PowerPoint window, where the Zoom slider and view buttons appear. You can customize what appears there by right-clicking the status bar and marking or clearing the check boxes on the menu that appears. See Figure B.5.

Appendix C

What's on the CD-ROM

This appendix provides you with information on the contents of the
CD that accompanies this book. For the latest and greatest information, please refer to the ReadMe file located at the root of the CD.

This appendix provides information on the following topics:

- Files on This CD
- Technical Support

Files on This CD

The CD-ROM included with *PowerPoint 2007 Bible* contains more than 500
PowerPoint templates and backgrounds that you can use to design your own
PowerPoint presentations. In addition, the author has included important
files that you will need to perform the Project Labs.

Templates and Backgrounds

If you aren't familiar with how to choose a background or template for your
presentation, be sure to read Chapter 3 in this book, which discusses templates, and Chapter 5, which includes the background discussion, before
attempting to use the CD-ROM.

These templates were provided for your use by several of the best-known
professional design firms and PowerPoint MVPs. They have additional templates available either for sale or free download from their Web sites. The
designers who supplied the templates and backgrounds for this book are:

- AwesomeBackgrounds:

  `http://www.awesomebackgrounds.com/templates.htm`

- Brainy Betty:

  `http://www.brainybetty.com/MENUPowerPoint.htm`

- GraphicsLand and MAKESIGNS.COM:

  `http://www.graphicsland.com/powerpoint-templates.htm`

- INDEZINE:

  `http://www.indezine.com/powerpoint/templates/`

- PoweredTemplates:

  `http://www.poweredtemplates.com`

- PresentationPro:

  `http://www.presentationpro.com/Products/Templates_Designs.asp`

- TemplateZone:

  `http://www.templatezone.com/microsoft-powerpoint-templates.php`

- ThemeArt:

  `http://www.themeart.com/products/powerpoint/`
  `powerpoint-templates.asp`

- ThemeGallery:

  `http://www.themegallery.com/english/themes/themes.asp?pt=8`

Some of the templates and backgrounds are single-slide files. Others contain many slides in one file with prebuilt designs for many different slides types (tables, charts, text, and so on) all using the same look.

If you somehow don't find templates or backgrounds you like on the CD and want to have more to choose from, these template and background sites would be excellent places to start. And if you do find templates from one of the suppliers on this CD you like, be sure to reward their good work by considering purchasing other templates from them for your future template needs.

The CD-ROM is organized with a directory for each vendor, and their templates are within that. Some of the vendor directories are further divided into subdirectories by category or for each template, and some include licensing and readme files you should read before using their templates. To use any of them, navigate to the CD-ROM drive and select the template or background you like using the methods described in Chapters 3 and 5. You can also copy the files from the CD-ROM to your local hard drive and use them from there. (Please note that the PresentationPro templates are not unzipped. To see previews of their files, please look in the PresentationPro subdirectory and open the samples.html file which provides links to their zipped templates on the CD-ROM.)

Project Lab Files

The author has provided files for use in the Project Labs that you find in Part IV of this book. The Project Labs provide an excellent way of practicing the information that you've learned from the book and show you how to use many of PowerPoint's features to create professional presentations. See Part IV for more information. The Project Labs contain the following exercises:

- Project Lab 1: Presenting Content Without Bulleted Lists
- Project Lab 2: Adding Sound and Movement to a Presentation
- Project Lab 3: Creating a Menu-Based Navigation System
- Project Lab 4: Creating a Classroom Game

System Requirements

Make sure that your computer meets the minimum system requirements listed in this section. If your computer doesn't match up to most of these requirements, you may have a problem using the contents of the CD.

- Microsoft Windows XP PC or later with Microsoft PowerPoint 2007
- A CD-ROM drive

Using the CD

To view the interface on the CD, follow these steps:

1. Insert the CD into your computer's CD drive. The license agreement appears.

NOTE The interface won't launch if you have autorun disabled. In that case, click Start ⇨ Run. In the dialog box that appears, type D:\start.exe. (Replace D with the proper letter if your CD drive uses a different letter. If you don't know the letter, see how your CD drive is listed under My Computer.) Click OK.

2. Read through the license agreement, and then click the Accept button if you want to use the CD. After you click Accept, the License Agreement window won't appear again.

The CD interface appears. The interface allows you to view the CD content with just a click of a button (or two).

Technical Support

If you have trouble with the CD-ROM, please call the Wiley Product Technical Support phone number at (800) 762-2974. Outside the United States, call 1(317) 572-3994. You can also contact Wiley Product Technical Support at **http://support.wiley.com**. John Wiley & Sons will provide technical support only for installation and other general quality control items. For technical support on the applications themselves, consult the program's vendor or author.

To place additional orders or to request information about other Wiley products, please call (877) 762-2974.

Index

G

W

Wiley Publishing, Inc.
End-User License Agreement

5. **Limited Warranty.**

   (a) WPI warrants that the Software and Software Media are free from defects in materials and workmanship under normal use for a period of sixty (60) days from the date of purchase of this Book. If WPI receives notification within the warranty period of defects in materials or workmanship, WPI will replace the defective Software Media.

   (b) WPI AND THE AUTHOR(S) OF THE BOOK DISCLAIM ALL OTHER WARRANTIES, EXPRESS OR IMPLIED, INCLUDING WITHOUT LIMITATION IMPLIED WAR-RANTIES OF MERCHANTABILITY AND FITNESS FOR A PARTICULAR PURPOSE, WITH RESPECT TO THE SOFTWARE, THE PROGRAMS, THE SOURCE CODE CONTAINED THEREIN, AND/OR THE TECHNIQUES DESCRIBED IN THIS BOOK. WPI DOES NOT WARRANT THAT THE FUNCTIONS CONTAINED IN THE SOFT-WARE WILL MEET YOUR REQUIREMENTS OR THAT THE OPERATION OF THE SOFTWARE WILL BE ERROR FREE.

   (c) This limited warranty gives you specific legal rights, and you may have other rights that vary from jurisdiction to jurisdiction.

6. **Remedies.**

   (a) WPI's entire liability and your exclusive remedy for defects in materials and workman-ship shall be limited to replacement of the Software Media, which may be returned to WPI with a copy of your receipt at the following address: Software Media Fulfillment Department, Attn.: *PowerPoint 2007 Bible*, Wiley Publishing, Inc., 10475 Crosspoint Blvd., Indianapolis, IN 46256, or call 1-800-762-2974. Please allow four to six weeks for delivery. This Limited Warranty is void if failure of the Software Media has resulted from accident, abuse, or misapplication. Any replacement Software Media will be warranted for the remainder of the original warranty period or thirty (30) days, whichever is longer.

   (b) In no event shall WPI or the author be liable for any damages whatsoever (including without limitation damages for loss of business profits, business interruption, loss of business information, or any other pecuniary loss) arising from the use of or inability to use the Book or the Software, even if WPI has been advised of the possibility of such damages.

   (c) Because some jurisdictions do not allow the exclusion or limitation of liability for conse-quential or incidental damages, the above limitation or exclusion may not apply to you.

7. **U.S. Government Restricted Rights.** Use, duplication, or disclosure of the Software for or on behalf of the United States of America, its agencies and/or instrumentalities "U.S. Government" is subject to restrictions as stated in paragraph (c)(1)(ii) of the Rights in Technical Data and Computer Software clause of DFARS 252.227-7013, or subpara-graphs (c) (1) and (2) of the Commercial Computer Software - Restricted Rights clause at FAR 52.227-19, and in similar clauses in the NASA FAR supplement, as applicable.

8. **General.** This Agreement constitutes the entire understanding of the parties and revokes and supersedes all prior agreements, oral or written, between them and may not be modi-fied or amended except in a writing signed by both parties hereto that specifically refers to this Agreement. This Agreement shall take precedence over any other documents that may be in conflict herewith. If any one or more provisions contained in this Agreement are held by any court or tribunal to be invalid, illegal, or otherwise unenforceable, each and every other provision shall remain in full force and effect.